INTEGRATED COMPUTER APPLICATIONS

MICROSOFT® OFFICE 2010 6e

Susie H. VanHuss, Ph.D.
Distinguished Professor Emeritus
University of South Carolina

Connie M. Forde, Ph.D.
Professor
Department of Instructional Systems
and Workforce Development
Mississippi State University

Donna L. Woo
Professor
Cypress College

Contributing Author:
Mark W. Lehman, Ph.D, CPA, CFE
Associate Professor Emeritus of Accountancy
Mississippi State University

SOUTH-WESTERN
CENGAGE Learning™

Australia • Brazil • Japan • Korea • Mexico • Singapore • Spain • United Kingdom • United States

SOUTH-WESTERN
CENGAGE Learning™

Integrated Computer Applications,
Sixth Edition
Susie VanHuss, Connie Forde, Donna Woo

Vice President of Editorial, Business: Jack W. Calhoun

Vice President/Editor-in-Chief: Karen Schmohe

Sr. Acquisitions Editor: Jane Phelan

Sr. Developmental Editor: Dave Lafferty

Consulting Editors: Catherine Skintik; Mary Todd, Todd Publishing Services

Associate Marketing Manager: Shanna Shelton

Sr. Content Project Manager: Martha Conway

Sr. Media Editor: Mike Jackson

CL Manufacturing Planner: Charlene Taylor

Production Service: PreMediaGlobal

Copyeditor: Gary Morris

Sr. Art Director: Tippy McIntosh

Cover and Internal Design: Grannan Graphic Design, Ltd.

Cover Illustration: Grannan Graphic Design, Ltd.

Rights Acquisition Specialist, Images and Text: Sam A. Marshall

Image Permission Researcher: Darren Wright

Text Permission Researcher: PreMediaGlobal

ISBN-13: 978-1-111-98809-8
ISBN-10: 1-111-98809-9

South-Western
5191 Natorp Boulevard
Mason, OH 45040
USA

Cengage Learning products are represented in Canada by Nelson Education, Ltd.

For your course and learning solutions, visit **www.cengage.com/highered**
Visit our company website at **www.cengage.com**

Printed in China
2 3 4 5 16 15 14 13

Contents

MODULE 1
Business Documents with Word

MODULE 2
Presentations with PowerPoint

MODULE 3
Spreadsheets with Excel

MODULE 4
Carolina Arts Federation: Integrating Word, PowerPoint, and Excel

MODULE 5

MODULE 6

Databases with Access

MODULE 7

Information Management with Outlook

MODULE 8

Digital Notebooks with OneNote

MODULE 9

Web Computing with Office Web Apps

MODULE 10

MarketAnalysis, Inc.: Integrating All Microsoft Office Applications

BUILDING WORKPLACE CONFIDENCE AND SKILLS

Integrated Computer Applications, 6E challenges you to learn all Microsoft® Office 2010 applications and integrate these tools to create relevant workplace solutions. Extensive practice, easy-to-learn commands, and numerous real-world projects will help you master each application and gain the confidence to take your skills to today's workplace.

Word *Excel* *PowerPoint* *Access*
Publisher *Outlook* *OneNote* *Office Web Apps*

NEW TO THIS EDITION

- ***OneNote*** (Module 8)
- ***Office Web Apps*** (Module 9) — will get you up and running on the SkyDrive
- ***Outlook and Publisher*** — extensively revised
- ***CourseMate*** — a value-added website
- ***New Projects*** — integrating OneNote and Office Web Apps

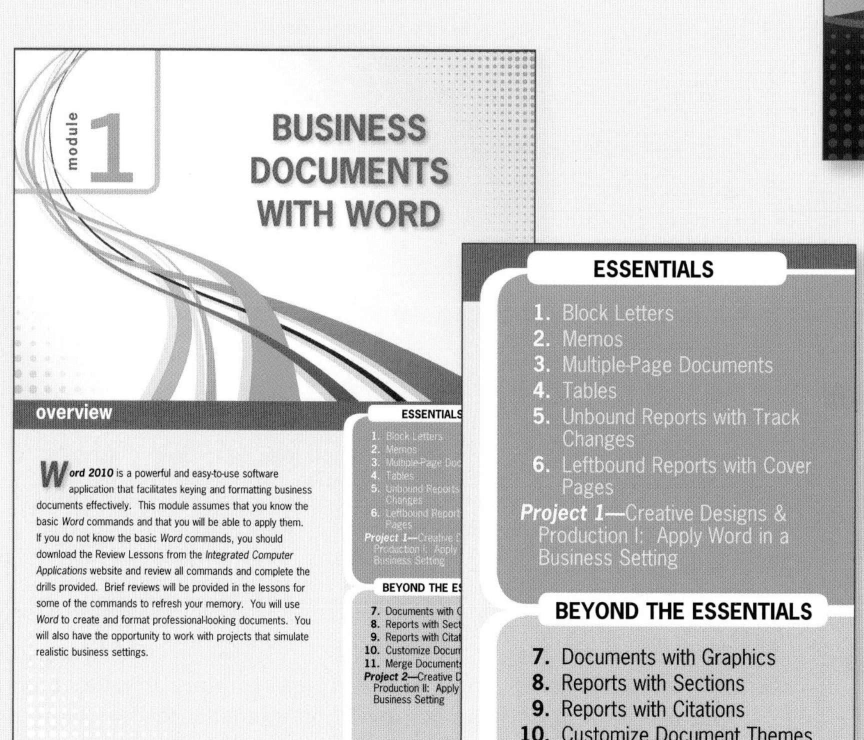

ORGANIZED FOR SUCCESS

Lessons in each module are grouped in two levels—**Essentials** and **Beyond the Essentials.** A project at the end of each level enables you to integrate the knowledge and skills just learned with other software applications.

EASY TO USE; EASY TO LEARN

Extensive practice and an easy-to-use format will give you the confidence to step into the world of work. Look for these features to bring you success.

- **Follow the Path** of the Ribbon to learn the steps of new commands.
- **Drills** apply each new command, making it easy to learn new concepts.
- **Quick Check** solutions let you know you're on the right track.

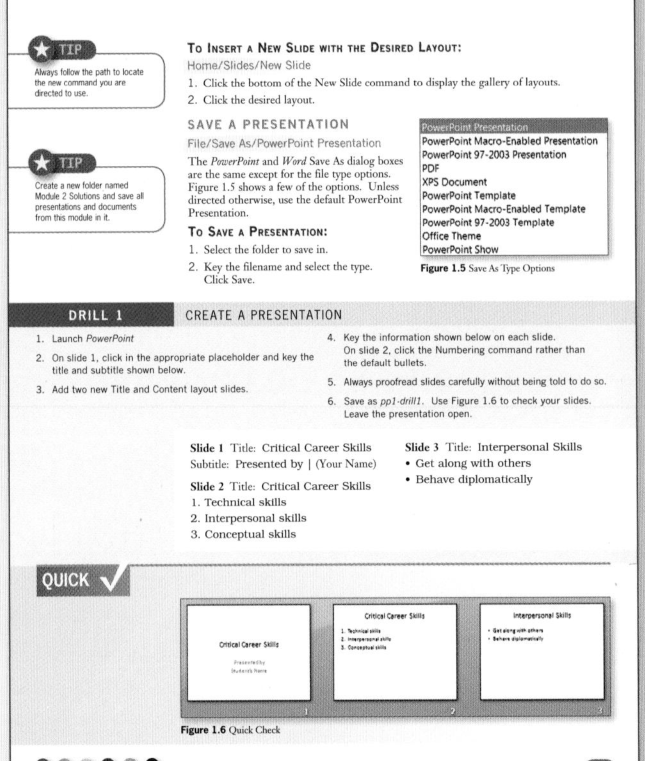

TIP

Always follow the path to locate the new command you are directed to use.

To Insert a New Slide with the Desired Layout:

Home/Slides/New Slide

1. Click the bottom of the New Slide command to display the gallery of layouts.
2. Click the desired layout.

TIP

Create a new folder named Module 2 Solutions and save all presentations and documents from this module in it.

SAVE A PRESENTATION

File/Save As/PowerPoint Presentation

The *PowerPoint* and *Word* Save As dialog boxes are the same except for the file type options. Figure 1.5 shows a few of the options. Unless directed otherwise, use the default PowerPoint Presentation.

To Save a Presentation:

1. Select the folder to save in.
2. Key the filename and select the type. Click Save.

Figure 1.5 Save As Type Options

DRILL 1 CREATE A PRESENTATION

1. Launch *PowerPoint*
2. On slide 1, click in the appropriate placeholder and key the title and subtitle shown below.
3. Add two new Title and Content layout slides.
4. Key the information shown below on each slide. On slide 2, click the Numbering command rather than the default bullets.
5. Always proofread slides carefully without being told to do so.
6. Save as *pp1-drill1*. Use Figure 1.6 to check your slides. Leave the presentation open.

Slide 1 Title: Critical Career Skills
Subtitle: Presented by | (Your Name)

Slide 2 Title: Critical Career Skills
1. Technical skills
2. Interpersonal skills
3. Conceptual skills

Slide 3 Title: Interpersonal Skills
- Get along with others
- Behave diplomatically

QUICK ✓

Figure 1.6 Quick Check

LESSON 1 CREATE PRESENTATIONS USING THEMES POWERPOINT 57

Apply It

Document 3
Memo from Template

ZAK MEMO

1. Click Sample Templates and preview the different types of templates shown. Scroll through the templates, noting the types that are featured. Note the categories of additional templates that may be downloaded from Office.com. Fax, letter, and resume templates are included. For this document, you will use the template in your data files.
2. Double-click *zak memo* to open the template file; save it as a *Word* document named *wd2-d3* in your solution files.
3. Key the memo on page 6 that you reviewed earlier in this lesson. Pay particular attention to the formatting information contained in the memo and the callouts on the full-page model.
4. Proofread and preview carefully. Check your document against the one in your textbook to ensure that you formatted it correctly. Use the Info command on Backstage view to check the information on this document.
5. Resave as *wd2-d3* and close.

Document 4
Memo from a Quick Part

ZAK MEMO

1. Use Recent in Backstage view to open the *zak memo* template again. Use Select All to select everything on the page (Home/Editing/Select/Select All) and save as a Quick Part named *Zak Memo*. Key **Memo heading** in the Description box.
2. Close the template; do not save it.
3. Open a new document and insert the *Zak Memo* Quick Part.
4. Key the memo shown below.
5. Preview, proofread, save as *wd2-d4*, and close.

TIP

Zak does not use a distribution list because it transmits all memos by e-mail. The e-mail distribution list contains the names of the Rex Project Team members.

TO: Rex Project Team | FROM: Jan Bennett | DATE: Current | SUBJECT: Client Follow-up

The plans and drawings for the Rex Project that were approved by our team at our last meeting were submitted to Bill Rex the next day. Bill called me today to indicate that his group was very pleased with the first draft. He indicated that they would like to meet with our team to go over a few changes that need to be made.

Bill requested that we meet at the Rex Plant to review some of the specifications that they have finalized. The meeting is tentatively scheduled for next Tuesday at 2:30 p.m. I will arrange to use the company van so that we can all go together. We will need to meet in the lobby of our building at about 1:45 p

Please
be an

xx

- **Apply It** exercises include extensive practice to reinforce new concepts.
- **Data files** are identified with an icon. Download these files to My Documents from the product website.

CDRC

- **Model documents** provide guides for applying the proper formats.

Zak and Associates

473 Kenton Drive | Irmo, SC 29063-2193 | 803-555-0144 | www.zakandassociates.com

TO: All Employees ↓ 1 after each heading

FROM: Lee Zak

DATE: Current date

SUBJECT: Memo Format

Most of you are aware that we have been working with Visual Image Consultants to help us improve our brand identity. The Executive Team has enthusiastically endorsed the standard document formats they proposed. This memo and the attached one illustrate the format that we will use for all memos. We elected to use our logo and headquarters address since we send memos to all of our offices in the region. Often our representatives share communications sent to them from headquarters with their customers.

PROJECTS BUILD CONFIDENCE AND EXPERTISE

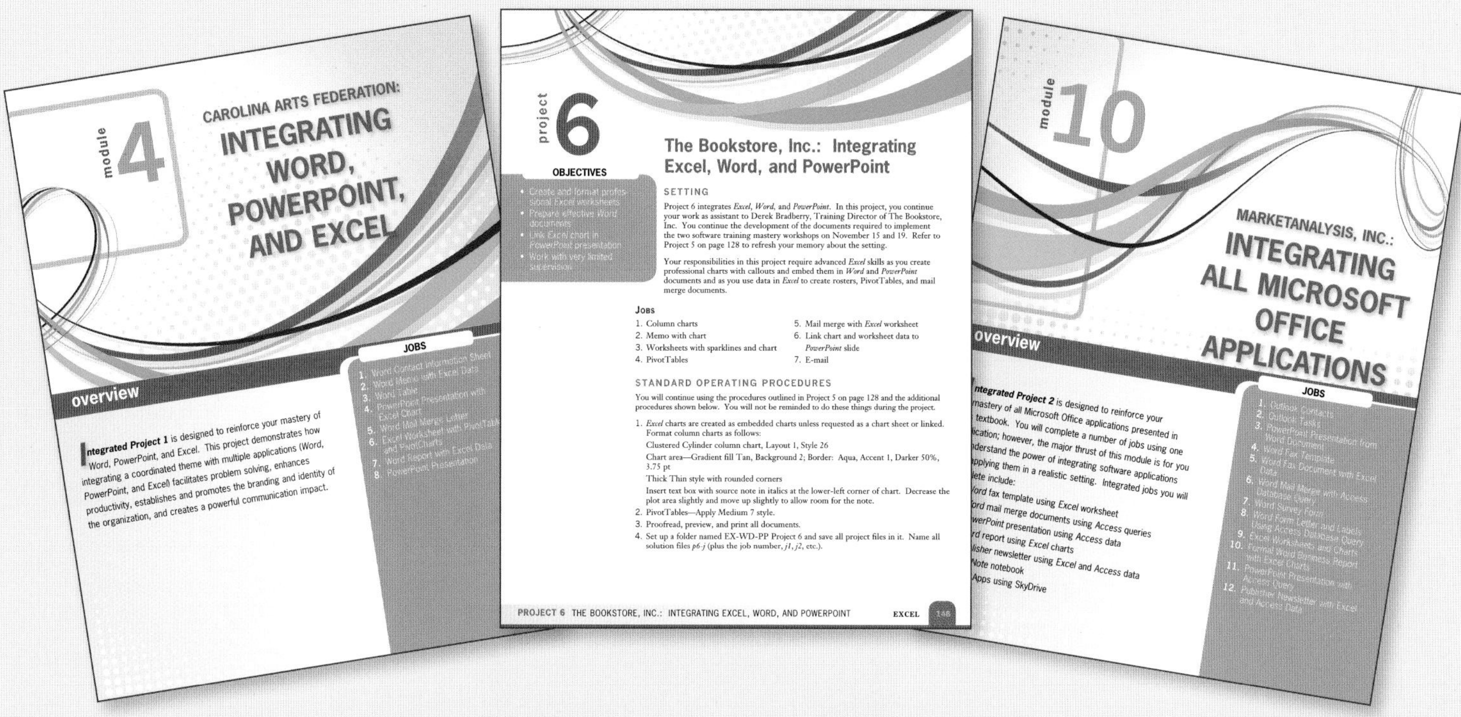

Projects feature realistic work settings, coordinated themes, and integrated applications to validate previous learning. Two projects are comprehensive (Modules 4 and 10). Modules contain projects after both the **Essentials** and **Beyond the Essentials** levels.

SPECIAL FEATURES POLISH WORKPLACE SKILLS

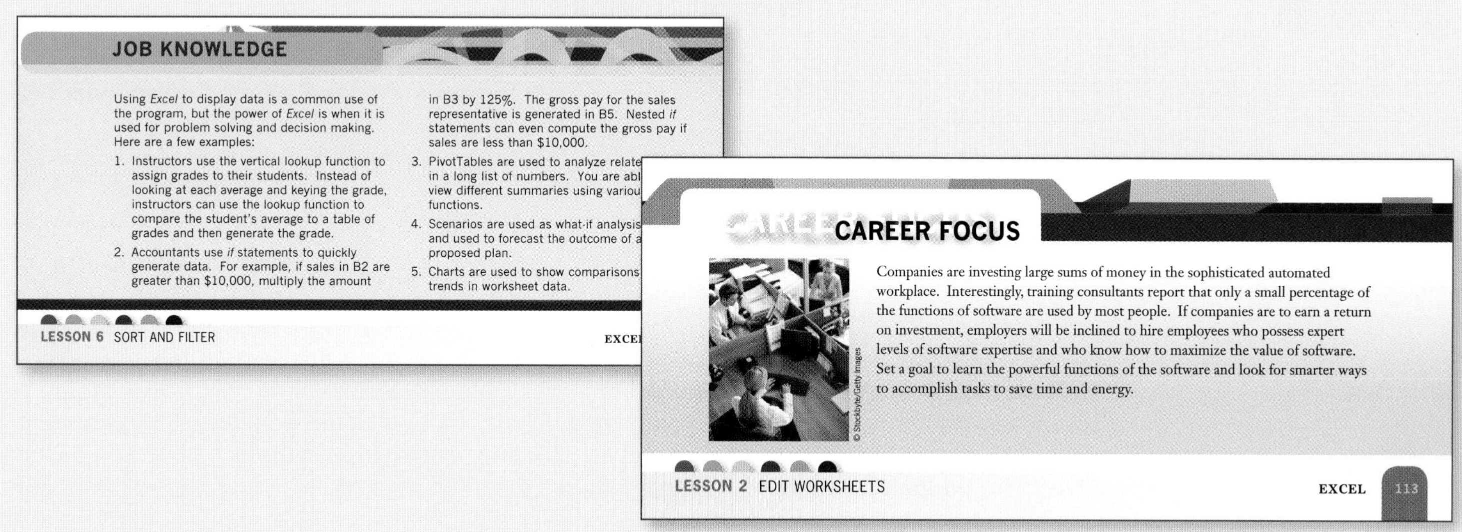

NEW VALUE-ADDED WEBSITE

Integrated Computer Applications, 6e offers a **CourseMate™** website with online learning and study tools to add another dimension. Students will have access to an interactive eBook, videos, flashcards, quizzing, and other tools to guide and encourage learning. The unique **Engagement Tracker** will enable instructors to monitor student interaction and outcomes. Experience it today. For more information about CourseMate: **www.cengage.com/coursemate**

Student Resources

- Learning Objectives
- Flashcards
- Interactive Quizzes
- Web Links
- Data Files
- Video Tutorials
- Enrichment Activities
- Interactive eBook

Instructor Resources

- Instructor's Manual
- ExamView®
- PowerPoint Presentations
- Engagement Tracker

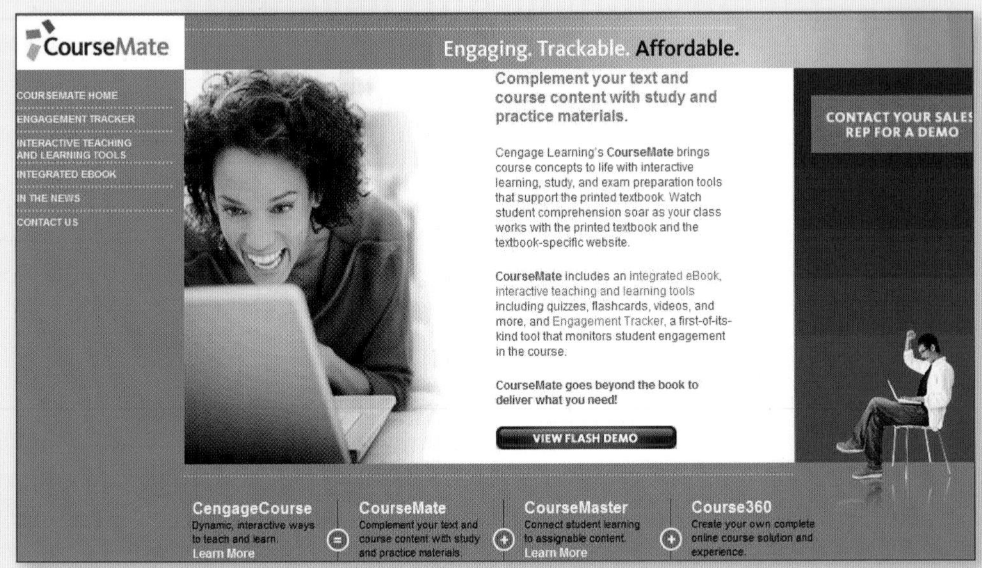

CENGAGEBRAIN

CengageBrain is your one-stop solution for textbooks, rentals, eTextbooks, eChapters, and online homework. Learn more at **www.cengagebrain.com**.

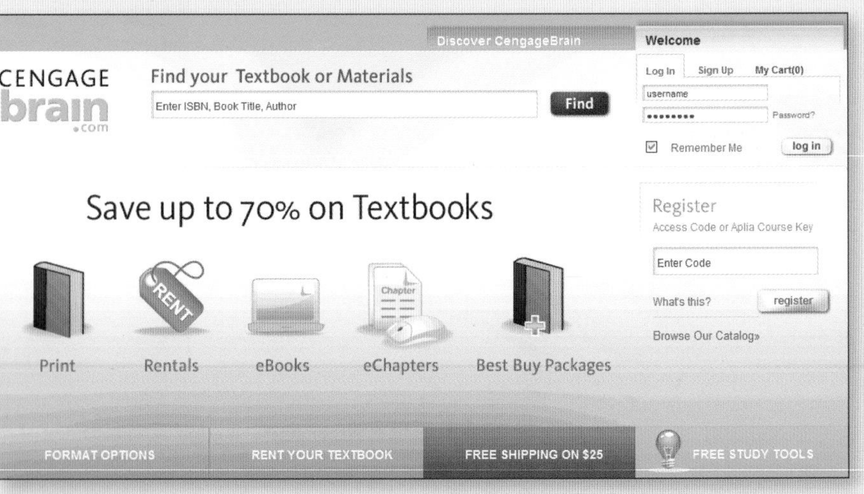

Also See Product Companion Site: **www.cengage.com/keyboarding/ica6e** and **www.collegekeyboarding.com**

BUSINESS DOCUMENTS WITH WORD

overview

W*ord 2010* is a powerful and easy-to-use software application that facilitates keying and formatting business documents effectively. This module assumes that you know the basic *Word* commands and that you will be able to apply them. Brief reviews will be provided in the lessons for some of the commands to refresh your memory. You will use *Word* to create and format professional-looking documents. You will also have the opportunity to work with projects that simulate realistic business settings.

ESSENTIALS

BEYOND THE ESSENTIALS

Job 12, continued

On July 1 the Miles for Health project was initiated at MarketAnalysis with 30 employees weighing in and receiving rules and procedures for logging miles for health. Accepting the challenge to improve their health, they agreed to walk at least 1 mile per day and increase the distance by 5 percent each week.

Our president Shane Veasley stepped up as the first participant to join the program. He stated, "We all must recognize the need to include exercise in our daily schedule. I want our company to be a leader in promoting health among our employees."

Three months have passed, and you have undoubtedly seen these Miles for Health members walking up stairs, running laps around the building at lunch, and working out at local fitness centers after hours. Let's celebrate their first-quarter progress. Thirty participants have walked a total of [key total from worksheet] miles, with the top award winner clocking [key from PivotTable] miles.

7. Save and print.
8. Attach your *Publisher* file to the *October* subpage under *Newsletters* in your *OneNote* notebook. Add the following To Do tag at top of the page: **Please be sure to update the link for the Top Ten Award Winners just prior to releasing the October newsletter.**
9. Add your MarketAnalysis notebook to your SkyDrive and share with two people.

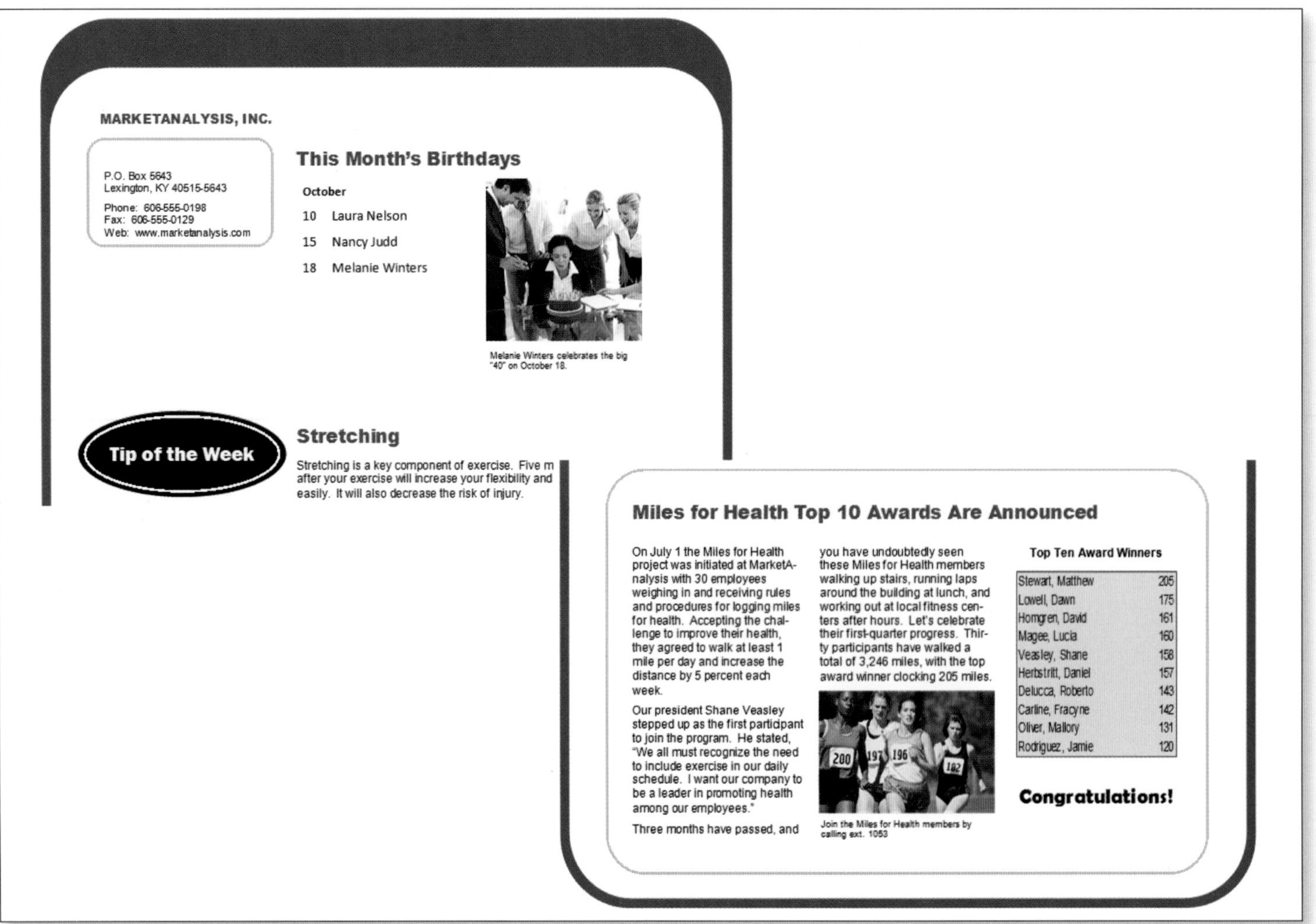

MARKETANALYSIS, INC.

P.O. Box 5643
Lexington, KY 40515-5643
Phone: 606-555-0198
Fax: 606-555-0129
Web: www.marketanalysis.com

This Month's Birthdays

October

10 Laura Nelson
15 Nancy Judd
18 Melanie Winters

Melanie Winters celebrates the big "40" on October 18.

Tip of the Week

Stretching

Stretching is a key component of exercise. Five m after your exercise will increase your flexibility and easily. It will also decrease the risk of injury.

Miles for Health Top 10 Awards Are Announced

On July 1 the Miles for Health project was initiated at MarketAnalysis with 30 employees weighing in and receiving rules and procedures for logging miles for health. Accepting the challenge to improve their health, they agreed to walk at least 1 mile per day and increase the distance by 5 percent each week.

Our president Shane Veasley stepped up as the first participant to join the program. He stated, "We all must recognize the need to include exercise in our daily schedule. I want our company to be a leader in promoting health among our employees."

Three months have passed, and you have undoubtedly seen these Miles for Health members walking up stairs, running laps around the building at lunch, and working out at local fitness centers after hours. Let's celebrate their first-quarter progress. Thirty participants have walked a total of 3,246 miles, with the top award winner clocking 205 miles.

Join the Miles for Health members by calling ext. 1053

Top Ten Award Winners

Name	Miles
Stewart, Matthew	205
Lowell, Dawn	175
Homgren, David	161
Magee, Lucia	160
Veasley, Shane	158
Herbstritt, Daniel	157
Delucca, Roberto	143
Carline, Fracyne	142
Oliver, Mallory	131
Rodriguez, Jamie	120

Congratulations!

Figure IP2.11 Page 2 of the Newsletter

LESSON

1

Block Letters

OBJECTIVES

- Create business letters using block format
- Review and apply *Word* commands
- Develop job knowledge and skills

STANDARD PROCEDURES

Data file: A data file may be required to complete some documents. The icon plus the filename appears next to these documents to alert you. Data files must be downloaded from the *Integrated Computer Applications* website; files are organized by module.

Solutions: Set up a folder for saving solutions for each module. For Module 3, for example, name the folder Module 3 Solutions. The filename for each document is shown in italic.

Follow the path: When commands are introduced, the path on the Ribbon is illustrated to help you locate the command easily. The path includes the tab ❶, the group ❷, and generally a third command ❸. Follow the path and then the step-by-step directions begin after the path. See the example below and in Figure 1.1.

REMOVE SPACE AFTER PARAGRAPH

Home/Paragraph/Line and Paragraph Spacing

Screen captures: Often steps to complete a command include a screen capture that is labeled to correspond to the steps as shown in the example.

❶ Home

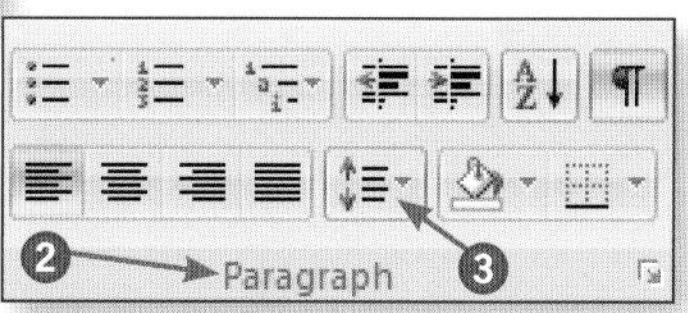

Figure 1.1 Example

LETTER FORMAT

Letters may be formatted in either block or modified-block format. In this module, you will format letters using block format, which is the one most frequently used. Most businesses research document design carefully and select a format that works well with their logo and trademarks. Visual design is a key part of corporate identity and image.

Business letters are usually printed on letterhead stationery. When letterhead is used, the date is inserted at about .5" below the letterhead or at about 2" from the top of the page. A very short letter may be centered on the page. Read the letter in Figure 1.2, which explains how to format a block letter.

TIP

Minor differences in appearance of screens occur depending on screen size and resolution and whether you are using *Vista* or the *Windows 7* operating system.

TIP

Keyboard shortcut: To move to the next line without space after the paragraph, press SHIFT + ENTER.

Word Skills

INSERT DATE

Insert/Date & Time

1. Click at the point the date is to be inserted.
2. Select Month, Day, Year format.
3. Deselect Update automatically; click OK.

REMOVE SPACE AFTER PARAGRAPH

Home/Paragraph/Line and Paragraph Spacing

1. Position the insertion point in the paragraph you wish to remove the space after.
2. Click Line and Paragraph Spacing and then Remove Space After Paragraph.

Job 12,
continued

Fundraising Ideas

- Donations of $1 for each gallon of gas purchased during the campaign were contributed.
- Bond donations received in return for being released from "jail" were contributed.
- Tips earned as servers at local restaurant were donated.
- Donations for "free" babysitting night were contributed.

Refer to Figure IP2.11 on page 328 as you design page 2 of the newsletter.

PAGE 2

1. Delete pages 2 and 3. On the new page 2, delete the logo placeholder near the top of the page.
2. Open the *Access* data file *marketanalysis*, and save as *ip2-j12b*. Complete the following directions to prepare the data required for the *This Month's Birthdays* section of the newsletter.
   a. Create a query that contains the fields Birth Date, First Name, and Last Name and will display all employees with a birth date of 10/*/*. The asterisks mean "any day, any year."
   b. Run the query. Three records should match your criterion. Save the query as **October Birth Date**. Select the three records in the query and copy. You will paste in the next step.
3. Expand the text box at the top of page 2 as shown in Figure IP2.11. Key the headline **This Month's Birthdays**. Use Paste Special to paste the birthday data. Remove the field names, and key the heading **October**. Display the correct day for each employee, and adjust tabs as shown in Figure IP2.11. Insert an appropriate clip art to accompany the birthday list, and add a caption.

Home/Clipboard/Paste/
Paste Special

1. Click New Text Box in the Paste As list.
2. Click OK.

4. Move the black oval shape to the left margin, and key **Tip of the Week** in the shape. Add text boxes for the heading and stretching tip shown in Figure IP2.11, or key a tip of your own.
5. Open the *Excel* data file *miles for health*, and save as *miles for health progress* in your solutions folder. Complete the following directions to prepare the data needed for the back page story.
   a. Compute total miles for each member and for each month. Compute the total miles for all three months and all members.
   b. Create a PivotTable on a new worksheet that displays Employee in the Row Labels box and Total in the Values box. The sum of total miles will display; sort in largest to smallest order.
6. Key the back page headline **Miles for Health Top 10 Awards Are Announced** and the following text for the story. Complete the steps below to complete the story.
   a. Insert an appropriate clip art to accompany this article, and add the caption shown in Figure IP2.11. Key the heading **Top Ten Award Winners** in the third column.
   b. From the PivotTable 1 prepared in step 5, copy the top ten walkers. Go to the back story, and use Paste Special to link this *Excel* data under the Top Ten Award Winners heading. Right-click the object, and format it with Accent 3 fill color and Accent 1 line color.
   c. Beneath the linked data, key **Congratulations!**, and format in Berlin Sans FB Demi font, 16 point.

You may need to click in the second column and break the link to the third column before you can click in the third column to add text.

Visual Image Consultants

864 Park Street
Columbia, SC 29201-2426

2"

Current date ↓ 2

Mr. Lee Zak
Zak and Associates
473 Kenton Drive
Irmo, SC 29063-2193 ↓ 1

} Remove extra space

Dear Mr. Zak ↓ 1

The block format with open punctuation illustrated in this letter is the format that we recommend for your company. This efficient format positions all lines at the left margin. With open punctuation, no punctuation is used after the salutation or the complimentary close. ↓ 1

Word 2010 and Word 2007 use the same defaults. The line spacing is 1.15, and the spacing after paragraphs is 10 points. With short lines such as the letter address and the name and title, the extra spacing after the paragraph needs to be removed. The spacing between the date and inside address and between the complimentary close and writer's name requires you to tap enter twice. Tap enter once after all other letter parts.

Please note the content and format of the closing lines. Sincerely is the complimentary close that we recommend, and the name and title illustrate the format we recommend. The initials xx represent the first and last initial of the person keying the letter. We also recommend that you standardize this format and ask all employees to use it. When we conduct the training session for your employees, we will teach them how to save the standard closing lines for their letters as a Quick Part that can be inserted with one click. Using this Word 2010 command can improve productivity significantly.

Mr. Zak, we look forward to meeting with you to finalize all of the design changes that we have discussed and to conducting the training for your staff.

Sincerely ↓ 2

Lynn T. Wells } Remove extra space
Managing Partner ↓ 1

xx

Figure 1.2 Block Letter Format

Job 12,
continued

3. Key the secondary story heading **Company to Host Business After Hours for Chamber**, and key the following text for the story.

Fayette and Clark County Chamber of Commerce members are invited to tour our facility and join us for food and beverages on November 15 from 5 to 7 p.m. We are requesting our employees to serve as volunteers.

Are you willing to serve as a volunteer for this event? We will need people to act as greeters, serve at the food stations, and distribute gift bags. We are hoping for a big turnout for this event, and we need you to make the evening a success.

To volunteer, simply go to www.marketanalysis.com/volunteer. Click one of the three volunteer areas and key your name and phone extension. Thank you for your service.

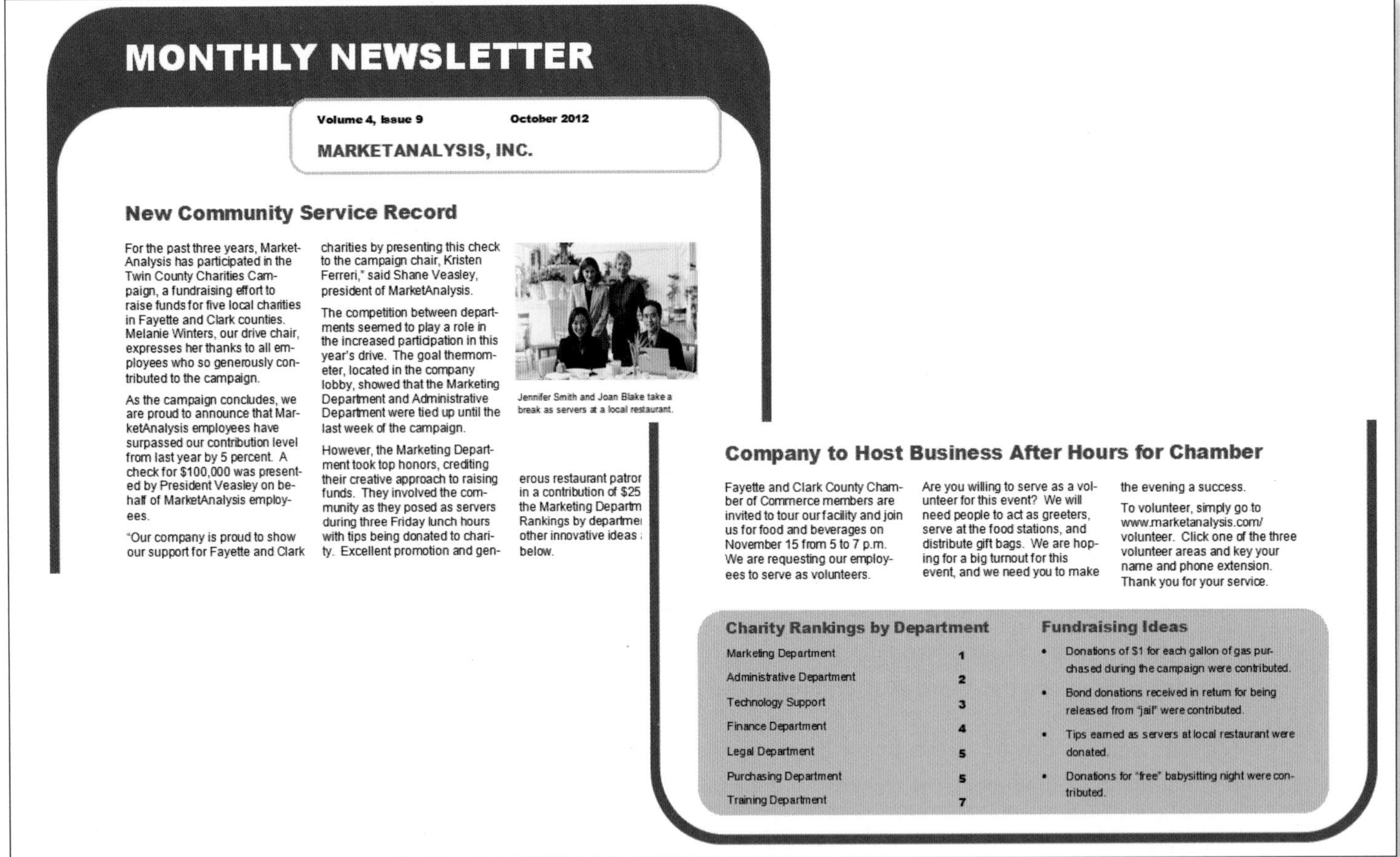

MONTHLY NEWSLETTER

Volume 4, Issue 9 **October 2012**

MARKETANALYSIS, INC.

New Community Service Record

For the past three years, MarketAnalysis has participated in the Twin County Charities Campaign, a fundraising effort to raise funds for five local charities in Fayette and Clark counties. Melanie Winters, our drive chair, expresses her thanks to all employees who so generously contributed to the campaign.

As the campaign concludes, we are proud to announce that MarketAnalysis employees have surpassed our contribution level from last year by 5 percent. A check for $100,000 was presented by President Veasley on behalf of MarketAnalysis employees.

"Our company is proud to show our support for Fayette and Clark charities by presenting this check to the campaign chair, Kristen Ferreri," said Shane Veasley, president of MarketAnalysis.

The competition between departments seemed to play a role in the increased participation in this year's drive. The goal thermometer, located in the company lobby, showed that the Marketing Department and Administrative Department were tied up until the last week of the campaign.

However, the Marketing Department took top honors, crediting their creative approach to raising funds. They involved the community as they posed as servers during three Friday lunch hours with tips being donated to charity. Excellent promotion and generous restaurant patror in a contribution of $25 the Marketing Departm Rankings by departmei other innovative ideas ; below.

Jennifer Smith and Joan Blake take a break as servers at a local restaurant.

Company to Host Business After Hours for Chamber

Fayette and Clark County Chamber of Commerce members are invited to tour our facility and join us for food and beverages on November 15 from 5 to 7 p.m. We are requesting our employees to serve as volunteers.

Are you willing to serve as a volunteer for this event? We will need people to act as greeters, serve at the food stations, and distribute gift bags. We are hoping for a big turnout for this event, and we need you to make the evening a success.

To volunteer, simply go to www.marketanalysis.com/volunteer. Click one of the three volunteer areas and key your name and phone extension. Thank you for your service.

Charity Rankings by Department

Department	Rank
Marketing Department	1
Administrative Department	2
Technology Support	3
Finance Department	4
Legal Department	5
Purchasing Department	5
Training Department	7

Fundraising Ideas

- Donations of $1 for each gallon of gas purchased during the campaign were contributed.
- Bond donations received in return for being released from "jail" were contributed.
- Tips earned as servers at local restaurant were donated.
- Donations for "free" babysitting night were contributed.

Figure IP2.10 Page 1 of the Newsletter

4. In the shaded area at the bottom of page 1, key the following information. Refer to Figure IP2.10.

Charity Rankings by Department

Marketing Department	1	Legal Department	5
Administrative Department	2	Purchasing Department	6
Technology Support	3	Training Department	7
Finance Department	4		

Apply It

Document 1
Block Letter

VIC LETTERHEAD

1. Open *vic letterhead* from the data files, and key the letter in Figure 1.2 on the previous page. Follow the illustrations in the letter for formatting. Use the current date. Replace the xx with your reference initials. Add your initials to each letter or memo you key.
2. Proofread carefully and preview the format.
3. Prepare an envelope (see *Word Skills* below).
4. Save as *wd1-d1* and close.

Document 2
Block Letter with Copy Notation

TAYLOR LETTERHEAD

1. Key the following letter on the *taylor letterhead*. Use the current date. Tap ENTER after the reference initials, key **c** for copy notation at the margin, and tap TAB to indent the name .5". Lines of the letter address and closing are separated by a vertical line | .
2. Proofread carefully and preview the format. Add an envelope to the document.
3. Save as *wd1-d2* and close.

Ms. Janice R. LeRuth | Manager, Human Resources | Marcus Tools, Inc. | 3764 W. Wall Street | Midland, TX 79703-7710 | Dear Ms. LeRuth

Thank you for inviting us to make a presentation on our new software designed to help your employees understand your benefits program and make informed decisions based on the options available to them. The latest version has new features that extend the capabilities of your current software significantly.

You suggested that we make the presentation on Thursday of next week at 2:30 p.m. That time works well for us. We plan to begin with an overview of the system followed by a complete demonstration of the new features. Then we will close with a cost analysis, recommendations for implementing the system, and a tentative schedule.

I will call you later this week to verify that this approach meets your needs. We look forward to meeting with your team next week.

Sincerely | Ralph C. Baker | Systems Manager | xx | c Lynn Fox, Systems Analyst

If the vertical page position does not display in your status bar, right-click the status bar and in the Customize Status Bar menu, click Vertical Page Position.

If your first reference initial or the c for copy is automatically changed to a capital letter, click the AutoCorrect Options button and select Undo Automatic Capitalization.

Word Skills

ENVELOPES
Mailings/Create/Envelopes

1. Select the letter address and then click Envelopes; the mailing address is automatically displayed in the Delivery ❶ address box (Figure 1.3).
2. Check the Omit box ❷ if there is a return address displayed; then click Print ❸.
3. Your instructor may prefer that you add the envelope to the top of the document containing the letter. If so, click Add to Document ❹.

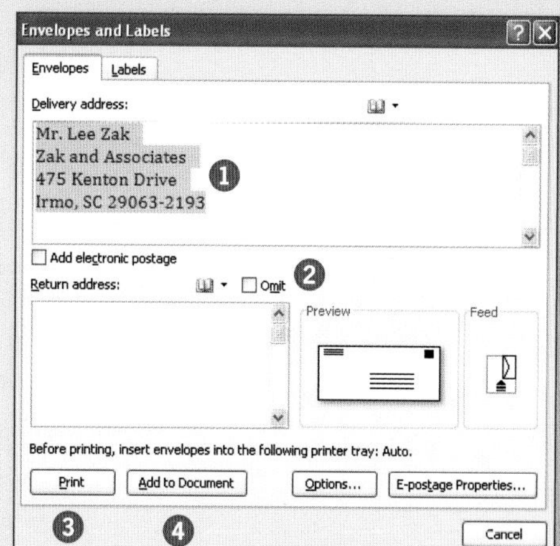

Figure 1.3 Create Envelopes

Job 11

PowerPoint Presentation with Access Query

KISNER
MAKISNER

Ms.Winters is preparing a *PowerPoint* presentation and needs a list of occupants for Florence, Covington, and Lexington in the Kisner Industrial study. She sends you the *PowerPoint* data file *kisner* so you can add this data. Save the presentation as *ip2-j11a*.

1. Open the *Access* data file *makisner*, and save as *ip2-j11b*. Create three queries, one for each city, that provide first name and last name for each occupant in the designated city. Do not show the city in the query results, and sort by last name in alphabetical order. Copy each query dynaset, and paste on the appropriate *PowerPoint* slide. Format the table attractively. Use Figure IP2.9 as a guide.
2. Attach your presentation file to the *PowerPoint Presentations* subpage under the *Kisner Industrial Co.* page under *Projects*.

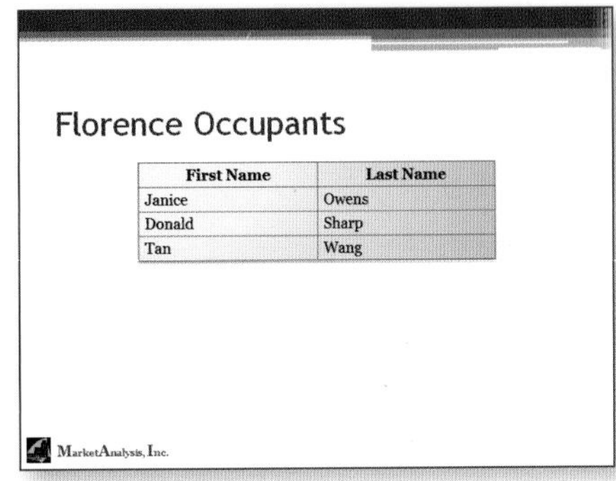

Figure IP2.9 *Access* Query Data Pasted on *PowerPoint* Slide

Job 12

Newsletter

MARKETANALYSIS
MILES FOR HEALTH

Refer to Figure IP2.10 on page 326 as you design page 1 of the newsletter.

MarketAnalysis publishes a two-page employee newsletter each month to highlight employee news. You have been asked to publish the October newsletter using the Studio template in *Publisher*. Use the default color scheme and fonts, and create business information for MarketAnalysis. Save the publication as *ip2-j12a*. Refer to Figures IP2.10 and IP2.11 as you work on the newsletter.

Page 1

1. Key the heading information as shown in Figure IP2.10 on the next page.
2. Key the lead story headline **New Community Service Record**, and key the following text for the story. Search for an appropriate clip art to accompany the content of this article. Add the caption.

For the past three years, MarketAnalysis has participated in the Twin County Charities Campaign, a fundraising effort to raise funds for five local charities in Fayette and Clark counties. Melanie Winters, our drive chair, expresses her thanks to all employees who so generously contributed to the campaign.

As the campaign concludes, we are proud to announce that MarketAnalysis employees have surpassed our contribution level from last year by 5 percent. A check for $100,000 was presented by President Veasley on behalf of MarketAnalysis employees.

"Our company is proud to show our support for Fayette and Clark charities by presenting this check to the campaign chair, Kristen Ferreri," said Shane Veasley, president of MarketAnalysis.

The competition between departments seemed to play a role in the increased participation in this year's drive. The goal thermometer, located in the company lobby, showed that the Marketing Department and Administrative Department were tied up until the last week of the campaign.

However, the Marketing Department took top honors, crediting their creative approach to raising funds. They involved the community as they posed as servers during three Friday lunch hours with tips being donated to charity. Excellent promotion and generous restaurant patrons resulted in a contribution of $25,000 by the Marketing Department. Rankings by department and other innovative ideas are shown below.

LESSON 2

Memos

OBJECTIVES

- Create memos
- Use a memo template
- Save Quick Parts
- Learn and apply *Word* commands

MEMOS

Memorandums (memos for short) are internal messages that may be printed on letterhead, plain paper, or paper with just a heading such as the company name. They may be sent electronically as e-mail or as an attachment to an e-mail. Memos were originally designed to stay within a company; however, e-mails are frequently sent outside the company.

TIP

The way that you open templates depends on where they are stored. The Word Skills instructions show first how to open templates installed on your computer and then how to open templates that you save in your solution files or that are provided in your data files.

Word Skills

TEMPLATES

File/New/Sample Templates or Office.com Templates

1. Click Sample Templates to display the options available.
2. Select the desired template and click Create.

TEMPLATES FROM DATA FILES

1. Double-click the template to display it.
2. Click Save As and note that the file has opened as a *Word* template rather than a *Word* document (Figure 2.1). Click the down arrow on Save as type and select Word Document.
3. In the Save in box, select the location to save the file (your solution folder); and in the File name box, key the filename such as *wd2-d1*; then click Save.

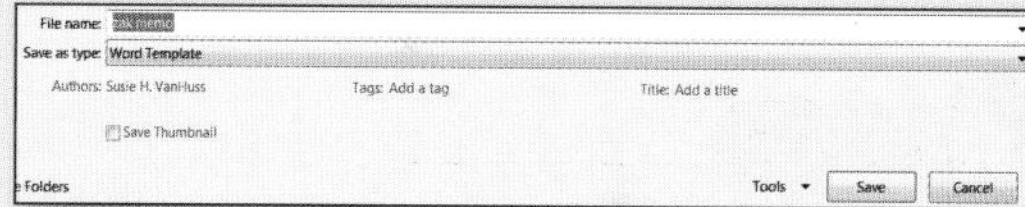

Figure 2.1 Save As Type

CAREER FOCUS

© Photoroller/Shutterstock.com

Companies expect employees to produce documents that create a positive image for the company. Many organizations provide employees with manuals or guides to follow when they prepare documents. Typically, the guides include samples of the various document formats used, guides for using logos and trademarks appropriately, procedures for preparing and distributing documents, and a variety of reference materials. Your project at the end of this module will require you to prepare a style guide for an organization.

Job 9,
continued

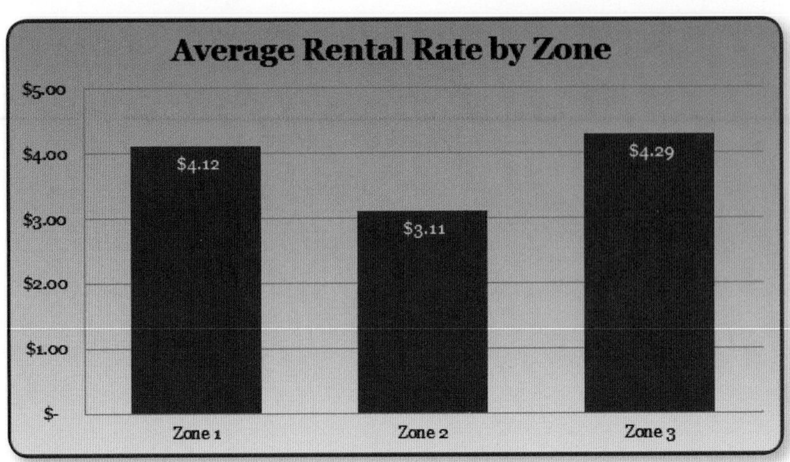

Figure IP2.8 Column Chart on Property Size Sheet

Job 10
Formal Business Report with Excel Charts

REPORT

Prepare a formal business report that includes several preliminary pages and the report body. Ms. Winters has given you the data file *report* that contains the report text with special instructions to you keyed in angle brackets < >. Delete the instructions in brackets when completed. Complete the following steps in the order shown.

1. Insert the Tiles cover page and add title: Industrial Space Report; subtitle: Fayette and Clark Counties; author: Melanie Winters; year: 2012; and the MarketAnalysis address.
2. Position the title on the correct line. Apply styles as instructed in the report.
3. Paste the three charts in the locations where instructed using the Picture Paste Option. Size each chart with a 2.25" height, and accept the resulting width. Add captions to all five charts in the report.
4. Add a caption to the table on page 2 of the report and center the label.
5. Number the preliminary and report pages. Follow directions carefully.
   a. Insert a Continuous section break on the first line of the first page of the report body.
   b. Position the insertion point on the second page (letter of transmittal). Number the preliminary pages of the report at the bottom center with lowercase Roman numerals. Start numbering at ii.
   c. Click Next twice to be in Section 2 footer. Then click Link to Previous to break link between the footers of Sections 1 and 2. Delete the page number displaying in the footer. Insert the Annual footer.
   d. Click Go to Header. Break the link between the headers in Sections 1 and 2. Insert the Annual header. Check the title of the report as inserted. Choose to start numbering the body of the report with page 1.
6. Create a table of contents using the Automatic 1 style. Position at 2" and apply the Title style to the title.
7. Create a table of tables and a table of figures as indicated. Key **Table of Tables** and **Table of Figures** at about 2", and apply the Title style. Select each title and choose Add Text to add to the contents page (References/Table of Contents/Add Text).
8. On the Contents page, key **Letter of Transmittal** as the first entry, tap TAB, and key **ii**. Click Update Table and update the table of contents.
9. Attach your report file to the *Reports* subpage under the *Kisner Industrial Co.* page under *Projects*.

TIP

Page numbering can be challenging when two number styles are used. Follow the substeps in step 5 carefully. Breaking the link between sections is essential.

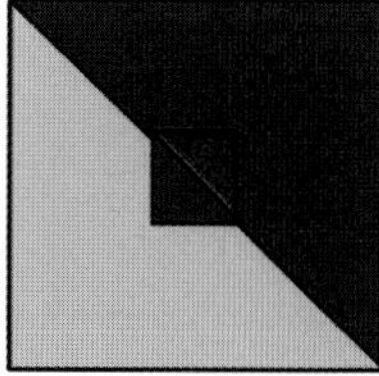

Zak and Associates

473 Kenton Drive | Irmo, SC 29063-2193 | 803-555-0144 | www.zakandassociates.com

TO: All Employees ↓ 1 after each heading

FROM: Lee Zak

DATE: Current date

SUBJECT: Memo Format

Most of you are aware that we have been working with Visual Image Consultants to help us improve our brand identity. The Executive Team has enthusiastically endorsed the standard document formats they proposed. This memo and the attached one illustrate the format that we will use for all memos. We elected to use our logo and headquarters address since we send memos to all of our offices in the region. Often our representatives share communications sent to them from headquarters with their customers.

Word 2010 has been installed on every computer. A few of you previously used Word 2003. We really like the 1.15 line spacing and the extra space after paragraphs. These defaults enhance the readability of our documents. To format the heading, we simply tap enter after each line. We also ask that each assistant who keys memos for our engineers and technical staff add their reference initials (first and last initials) as shown at the bottom of this memo. Enclosures, attachments, and copy notations are also positioned below the reference initials as shown on this illustration.

Our executive assistant, Leslie West, will provide each of you with a template that has the heading so that you will not have to key it each time you prepare a memo. At our training session, you will also learn how to save the heading as a Quick Part so that you can insert the heading with just one click. The schedule is also attached. One of our goals is to increase our productivity as well as enhance the image of our documents.

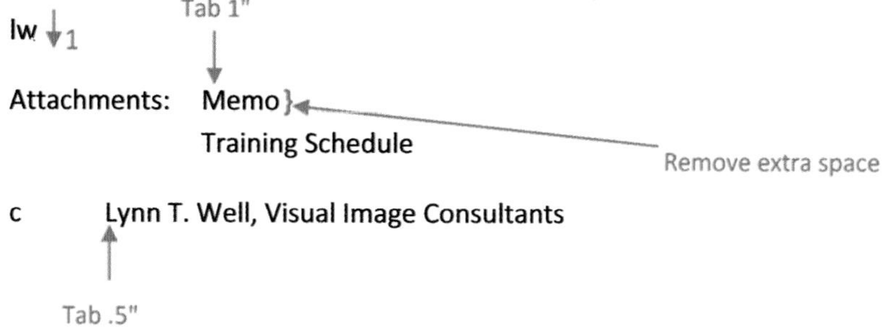

Figure 2.2 Memo

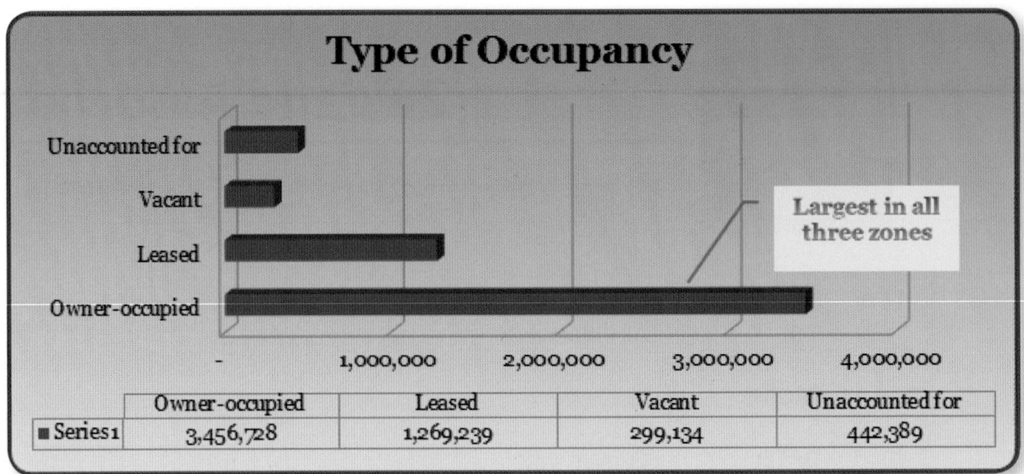

Figure IP2.7 Bar Chart on Occupancy Sheet

3. Complete Sheet3 of the workbook.
   a. Rename the third sheet tab **Property Size**, and change tab color to Orange, Accent 4. Key the worksheet data shown below. Format the headings the same as on the Occupancy worksheet.
      In B8, enter a function to calculate the average lease rate for Zone 1; copy to remaining zones. Format the number cells in rows 4–7 as Comma style with two decimals. Format rows 3 and 8 as Accounting style.

Average Lease Rate by Property Size			
	Zone 1	Zone 2	Zone 3
Less than 5,000	$6.83	n/a	$2.74
5,000 – 10,000	3.22	4.57	5.41
10,001 – 50,000	3.17	2.40	4.73
50,001 – 100,000	3.25	2.47	n/a
Over 100,000	n/a	3.00	n/a
Average			

   b. Select B2:D2 and B8:D8, and create a clustered column chart to show the average lease rate by zone. Embed at A10 and drag to fill the range A10:G27. Use Figure IP2.8 as a guide. Use Layout 10, do not include a legend, add a chart title, and change the major unit to 1.0 on the vertical axis options. Format chart area as for other charts.

4. Attach your *Excel* file to the *Reports* subpage under the *Kisner Industrial Co.* page under *Projects*.

DISCOVER

Chart Tools Layout/Axes/Axes

1. Click Primary Vertical Axis.
2. Click More Primary Vertical Axis Options.
3. In Axis Options list, click Fixed for Major unit and then key **1.0**.

BACKSTAGE VIEW

The File tab displays the Backstage view, which is used to manage documents and data that relates to them. You have already used many of the commands shown in Figure 2.3.

Recent: Lists documents that you have recently worked with; click a file listed to open it. Click the pin at the right to engage it as shown on the first two files. Pinned files remain on the list; other files rotate off.

Info: Provides a wide range of data about a document. Open a document and click Info to view the types of data shown.

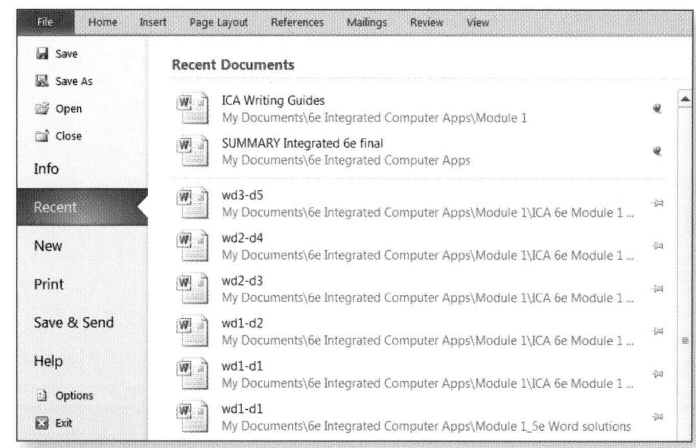

Figure 2.3 File Menu

QUICK PARTS

Quick Parts are preformatted segments of text and graphics saved as Building Blocks. Text and graphics can be saved in the Quick Parts gallery and inserted in documents as needed.

Word Skills

CREATE QUICK PARTS

Insert/Text/Quick Parts

1. Select the text you wish to save as a Quick Part, and click Quick Parts.
2. Click Save Selection to Quick Parts Gallery to display the Create New Building Block dialog box (Figure 2.4).
3. Key the name of the Quick Parts, such as **Zak Memo** ❶, and a description such as **Memo heading** ❷. Accept the defaults in the other boxes and click OK.

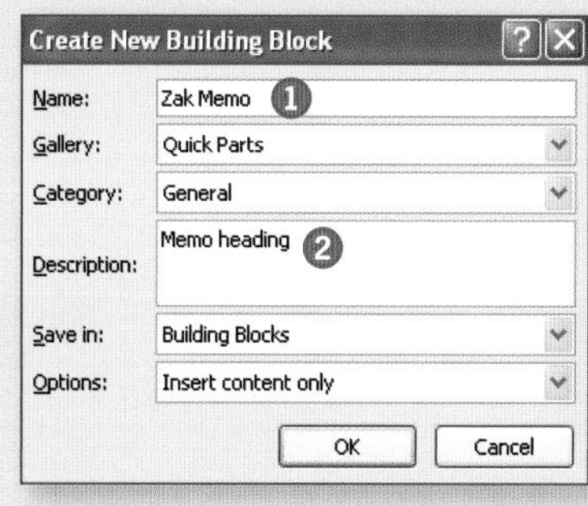

Figure 2.4 Create Building Block

INSERT A QUICK PART

1. Click Quick Parts.
2. Click the Quick Part ❸ you wish to insert from the gallery (Figure 2.5).

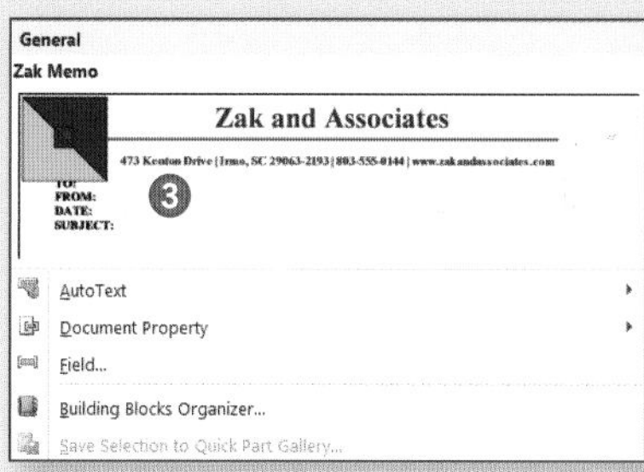

Figure 2.5 Insert Quick Part

Job 9

Excel Worksheets and Charts

KISNER INDUSTRIAL CO

Your next task is to complete an *Excel* workbook for Kisner Industrial Co. Complete the tasks for this job in the following order.

1. Open the *Excel* data file *kisner industrial co.* Save the file as *ip2-j9.* Complete Sheet1 of the workbook.
   a. Rename the sheet tab **Zone**, and change tab color to Purple, Accent 3. In B6, enter a function to calculate the total square feet. Format B3:B6 using the Comma style with no decimals. Apply the Total style to A6:B6.
   b. Create a 3-D pie chart, and embed at A8; drag to fill the range A8:G23. Use Figure IP2.6 as a guide to format the pie chart. Choose Layout 6 with data labels and legend, add chart title, format chart area with gradient fill and thick rounded borders, add text box with same fill as chart area and border and shadow effect of your choice, and change font of data labels to light color for contrast.

TIP

If the plot area is too large, select it and drag the corner handles to make it smaller. Then move the plot area to center it in the chart area.

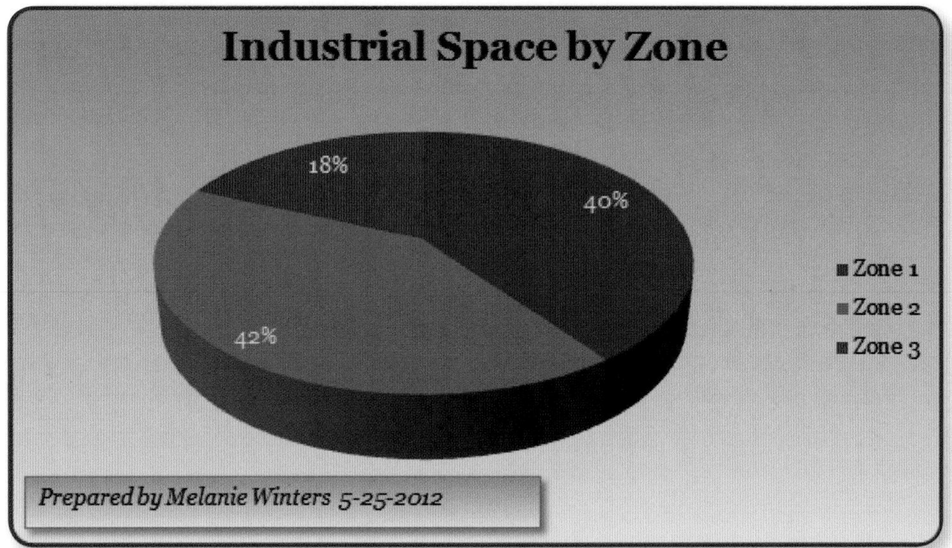

Figure IP2.6 Pie Chart on Zone Sheet

2. Complete Sheet2 of the workbook.
   a. Rename the second sheet tab **Occupancy**; change tab color to Teal, Accent 2.
      Merge and center the title in A across columns A–E, and center the text vertically in the cell. Apply Title style and change the row height of row 1 to 36.00 points.
      Merge and center the column heading Square Footage Surveyed across columns B–E. Apply Heading 4.
      Apply the Heading 3 style to the column headings in B3:E3.
      Format all cells with numbers with the Comma style and no decimal places. Apply the Total style to the total row. Size columns attractively.
      Insert the Column sparkline to display in F4:F7. In F3, key the column heading **Trend**.
      Enter a function in E4 and B8 to calculate the totals. Copy to appropriate cells.
   b. Select A4:A7 and E4:E7, and create a 3-D bar chart. Embed at A11 and drag to fill the range A11:F25. Use Figure IP2.7 as a guide to format the bar chart. Choose Layout 5, add a chart title, format chart area with gradient fill and thick rounded borders, and add callout shape with WordArt text.

TIP

When selecting nonadjacent range, press CTRL and select the second range.

Apply It

Document 3
Memo from Template

ZAK MEMO

1. Click Sample Templates and preview the different types of templates shown. Scroll through the templates, noting the types that are featured. Note the categories of additional templates that may be downloaded from Office.com. Fax, letter, and resume templates are included. For this document, you will use the template in your data files.
2. Double-click *zak memo* to open the template file; save it as a *Word* document named *wd2-d3* in your solution files.
3. Key the memo on page 6 that you reviewed earlier in this lesson. Pay particular attention to the formatting information contained in the memo and the callouts on the full-page model.
4. Proofread and preview carefully. Check your document against the one in your textbook to ensure that you formatted it correctly. Use the Info command on Backstage view to check the information on this document.
5. Resave as *wd2-d3* and close.

Document 4
Memo from a Quick Part

ZAK MEMO

1. Use Recent in Backstage view to open the *zak memo* template again. Use Select All to select everything on the page (Home/Editing/Select/Select All) and save as a Quick Part named *Zak Memo*. Key **Memo heading** in the Description box.
2. Close the template; do not save it.
3. Open a new document and insert the *Zak Memo* Quick Part.
4. Key the memo shown below.
5. Preview, proofread, save as *wd2-d4*, and close.

TIP

Zak does not use a distribution list because it transmits all memos by e-mail. The e-mail distribution list contains the names of the Rex Project Team members.

TO: Rex Project Team | FROM: Jan Bennett | DATE: Current | SUBJECT: Client Follow-up

The plans and drawings for the Rex Project that were approved by our team at our last meeting were submitted to Bill Rex the next day. Bill called me today to indicate that his group was very pleased with the first draft. He indicated that they would like to meet with our team to go over a few changes that need to be made.

Bill requested that we meet at the Rex Plant to review some of the specifications that they have finalized. The meeting is tentatively scheduled for next Tuesday at 2:30 p.m. I will arrange to use the company van so that we can all go together. We will need to meet in the lobby of our building at about 1:45 p.m.

Please let me know if you will be able to attend the meeting. This meeting will be an important one, and I hope everyone will be able to attend.

xx

Job 8

Merge Form Letter and Labels with Access Database Query

MAKISNER
MARKETANALYSIS LETTERHEAD

Review Module 6, Lessons 3 and 5, to create queries and use a database to create labels.

In this job, you will create a query in the *makisner* database that you will use in a form letter, which will be sent to Zone 2 occupants. The form letter solicits information regarding a landuse market survey. You will also use the query to create the mailing labels for this mailout. Complete the tasks for this job in the following order.

1. **Create query.** Open the *Access* data file *makisner*. Save the database as *ip2-j8a*. Using the Occupants table, create a query for occupants located in Zone 2. Since this query will be used for a mail merge letter, insert in the query the fields that will be used for a letter address, and use the Zone field to identify Zone 2 occupants. Sort the query by postal code in ascending order, and do not show the Zone field in the query results. Name the query **Zone 2 Survey Request**.
2. **Complete mail merge letters.** Open the *Word* data file *marketanalysis letterhead*, and save as *ip2-j8b main*. Prepare the main document for the mail merge using the text shown below. Select the Zone 2 Survey Request as the recipient list. Insert the letter address merge fields and the City merge field as indicated below. Save the merged document as *ip2-j8b*.
3. **Create mail merge mailing labels in *Access* for the Zone 2 letters.** Choose the Labels report (Create/Reports/Labels) to create mailing labels (Avery 5160) using the Zone 2 Survey Request query. Insert the appropriate merge fields on the label. Sort the labels by postal code. Use the default report name for the labels report. Ignore any error messages regarding lost data. Remember, the labels are saved as a report in the *Access* database.

Text for form letter:

MarketAnalysis, Inc. is conducting a survey of industrial manufacturing, warehouse, and distribution space in Fayette and Clark counties. The goal of this market study is to provide information on trends in the industrial real estate market. This information is not currently available in «City» through any other source.

Your property has been identified as an industrial property by your county assessor's office. To assist us in making this study as complete as possible, please take a few minutes to fill out the survey in one of the following ways:

1. Return the enclosed survey in the preaddressed, postage-paid envelope.
2. Fax the completed survey to 606-555-0129.
3. Complete the survey form online at www.marketanalysis.com.

While the specific information you provide in the survey will not be published, the aggregate results of this study will be available to you through various reports such as the Thoroughbred Real Estate Report.

Since our time is relatively short, please respond as quickly as possible so that we can include your property in our survey.

Sincerely

In addition, you may view an abstract of this study at the website www.marketanalysis.com/market_surveys.htm.

LESSON

3

Multiple-Page Documents

OBJECTIVES

- Create multiple-page letters
- Create multiple-page memos
- Create second-page headers
- Learn and apply *Word* commands

SECOND-PAGE HEADINGS

The majority of letters and memos are one-page documents, but a substantial number may have two or more pages. A heading should be keyed on the second and subsequent pages consisting of the recipient's name, the page number, and the date. See Figure 3.1.

Ms. Margaret V. Glenn, Director
Page 2
June 11, 20--

Even Page Header

Figure 3.1 Second-Page Heading

Companies may use the header area of a document to insert letterhead elements, such as company logo, name, or address. This header automatically displays on subsequent pages, in the space you would use to insert the second-page heading. To solve this problem, you must create different headers for the first and second pages of the document.

One way to do this is to use different odd and even page headers. However, this does not work for documents longer than two pages. For long documents, you must create sections so you can use different types of headers and footers.

Word Skills

DIFFERENT ODD & EVEN PAGES

Header & Footer Tools Design/Different Odd & Even Pages

1. When text flows to the second page of a letter or memo, double-click in the header area to open the header and display the Header & Footer Design tools. See Figure 3.2.
2. Click Different Odd & Even Pages to check it. Note that if letterhead was included in the header, it disappears.
3. Key recipient's name. On the next line, key **Page** and then insert the page number: click Page Number and then Current Position to display the options. See Figure 3.3.
4. Click Plain Number to insert the page number.
5. Insert the current date on the third line. Do not update automatically unless the date on the first page of the letter or memo is updated automatically.
6. Close the header and finish keying the document.

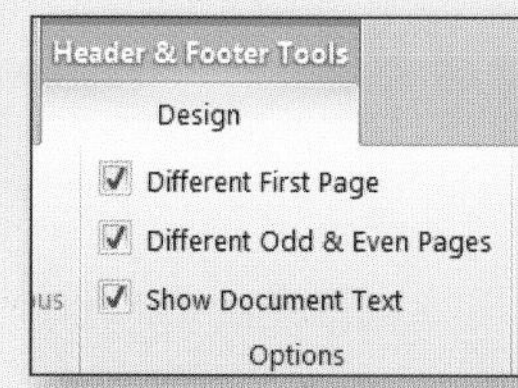

Figure 3.2 Design Tools

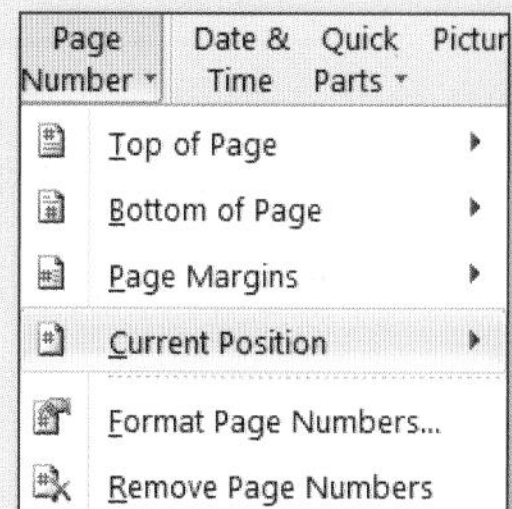

Figure 3.3 Insert Page Number

Margins: .75" top and bottom; .5" left and right

Industrial Distribution, Warehouse, and Manufacturing Space

3 pt line

Fayette and Clark Counties

6.25" underline tab

1.0 line spacing *3.0" underline tab* *3.25" left tab*

Property Address

Street: ____________ City: ____________
9-pt Georgia
ZIP Code: ________ County: ________ Industrial Real Estate Zone: ________

11-pt Georgia Bold

Building

Square footage: ________ ______% Owner-occupied ______% Leased ______% Vacant

10-pt Georgia

Occupants ☐ Single occupant in building ☐ Multiple occupants in building

Space requirements

Next 12 months ☐ Increase expected ☐ Decrease expected ☐ No change expected

Rental rate per square foot per year $ ____________ ☐ Net ☐ Gross

6.25" underline tab

Lease expiration date Month/Year ______/______ Square footage that becomes available ________

6 pt line

Future rental needs: *←11-pt Georgia Bold→* **Property contact:**

1.5 line spacing *1.15 line spacing*

3.0 underline tab *4.25" underline tab*

8 pt *8 pt*

Name: ____________
Title: ____________
Organization: ____________
Telephone: ____________
E-mail: ____________
Street: ____________
City: ____________
State: ______ ZIP Code: ____________

☐ **Please send me a copy of the completed study results.**

Thank you for completing this survey. Send completed forms to:

Small caps

MarketAnalysis, Inc.
P. O. Box 5643
Lexington, KY 40515-5643

OR

FAX: 606 555-0129

Figure IP2.5 Survey Form

Apply It

Document 5
Two-Page Letter

R&M LETTERHEAD

1. Open the *r&m letterhead* template from the data files, and save as a *Word* document named *wd3-d5*. Date the letter June 11, 20--
2. Key the letter shown below to:

Ms. Margaret V. Glenn, Director | Mountain View College Foundation | 586 West Elk Avenue | Elizabethton, TN 37643-2528 | Dear Ms. Glenn

3. Use the following closing lines:

Sincerely | Russell M. Rockafellow | Partner | xx | Enclosure: Description of Properties | c Richard R. Meekins

4. Add an appropriate second-page heading using Different Odd & Even Pages.
5. Proofread, preview, and print. Resave as *wd3-d5*.

This letter provides a report of my June 7 trip to Roan Mountain, Watauga, and Johnson City to evaluate the three parcels of property that donors have proposed giving to the Mountain View College Foundation.

Roan Mountain Property—this 200-acre tract of land is located near Roan Mountain State Park with its famed Rhododendron Gardens. The property has been in the family of the proposed donor for several generations and has never been placed on the market. Portions of the property have been used for tree farms in the past. The trees on these farms have not been tended or harvested since the donor became a widow approximately ten years ago.

Considering its location, it is not likely to have any environmental problems nor does it have any wetlands on the property. The property appears to have significant value as a tree farm or for future development. East Tennessee Appraisal Services has been commissioned to appraise the property and provide us with a current appraisal based on its highest and best use. This property should be accepted.

Watauga Property—this 25-acre tract has approximately one thousand feet of frontage on deep water on the Watauga Lakes. The setting for this tract of land is breathtaking. It would be ideal for development, and if developed properly, could be very valuable. Local citizens indicated that the family had been approached on numerous occasions to sell the property, but they declined all offers.

East Tennessee Appraisal Services has been commissioned to appraise the property and provide us with a current appraisal based on its highest and best use. This property should be accepted immediately. There is no downside to accepting this property.

Job 6,
continued

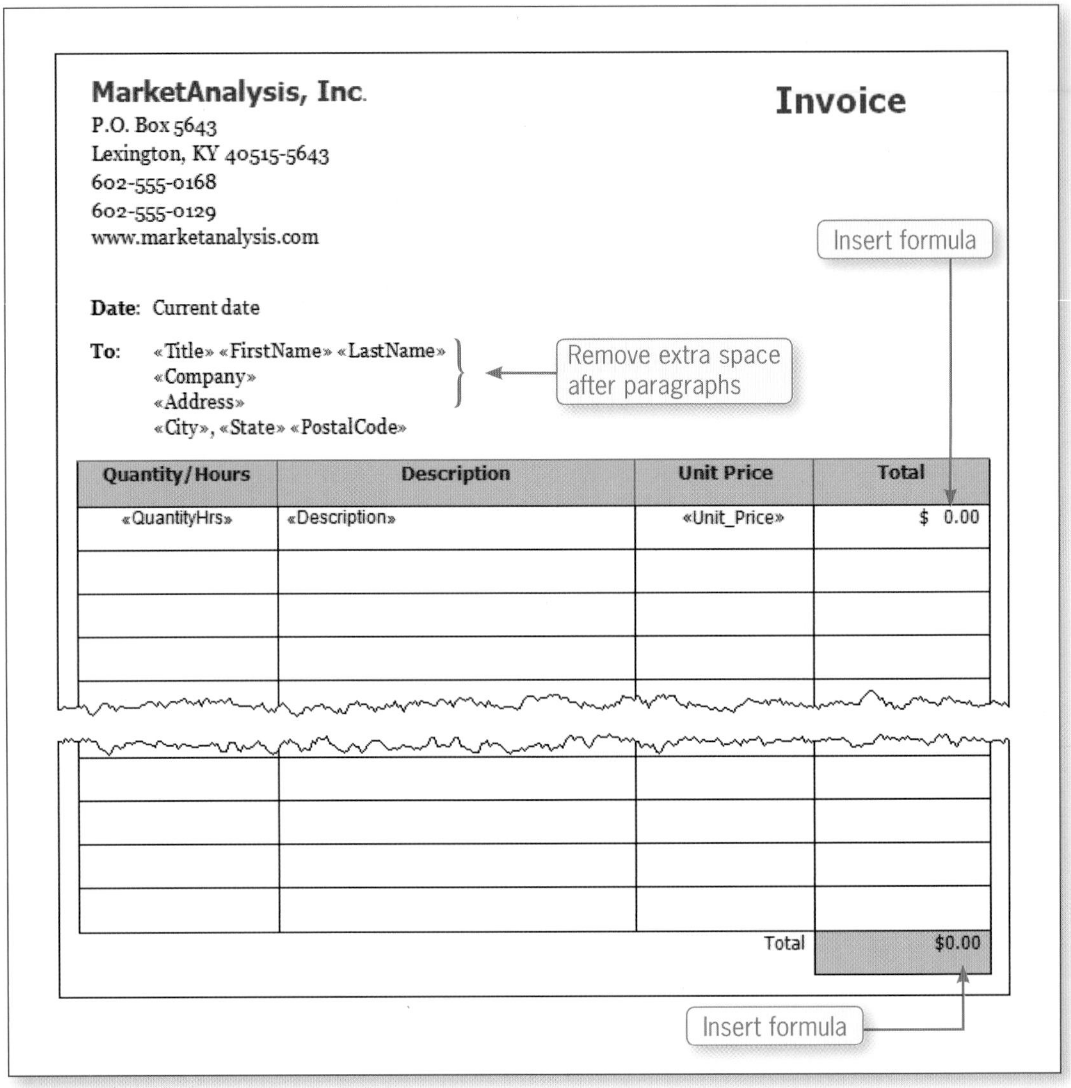

MarketAnalysis, Inc.
P.O. Box 5643
Lexington, KY 40515-5643
602-555-0168
602-555-0129
www.marketanalysis.com

Invoice

Insert formula

Date: Current date

To: «Title» «FirstName» «LastName»
«Company»
«Address»
«City», «State» «PostalCode»

Remove extra space after paragraphs

Quantity/Hours	Description	Unit Price	Total
«QuantityHrs»	«Description»	«Unit_Price»	$ 0.00
		Total	$0.00

Insert formula

Figure IP2.4 Invoice with Merge Fields

Job 7
Survey Form

MA LOGO

Create the survey form shown in Figure IP2.5 on the following page. Use the handwritten notes on the form to guide you.

Reminders:

1. Use WordArt to create the form title.
2. Adjust space before and after paragraphs to make fine adjustments.
3. Set underline tab leaders to ensure that blank lines at the end of the lines end at the same place.
4. Change line spacing as indicated.
5. After inserting the *ma logo* graphic from the data files in the upper-left corner of the form, change text wrapping to square, and position the logo and text as shown.
6. Attach your *Word* file to the *Kisner Industrial Co.* page under *Projects* in the *OneNote* notebook. Reposition the sections in the MarketAnalysis notebook so that they display in alphabetical order.

Document 5, continued

Johnson City Property—this property consists of four lots that were acquired through foreclosure proceedings. The lots are located near an industrial area that could easily have environmental contamination. The property could best be described as depressed. Area citizens indicated that the property had been on the market for approximately two years and appeared to attract very little interest from potential buyers.

The property should not be accepted without appropriate environmental testing. It is also doubtful that a clear title could be obtained. Based on the poor condition of the property, it did not appear prudent to order an appraisal of the property. The best course of action may be to decline this proposed gift.

A more complete description of the properties is attached. As soon as I receive the appraisals of the Roan Mountain and Watauga Lakes properties, I will schedule an appointment to provide you with my recommendations for the properties.

Document 6

Two-Page Memo

XYZ MEMO

1. Open the *xyz memo* template from the data files, and save as a document named *wd3-d6*.
2. Key the memo shown below to **Mason M. McLendon** from you; copy Lee Sanderson.
3. Use the current date and the subject **Effective Time Management**.
4. Include an appropriate second-page header using the Different Odd & Even Pages option. Include the attachment notation for the handout. When you key documents for yourself, do not include reference initials.
5. Preview and proofread carefully. Resave as *wd3-d6* and close.

At our last meeting, you asked me to share my thoughts on ways to manage time effectively and to summarize guides that I believe should be incorporated in our new Management Training Program. This memo contains my thoughts on the topic and the key elements that I believe we should emphasize in the program. I have also attached a handout that Lee Sanderson and I used in a previous training program.

Time is an interesting concept to study because it is one of the few resources that is distributed equally. Everyone has exactly the same amount of time. Effective time management focuses on how time is used.

Successful people often share a common trait—they use their time effectively and they respect the time of others. Using time effectively requires both a healthy attitude about time and many time management skills.

Good time managers understand and appreciate the value of time and desire to use it effectively. Respecting the time of others is a part of that attitude. If you cannot meet a deadline, letting the person involved know ahead of time enables him or her to take action to minimize the effects of your being late. Being proactive and informing people before a deadline takes far less time than being reactive and trying to explain why you did not do what was expected.

Job 5

Fax with Excel Data

MARKETANALYSIS THIRD QUARTER

Use the fax cover sheet template created in Job 4 to create a fax to Hiren Patel. Save as *ip2-j5a*.

Figure IP2.2 Patel Business Card

1. Complete the heading information using the data from the business card as shown in Figure IP2.2 with the subject **Third Quarter Sales**. In the CC row, key Whitney Rice. Key an **x** in the box to the left of *Please review* at the bottom of the form. Then key the following body text.

   Here are the latest sales figures. As you can see, we are up 4 percent over last quarter. Let's get together and discuss the numbers in greater detail over lunch. Give me a call when you get back in town.

2. Edit the *Excel* data file *marketanalysis third quarter* by inserting a function in E3 to calculate a total. Copy the formula down through E14. Save the file as *ip2-j5b*. Copy A2:E14 and use Paste Special to embed the copied data on the fax sheet below the paragraph as shown in Figure IP2.3. Adjust the size as necessary to fit the table on the page, and center the table horizontally on the page.

DISCOVER

Home/Clipboard/Paste

1. Click arrow on Paste command.
2. Click Paste Special.
3. Click Microsoft Office Excel Worksheet Object in As list.
4. Click OK.

RE: Third Quarter Sales

COMMENTS:
Here are the latest sales figures. As you can see, we are up 4 percent over last quarter. Let's get together and discuss the numbers in greater detail over lunch. Give me a call when you get back in town.

	July	Aug	Sept	Total
Stewart, Matthew	67,580	65,790	65,790	199,160
Lowell, Dawn	65,990	58,670	67,590	192,250
Homgren, David	65,450	67,555	56,440	189,445
Magee, Lucia	65,450	76,565	45,675	187,690
Delucca, Roberto	65,450	56,565	56,675	178,690
Carline, Fracyne	55,565	45,340	65,455	166,360
Rodriguez, Jamie	65,450	46,450	50,400	162,300
Caminski, Laurel	50,000	45,000	47,000	142,000
Johnson, Davita	46,000	45,000	50,000	141,000
Wilson, Elvira	47,000	45,705	46,590	139,295
Hiren, Daniel	45,555	35,600	45,600	126,755
Lafrence, Charles	36,000	37,000	38,000	111,000

Figure IP2.3 *Excel* Data Inserted in Fax

Job 6

Mail Merge with Access Database Query

INVOICE
MAKISNER

It is time to bill the customers in Zone 4. You have been asked to create the mail merge document for merging the invoices for these customers. Open the *Word* data file *invoice* and save it as *ip2-j6a main*. Open the *Access* data file *makisner*, and save it as *ip2-j6b*. Select the Zone 4 query from the database as the recipient list for the mail merge. Refer to Figure IP2.4 for the location of the merge fields.

In D2, insert a formula to multiply Quantity/Hours times Unit Price. In D14, insert a formula to sum all the rows above. Choose the Currency format for both formulas.

Save the merged invoices as *ip2-j6a*.

Document 6,
continued

The skills needed to manage time are being able to assess what is really important, being able to judge how much time to spend on something, and being able to prioritize. Effective use of time requires you to focus on the top priority at the moment and to avoid distractions, even when they are interesting and enticing.

How much time it takes to complete a given task often depends on the resources that are available and how effectively those resources are used. Resources include people, tools, information, money, and a host of other assets. Too often people spend time trying to figure out how to do something rather than seeking help from someone who has the requisite knowledge or tools and would willingly assist with the task.

Good planning and organization enhance the ability to accomplish a task. Working smarter produces better results than just working faster or harder.

Specific guides for managing time effectively are summarized below.

1. List the things that have to be done. List everything that is important.
2. Classify the things that have to be done into three or four groups based on their priority.
3. Complete the tasks with the highest priority first. Then move to the next level and do those things. Follow this procedure until you have completed all tasks.
4. Handle paper only once. Going through documents and putting them back on the desk to deal with later often requires more time than completing the tasks right away.
5. Be organized. Much time is wasted looking for things.
6. Prepare a schedule and stick to it.

Good time management is important. It ensures that we do the important things first and that we plan time for all the things that are truly important to us, including leisure and fun activities.

JOB KNOWLEDGE

Use these guides to select an appropriate salutation or greeting:

- Use a person's last name plus a courtesy title when you know the name (*Dear Mr. Ray; Dear Ms. Bass*).
- Use *Ladies and Gentlemen* when a letter is addressed to a company.
- Use *Dear* plus the position name when you do not know the individual's name (*Dear Sales Manager*).

Use these guides to select an appropriate complimentary close (only the first word is capitalized):

- Generally use *Sincerely*; to be less formal, use *Cordially* or similar closings.
- For very formal documents, use *Very truly yours* or *Sincerely yours*.
- To pay special respect to an older or very high ranking person, use *Respectfully yours*.

Job 3
Presentation

OUTLINE
MARKETANALYSIS LETTERHEAD

Ms.Winters requests that you create a *PowerPoint* presentation using her outline. Open the *Word* data file *outline* in *PowerPoint*, and edit this presentation that explains the market study of Fayette and Clark counties. Ms. Winters will add additional information to the slide show after your work is completed.

Requirements for the presentation:

1. Display each slide and click Reset in the Slides group on the Home tab to apply the correct theme formats.
2. Change the layout of slide 1 to Title Slide. Add a text box and key **Presented by Melanie Winters | Project Coordinator**.
3. Customize the Slide Master layout by inserting the logo and company name at the bottom left of the slide. Copy the company name from the *marketanalysis letterhead* data file. Size the logo and text appropriately. Then copy the graphic and text to the Title Slide layout.

4. Insert clip art (may include photographs) of your choice on two slides. Apply a picture style and border on at least one clip.
5. Cut the bulleted text on slide 2. Create a text box with a gradient fill and an attractive border, and paste the cut text in it. Format text as desired.
6. Convert two of the bulleted lists to SmartArt.
7. Use the Rehearse Timings command to apply automatic timings. Then run the slide show to make sure timings are adequate.
8. Print handouts nine per page.
9. Attach the *PowerPoint* file to the *PowerPoint Presentations* page under *Projects* in the *OneNote* notebook.

Job 4
Customize Fax Template

MARKETANALYSIS LETTERHEAD

You have been asked to create a customized fax cover sheet template for Melanie Winters. Begin by downloading the Urban Fax cover sheet template from *Word*'s Sample templates folder on the New tab in Backstage view. In the top portion of the fax and in the heading, key information requested with appropriate MarketAnalysis information from the *marketanalysis letterhead* data file, as shown in Figure IP2.1. Delete the blank table row after the phone number. Save as a template with the name *marketanalysis fax*.

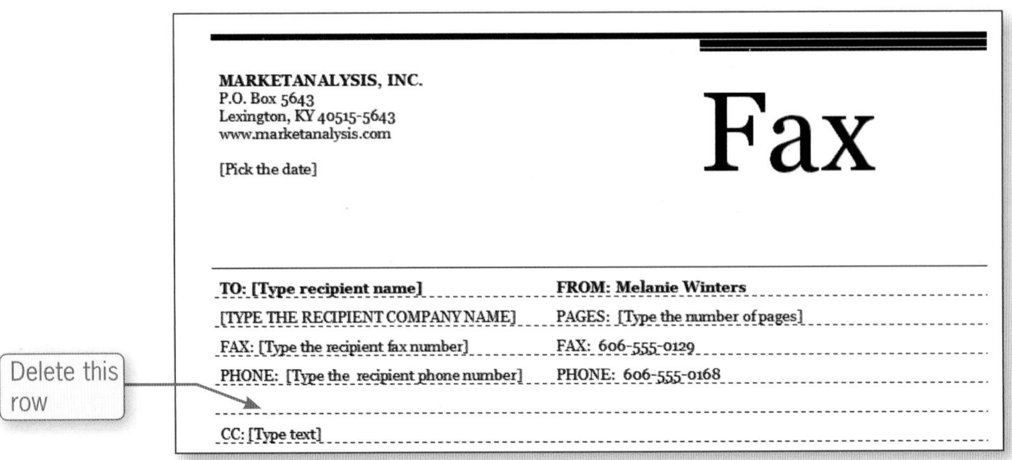

MARKETANALYSIS, INC.
P.O. Box 5643
Lexington, KY 40515-5643
www.marketanalysis.com

[Pick the date]

Fax

TO: [Type recipient name]	**FROM: Melanie Winters**
[TYPE THE RECIPIENT COMPANY NAME]	PAGES: [Type the number of pages]
FAX: [Type the recipient fax number]	FAX: 606-555-0129
PHONE: [Type the recipient phone number]	PHONE: 606-555-0168
CC: [Type text]	

Figure IP2.1 Fax Heading

LESSON 4

Tables

OBJECTIVES

- Create and format tables
- Use table tools for design and layout
- Learn and apply *Word* commands

TABLE STRUCTURE

Tables consist of columns ❶ (vertical lists) and rows ❷ (horizontal lists) that contain alphabetic and/or numeric data. The points at which they intersect are called cells ❸. Columns are referred to by letter and rows by number (Figure 4.1). Tables can be moved using the table move handle ❹ or sized by clicking in the table and then dragging the table size handle ❺.

❹

	❶ Column A	❶ Column B	❶ Column C
❷ Row 1	A1 ❸ Cell A1	B1	C1
❷ Row 2	A2	B2	C2
❷ Row 3	A3	B3	C3 ❸ Cell C3

❺

Figure 4.1 Table Structure

Tables can be created and formatted in several different ways. In this module, you will create tables using the Insert Table command. Then you will use Table Design tools to change the appearance of a table, and the Table Layout tools to add and delete or merge and split rows and columns.

Word Skills

CREATE A TABLE

Insert/Tables/Table

1. Click Table to display the Insert Table grid. Under Insert Table, drag to select the number of rows and columns needed (Figure 4.2). Note that Insert Table changes to the size of the table.
2. Click the left mouse button to display the table in the document.

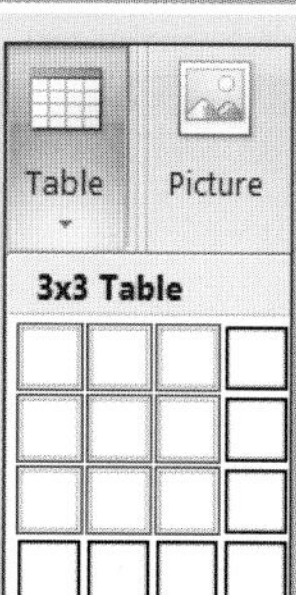

Figure 4.2 Insert Table

DESIGN AND FORMAT A TABLE

1. Click in the table to display the Table Tools tabs. To change the design or format of a table, always begin by clicking in the table.
2. The Design and Layout tabs display below the Table Tools tab (Figure 4.3). Click the Design tab to change the appearance of a table or the Layout tab to change the structure of the table.

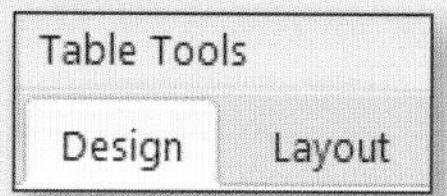

Figure 4.3 Table Tools

Job 1
Outlook Contacts

MarketAnalysis, Inc. uses *Outlook* to keep track of all its contacts. Create a new folder in the Contacts window called Your Name - MA (right-click Contacts folder and choose New Folder). In the Navigation Pane, click the *Your Name* icon.

Key telephone numbers with no hyphens, spaces, or parentheses; *Outlook* automatically inserts them.

1. Add the following contacts to your new folder.

Mr. Jerry Chitturi	Mr. Craig Stern	Ms. Alison Francisco
President	Administrative Assistant	Marketing Manager
Kisner Industrial Co.	MarketAnalysis, Inc.	MarketAnalysis, Inc.
1783 Portland Drive	P.O. Box 5643	P.O. Box 5643
Lexington, KY	Lexington, KY	Lexington, KY
40503-1783	40515-5643	40515-5643
(606) 555-0132	(606) 555-0168	(606) 555-0168

2. Create a business card for yourself and save it in the Your Name - MA contact folder.
3. Send an e-mail to your instructor telling him/her that you are working as an Administrative Assistant for MarketAnalysis. Attach your business card to the e-mail.
4. Print the contact list in Card style.

Job 2
Outlook Tasks

All employees at MarketAnalysis are required to keep their calendars current on *Outlook*. They are also encouraged to keep their "to-do" lists in *Outlook* as items from the Tasks list can easily be converted to calendar items.

1. Create a new folder in Tasks called Your Name - MA. Add the tasks listed below; the tasks are due in July and August of 2012.

Task	Due Date	Special Instructions
Revise survey form	7/2/2012	High Priority
Revise form letter to accompany survey form	7/2/2012	Set a reminder for 9 a.m. on 7/2/2012
Mail survey form with cover letter	7/9/2012	Assign Key Customer category
Finalize script for phone survey	7/16/2012	Assign Urgent category
Compose draft of report	8/3/2012	
Print final copy of report	8/6/2012	Set a reminder for 11 a.m. on 8/6/2012
Compose draft of PowerPoint presentation	8/13/2012	

TIP

Tasks can be placed in ascending or descending order according to due date by clicking on the words *Due Date* in the header row.

2. Update the status of the tasks as follows:
   - *Revise survey form* is now In Progress and is 50 percent complete. The start date on this was 6/25/2012.
   - *Revise form letter to accompany survey form* is now In Progress and is 25 percent complete. This was started on 6/29/2012.
   - *Compose draft of report* is now completed. This was started on 7/30/2012.
3. Display the task list in Detailed List View with tasks listed in ascending order according to Due Date. Print in Table style.

Tables

Region	Quarter 1	Quarter 2	Quarter 3	Quarter 4
North	3,985,678	2,489,956	3,563,098	2,639,034
South	4,140,842	3,987,042	2,845,016	3,092,587
East	2,536,820	3,750,023	5,092,120	3,062,034
West	3,712,083	2,435,762	3,742,831	2,985,824
Totals				

Figure 4.4 Table Created

ANNUAL SALES BY REGION					
Region	Quarter 1	Quarter 2	Quarter 3	Quarter 4	Annual
North	3,985,678	2,489,956	3,563,098	2,639,034	12,677,766
South	4,140,842	3,987,042	2,845,016	3,092,587	14,065,487
East	2,536,820	3,750,023	5,092,120	3,062,034	14,440,997
West	3,712,083	2,435,762	3,742,831	2,985,824	12,876,500
Totals	14,375,423	12,662,783	15,243,065	11,779,479	54,060,750

Figure 4.5 Table Formatted

Word Skills

ADD A COLUMN OR ROW

Table Tools Layout/Rows & Columns

1. Click in the column where you want to add another column, and then click Insert Left (or Insert Right) (Figure 4.6).
2. Click in the row where you want to add another row, and then click Insert Above (or Insert Below).

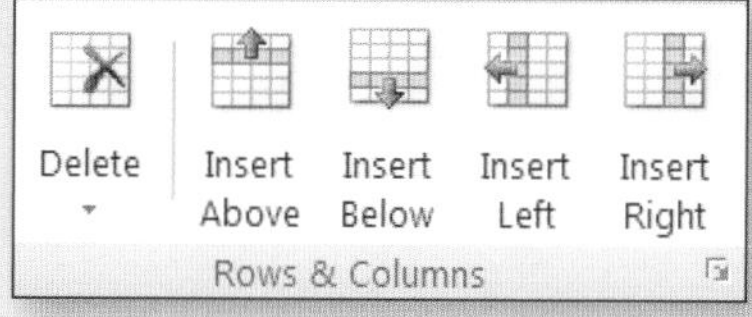

Figure 4.6 Rows & Columns

MERGE OR SPLIT CELLS

Table Tools Layout/Merge/Merge Cells or Split Cells

1. Select the cells you want to merge and click Merge Cells (Figure 4.7).
2. Click in the cell you wish to split, and click Split Cells; then indicate the number of columns and rows, and click OK.

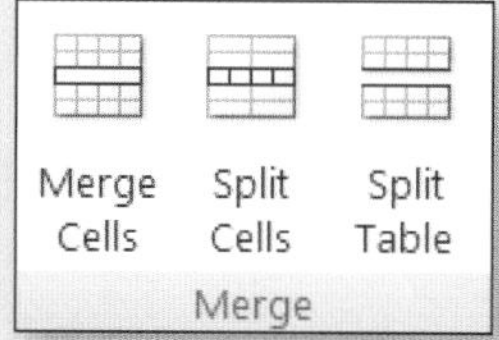

Figure 4.7 Merge

SUM A COLUMN OR ROW

Table Tools Layout/Data/Formula

1. Click in the cell below the column you want to sum, and then click Formula to display the Formula dialog box with the SUM formula in the Formula text box (Figure 4.8).
2. Select the number format desired, and click OK.
3. Click in the cell to the right of the row you want to sum, and then click Formula to display the Formula dialog box. The formula changes to =SUM(LEFT); click OK.

Figure 4.8 Sum Above

To sum left for a series of rows, start with the bottom row and move up the rows to sum them. If you start with row 1, the formula will change to SUM(LEFT) for that row. However, in row 2, the formula will be SUM(ABOVE) and you will have to change it for each remaining row to SUM(LEFT).

integrated project 2

MarketAnalysis, Inc.: Integrating All Microsoft Office Applications

OBJECTIVES

- Create effective *Word, PowerPoint, Excel, Access,* and *Publisher* documents
- Use *Outlook* to maintain contact lists and manage tasks
- Use *OneNote* to maintain and share company files on the SkyDrive
- Create integrated documents using the *Microsoft Office* suite
- Work with very limited supervision

SETTING

MarketAnalysis, Inc., located in Lexington, Kentucky, is a management consulting firm with an outstanding statewide reputation in analyzing market data. The company assigns each project to a team led by a project coordinator. The Kisner Industrial Co. has commissioned MarketAnalysis, Inc. to conduct a study to determine real estate trends in Fayette and Clark counties. Melanie Winters, project coordinator, asked you to work on the part of the study that deals with commercial manufacturing real estate utilization in these two counties.

JOBS

1. *Outlook* contacts and tasks
2. *Word* templates
3. *PowerPoint* presentations with handouts and data using an *Access* query
4. Mail merge invoice, letters, and labels using *Access* database
5. *Excel* worksheets and charts
6. Report with preliminary pages and embedded *Excel* charts with captions
7. Forms
8. Newsletter using *Publisher*
9. *OneNote* notebook shared on SkyDrive

STANDARD OPERATING PROCEDURES

Use these procedures for all documents you prepare. You will not be reminded to do these things during the project.

1. Use Urban theme for all documents.
2. Format reports as leftbound reports.
3. Use MarketAnalysis letterhead from the data files, block letter format with open punctuation, and an appropriate salutation and closing.
4. Proofread, preview, and print all documents.
5. Set up a folder named Integrated Project 2, and save all project files in it. Name all solution files *ip2-j* (plus the job number, *j1*, *j2*, etc.) unless another solution name is provided.
6. Prepare the notebook described in the *request* data file.

REQUEST
NEWSLETTER
ASSIGNMENTS

APPLY A TABLE STYLE

Table Tools Design/Table Styles

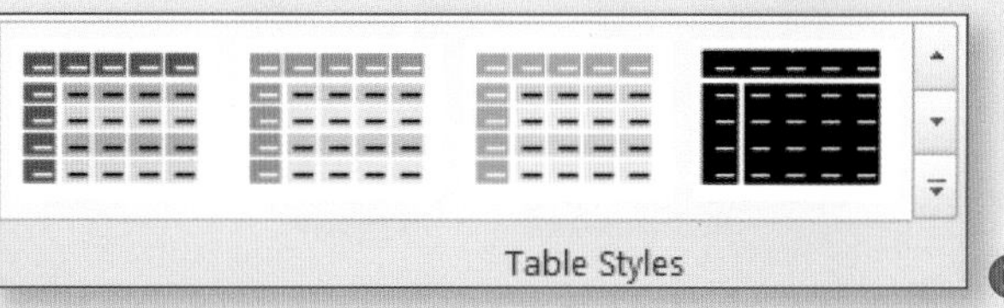

Figure 4.9 Table Styles

1. Click in the table, and then click the More button 1 at the right side of Table Styles. Scroll down to the desired style such as Medium Grid 3 – Accent 5 (Figure 4.9).
2. Hover the mouse over the style to preview it and then click to apply it.

AUTOFIT CONTENTS OF A TABLE

Table Tools Layout/Size/AutoFit

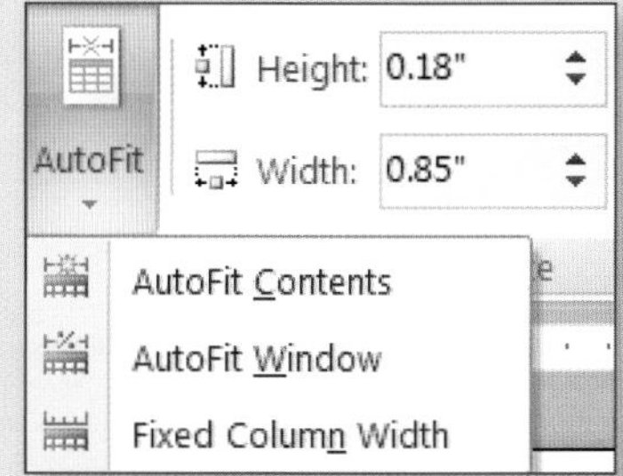

Figure 4.10 AutoFit Contents

1. Click in the table and then click the AutoFit command.
2. Click Autofit Contents (Figure 4.10).

Apply It

Document 7

Create and Format Table

TIP

Note that if you format cells using features such as bold or alignment, when you apply a table style those formats are likely to change. If you want specific formats such as headings bold and centered, apply the formats after you have applied the style.

1. Key the five-column, six-row table shown in Figure 4.4 on the previous page; position at about 2".
2. Click in column E (Quarter 4) and insert a column on the right. Key **Annual** as the column heading.
3. Click in row 1 and insert a row above it; select and merge all cells in the row. Key the title **ANNUAL SALES BY REGION**; center and bold it.
4. Click in each blank cell in the bottom row and sum the column; use whole number format.
5. Click in each blank cell in the last column and sum the row; use whole number format.
6. Click in the table and apply Medium Grid 3 – Accent 5, from the table styles. Center and bold the headings in columns B through F.
7. Click in the table and use AutoFit Contents to size it.
8. Preview and proofread; check numbers (Figure 4.4) and the style (Figure 4.5). Save as *wd4-d7* and close.

Word Skills

ALIGNMENT

Table Tools Layout/Alignment

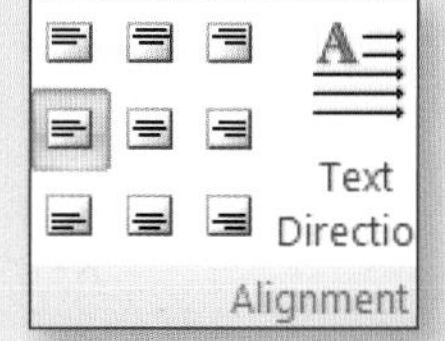

Figure 4.11 Alignment

1. Select the cells you wish to align vertically and horizontally. Hover the mouse over each illustration (Figure 4.11) to display the ScreenTip.
2. Click the alignment desired.

ROW HEIGHT

Table Tools Layout/Cell Size

1. Click in the row whose height you want to change.
2. Click the up or down arrows to increase or decrease row height.

MARKETANALYSIS, INC.: INTEGRATING ALL MICROSOFT OFFICE APPLICATIONS

overview

Integrated Project 2 is designed to reinforce your mastery of all Microsoft Office applications presented in this textbook. You will complete a number of jobs using one application; however, the major thrust of this module is for you to understand the power of integrating software applications and applying them in a realistic setting. Integrated jobs you will complete include:

- *Word* fax template using *Excel* worksheet
- *Word* mail merge documents using *Access* queries
- *PowerPoint* presentation using *Access* data
- *Word* report using *Excel* charts
- *Publisher* newsletter using *Excel* and *Access* data
- *OneNote* notebook
- Web Apps using SkyDrive

JOBS

1. Outlook Contacts
2. Outlook Tasks
3. PowerPoint Presentation from Word Document
4. Word Fax Template
5. Word Fax Document with Excel Data
6. Word Mail Merge with Access Database Query
7. Word Survey Form
8. Word Form Letter and Labels Using Access Database Query
9. Excel Worksheets and Charts
10. Formal Word Business Report with Excel Charts
11. PowerPoint Presentation with Access Query
12. Publisher Newsletter with Excel and Access Data

Document 8
Format Table

RESTAURANT ANALYSIS

1. Open *restaurant analysis* and format the table as shown in Figure 4.12.
2. Apply Medium Grid 3 – Accent 1 from Table Styles to the table.
3. Split rows 2–7 in column C into four columns. Key the ratings shown in Figure 4.12; apply Align Center to everything in the table except column A. Apply Align Center Left to column A.
4. Select cells A1 and A2 and merge them; do the same for cells B1 and B2.
5. Click in row 1 and insert a row above it. Key the title **COMPETITIVE RESTAURANT ANALYSIS**. Increase the font size to 14 point, and apply Align Center.
6. Bold all column heads except for *Restaurant*, which is already bold.
7. Increase the height of row 1 to .5"; select all the other rows, and increase the height to .3".
8. Preview and proofread carefully. Save as *wd4-d8* and close.

COMPETITIVE RESTAURANT ANALYSIS					
Restaurant	**Number of Ratings**	**Quality Rating (High 4)**			
		4	**3**	**2**	**1**
Abbott Seafood	38	20	12	6	0
Chez Patrick	34	24	10	0	0
Ristorante LaMarca	40	26	11	2	1
Redman Steak House	32	10	12	6	4
Yen's Garden	38	14	12	8	4

Figure 4.12 Document 8 Illustration

Document 9
Format Table

1. Key and format the following table in an attractive, effective style of your choice.
2. Use the SUM function to complete all of the blank cells; apply AutoFit to Contents.
3. Save as *wd4-d9* and close.

SALES SUMMARY			
Quarter	Equipment	Supplies	Total Sales
First	219,475	108,963	
Second	238,907	125,872	
Third	240,106	138,760	
Fourth	230,437	132,694	
Total			

Job 4

Attach Word File

RECOMMENDATIONS

1. Add the *recommendations* file from your data files to the ICA Module 9 Solutions folder in My Documents on the SkyDrive. Rename it *p12-j4*.
2. Double-click the file to open it; copy it; then open the notebook in *OneNote*, and paste the content on the Recommendations page.
3. Add a new page under the *Trip* section named *Schedule*. At the top of the page, create a "To Do" tag, and key short reminders of the three items listed under *Transportation and Scheduling* on the Recommendations page.

Job 5

Create PowerPoint File and View on SkyDrive

BAILEY
BEDENBEAU LOGO
SHARON SCHMOHE
TOP SALES TEAM
TRAVIS DAVIS

1. Use the information in the *bailey* data file to create a *PowerPoint* presentation for Carolyn Bailey.
2. Save it in your solutions folder as *p12-j5*.
3. Add it to the ICA Module 9 Solutions folder in My Documents on the SkyDrive.
4. View the presentation using Slide Show on the View tab.

Unbound Reports with Track Changes

LESSON 5

OBJECTIVES

- Format unbound reports
- Apply document themes and styles
- Work with comments and tracked changes
- Learn and apply *Word* commands

REPORTS

Reports are used to provide a record of activities, events, and actions or to transmit information for decision making within or outside an organization. Typically, business reports contain a cover page, a title, a subtitle, and side headings. The appearance of the headings is determined by the document theme and styles applied.

The default 1" margins are used for unbound reports. The first page begins about 2" from the top of the page. Review the full-page report on the next page that illustrates the title, headings, and other formats of the default Office theme. The document was formatted using the Office default document theme. The title and headings are the default headings with the Office document theme. If you select a different document theme, the color and fonts will change to the new color and theme fonts.

DOCUMENT THEMES AND STYLES

Document themes consist of coordinated color themes, heading and body fonts, and effects. Documents created in *Word*, *Excel*, *PowerPoint*, and *Publisher* can use the same themes. The Office theme is used unless you change it.

Preformatted styles such as title and heading styles can be easily applied to text. The size and resolution of your screen determine how many styles display in the Styles gallery.

Word Skills

APPLY DOCUMENT THEMES

Page Layout/Themes/Themes

1. To select a built-in theme, click Themes (Figure 5.1) to display the Themes gallery.
2. Preview the themes and click the one that you want to apply.

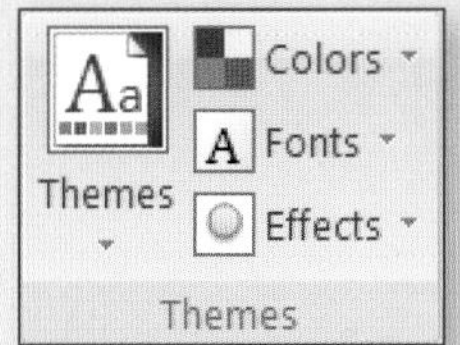

Figure 5.1 Themes

APPLY STYLES

Home/Styles

1. To apply a style, click in the text in which you want to apply the style, and then click the desired style in the Styles gallery (Figure 5.2).
2. To view additional styles, click the More button ❶ to expand the Styles gallery.

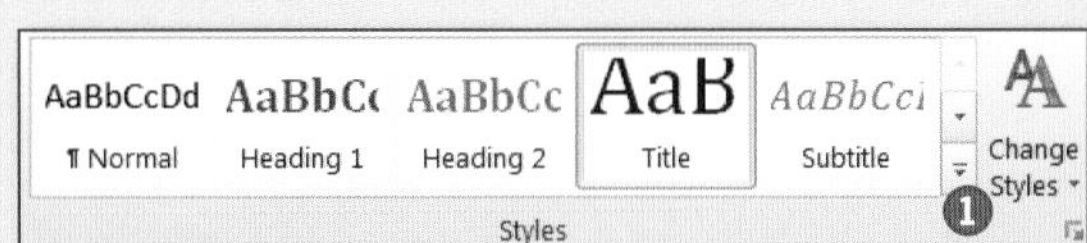

Figure 5.2 Styles

Job 2

Collect and Organize Content

BEDENBEAU MEETING NOTES

1. Open the *Bedenbeau* notebook in *OneNote*, and attach the *Word* data file *bedenbeau meeting notes* to the *Client Meeting* page under the *Planning* section. Open the document, and review all of it very carefully.
2. Several sections in the *bedenbeau meeting notes* document have headings that are the same as a page name in the notebook. Copy the information from each section, and paste it to the page with the same name to organize and simplify the use of the notebook.

Job 3

Create Budget, Add File to SkyDrive, and Add Links

1. In *Excel*, use the information below to create a worksheet. Save it as *p12-j3* in your solution folder.
   a. Use the same general format that was used for the BEI Conference budget you worked with in Module 8.
   b. Complete the totals for column C; after the event, the actual amount and totals will be added to columns D and E.
2. Add the file to the ICA Module 9 Solutions folder in My Documents on the SkyDrive.
3. Open the *Bedenbeau* notebook in *OneNote* on the SkyDrive, and attach the *p12-j3* file to the *Budget* page of the notebook.
4. Click near the top of the *Group Activities* page, and add a link to the *Budget* page; do the same for the *Individual Activities* page.

Budget for President's Club Trip				
Budget Item	**Amount**	**Totals**	**Actual**	**Totals**
Individual Activities				
Allowance 12 @ 300	3,600			
Resort package 14 @ 750	10,500			
Hospitality room	850			
Group Activities				
Welcome reception	450			
Low Country Seafood	1,125			
Awards reception	600			
Awards banquet	1,800			
Band	1,200			
Total				

2"
Tap ENTER 3 times

Title Style →

Business Reports

Subtitle Style → *Writing and Formatting*

1" default margin

Reports provide information used to make decisions or to document activities, events, or transactions. Organizations use both internal and external reports for problem solving. Appropriate formatting not only makes a good first impression; it enhances the readability of a report. Internal reports should be written and formatted with the same care and attention that external reports receive. Reports move up the organizational hierarchy and can have a very positive impact on career upward mobility.

1" default margin

Heading 1 Style →

Components of a Report

Reports typically contain the following components: identifying information, purpose, methods, data analysis, conclusions, recommendations, and a summary. Depending on the length of the report these components may be separate, or they may be combined.

Heading 2 Style →

Identifying Information

Most of the identifying information is contained on the cover page of a report. It may also be placed in a cover letter or in the body of the report.

Purpose

The purpose explains why the report is being written and what objectives are expected to be achieved by writing the report. A purpose clearly stated sets the tone for the remainder of the report.

Methods and Data Analysis

The methods section describes the process used to collect data and analyze the data. The data analysis consists of a discussion of the facts and how they can be interpreted to solve the problem.

Conclusions, Recommendations, and Summary

Conclusions are the results obtained by analyzing and interpreting the data. Recommendations are actions suggested based on the conclusions. The summary presents the highlights of the report.

Heading 1 Style →

Cover Page

A gallery of preformatted cover pages is available in your software. Cover pages can be customized to match an organization's branding and saved for future use.

Figure 5.3 Unbound Report Format

project 12

VanHuss & VanHuss, Inc.: Integrating Word, Excel, PowerPoint, and OneNote

OBJECTIVES

- Create a new notebook and share it on SkyDrive
- Collect and organize content
- Work with *Word, Excel, PowerPoint*, and *OneNote* files on the SkyDrive
- Work independently with few instructions

SETTING

You worked with VanHuss & VanHuss, Inc. in the previous project, and you will have the same position in this project. You will be working with a different client, Bedenbeau, Inc., a company based in Savannah, Georgia, that is contracting with VanHuss & VanHuss, Inc. to host a special event for President's Club winners. As the event manager, you have already met with Mr. Cameron Martinez, Bedenbeau President and CEO, and Ms. Carolyn Bailey, Bedenbeau National Sales Manager, for the initial planning of the President's Club trip.

JOBS

1. Create a new notebook with sections, pages, and subpages and share it on SkyDrive
2. Attach a *Word* document and add content to the notebook
3. Create an *Excel* worksheet for the budget
4. Attach a *Word* document and add content and tags to the notebook
5. Create a *PowerPoint* presentation and view on SkyDrive

Job 1

Share Notebook

1. Use *OneNote* to create a new notebook named **Bedenbeau**; save it in your solution folder.
2. Create two sections, *Planning* and *Trip*, and add the pages and subpages shown below. The pages on the left belong in the *Planning* section, and those on the right belong in the *Trip* section.
3. Then share the notebook on the SkyDrive in a new subfolder under *Office* (not My Documents) named **VanHuss & VanHuss**.

Client Meeting
Event Plans
    Budget
    Recommendations

Events
    Group Activities
    Individual Activities

Apply It

Document 10
Unbound Report

1. Key the report shown on the previous page. Format the title, subtitle, and side headings using the styles illustrated.
2. Preview, proofread, and print. Save as *wd5-d10* and close.

Document 11
Unbound Report

1. Open Document 10 (*wd5-d10*).
2. Preview several themes; note that with some themes the report becomes a two-page report because of the larger font size the theme uses. Apply Grid theme.
3. Preview the report to make sure it fits on one page. Save as *wd5-d11* and close.

COMMENTS

Comments enable multiple reviewers to critique a document and insert comments about it. Comments usually are displayed in balloons. The Comments group provides options for inserting a comment, moving from one comment to another, and deleting a comment.

Word Skills

INSERT A COMMENT
Review/Comments/New Comment

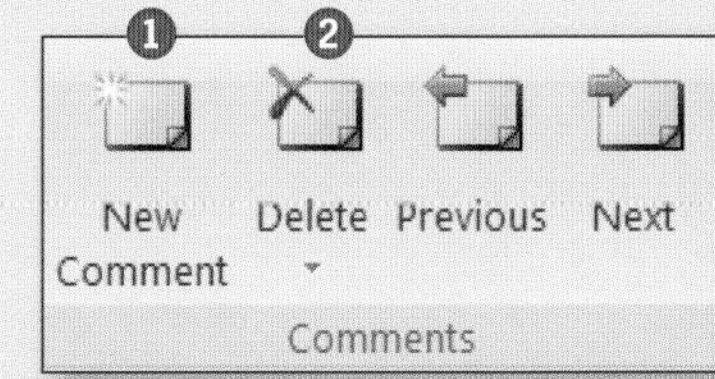

Figure 5.4 Comments Group

1. Select the text or click at the end of the text on which you want to comment.
2. Click New Comment ❶ (Figure 5.4), and key the comment you want to make in the balloon.

RESPOND TO A COMMENT

1. Click the balloon containing the comment to which you want to respond.
2. Click New Comment, and key your response in the New Comment balloon.

DELETE A COMMENT
Review/Comments/Delete

1. Click the balloon containing the comment you want to delete.
2. Click Delete ❷.

File/Options

Before you enter comments or track changes, check to see that your name and initials are in the User Name and Initials boxes on your computer.

TRACK CHANGES

The Track Changes feature is used to track the revisions made in a document. It enables a reviewer to make suggested changes in the form of insertions, deletions, and formatting to text without changing the document. Tracked changes can be accepted into a document or rejected. Comments cannot be accepted and made a part of a document.

Review Changes and Comments

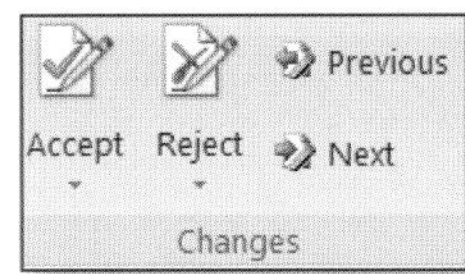

Changes and comments can be reviewed in sequence, and each change can be accepted or rejected using tools in the Changes group. Comments should be deleted because the suggestions do not convert to text. All changes can also be accepted or rejected at one time.

DRILL 1 DOCK TO DESKTOP

1. Select the *Training Program* notebook and the *Training Programs* section; create a subpage under the *Management Development* page and name it *Types of Programs*; then dock the *Management Development* page to the desktop.
2. Open *Internet Explorer* and use *management development program* as keywords to locate content about management development programs.
3. Select an article that describes a management development program. Select the information, and drag it to the *Management Development Programs* page. Note the content may be different from that shown in Figure 3.2.
4. Find one or two articles that relate to types of management development programs and copy content from each to the *Types of Programs* subpage.

SHARE AN EXISTING NOTEBOOK

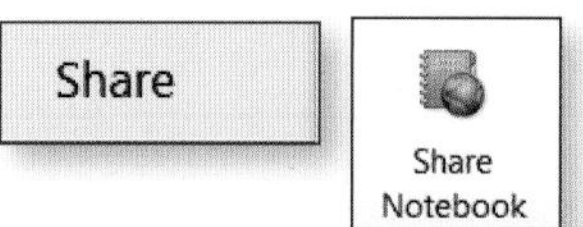

Both new and existing notebooks can be shared with other people or on different computers that you use.

To Share a Notebook:

File/Share/Select Notebook

1. Follow the path and select the notebook that you wish to share.
2. Under Share On, click either Web or Network. To share on SkyDrive, click Web.
3. Under Web Location, click Sign In -or- Windows Live SkyDrive if you have already signed in.
4. Click the desired folder, such as My Documents, and then click Share Notebook.

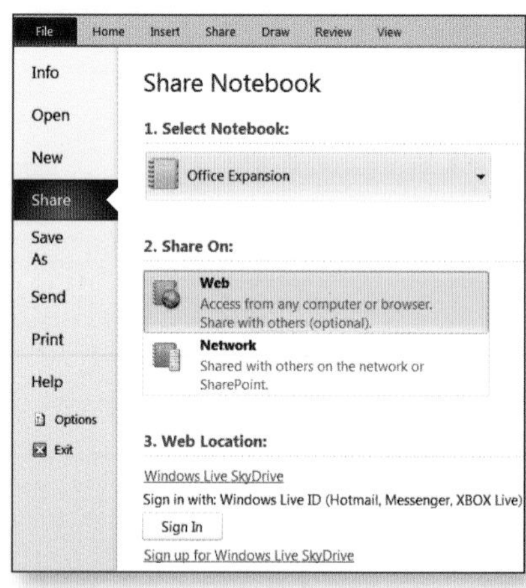

Figure 3.5 Share Notebook

DRILL 2 SHARE A NOTEBOOK

1. Share the *Office Expansion* notebook on your SkyDrive. Place it in the My Documents folder.
2. View the various pages of the notebook.

Apply It

Task 5
Copy Content to Docked Note Pages

MANAGEMENT DEVELOPMENT

1. Share the *Training Program* notebook on your SkyDrive.
2. Open the *Training Program* notebook on the SkyDrive in *OneNote* (not in your browser).
3. Go to the *Management Development* page of the notebook, and dock it to your desktop.
4. Open the *management development PowerPoint* file. Review your notes on the *Management Development* page and review slide 2 of the presentation. If the notes are not visible in the *OneNote* window, remember to use the scroll bar and arrows at the bottom of the *OneNote* window to access them.
5. Use the Next Page command to go to the *Types of Programs* page, and then display slide 3. Note that these two slides contain content similar to the information on the two pages in *OneNote*.

Word Skills

TURN TRACK CHANGES ON OR OFF

Review/Tracking/Track Changes

1. Click Track Changes to turn it on; it turns orange and all changes made in a document will be tracked.
2. To turn Track Changes off, click the highlighted Track Changes command.

ACCEPT OR REJECT CHANGES

Review/Changes/Next or Previous

1. Click Next or Previous.
2. To accept a change, click Accept and Move to Next (Figure 5.5); to reject a change, click Reject and Move to Next.
3. To reject a comment, click Delete in the Comments group.
4. To accept or reject all changes, click Accept All Changes in Document or Reject All Changes in Document.

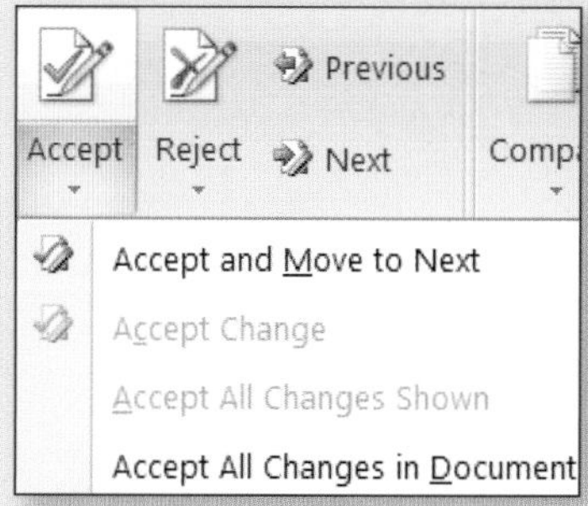

Figure 5.5 Accept Changes

Apply It

Document 12

Report with Track Changes

RECREATION COMPLEX

1. Open *recreation complex* and save it as *wd5-d12*. Click the Review tab and check to see that Track Changes is turned on; apply Adjacency theme.
2. Read the first comment. Then proofread and locate the five uncorrected errors in the document. Correct the errors. Note how Track Changes displays the corrections.
3. Review the changes that are tracked in the document. Accept each insertion and deletion individually. Then delete both comments. Turn Track Changes off.
4. Apply Title style to the title and Heading 1 style to the side headings.
5. Format the table using Light List – Accent 1. Center the title horizontally and vertically. Increase the font to 14 points and the row height to .3". Select the remaining rows and increase the height to .2".
6. Sum columns B and C. Add a $ sign to the totals. Bold the headings. Then select both columns including the heading and click Align Center Right. Select column A and click Align Center Left.
7. Insert the page number using Plain Number 3 positioned at the top right side of the page. Click Different First Page.
8. Proofread and preview. Resave as *wd5-d12* and close.

Document 13

Report with Comments

PROFESSIONAL ATTIRE

1. Open *professional attire* and save it as *wd5-d13*; read the entire report carefully.
2. Follow all directions in comments for formatting the report.
3. Proofread carefully and preview the report. Resave as *wd5-d13*.

LESSON 3

OneNote on the SkyDrive

OBJECTIVES

- Dock *OneNote*
- Linked note taking
- Share notebook on SkyDrive

DOCK ONENOTE

You can take notes in a *OneNote* window about a *Word* or *PowerPoint* document by docking the desired *OneNote* page to the desktop. Notes taken in the *OneNote* window are automatically linked to the material in *Internet Explorer*, *Word*, or *PowerPoint*. The source is automatically added to the *OneNote* page.

To Dock to the Desktop:

View/Views/Dock to Desktop

1. Select the page in a *OneNote* notebook to which you want to add notes.
2. Follow the path to display the *OneNote* page in a window at the side of your desktop (Figure 3.1).

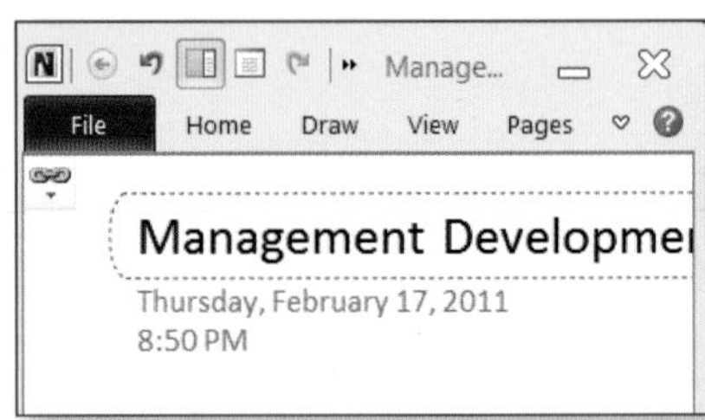

Figure 3.1 Docked *OneNote* Page

To Work with Linked Notes:

1. Locate the content from the Internet in your browser, in a *Word* document, or in a *PowerPoint* presentation which you want to link to the note page in the window.
2. Select the specific text you want to copy for further reference, and drag it to the text box on the docked *OneNote* page. The reference is added automatically to the text box (Figure 3.2).
3. If all of the notes pasted are not visible, use the arrows and scroll bar at the bottom of the window to view the content (Figure 3.3). To navigate pages, click Previous Page or Next Page on the Pages tab (Figure 3.4).

TIP

You can also use Copy and Paste to transfer the content to the note page or use the Send to OneNote command.

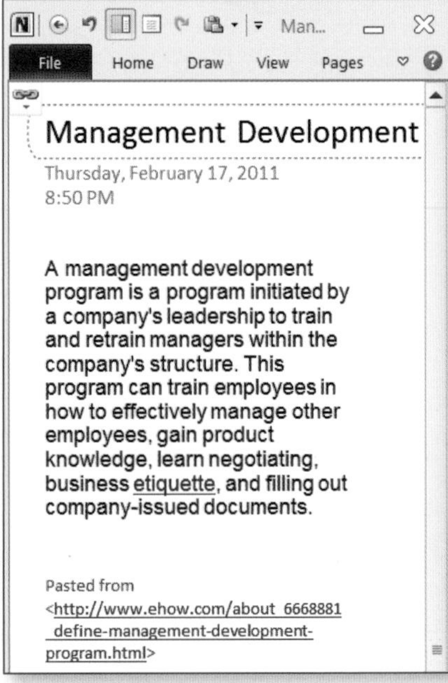

Figure 3.2 Linked Notes

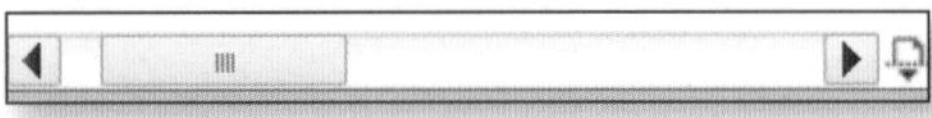

Figure 3.3 Scroll Bar and Arrows

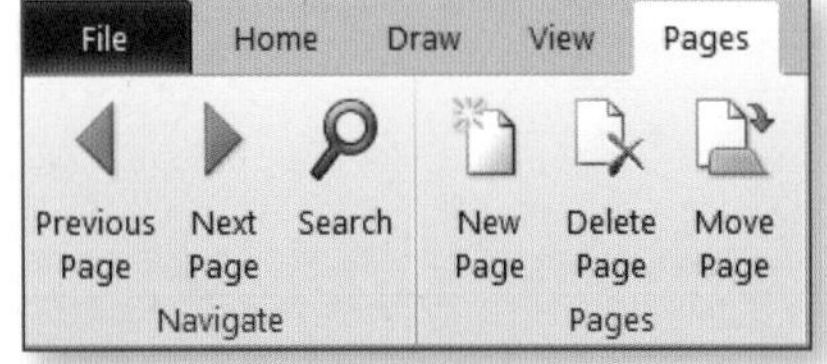

Figure 3.4 Navigate Pages

Leftbound Reports with Cover Pages

LESSON 6

OBJECTIVES

- Format leftbound reports
- Create cover pages
- Learn and apply *Word* commands

REPORTS

The difference between a leftbound report and unbound report is that space in the left margin must be allowed for the binding of the report. With leftbound reports, an extra half inch is provided in the left margin for the binding. Adding a preformatted cover page is simple; formatting page numbers following it takes more care. See Figure 6.4.

Remove page numbers from a document before setting a section break to format the page numbers. Close headers and footers before setting the section break.

Word Skills

SET CUSTOM MARGINS

Page Layout/Page Setup/Margins

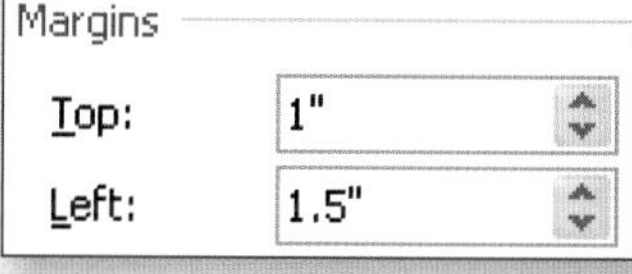

Figure 6.1 Margins

1. Click Custom Margins at the bottom of the Margins gallery to display the Page Setup dialog box.
2. In the Margins section (Figure 6.1), click the arrow on Left to increase it to 1.5" and click OK.
3. Preview the Margins gallery again; note that the custom margin you set is now shown as the Last Custom Setting (Figure 6.2). For the next leftbound report, click that option.

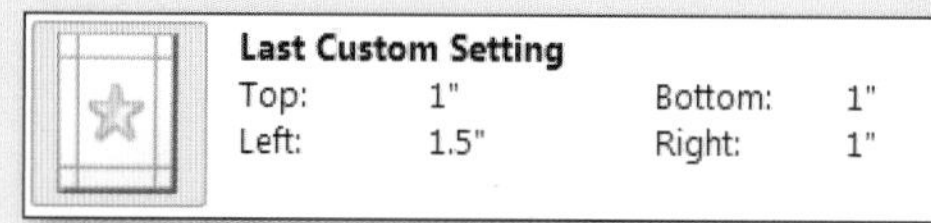

Figure 6.2 Last Custom Setting

INSERT COVER PAGE

Insert/Cover Page

1. Click Cover Page and preview some of the cover pages in the Cover Page gallery that displays.
2. Click the one that you want to insert.

REMOVE PAGE NUMBERS

Insert/Header & Footer/Page Number

1. Click Page Number to display options.
2. Click Remove Page Numbers.

INSERT SECTION BREAK

Page Layout/Page Setup/Breaks

Breaks

1. To insert a Next Page section break, click where you wish to position the break and click Breaks.
2. Then select Next Page in Section Breaks. Note that the section number changes in the status bar.

Apply It

Task 3
Add Slide and Notes to Presentation

1. Copy the *wa2-drill2* file to the My Documents folder. Rename it **wa2-t3** and move it to the *ICA Module 9 Solutions* folder.
2. Add a new slide after slide 4 with Title and Content layout. Key the title **Prepare Effective Presentations**. Insert a Basic Chevron Process SmartArt diagram with three shapes. Key **Opening, Body, Closing**.
3. Key the notes shown below in the Notes section:

Use the opening to set the tone and make a good first impression. Use the body to present the bulk of your presentation. Use the closing to summarize key points made or to call for specific action.

4. View the presentation using Slide Show on the View tab. Note that the last slide has no animation.
5. Open the presentation in *PowerPoint* on your computer. View the Transition tab and note that the Rotate transition has been applied. Animate the last slide using Wipe from Bottom Effect Options and One by One sequence.
6. Open the presentation in your browser. View the Slide Show. Note that the Rotate transition was converted to Fade. Then view the notes on each slide.

Task 4
Edit a Worksheet on SkyDrive

CONFERENCE BUDGET

1. Add the *conference budget* file from the data files to the ICA Module 9 Solutions folder. Rename it **wa2-t4**.
2. Make the following edits to the worksheet:
   a. Delete *Draft* from the title.
   b. Change the cost of rental display units to **1,200**.
   c. Change the equipment cost to **300**.
   d. Change the cost of food and beverages to **2,250**.
   e. Check the final total. It should be 15,700.

CAREER FOCUS

© Photodisc/Getty Images

The higher you move up in an organization in your career, the more likely it is that you will travel for business purposes and the more likely you are to work with individuals who live in other geographic areas. Web Apps facilitate working in both of these scenarios. In the business setting, Web Apps are more likely to be hosted on a *SharePoint* server than on the SkyDrive. You will be able to access the documents you need as you travel. You will also be able to share documents very easily with individuals in other geographic areas.

BREAK LINKS

Header & Footer Tools Design/Navigation

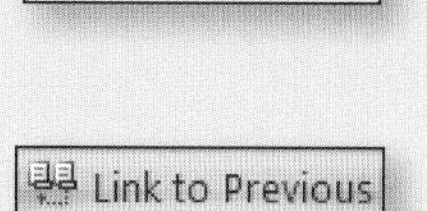

1. Double-click in the Header area on the first page of the new section. Note that it has Same as Previous, indicating the header will be the same as in the previous section.
2. In the Navigation group, click Link to Previous to break the link to the header in Section 1; then do the same to break the link for the footer.

INSERT PAGE NUMBERS

Insert/Header & Footer/Page Number

1. Click Page Number and then select Top of Page.
2. Preview options for type of page number, and click to apply the one selected.

FORMAT PAGE NUMBERS

Insert/Header & Footer/Page Number

1. On the first page of Section 2 of the report after the cover page, click Format Page Numbers to display the Page Number Format dialog box.
2. In the Page numbering section (Figure 6.3), click Start at and use the arrow to set at 1.

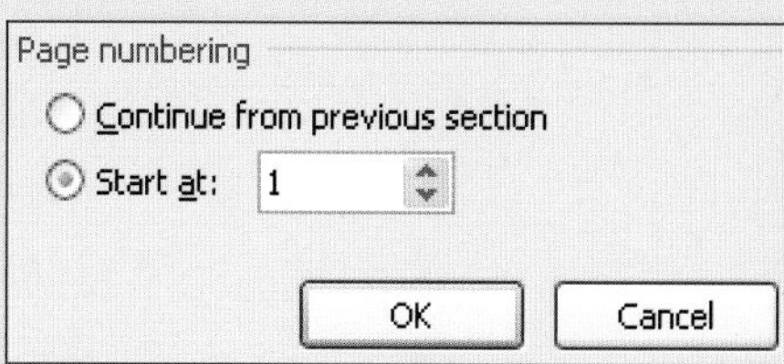

Figure 6.3 Set Page Numbering

Apply It

Document 14

Leftbound Report with Cover Page

1. Open *wd5-d13* and save as *wd6-d14*. Apply 1.5" left custom margin. Remove the page numbers.
2. Insert a Cubicles cover page; add title, company name, and the current year; subtitle: **Client Expectations—A Professional Image from Glenn and Hess Associates.** Delete the Author placeholder.
3. Insert a Next Page section break at the top of the second page; in the header and footer areas, break the links to previous header and footer.
4. Insert Accent Bar 2 page numbers at the top of the second page of the report; apply Different First Page; set page number on first page of the report to 1.
5. Resave as *wd6-d14* and close.

Use Figure 6.4 to check your document.

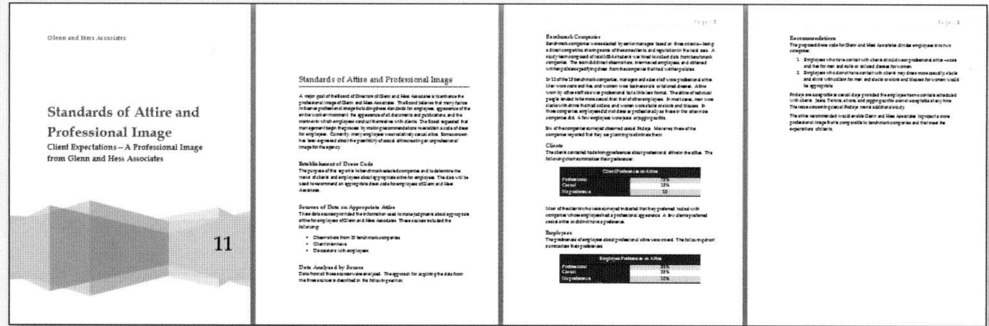

Figure 6.4 Leftbound Report with Cover Page

DRILL 2 VIEW SLIDE SHOW AND NOTES

CAREER SKILLS

1. Add the *career skills* file from your data to the ICA Module 9 Solutions folder.
2. Start the Slide Show and view each slide.
3. View the notes on each slide.
4. Close the file and rename it **wa2-drill2**.

INSERT GRAPHICS

Generally, graphics are inserted using commands on the Insert tab (Figure 2.7). You already know how to apply many of these commands.

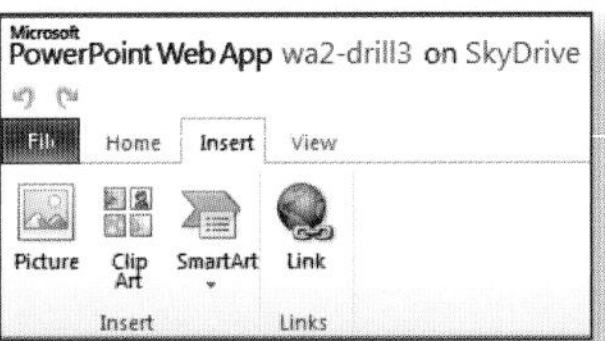

Figure 2.7 Insert Tab

To Insert a Picture:

Insert/Insert/Picture

1. Click where you want to insert the picture.
2. Browse and select desired picture. Click Insert.

To Create SmartArt:

Insert/Insert/SmartArt

1. Click where you want to insert the SmartArt.
2. Follow the path and select the desired SmartArt diagram.
3. Key the text for the shapes in the bulleted list.

DRILL 3 INSERT GRAPHICS

SALES CHART

1. Create a four-slide presentation named **wa2-drill3** using the Pushpin theme. The first slide is the title slide. Key **Graphics** as the title and your name as the subtitle. Use Title and Content layout for slides 2–4.
2. On slide 2, key **Top Sales Associates** as the title, and search clip art using the keywords *male and female* for a picture of a professionally dressed male and female. Insert in the content area.
3. On slide 3, key **Sales by Product Line** as the title, and insert the picture *sales chart* from the data files.
4. On slide 4, key **Sales Priorities** as the title, and insert a Continuous Block Process SmartArt diagram. Key the following items in the bulleted list for the three shapes:

   Increase software sales
   Maintain focus on hardware sales
   Transfer supplies product line to internal sales

5. Change colors to Colorful Range – Accent Colors 2 to 3.
6. Close the file.

QUICK ✓ Use Figure 2.8 to check your solution.

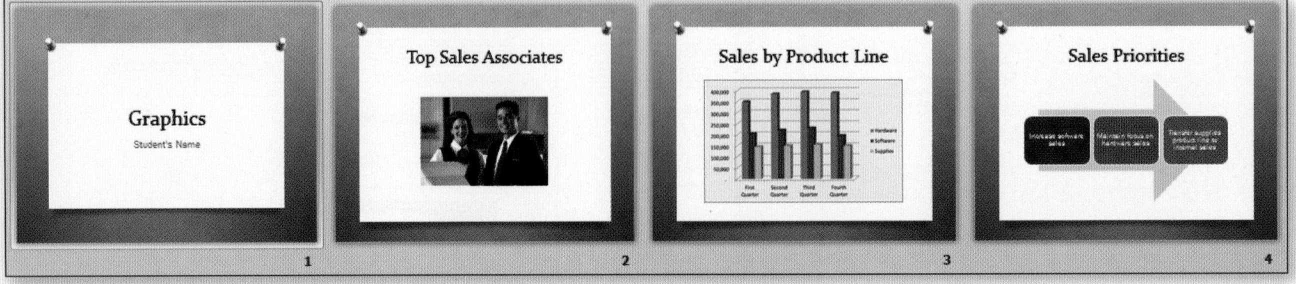

Figure 2.8 Quick Check

Document 15
Leftbound Report

TIP

The Last Custom Setting in the Margins gallery should have the 1.5" left margin setting that can be clicked if you did not change margins after preparing Document 14.

1. Open *wd5-d12* and save as *wd6-d15*. Apply 1.5" left custom set margin. Remove page numbers from the document.
2. Insert a Mod cover page from the Cover Page gallery. Add the title, subtitle **Project Status**, and pick the date 5/4/20--. Your name should display as the author; if not, insert it. Delete the abstract section.
3. Insert a Next Page section break at the beginning of the second page; break the links for the header and the footer.
4. Insert Motion (Odd Page) header at the top of the second page of the report; apply Different First Page; set page number on first page of the report to 1. Save as *wd6-d15* and close.

FOOTNOTES

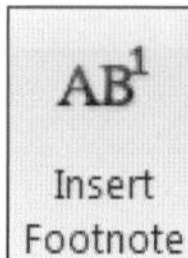

Insert Footnote

In industry, footnotes are used to document reference sources and to provide supplementary information. In this lesson, you will use footnotes to provide supplementary information.

TIP

Work in Print Layout view when you work with footnotes.

Word Skills

INSERT FOOTNOTES

References/Footnotes/Insert Footnote

1. Position the insertion point in the document where the footnote reference is to be inserted.
2. Click Insert Footnote to insert the reference number in the document and at the bottom of the page. The insertion point appears at the point where the footnote needs to be keyed.
3. Key the footnote; then click above the footnote divider line to return to the document.

DELETE FOOTNOTES

1. Select the reference number in the text.
2. Tap DELETE.

Apply It

Document 16
Report with Footnotes and Track Changes

TELEMEDICINE CENTER

1. Open *telemedicine center* and format it as a leftbound report. Save as *wd6-d16*. Apply Solstice theme.
2. Read the comments and follow the directions contained in them. Be sure to locate the five uncorrected errors and correct them with Track Changes turned on.
3. Insert the footnotes where indicated in the comments. Key the footnote information shown below.
4. Accept changes individually; after you have finished, delete all comments.
5. Add a cover page of your choice; number the pages appropriately using the page number format of your choice. Use the subtitle **Todd Medical Center Project** and the current date. Resave as *wd6-d16* and close.

[1] All data were collected and analyzed by the Rexmere Market Research firm.

[2] Todd Medical Center has its share of the costs allocated in the budget. Both communities have raised almost all of the funds required for their investment in the project.

Add a Friend

1. Click Messenger and select Add friends.
2. Key the e-mail address, click Next, and then click Invite.

Copy a Document

1. Click the folder and then point at the document to be copied.
2. Select More and then Copy.
3. Select the folder where you want to place the document, and click Copy this file into (folder name).

3. Note that you can ❶ clear the settings, including whether they can only view files ❷ or edit them ❸. Add people by keying their e-mail addresses.
4. You can also send a link to a folder to share it. Click the Send a link option under Share (Figure 2.3).
5. Key the e-mail address(es) and a message if desired. Check the box Require recipients to sign in with Windows Live ID. Click Send.

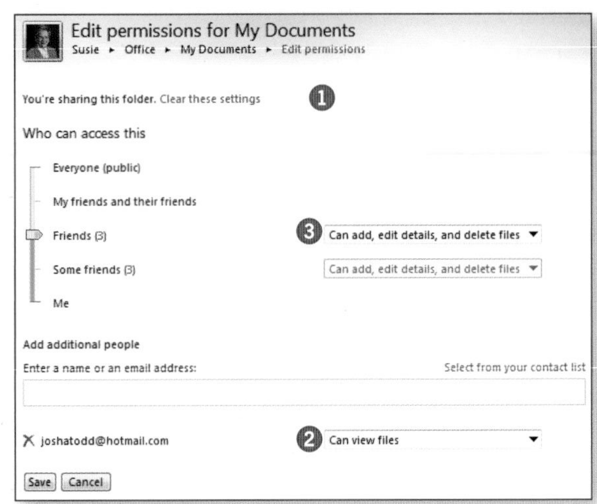

Figure 2.4 Edit Permissions

DRILL 1 SHARE FOLDERS

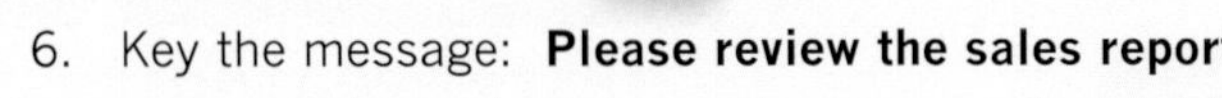

1. Add at least one friend and obtain the e-mail addresses of one or more individuals who have a Windows Live ID.
2. Share your My Documents folder with the friend you added.
3. Click Office on your SkyDrive, and then click New to create a new folder. Name it **Excel Documents**.
4. Click *Excel Documents* and then click Add files. Double-click *sales report* in your data files to upload the file.
5. Send a link to two individuals to share the *Excel* folder by keying their e-mail addresses in the Send to box.
6. Key the message: **Please review the sales report**.
7. Check the Require recipients to sign in with Windows Live ID box. Click Send.
8. Edit the *sales report* file in your browser by changing the sales for Josh Todd in Qtr 4 from 1,258,921 to **1,285,291**. Note the change in the Sparkline.
9. Rename the file **wa2-drill1**.
10. Copy the file to *ICA Module 9 Solutions*.

POWERPOINT PRESENTATIONS

Presentations can be created in the *PowerPoint Web App* or can be added from files. Files that are added can be edited in the browser or in *PowerPoint* on your computer. A presentation can be viewed in Slide Show View. Notes pages can also be viewed.

To Upload a Presentation and Use *PowerPoint* Slide Show:

1. Select the folder to which you want to add the presentation, click Add files, select the presentation you want to upload, and double-click it or click Open.
2. After the presentation uploads, click Continue. Then click the presentation to open it.
3. Click Start Slide Show (Figure 2.5) and view it.

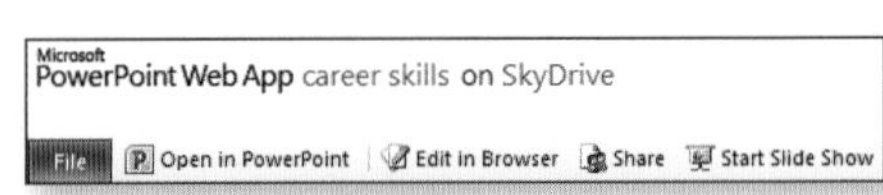

Figure 2.5 Start Slide Show

To View Notes:

View/Show/Notes

1. Click Notes at the bottom of the slide that is displayed (Figure 2.6).
2. View the notes on each slide. -or-
3. Click Edit in Browser and follow the path to view the notes.

Figure 2.6 View Notes

project 1

Creative Designs & Production I: Apply Word in a Business Setting

OBJECTIVES

- Create effective *Word* documents
- Use a coordinated document theme for all documents
- Apply *Word* commands
- Work independently with few instructions

SETTING

Creative Designs & Production, LLC (CDP) is a small, award-winning company that designs and produces creative visual, audio, and print products including public service announcements and commercials for television and radio, training films, brochures, advertising, and other print products. In its ten years of business, CDP has won more than forty major awards for its creative designs and productions. As events coordinator, you work closely with the three owners of the company—Lori Maxwell, Creative Director and Manager; Jeff Maxwell, Producer; and Steve Johnson, Business Manager. As you might expect in a small business, the environment is casual, everyone is on a first-name basis, and everybody has a wide range of responsibilities.

Company Information

Address:	Creative Designs & Production, LLC 1776 Robin Hood Road Richmond, VA 23220-1012
Telephone:	804-555-0134
Fax:	804-555-0196
Website:	www.cdp-va.net
E-mail:	Firstname.Lastname@cdp-va.net

Jobs

1. Memo
2. Letter
3. Table
4. Two-page letter
5. Unbound project report with track changes
6. Leftbound report with cover page

STANDARD OPERATING PROCEDURES

1. CDP uses a customized document theme and standard format for documents. Use the *blank cdp theme* file in the data files with the theme applied for each document that does not require a template.
2. Use the *cdp letterhead* template for letters. CDP uses block style. Use the current date; supply an appropriate salutation and closing lines if they are not provided.
3. Use the *cdp memo* template to create a Quick Part for CDP memos.

Excel and PowerPoint on the SkyDrive

LESSON 2

OBJECTIVES

- Share folders
- Open and view *PowerPoint* slide show

WORK WITH EXCEL AND POWERPOINT

In this lesson, you will work with *Excel* workbooks and *PowerPoint* presentations. You can create new documents or add files for these applications in the same way that you created *Word* documents and added *Word* files. The *Excel* Ribbon is shown in Figure 2.1.

TIP

Web Apps enable you to access files remotely and to share files with others. To share files, you need to add at least one person as a friend and to share files with at least two other people. Your instructor may want to be the friend with full editing access to your files. These individuals must have a Windows Live ID.

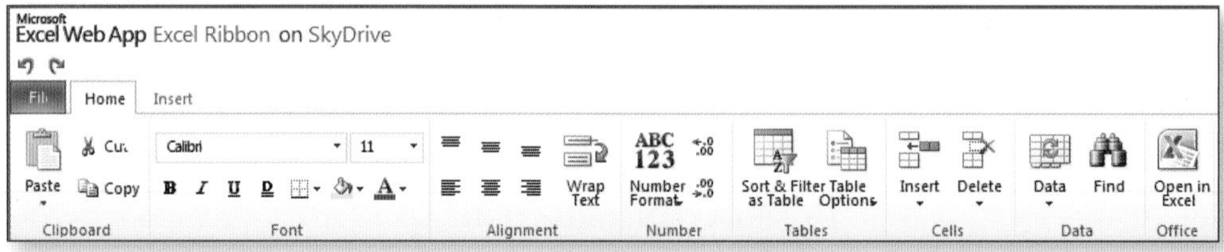

Figure 2.1 *Excel* Home Tab

Excel has two tabs plus the File menu, which is available on all tabs. The Home tab is illustrated above. The Insert tab includes tables, charts, and links. The commands are the same as those you used in *Excel*.

The *PowerPoint* Ribbon in Figure 2.2 illustrates the SmartArt Tools tab.

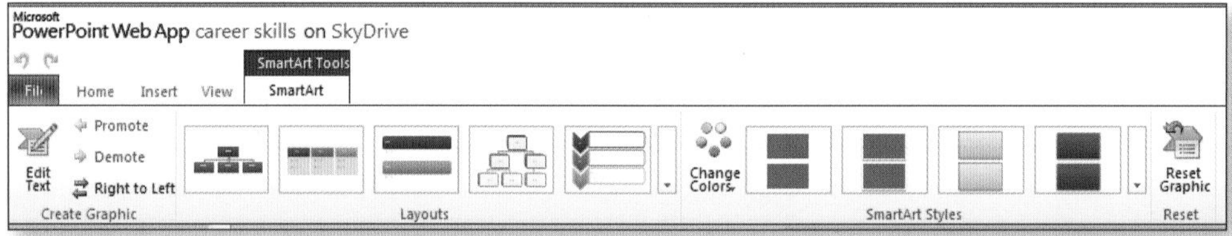

Figure 2.2 *PowerPoint* SmartArt Tools

The *PowerPoint* Ribbon has the same three tabs as *Word*. The Insert tab includes Picture, Clip Art, SmartArt, and Link. The View tab includes Editing View, Reading View, Slide Show, and Notes. The commands are the same as those you used in *PowerPoint*.

SHARE FOLDERS

You can share folders with others. More than one person can work on shared files. If a folder has been shared, all files in that folder are shared.

To Share a Folder:

1. To share a folder, click the folder.
2. Click the Share down arrow (Figure 2.3) and click Edit permissions to display the Edit permissions for (Name of Folder) screen (Figure 2.4).

Figure 2.3 Share a Folder

4. Prepare a subfolder in your solution files to save all work for this project. You will work for this company again in Projects 2 and 7. Save the file for each job as *p1-j* (plus the job number, such as *j1*, *j2*, etc.), and then close the file.
5. Preview, proofread, and print each document. You will not be reminded to do this.

Job 1

Memo

CDP MEMO

1. Open the *cdp memo* template from the data files. Use the Select All feature (or the keyboard shortcut CTRL + A) to select the memo head and save it as a Quick Part named *CDP Memo*. In the description, key **Heading for CDP memo**. Close the template.
2. In a new document, insert the *CDP Memo* Quick Part and prepare a memo from you to Lori Maxwell and Jeff Maxwell; copy Steve Johnson. Use the current date and the subject **Site for the School Spirit PSA Filming**. Key the text shown below.
3. Save the document as *p1-j1* and close.

The Coastal Virginia University advancement administrators recommended that we contact Dr. Joyce Martinez and her husband, Esteban, about using their home as the setting for the filming of the School Spirit public service announcement that will be shown during the half-time of all televised football and basketball games as well as during other sporting events.

Dr. Martinez, executive director of the CVU Foundation that is contracting with us for the filming of the PSA, had been briefed by her colleagues about the PSA story line and that the Martinez home had been suggested as a potential site for the filming if they were willing to make it available. She was most cordial when I contacted her and agreed to our request to send Dan Holland to take pictures to determine if the site met the technical specifications. I arranged for Dan to make the site visit today and take the pictures. They have been posted on his website along with his scouting notes. He is very enthusiastic about the potential of this site.

Esteban Martinez will coordinate all activities at the Martinez home for this project. He understands that the preliminary work on the set will require about four hours on one day and that the filming will require eight to ten hours on the next day. He is also aware that the project is scheduled to be filmed within ten days. This schedule is acceptable to him.

Job 2

Letter

CDP LETTERHEAD

1. Use the *cdp letterhead* template to prepare a letter to Dr. Joyce Martinez from Steve. Use appropriate names, titles, salutation, and complimentary close. The Coastal Virginia University Foundation address is: 1164 King Carter Drive | Irvington, VA 22480-2504.
2. Enclose the contract.
3. Save as *p1-j2* and close the document.

Our discussions were most productive, and we have finalized the contract for the filming of two 30-second public service announcement spots for Coastal Virginia University. All of the changes that you requested have been implemented in the contract.

Apply It

Task 1
Create Word Document in SkyDrive

1. Create a new document in the ICA Module 9 Solutions folder on the SkyDrive and name it **wa1-t1**.
2. Key and format the document shown below using the following guides:
   a. Tap ENTER three times and key the title.
   b. Click the More Styles button, and apply Title style.
   c. Key the subtitle, click the More Styles button, and apply Subtitle style.
   d. Apply Heading 1 style to headings shown in bold.
   e. Use the keyword *dogs* to search for clip art, and insert clip art where indicated.
   f. Display the Picture Tools Format tab, and click Shrink twice to reduce the size of the clip art.
3. Save, preview, print, and close the document.

Working on the SkyDrive

Student's Name

Working on the SkyDrive is different from working on my computer. The Ribbon on the SkyDrive has only four tabs--File, Home, Insert, and View.

Home Tab

One of the new commands on the Home tab is Open in Word. This command enables you to work in Word on your computer. The advantages of working on your computer at home are:

- More tabs and commands are available.
- Computer speed is faster than the Internet speed.
- Creating documents in the full version of Word is easier than in the Web Apps version.

Insert Tab

Only three options are available on the Insert tab:

1. Tables
2. Pictures--including those from files and those from Clip Art
3. Links

A sample of clip art available is shown below.

View Tab

Views available include:

- Reading View
- Editing View

Task 2
View Document on SkyDrive

RECREATION COMPLEX

1. Add the file *recreation complex* to the ICA Module 9 Solutions folder.
2. Rename the file **wa1-t2**.
3. Use Edit in browser to open the document. Note the way the document displays.
4. On the View tab, click Reading View and note that the document displays as it would on your computer. Then close the document.

Job 2,
continued

Please note that 50 percent of the contract cost is due when the contract is signed, and the remaining 50 percent is due when you approve and accept the final product. Please return the contract within three days with your check for $44,000. You were provided a significant discount as a nonprofit organization and because you agreed to using your home as the set for these spots.

We look forward to working with you to produce a public service announcement that we believe will change the standard the industry uses for these unique opportunities to showcase your university on regional or national television. We appreciate your willingness to grant us the latitude to be truly creative with this exciting venture.

Job 3
Table

BLANK CDP THEME

The *blank cdp theme* data file is a blank document that has the CDP customized document theme applied. In Project 2, you will create the customized theme on your computer.

Table Tools Layout/Cell Size/ Distribute Columns

1. Open *blank cdp theme* from the data files and save it as *p1-j3*.
2. Apply Landscape orientation; tap ENTER twice and insert a 4-column, 14-row table.
3. Apply Medium Grid 3 – Accent 1 table style. Merge the cells in row 1, increase the cell height to .5", and key the title: **Schedule for Filming School Spirit PSA**. Apply uppercase, increase the font size to 20 point, and apply Align Center.
4. Select all four columns, rows 2–14, increase the row height to .3", and apply Align Center Left. Key the headings in row 2: **Time, Activity, Participants,** and **Person Responsible**. Increase the font size to 14 point.
5. Select column A, rows 2–14, and set the width or drag the border to about 1".
6. Select column D, rows 2–14, and set the width or drag the border to about 1.75".
7. Select columns B and C, rows 2–14, and click Distribute Columns. These two columns should be about 3.2" wide. Adjust columns if text in any row wraps to a second line.
8. Review the table shown below for format; then key the table content shown on the next page.
9. Resave as *p1-j3* and close.

SCHEDULE FOR FILMING SCHOOL SPIRIT PSA			
Time	Activity	Participants	Person Responsible
8:00–10:00	Set preparation	Technical crew	Todd Marshall
8:30–10:00	Lighting assessment and implementation	Lighting crew, film director, creative director	Josh Feldstein
8:30–10:00	Sound assessment and implementation	Recording crew, film director, creative director	Lisa Sexton
9:00–10:00	Final rehearsal	Actors and producer	Jeff Maxwell
10:00–10:30	Break	All	Student's Name
10:30–11:00	Final check	All technical crews, wardrobe and make-up crew	Lori Maxwell
11:00–11:30	Rehearsal filming PSA Spot 1	All	Jeff Maxwell
11:30–1:30	Film PSA Spot 1	All	Jeff Maxwell
1:30–2:15	Lunch	All	Student's Name
2:15–2:45	Rehearsal filming PSA Spot 2	All	Jeff Maxwell
2:45–4:00	Film PSA Spot 2	All	Jeff Maxwell
4:00–5:30	Tear down set and restore environment	All	Todd Marshall

Figure P1.1 Job 3 Illustration

NEW FOLDERS AND DOCUMENTS

TIP

If you get a security warning while working on files, click No.

Generally, documents are stored in the My Documents folder. To organize documents, create subfolders for new documents.

To Create a New Folder:

New/Folder

1. Click My Documents so that you can add a subfolder in the My Documents folder.
2. Click New and select Folder (Figure 1.3).
3. Key the name of the folder and click Create folder.

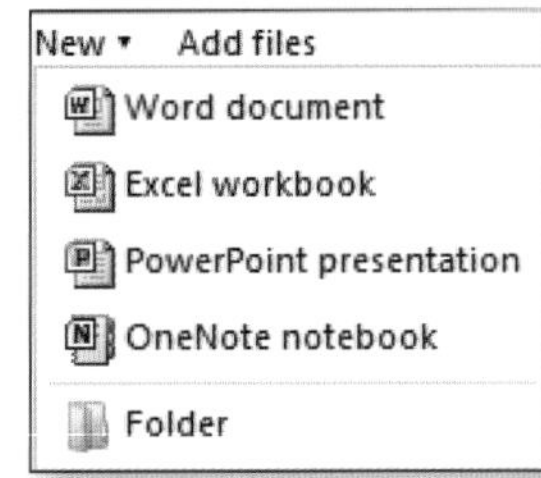

Figure 1.3 New Document or Folder

To Create a New Document:

TIP

If you get a reminder to save a document prior to moving to Reading View or some other area, click Save. If you get a warning to enable editing, click it.

New/Word document

1. Click in the folder in which you wish to save the document.
2. Follow the path, key the name of the new document, and click Save.
3. Key the document.
4. Use Reading View (View/Reading View) to preview the document.
5. Close the document.

DRILL 1 CREATE FOLDER AND NEW DOCUMENT

1. Create a new subfolder in the My Documents folder named **ICA Module 9 Solutions**.
2. Create a new document named **wa1-drill1**.
3. Key the information shown at the right.
4. Preview the document; then close it.

This document is the first one that I have prepared using the SkyDrive. Working in the "cloud" is a fun, new experience.

To Add or Upload Files:

DISCOVER

File/Print

To print a document, click Print on the File menu.

1. Click in the folder in which you want to add files.
2. Click Add files and then click the *select documents from your computer* link; browse and select the file you wish to add. Click Continue after it loads.
3. To rename the file, hover the mouse over the filename; then click More, select Rename (Figure 1.4), and key the new name.
4. To edit the file, click Edit in browser.
5. To edit the file using *Word* on your computer, click Open in Word on the Home tab.

Figure 1.4 Rename

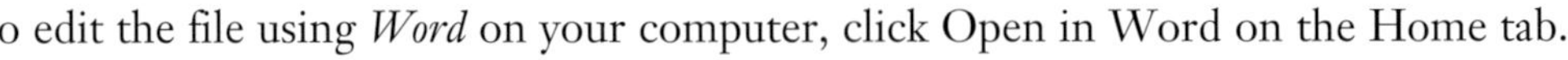

DRILL 2 ADD A FILE

WEB APPS IN PERSPECTIVE

1. Click Add files and select *web apps in perspective*; click Continue. Rename the file **wa1-drill2**.
2. Open the document using Edit in browser and key the following sentence as a new paragraph at the end of the document: **Also note that the File menu is available from all tabs.**
3. Open the document using Open in Word on the Home tab.
4. After the first sentence, tap ENTER, key **SharePoint Server**, and tap ENTER. Apply Heading 1 style.
5. After the second sentence under the heading, tap ENTER, key **Web Apps on SkyDrive**, and tap ENTER. Apply Heading 1 style.
6. Save the document; then preview, print, and close it.

8:00–10:00	Set preparation	Technical crew	Todd Marshall
8:30–10:00	Lighting assessment and implementation	Lighting crew, film director, creative director	Josh Feldstein
8:30–10:00	Sound assessment and implementation	Recording crew, film director, creative director	Lisa Sexton
9:00–10:00	Final rehearsal	Actors and producer	Jeff Maxwell
10:00–10:30	Break	All	Student's Name
10:30–11:00	Final check	All technical crews, wardrobe and make-up crew	Lori Maxwell
11:00–11:30	Rehearsal filming PSA Spot 1	All	Jeff Maxwell
11:30–1:30	Film PSA Spot 1	All	Jeff Maxwell
1:30–2:15	Lunch	All	Student's Name
2:15–2:45	Rehearsal filming PSA Spot 2	All	Jeff Maxwell
2:45–4:00	Film PSA Spot 2	All	Jeff Maxwell
4:00–5:30	Tear down set and restore environment	All	Todd Marshall

Job 4

Two-Page Letter

CDP LETTERHEAD
FELDSTEIN LETTER

1. Use the *cdp letterhead* template to prepare a letter from Lori to Josh Feldstein. Open the *feldstein letter* data file and transfer the text to the letterhead document. Save as *p1-j4*.
2. Address: Mr. Josh Feldstein | Feldstein Productions, Inc. | 587 N. Rodeo Drive | Beverly Hills, CA 90210-3206. Add a second-page heading.
3. Key the paragraphs shown below and on the next page at the bottom of the letter.
4. Resave as *p1-j4* and close.

You were correct in your assessment that the large, comfortable recreational room on the lower level of the Martinez home provided a better setting than the upscale main floor. Rarely do we have the luxury of more space than we need when we film in a "home" setting. The simple set of the old, gold couch that had been hidden away, the small coffee table, a bowl of popcorn, and cold drinks added more realism of watching a sporting event than we thought possible.

The last-minute change to include Andy in the spot with the three actors worked out beautifully. He is a precious dog and will be a hit with the audience. We were amazed as were Mr. and Mrs. Martinez that he wore the bandana and sat still during the many hours of filming.

LESSON 1

Word on the SkyDrive

OBJECTIVES

- Set up your SkyDrive
- Upload, view, and edit *Word* documents
- Create *Word* documents on SkyDrive

GETTING STARTED

To access Web Apps, you must first create a Windows Live ID if you do not already have one. Once you have the ID, you can sign in and work with any of the four available applications.

To Create a Windows Live ID and Go to the SkyDrive:

1. Go to www.windowslive.com and click *Sign up* to create an ID, or you can sign in if you already have an ID (Figure 1.1).
2. Complete the form that displays and click *I accept*.
3. If you already have an ID, your name and e-mail address should display; click it to sign in.

Figure 1.1 Create ID and Sign In

4. When you sign in, your SkyDrive will display with your name (Figure 1.2). Note that you can add your picture if desired. You can access the applications, such as *Hotmail* or *Office*, listed across the top of the screen ❶.
5. To create new documents in any application or to create folders, click the New command ❷.
6. You can also click the software icon, such as *Word*, to create a new document ❸.

Figure 1.2 Your SkyDrive

The second spot was really a bonus. I was astounded that Lisa was able to play both the younger sister of a college student and his grandmother with only a 30-minute makeup and wardrobe change. Bringing the talent in from Atlanta and Charlotte proved to be a very good investment.

Again, thank you for the excellent work you did on this project. We look forward to receiving your critique of the final product.

Job 5

Unbound Report

SCHOOL SPIRIT

1. Open *school spirit* from the data files and save it as *p1-j5*. Make sure Track Changes is turned on and your name and initials are listed on your computer. Use the following directions to prepare the unbound report.
2. Use the title **School Spirit Project**. Apply Title style. Position it at about 1.7" so that the report will fit on one page.
3. Proofread, locate, and correct the five errors that have not been marked by Track Changes. Add the footnote as indicated in the comment; then delete the comment.
4. Accept all changes except the insertion: "*representing a substantial profit*."
5. Navigate to the end of the report, and key the paragraph shown below.
6. Resave as *p1-j5* and close.

The client expressed complete satisfaction with the product and considered the second spot that was filmed at no extra cost to be a significant bonus. Several invoices are outstanding; therefore, the final budget has not been prepared. However, since rental costs for a studio were not incurred and all phases of the project were completed in less time than budgeted, this project will definitely be under budget with no sacrifice in quality whatsoever. This project is the third one completed for Coastal Virginia University, and CDP can expect to contract with them for another project with two spots within the next six months.

Job 6

Leftbound Report with Cover Page

Remember to use a Next Page section break after you add the cover and to break the links for both the header and footer before inserting the footer with page numbers. Change the number on the first page of the report to 1.

1. Open *p1-j5* and save as *p1-j6*. Position the title at about 2". Key the following headings in the document; apply Heading 1 style to each heading.

   Project Description (Position after paragraph 1)

   Pre-Production Plan (Position after paragraph 2)

   Production (Position after paragraph 3)

   Post-Production Work (Position after paragraph 5)

   Potential for Future Business (Position after paragraph 6)
2. Add a Tiles cover page with the subtitle **Project Completed and Delivered**. Complete other information and change author name to your name. Then add Tiles footer and key the company name if it does not appear automatically.
3. Resave as *p1-j6* and close.

module 9

WEB COMPUTING WITH OFFICE WEB APPS

overview

This short module is designed as an introduction to *Office Web Apps* using Windows Live SkyDrive. *Web Apps 2010* enable you to work with four applications—*Word, PowerPoint, Excel,* and *OneNote.* Windows Live SkyDrive provides you with 25 GB of free online storage. You do not need *Office 2010* on your computer to use Web Apps; however, only very basic commands are available in the four applications. You can also work with the full applications on your computer from the SkyDrive. You will have the opportunity to work with the same company in Project 12 that you worked with in Project 11, simulating a realistic business.

ESSENTIALS

1. Word on the SkyDrive
2. Excel and PowerPoint on the SkyDrive
3. OneNote on the SkyDrive

Project 12—VanHuss & VanHuss, Inc.: Integrating Word, Excel, PowerPoint, and OneNote

LESSON
7

Documents with Graphics

OBJECTIVES

- Format documents with pictures, shapes, SmartArt, drop caps, clip art, and WordArt
- Format documents with equal-size columns
- Learn and apply *Word* commands
- Develop job knowledge and skills

GRAPHICS

A wide variety of graphics—shapes, SmartArt, clip art, pictures, drop caps, and WordArt—can be used to provide illustrations and to enhance text. Graphics are inserted from the Insert tab, and each type has a set of tools that are very similar to the table tools that you worked with in previous lessons. The same principle applies: To format the graphic, click in it and apply the appropriate design or format from the tools that display.

Word Skills

SHAPES

Insert/Illustrations/Shapes

1. Position the insertion point where you want to add a shape, and click Shapes to display the Shapes gallery.
2. Click the shape desired and drag to draw it.
3. Click the shape to display the drawing tools used to apply a style or to format it. You also can add text to it (Drawing Tools Format/Insert Shapes/Edit Text or right-click and select Add Text).

SMARTART

Insert/Illustrations/SmartArt

1. Position the insertion point where you want to add the graphic, and click SmartArt to open the Choose a SmartArt Graphic dialog box shown in Figure 7.1. Categories of SmartArt are listed at the left, the layouts for each category display in the center, and the preview and description of the appropriate use appear in the right pane.
2. Preview the SmartArt and click the one you want to insert.
3. To add text, click in each shape on the graphic and key the text. (See Figure 7.2.) -or-
4. In the SmartArt Design Tools, click Text Pane and key your text in the text pane.

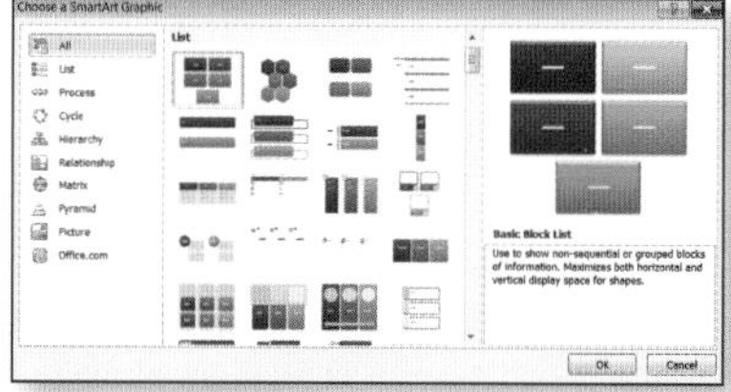

Figure 7.1 Choose a SmartArt Graphic

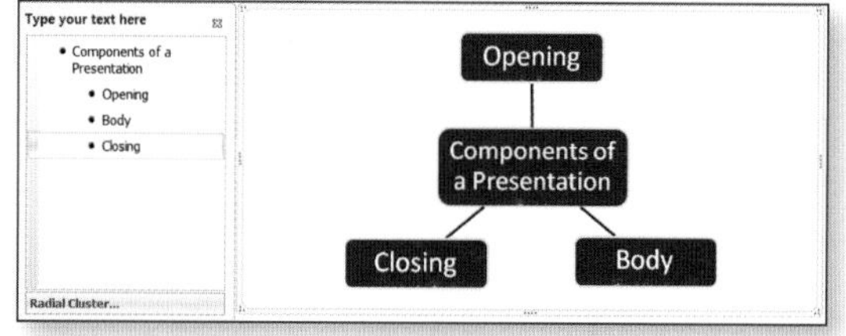

Figure 7.2 Add Text to SmartArt

Job 2
Collect and Organize Content

CLIENT MEETING NOTES

1. Attach the *Word* data file *client meeting notes* to the Client Meeting page under the General Information section. Open the document and review all of it very carefully.
2. Note that several sections in the *client meeting notes* document have a heading that has the same name as a page in the notebook. Copy the information from each section and paste it to the note page with the same name to organize and simplify the use of the notebook.

Job 3
Attach Budget and Link to Note pages

CONFERENCE BUDGET

1. Attach the *Excel* data file *conference budget* to the General Information page. Link each major heading (shown in bold on the budget) to the first page in the appropriate section of the notebook.
2. Add a tag at the top of the General Information page with the budget. Select *Important* tag and key: **Request final budget approval from BEI**

Job 4
Key Recommendations

Key the recommendations shown below on the Summary of Recommendations page.

VanHuss offers the following recommendations to BEI for the Business and Technology Conference:

1. Select the Sponsorship package at a cost of $10,000, which provides two premium booths with better amenities than the standard booths, a full-page ad in the program, a 50 percent discount on the cost of seminar rooms, and priority in booth and seminar room locations.
2. Select exhibit booths 12 and 14. These booths are across the aisle from each other and are located near both the main entrance to and the exit from the exhibit hall.
3. Select the Palmetto Room for the two seminars and the Thursday morning time options from 8:30 to 10:00 and 10:30 to 12:00 for the programs. The Palmetto Room is a corner that is larger than the other seminar rooms and has nicer furnishings. The time slots do not conflict with major program offerings.
4. Select the McLagan Restaurant as the venue for the dinner. It gets outstanding ratings and is located three blocks from the Conference Center. This option eliminates providing transportation. The best alternative for the menu is to offer the choice of salad, entrée, and dessert from a limited menu provided by Chef Leone.

Job 5
Add Tags

Review each page of the notebook. Determine if any items on the page have not yet been done. If so, add a To Do list tag at the top of the page and list items that still need to be done.

For example, on the Summary of Recommendations page, add to the tag: **Request approval of recommendations**. On the Client Dinner Venue page, add: **Determine number of guests, make final reservations, make arrangements for reception prior to dinner, and select gifts for attendees**.

Apply It

Document 17
Memo with SmartArt and Shapes

TRAINING GRAPHICS

1. Open *training graphics* and save it as *wd7-d17*; complete the memo by adding the three graphics shown at the positions indicated in the memo.

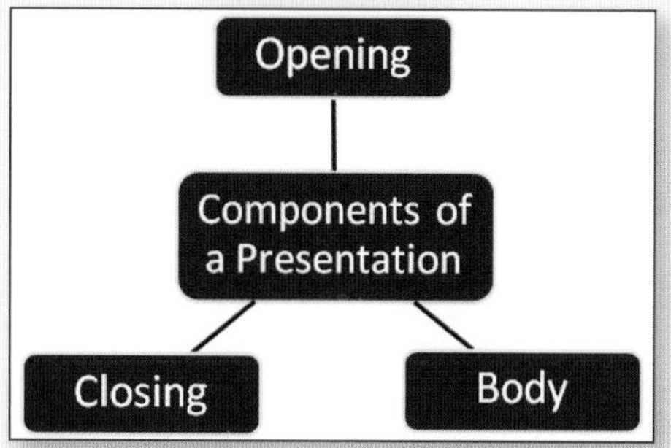

Figure 7.3 Radial Cluster SmartArt

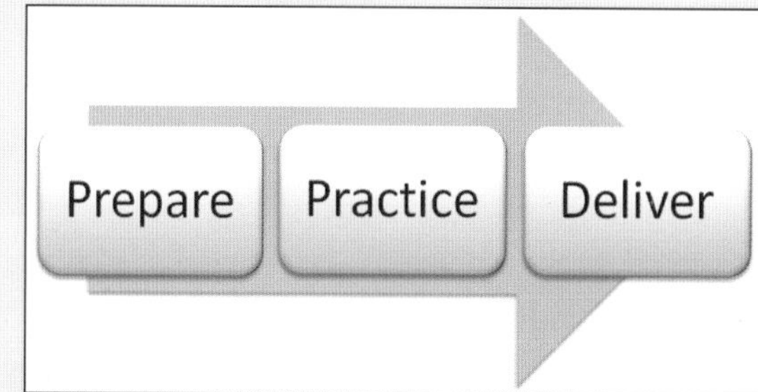

Figure 7.4 Continuous Block Process SmartArt

Figure 7.5 Grouped Smiley Face, Octagon, and Star

2. Select the Radial Cluster SmartArt and change to Primary Theme Colors, Dark 2 Fill; size center shape 0.8" high × 2" wide; size other shapes .5" high × 1.5" wide; add text shown in Figure 7.3. Overall size of the graphic should be 3" high × 6" wide.
3. Select the Continuous Block Process SmartArt and change to Primary Theme Colors, Dark 2 Outline, Intense Effect style; size graphic 3" high × 6" wide; add text shown in Figure 7.4.
4. Draw and position Shapes as shown in Figure 7.5. Apply Light, Outline, Colored Fill with the color accents illustrated; size each shape 1.7" × 1.7".
5. Add text **Stop and Focus on the Audience** to the Octagon and **You** to the star. Select the shapes by holding down SHIFT as you click each shape and then click Group (Drawing Tools Format/ Arrange/Group).
6. Preview, resave the document, and close.

TIP

Remember to add an appropriate second-page header using the Different Odd & Even Pages option.

TIP

Group multiple shapes so they can be moved as one object.

Word Skills

FORMAT PICTURES OR CLIP ART

Picture Tools Format/Adjust/ Corrections, Color, Artistic Effects, or Compress Picture

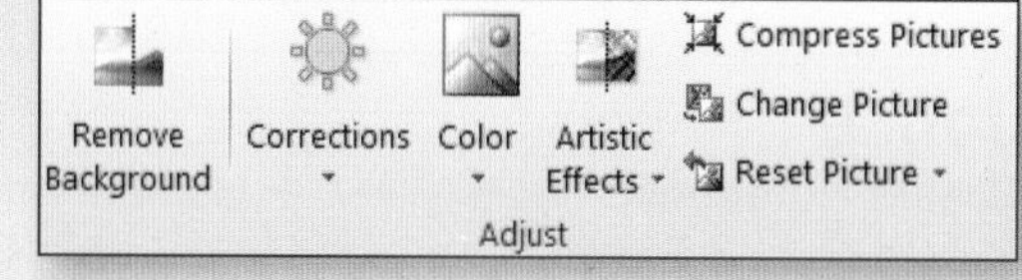

Figure 7.6 Adjust Pictures or Clip Art

1. Click the down arrow on each icon to see the types of adjustments that can be made.
2. Select an image and click the down arrow on Corrections, Color, or Artistic Effects and select desired adjustment. See Figure 7.6.
3. To reduce file size of a picture, select it and click Compress Pictures; accept the defaults and click OK.

TIP

Both pictures and clip art are formatted with Picture Tools. To use a Picture Tools Format command, you must always click the picture or clip art first.

project **11**

VanHuss & VanHuss, Inc.: Integrating Word, Excel, and OneNote

OBJECTIVES

- Create a notebook with appropriate sections, pages, and subpages
- Collect and organize content
- Link to content
- Work independently with few instructions

SETTING

VanHuss & VanHuss, Inc., (VanHuss) is a consulting and professional services firm that has been in business for twenty years. It is located at 2005 Main Street, Suite 2001, Columbia, SC 29201-3204. One of the services VanHuss provides is to manage a variety of projects and events for clients. In your position as Manager, Professional Services, one of your responsibilities is to manage special events and trade shows for clients. In this project, the client you will be working with, BEI, Inc., a publisher of business books, located at 300 Spring Street, NW, Atlanta, GA 30308-3008. Your contact will be David Blackmon, President and CEO.

JOBS

1. Create a notebook with sections, pages, and subpages
2. Collect and organize content
3. Attach *Excel* budget and link to note pages
4. Key recommendations
5. Add "To Do List" tags

STANDARD OPERATING PROCEDURES

1. VanHuss manager meets with each client and collects information about the project.
2. VanHuss organizes all information for the project in a *OneNote* notebook and shares it with the client.
3. Save the notebook in your solution files and leave it open.

Job 1

Create Notebook, Sections, and Pages

Use the information below to create a new notebook named **BEI Conference** with four sections—**General Information, Exhibit, Professional Seminars,** and **Client Dinner**. Add the pages and subpages listed below for the four tabs.

Client Meeting
Event Plans
Summary of Recommendations

Exhibit Plan
    Space, Setup, and Drayage
    Schedule

Arrangements

Venue
    Arrangements
    Menu Options

Cropping handles appear on the four corners and on the center of each side of a picture.

SIZE PICTURES OR CLIP ART

Picture Tools Format/Size/Crop or Height and Width

1. To remove unwanted portions of a picture or clip on one side, click Crop and drag the cropping handle on the side inward.
2. To crop the same amount on two sides, press CTRL while you drag the handle. The cropping line illustrates what is being cut off. Click off the picture to finish.
3. To increase or decrease the size of a picture, use the Height and Width spin arrows.

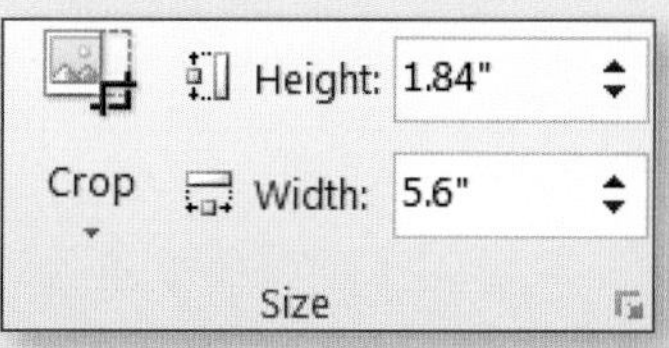

Figure 7.7 Size Pictures or Clip Art

Click the down arrow on each icon to see Arrange options available.

ARRANGE PICTURES OR CLIP ART

Picture Tools Format/Arrange

1. To move a picture or clip, click Wrap Text. Select a style and drag to the desired position.
2. To position a picture, click Position and select the desired position with text wrapping.
3. To rotate a picture, click Rotate and select the desired option.

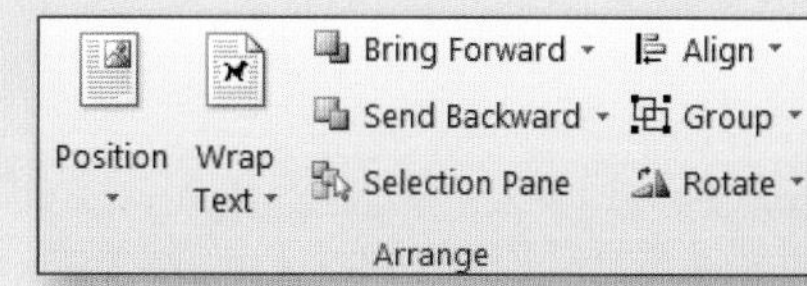

Figure 7.8 Arrange Pictures or Clip Art

PRACTICE USING PICTURE FORMAT TOOLS

ANDY II

In a new document, insert *Andy II* from the data files; preview several options in each group and then apply the following commands; do not save the document.

a. Rotate: Flip Horizontal
b. Crop: Close to puppy's image
c. Correction: Brightness: +40% Contrast: +20%
d. Color: Saturation: 200%
e. Artistic Effects: Texturizer
f. Position: Top Center with Square Wrapping

Document 18

Memo with Pictures and Clip Art

PICTURES FOR ARTICLE
BUSINESS ENTERTAINING
HOME

1. Open *pictures for article* and save as *wd7-d18*.
2. Read the memo; insert both pictures, apply Top and Bottom wrapping and use the format described in the memo. Position the second picture at the top of the second page. See Figure 7.9.
3. Search for clip art using *set table in restaurant* as the keywords; insert a clip similar to the one shown in Figure 7.6; apply Top and Bottom wrapping. Size as noted in the memo.
4. Resave as *wd7-d18* and close.

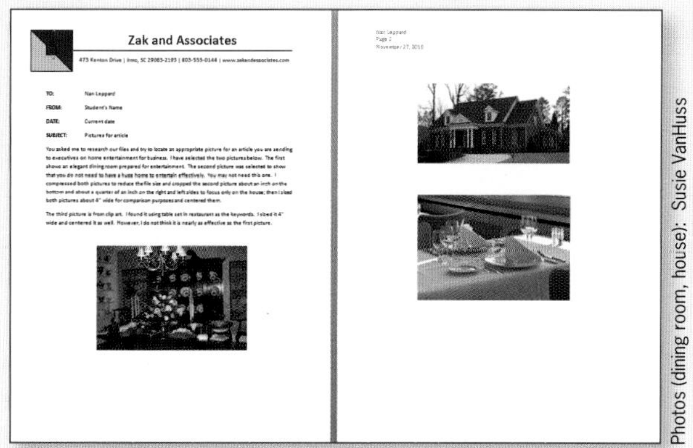

Photos (dining room, house): Susie VanHuss

Figure 7.9 Memo with Pictures and Clip Art

DRILL 3 SEARCH FOR CONTENT

1. Key **Task Force Chair** in the search box on any note page.
2. Accept the defaults and click the Search icon.
3. Click the highlighted page to access the Chair's name.

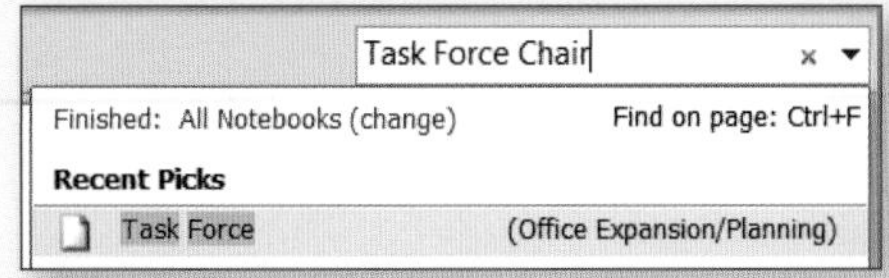

Figure 3.6 Search Results

PRINT A PAGE

File/Print/Print or Print Preview

The Backstage view is used to print a page in *OneNote*. The process is very similar to the way you printed in *Word*.

To Print a Note Page:

1. Follow the path to display the Print options.
2. Select Print Preview to view the document as it will be printed; then click print.

DRILL 4 PRINT A NOTE PAGE

1. Click on the Communication Skill Schedule page of the Training Program notebook; preview and print it.
2. Click on the Timeframe page of the Training Facilities section in the Office Expansion notebook; preview and print.

Apply It

Task 5

Attach and Link Files and Send Content to OneNote

BUDGET

1. Attach the *budget* data file to the Budget note page in the Planning section of the Office Expansion notebook.
2. Select the Interior Design note page heading and link it to the Budget page.
3. Add a new subpage under Interior Design and name it **Training Room Layout**.
4. Find sample layouts on the Internet using the keywords *training room layout* and send them to *OneNote*. Position them on the Training Room Layout page.

CAREER FOCUS

© StockLite/Shutterstock.com

The ability to organize and manage projects and events is a very important career skill. Even relatively simple projects and events entail many details. To manage projects and events successfully, paying careful attention to the details is critical. Typically, a project or event is one of many tasks an employee must complete. *OneNote* provides an effective way to retain and organize all of the information about a project in one location. Using a digital notebook rather than a paper-based file simplifies the task and makes it easy to access the information.

WordArt is frequently used for a banner or masthead at the top of a newsletter or flyer. Size and position the banner as desired.

WORDART AND DROPPED CAPS

Text can be formatted graphically using WordArt or Drop Caps. The WordArt gallery provides a number of styles for WordArt. To format WordArt, use the tools on the Drawing Tools Format tab to change Styles, Text Fill, Text Outline, or Text Effects.

A drop cap is a large capital letter at the beginning of a text block that is used to draw the reader's attention. It usually extends from the top line of the paragraph down two or three succeeding lines. A drop cap can also be positioned in the margin.

COLUMNS

Programs, newsletters, flyers, and brochures are typically formatted in columns of varying widths. You will work extensively with these documents in *Publisher*. In this lesson, you will format documents with equal-width columns. Column format can be applied before or after keying text. Generally, it is easier to format text in columns after it has been keyed.

TEXT BOXES

A gallery of preformatted text boxes called pull quotes and sidebars is available. A pull quote is a text box that contains a quote that you would like to emphasize. A sidebar is used to add supplementary text to an article.

Word Skills

INSERT WORDART

Insert/Text/WordArt

1. Click WordArt to display the WordArt gallery. Then select the style desired.
2. Select the text in the text box that displays and replace it with your text.
3. Format the text as desired using the Drawing Tools Format tab.

INSERT DROP CAP

Insert/Text/Drop Cap

1. Click in the paragraph that you want to begin with a drop cap.
2. Click Drop Cap and then select Dropped or In margin.

You will work with very simple equal-size columns and newsletters in this lesson. In *Publisher*, you will work more extensively with text boxes and documents with columns.

CREATE COLUMNS OF EQUAL WIDTH

Page Layout/Page Setup/Columns

Columns

1. Select the text you want to format in columns; click Columns, and select the desired number of columns.
2. To balance columns on a page, click at the end of the columns and insert a Continuous section break.

INSERT TEXT BOX

Insert/Text/Text Box

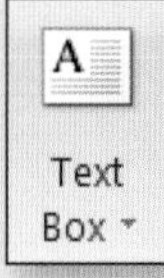

1. Click Text Box and select the desired type and style from the gallery.
2. Key or paste the text that you want to emphasize in the text box.

To Send Content from *Internet Explorer* to *OneNote*:

1. Click on the location in *OneNote* to which you want to add notes or graphics from the Internet. If desired, check the box to always send to the selected location.
2. Locate and select desired text or graphics.
3. Right-click the content and select Send to OneNote (Figure 3.3).
4. Select the location if you did not check the box to send it to selected location (Figure 3.4). Click OK.

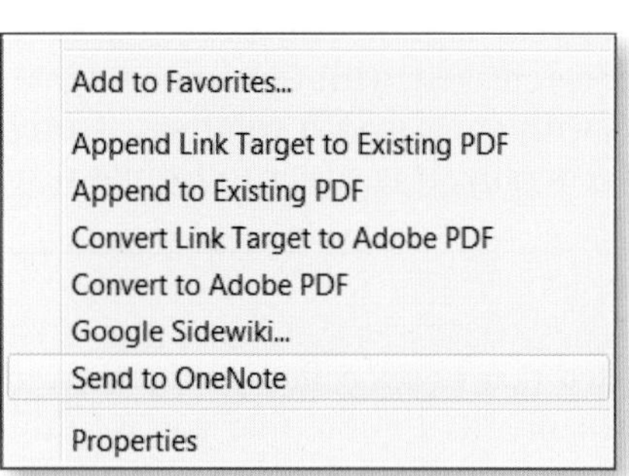

Figure 3.3 Send to OneNote

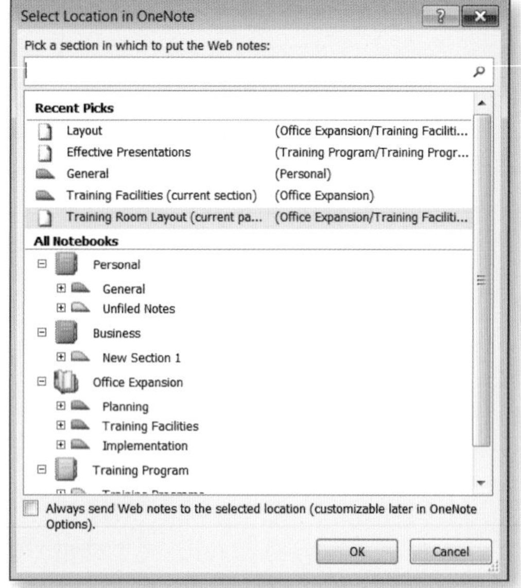

Figure 3.4 Select Location for Content

DRILL 2 SEND CONTENT FROM INTERNET EXPLORER

1. Locate a picture of a conference table on the Internet and send it to *OneNote*.
2. Position it on the Furnishings Page below the picture of the conference table that is already on the page.
3. Keep the picture and the link. Delete any other materials that may have been sent with the picture.

SEARCH FOR CONTENT

The Search box is located on the right side of the section tabs that appear at the top of the note page window. The drop-down arrow provides a list of search options as shown in Figure 3.5. The default option is to search all open notebooks.

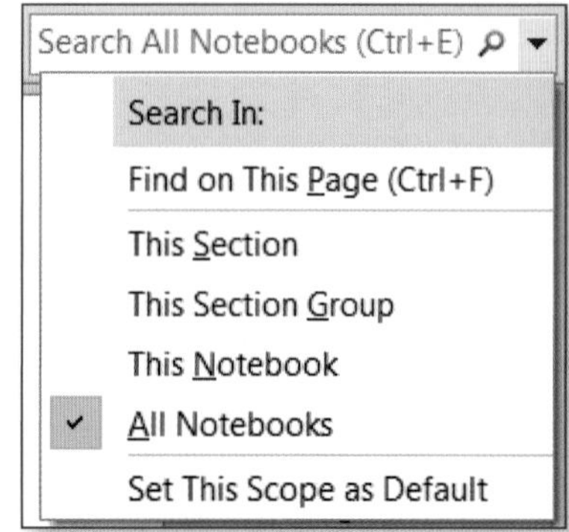

Figure 3.5 Search for Content

To Search for Content:

1. Enter the keywords in the Search box on any note page in any notebook to locate specific content.
2. Select the scope of the search from the drop-down list, and click the Search icon.
3. When the results display, click the highlighted page to access the content. (See Figure 3.6 on the next page).

Apply It

Document 19

Newsletter with Columns and WordArt

ARTICLE
BUSINESS ENTERTAINING

Picture Tools Format/ Arrange/Position

1. Click Position.
2. Select Position in Middle Center.

1. Open *article* and save as *wd7-d19*. Use the Office theme. Format the text in two equal-size columns.
2. Add a WordArt banner at about 1.5". Select Gradient Fill – Blue, Accent 1, Outline – White style from the WordArt gallery. Replace the text in the text box with **Business Entertaining**.
3. Use the tools on the Drawing Tools Format tab to add an Art Deco Bevel Text Effect and a Triangle Up Transform Text Effect.
4. Click in the first paragraph and apply Drop Cap. Select the drop cap and apply Blue, Accent 1 color.
5. Insert the picture *business entertaining*; apply Square wrapping and size it about 2" × 3". Position the picture in the Middle Center. Insert a Continuous section break at the end of the document to balance the columns. See Figure 7.10.
6. Resave as *wd7-d19* and close.

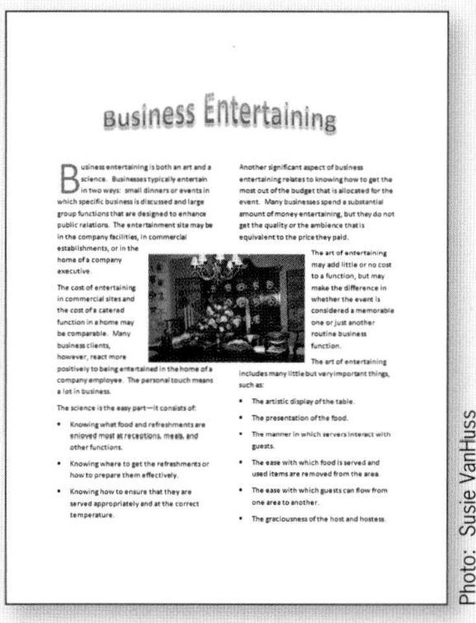

Figure 7.10 Document 19 Illustration

Document 20

Article with Pull Quote and Sidebar

NEWSPAPER COLUMNS

1. Open *newspaper columns* and save it as *wd7-d20*.
2. Replace the heading that is keyed with WordArt using the same style and format as you used for Document 19 except use Square Transform Text Effect rather than Triangle Up Transform Text Effect.
3. Position the WordArt so that the column text can start at about 2.8".
4. Select the text and format it in two columns.
5. Insert a Braces Quote 2 text box, and copy the first sentence of the third paragraph and paste it as a pull quote. Change the text color to White. Position it as shown at the right. The text box size should be about 2.6" high × 1.7" wide.
6. Insert an Annual Sidebar. Change Fill color to the same as the banner. Drag to the approximate size (3.2" high), and position as shown in Figure 7.11. Then increase font to 11 points, and key the following text in it:

   Visual Image Consultants provided the information in this newsletter to us as an example to show our staff. We have retained Visual Image Consultants to assist us with standardizing our document formats and improving our image.

   Visual Image Consultants is currently custom designing several pull quote and sidebar text boxes that we can save as Quick Parts.
7. Resave as *wd7-d20* and close.

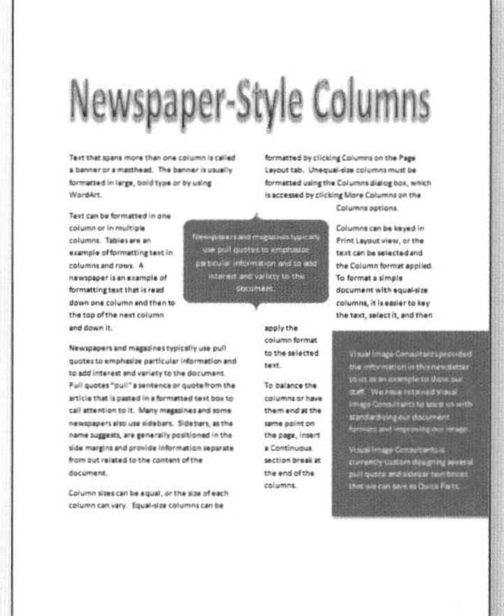

Figure 7.11 Document 20 Illustration

LESSON 3

Access and Print Content

OBJECTIVES

- Attach files and link to content
- Send content from Internet to *OneNote*
- Search for content
- Print a page

ATTACH FILES AND LINK TO CONTENT

Insert/Files/Attach File

OneNote serves as a location for all content about a particular project or event. *Word, PowerPoint*, or *Excel* files can be attached to *OneNote* pages. The page containing the file can be linked to other content in *OneNote*.

To Attach a File:

1. Select the page to which you want to attach the file.
2. Follow the path to display the Choose a file or set of files to insert dialog box; browse to select the file desired, and click Insert.

To Link the Attached File to Content:

Insert/Links/Link

1. Select the content to which you want to link the file.
2. Follow the path to display the Link dialog box (Figure 3.1).
3. Select the section or page to which you want to link the file and click OK (Figure 3.2).

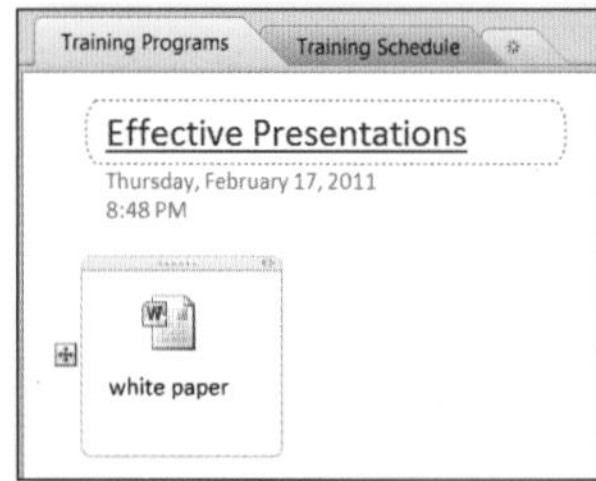

Figure 3.2 File Attached and Pages Linked

Figure 3.1 Link to Content

DRILL 1 ATTACH FILE AND LINK TO CONTENT

 WHITE PAPER

1. Click on the Effective Presentations page in the Training Programs section and insert *white paper* data file.
2. On the Training Schedule section, select the Effective Presentations heading in the table.
3. Click Link to display the Link dialog box; select Training Programs and click OK.
4. Select the Effective Presentations page heading and click Link to display the Link dialog box; select Training Schedule and click OK.
5. Check to see that the pages are linked. See Figure 3.2.

LESSON 8

Reports with Sections

OBJECTIVES

- Format reports with sections and a table of contents
- Update a table of contents
- Copy and paste an *Excel* chart in a report
- Learn and apply *Word* commands
- Develop job knowledge and skills

REPORTS WITH SECTIONS

Page Layout/Page Setup/Breaks

TIP

Do not insert page numbers until you have broken the links between the headers and footers in each section that will have different formatting.

In Lesson 6, you learned to use section breaks and to break the links between sections when you prepared reports with cover pages and numbered the report pages. You may want to review the *Word Skills* in Lesson 6. In this lesson, you will use the same type of breaks to prepare reports that have cover pages (Section 1), preliminary pages (Section 2), and the body of a report (Section 3). In this lesson, the preliminary pages (Section 2) are numbered in the footer with lowercase Roman numerals, and the pages in the body of the report (Section 3) are numbered as headers using Arabic numerals.

Preliminary pages of a report may include a letter of transmittal, table of contents, table of figures, or other types of information. In this lesson, you will insert a table of contents and number the preliminary pages.

Word Skills

ADD MULTIPLE SECTION BREAKS TO A REPORT

1. To insert a Next Page break, position the insertion point where you want to insert the break and click Breaks.
2. Select Next Page in Section Breaks. Repeat these steps if you want to add both a cover page and preliminary pages to a report.

BREAK LINKS

Header & Footer Tools Design/Navigation

1. Click in the header on the first page of the new section (Section 2); in the Navigation group, click Link to Previous to break the link. Then move to the footer and break the link.
2. Repeat step 1 to break the links in the next section (Section 3).

INSERT AND FORMAT REPORT PAGE NUMBERS

Insert/Header & Footer/Page Number

1. Click in the header of the report (Section 3) on the second page. Insert Plain Number 3 numbers at the top of the page.
2. On the first page of the report, click Format Page Numbers. In the Page numbering section, click Start at and use the arrows to set the number to 1.

ORGANIZE CONTENT

Home/Clipboard/Cut, Copy, or Paste

Both text and graphic content can be moved or copied from one section or one notebook to another. Content can be moved or copied in the same way you moved or copied it in *Word*—by dragging; by using the Cut, Copy, and Paste commands; or by right-clicking it and selecting Move or Copy and Paste.

To Move Sections from One Notebook to Another:

1. Select the section, such as Training Facilities, that you want to move from the Row of Section tabs in one notebook to a new notebook, such as Office Expansion.
2. Drag the section to the new notebook on the Navigation bar. Make sure the black locator line is where you want to position the new section, and then release the mouse button.

To Move a Section from Within a Notebook:

1. Select the section and drag it to the new location.
2. Release the mouse button to drop it.

Figure 2.5 Move Section to New Notebook

DRILL 4 MOVE A SECTION TO ANOTHER NOTEBOOK

1. Select the Training Facilities tab in the Training Program notebook.
2. Drag the Training Facilities section to the Office Expansion notebook. Drop it between the Planning and Implementation Sections.

Apply It

Task 3
Revise Notebook

SMALL CONFERENCE ROOM

1. Key the following information on the Task Force page; add bullets to the members list.

Task Force Chair (Heading 1)
Jan Johnson

Task Force Members (Heading 1)
Mike Burge
Judy Jones
Jane Martin
Mark West

2. Add a new section to the Office Expansion notebook, and name it **Training Schedule**.
3. Add two new pages in the Training Schedule named **Communication Skill Schedule** and **Management Development Schedule**.
4. Click below the Office Furnishings picture on the Furnishings page, and add the *small conference room* picture from the data files.

Task 4
Move a Section and Organize Content

COMMUNICATION SKILL SCHEDULE

1. Move the Training Schedule section from the Office Expansion notebook to the last section in the Training Program notebook.
2. Paste the *communication skill schedule* from the data files to the Communication Skill Schedule page. Extend the width of the table so that text fits on one line.

INSERT AND FORMAT PRELIMINARY PAGE NUMBERS

Insert/Header & Footer/Page Number

1. Click in the footer of the preliminary pages (Section 2) on the first page. Insert Plain Number 2 numbers at the bottom of the page.
2. Click Format Page Numbers to display the Page Number Format dialog box. In the Number format section, click lowercase Roman numerals (Figure 8.1).
3. Do not change the page number. The first section contains the cover page, which is not numbered; however, it is counted as a page in the preliminary pages. The first page of Section 2 will be numbered ii.

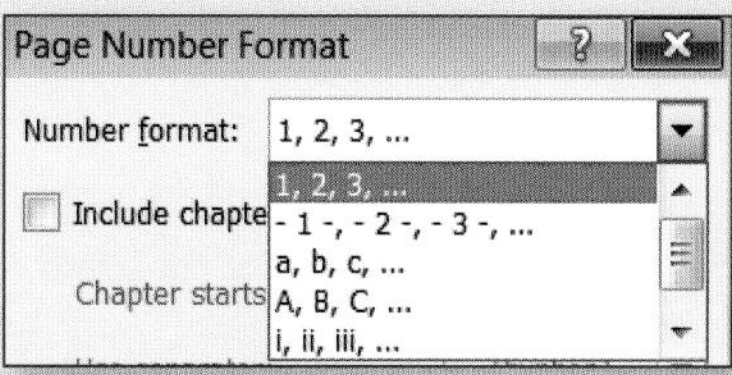

Figure 8.1 Page Number Format

TABLE OF CONTENTS

A table of contents is a listing of all the headings in a document with the page numbers on which they appear. The table of contents can be generated automatically if the headings are formatted using styles. Once a table of contents has been generated, either the page numbers or the entire table of contents can be updated when document content changes.

Word Skills

TABLE OF CONTENTS

References/Table of Contents/Table of Contents

1. Position the insertion point at the beginning of a blank page where the table of contents is to be inserted.
2. Click Table of Contents to display the Built-In gallery, and click the desired style to generate the table of contents.
3. Apply Title style to the title.
4. To update a table of contents, select it and click Update Table; then select Update entire table. Check to see that new headings and page numbers are added.

COPY AND PASTE EXCEL CHARTS

1. Open the *Excel* file, select the chart you want to copy, and click Copy.
2. Position the insertion point in the *Word* file where you want to place the chart and click Paste. The Paste Options button appears at the lower-right corner of the chart.
3. Click the down arrow on the Paste Options button, and select the desired options—usually the defaults shown.

Figure 8.2 Paste Options

To Format Text:

Home/Basic Text/select command

1. Select the text.
2. Click the command on the Ribbon. -or-
3. Point to the Mini toolbar and click the command.

DRILL 2 FORMAT TEXT

1. In the Training Facilities section on the Interior design page in the Training Program notebook, select *Designs by Rae Bradwell* and apply Italic to the text.
2. In the Planning Section on the Project Approval page in the Office Expansion notebook, key **Status** above the current text and apply Heading 1 Quick Style.
3. On the same page below the current text, key and format the text shown at the right.

Tasks to Be Completed (Heading 1)
The Executive Committee is waiting on additional information concerning project completion.

Task Force (Heading 2)
The announcement of members will be made next week.

Budget (Heading 2)
The CEO is waiting on the construction costs and on information from Rae Bradwell on several cost items.

INSERT PICTURES, TABLES, AND GRAPHICS

Generally, pictures, tables, and graphics are inserted using commands on the Insert tab (Figure 2.4). Graphics from other applications can also be pasted into *OneNote*. You already know how to apply many of these commands, such as Picture, Table, Symbol, and Date & Time.

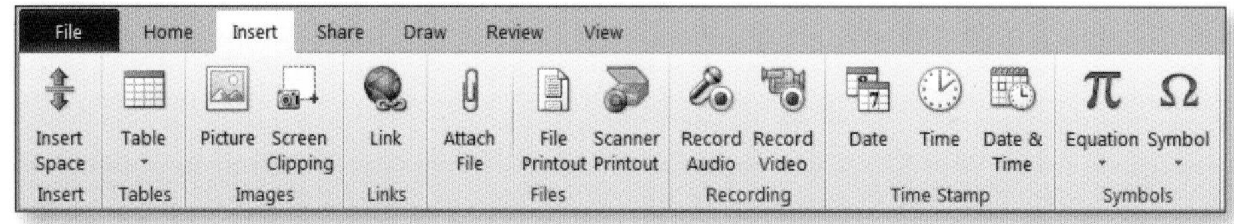

Figure 2.4 Insert Tab Ribbon

To Insert a Picture:

Insert/Images/Picture

1. Click where you want to insert the picture.
2. Browse and select desired picture. Click insert.

To Paste a Graphic from Another Application:

1. Select the graphic and click Copy.
2. Click on the note page to which you want to add the graphic and click Paste.
3. Move the graphic to the desired position.

DRILL 3 INSERT GRAPHICS AND SYMBOLS

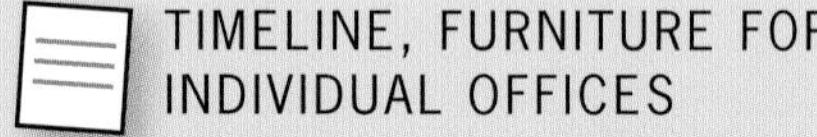

1. Copy the SmartArt graphic from the *timeline* data file, and paste it on Timeframe subpage in the Training Facilities section in the Training Program notebook. Move it to the horizontal center of the page. Click the To Do tag to add a check mark to it to show that the task was completed.
2. In the Training Facilities section on the Interior Design page, insert the trademark symbol (™) after *Bradwell*.
3. In the Training Facilities section on the Furnishings subpage, insert *furniture for individual offices* from the data files.

Apply It

Document 21
Report with Sections and Table of Contents

PORTFOLIO STRUCTURE
ASSET ALLOCATION

1. Open *portfolio structure* and save as *wd8-d21*. Then open the *Excel* file *asset allocation*.
2. Format the report using the styles indicated in the comments, and copy and paste the chart where indicated. Check your solution to ensure that all instructions have been followed, and then delete all comments. Close *Excel*.
3. Insert a Next Page break at the beginning of the document and insert a Cubicles Cover Page. Your name should already be inserted as the author. Complete the other placeholders with information from the report. Use the current date.
4. Insert another Next Page break at the first page of the report. Then double-click in the header area of Section 2 (the blank page), and break the link between Section 2 and Section 1. Do the same for the footer.
5. Click in the header on the first page of the report, and break the link between Sections 3 and 2. Do the same for the footer.
6. Close the header and go to the second page of the body of the report; insert Plain Number 3 numbers at the top of the page. Click Different First Page. Go to the first page of the report, and format the page numbers to begin at 1.
7. Click in the footer of the blank page (Section 2), and insert Plain Number 2 numbers at the center bottom. Format the page numbers using lowercase Roman numerals.
8. Preview the report to make sure the cover page is not numbered. The blank page is numbered ii at the center bottom, and the report body is numbered at the top right with no page number showing on the first page. The second page is numbered 2.
9. Position the insertion point at about 2" on the blank page, and insert a table of contents using Automatic Table 2. Apply Title style to the title.
10. In the body of your report, add **Additional Considerations** above the last paragraph in the report and apply Heading 1 style. Then update the entire table of contents.
11. Resave as *wd8-d21*, and close.

TIP

Preview your solution to make sure all instructions have been followed and the pages are numbered correctly before deleting comments.

Document 22
Report with Sections and Table of Contents

1. Open *wd6-d14* from your solution files, and save as *wd8-d22*.
2. Remove all page numbers; then follow the directions from the previous document to insert a table of contents on a blank page after the cover page. Use plain numbers and number the document the same way you did with the previous document.
3. Preview the document and check page numbering.
4. Resave as *wd8-d22*.

LESSON 2

Collect and Organize Content

OBJECTIVES

- Add a tag
- Format text
- Insert pictures, tables, and other graphics
- Organize content

NOTE TAGS

To Do (Ctrl+1) Notes entered in *OneNote* can be marked with tags. Tags serve as reminders to do a task or to provide additional information. You can search for tags in all open notebooks, and you can add a check to indicate that you have completed the task. Figure 1.1 shows some of the tags available. Tags can also be customized.

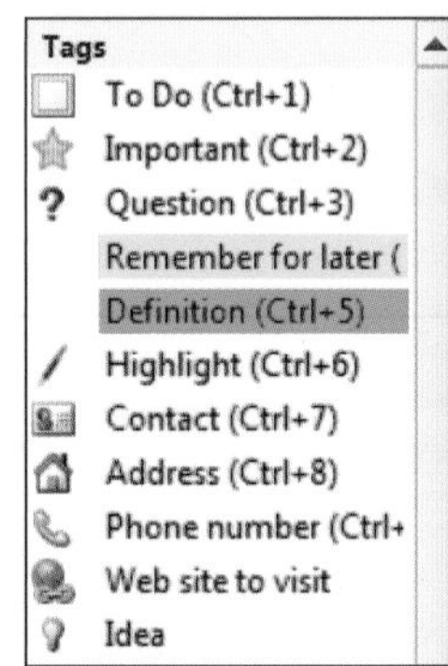

Figure 2.1 Tags

To Insert a Tag:

Home/Tags/To Do

1. Click on the page where you want to add a tag. Tags may be more visible if you position them near the top of a page.
2. Scroll and select the desired tag.
3. Key the information in the tab box that displays.

DRILL 1 ADD TAGS

1. Add a To Do List tag on the Training Facilities Timeframe page.
2. Key the information shown at the right in the tab box.

Get a more specific timeframe from Rae.

FORMAT TEXT

Text can be formatted from the Home tab ribbon or the Mini toolbar with many of the same commands you used in *Word* (Figures 2.2 and 2.3). Note that Tag and Quick Styles have been added to the Mini toolbar. Most of the formatting used in *OneNote* can be done from the Mini toolbar.

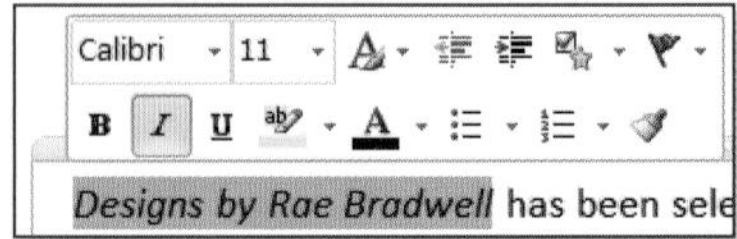

Figure 2.2 Mini Toolbar

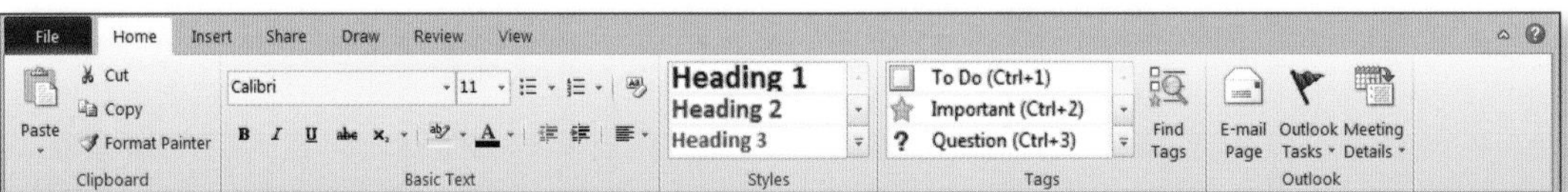

Figure 2.3 Home Tab Ribbon

LESSON 9

Reports with Citations

OBJECTIVES

- Format reports with citations
- Format reports with bibliography
- Learn and apply *Word* commands
- Develop job knowledge and skills

REPORTS WITH CITATIONS

References/Citations & Bibliography/Insert Citation

TIP

Use Print Layout view to work with citations.

A citation provides documentation of sources of work cited or used in a document such as a report. A bibliography is a list of all of the work cited in a document. Citations are positioned at the location in which the work is cited. The bibliography is positioned at the end of the document. The steps for documenting work cited include selecting the style (MLA), selecting a previously used source or creating a new source, inserting the citation, and generating the bibliography, which is called Works Cited when MLA style is used.

Word Skills

ADD CITATION AND CREATE A SOURCE

References/Citations & Bibliography

Figure 9.1 Citations & Bibliography Group

1. Position the insertion point where the reference is to be inserted.
2. Click the down arrow on the Style ❶ box, and select the style.
3. Click Insert Citation ❷ (Figure 9.1), and select Add New Source.
4. Click the down arrow in the Type of Source ❸ box, and select one of the choices, e.g., book, journal article, etc. (Figure 9.2).

TIP

Click the Show All Bibliography Fields checkbox to show more fields in the Create Source dialog box for more complete citations.

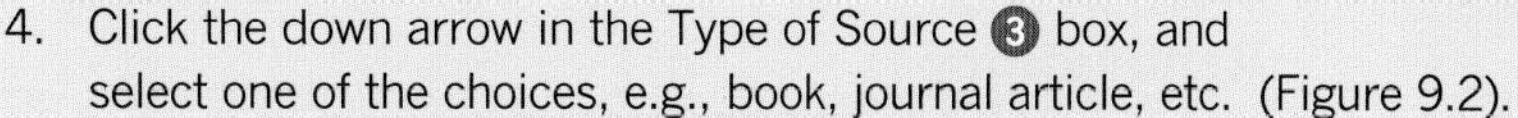

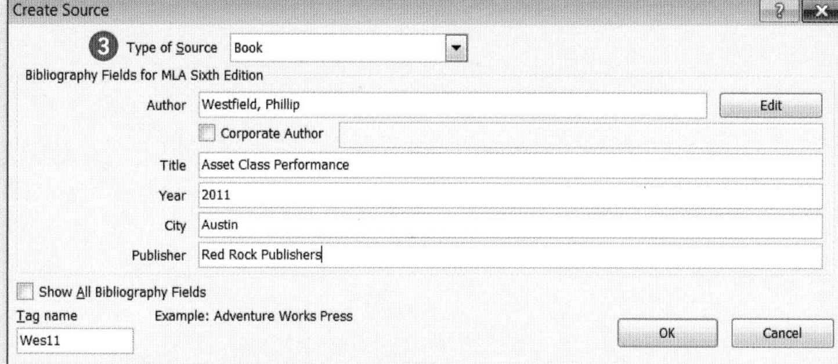

Figure 9.2 Create Source Dialog Box

5. Complete the Bibliography Fields for MLA style, and click OK.

ADD TEXT

To add text to a page, click anywhere on the page. *OneNote* adds a note container for each block of text that you type or write.

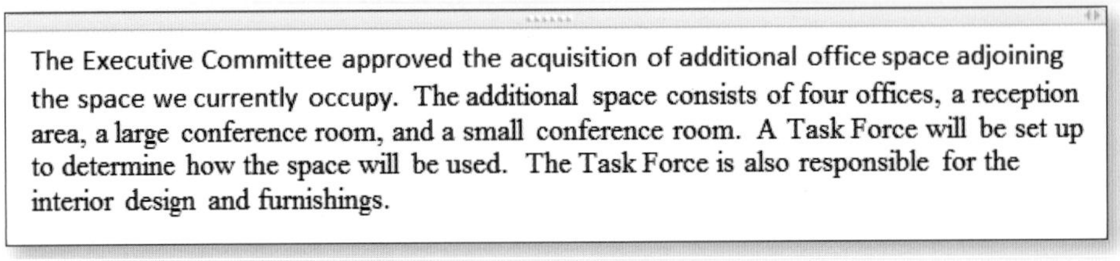

The Executive Committee approved the acquisition of additional office space adjoining the space we currently occupy. The additional space consists of four offices, a reception area, a large conference room, and a small conference room. A Task Force will be set up to determine how the space will be used. The Task Force is also responsible for the interior design and furnishings.

Figure 1.4 Container for Text

DRILL 3 ADD TEXT

1. Click anywhere on the page to add a note container.
2. Key the text shown at the right in the container.

The Executive Committee approved the acquisition of additional office space adjoining the space we currently occupy. The additional space consists of four offices, a reception area, a large conference room, and a small conference room. A Task Force will be set up to determine how the space will be used. The Task Force is also responsible for the interior design and furnishings.

Apply It

Task 1
Set Up New Notebook with Sections, Pages, and Subpages

1. Set up a new business notebook named **Training Program**.
2. Create two sections named **Training Facilities** and **Training Programs**.
3. Under the Training Facilities tab, add the following pages and subpages (subpages are indented).

Space Allocation
Interior Design
   Renovations
   Furnishings

4. Add a subpage between the Space Allocation page and the Interior Design page. Name it **Timeframe**.
5. Under the Training Programs tab, add the following pages and subpages.

Communication Skill
   Effective Presentations
   Effective Letters and Reports
Management Development

Task 2
Add Text to Pages

TASK 2 NOTES

6. Copy the notes from the *task 2 notes* data file and paste to the appropriate *OneNote* pages.

EDIT CITATION

1. Click the citation you want to edit, click the down arrow at the right of the field that is highlighted, and then click Edit Citation (Figure 9.3).
2. Make the needed corrections to the current citation such as adding page numbers to indicate the pages from which material was quoted (Figure 9.4). Click OK.

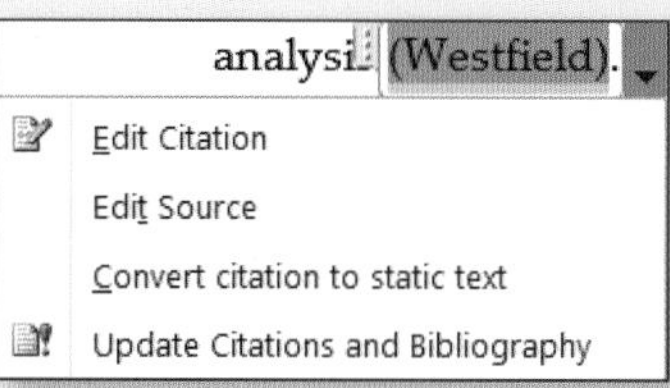

Figure 9.3 Citation Field Menu

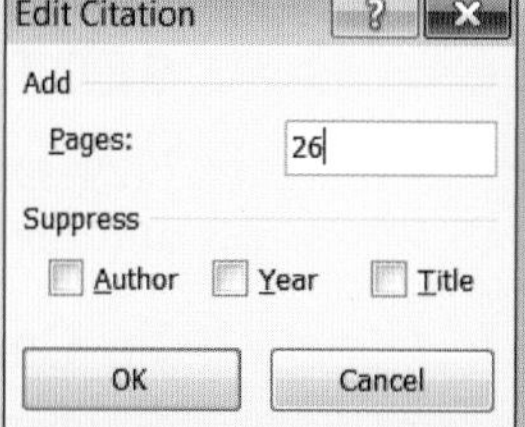

Figure 9.4 Edit Citation

DISCOVER

Add Works Cited Title to Table of Contents

References/Table of Contents/Add Text

1. Select the text of the Works Cited title.
2. Click Add Text.
3. Choose the desired table of contents level for the selected text.

CREATE THE BIBLIOGRAPHY

References/Citations & Bibliography/Bibliography

1. Add a page break below the last line of the report. Position the insertion point at 2".
2. Click Bibliography to display the gallery of bibliography styles. Select Works Cited for MLA.
3. Click in the title and apply Title style as shown in Figure 9.5.
4. Use Add Text command to add the Works Cited title to the table of contents as Level 1, and then update the table of contents.

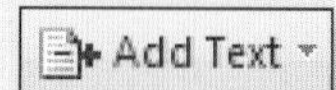

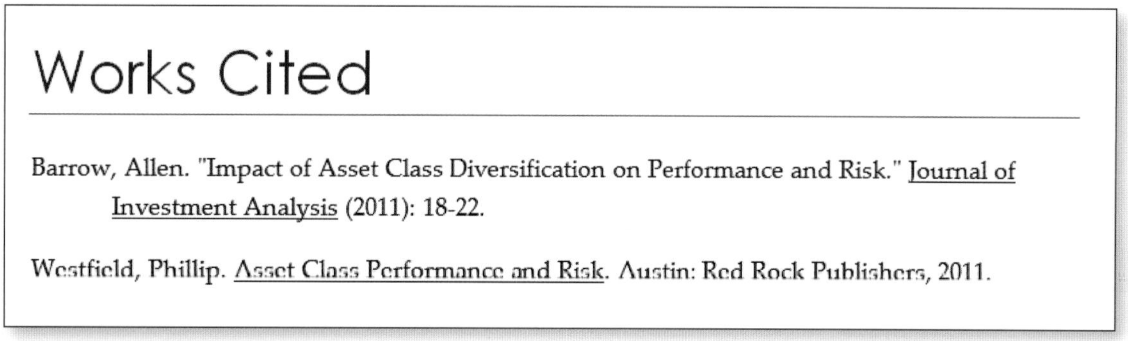

Works Cited

Barrow, Allen. "Impact of Asset Class Diversification on Performance and Risk." Journal of Investment Analysis (2011): 18-22.

Westfield, Phillip. Asset Class Performance and Risk. Austin: Red Rock Publishers, 2011.

Figure 9.5 Works Cited

JOB KNOWLEDGE

Effective document design does far more than just make a document attractive. It accomplishes a number of objectives:

- Supports document content
- Denotes formality
- Adds organizational structure
- Enhances readability
- Provides a consistent image
- Emphasizes important points

DRILL 1 CREATE A NOTEBOOK

1. Launch *OneNote*.
2. Create a new business notebook; store it in your solution files.
3. Name the notebook **Office Expansion**.
4. Leave the notebook open.

★ TIP

You can leave all notebooks open in *OneNote*, and all work in *OneNote* is saved automatically. You do not need to save any of the drills or applications.

★ TIP

The thick black line shows where the new page will be positioned.

SECTIONS AND PAGES

New sections are created by renaming New Section 1 and then using the Create a New Section tab.

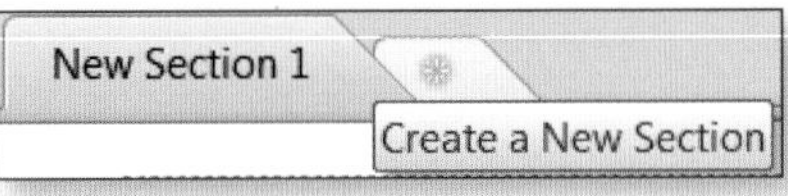

To Create New Sections:

1. Click the notebook in the Navigation bar that you want to add sections.
2. Right-click New Section 1 tab and click Rename. Key the desired name.
3. Click the Create a New Section tab; when the New Section 2 tab appears, rename it following directions in step 2.

To Create New Pages and Subpages:

1. Click the notebook in the Navigation bar and the section to which you want to add pages.

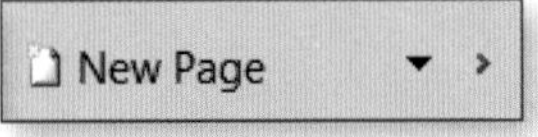

2. At the top of the page tab list, click the New Page button to display an untitled page.
3. Repeat the process to add additional pages.
4. To name the page, click in the text box that displays at the left top of the page and key the name.
5. To add a subpage, right-click the Page tab and click Make Subpage. The page will appear in the page tab list and will be indented at the first position.
6. To add a new page within the list of pages, point to the page tab list until the little New Page icon with an arrow appears. Point to the icon and move it up or down by moving the mouse pointer to the desired location, and then click the icon.

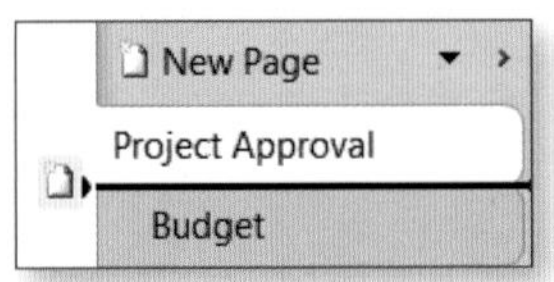

DRILL 2 CREATE SECTIONS, PAGES, AND SUBPAGES

1. Click the Office Expansion notebook and create two new sections.
2. Name the first section **Planning** and the second section **Implementation**.
3. In the Planning section, add two new pages named **Project Approval** and **Budget**. Make *Budget* a subpage.
4. Add a new page between the project approval and budget pages. Make it a subpage named **Task Force**.

Use Figure 1.3 to check your solution.

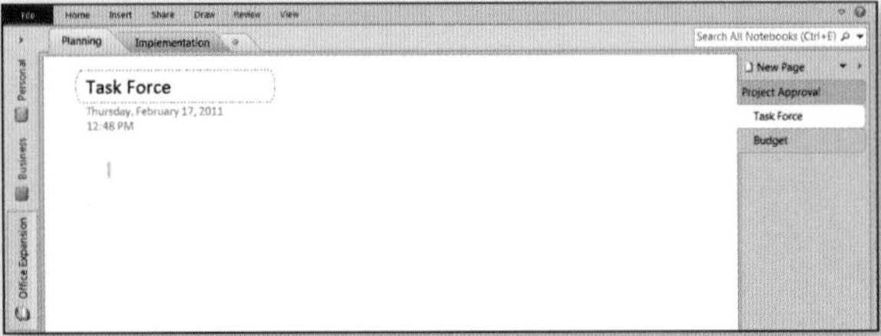

Figure 1.3 Drill 2 Quick Check

Apply It

Document 23
Report with Citations and Bibliography

1. Open *wd8-d21* and save as *wd9-d23*.
2. On page 1 below the heading *Historic Asset Class Analysis*, position the insertion point before the period at the end of the second sentence. Use the information below to insert the Westfield citation and add the new source information. Use MLA style.
3. Position the insertion point in the next paragraph before the period at the end of the Barrow quote. Use the information shown below to insert the Barrow citation and add the new source information.

Make any adjustments in the position of the charts or in the document that might be needed.

Citation 1: Book	Citation 2: Journal Article
Author: Westfield, Phillip	**Author:** Barrow, Allen
Title: Asset Class Performance and Risk	**Title:** Impact of Asset Class Diversification on Performance and Risk
Year: 2011	**Journal Name:** Journal of Investment Analysis
City: Austin	**Year:** 2011
Publisher: Red Rock Publishers	**Pages:** 18–22

4. Add a page break at the end of the report, and position the insertion point at about 2".
5. Generate the bibliography and select the Bibliography style (Works Cited for MLA).
6. Click in the title and apply Title style.
7. Add the title text to the table of contents at Level 1, and update the entire table of contents. Resave as *wd9-d23* and close.

MANAGE SOURCES

References/Citations & Bibliography/Manage Sources

Manage Sources The Source Manager maintains a master list of all references keyed in *Word 2010*. The Master List is shown in the left pane of the Source Manager, and the references you are using in the open document are shown in the Current List in the right pane. References may be copied from the Master List to the Current List. The Source Manager can be used to copy, delete, edit, or create new sources.

Word Skills

USE THE SOURCE MANAGER

References/Citations & Bibliography/Manage Sources

1. Open a document and click Manage Sources to display the Source Manager. See Figure 9.6 on the next page.
2. To use an existing source, locate it in the Master List, select it, and click Copy to move it to the Current List.

LESSON 1

Create Notebooks

OBJECTIVES

- Create and save a notebook
- Add sections, pages, and subpages
- Key notes on a page

GETTING STARTED

The top portion of the opening screen is shown in Figure 1.1. Note that the tabs on the Ribbon are displayed in minimized form. The Ribbon will display the groups and commands when the Maximize button is clicked or the tab is clicked. Many of the commands are the same as those you used in *Word 2010*. The Quick Access Toolbar is also available and can be customized.

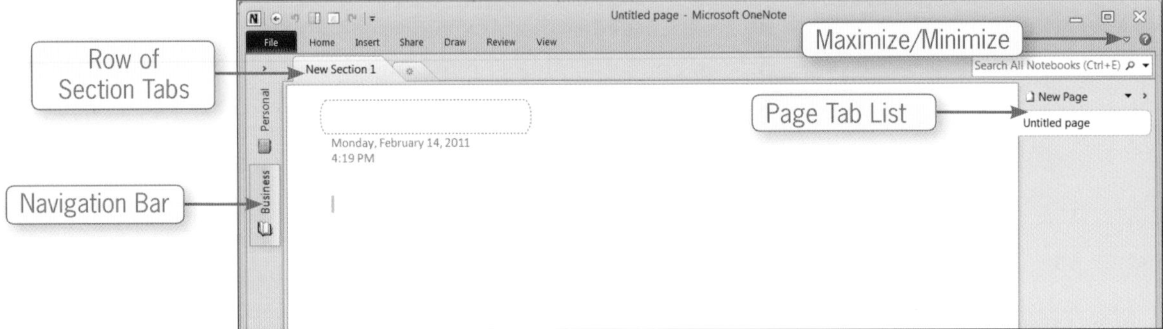

Figure 1.1 Minimize/Maximize Ribbon Command

CREATE A NOTEBOOK

File/New

Multiple notebooks can be created for a variety of business or personal uses. As a student, you may want to create a notebook for each class with sections and pages for class notes, research papers, and various projects. Businesses may create notebooks for different types of projects, events, presentations, or research work. Each project can be divided into sections, pages, and subpages. You can set up sections and pages when you create a notebook, or you can add them as you need them.

To Create a New Notebook:

1. Follow the path to display the New Notebook dialog box.
2. Indicate where to store the notebook.
3. Key the name of the notebook.
4. Browse to select the location and click Create Notebook.

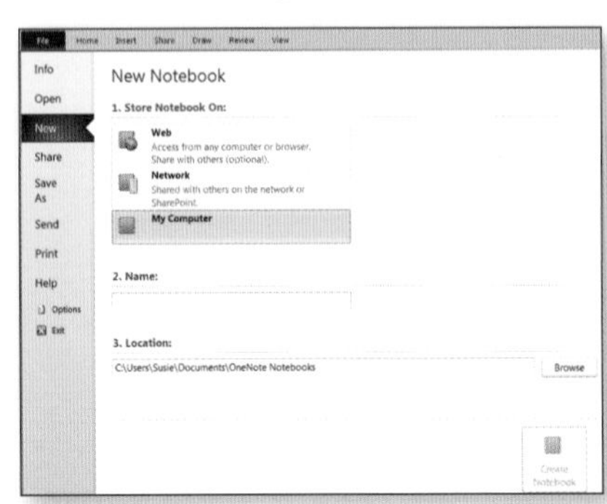

Figure 1.2 Create New Notebook

3. To edit a source, click it and then click Edit. Make the revisions desired.
4. To create a new source, click New, select the type of source, and key the information in the text boxes.
5. To delete a source, select it and click Delete.

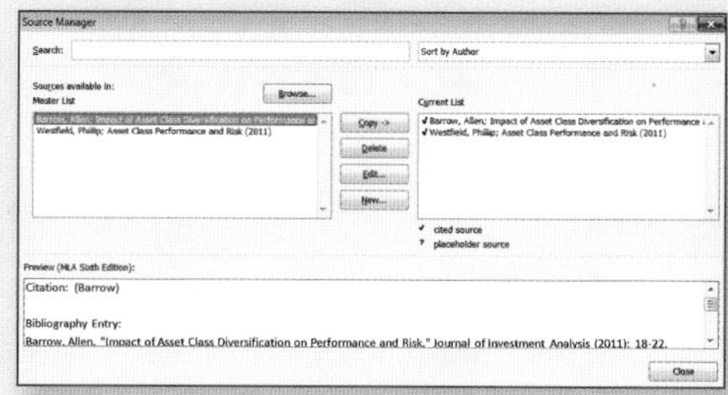

Figure 9.6 Source Manager

Apply It

Document 24

Report with Citations and Bibliography

IMAGE

TIP

Position citations before the period at the end of sentences.

1. Open the *image* data file and save as *wd9-d24*.
2. Use the information below to create two new sources using MLA style.

Citation 1: Interview	**Citation 2:** Interview
Interviewee: Glenn, Patrick	**Interviewee:** Quick, Jennifer
Title: Chairman and CEO	**Title:** Client
Interviewer: Metz, Julie	**Interviewer:** Wheeler, Robert
Year: 2011	**Year:** 2011
Month: September	**Month:** October
Day: 22	**Day:** 6

3. Insert the Glenn citation at the end of the first sentence of the report.
4. Insert the Quick citation at the end of the first sentence after the Clients heading.
5. On a new page at the end of the report, create a bibliography using Works Cited style. Position the title at about 2", and apply Title style.
6. Add the title text to the table of contents, and update the table of contents.
7. Resave as *wd9-d24* and close.

CAREER FOCUS

© Stockbyte/Getty Images

Participating in professional organizations is important for both students and business professionals. These occasions to network with peers in the same field provides numerous learning opportunities. Seminars and conferences sponsored by professional organizations provide the most current information available on topics related to your career. Professional organizations also provide great leadership experiences for those who actively participate in the organization.

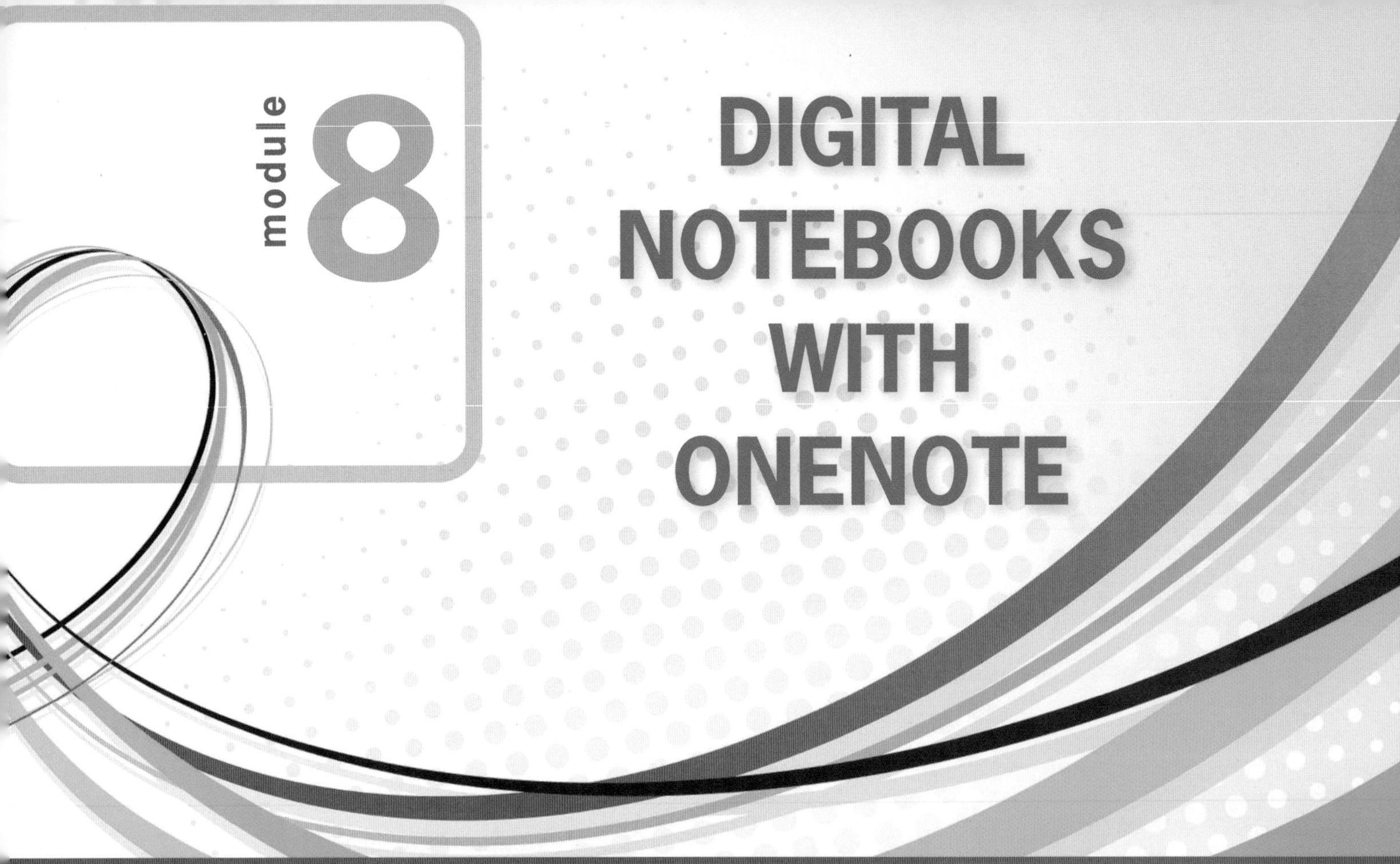

DIGITAL NOTEBOOKS WITH ONENOTE

overview

This short module is designed as an introduction to *OneNote*. *OneNote 2010* enables you to use digital notebooks to collect and store a variety of information in one location. You can collect and organize text, pictures, digital handwriting, audio, video, links to information, and more in a digital notebook. You can create as many digital notebooks as you need for different projects, tasks, or events. Digital notebooks can be shared on networks, SharePoint Server, or on the SkyDrive. You will share a notebook you create in this module on the SkyDrive in the next module. You will also have the opportunity to work with a project that simulates a realistic business setting.

ESSENTIALS

1. Create Notebooks
2. Collect and Organize Content
3. Access and Print Content

Project 11—VanHuss & VanHuss, Inc.—Integrating Word, Excel, and OneNote

Customize Document Themes

LESSON 10

OBJECTIVES

- Create custom themes
- Apply customized document themes
- Learn and apply *Word* commands
- Develop job knowledge and skills

DOCUMENT THEMES

In this lesson, you will create a new theme by customizing an existing one. Customizing a theme enables a company to select colors and fonts that match its branding and corporate identity. Themes can be shared across *Office* programs so that all documents have a coordinated, uniform appearance.

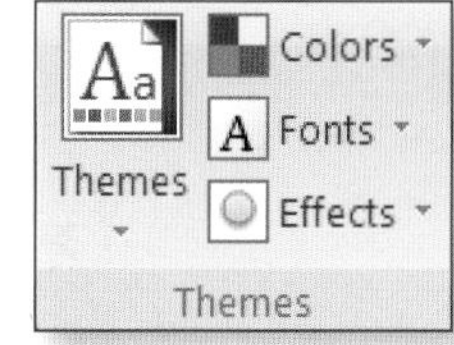

Figure 10.1 Themes

To customize a theme, you first create the colors, choose fonts, select the effects, and then save the theme. These actions can be handled by the commands in the Themes group (Figure 10.1).

Word Skills

CREATE NEW THEME COLORS

Page Layout/Themes/Colors

1. To customize colors, click the Colors down arrow to display the gallery of Built-In colors for each theme. Then click Create New Theme Colors gallery to display the Create New Theme Colors dialog box. Any colors can be changed.
2. Click the down arrow button ❶ on each theme color you wish to change to display a palette showing theme colors ❷, standard colors ❸, and custom colors ❹ that can be selected, as shown in Figure 10.2.
3. Select the desired color and repeat the step until all colors that you want to change have been changed.
4. Select Custom 1 in the Name box, and key a name for the new theme colors. Then click Save.

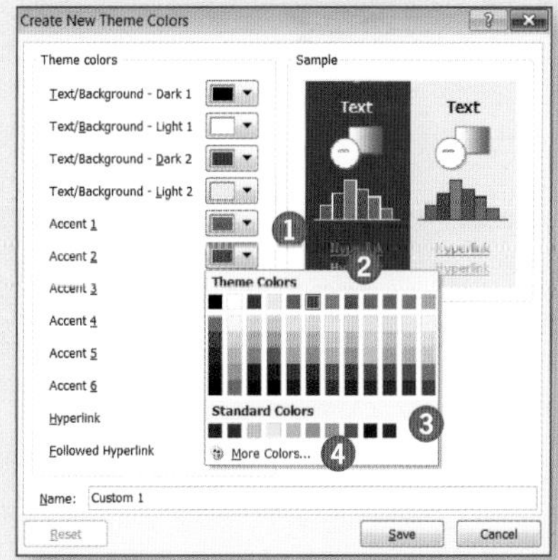

Figure 10.2 Create New Theme Colors

Job 8,
continued

4. Select the Subject and Priority lines in the Contact form's Notes box; press CTRL + C to copy the text. Click the *Word* document button on the taskbar to display your document; click CTRL + V to paste the two lines on the page.
5. Point to the *Outlook* icon on the taskbar and then click the First Quality Print Shop - Contact form. Click Save & Close to save the contact. Click the *Outlook* button on the taskbar. In Contacts, change to Business Card view if necessary, select the First Quality Print Shop business card, and press CTRL + C. Click the *Word* document button on the taskbar and press CTRL + V to place the contact icon on the page. Double-clicking the icon will display the Contact form.
6. Create a task to call Marconi Catering on 5/4/20-- to confirm the delivery of continental breakfast and lunch for both May 7 and 8. Assign the category Open House to this task and make it high priority. Drag this task to the Contacts folder and insert the following information in the Contact form:

   Marconi Catering | (714) 555-0121
   9021 Garden Drive | Garden Grove, CA 92840-0109

   Copy the subject, due date, and priority lines from the Contact form Notes box and paste it in the *Word* document. Embed a copy of the Marconi Catering business card in the *Word* document.
7. Format the document attractively. Figure P10.2 shows one formatting option. Save the *Word* document as *p10-j8*.

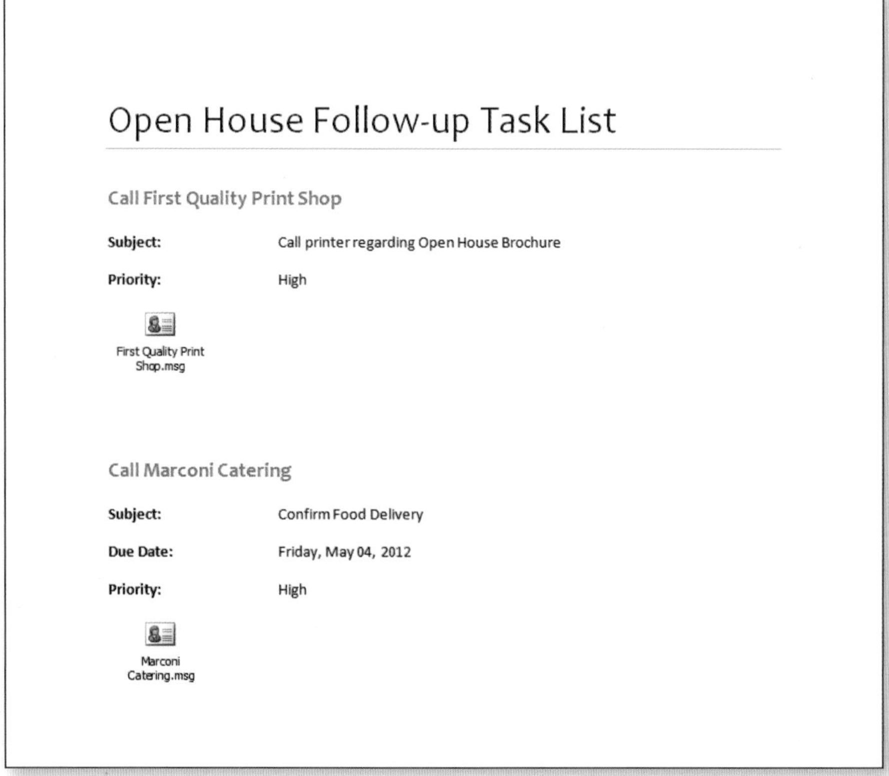

Figure P10.2 Embedded Icons

You cannot create effects. You can select the effects you want to apply with your custom theme. Effects apply only to some graphics.

SELECT EFFECTS

Page Layout/Themes/Effects

1. Click the Effects down arrow to display the gallery of effects.
2. Preview and select the desired effect scheme and apply it to the open document.

CREATE NEW THEME FONTS

Page Layout/Themes/Fonts

1. Click the Fonts down arrow to display the Create New Theme Fonts dialog box.
2. Click the arrow next to Heading font, and select the heading font desired; then click the arrow next to Body font, and select the body font desired.
3. Select Custom 1 in the Name box, key a name for the theme fonts, and click Save.

CREATE NEW DOCUMENT THEME

Page Layout/Themes/Themes

1. Click Themes to display the gallery of themes.
2. Click Save Current Theme to display the Save Current Theme dialog box.
3. Select Theme 1, key the name for your custom document theme, and click Save.

Apply It

Document 25

Customize Document Theme

1. Open *wd9-d25* and save as *wd10-d25*.
2. Create new theme colors by changing to the following colors:

Text/Background – Dark 2: Standard Dark Blue

Accent 1:	Standard Blue	**Accent 4:**	Standard Yellow
Accent 2:	Standard Dark Red	**Accent 5:**	Standard Light Blue
Accent 3:	Custom RGB 50, 150, 25	**Accent 6:**	Orange, Accent 3, Darker 25%

3. Save as **My Colors**. The colors are applied to the open document.
4. Create new theme fonts using Corbel as the heading font and Constantia as the body font.
5. Save as **My Fonts**. The fonts are applied to the open document.
6. Apply Oriel effects to the open document. Save the current theme as **My Theme**.
7. Resave as *wd10-d25* and close.

Document 26

Apply Custom Theme

1. Open *wd6-d15* and save as *wd10-d26*.
2. Apply My Theme to the document. Preview and adjust the table by positioning the report title at 1.7" rather than at 2" (position insertion point at the top of the page and tap DELETE once).
3. Resave as *wd10-d26* and close.

Job 7

Mail Merge with Contacts List

LETTERHEAD

You will use the *Word* Mail Merge feature to merge a letter to each client in your contacts list.

1. Open the revised *letterhead* template and save it as a *Word* document named *p10-j7 main*. In the Mailings tab, click Start Mail Merge, and select Step by Step Mail Merge Wizard to display the Mail Merge task pane.
2. Select Letters, click Next, and choose to use the current document to set up the letter. Click Next.
3. Choose Select from Outlook contacts. Click Choose Contacts Folder. The Select Contacts dialog box displays. Contacts should be selected. Click OK. The Mail Merge Recipients dialog box displays. Click OK. Click Next.
4. Insert the date April 2, 20-- and then tap ENTER twice. Click Address block in the Mail Merge task pane to display the Insert Address Block dialog box. Click OK. Tap ENTER.
5. Click Greeting line in the Mail Merge pane. Change the punctuation following the greeting line to none, and then click OK. Tap ENTER.
6. Key the following text in the body of the letter:

   Aldrin Glenn Aircraft will be sponsoring its Annual Open House at the Huntington Beach facility on May 7-8, 20--, in Exhibition Hall. Divisions from Aldrin Glenn Aircraft, nationwide, are invited to display special accomplishments and innovations.

   All vendors and suppliers are invited to set up a display and provide demonstrations on new products. If you are interested in being an exhibitor, please complete and return the enclosed *Exhibitor Reservation Form* by May 1, 20--.

   We look forward to having you join us at our 20-- Open House. Please call me if you have questions or if I can be of assistance to you.

7. Insert an appropriate closing and sign the letter from you, Open House Committee Chair. Click Next to preview your letter. Remove the extra space between lines in the address block.
8. Click Next and complete the merge. Choose to edit individual letters. Merge all records. Save the merged letters document as *p10-j7*.

Job 8

Embed Contacts Icon in Word Document

Prepare a list of items for your assistant to follow up on in preparation for the Open House. The easiest way to prepare this list is to copy the tasks in your task list into a *Word* document. Because some of the tasks require calling people in your contact list, you will insert an icon after the task so that your assistant can double-click the icon and access the contact information.

Embed or insert an icon by selecting the business card in the Contacts folder; then copy (CTRL + C) the item and paste it in the *Word* document.

1. In a new *Word* document, key **Open House Follow-up Task List** and apply the Title style; tap ENTER. Leave the document displayed on the screen.
2. In *Outlook*, create a new task with the subject **Call printer regarding Open House Brochure**. Category: Open House. High priority. Message: **Confirm with First Quality Print Shop that Open House brochures will be delivered no later than May 2, 20--.**
3. Drag the task to the Contacts button; if information is displayed in the name and e-mail address fields in the Contact form, delete it. Key the following information in the Contact form:

   First Quality Print Shop | (714) 555-0113
   7001 Shadwell Drive | Huntington Beach, CA 92646-0531

Merge Documents

LESSON 11

OBJECTIVES

- Merge form letters
- Learn and apply *Word* commands

A data source can be a *Word* file, *Access* database table, or *Excel* worksheet data.

MAIL MERGE

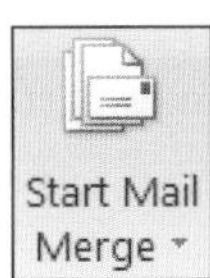

Mail merge is used to prepare a document such as a form letter that is sent to multiple recipients. With form documents, most of the content information is sent to all recipients. However, some information varies with each recipient such as the address and salutation. The variable information is contained in the data source. Use the following steps and the Mail Merge Wizard to complete mail merge:

1. Set up the main document. The main document contains the letterhead and the content that remains the same for each version of the merged document. Merge fields are inserted as placeholders for the variable information that comes from the data source file.
2. Prepare the data source or use an existing data source. This file contains all of the variable information that will be merged into the fields in the main document.
3. Edit or refine the list of recipients of the document.
4. Add the merge fields to the main document. These are the placeholders for the variable information that will be added to the document.
5. Preview the documents and complete the merge.

Data Source

Main Document

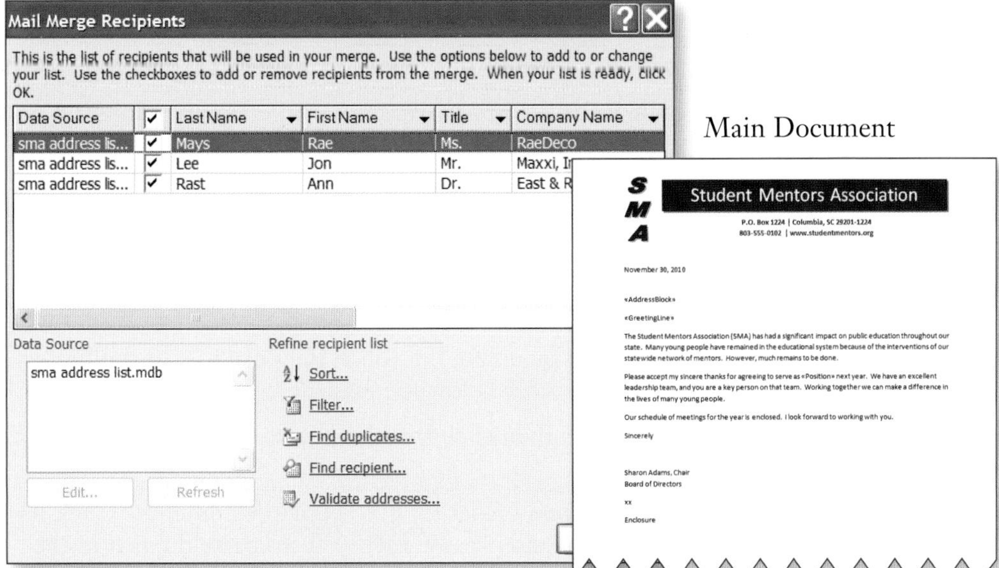

SMA
Student Mentors Association
P.O. Box 1224 | Columbia, SC 29201-1224
803-555-0102 | www.studentmentors.org

November 30, 2010

«AddressBlock»

«GreetingLine»

The Student Mentors Association (SMA) has had a significant impact on public education throughout our state. Many young people have remained in the educational system because of the interventions of our statewide network of mentors. However, much remains to be done.

Please accept my sincere thanks for agreeing to serve as «Position» next year. We have an excellent leadership team, and you are a key person on that team. Working together we can make a difference in the lives of many young people.

Our schedule of meetings for the year is enclosed. I look forward to working with you.

Sincerely

Sharon Adams, Chair
Board of Directors

xx

Enclosure

Merged Document

SMA
Student Mentors Association
P.O. Box 1224 | Columbia, SC 29201-1224

December 1, 2010

Ms. Rae Mays
RaeDeco
426 Trade Street
Greer, SC 29651-3734

Dear Ms. Mays

The Student Mentors Association (SMA) has had a significant impact on public education throughout our state. Many young people have remained in the educational system because of the interventions of our statewide network of mentors. However, much remains to be done.

Please accept my sincere thanks for agreeing to serve as a Board member next year. We have an excellent leadership team, and you are a key person on that team. Working together we can make a difference in the lives of many young people.

Our schedule of meetings for the year is enclosed. I look forward to working with you.

Sincerely

Sharon Adams, Chair
Board of Directors

xx

Enclosure

Figure 11.1 Mail Merge Documents

Job 4

E-mail Signature and Theme

1. Create a new e-mail signature named **Open House**. Key **Your Name | Open House Committee Chair**. Make this the default signature for all new messages and Replies/forwards. Apply the Ice theme.
2. Create a new mail message to **Dr. Thomas Schwartz**. Key the following message:

   Please review the attached *Exhibitor Reservation Form*. This is a draft.

   Please send me your suggestions and recommendations for changes by this Friday.
3. Insert the business card you created in Job 3 below your signature. Print the message and send.

Job 5

Use Quick Steps

You will create a subfolder in your Inbox to hold all messages pertaining to the Open House. Then you will create a Quick Step to move the message to the Open House folder.

1. Right-click the Inbox folder.
2. Choose New Folder to display the Create New Folder dialog box. Key **Open House** for the name of the new folder and click OK.
3. Click Create New to display the Edit Quick Step dialog box.
4. Name the Quick Step **Move to Open House**.
5. Click the Choose an Action drop-list arrow and click Move to folder. Click the Choose folder drop-list arrow and click Open House. Click Finish.
6. Open the Sent Items folder and select the e-mail that you created in Job 4 to Dr. Thomas Schwartz.
7. Click the *Move to Open House* Quick Step. Check to see that the message has been moved to the Open House folder.

Job 6

Outlook Note in Word Document

You receive a phone call from an Aldrin Glenn Steering Committee member recommending that you include a liability insurance clause on the Exhibitor Reservation Form. You key this information in a note as you are on the phone:

Exhibitor's Liability Insurance

Exhibitors must carry their own liability insurance coverage for any loss or damage resulting from demonstrating their products.

Apply the Open House category to the note, and then follow these procedures to copy the contents of the note into the footer of the form.

1. In Notes, double-click the Exhibitor's Liability Insurance note if necessary so that it is displayed on the screen. Do not close Notes or *Outlook*.
2. Open the Exhibitor Reservation Form you created in Job 2. Choose to edit the footer and position the insertion point in the footer below the existing content.
3. Click the *Outlook* button on the taskbar; then click the note to display the note on the same screen as the form.
4. Select the body of the note, and then press CTRL + C to copy the contents. Click the insertion point in the footer of the form and press CTRL + V to paste the text in the footer. Choose the Merge Formatting Paste option.
5. Save the form as *p10-j6*.

You may want to include the word *main* in your main document name so you can easily identify it.

In this lesson, you will use letterhead templates from the data files that you open and save with an appropriate name. Because your data files are not accessed from My Templates, select the option. Use the current document rather than Start from a template.

The variable information for each recipient is called a record.

MAIL MERGE WIZARD

Mailings/Start Mail Merge/Start Mail Merge

1. Open a new document and save it with a meaningful name.
2. Click Start Mail Merge, and select Step by Step Mail Merge Wizard; then follow the six steps of the Mail Merge Wizard as explained below.

Step 1. Select document type

1. Select one of the five document types (Figure 11.2).
2. Click Next: Starting document at the bottom of the Mail Merge task pane.

Step 2. Select starting document

1. Click one of the options shown in Figure 11.3.
2. Click Next: Select recipients at the bottom of the Mail Merge task pane.

Step 3. Select recipients

1. Select one of the options shown in Figure 11.4.
2. If you select Type a new list, click Create to display the New Address List dialog box.
3. Click Customize Columns and leave the fields that you want to include. Delete those not needed, and add new fields if needed or rename a field on the list (Figure 11.5).
4. For letters, you would typically use Title, First Name, Last Name, Company Name, Address Line 1, City, State, and ZIP Code.

   Add fields for variable information that will be inserted in the body of the letter.
5. Click OK after the fields have been customized.
6. Key records in the table. Tap TAB to move from one column to the next.
7. After you have keyed all records, click OK to display the Save As dialog box. Note the default directory is My Data Sources in the My Documents folder. Your instructor may direct you to save your files to your solutions folder.
8. Key the filename. The file type is Microsoft Office Address Lists. Click Save.
9. Click Next: Write your letter at the bottom of the Mail Merge task pane.

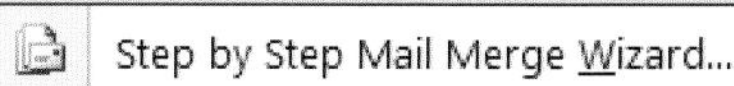

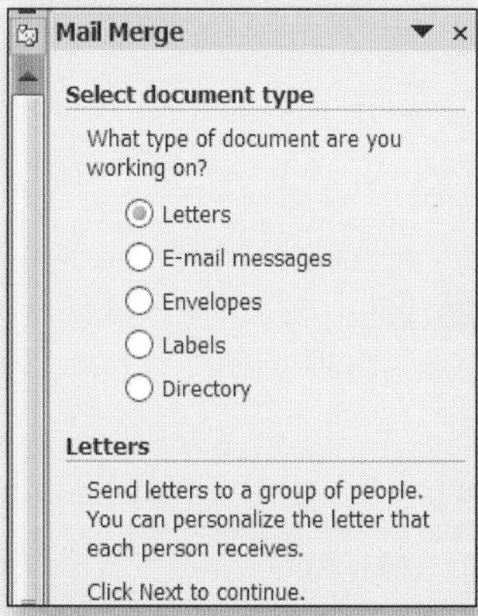

Figure 11.2 Document Type

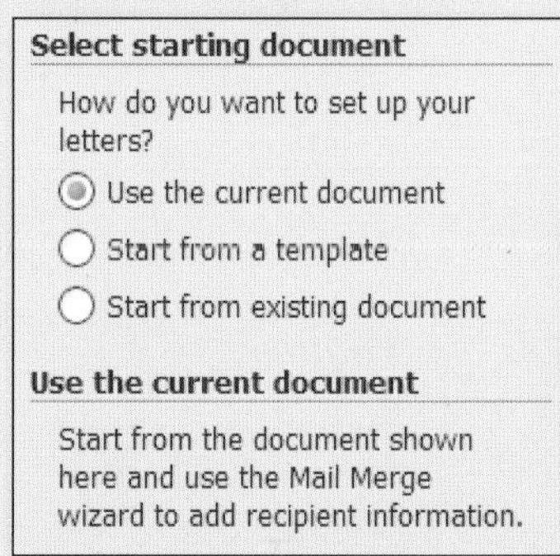

Figure 11.3 Starting Document

Figure 11.4 Select Recipients

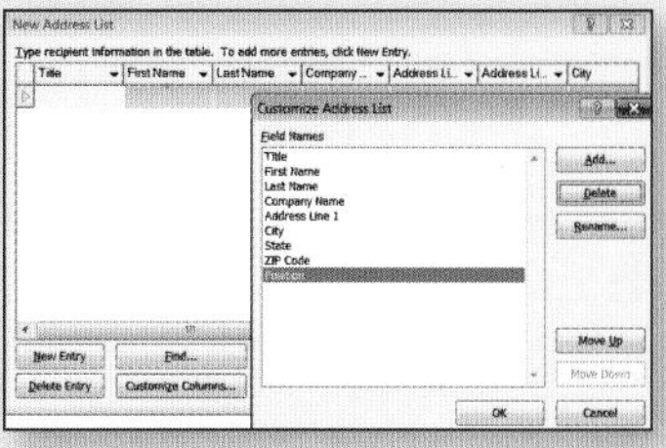

Figure 11.5 Customize Address List

Job 1,
continued

3. Display Tasks. Drag the Open House task to the Calendar button in the Navigation Pane. This opens an Appointment form with Open House inserted in the Subject box. Indicate the time of the meeting from 2:00 to 2:30; the meeting will take place in the Facility Manager's Office.
4. You and the Facility Manager decided on May 7–8, 20-- for the Open House. Schedule this event on your calendar.

Job 2
E-mail Attachment

LETTERHEAD

Create the Exhibitor Reservation Form that will be used as an e-mail attachment.

1. Open the data file *letterhead* and apply the Waveform theme. Save the revised template in your solutions folder with the same name.
2. Using the revised *letterhead* template, key the document shown in Figure P10.1. Use appropriate size fonts and spacing to attractively display the document. Insert a text box for the boxed text and format attractively.
3. Save as a *Word* document with the name *p10-j2*.

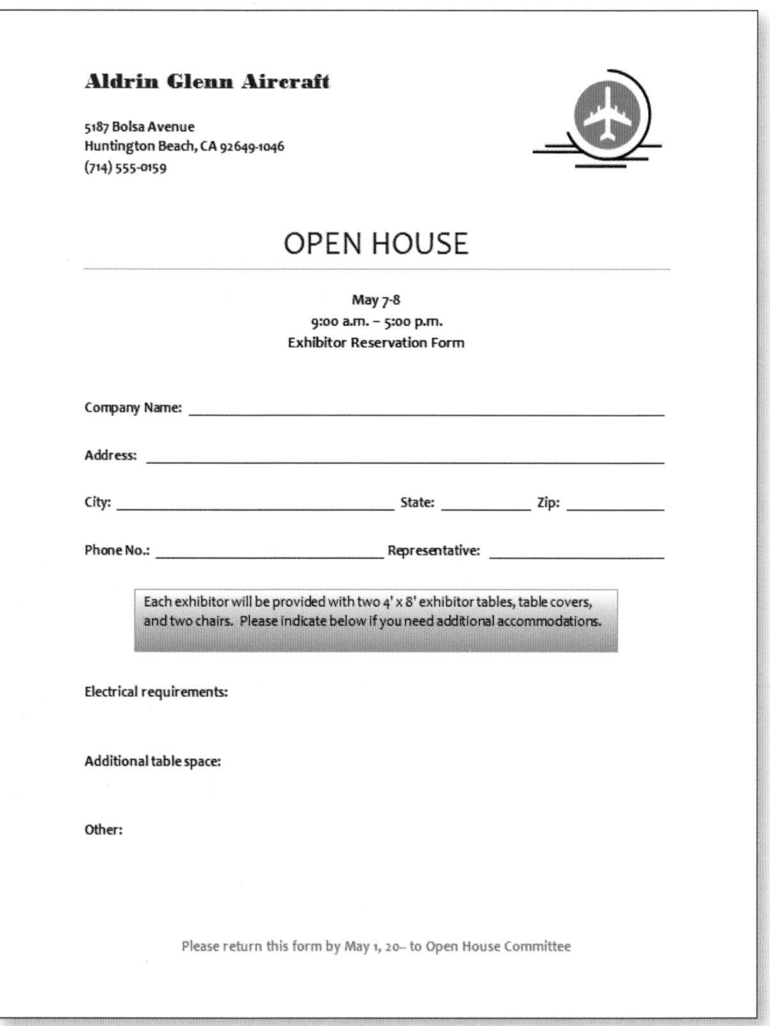

Aldrin Glenn Aircraft

5187 Bolsa Avenue
Huntington Beach, CA 92649-1046
(714) 555-0159

OPEN HOUSE

May 7-8
9:00 a.m. – 5:00 p.m.
Exhibitor Reservation Form

Company Name: ______________________

Address: ______________________

City: ______________ State: ________ Zip: ________

Phone No.: ______________ Representative: ______________

Each exhibitor will be provided with two 4' x 8' exhibitor tables, table covers, and two chairs. Please indicate below if you need additional accommodations.

Electrical requirements:

Additional table space:

Other:

Please return this form by May 1, 20-- to Open House Committee

Figure P10.1 Exhibitor Reservation Form

Job 3
Create Business Card

Create a business card for yourself using the title **Open House Committee Chair**. Include the name, address, and phone number of Aldrin Glenn Aircraft on your business card.

Mailings/Write & Insert Fields/ Address Block

Alternate method: Insert the Address Block or the Greeting Line from the Mailings tab.

Should you need to edit one of the letters, click Edit recipient list and make the necessary changes to the data source file.

Step 4. Write your letter

1. Insert the date if it is not included in your letterhead template. Select Update automatically. Tap ENTER twice.
2. Click Address block on the Mail Merge task pane (Figure 11.6). Click OK to accept the defaults for the recipients' name, company name, and postal address. Tap ENTER once.
3. Click Greeting line, click the down arrow on the punctuation field, and select None (Figure 11.7). Click OK and Tap ENTER once.
4. Key the body of the letter. Insert fields where appropriate (Mailings/Write & Insert Fields/Insert Merge Field). Insert only those fields that are not part of the address or greeting line, such as Position.

Step 5. Preview your letters

1. Remove the extra spacing between the lines of the letter address.
2. Click the navigation buttons to preview each of the letters (Figure 11.8).
3. Click Next: Complete the merge.

Step 6. Complete the merge

1. Click Edit individual letters (Figure 11.9). Click All; then OK.
2. Save the document that contains the merged letters and close.

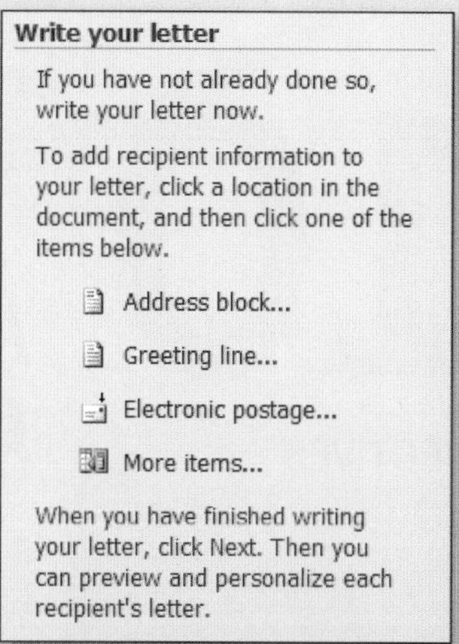

Figure 11.6 Write Your Letter

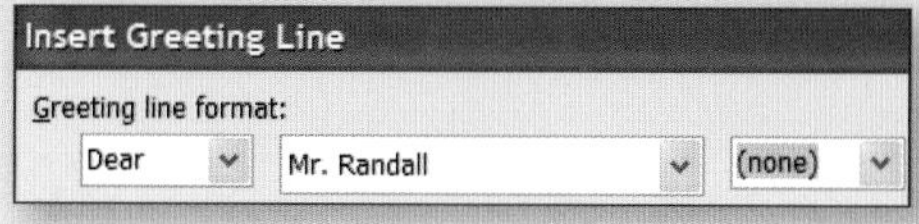

Figure 11.7 Greeting Line

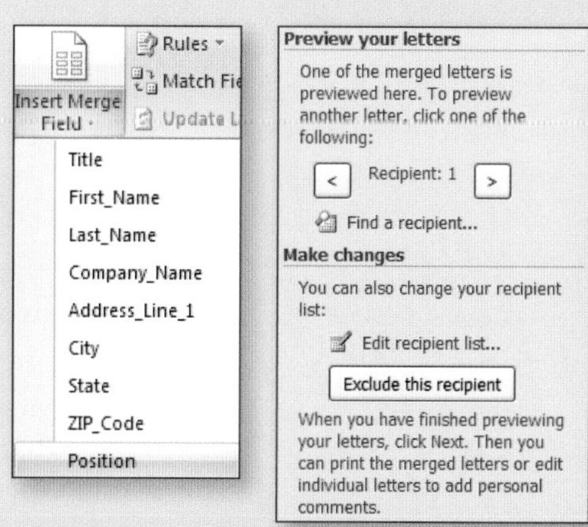

Figure 11.8 Preview Letters

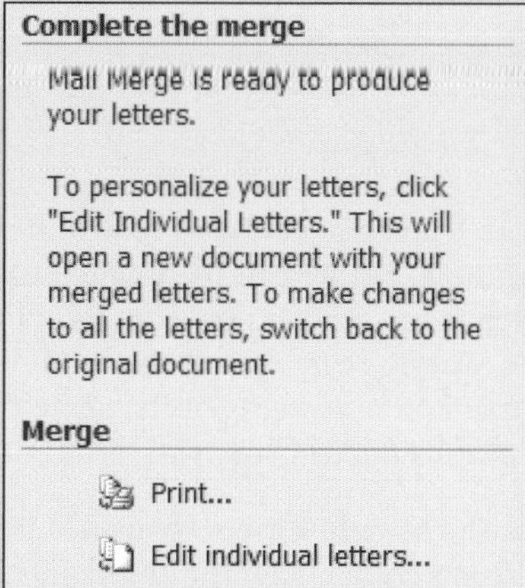

Figure 11.9 Complete the Merge

project 10

Aldrin Glenn Aircraft: Integrating Outlook and Word

OBJECTIVES

- Use *Outlook* components
- Use AutoCreate
- Perform mail merge using *Outlook* contact list
- Embed *Outlook* items in *Word* document

SETTING

You are in charge of planning the Annual Open House for Aldrin Glenn Aircraft. Various divisions of Aldrin Glenn Aircraft from across the nation will display special projects and accomplishments. Vendors, suppliers, and manufacturers are invited to demonstrate their new products. Guests from all the Aldrin Glenn Aircraft facilities nationwide and key customers are invited to the Open House.

JOBS

1. AutoCreate items
2. E-mail attachment
3. Create business card
4. Apply e-mail signature and theme
5. Use Quick Steps
6. Embed *Outlook* note in *Word* document
7. Mail merge using *Outlook* contact list
8. Embed contacts in *Word* document

STANDARD OPERATING PROCEDURES

1. Use the Ice theme for all e-mail messages and the Waveform theme for all *Word* documents.
2. Use the *letterhead* template for all letters and forms.
3. Prepare a subfolder in your solution files to save all work for this project. If a job has a file that can be saved, name each file as *p10-j* (plus the job number, such as *j1*, *j2*, etc.), and then close the file.
4. Preview, proofread, and print documents.

Job 1

AutoCreate

Outlook's AutoCreate feature generates a new item when an item is dragged from one folder to another. For example, a note can be dragged to Tasks to create a new task, or a note can be dragged to Contacts to create a new contact. Tasks can be dragged to Calendar to create a new appointment. AutoCreate works only with items of different types. If you drag an item into a folder that contains items of the same type, the item is copied or moved. In this job, you will drag various *Outlook* items to different folders to create new items.

Display the To-Do Bar to the right of the Notes window. After completing steps 2 and 3, you should see the task and the appointment listed in the To-Do Bar.

1. Create a note with the title **Open House.** Create a new category called **Open House** and apply the Peach color. Key the following message in the note:

   Make an appointment with the Facility Manager to set date for this year's Open House.

2. Drag the note that you just created to the Tasks button in the Navigation Pane. An Open House Task form opens with the information from the note. Insert tomorrow's date for the due date. Indicate the priority of the task as High.

Apply It

Document 27
Mail Merge

SMA LETTERHEAD

1. Open *sma letterhead* and save as *sma board main.* Use the Mail Merge Wizard and the information below to complete a mail merge.
2. Use the fields and key records shown for the address list; save as *sma address list* in your solutions folder.

Field Name	Record 1	Record 2	Record 3
Title	Ms.	Mr.	Dr.
First Name	Rae	Jon	Ann
Last Name	Mays	Lee	Rast
Company	RaeDeco	Maxxi, Inc.	East & Rast, PA
Address Line 1	426 Trade Street	194 Skyhawk Road	468 Boykin Avenue
City	Greer	Irmo	Lamar
State	SC	SC	SC
ZIP Code	29651-3734	29063-7960	29069-8870
Position	a Board member	an officer	an officer

3. Key the letter shown below; format it appropriately. The field to insert in the body of the letter is shown in bold.

«AddressBlock»

«GreetingLine»

The Student Mentors Association (SMA) has had a significant impact on public education throughout our state. Many young people have remained in the educational system because of the interventions of our statewide network of mentors. However, much remains to be done.

Please accept my sincere thanks for agreeing to serve as **«Position»** next year. We have an excellent leadership team, and you are a key person on that team. Working together we can make a difference in the lives of many young people.

Our schedule of meetings for the year is enclosed. I look forward to working with you.

Sincerely

Sharon Adams, Chair

Board of Directors

xx

Enclosure

4. Complete the merge and save the merged letters as *wd11-d27.* Save and close all documents.

2. Under Choose default signature, insert your e-mail address for E-mail account. Click the New messages drop-list arrow and choose **Your Name**. Click OK until you return to your Inbox.
3. Select a stationery for your e-mail.
4. Send an e-mail message to yourself using the stationery and signature you just created. Insert an appropriate subject line. Key the message:

This stationery will be applied to all my e-mail. The signature will be the default signature for all new messages until I change it.

5. Print the e-mail message. The printed copy will show your signature but may not include the stationery design.

Job 12
Create and Use Quick Steps

1. Compose and send an e-mail to yourself explaining the advantages of using Quick Steps.
2. Use the *Complete xx* Quick Step to delete the message. Move the message from the Deleted Items folder back to your Inbox.
3. In the Navigation Pane, right-click the Inbox folder and choose New Folder. The Create New Folder dialog box displays.
4. Key **Outlook Class (xx)** in the Name box; replace xx with your initials. Click OK. The Outlook Class folder displays in the Navigation Pane below the Inbox.
5. Create a New Quick Step that moves class assignments to the Outlook Class folder: Name the Quick Step **Class Assignments xx**.
6. Select Move to folder as the action. The messages will be moved to the Outlook Class folder.

Job 13
Use Conversation View

1. Set *Outlook* to display your messages in Conversation view.
2. Select all the options in the Conversation Settings drop list.
3. Click on message threads to see how *Outlook* grouped the messages in Conversation view.

Job 14
Set AutoArchive Options

1. Display the AutoArchive dialog box. Click the checkbox to select *Run AutoArchive every*; change the number of days to 1.
2. Click the checkbox to prompt before AutoArchive runs if necessary.
3. Remove the check mark in the checkbox for *Delete expired items (e-mail folders only)*.
4. Click the checkboxes for *Archive or delete old items* and *Show archive folder in folder list* if necessary.
5. Change *Clean out items older than* to 2 days (set this option so that e-mail messages from the first day of class will be moved).
6. By default, *Move old items to:* is selected and the default location for moving old items is to the Archive folder. No changes need to be made.
7. The next time you sign on to your computer, you will be asked whether you want to archive old items. If you wish to do so, messages older than the specified time will be moved to the Archive folder. If you do not want to archive the messages, click Cancel.

Document 28

Mail Merge

MV LETTERHEAD

1. Open *mv letterhead* and save as *mv regional meetings main*.
2. Use the Mail Merge Wizard and the information below to complete a mail merge. Format the letters appropriately. The fields to add to the address list and insert in the letters are shown in bold. Save the address list as *mv regional managers*.
3. Save the merged letters as *wd11-d28* and close.

Field Name	**Record 1**	**Record 2**	**Record 3**
Title	Ms.	Mr.	Ms.
First Name	Sonya	Steve	Robin
Last Name	Hayward	Mulvaney	Crider
Company	All are regional managers of MelView Advertising, Inc.		
Address Line 1	468 N. Orange Avenue	207 14th Street NE	4842 S. Tryon Street
City	Orlando	Atlanta	Charlotte
State	FL	GA	NC
ZIP Code	32801-4756	30309-3606	28217-2402
Meeting Date	March 20	July 8	October 15
Location	Orlando	Atlanta	Charlotte

«AddressBlock»

«GreetingLine»

Last year the senior management team began a pilot program of rotating its quarterly planning meeting among the regional offices. The feedback from the regional managers was outstanding, and our senior managers benefited immensely from the input they received. Therefore, we plan to continue this practice.

Would you please host our **«Date»** meeting in **«Location»**? The meeting you hosted last year worked extremely well, and we would like to use the same format.

We look forward to a very productive meeting in your region.

Sincerely

Robert A. Mazingo

xx

DRILL 2 CREATE QUICK STEPS

1. Create a new Quick Step that will move messages to the Deleted Items folder. Name the Quick Step **Complete xx** (replace xx with your initials).
2. Select Delete message from the Choose an Action drop list.
3. Click Finish.

USE AUTOARCHIVE

In a busy office, old messages, tasks, and other items will accumulate very quickly unless you clean them out or archive them. The AutoArchive feature in *Outlook* lets you specify how often the items should be archived, where the archived items should be placed, and other criteria for archiving. Items are archived every 14 days by default. *Outlook* places archived items in the Archive folder unless you specify otherwise.

To Set AutoArchive Options:

File/Options/Advanced

1. Click Advanced in the left pane (Figure 6.7) and then click AutoArchive Settings to display the AutoArchive dialog box (Figure 6.8).

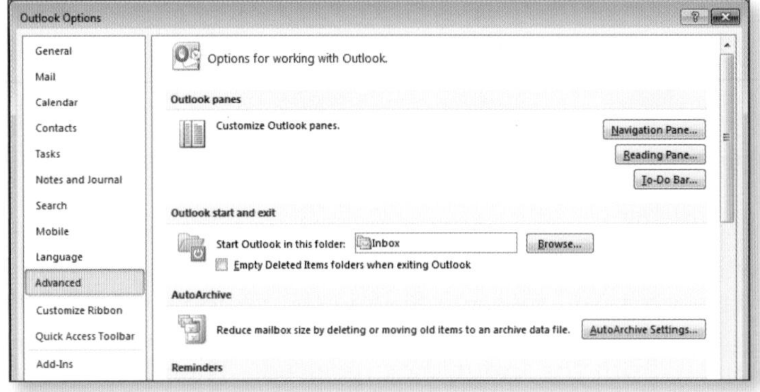

Figure 6.7 Outlook Options

Figure 6.8 AutoArchive Dialog Box

2. Change the AutoArchive settings as needed. Select the frequency that you want items archived, whether you want the items to be deleted, how old items should be when they are archived, and the folder that the archived items will be moved to.
3. Click OK twice.

Apply It

Job 11
Create Signature and Use Stationery

1. Create a new signature; name the file using your first and last name. Key the following text in the Edit signature box. Select a font and a color for your signature.

Your Name

[Insert the name of your class]

project **2**

Creative Designs & Production II: Apply Word in a Business Setting

OBJECTIVES

- Create effective *Word* documents
- Use a coordinated document theme for all documents
- Work independently with few instructions

SETTING

In this project, you continue your work as Events Coordinator for Creative Designs & Production, LLC. You may wish to refer to Project 1 on page 24 to refresh your memory about the setting and for contact information.

Jobs

1. Contact sheet (Quick Part)
2. Memo
3. Customize and prepare fax
4. Mail merge (letters)
5. Report
6. Creative Designs & Production style guide

STANDARD OPERATING PROCEDURES

It is your responsibility to follow the three instructions listed below as well as the Standard Operating Procedures from Project 1 without being reminded to do so.

1. Use the CDP custom theme and standard document formats for all jobs. Use the *cdp letterhead* for letters, the CDP Memo Quick Part for memos, and the current date unless directed otherwise.
2. Preview, proofread, and print each job.
3. Create a subfolder for Project 2 in your *Word* solutions file. Save the file for each job as *p2-j* (plus the job number, such as *j1*, *j2*, etc.), and then close the file.

Job 1

Contact Information

CDP LETTERHEAD

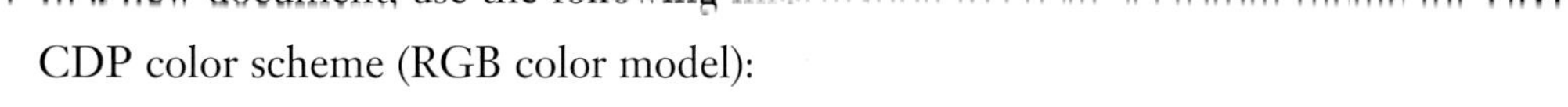

1. In a new document, use the following information to create a custom theme for CDP.

   CDP color scheme (RGB color model):

   Accent 1: Red—204 | Green—102 | Blue—0
   Accent 2: Red—50 | Green—50 | Blue—255
   Accent 3: Red—255 | Green—205 | Blue—100
   Accent 4: Red—153 | Green—153 | Blue—245

   Followed Hyperlink: Red—204 | Green—102 | Blue—0

   You will save the default Office fonts and effects as part of the theme.

2. Use the information and Figure P2.1 to design a contact sheet that CDP can use to attach to each proposal and contract it sends to clients.
3. Logo and company name: Copy from letterhead and increase font to 26 point.
4. Contact Information: Heading 1; increase font to 16 point and change text color to White; apply Dark Red shading (Home/Paragraph/Shading).

TIP

Use Contact information provided in Project 1.

CONVERSATION MANAGEMENT

Outlook's Conversation view can help you better manage your messages. This new feature organizes message threads into conversations so that you will see the original message with all the replies to that message grouped together. This pulls together related messages regardless of the folder in which they are stored.

To Use Conversation View:

View/Conversations/Show as Conversations

1. Click the message header in the Inbox folder.
2. Follow the path and select the Show as Conversations checkbox. Choose All folders or This folder.
3. Click the Conversation Settings drop-list arrow to show options (Figure 6.3).
4. Check the options on how you want the conversation displayed. (Check all items.) Selecting the option Show Messages from Other Folders will include Sent Items, Calendar items, and Tasks.
5. With Conversation view selected, you can click on any message in the Inbox folder, and it will display the conversations regarding the topic (Figure 6.4).

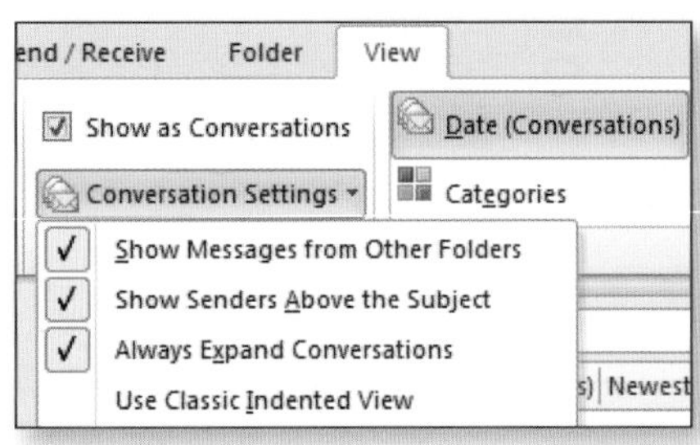

Figure 6.3 Conversation Settings

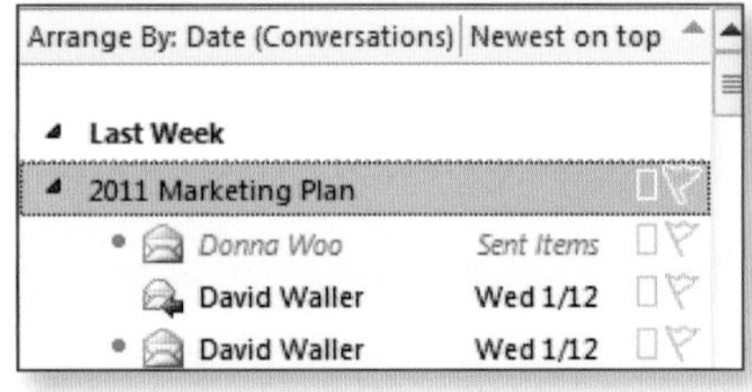

Figure 6.4 Conversation View

USE QUICK STEPS

Quick Steps are designed to help you process messages easier and faster (Figure 6.5). Quick Steps will perform several actions and execute them in one step. For example, you can mark a message as read and move the message to the Deleted Items folder with just one click on a Quick Step.

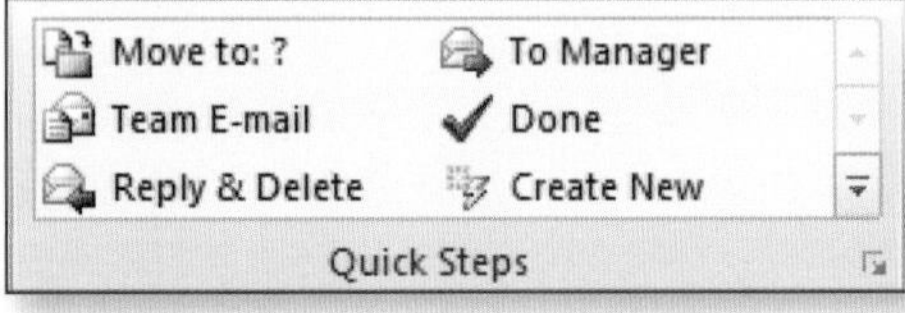

Figure 6.5 Quick Steps

To Create New Quick Steps:

Mail/Home/Quick Steps

1. In the Quick Steps group, select Create New to display the Edit Quick Step dialog box (Figure 6.6).
2. Key a name for the new Quick Step.
3. Click the Choose an Action drop-list arrow and select an action. Provide any other information, such as a folder name.
4. Click Finish.

To Use Quick Steps:

1. Select the message header or open the message.
2. Click the Quick Step that is to be applied.

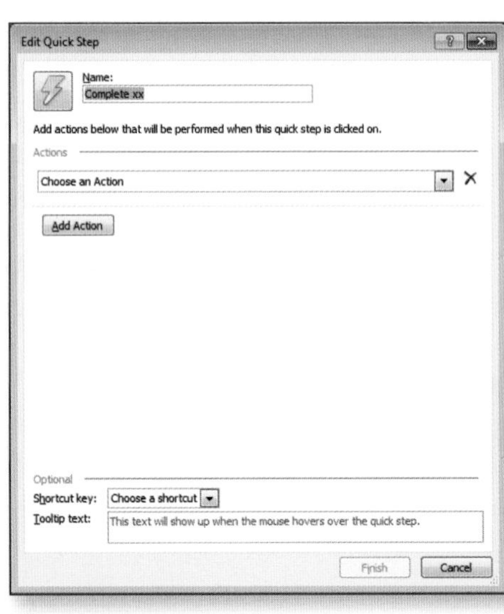

Figure 6.6 Edit Quick Steps

DISCOVER

Remove Hyperlink

Right-click the hyperlink and select Remove Hyperlink. Note that the hyperlink color and line are removed.

Category and Options

Insert/Quick Parts/Save Selection to Quick Part Gallery

1. Click Category down arrow and select Create New Category; in the Name box, key **CDP** and click OK.
2. Click Options down arrow and select Insert content in its own page. Then click OK.

5. Corporate Headquarters: Heading 2 style; include address, telephone, fax, website, and e-mail format for all employees. E-mail address should be: **Firstname.Lastname @cdp-va.net**. Remove the hyperlink from the standard employee e-mail format.
6. Key Contacts: Format same as Contact Information. Include the three owners and their names, titles, telephone extensions, and personal e-mail. Extensions are: Lori, 0174; Jeff, 0175; and Steve, 0176.
7. Select all information and save as a Quick Part. Use CDP Contact Information for both the name and description. Create a new category named CDP, and choose to Insert content in its own page.
8. Close the document you used to create the Quick Part; do not save it.
9. In a new document, insert the Quick Part and use Figure P2.1 to check your document.

Creative Designs & Production, LLC

Contact Information

Corporate Headquarters
1776 Robin Hood Road
Richmond, VA 23220-1012

Telephone: 804-555-0134

Fax: 804-555-0196

Website: www.cdp-va.net

E-mail: Firstname.Lastname@cdp-va.net

Key Contacts

Owners
Lori Maxwell
Creative Director and Manager
Telephone Extension: 0174
Lori.Maxwell@cdp-va.net

Jeff Maxwell
Producer
Telephone Extension: 0175
Jeff.Maxwell@cdp-va.net

Steve Johnson
Business Manager
Telephone Extension: 0176
Steve.Johnson@cdp-va.net

Figure P2.1 CDP Contact Information

Job 2

Memo

1. Use the CDP Memo Quick Part you saved in Project 1 to prepare a memo to Lori from you. If the Quick Part has been deleted from your computer, use the *cdp memo* template that is in the data files for Project 1 to create a new Quick Part.
2. Subject: CDP Contact Information. Key the memo shown below.

The CDP Contact Information that you asked me to design and prepare using our custom theme is attached. Please review it and let me know if you would like to make any changes. Once you have approved it, I will provide all employees with the file so that they can copy it and save it as a Quick Part on their computers.

All of our employees now have Office 2010 installed on their computers. I have spent some time talking with all employees who prepare client documents about the importance of coordinating all documents using the custom theme. Several short training sessions have been scheduled to ensure that our employees can produce publications, worksheets, slide presentations, and documents designed to complement our logo and to promote our corporate identity and branding efforts.

I will give you an update once the training begins. Please let me know if you want to participate in any of the training sessions. Steve has indicated he would like to talk with our employees during the training sessions about changes he is making in our proposals and contracts.

DRILL 1 DISPLAY OUTLOOK TODAY

1. Launch *Outlook* and display Outlook Today.
2. View your appointments for the day, if any have been scheduled.
3. Schedule an appointment for today to begin in one hour. The subject is Marketing Strategy Meeting; it will be held in Conference Room 2. Add a note to bring a copy of the draft plan.
4. Save and close the appointment window.
5. Display the Outlook Today screen; the appointment is listed under Calendar.
6. Click the appointment to see the Appointment form. The note to bring the draft plan displays. Close the Appointment form.

CREATE SIGNATURES AND USE OFFICE THEMES

People often conclude an e-mail message with their name, title, company name, and perhaps their telephone number. If you use the same closing lines each time, you can create a signature that will automatically insert the text for you and provide a consistent closing for each message.

You can also apply an *Office 2010* theme to a message, identical to themes you have used in other *Office* applications. Using a theme for e-mail messages that matches themes used for other company documents can strengthen branding and ensure consistency. You can apply a theme, select theme colors or fonts, or apply page color to improve the look of your messages.

To Create a Custom Signature:

File/Options/Mail

1. Click the Signatures button in the right pane to open the Signatures and Stationery dialog box.
2. Click New to open the New Signature dialog box (Figure 6.2).
3. Key a name for the signature; click OK.
4. In the Edit signature box, key the text you want to appear in the signature. Format the text as needed.
5. In the Choose default signature section of the dialog box, select the e-mail account that will have the automatic signature. In the New messages and Replies/forwards lists, select the signature you want to appear. Click OK twice to return to the Inbox.

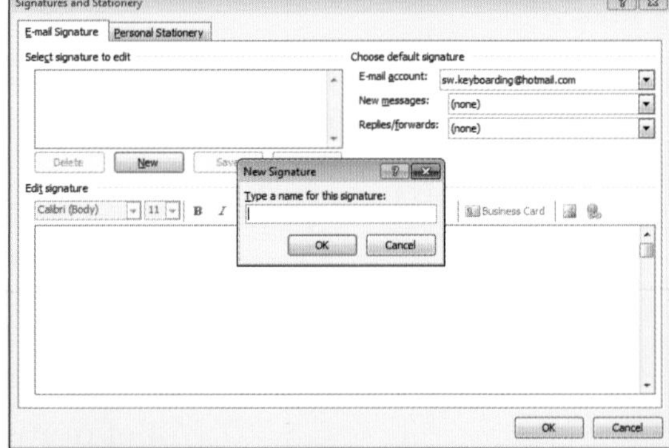

Figure 6.2 Create New Signature

To Apply a Stationery Theme:

File/Options/Mail

1. Click Stationery and Fonts to open the Signatures and Stationery dialog box.
2. Click Theme and select the theme you want to use. Click OK three times.

Job 3
Fax

If you do not have access to the Internet to download the fax, use the *business fax* document from your data files and begin following directions with step 2.

Do not apply the CDP document theme to this template. Many fax machines transmit a black and white copy, and using a larger font for a fax cover is preferable.

1. Download the Business Fax Cover Sheet from (File/New/Office.com/Faxes/Business Fax Cover Sheet/Download).
2. The fax is in Compatibility Mode, meaning that it is not in *Word 2010* file format. Convert it to a *Word 2010* document (File/Convert).
3. Increase the height of the text box below FAX to allow room for the two-line company name.
4. Key the company information in the text box. Remove the clip art and copy and paste the CDP logo in the lower-left corner of the FAX box. Size it about .75" × .75".

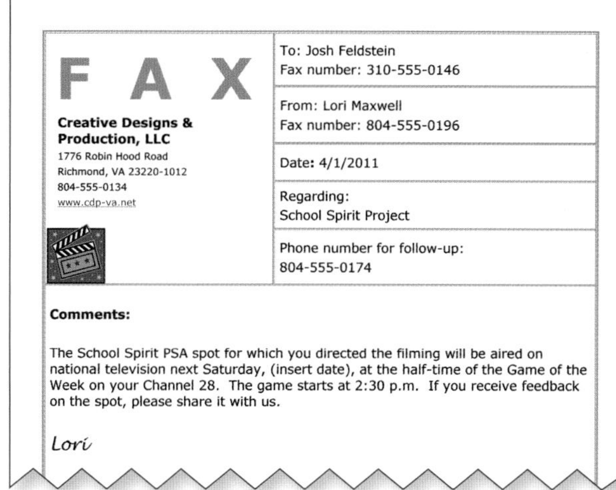

FAX

Creative Designs & Production, LLC
1776 Robin Hood Road
Richmond, VA 23220-1012
804-555-0134
www.cdp-va.net

To: Josh Feldstein
Fax number: 310-555-0146

From: Lori Maxwell
Fax number: 804-555-0196

Date: 4/1/2011

Regarding:
School Spirit Project

Phone number for follow-up:
804-555-0174

Comments:

The School Spirit PSA spot for which you directed the filming will be aired on national television next Saturday, (insert date), at the half-time of the Game of the Week on your Channel 28. The game starts at 2:30 p.m. If you receive feedback on the spot, please share it with us.

Lori

Figure P2.2 Fax

5. Save as a template in your solution files named *cdp fax* and close it.
6. Use the template and the information below to prepare a fax from Lori to Josh Feldstein (310-555-0146) regarding the School Spirit Project. Use Lori's direct number (804-555-0174) for follow-up.
7. Add comments:

   The School Spirit PSA spot for which you directed the filming will be aired on national television next Saturday, (insert date), at the half-time of the Game of the Week on your Channel 28. The game starts at 2:30 p.m. If you receive feedback on the spot, please share it with us.

   Lori

Job 4
Mail Merge

CDP LETTERHEAD

1. Use the *cdp letterhead* from the data files, the information below, and the Mail Merge Wizard to complete a mail merge.
2. Use the following fields and records to key the address list. Save it as *cdp focus group list*.

Field Name	Record 1	Record 2	Record 3
Title	Ms.	Mr.	Dr.
First Name	Zoe	Max	Lee
Last Name	Davis	Reed	Lane
Address Line 1	3542 Pump Road	687 E. Main Street	3524 W. Cary Street
City	Richmond	Richmond	Richmond
State	VA	VA	VA
ZIP Code	23233-1115	23219-2405	23221-2729
Area	arts	education	business

3. Key the letter on the next page; insert the fields. Format the letter appropriately. Position the date at about 2.3" for this short letter.
4. Save the main document as *cdp focus group main* and the final merged document after you have edited all letters as *p2-j4*.

LESSON 6

Manage Messages

OBJECTIVES

- Use Outlook Today
- Create signature and apply theme
- Use Conversation view
- Use Quick Steps
- Use AutoArchive

MANAGE MESSAGES

Outlook provides methods of customizing and organizing messages. With e-mail being the dominant form of communication, it is not unusual for people to be inundated with messages. Outlook Today, creating signatures, conversation management, Quick Steps, and AutoArchive are features that will help you manage your messages more efficiently.

USE OUTLOOK TODAY

Outlook Today is the first screen that displays when you open *Outlook*, unless the default was changed. Outlook Today provides a summary of the current day's schedule, tasks, and e-mail. If Outlook Today is not displayed on your screen, click Outlook Data File or Mailbox – Your Name in the Folder List of the Navigation Pane to display it.

The Calendar section (Figure 6.1) contains all the appointments for the day. If you need to view the details of the appointment, click the appointment time or title to open the appointment detail form. The Tasks section lists the tasks for the current day and their due date. You can mark a task completed by selecting the checkbox. Tasks that are past due are displayed in red. The Messages section lists the number of unread messages in your Inbox and the number of messages in the Drafts and Outbox folders.

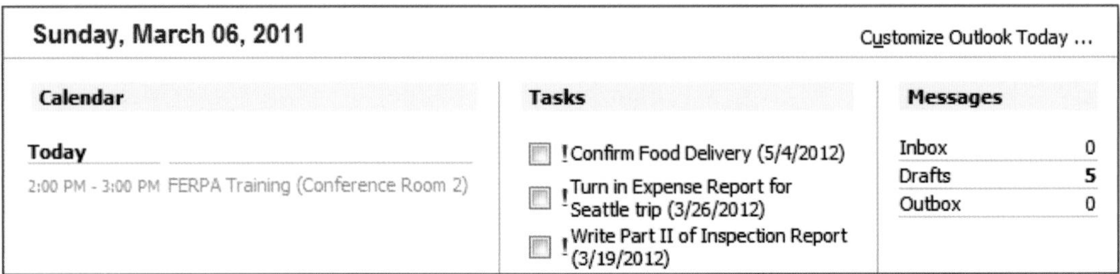

Figure 6.1 Outlook Today

Remember to remove extra space from address lines when you preview the letter.

Current date

«AddressBlock»

«GreetingLine»

Public service announcements provide visibility for many of the leading nonprofit organizations that serve our community. Focus groups are a very effective way of making sure that these spots are appropriate and effective.

Thank you for agreeing to represent the «**Area**» community next year on our community focus group panel. Your input will be extremely valuable to those organizations that serve our community so well.

Information about the way the focus group panel is structured and about the members who will be serving with you on the panel is enclosed. More detailed information will be presented at the orientation meeting.

We look forward to working with you.

Sincerely

Lori Maxwell | Creative Director and Manager

Job 5

Unbound Report

1. Open *p1-j6* and save as *p2-j5*.
2. Change margins from leftbound report format to unbound report format.
3. Make the following modifications in the report.
   - Change the last sentence of the first paragraph to read:

   This report provides the required project summary with all components including the final budget analysis.

   - Modify the last paragraph. Keep the first sentence and the last sentence. Insert the following text between the two sentences:

   This gesture was made because rental costs for a studio were not incurred and all phases of the project were completed in less time than budgeted with no sacrifice in quality whatsoever.

   - Add the following heading and paragraph between Post-Production Work and Potential for Future Business.

   Budget Analysis

   The following budget summary shows the estimated and actual costs for this project. Even though Coastal University of Virginia was given a major discount in our fixed bid, the project was completed significantly under the estimated cost ($20,565).
4. Key the table shown in Figure P2.3. Apply Table Colorful 2 style. Format the last column.
5. Merge the cells in the first row and set row height at .5"; key the title: **SCHOOL SPIRIT PROJECT BUDGET ANALYSIS**. Align Center and apply Cambria 14-point font; remove italic formatting. Set column height for all other rows at .3".

Last Column Format

Table Tools Design/Table Style Options/Last Column

Click Last Column to select it and apply shading to the last column.

Title	Category	Message
Excess Cable	Business Vendor	Call Christina Lopez regarding returning excess cable.
Upholstery Samples	Business Supplier	Ask Ms. Truong to send new upholstery samples.
Hinkson Speech	Business	Call Ken Hinkson regarding modifications to his speech.
Upgrade Software	Business	Call the Information Technology Department to upgrade operating system on business laptop computer to Windows 7.
Engine Modifications	Business Urgent	Call for new specifications on engines.

4. Add the following text to the *Hinkson Speech* note: **Wish Ken a belated happy birthday.**
5. Print the Notes by category in Table Style (View/Change View/Notes List/Categories) and label the printout.

Job 10
Use Journal

1. Activate Journal to track E-mail message, Meeting cancellation, Meeting request, Meeting response, Task request, and Task response on two of your classmates and your instructor. Your classmates and your instructor must be in your main Contacts folder.
2. E-mail your classmates and your instructor an invitation to a Business Club meeting that you will be hosting next week; specify location and time.
3. After you receive the responses, use the Entry List view to see the journal recordings. Print a copy in Table Style and label.

CAREER FOCUS

© AVAVA/Shutterstock.com

Integrating Outlook with Mobile Devices

Outlook 2010 has mobility features that allow you to integrate *Outlook* with your mobile devices. The mobility features help business people who need to be away from the office remain current with important e-mail and be on time for meetings.

You can configure *Outlook* to send alerts to your cell phone or PDA when you receive important e-mail or voice messages. *Outlook* can also send a daily summary of your schedule to your mobile device, as well as send reminders for meetings and appointments. If you have an assistant who schedules meetings for you while you are out of the office, you can configure Exchange Server to send new and updated calendar items to your cell phone.

6. Merge the cells in columns B, C, and D of row 2. Merge rows 2 and 3 of column A. Key the headings shown below; apply Cambria font, bold and Align Center.

   Headings:

	Estimated Costs			Final Costs
Budget Categories	**Fixed Costs**	**Variable Costs**	**Total Costs**	**Actual Costs**

7. Adjust column widths so that text does not wrap in any column. Alignment: column A, rows Align Center Left; columns B, C, D, and E, rows 4–17, Align Center Right.
8. Use the SUM(ABOVE) or SUM(LEFT) formula to fill all blank cells. Apply whole number format; add a $ sign to the first row of numbers and to the total rows.
9. Key the following text for the budget categories Fixed Costs, Variable Costs, and Actual Costs. Sum rows to the left for the Total Costs, and sum rows above for the totals.

SCHOOL SPIRIT PROJECT BUDGET ANALYSIS

Budget Categories	Estimated Costs			Final Costs
	Fixed Costs	Variable Costs	Total Costs	Actual Costs
Pre-production crew	$1,500	$10,250	$11,750	$7,390
Location and casting expenses	2,500	5,875	8,375	3,692
Filming crew	1,350	11,925	13,275	9,148
Studio and set construction	0	2,500	2,500	0
Props, wardrobe, animals	125	1,000	1,125	980
Equipment and rental costs	2,250	7,000	9,250	6,350
Consumables and miscellaneous	0	1,250	1,250	1,400
Directors/creative fee	8,000	0	8,000	8,000
Talent and expenses	1,000	7,000	8,000	7,500
Production fees	10,000	0	10,000	10,000
Editorial/finishing	3,000	7,000	10,000	8,500
Totals	$29,725	$53,800	$83,525	$62,960
Bid and final costs			$83,525	$62,960

Figure P2.3 Table

TIP

Display gridlines to work with the table (Table Tools Layout/View Gridlines).
To sum rows to the left, start with the bottom row and work up to avoid having to change SUM(ABOVE) to SUM(LEFT).

Pre-production crew | $ 1,500 | $10,250 | $ 7,390
Location and casting expenses | 2,500 | 5,875 | 3,692
Filming crew | 1,350 | 11,925 | 9,148
Studio and set construction | 0 | 2,500 | 0
Props, wardrobe, animals | 125 | 1,000 | 980
Equipment and rental costs | 2,250 | 7,000 | 6,350
Consumables and miscellaneous | 0 | 1,250 | 1,400
Directors/creative fee | 8,000 | 0 | 8,000
Talent and expenses | 1,000 | 7,000 | 7,500
Production fees | 10,000 | 0 | 10,000
Editorial/finishing | 3,000 | 7,500 | 8,500
Bid and final costs | | $83,525 | $62,960

Remember to break the links between the first page of the report and the previous section for both the header and the footer. Since you want the footer to display on the first page, deselect Different first page.

10. Insert a blank page after the cover page and create a Table of Contents using Automatic Table 2. Apply Title style; number center bottom using lowercase Roman numerals. Show the footer on the first page of the report.

Job 6

Style Guide

Use Title style for Creative Designs & Production Style Guide. Add a note for documents that should be saved as Quick Parts.

Lori asked you to prepare a style guide for all employees.

Key titles and the filenames of both sample documents and templates you prepared in Projects 1 and 2 that will be saved in a folder named Style Guide. Format the list attractively; use Title style and Heading 1 style for documents; copy all files to the Style Guide folder. Include all templates plus the following documents:

Memo Format | Letter Format | Multiple-Page Letter | Schedule Table | Fax | Contact Information | Project Report with Budget Analysis Table

USE THE JOURNAL TO RECORD CONTACT INFORMATION

The Journal is used to record activities based on any contact. The activities can be any *Outlook* item or an *Office* document. *Outlook* can create automatic journal entries for e-mail messages, task requests, or *Office* files that you create or open.

To Set Options for Recording Journal Items:

File/Options/Notes and Journal/Journal Options

1. Follow the path to display the Journal Options dialog box (Figure 5.2).
2. Check the boxes of the items and files you want to track in the Journal.
3. Select the contacts on whom you want this information recorded. Only contacts in your main Contacts folder can be selected for automatic journaling.
4. Click OK two times to close the dialog boxes.

View the recorded entries by opening the Journal folder. If you do not see the Journal folder, click the Folder List button to display it in the Navigation Pane.

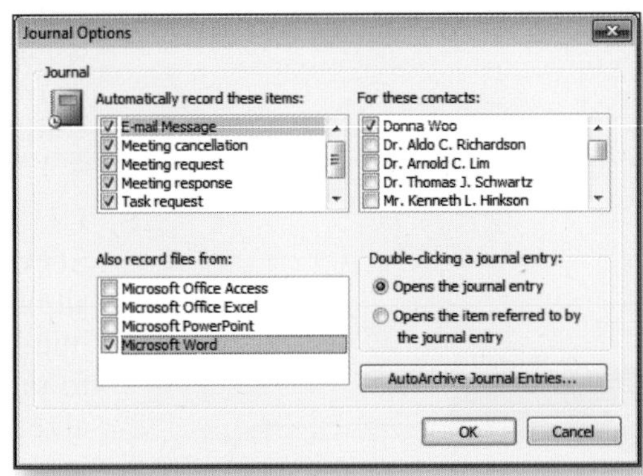

Figure 5.2 Journal Options

To View Journal Activities:

Home/Current View

Choose the desired view, such as Timeline (Figure 5.3), Entry List (Figure 5.4), or Last 7 Days to see the Journal recordings.

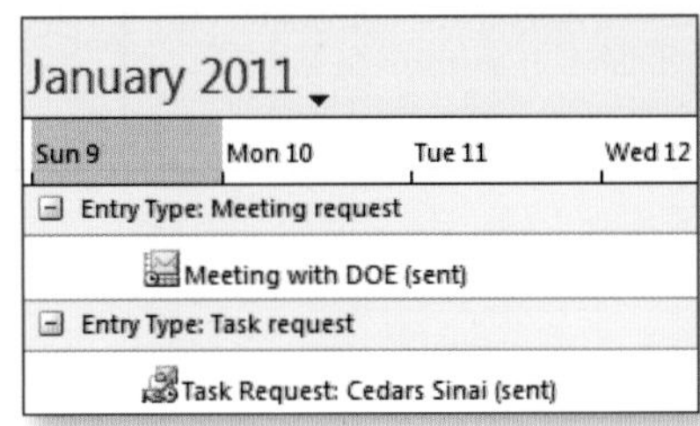

Figure 5.3 Timeline

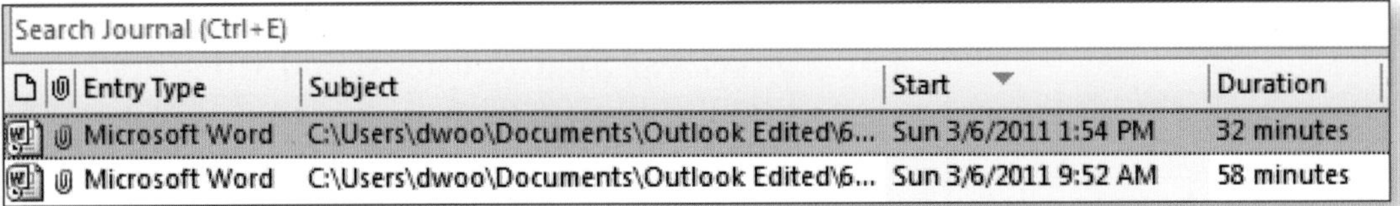

Figure 5.4 Journal Entry List

Apply It

Job 9

Working with Notes

1. Open the Reserve Microphone note. Create a new color category for notes using the Dark Red color. Name the category **Urgent**.
2. Apply the Urgent category to the Fix Photocopier note.
3. Create the notes shown on the next page.

PRESENTATIONS WITH POWERPOINT

overview

***P**owerPoint 2010* is a powerful and easy-to-use presentation software application that facilitates communicating effectively with an audience. You may be familiar with some of the basic functions of *PowerPoint*. If so, you will be able to work through the lessons quickly. You already know many *PowerPoint* commands because they are the same commands that you used in the *Word* module that you just completed. However, this module assumes that you have had little or no formal instruction in using *PowerPoint*.

ESSENTIALS

1. Create Presentations Using Themes
2. Work with Tables and Graphics
3. Add Transitions and Animations
4. Print Notes, Handouts, and Slides
Project 3—Riverfront Enterprises: Integrating PowerPoint and Word

BEYOND THE ESSENTIALS

5. Customize Presentations
6. Embed and Link Files
7. Manage and Deliver Presentations
Project 4—The Leadership Group: Integrating PowerPoint and Word

To Edit a Note:

1. Double-click the note to be edited.
2. Make the necessary changes. Click the Close box in the upper-right corner to save and close the note.

To Resize a Note:

1. Resize the note by dragging on the bottom border to lengthen it or on the side borders to widen it.
2. Drag the resize area in the lower-right corner outward to make the note larger diagonally. Dragging away from the note enlarges it; dragging toward the note reduces it.

To Delete a Note:

1. Select the note that is to be deleted.
2. Tap DELETE. You can also right-click the note and select Delete from the shortcut menu.

DRILL 1 CREATE, EDIT, AND DELETE NOTES

1. Display Notes. Create the following notes. Use the Notes menu to apply categories.

Title	Category	Message
Call John Doe	Business	Call John Doe to order more printer paper.
Artist Brochure	Supplier	Call graphic artist to design new brochure.
Time Card	Business	Remember to turn in time card.
Print Quotes	Supplier	Call for print quotes on new brochure.
Add Phone	Business	Send memo to Hillary Richardson requesting a telephone for John Ramirez, a new employee.
Reserve Microphone		Reserve a microphone for next Tuesday's meeting in Rambler Hall. URGENT!
Fix Photocopier		Put in a service request to have the photocopier repaired. URGENT!

2. Edit the Call John Doe note by adding the telephone number to the message: 555-555-0192.
3. Enlarge each of the notes. Restore them to normal size.
4. Click the Notes List button on the Home tab, in the Current View group. The notes display with the contents, categories, and creation date and time displayed. Print a copy of your notes in Table Style. Label the printout as OL5-drill1-4.
5. Print the notes displayed by category in Table Style. The notes should still be displayed in Notes List view; click the View tab and then Categories. Label the printout as OL5-drill1-5.

Create Presentations Using Themes

LESSON 1

OBJECTIVES

- Create presentations
- Choose a theme
- Use effective slide layouts
- Add content
- Format slides

OVERVIEW

A presentation consists of a series of slides designed to communicate effectively to an audience. Slides may contain text, SmartArt, clip art, pictures, charts, graphs, video clips, audio, WordArt, and a variety of other elements. In addition to the slides, you may also create handouts and notes pages to assist with the delivery of the presentation.

PowerPoint presentations may be used to support a speaker, or they may be designed to stand alone. Self-running presentations may be broadcast using a Web browser, or they may be used in kiosks, booths, or in exhibit areas at trade shows. Presentations used by speakers typically have less text because the speaker provides the message.

The applications in *Microsoft Office 2010* share many common commands. Therefore, you will be able to use those commands that you learned in *Word* in *PowerPoint*, *Excel*, *Publisher*, and other applications without needing further instruction.

GETTING STARTED

You can launch *PowerPoint* in the same way that you launch *Word*. The opening screen consists of a ribbon and a workspace that you will use to create presentations. Note in Figure 1.1 below how similar the *PowerPoint* Home tab ribbon is to the *Word* Home tab ribbon. You already know many of the commands in the Clipboard, Font, Paragraph, and Editing groups as well as those on the File menu and the Quick Access Toolbar.

When *PowerPoint* opens, the icon displays in the taskbar. To make it easier to launch *PowerPoint* in the future, pin it to the taskbar if you are using *Windows 7*.

1. Right-click the *PowerPoint* icon.
2. Click Pin this program to taskbar.

PATH

Home/Slides/New Slide

In the *Word* module, you were provided with the path to help you locate new commands quickly and easily. The path is also provided to help you locate commands in *PowerPoint*. If you are directed to click the New Slide command, you automatically know by following the path that it will be located on the Home tab in the Slides group.

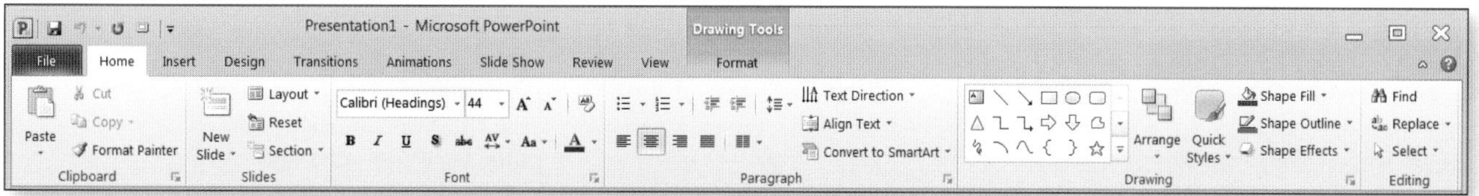

Figure 1.1 Home Tab

LESSON
5

Use Notes and Journal

OBJECTIVES

- Create and edit notes
- Assign categories to notes using Notes menu
- Use Journal

CREATE AND EDIT NOTES

The *Outlook* Notes feature is often referred to as electronic sticky notes because of its appearance. Notes provide all the convenience of sticky notes without the clutter. Information stored on notes can easily be transferred to a more permanent area such as Contacts, Tasks, or Calendar.

Notes are simple to create; there are no boxes to fill or options to select. Notes have limited text-editing ability. Wordwrap, cut, copy, and paste commands are available in the Notes feature. Because notes are meant to be informal and quick, font attributes and formatting features are not available. As you key your message, the note expands to hold all text; you do not need to worry about condensing the message to a few lines. To scroll through your note, use the up and down arrow keys on your keyboard. The PgUp and PgDn keys can also be used to scroll through the note. Click the Close button in the upper-right corner to save and close the note.

To Create a Note:

Home/New/New Note

1. Click the Notes icon in the Navigation Pane to display the Notes window.
2. Click New Note to display a blank note. Begin by keying a title for the note ❶ (Figure 5.1); then tap ENTER. Keep the title short and descriptive of the contents of the note. The title will display below the note item in Notes.

3. Key the text for the body of the note ❷; the note adds new lines as you need them. If you keyed more text than the note displays, you can maximize the note by double-clicking on the note's title bar. Double-click the title bar again to restore the note to its original size.
4. When you are finished with the note, click the Close box ❸ in the upper-right corner to close the note. Closing the note automatically saves it. The note now displays in the Notes window; the title of the note displays to identify it.

DISCOVER

Click the Notes menu icon to display a menu that allows you to apply a category to the note, as well as save with a new name or cut, copy, and paste text.

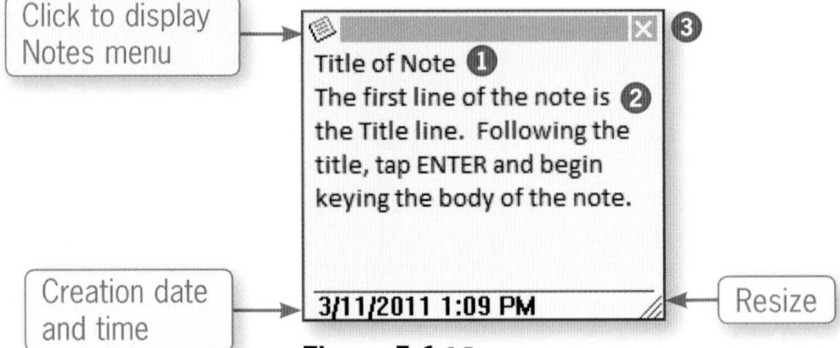

Figure 5.1 Note

WORKSPACE

A presentation by default opens in Normal view with the title slide. The three main components of the workspace as shown in Figure 1.2 are the Slides/Outline pane ❶, the Slide pane ❷, and the Notes pane ❸. These panes are described in detail below. Note that the status bar at the bottom of the screen also provides additional information—number of slides, theme, view buttons, and the Zoom slider. Once text has been entered, the Spelling status button appears. The views in *PowerPoint* are different from those in *Word*. You will learn how to use these views later in this lesson. Note that the Zoom slider has an additional button on the right side that was not included in *Word*. This button resets the slide to its original size or fits it to the window. The *PowerPoint* opening screen also contains the Horizontal and Vertical Rulers.

❶ Slides/Outline pane. The Slides tab shows a miniature version, called a thumbnail, of the text and graphics on the slide. The Outline tab shows the text of the presentation in Outline format.

❷ Slide pane. The Slide pane shows a large view of the current slide. This pane is used for adding the slide title, text, and graphics. The boxes with dotted line borders containing instructions are called placeholders. The layout shown below is for the title slide only. A variety of different slide layouts are available.

❸ Notes pane. The Notes pane is used to key information about the slides. The speaker can use the information as notes when delivering the presentation. On a self-running presentation, supplementary information can be provided.

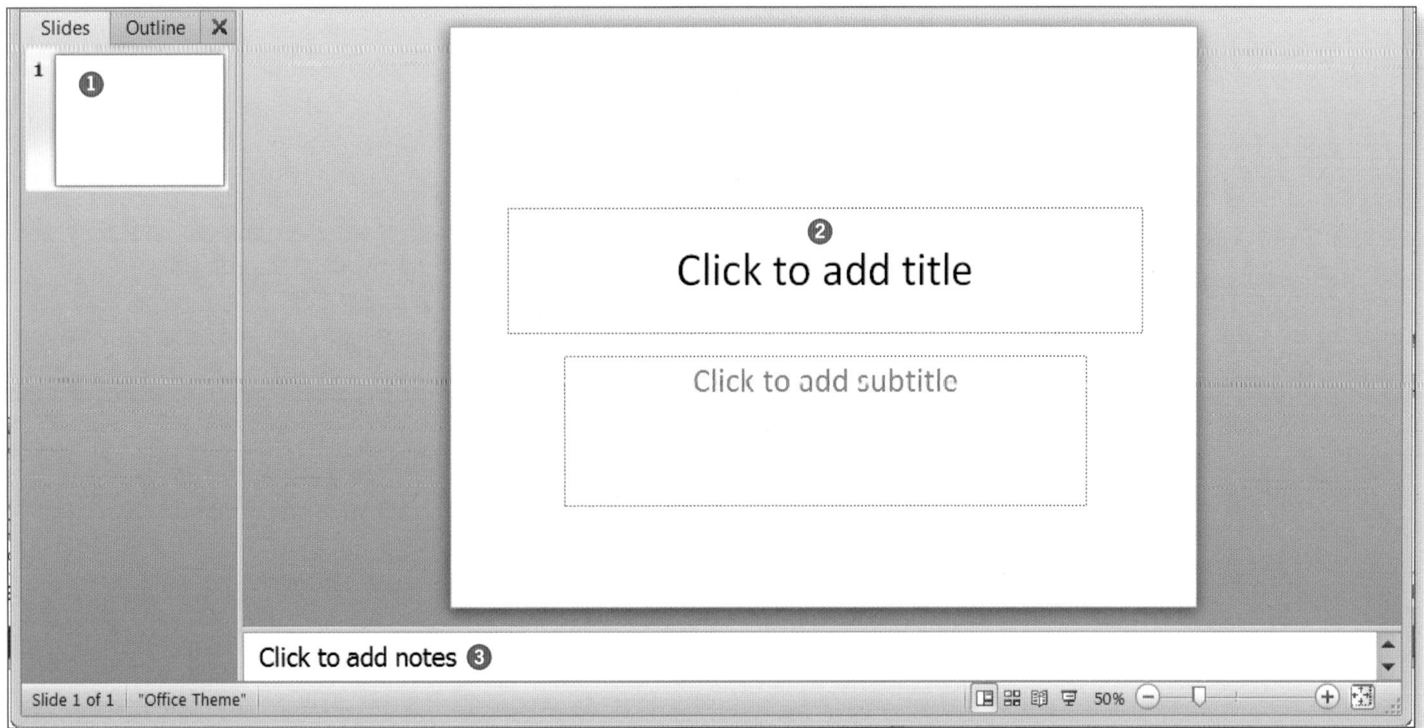

Figure 1.2 Workspace

Apply It

Job 8
Tasks

1. Create a new category called **Personal**; select the Dark Blue color. Add the following tasks to your task list. Do not key the letters in parentheses; they will be used for reference only.

Subject	Due Date	Special Instructions
(A) Write Part I of Inspection Report	In two weeks	High Priority
(B) Pick up maps of Seattle	3/2/20--	Set reminder for 3/2 at 10:00 a.m.
(C) Pick up dry cleaning	Tomorrow	Categorize as Personal
(D) Turn in Expense Report for Seattle trip	3/3/20--	High Priority. Set reminder for 3/3 at 8:00 a.m.
(E) Write Part II of Inspection Report	In four weeks	High Priority
(F) Call Jacob Smith	3/5/20--	Key note: **Need new electrical specifications.**
(G) Pick up new brochures on Space Station 6	3/9/20--	Set reminder for 3/9 at 10:00 a.m.

2. Display Tasks in Detailed view. Print in Table Style. Label printout.
3. Mark task (C) as being complete.
4. Mark the task to repair the printer as being complete.
5. Update task (A) with the following information: Indicate the current date for the Start date. Change the status to "In Progress." Show 25% completion.
6. Update the task to send the sales report to Ken Hinkson. Use today's date for the start date. Change the status to In Progress and indicate that it is 75% complete.
7. Delete task (C) from the list.
8. Assign the Personal category to the task to shop for coat and boots.
9. Display the To-Do List in Detailed view, print in Table Style, and label.
10. Display Tasks in Simple List view by categories (View/Arrangement/Categories); print in Table Style, and label.
11. Display the tasks that are completed (Home/Current View/Completed). Print in Table Style, and label.
12. Display Tasks in Active view, print in Table Style, and label.
13. Expand the To-Do Bar to view the appointments and tasks.
14. Send a Task Request to one of your classmates asking him or her to create and post flyers regarding the next Business Club meeting.
15. Send a Task Request to a second classmate asking him or her to purchase and set up refreshments for the next Business Club meeting.

CREATE A NEW PRESENTATION

Once you launch *PowerPoint*, you have begun the process of creating a new presentation. The presentation opens with the title slide displayed, and you are ready to begin. You can open another presentation with the New command.

Follow this path to open a new presentation if you already have one open:

File/New/Blank presentation or Available Templates and Themes/ Create

To Add Text to a Slide:

1. Click the placeholder on the slide.
2. Key the desired text.

NEW SLIDE

Home/Slides/New Slide

Note that the New Slide button has two parts—clicking the top part of the New Slide button adds a new slide with a pre-selected layout (Title and Content) immediately. Clicking the bottom part of the command displays the gallery of slide layouts shown in Figure 1.3. You can select the desired layout of the new slide from the gallery.

When you first click the top of the New Slide button in a new presentation, the Title and Content layout displays. After that when you click the top of the New Slide button, the layout of the current slide will display.

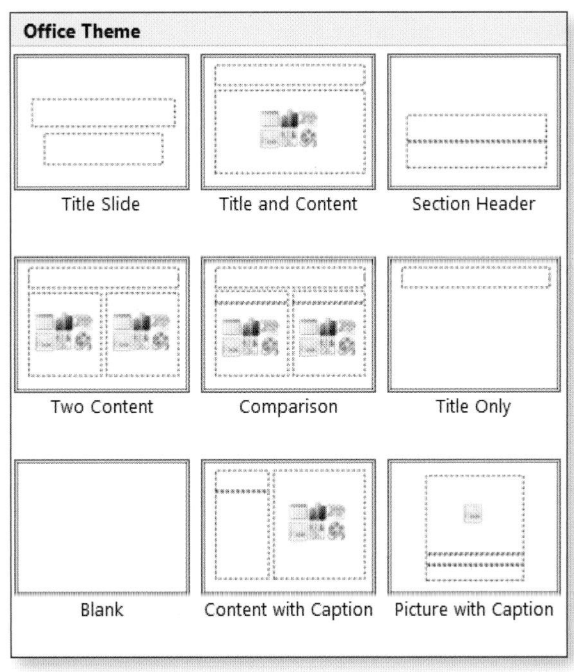

Figure 1.3 Slide Layouts

Figure 1.4 Content Icons

SLIDE LAYOUTS

Note that many of the layouts contain a series of six content icons in placeholders as shown in Figure 1.4 above. When you hover the mouse over one of the content icons, the icon darkens and a ScreenTip indicates the type of content that will be inserted as shown above with the SmartArt icon in Figure 1.4. The other types of content that can be inserted are table, chart, picture, clip art, and media clip. Text can also be inserted in addition to the content icons pictured. The default for text is a bulleted list.

Many of the slides have a placeholder to key the title of the slide. Other slides with graphics provide a placeholder for a caption such as the one shown below the illustrations in this textbook. Some slides also have placeholders for two segments of content as shown in the second row of the gallery. The second layout in that row provides a placeholder for text to be placed above the content. In Lesson 5, you will learn how to rearrange, delete, and add new placeholders.

Assign a Category to a Task

Task/Tags/Categorize

Categories can be assigned to tasks, just as they were assigned to contacts and appointments.

CHANGE TASK VIEWS

Depending on the task you are working on, changing the view may provide you with more meaningful detail. Options in the Current View group of the Home tab make it easy to switch to a different view of the task list. The Detailed view provides additional information such as status, modified, date completed, and categories. Current View and Arrangement groups in the View tab provide additional helpful views.

ASSIGN A TASK TO ANOTHER PERSON

You can use *Outlook's* Task Request to assign a task to someone else. The task assignment is sent as an e-mail message, and the assignee has the option of accepting or declining the task.

To Create a Task Request:

Home/New/New Items/Task Request

1. Follow the path to display the Task form. Complete the form with the task information and the assignee's e-mail address (Figure 4.3).
2. The options to keep an updated copy of the task on your task list and sending a status report when the task is completed are selected by default to keep you informed of the progress on the task.
3. Click Send. The assignee can either accept or decline the task.

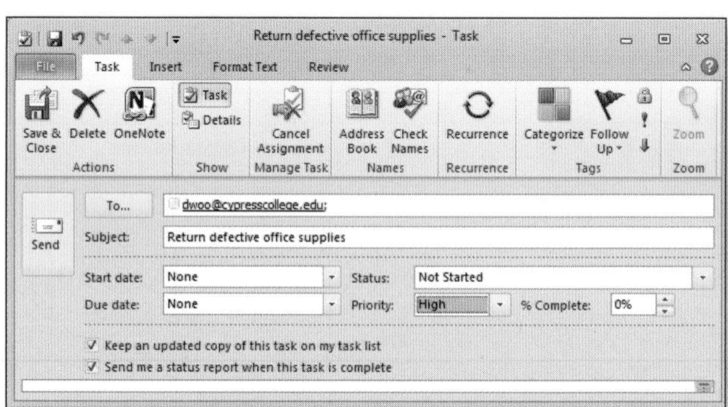

Figure 4.3 Task Request

VIEW THE TO-DO LIST AND TO-DO BAR

In the Navigation Pane, under My Tasks, click the To-Do List icon to display the To-Do List in the middle pane. The list displays according to due date; those items with no due date are listed on top. Click the other view options to see the different ways that information is displayed.

Click the expand button, located above the calendar icon at the right, to display the To-Do Bar. The To-Do Bar consists of three sections, as shown in Figure 4.1. The Date Navigator displays at the top, the appointment list shows a few of the upcoming appointments, and the task list displays below.

DRILL 2 UPDATE TASKS AND USE TASK VIEWS

1. Update the task of signing employment contracts. Insert today's date for the start date. Change the status to In Progress and the % Complete to 25%.
2. Indicate that the task to return the books to the resource center is complete.
3. Assign the Business category to the task to call for printer repair.
4. Display the task list in Detailed view. Print the list in Table Style. Label the printout OL4-drill2-4.

Always follow the path to locate the new command you are directed to use.

To Insert a New Slide with the Desired Layout:

Home/Slides/New Slide

1. Click the bottom of the New Slide command to display the gallery of layouts.
2. Click the desired layout.

Create a new folder named Module 2 Solutions and save all presentations and documents from this module in it.

SAVE A PRESENTATION

File/Save As/PowerPoint Presentation

The *PowerPoint* and *Word* Save As dialog boxes are the same except for the file type options. Figure 1.5 shows a few of the options. Unless directed otherwise, use the default PowerPoint Presentation.

PowerPoint Presentation
PowerPoint Macro-Enabled Presentation
PowerPoint 97-2003 Presentation
PDF
XPS Document
PowerPoint Template
PowerPoint Macro-Enabled Template
PowerPoint 97-2003 Template
Office Theme
PowerPoint Show

Figure 1.5 Save As Type Options

To Save a Presentation:

1. Select the folder to save in.
2. Key the filename and select the type. Click Save.

DRILL 1 CREATE A PRESENTATION

1. Launch *PowerPoint*
2. On slide 1, click in the appropriate placeholder and key the title and subtitle shown below.
3. Add two new Title and Content layout slides.
4. Key the information shown below on each slide. On slide 2, click the Numbering command rather than the default bullets.
5. Always proofread slides carefully without being told to do so.
6. Save as *pp1-drill1.* Use Figure 1.6 to check your slides. Leave the presentation open.

Slide 1 Title: Critical Career Skills
Subtitle: Presented by | (Your Name)

Slide 2 Title: Critical Career Skills
1. Technical skills
2. Interpersonal skills
3. Conceptual skills

Slide 3 Title: Interpersonal Skills
- Get along with others
- Behave diplomatically

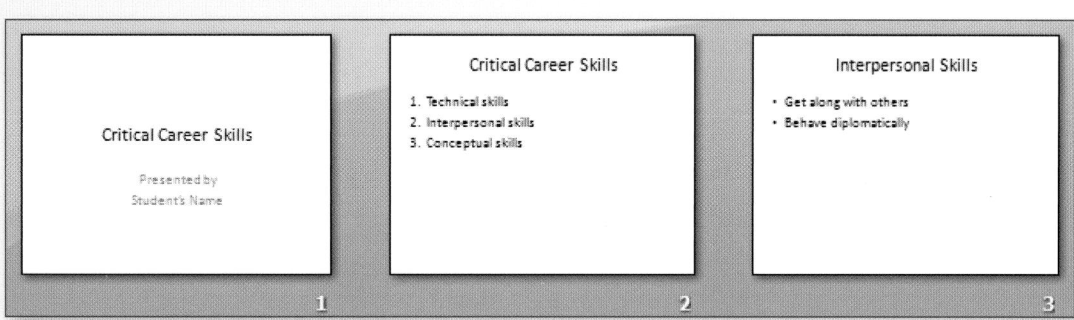

Figure 1.6 Quick Check

To Add a Task Using the Task Form:

Home/New/New Task

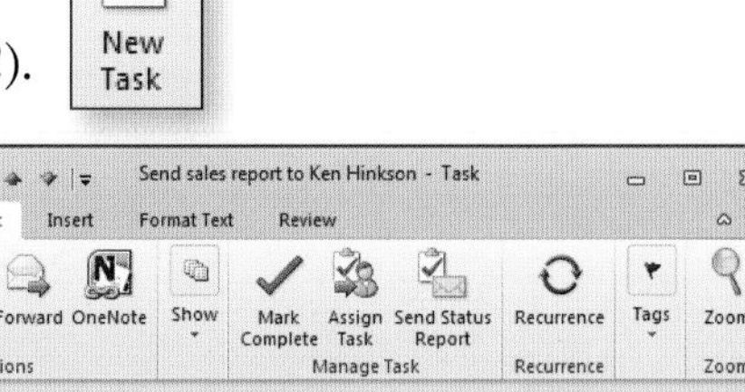

1. Click New Task to display a Task form (Figure 4.2).
2. Key the subject of the task ❶. Key the due date or click the drop-list arrow to select a date from the calendar ❷.
3. If applicable, select a priority ❸ and key information in the note box ❹.
4. If a reminder is needed, click the Reminder checkbox ❺ and select a date and time ❻. The Start date, Status, and % Complete fields can be edited when the task is in progress.
5. Click Save & Close to return to Tasks.

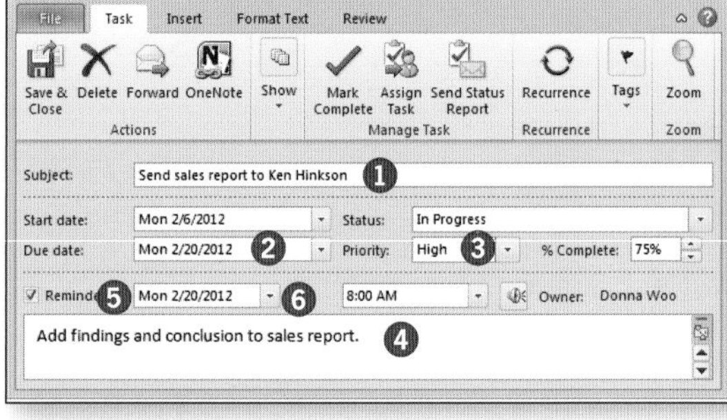

Figure 4.2 Task Form

DRILL 1 ENTER TASKS

1. Key the following tasks in the task list.

   Shop for winter coat and boots for Vermont trip

   Return books to the company resource center [insert tomorrow's date in the Due date field]

   Call to have printer repaired today

2. Key the following tasks using Task forms. (Insert due dates for next year.)

Subject	Due Date	Special Instructions
Schedule appointment with Grayson Huyn	2/6/20--	Key note: **Need to allocate two hours for this meeting to view new software.**
Send sales report to Ken Hinkson	2/20/20--	Set a reminder for 2/20 at 8:00 a.m. Set as high priority.
Call Laura Brown regarding Aviation Conference	2/21/20--	Set a reminder for 2/21 at 9:00 a.m. Key note: **Prepare handouts for Aviation Conference.**
Sign employment contracts	2/22/20--	Set a reminder for 2/22 at 9:00 a.m. Set as high priority.

COMPLETE A TASK

You can show that a task is completed in the Tasks window by clicking the checkbox immediately to the left of the task or by clicking Mark Complete in the Home tab. A line is drawn through the task to show that it has been completed. If you no longer need the task to display on the task list, select it and tap DELETE or choose Remove from List on the Home tab. You can also indicate that a task is completed in the Task form by clicking Mark Complete in the Task tab or by choosing Completed in the Status list. Partial completion of a task can be indicated in the % Complete box.

SLIDE VIEWS

View/Presentation Views/Slide Sorter or Slide Show

You have been working with Normal view. You can change the view by (1) clicking one of the View buttons at the right side of the status bar or (2) changing the view on the View tab in the Presentation Views group (Figure 1.7).

In this lesson you will also work with Reading, Slide Sorter, and Slide Show views. Reading View is used to review a presentation within a computer window with simple controls to make it easy to review.

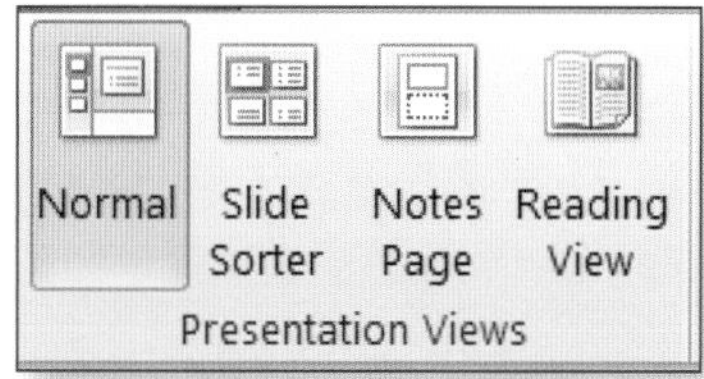

Figure 1.7 Presentation Views

Slide Sorter view uses thumbnails of slides to display all of the slides in a presentation. The Quick Check in Figure 1.6 illustrates Slide Sorter view. This view is especially helpful in rearranging slides in a presentation or to provide a quick overview of the entire presentation. To rearrange slides, display them in Slide Sorter view and drag slides to the desired position.

Slide Show view uses the full computer screen to display only the Slide pane of each slide. You can view selected slides or an entire presentation in this view. This view shows what the audience will see when the presentation is projected on a screen.

DISCOVER

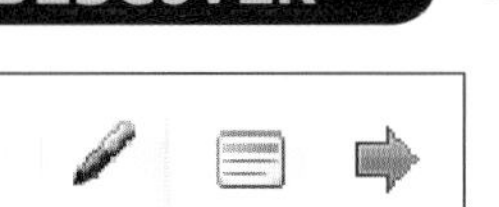

Hover the mouse over the lower-left corner of the screen in Slide Show view to locate buttons to move backward, use a pen, exit the show, or move forward.

NAVIGATING A PRESENTATION IN SLIDE SHOW VIEW

You can move forward from one slide to the next by clicking the mouse or by tapping the Space Bar. To move back a slide, tap the BACKSPACE key. You can also right-click the mouse for navigation options. At the end of the presentation, click when the option to exit appears (Figure 1.8).

Additional navigation options and presentation tools are also available in Slide Show view.

End of slide show, click to exit.

Figure 1.8 Exit Slide Show

DRILL 1, continued — MODIFY AND NAVIGATE A PRESENTATION

1. With *pp1-drill1* open, click the thumbnail of the first slide in the Slides/Outline pane.
2. Click Slide Sorter view to view the three slides.
3. Click Slide Show view, move through the three slides, and then click to return to Normal view.
4. On slides 2 and 3, change *Interpersonal* to **Soft**. On slide 3, add bullet item: **Communicate effectively**.
5. Add slides 4 and 5 and key the text shown below.
6. Use Slide Sorter view to rearrange the last three slides in the same order as the topics on slide 2.
7. Resave *pp1-drill1* and keep it open. Use Figure 1.9 on the next page to check the content and order of your slides.

Slide 4 Title: Conceptual Skills
- Ability to see the big picture
- Understand how your job fits into the business strategy
- Understand that businesses operate in a global context

Slide 5 Title: Technical Skills
- Knowledge
- Expertise
- Ability to do the job

LESSON 4

Create and Use Tasks

OBJECTIVES

- Create, update, and view tasks
- Assign tasks to others
- View To-Do List, To-Do Bar, and Daily Tasks List

STARTING TASKS

The Tasks feature in *Outlook* helps you keep track of things that you need to do. A task is an item that you can track. For example, you can track the status of the task, change the percentage completed, assign the task to someone else, or have it recur over time. Incomplete tasks or other items you marked for follow-up will display in the To-Do Bar. You can create to-do items from other *Outlook* items such as messages or contacts. Whenever you create a task, *Outlook* also creates a to-do item with the same name.

In the Navigation Pane, click the Tasks button ❶ and then the Tasks icon ❷ under My Tasks to display the Tasks window. The task list is displayed in Figure 4.1 in the default Simple List view. The task list is divided into columns such as the Subject column ❸ and the Due Date column ❹. Tasks that are overdue are displayed in red; tasks that have been completed display with a strikeout line through them.

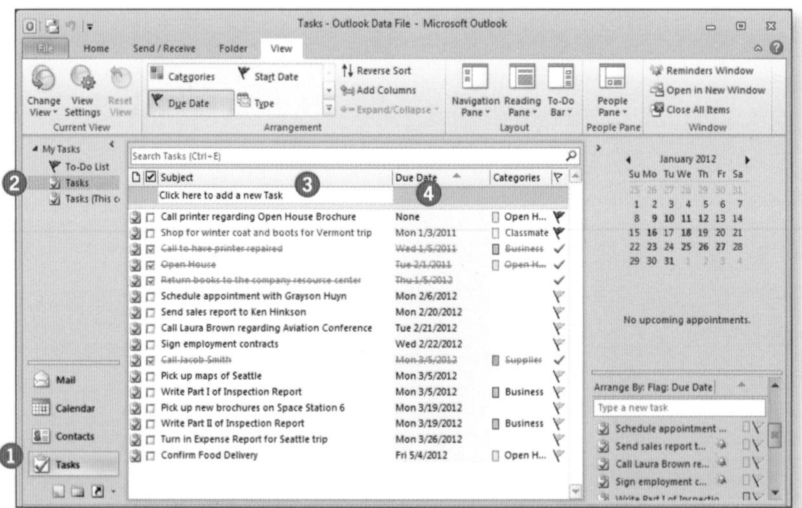

Figure 4.1 Tasks Window with To-Do Bar

The To-Do Bar is displayed at the right of your screen; it can be minimized to allow more space for the task list.

Tasks can be added to the task list by clicking on the words "Click here to add a new Task" and then keying the task. If you need to include a due date, tap TAB to move to the Due Date column and key a due date, or click the drop-list arrow and select a date from the calendar. If you wish to enter more detailed information, such as start date, status, priority, percentage completed, or other notes, you need to use the Task form.

QUICK ✓

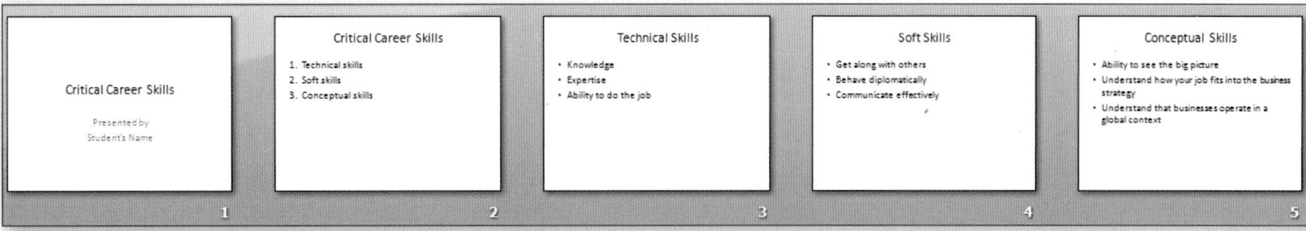

Figure 1.9 Quick Check

With your presentation open, hover the mouse over each theme thumbnail to preview how it will look with your presentation.

PRESENTATION THEMES

Design/Themes

You used the default theme for the presentation you prepared in Drill 1. The same document themes you used in *Word* are also available in *PowerPoint*. Themes in *PowerPoint* include: (1) a color scheme, (2) font types and sizes, (3) background design, and (4) placeholder positions. Figure 1.10 shows the title and first slides of the presentation using three different themes: Angles, Hardcover, and Waveform.

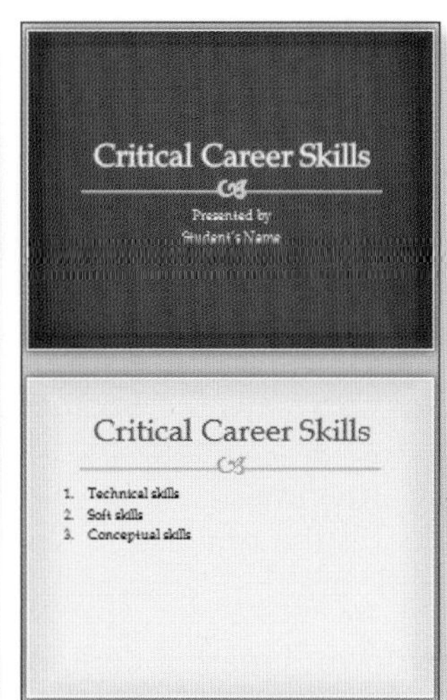

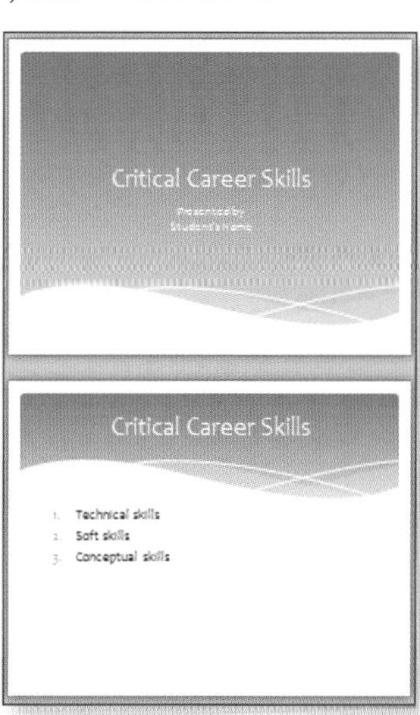

Figure 1.10 Angles, Hardcover, and Waveform Themes

To Apply a Theme:

Design/Themes

1. Hover the mouse over theme thumbnails to preview the theme on the current slide. Click the More down arrow in the Themes gallery to see additional themes.
2. Click the thumbnail of the theme you want to apply.

DRILL 2 APPLY PRESENTATION THEME

1. With *pp1-drill1* open, click the title slide and hover the mouse over each theme to preview it.
2. Click one of the other slides and preview several themes.
3. Click the Waveform theme to apply it. Compare your slides to those in Figure 1.9 at the top of the page.
4. Save as *pp1-drill2* and close the file.

Job 7

Edit Appointments and Schedule a Meeting

1. Move the China 797 Order appointment from 1/24/20-- to the same time on 1/31/20--: Select the appointment on the Day calendar and drag it to the 1/31 date on the Date Navigator. The appointment is automatically moved to the same time on 1/31.
2. You are scheduled for jury duty from 2/13 to 2/17; location is Harbor Court. Show the time as Out of Office.
3. You will need to cancel the Weekly Planning Meeting on 2/15 because you will be on jury duty. On the Day calendar, select the Weekly Planning Meeting appointment and tap DELETE. A Confirm Delete dialog box displays asking whether you want to delete this occurrence or whether you want to delete the entire series. Delete only the occurrence.
4. Send a meeting invitation to two of your classmates inviting them to a student government meeting next week in the lecture hall. Ask one of your classmates to accept the invitation and the other classmate to decline the invitation.
5. Send an e-mail to a classmate asking him/her to stop by and see you on either 1/11 or 1/12. Include a copy of your calendar for both those days and include limited details in the calendar.
6. Print the calendar for the months of January and February in Calendar Details Style. Label the printout.

JOB KNOWLEDGE

You can send your business card or vCard with your e-mails. *Outlook* displays the business card in the signature and as an attachment. When the recipient clicks the attachment, the business card information is added to the recipient's Contacts folder.

1. Using a Contact form, create a contact record for yourself. Key information only in the fields you want included in the business card. Click Business Card in the Options group to view your business card. Click OK. Save and close the Contact form.
2. Create a new e-mail. After keying your e-mail message, tap ENTER a couple of times to place the insertion point below the message.
3. Click Insert/Include/Insert Business Card. If your name does not display in the drop list, click Other Business Cards. Choose the desired name from the list, and then click OK. The business card displays in the e-mail.

Apply It

Presentation 1

Presentation with Theme

1. Prepare the following presentation for your instructor using the Clarity theme.
2. Use Slide Sorter to move slide 4 last; then preview using Slide Show view and appropriate navigation techniques. In slide 2, replace *Diversity needed* with **Diversity required**.
3. Save as *pp1-p1* and close.

Slide 1 Title: Student Projects

Subtitle: Instructor's Name

Slide 2 Title: Team

Bulleted text: Minimum 4 members | Maximum 6 members | Diversity needed | Instructor appoints | Team selects leader

Slide 3 Title: Project Topic

Bulleted text: Team proposes topic | Business-related requirement | Instructor must approve

Slide 4 Title: Project Work

Bulleted text: About 25 percent in class | About 75 percent outside of class | Student managed and directed

Slide 5 Title: Requirements

Bulleted text: Written report | PowerPoint presentation | All members participate

Presentation 2

Presentation with Theme

1. Create a new presentation.
2. Key the slides shown below and apply the Flow theme.
3. Save as *pp1-p2*.

Slide 1 Title: Career Options

Subtitle: Presented by | (Your Name)

Slide 2 Title: Career Options

- Business
- Professional
- Technical
- Other

JOB KNOWLEDGE

Designing effective slides requires using good judgment. Try to keep the text on each slide to a minimum. Too much text can be very dull and boring. In the next lesson, you will learn to use graphic design elements to add variety to your presentation.

Always consider the audience when selecting themes and make a careful, strategic selection. Matching the style of the presentation to the audience is important. A colorful and lively presentation may be very effective for a student group, whereas a more subtle and formal presentation would be more effective for a board of directors.

Apply It

Job 6

Schedule Appointments and Events

1. Add the following appointments and events to your calendar. You have just been elected to your company's labor negotiations committee representing management. Your duties for the coming year will include attending union meetings.

Date/Time	Appointment/Location	Special Instructions
1/3–1/4 All day	New Labor Laws for 20-- Seminar Arco Towers, Los Angeles	Key in note area: **Bring copy of labor contract.**
1/10 9:00–11:30	New Labor Laws Meeting General Assembly Hall	Set a reminder for 30 minutes.
1/11 2:00–5:00	Negotiations Meeting Conference Room 3	Key in note area: **Meeting with union leaders.**
1/23 1:30–4:30	CPR, First Aid & Disaster Preparation Seminar, American Heart Association, Irvine	Show this appointment as Tentative.
1/24 9:00–11:00	China 797 Order Conference Room A	Key note: **Meet with buyers from China.** Tag as High Importance and apply the category Key Customer.
2/21 9:00–11:00	Union Meeting Town Hall	Recurring meeting that meets the same day during the third week of each month with no end date.

2. Add the following appointments to your personal calendar.

1/26 9:00–12:00	Laser Eye Surgery, Expert Eye Center	Key note: **Arrange for Robert to drive.**
1/27 2:00–3:00	Follow-up eye doctor appointment	Set reminder 30 minutes before.

3. Mark 1/26 and 1/27 on the work calendar as being Out of Office All day event. Key **Medical Leave** in the Subject line.
4. Print all appointments grouped by category (View/Current View/Change View/List/Categories). Click Reverse Sort to place the appointments with a category tag at the top of the list. Label the printout as OL3-job6-4. Click Reset View and confirm resetting view to original settings.
5. Print all recurring appointments in Table Style (View/Current View/Change View/List/Recurrence). Click Reverse Sort to place the appointments with recurrence patterns at the top of the list. Label the printout as OL3-job6-5.
6. Change to Calendar view in the View tab. Print the calendar in Weekly Agenda Style between the dates of 1/3 and 2/24 (File/Print/Weekly Agenda Style/Print Options/Print range Start 1/3/20-- End 2/24/20--). Label the printout.

LESSON 2

Work with Tables and Graphics

OBJECTIVES

- Create effective presentations
- Add tables to slides
- Add graphics to slides

TABLES AND GRAPHICS

Tables and graphics can be inserted in two different ways. You can click one of the six content icons to insert a table, chart, SmartArt graphic, picture, clip art, or media clip. When you hover the mouse over an icon, it darkens and a ScreenTip displays indicating the type of content that will be inserted as shown in Figure 2.1. The second way to insert tables or graphics is from the Insert tab just as you did when you inserted tables and graphics in *Word*. You will use both options in this lesson.

Figure 2.1 Content Icons

Table Tools Layout/Merge/Merge Cells

1. Select cells in row 1.
2. Click Merge Cells.
3. Key content.

To Insert a Table Using the Table Icon:

1. In an open presentation, insert a new slide that includes a content placeholder, such as Title and Content.
2. Click the Table icon to display the Insert Table dialog box; indicate the number of columns and rows desired as shown in Figure 2.2.
3. Merge the cells in the first row if you wish to add a title to the table.
4. Key the content in the table.

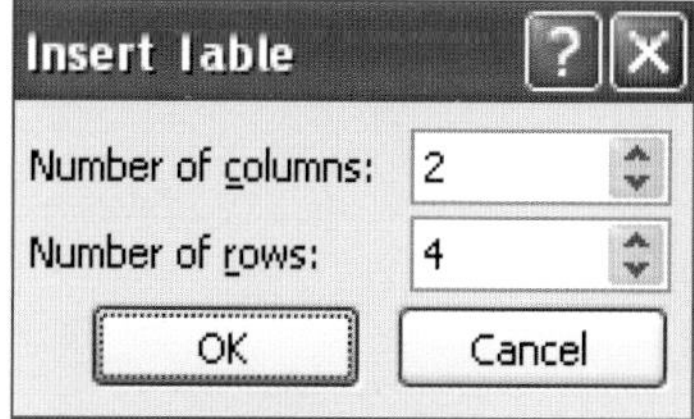

Figure 2.2 Insert Table

DRILL 1 TABLE

DISCOVER

Table Tools Layout/Alignment/Center or Center Vertically

1. In a new presentation, key the title **Career Skills** and the subtitle **Presented by | *Your Name*.**
2. Add a new Title and Content layout slide. Key the title **Communication Skills**.
3. Insert a two-column, four-row table.
4. Merge the cells in the top row; key the content; center the title horizontally and vertically; align columns as shown.

Estimated Distribution of Communication Time	
Writing	10%
Reading	15%
Speaking	32%

5. Add a row at the bottom; key **Listening 43%**.
6. Apply the Civic theme, and save as *pp2-drill1*. Keep the presentation open.

3. Key the subject, location, date, time, and any message that needs to be included; then click the Send button.

4. The buttons to accept, decline, or propose a new time for the meeting display at the top of the recipients' meeting invitation (Figure 3.8). Once the recipient clicks on the response button, an e-mail is automatically sent to the person setting up the meeting (Figure 3.9).

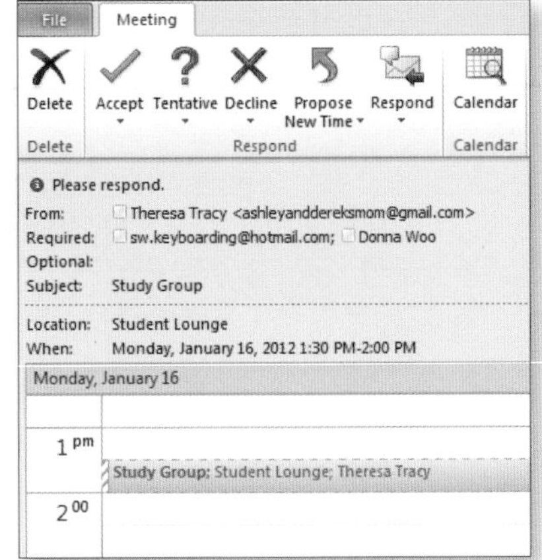

Figure 3.8 Meeting Invitation

Figure 3.9 Accepted Meeting Invitation

DRILL 5 SCHEDULE A MEETING

1. Send a meeting invitation to a classmate inviting him or her to a study group session next week in the student lounge.
2. Ask the classmate to accept the invitation; the meeting will be placed on your calendar.

SEND CALENDAR IN E-MAIL

You can send your calendar in the body of an e-mail message to another person. If the e-mail recipient uses *Outlook 2010*, he or she can display the calendar side by side or overlay it with other calendars. The calendar will not be updated as you make changes to your schedule.

To E-mail a Calendar:

Home/Share/E-mail Calendar

1. Follow the path to display the Send a Calendar via E-mail dialog box (Figure 3.10).
2. If you work with multiple calendars, click the Calendar down arrow and select the calendar you want to e-mail.
3. Click the Date Range down arrow and specify the time period of the calendar.
4. Click the Detail down arrow and specify the amount of information you want included in the calendar. Click OK.

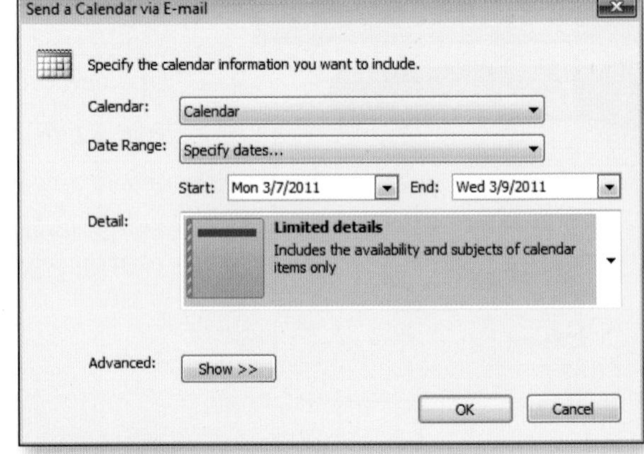

Figure 3.10 Send Calendar

Always follow the path to locate the new command you are directed to use.

You can also click More SmartArt Graphics at the bottom of the Convert to SmartArt gallery to open the Choose a SmartArt Graphic dialog box where you can select any SmartArt graphic. Always preview the desired graphic from the gallery that displays.

SMARTART

A text list can be converted to a SmartArt graphic, or SmartArt can be inserted in a new slide. You can key text directly into a SmartArt graphic, or you can key your text in a text pane. Select a graphic that illustrates your content effectively. Read the description of a graphic before inserting it to determine if it is appropriate and then hover the mouse over the graphic to provide a live preview of it. SmartArt should be used judiciously.

To Convert a Text List to a SmartArt Graphic:

Home/Paragraph/Convert to SmartArt

1. Select the text to be converted.
2. Click Convert to SmartArt ❶ to display the gallery (Figure 2.3).
3. Click the graphic ❷ to apply it.

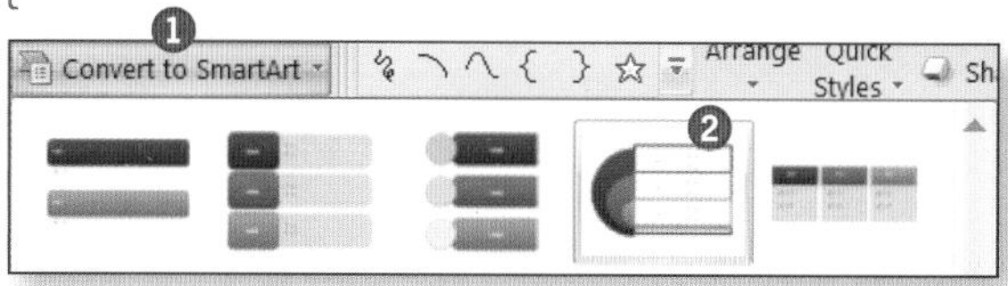

Figure 2.3 Convert to SmartArt

To Create a SmartArt Graphic:

Insert/Illustrations/SmartArt

1. Follow the path or click the SmartArt icon in a content placeholder to open the Choose a SmartArt Graphic dialog box.
2. Preview the desired graphic, such as a Target List; then click OK to insert it.

To Add Text or a Shape to a SmartArt Graphic:

SmartArt Tools Design/Create Graphic/Text Pane or Add Shape

1. Click in the graphic to display the SmartArt Tools; click the Design tab ❶ as shown in Figure 2.4.

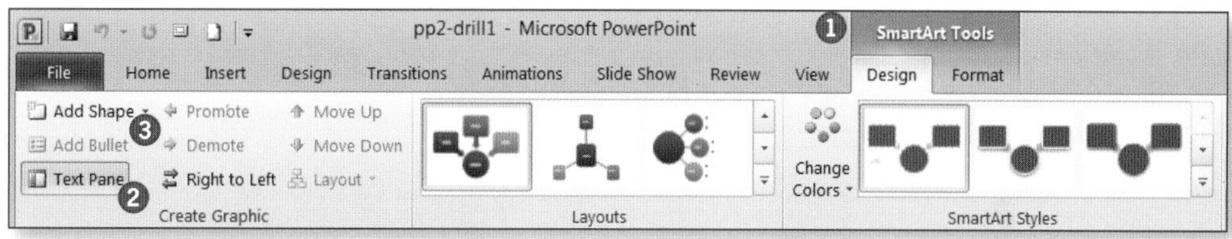

Figure 2.4 SmartArt Tools Design Tab

2. To add text, click in the text boxes or click Text Pane ❷ and key the text (Figure 2.5.)

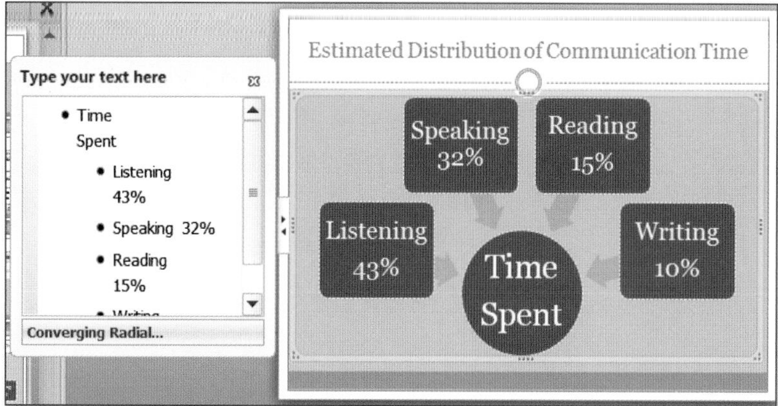

Figure 2.5 Text Pane

3. To add a shape, click Add Shape ❸; then choose an option to insert the shape before or after the selected shape.

MAINTAIN MULTIPLE CALENDARS

You may have a need to create separate calendars if you are scheduling for multiple people, or you may choose to create a separate personal calendar. You can display multiple calendars side by side to compare schedules or overlay them to find a common free time slot.

To Create and View a New Calendar:

Folder/New/New Calendar

1. Follow the path to display the Create New Folder dialog box.
2. Key the name of the folder.
3. Select Calendar Items in the Folder contains drop list, if necessary.
4. In the Select where to place the folder list, select Calendar. Click OK.
5. The new Personal folder is now listed in the Navigation Pane. Click the checkbox to the left of Personal folder to display the personal calendar side by side with your original calendar.
6. To overlay the calendars, click the View tab. In the Arrangement group, click Overlay. The calendars become transparent and are now stacked to display common free time slots.

DRILL 4 CREATE PERSONAL CALENDAR

1. Create a personal folder named **Personal—xx** (use your initials in place of the xx).
2. Place the new folder in the Calendar folder.
3. Click the checkbox to the left of your personal folder to display the calendars side by side.
4. Add a dentist appointment from 4:30 to 5:30 on January 9 of next year to your personal calendar.
5. Overlay the calendars (View/Arrangement/Overlay).

SCHEDULE A MEETING

A meeting is an activity that involves other people. A meeting invitation is sent by e-mail to all prospective attendees. The recipient can either accept, decline, or propose a new time for the meeting. *Outlook* automatically adds the meeting to your calendar and to the calendar of all who accept your meeting invitation.

To Schedule a Meeting:

Home/New/New Meeting

1. Follow the path to display the Meeting form.
2. Key the e-mail addresses of people who will be invited to the meeting.

DRILL 1, continued — SMARTART

Hover the mouse over a SmartArt graphic to display its name in a ScreenTip.

1. Insert a new slide between the Title slide and slide 2 with the table.
2. Key the title **Career Skills** and the following bulleted text:
   - Communication skills critical for all professions
   - Presentation skills essential
   - PowerPoint enhances many types of presentations
3. Select the bulleted text and convert it to a Target List SmartArt graphic (Home/Paragraph/Convert to SmartArt).
4. Insert a new slide with a Title and Content layout after slide 3. Key the title **Estimated Distribution of Communication Time**.
5. In the content area, add a Converging Radial SmartArt graphic. Add a new shape after the third shape on the right.
6. Display the Text pane and key the following text. If necessary, tap ENTER to position the percentage on a second line.
   - Time Spent
     - Listening 43%
     - Speaking 32%
     - Reading 15%
     - Writing 10%
7. Resave as *pp2-drill1* and close.

HIDE SLIDES

Slide Show/Set Up/Hide Slide

Sometimes it is desirable to show a slide to some individuals but not to others. For example, if you had a slide with appraised property values, you might want to show it to those in your own organization. However, you would not show it to developers who might bid on the property. In the presentation you just created, slides 3 and 4 present the same information. You would only want to show one of these slides.

To Hide a Slide:

1. Select the slide you want to hide.
2. Click Hide Slide. (*Option*: Right-click the slide in the Slides tab and select Hide Slide.)
3. The slide number in the Slides/Outline pane displays the Hidden Slide icon (Figure 2.6).

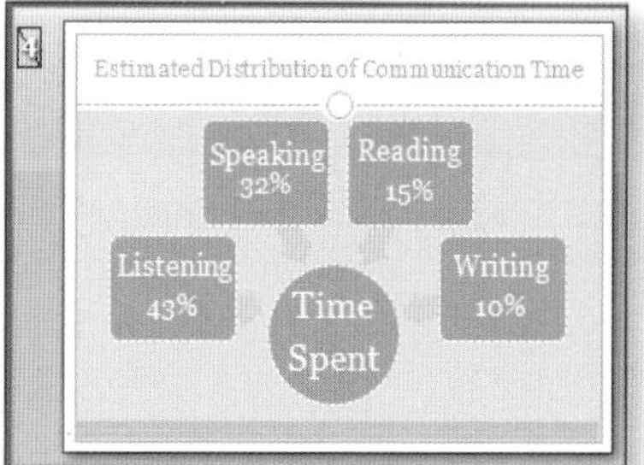

Figure 2.6 Hidden Slide

To Unhide a Slide:

1. Right-click the Hidden Slide icon in the Slides/Outline pane.
2. Click Hide Slide again to show the slide.

DRILL 2 — HIDE SLIDES

1. Open *pp2-drill1*.
2. Hide slides 3 and 4.
3. Unhide slide 3.
4. Save as *pp2-drill2* and leave the presentation open.

3. A reminder displays on the screen as shown in Figure 3.6. Click the Dismiss button to remove the reminder ❶. To have a reminder display again at a later time, select the time from the list ❷ and then click the Snooze button ❸. Click Open Item to display the Appointment form.

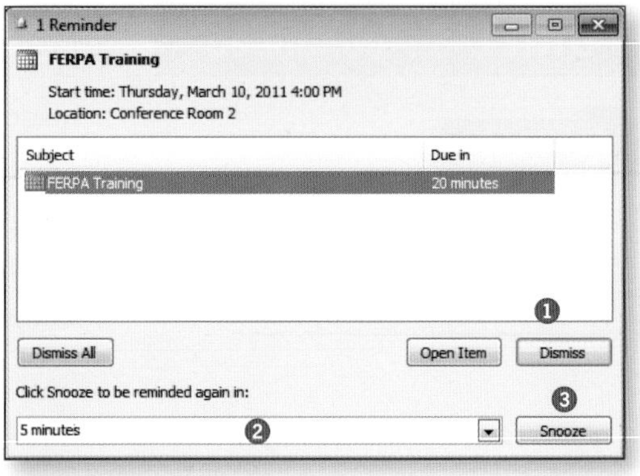

Figure 3.6 Reminder

SCHEDULE RECURRING APPOINTMENTS

Appointments are often scheduled on a regular basis, perhaps weekly, monthly, quarterly, etc. By designating an appointment as recurring in *Outlook*, you can enter the appointment once and then specify the pattern of recurrence.

To Schedule Recurring Appointments:

1. Key the appointment information in the Appointment form.
2. Click the Recurrence button to display the Appointment Recurrence dialog box, as shown in Figure 3.7.
3. Select the recurrence pattern—whether the appointment is to occur daily, weekly, monthly, or yearly ❶. Select the day the appointment will take place ❷.
4. Select the range of recurrence. If the recurring appointment is ongoing, such as a lunch hour, you can select the No end date option. You can also select the number of times of recurrence or give an end date for the recurring appointments ❸.

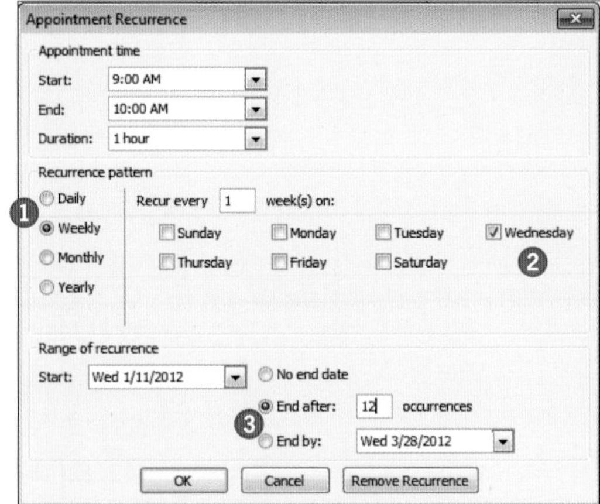

Figure 3.7 Appointment Recurrence

5. Click OK to close the Appointment Recurrence dialog box. Click Save & Close to close the Appointment form.

DRILL 3 SET RECURRING APPOINTMENT AND REMINDER

1. Double-click the Weekly Planning Meeting set for 1/11. Make this a recurring appointment that will meet on the same day of the week for the next 12 occurrences. Set a reminder to display 15 minutes before the meeting.
2. Double-click the Luncheon Meeting at the Chamber of Commerce scheduled for 1/11.
3. Make this a recurring appointment that will meet the same day, in the second week of every month. The end of the range of recurrence will be in December.
4. Click OK to close the Appointment Recurrence dialog box. Set a reminder to display 30 minutes before the appointment. Click Save & Close to close the Luncheon Meeting Appointment form.

Picture tools are used to format both clip art and pictures.

CLIP ART AND PICTURES

Insert/Illustrations/Clip Art

Clip art and pictures from files can be inserted and formatted in *PowerPoint* in the same way that you did in *Word* documents. Clip art files include illustrations, photographs, video, and audio.

To Insert and Format Clip Art:

1. Click the Clip Art icon (or Clip Art on the Insert tab) to display the Clip Art task pane.
2. Key a keyword, such as *conference*, in the Search for box, and then click Go.
3. Review the search results as shown in Figure 2.7 and click the desired clip art to insert it.
4. Select the clip and drag the corners to size it appropriately.
5. Select the clip and apply the desired correction, color, or artistic effect.

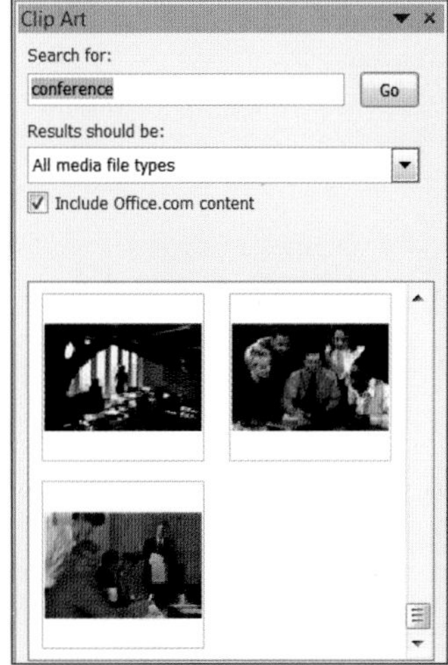

Figure 2.7 Clip Art

DRILL 2, continued CLIP ART

1. In the open presentation, select slide 3, click Layout on the Home tab, and select Two Content layout. The table will be in the left content area.
2. In the right content area, search for a photograph in clip art using the keyword *conference*. Look for a small group of people communicating in a conference setting. Select a clip that reflects diversity.
3. Insert it in the right content area, size it about the same size as the table, and drag it to the top of the placeholder.
4. Resave as *pp2-drill2* and close.

QUICK ✓ Check to see that slide 4 has the hidden icon as shown below the slide in Figure 2.8.

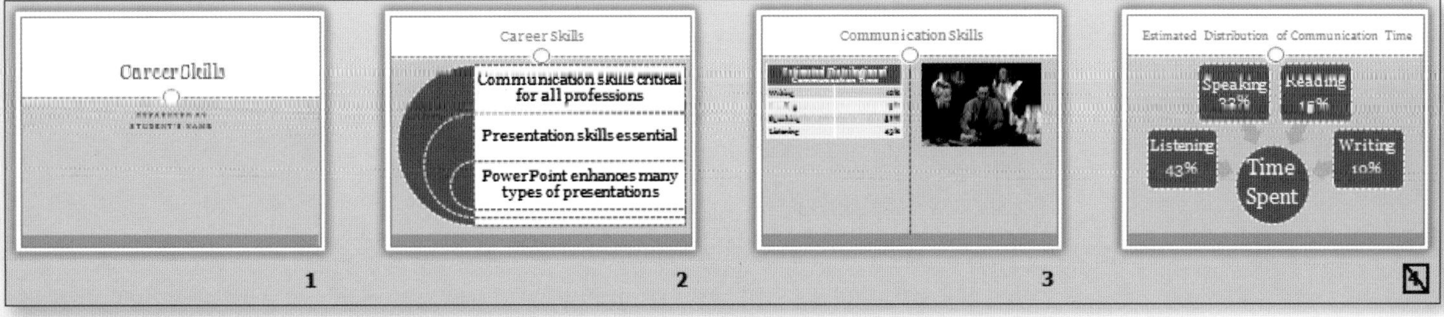

Figure 2.8 Quick Check

3. Key the following appointments using Appointment forms.

Date	Time	Subject/Location
1/9/20--	9:00–9:30	Meet with Heather Valdez, B-47 Project. Tag as High Importance and apply Key Customer category.
1/10/20--	1:00–4:00	Meet in C-144 to plan B787 Project.
1/10/20--	4:30–5:30	Front-end Electrical Webinar—add note: Meeting ID: 1289 Password: C25RW
1/11/20--	9:00–10:00	Weekly Planning Meeting, Conference Room 1 Print 15 copies of the agenda.
1/11/20--	11:30–2:00	Luncheon Meeting at the Chamber of Commerce; tag this item as Low Importance.
1/12/20--	9:30–11:30	Meet with Process Engineering, Room C59
1/12/20--	2:00–4:00	Arbitration Meeting, City Hall
1/16/20-- to 1/20/20--	All day event	Aeronautic Electrical Engineering Conference, Las Vegas, Nevada. Show as Out of Office.

4. Edit the 10:00 meeting with Jet Propeller and apply Vendor category. Apply the Key Customer category to the 12:00 luncheon with Susan Gray.

SET REMINDERS

Reminder: 15 minutes

You can set a reminder that displays on your screen to remind you of an upcoming appointment. The reminder is similar to setting an alarm clock; you determine the time the reminder will display, and you have the option of clicking the "snooze" button.

To Set a Reminder:

1. Key the appointment in the Appointment form.
2. Click the Reminder drop-list arrow and select the time frame in which the reminder is to display prior to your appointment.

PICTURES

Insert/Illustrations/Picture

Carefully selected and formatted pictures that complement a presentation's theme make it interesting. Compressing high-resolution pictures to reduce the file size is very important. In the *Word* module, you learned to adjust, size, arrange, and apply picture styles to pictures. You will apply these same commands in *PowerPoint*.

To Insert a Picture:

1. Click the Picture content icon or Picture on the Insert tab.
2. Browse and select the desired file; then click Insert.

To Format Pictures or Clip Art:

Picture Tools Format/Adjust/Corrections, Color, Artistic Effects, or Compress Picture

TIP

To use a Picture Tools Format command, you must select the picture or clip art first.

1. Review the types of adjustments that can be made as shown in Figure 2.9.
2. Select the picture and click the down arrow on Corrections, Color, or Artistic Effects and select the desired adjustment.
3. To reduce file size of a picture, select it and click Compress Pictures; accept the defaults and click OK. As a standard procedure, compress each picture inserted in presentations.

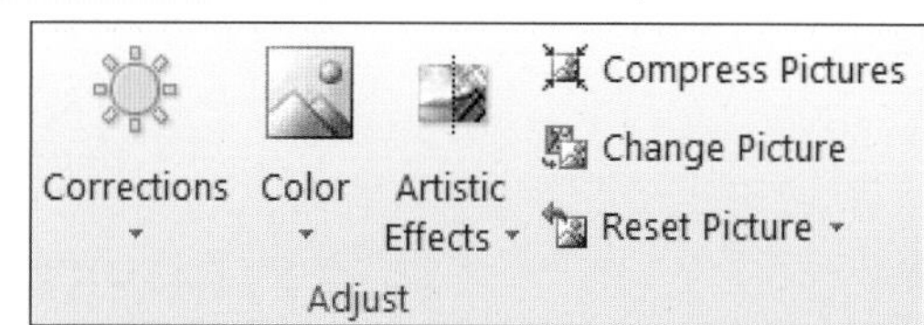

Figure 2.9 Adjust Pictures

To Size Pictures or Clip Art:

Picture Tools Format/Size/Crop or Height and Width

1. To remove unwanted portions of a picture or clip on one side, click Crop and drag the cropping handle on the side inward.
2. To crop the same amount on two sides, press CTRL while you drag the handle. The cropping line illustrates what is being cut off. Click off the picture to finish.
3. To increase or decrease the size of a picture, use the Height and Width spin arrows as shown in Figure 2.10.

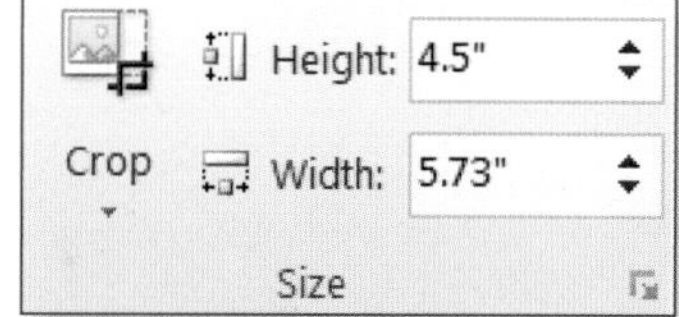

Figure 2.10 Size Pictures

To Arrange Pictures or Clip Art:

Picture Tools Format/Arrange/Align or Rotate

1. To move a picture or clip, drag to the desired position or click Align and select the desired alignment.
2. To rotate a picture, click Rotate and select the desired option. See Figure 2.11.

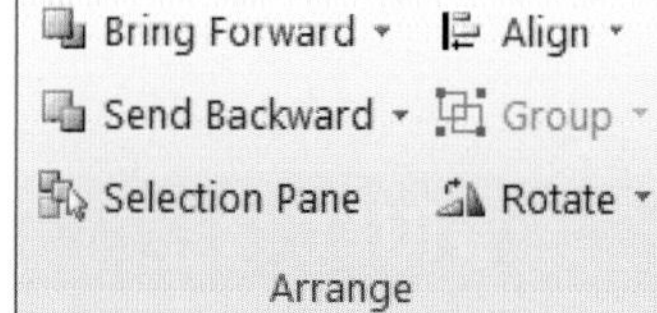

Figure 2.11 Arrange Pictures

To Apply Picture Styles:

Picture Tools Format/Picture Styles

1. Hover the mouse over the options in the Picture Styles gallery to preview the styles before selecting one. See Figure 2.12.
2. Click the desired style to apply it.

Figure 2.12 Picture Styles

To Schedule an Appointment Using the Appointment Form:

Home/New/New Appointment

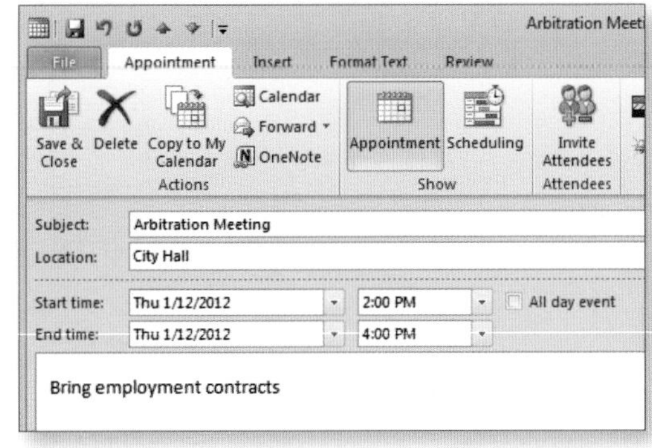

Figure 3.4 New Appointment Form

1. Click the New Appointment button to display the Appointment form (Figure 3.4).
2. Key the Subject and Location of the appointment.
3. Click the drop-list arrow for Start time and choose the date. Click the time drop-list arrow and select the time.
4. If the End time needs to be changed, click the appropriate drop-list arrow and choose the new date and time.
5. Notes regarding the appointment can be keyed in the window below.
6. Click Save & Close to return to the main Calendar screen.

SCHEDULE EVENTS

Events are activities that last 24 hours or longer. A multiday conference or vacation time is an example of an event. When an event is scheduled, a description of the event displays in a banner below the day heading. If an event lasts more than one day, the beginning and end dates are also shown on the event banner (Figure 3.5).

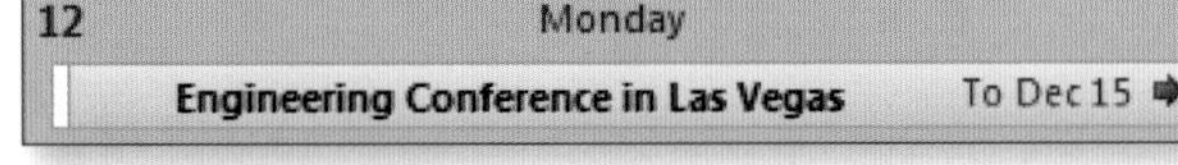

Figure 3.5 Event Banner

Changes can be made to scheduled appointments and events by double-clicking the appointment or event. The Appointment or Event window displays so that changes can be made.

To Schedule an Event:

Home/New/New Items/All Day Event

1. Follow the path to display the Event window.
2. Key the subject and location of the event. Key the start and end dates of the event. The start and end times are dimmed because the All day event checkbox is selected.
3. Click Save & Close to view the event banner.

DRILL 2 SCHEDULE APPOINTMENTS AND EVENTS

1. Click the Go To dialog box launcher and key the date for January 9 of next year; tap ENTER.
2. Key the following appointments in the Day view of the calendar.

Date	Time	Description
1/9/20--	10:00–11:00	Meet with Jet Propeller representative
1/9/20--	12:00–1:00	Lunch with Susan Gray
1/9/20--	2:00–4:00	Meet with Aeronautic Engineering

DRILL 3 PICTURES

The picture must be selected to use any of the Picture tools. Remember to compress all pictures.

This presentation is designed as part of a sales presentation to interest clients in taking a private safari tour. Design the slides to emphasize the five "must see" animals clients will see on the tour.

1. Open *african safaris* and add five new slides using the Title and Content layout.
2. Insert pictures in the slides in the following order: *rhinoceros, elephant, lion, leopard, cape buffalo*. Key the animal name in the title placeholder.
3. Crop each picture so that roughly 1" remains between the animal and each side of the picture. If a side is less than 1" from the animal, do not crop that side.
4. Size the picture to approximately 4.5" high.
5. In the Arrange group, click Align and then Align Center to center the picture horizontally.
6. Drag the picture to position it at approximately the vertical center of the content portion of the slide. *Note:* Align Middle centers an object on the entire slide, not in the content portion.
7. From the Picture Styles, add a Simple Frame, White.
8. Select the leopard and apply the Correction: Sharpen: 25%.
9. Select the lion and change the Color Tone to Temperature: 5900 K.
10. Use Slide Sorter view to arrange the five animal pictures in alphabetical order.
11. Preview the presentation using Slide Show view.
12. Save as *pp2-drill3* and close.

Use Figure 2.13 to check your slides. Note the way the pictures are cropped and positioned.

QUICK ✓

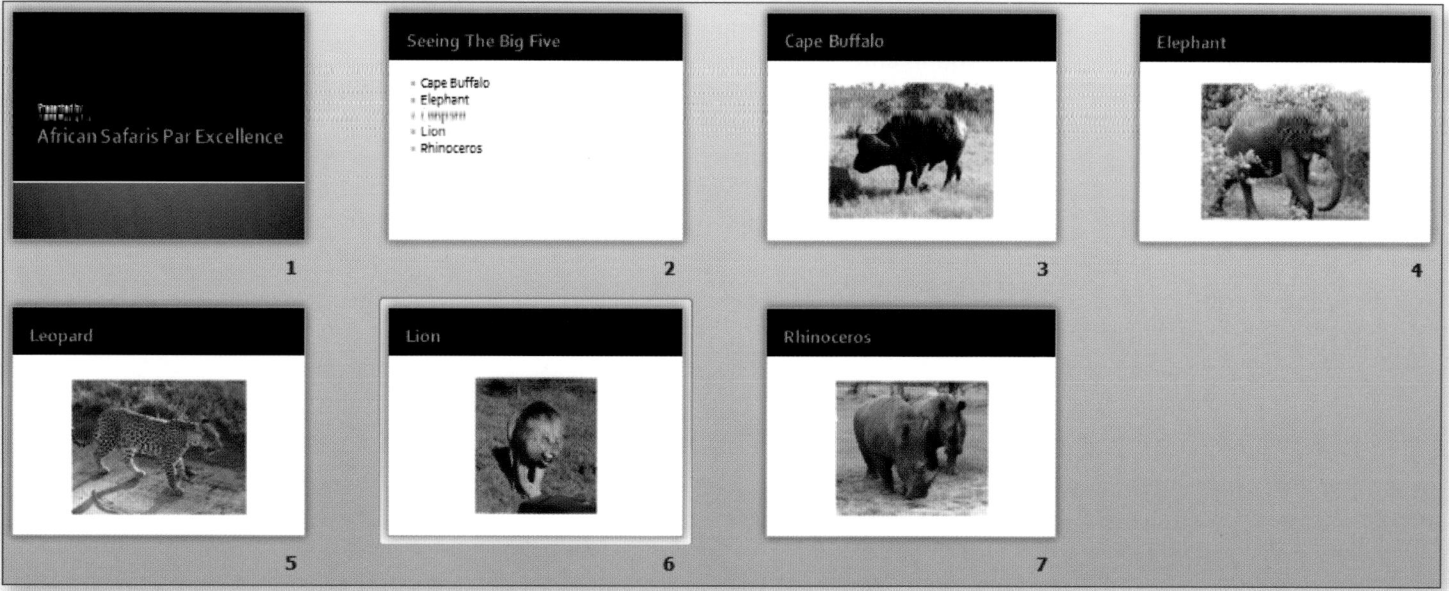

Photos: Susie VanHuss

Figure 2.13 Quick Check

DRILL 1 NAVIGATING CALENDAR VIEWS

1. Display the Calendar window in default view if necessary (Home/Arrange/Day).
2. Click the Week button to display the calendar for the week. Click the Month button to display the calendar for the month. Click the Day button to return to default view.
3. Click the last day of the month in the Date Navigator; the Calendar window displays the last day.
4. Click the Forward button located to the left of the date; the next day's calendar displays. Click the Back button twice to display the previous day's calendar.
5. Click the first day of the month in the Date Navigator.
6. In the Date Navigator, move the mouse pointer over the name of the month and hold down the left mouse button. Several months before and after the current month display. Select the month that is two months ahead of the current month.
7. In the Date Navigator, click the right arrow to the right of the month and year. Next month's calendar displays. Click the left arrow to display the previous month.
8. Click the Go To dialog box launcher, key **1/9/12** in the date box, and click OK. This takes you to a specific date.
9. Click the Today button in the Go To group to return to the current date.

SCHEDULE APPOINTMENTS

Calendar allows you to schedule appointments, meetings, events, and resources. An appointment is an activity that does not involve inviting other people or reserving resources.

Appointments can be set in the Day view of the calendar. Begin by using the Date Navigator to select the month and day of the appointment. Then click the time slot, key a description of the appointment, and tap ENTER. Appointments are set for 30 minutes. If you need to allocate more than 30 minutes for the meeting, drag the bottom border of the appointment box down to add the needed time, as shown in Figure 3.2.

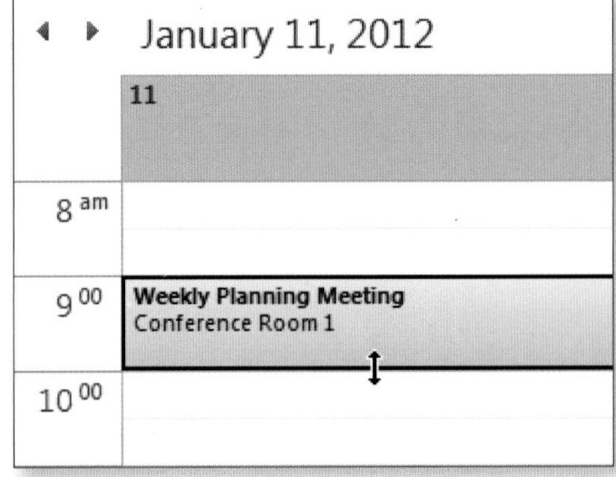

Figure 3.2 Add Appointment in Day View

Appointments can also be set in the Appointment form. The Appointment form allows you to enter more details about the appointment. The Tags group contains options for labeling appointments as Private, High Importance, Low Importance, or assigning a category to the calendar item. If you are connected to Exchange Server, others may be able to view your calendar to schedule a meeting. Therefore, you may want to mark your calendar items using the Show As designation (Figure 3.3) in the Options group as being Busy or Out of Office as appropriate.

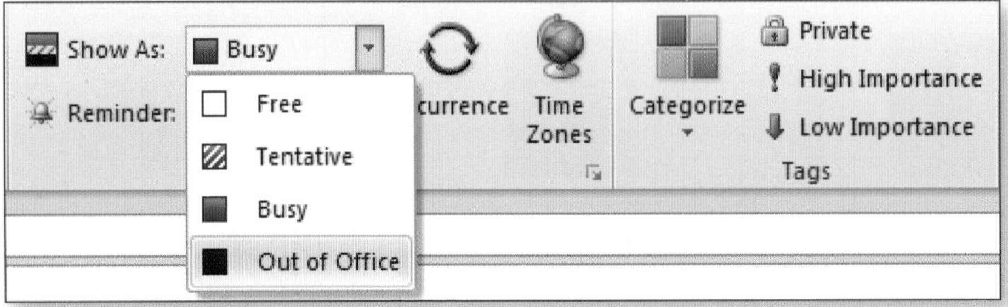

Figure 3.3 Appointment Options

Apply It

Presentation 3
Presentation with Graphics

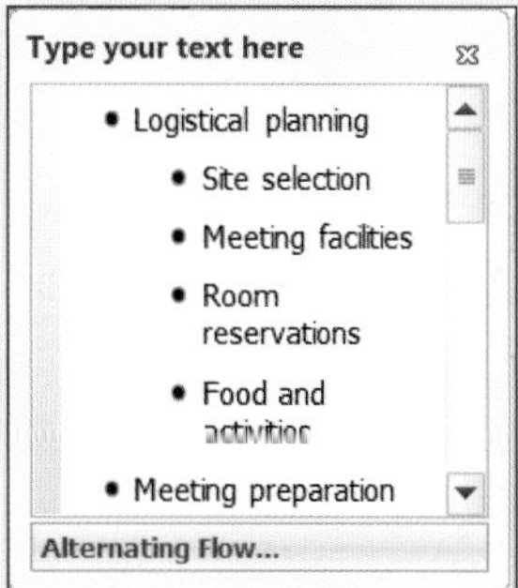

Figure 2.14 Text Pane

1. Prepare the following presentation using the Waveform theme.

Slide 1 Title: Spring Retreat Subtitle: The Leadership Group

Slide 2 (Use Comparison layout.)

Title: Proposed Site Options

Content titles: Beach Option | Mountain Option

Contents: Insert clip art. Select a beach scene and a mountain scene. Size pictures so they will be approximately the same size. Add an artistic effect to the beach clip and a correction to the mountain clip.

Slide 3 (Use Title and Content layout.)

Title: Planning Process

Bulleted text: Logistical planning | Meeting preparation | Retreat | Follow-up

Convert text to an Alternating Flow SmartArt graphic. Use the Text pane and tap ENTER and then TAB under each heading to add four bulleted items. See Figure 2.14.

Logistical planning	Meeting preparation	Retreat	Follow-up
Site selection	Retreat objectives	On-site coordination	Retreat evaluation
Meeting facilities	Agenda	Presentations	Review action plans
Room reservations	Program participants	Group discussions	Determine feasibility
Food and activities	Meeting materials	Action plans	Implement plans

Slide 4 (Use Title and Content layout.)

Title: Group Leadership

Contents: Insert Organization Chart SmartArt graphic. Key directly in the graphic. Delete the Assistant shape between the top shape and the next three shapes.

Top shape: Your Name | Group Leader | Agenda

Three shapes starting from left: (The second line in each shape is the area of responsibility.)

Marcus Lee | Logistics | Ann Morris | Retreat | Jan Cox | Follow-up

2. Save as *pp2-p3* and close.

CAREER FOCUS

Communication skills are critical for success in virtually every career. Most people spend far more time developing reading and writing skills than speaking skills. However, they use their speaking skills on the job far more than their reading and writing skills. Developing the ability to make presentations to groups is important for upward mobility. Many people have a tremendous fear of speaking before a large group. You can be an effective speaker if you:

1. Know your topic, organize the content, and prepare good supporting visuals.
2. Learn effective delivery techniques.
3. Practice and develop confidence in your ability to make presentations.

Use Calendar to Schedule Appointments

LESSON 3

OBJECTIVES

- Schedule appointments, events, and meetings
- Set reminders and recurring appointments
- Create multiple calendars and send calendar by e-mail

The Calendar feature is an essential tool for organizing both business and personal activities. You can schedule appointments, events, and meetings with *Outlook*. *Outlook* provides many ways to view the calendar, as well as allowing you to share the calendar with others.

THE CALENDAR WINDOW

Click the Calendar button in the Navigation Pane to display the Calendar window. Figure 3.1 shows Calendar's default view. If your calendar does not look like this, click the Day button in the tab (Home/Arrange/Day).

You can display the calendar in daily, weekly, or monthly view by clicking the appropriate button in the Arrange group on the Home tab. Appointments for each day are displayed in the calendar grid. The Daily Task List at the bottom displays the tasks for each day.

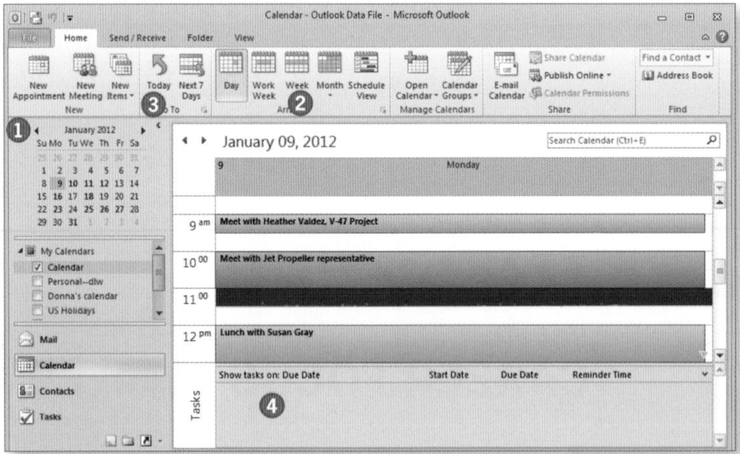

Figure 3.1 Calendar Window

❶ **Date Navigator:** Click the left or right arrow on either side of the month to display previous or next month. Click a date and the calendar displays that day in the View Pane.

❷ **Day, Week, Month buttons:** Buttons in the Arrange group on the Home tab allow the user to quickly switch between *Outlook*'s built-in views.

❸ **Today button:** Allows you to quickly return to today's calendar.

❹ **Daily Task List:** Scheduled tasks display at the bottom of each day in the Day and Week views.

Add Transitions and Animations

LESSON 3

OBJECTIVES

- Create effective presentations
- Add transitions to slides
- Add animations to slides

TRANSITIONS

Transitions/Transition to This Slide

Transitions are effects that occur when one slide replaces another. Transitions can be added to individual slides, but they are generally applied to all slides. See Figure 3.1. Transitions should be used judiciously; preview them carefully. Most speakers prefer to use a smooth transition and to avoid a lot of motion that can be distracting to the audience. In self-running presentations, slides are set to move automatically after a certain amount of time.

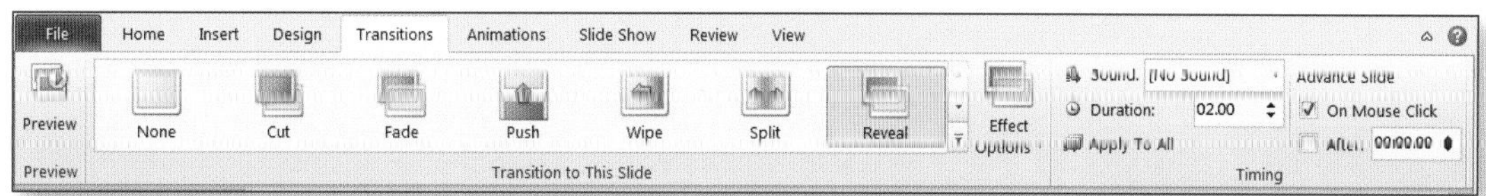

Figure 3.1 Transitions

To Add Transitions to Slides:

Transitions/Transition to This Slide

1. To add a transition to one slide, select the slide in the Slides/Outline pane.
2. To preview the transition to or the animation effects on a slide, click the Preview button.
3. Preview and select the desired transition; click to apply. Change duration if desired.
4. To add a transition to all slides, click the desired transition, and then click Apply To All.

DRILL 1 TRANSITIONS

1. Open *pp2-drill3* and save it as *pp3-drill1*.
2. Apply Reveal transition to all slides. Use 2:00 duration.
3. Click the Preview button to preview slide 2; use Slide Show view to preview all slides.
4. Resave as *pp3-drill1* and close.

ANIMATIONS

Animations/Animation/Select Animation Effect

Animations are visual or audio effects added to text or objects on slides. For example, you can use preset animations to make bulleted items or elements of a SmartArt graphic display one at a time as you click the mouse (Figure 3.2). Always select animations that set the proper tone for the presentation.

You can display contact information in any *Outlook* component by clicking Find a Contact in the Find group on the Home tab. Simply click Find a Contact, key the name of the contact, and *Outlook* will display the Contact form.

Apply It

Job 4
Create Contacts

CONTACTS

1. Change the view to Business Card view.
2. Add the contacts in the *contacts* data file to your Contacts folder.
3. Rename the purple category as Vendor.
4. Print the contacts by category in Table Style (List View/Categories arrangement, Print). Label the printout OL2-job4-4.

Job 5
Search and Edit Contacts, Use Map It, and Display People Pane

1. Use Search Contacts to find Judith Englewood. Add her home phone **(310) 555-0110** to her contact record.
2. Use Find a Contact to find the contact information for Hillary Richardson. Add a home address for her: **43 Niguel Village Drive, Laguna Niguel, CA 92677-4027**.
3. Add your name, home address, and e-mail address to Contacts. Remember to change the address button to Home. Click the up arrow in the lower-right corner to expand the People Pane. A list of recent messages sent to you displays. Click on one of the messages to display the message in the e-mail window. View your address on the map by clicking the Map It button, located at the right of the address box in the Contact form. Close your browser.
4. Add one of your classmates to Contacts, including his or her name, address, phone number, and e-mail address. Rename the yellow category **Classmate**. Assign the Classmate category to your classmate. Save the contact. Use Search Contacts to find and open the contact. Send an e-mail from the Contact form to your classmate, giving him or her the directions on how to send an e-mail directly from the Contact form.
5. Add a second classmate to Contacts. Assign the Classmate category. Use Map It to locate the classmate's address on the map.
6. Click the Search Contacts box in the Contacts window; the Search tab displays. Click the Categorized button, and then click Classmate. The two classmates that you entered in steps 4 and 5 display. Close the search.
7. In *Outlook* Mail, click Sent Items. Click in the Search Sent Items box. In the Search tab, click the Sent To drop-list arrow and choose Sent To: Me or CC: Me. The e-mails that you sent to yourself display. Close the search.
8. Display your Mail Inbox screen. On the Home tab, in the Find group, click Find a Contact. Key your name and tap ENTER. Your Contact form displays. Close the search.
9. Click the Search box in the Inbox screen and search for all e-mails from one of your classmates. Close the search.
10. Display all the contacts that have been categorized as Vendors. Close the search.
11. Display all contacts that have a job title of Buyer. (Click Search box, More, Job Title, key **Buyer** in the Job Title box; tap ENTER.) Close the search.
12. Print all the contacts by category in Table Style and label the printout.

DISCOVER

An e-mail can be sent from the Contact form. With the Contact form open, follow the path to display the e-mail screen:

Contact/Communicate/E-mail

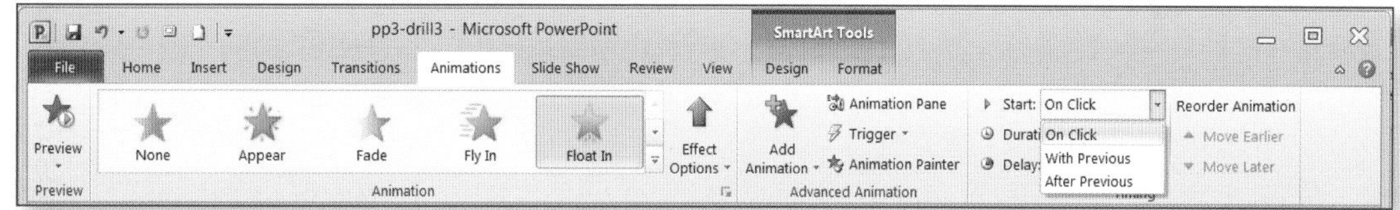

Figure 3.2 Animations

To Animate Slides:

Animations/Animation/Select Animation Effect

1. To animate a slide, click in the placeholder or object you want to animate.
2. Select the animation effect desired and click the Start option desired.
3. To animate bulleted text or a SmartArt element to appear one at a time, click that option on the Effect Options menu (Figure 3.3).
4. Use the Preview button or Slide Show to preview slides.

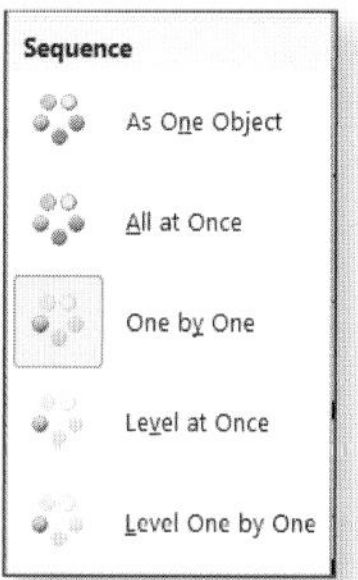

Figure 3.3 Effect Options

DRILL 2 ANIMATIONS

SNOW

1. Open *snow* from the data files and save it as *pp3-drill2*.
2. Apply Couture design theme.
3. Apply Rotate transition with 2:00 duration to all slides.
4. Select the picture on each slide and apply Zoom animation; select Start On Click.
5. Resave as *pp3-drill2* and close.

DRILL 3 ANIMATE ITEMS ONE AT A TIME

1. Open *pp2-drill2* and save it as *pp3-drill3*.
2. Apply Fade transition with 2:00 duration to all slides.
3. Click in the SmartArt graphic on slide 2 and apply Float In animation and One-by-One sequence. All slides will use the Float Up animation version.
4. On slide 3, select the table and then the picture and apply the animation as one object.
5. On slide 4, click in the SmartArt graphic and apply One-by-One sequence.
6. Resave as *pp3-drill3* and close.

Apply It

Presentation 4

Presentation with Transitions and Animations

CDRC

1. Open *pp2-p3* and save as *pp3-p4*.
2. Add the new slides and make the changes to existing slides described on the next page.
3. Add Push transition to all slides.
4. Add to the slides the animations indicated on the next page.
5. After all additions and changes indicated on the next page are made, proofread carefully and then preview using Slide Show view. Resave as *pp3-p4* and close.

DRILL 3 RENAME AND ADD CATEGORIES

1. Rename the categories as follows:

Color	Category Name
Blue	Business
Green	Supplier
Orange	Key Customer
Red	Important Contact

2. Assign the following categories to your contacts.

Name of Contact	Category
Hinkson	Business
Smith	Business, Key Customer
Ramirez	Business, Important Contact
Truong	Business, Supplier

3. View the contacts by category (View/Current View/Change View/List/Arrangement/Categories). Print the list in Table Style; label the printout.

PEOPLE PANE

When a contact is open, useful information about the person displays in the People Pane. Expand the People Pane by clicking the up arrow in the lower-right corner. You can see recent e-mail messages, upcoming scheduled meetings, attachments, and activity feeds from business and social networks, such as Facebook and LinkedIn. Click the appropriate category ❶ to display the list of items ❷. Click the item to view it. When you finish viewing the People Pane, click the down arrow to collapse it.

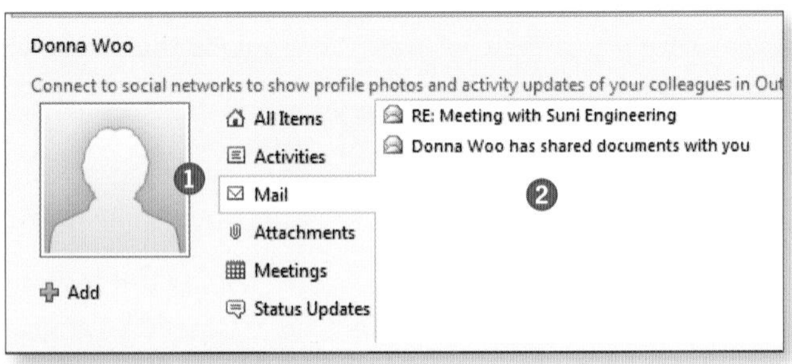

Figure 2.5 People Pane

FIND CONTACTS AND USE INSTANT SEARCH

Outlook's Search feature helps you find *Outlook* items quickly. Every *Outlook* component contains a Search box above the main display of items on the Home, Send/Receive, Folder, and View tabs. Figure 2.6 shows the Search Contacts box. Click the box and key the name of the Contact; as you key, *Outlook* finds contacts that match. When you click in the Search box, the Search Tools Search tab (Figure 2.7) also displays, containing additional tools that help you refine the search. For example, clicking the Categorized button allows you to narrow your search by looking only in a specific category. The More drop list displays additional properties that can be used for searching.

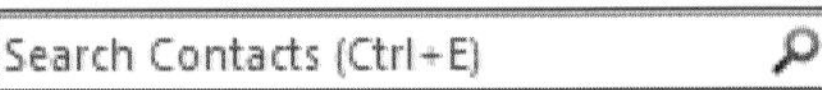

Figure 2.6 Search Contacts

TIP

Click the Close Search button on the Search tab to remove the results of a search from the window and restore the view of the component you were searching.

Figure 2.7 Search Tab

Presentation 4,
continued

Slide 2: Modify by changing *Beach Option* to **Palmetto Isle Beach Resort** and *Mountain Option* to **Westwego Mountain Resort**. Decrease the font of both to 20 points; Align Left. Animate the left clip to fly in from the left and the right clip from the right.

Slide 3: Insert a new slide after slide 2. (Use Title and Content layout.)

Title: Cost Comparison

Table:

Cost Item	Westwego Mountain Resort	Palmetto Isle Beach Resort
Room and tax	$105	$120
Meeting room	$100	No charge with food
Luncheon buffet	$18	$20

Format: Center text vertically in all cells; center text horizontally in columns 2 and 3.

Row 1: Increase height to 1", increase font to 24 points, center headings horizontally.

Rows 2–4: Increase height to .7".

Select the table and animate by clicking Fly In. Use default From Bottom unless directed otherwise.

Table Tools Layout/Cell Size/Height

1. Click in a row or select rows for which you wish to change the height.
2. Click Up arrow in Height box to increase row height

Slide 4: Select the content area and animate by clicking Fly In, One by One.

Slide 5: Select the content area and animate by clicking Fly In, By level at once.

Slide 6: Insert a new slide after slide 5. (Use Title and Content layout.)

Title: Retreat Focus

- Strategic plan for child development center
  - Recommended by Employee Benefits Team
  - Approved by Executive Committee
- Work with strategic partner
  - Palmetto University agreeable
  - Consider adding research center

Convert to SmartArt Chevron List. Animate content area using Fly In, One by one.

Home/Paragraph/ Increase Indent

1. To indent bullets to second level, click Increase Indent.
2. To return to first level, click Decrease Indent.

Slide 7: Insert a new slide after slide 6. (Use Title and Content layout.)

Title: Model Design

Picture: Insert the *cdrc* data file; crop about .5" from top, bottom, and left side. Increase height to 4"; center at about the vertical and horizontal center of content area; compress picture. Animate object using Fly In.

Slide 8: Insert a new slide after slide 7. (Use Comparison layout.)

Title: Target Profile

Left heading and content:

Full-Care Target: 150
Infants: 40
Toddlers: 50
Preschool: 60

Right heading and content:

After-School Target: 50
Below age 9: 30
Ages 9–12: 20

Animate each content area by using Fly In, All at Once.

ORGANIZE CONTACTS

A major advantage of keeping a contact list in *Outlook* rather than a paper address book is the ability to organize and reorganize contacts quickly. Categories can be assigned to contacts as a method of organizing the contacts. You can rename or create new categories.

> **DISCOVER**
>
> **Create New Categories**
> 1. In the Color Categories dialog box, click New.
> 2. Key a name for the new category.
> 3. Click the Color drop-list arrow and select the desired color.
> 4. Click OK.

To Rename a Category and Assign a Category to a Contact:

Contact/Tags/Categorize

1. Double-click the contact to display the Contact form.
2. Click the Categorize drop-list arrow. A list of the color categories displays.
3. Click All Categories to display the Color Categories dialog box. To rename the category; click on the desired color and then click the Rename button. Key the new category name. The new name displays in the categories list as shown in Figure 2.4.
4. More than one category can be assigned to a contact by clicking the checkbox to the left of each category you want to assign to the contact. Then click OK. The Contact form displays all the chosen categories below the Ribbon.

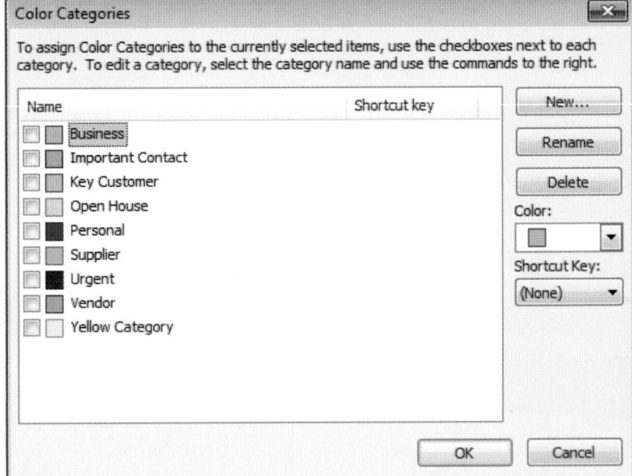

Figure 2.4 Color Categories

You can apply categories in other *Outlook* components, such as Calendar appointments, tasks, or notes, to help you keep these items organized.

CHANGE VIEWS

Outlook allows you to change the way in which the data is displayed, which may make it easier for you to find the information you need. For example, if you need to call one of your suppliers, but cannot remember the person's name, rather than scroll through all your contacts, you can display the contacts according to category and then easily view those listed under supplier.

Contacts are displayed in Business Card view by default. You can quickly change the view on the Home tab, in the Current View group. Click the More button or click the up and down scroll arrows to display all the views.

The view can be further defined by changing settings on the View tab. For example, you can view contacts by category, by company, or by location.

To Display Contacts in List View by Category or Company:

View/Current View/Change View

1. Click Change View and select List.
2. In the Arrangement group, choose Categories to view the contacts arranged by categories. Choose Company to display the list alphabetically by company.

Print Notes, Handouts, and Slides

LESSON 4

OBJECTIVES

- Create effective presentations
- Add notes to slides
- Print slides, notes, and handouts

NOTES

View/Presentation Views/Notes Page

In Normal view, the Notes pane is the area located below the Slide pane. To add one or two lines of notes, you can click in the Notes pane and key the information. To add more extensive notes, use Notes Page view. Many speakers prefer to use a larger-than-normal font size to make the notes easier to read.

To Prepare Notes:

1. To add notes to a slide, click Notes Page to display the first slide with a placeholder for keying notes.
2. Key the desired notes as shown in Figure 4.1. Increase the font size as desired.
3. Click the Next Slide button on the scroll bar to move to the next slide and key the information for that slide. Repeat this step until all the notes have been keyed.

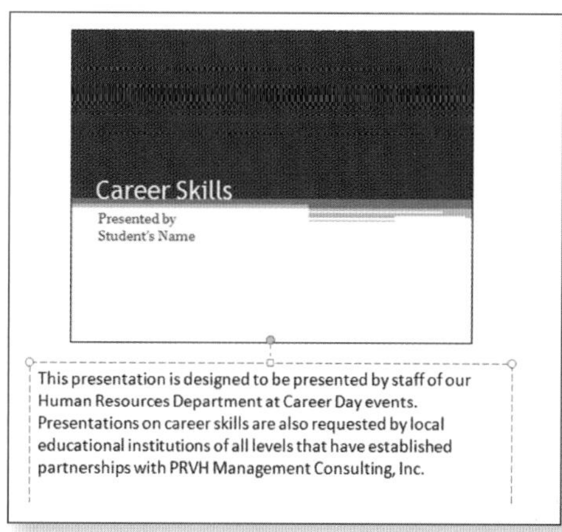

Figure 4.1 Notes Page

DRILL 1 PREPARE NOTES PAGES

CAREER SKILLS

1. Open *career skills*, click Notes Page to display the notes page for the first slide, and key the information shown on the next page. Increase the font size to 16 points.
2. Do the same for slides 2, 3, and 4.
3. Modify the information in slide 4 for slide 5 by changing *table* to **diagram** in the second sentence and by deleting *as illustrated in this slide* from the last sentence. One of these slides (4 or 5) will be hidden when the presentation is used.
4. Proofread notes carefully. Save as *pp4-drill1* and leave the presentation open.

Home/Font/Increase Font Size

1. To increase the font size, select the text.
2. Click Increase Font Size until the text reaches the desired size.

ADD CONTACTS FROM THE SAME COMPANY

Often, you will need to enter more than one contact from the same company. After one contact has been created from the company, additional contacts can be entered without having to rekey the company name, address, and telephone number.

To Add Another Contact from the Same Company:

Home/New/New Items/Contact from the Same Company

1. In Contacts, select a contact from the same company by clicking on the business card. Then follow the path and select Contact from the Same Company (Figure 2.3).
2. A new Contact form displays with the company name, address, and phone numbers already filled in. Key the necessary information on the new contact. Click Save & Close or Save & New as appropriate.

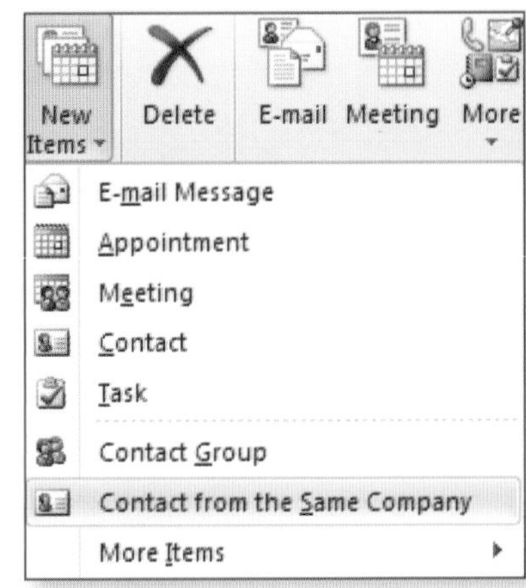

Figure 2.3 Contact from the Same Company

DRILL 2 EDIT, ADD, AND PRINT CONTACTS

1. Change Susan Smith's mobile phone number: Double-click Susan's business card to open her Contact form. Change the mobile phone number to (949) 555-0130.
2. Add the following contacts. These people are from the same companies as previous contacts, so you can use the Contact from the Same Company feature.
3. After you finish adding all the contacts, view them in the Contacts window. Print all the contacts in Medium Booklet Style. Label the printout as OL2-drill2-3.

Field Name	Contact 3	Contact 4
Title	Ms.	Mr.
First	Lucille	Robert
Middle	M.	C.
Last	Truong	Ramirez
Company	Aldrin Glenn Aircraft	Dansford International
Job title	Purchasing Manager	IT Specialist
E-mail	ltruong@aldrin.com	robert.ramirez@dansfordintl.com
Phone/Mobile	(714) 555-0189	(949) 555-0114

Slide 1 Notes:

This presentation is designed to be presented by staff of our Human Resources Department at Career Day events. Presentations on career skills are also requested by local educational institutions of all levels that have established partnerships with PRVH Management Consulting, Inc.

Slide 2 Notes: (Tap ENTER twice between each item.)

Business: Emphasize the wide range of industries and the levels of jobs from low- to mid- to high-level positions in the various businesses within each industry.

Professional: Give examples such as physicians, musicians, teachers, lawyers, and scientists.

Technical: Give examples such as computer experts, medical technicians, graphic illustrators, and physical therapists.

Other: Give examples such as farmers, lifeguards, barbers, and oil field workers.

Slide 3 Notes:

Every career requires good communication skills. The ability to make effective presentations is clearly a skill needed for upward mobility.

Slide 4 Notes:

The percentages were reported in a survey our Human Resources Department conducted with a number of our large clients. This table makes it even more obvious how important good listening and speaking skills are in careers. Note that speaking differs from making presentations. Speaking includes making presentations as well as conversations used in conducting business as illustrated in this slide.

Slide 5 Notes: Follow directions on previous page.

HANDOUTS

File/Print

Use landscape orientation with four slides per page to increase readability of handouts. See Figure 4.3 on the next page.

Handouts are pages that contain small versions of all slides in a presentation. Slides can be printed 1, 2, 3, 4, 6, or 9 per page. Click Full Page Slides to display the list of print options shown in Figure 4.2 Print Options. To print a border around the slides, click Frame Slides. Note that the handout with three slides per page provides lines for notes. Printing a larger number of slides per page costs less to provide handouts. However, readability of the slides should be considered before determining how many slides should be printed per page.

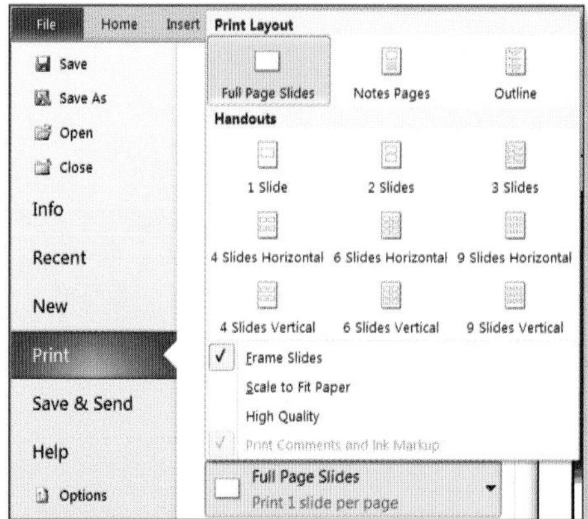

Figure 4.2 Print Options

5. Key the information as needed in the field boxes in the Contact form. Click buttons in the Phone numbers and Addresses sections to add more detailed information. The arrows to the right of the buttons open menus from which you can select other button names to store additional information, such as a home phone or address.
6. Key any additional information regarding the contact in the Notes box. A picture of the person can be added by clicking the Add Contact Picture button. The business address can be mapped by clicking the Map It button, if your computer is connected to the Internet.
7. When finished, click Save & Close. If you need to add more contacts, click Save & New and then choose Save & New from the menu. A new Contact form displays.

DRILL 1 ENTER CONTACTS

1. Display Contacts in *Outlook*.
2. Click New Contact and key the information for Contact 1 below; when finished, click the Save & New button to add Contact 2. Use the Check Full Name box to key the name details.

Field Name	Contact 1	Contact 2
Title	Mr.	Ms.
First	Kenneth	Susan
Middle	L.	B.
Last	Hinkson	Smith
Company	Aldrin Glenn Aircraft	Dansford International
Job title	Engineer	Buyer
E-mail	khinkson@aldrin.com	susan.smith@dansfordintl.com
Web page address	www.aldrin.com	www.dansfordintl.com
Phone/Business	(714) 555-0159	(949) 555-0155
Business Fax	(714) 555-0160	(949) 555-0156
Phone/Mobile	(714) 555-0102	(949) 555-0132
Address/Business	5187 Bolsa Avenue Huntington Beach, CA 92649-1046	1150 Jamboree Road Newport Beach, CA 92660-1219

Key telephone numbers with no hyphens, spaces, or parentheses; *Outlook* automatically inserts them.

3. Return to the Contacts window; the contacts display in Business Card view.
4. Click the business card for Kenneth Hinkson; the first line of the card is now orange, indicating that the card is selected. Double-click the card to display the Contact form; changes to the form can be made as needed.
5. Print the contacts in Card Style (File/Print/Card Style). Label the printout OL2-drill1-5.

To Print Notes Pages, Handouts, or Slides:

File/Print/Full Page Slides

1. Click Full Page Slides and select the appropriate option: Full Page Slides, Notes Pages, Outline, or Handouts.
2. If you are printing handouts, select the number of copies, desired layout, and number of slides per page. Click Frame Slides if desired.
3. To print handouts using landscape orientation, click View, Handout Master View, Handout Master, Handout Orientation, and select Landscape. Then click Close Master View.
4. Click file and then click Print.

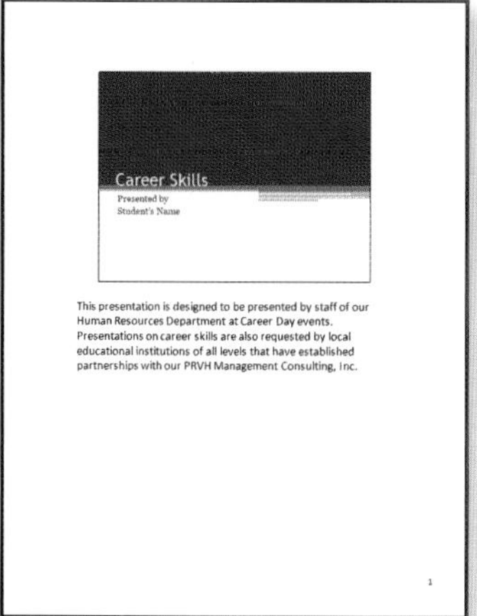

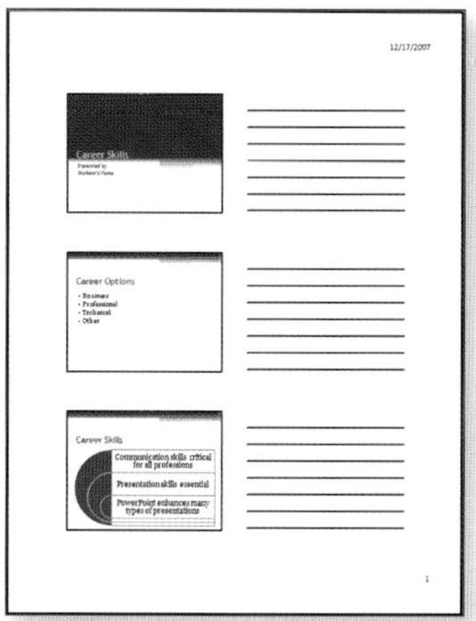

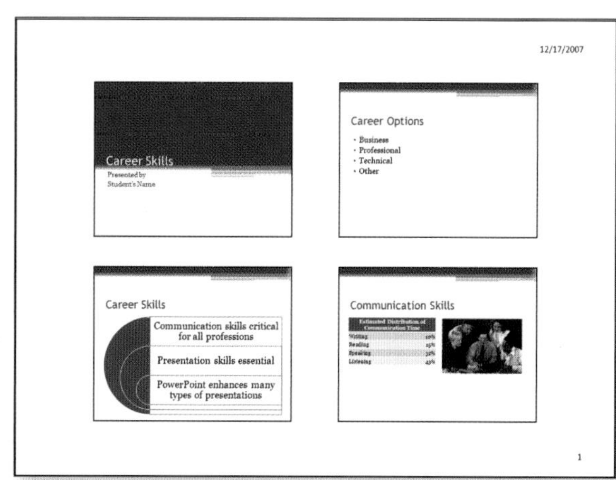

Figure 4.3 Notes Pages, Handouts 3 Per Page, and Handouts 4 Per Page with Landscape Orientation

DRILL 1, continued — PRINT NOTES PAGES, SLIDES, AND HANDOUTS

1. Preview the notes pages of the open presentation, and print one copy of each page.
2. Preview the handouts using three slides per page and then preview the handouts using four slides per page and landscape orientation. Print the handouts using four slides per page and landscape orientation.
3. Print one copy of all slides.
4. Resave as *pp4-drill1* and close.

Apply It

Presentation 5

Presentation with Notes and Handouts

MASTER PLAN NOTES (WORD DOCUMENT)
MASTER PLAN (POWERPOINT PRESENTATION)

1. Open *master plan notes* in *Word* and *master plan* in *PowerPoint*. Review the rough notes for each slide; edit, correct errors, and add notes to the slides using complete sentences and 14-point font.
2. Apply Oriel theme and Uncover From Right transition, 2:00 duration to all slides.
3. Animate slides 2 and 3 using Wipe From Left, By Paragraph.
4. Convert slide 4 to Vertical Box List SmartArt and move after slide 5. Animate using Wipe from Bottom, One by One.
5. Print Notes Pages and Handouts, 3 per page.
6. Save as *pp4-p5* and close.

LESSON
2

Create and Manage Contacts

OBJECTIVES

- Create and edit contacts
- Display the People Pane
- Use Search Contacts

GETTING STARTED WITH CONTACTS

The Contacts feature serves as an electronic address book. All the information that you need to communicate and conduct business—such as name, address, telephone number, e-mail address, and Web page address—is stored in database fields in Contacts (Figure 2.1). Storing the information in fields allows you to group contacts, arrange them in a variety of views, and find information very quickly.

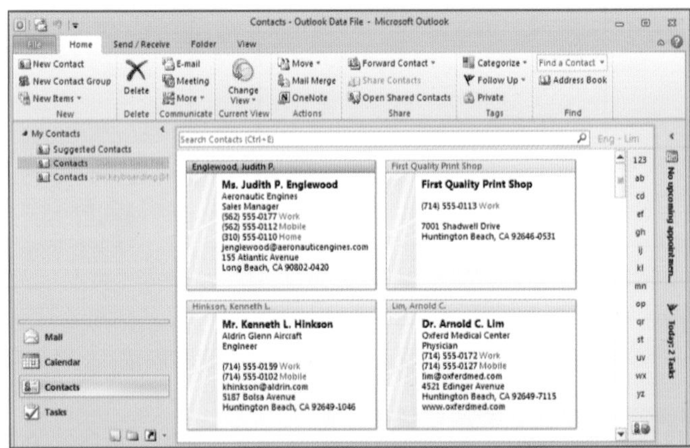

Figure 2.1 Contacts Window

To Add a Contact:

Home/New/New Contact

1. Click the Contacts button in the Navigation Pane to display Contacts; the window is empty because you have not entered any contacts.
2. Click New Contact to display the Contact form.
3. Key the contact's name in the Full Name text box. To add more detailed information for the name, click the Full Name button to display the Check Full Name dialog box (Figure 2.2). Select a title from the Title list. Key the first, middle, and last names. (Tap TAB to move from field to field.) Choose a suffix, if appropriate. Click OK to return to the Contact form.
4. The File as box shows the contact being filed by last name; if this is not appropriate, click the drop-list arrow to select another method of filing.

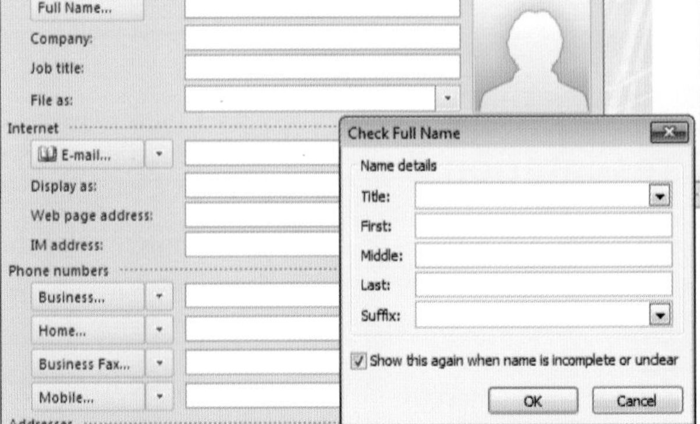

Figure 2.2 Contact Form

project 3

Riverfront Enterprises: Integrating PowerPoint and Word

OBJECTIVES

- Create effective *PowerPoint* presentations
- Prepare effective *Word* documents
- Coordinate themes and designs in presentations and documents
- Work with very limited supervision

SETTING

Project 3 integrates *PowerPoint* and *Word*. In this project, you are an assistant in the Human Resources Division of Riverfront Enterprises located at 391 Grand Avenue, St. Paul, Minnesota 55102-2679. You will work closely with Mr. DeShawn R. Taylor, Senior Vice President; Ms. Larissa Nottingham, Director of Employment; and Mr. David Walvius, Director of Employee Benefits. Your assignments will require you to complete jobs that include both *Word* documents and *PowerPoint* presentations.

JOBS

1. Block letter
2. Memo
3. *PowerPoint* presentation
4. Handout formatted as an unbound report
5. Notes pages and slide handouts

STANDARD OPERATING PROCEDURES

Use these procedures for all documents you prepare. You will not be reminded to do these things during the project.

1. Use Module theme for all *Word* and *PowerPoint* documents.
2. Use *riverfront enterprises letterhead* template from the data files, block letter format with open punctuation, an appropriate salutation and closing, and prepare envelopes.
3. Use the *riverfront enterprises memo* template from the data files for memos.
4. Proofread, preview, and print all documents.
5. Set up a folder named PP-WD Project 3 and save all project files in it. Name all solution files *p3-j* (plus the job number, *j1*, *j2*, etc.).

Apply It

Job 1
Create Word Attachment

1. Key the following document in *Word 2010*. Format the heading as Heading 1 and apply the Flow theme to the document.
2. Save it as *Tracking and Flagging Messages*. Print and label, following labeling directions at left.

DISCOVER

Follow this style for labeling printouts in all jobs:

OL1-job1-2

OL1 indicates Lesson 1
job1 indicates job number
2 indicates step 2 in job

Tracking and Flagging Messages

Many of the e-mail messages that you receive are read and then discarded. Some messages can be responded to immediately. Other messages may require that you deal with them at a later time.

Outlook 2010 has a feature that allows you to flag messages to draw your attention to them. It even takes this concept one step further by creating the message as a task with a due date. It then automatically places the item in your To-Do List with the follow-up date you assigned.

Job 2
Create E-mail and Save as Draft

1. Create the following e-mail message to yourself. Mark the message as being of low importance. The subject of the e-mail is **Tracking and Flagging Messages**. Include the following message:

Download this attachment and read about the follow-up flagging feature.
I tried it and really find it to be useful.

2. Save the e-mail by clicking the Save button on the Quick Access Toolbar. The message has been saved as a draft.
3. Close the message.

Job 3
Attach File, Forward, Delete, and Move Messages

1. Find the e-mail *Tracking and Flagging Messages* in your Drafts folder. Double-click the message to open it.
2. Attach the *Word* file that you created in Job 1 to the message. Print and send the message.
3. Open the e-mail and forward a copy to a classmate or your teacher.
4. Delete the messages *Meeting with Suni Engineering* and *Tracking and Flagging Messages*. Display the Deleted Items folder. Move both messages back to the Inbox folder. Print the messages in your Inbox folder in Table Style and label the printout.
5. Click the Sent Items folder; print the messages in Sent Items in Table Style.

Job 1
Letter

RIVERFRONT ENTERPRISES LETTERHEAD

Mr. Taylor asked you to prepare the following letter to Ms. Krawczyk. Include her title in the address.

TIP

To remove the extra space after paragraphs with short lines, such as the inside address, use the keyboard shortcut SHIFT + ENTER to move directly to the next line.

Thank you very much for inviting Riverfront Enterprises to make one of the major presentations at the Minnesota State Career Fair on (one month from today) from 10:30 to 11:30 a.m. at the Westfield Convention Center. We are delighted to accept your invitation. We appreciate the opportunity to talk about the skills we expect in the candidates we hire for positions in our organization.

We plan to hire new employees in every division of our company this year, and we consider it a privilege to talk with students from across the state who are preparing to enter the workforce. I plan to include on the program with me two of our relatively young employees who are on the fast track and have senior-level positions in the Human Resources Division. I believe they will relate very well to your audience.

Thank you for offering to provide a computer projector for us. We plan to bring our own laptop computer, but it would save time to use the projector that is already set up for the day. I will send you the information you requested for the program in a few days.

We look forward to working with you at this exciting event.

Job 2
Memo

RIVERFRONT ENTERPRISES MEMO

Prepare a memo from DeShawn Taylor to Larissa Nottingham and David Walvius. Send a copy to President Norah Demars. Use an appropriate subject line.

Ms. Marina Krawczyk invited Riverfront Enterprises to make one of the major presentations at the Minnesota State Career Fair on (use date from Document 1) from 10:30 to 11:30 a.m. at the Westfield Convention Center. This presentation provides us with an excellent opportunity to showcase Riverfront Enterprises and to recruit some outstanding new employees.

Hopefully, the two of you will be able to join me in making this presentation. Ms. Krawczyk asked us to address the skills that we expect in the candidates we hire for positions in our organization. Please check your calendars and let me know if your schedule permits you to be on the program. Unless you have a major conflict, please try to make yourself available for this opportunity.

I look forward to working with you on this project.

DRILL 3 READ, REPLY, AND FORWARD A MESSAGE

1. Display your Inbox. If you do not see the message that you sent to yourself, click the Send/Receive tab and click Send/Receive All Folders. The e-mail should be displayed with a red exclamation mark. Double-click the message to open it.
2. Click the Reply button and key **I will be able to attend**. Print the e-mail and send it.
3. Forward a copy of the e-mail to your teacher or another student in the class. Add the following message to the e-mail: **FYI, just wanted to let you know that we are working on resolving the issues**.
4. Print the e-mail and send it.
5. Close the *Meeting with Suni Engineering* message.

SEND A MESSAGE WITH AN ATTACHMENT

A quick and inexpensive method of transferring a file to another location is to send it as an attachment to an e-mail. You can send files created in *Word*, *Excel*, *PowerPoint*, or other software applications as attachments to e-mail.

To Attach a File to an E-mail:

Message/Include/Attach File

1. Key the message.
2. Click Attach File to display the Insert File dialog box. Select the folder and then the file that is to be attached. Click Insert. The name of the file appears in the Attached box in the message header. The icon next to the filename indicates the program in which the attachment was created.
3. Click the Send button.

DISCOVER

Follow this style for labeling printouts in all drills:

OL1-drill4-5

OL1 indicates Lesson 1 of the *Outlook* module; **drill4** indicates the number of the drill in the lesson; **5** indicates the number of the step in the drill in which the item is printed.

PRINT MESSAGES

You can print your messages and attachments in *Outlook*. To print an attachment, double-click the attachment icon, choose to open the file, and then send it to print. You can also right-click the attachment icon in the preview or message window and select Quick Print on the shortcut menu.

Outlook provides several options for printing e-mail messages from the Inbox. Messages can be printed in Table Style or Memo Style. Table Style prints the messages in a table format, similar to the way they appear in the Inbox. Memo Style prints the message in memo format; the heading lists who the message is from, when it was sent, who it was sent to, and the subject line. The message is printed below the heading.

DRILL 4 SEND MESSAGE WITH ATTACHMENT

E-MAIL ATTACHMENT

1. Create a new e-mail and address it to yourself. The subject of the e-mail is **E-mails with Attachments**. Indicate that this e-mail is of high importance.
2. Include the following message:

   I am attaching a file that contains some helpful information on viewing e-mail attachments. You should download the file, save, and print it. The attachment was keyed in Microsoft Word.

3. Attach the data file *e-mail attachment*. Send the e-mail. Print the messages in your Inbox in Table Style. Label the printout OL1-drill4-3.
4. Display your Inbox. Select the message *E-mails with Attachments*. Tap DELETE to remove it from the Inbox. Click the Deleted Items folder. Right-click the message you just deleted, and choose Move and then Inbox to move the message back to your Inbox. Click the Inbox folder to verify that the message has been restored.

Job 3

PowerPoint Presentation

Remember to use the theme specified in the standard operating procedures.

The Quick Check on page 80 contains a thumbnail of each slide. Use it for reference.

You met with the team and everyone agreed on the content of 14 slides. You will now prepare the presentation for the team. General instructions are provided below.

1. Apply Fade; Effect Options: Smoothly with 0.50 duration transition to all slides; animate content areas only—not slide titles.
2. Text, notes, and specific instructions for formatting each slide are presented on the following pages. Use a 16-point font for notes. After the presentation has been completed, print notes pages and handouts four to a page using landscape orientation.

Slide 1 (Title Slide)

Copy the Riverboat logo from the letterhead or memo head and paste it at the top right corner of the slide.

Title: The Ideal Hire for Riverfront Enterprises

Subtitle: DeShawn Taylor | Larissa Nottingham | David Walvius

Animation: None

Notes: Introduce the presenters and indicate what each will talk about. Give a very quick overview of Riverfront Enterprises.

Slide 2 (Title and Content)

Title: Key Questions

- What do we as employers expect?
- How do you prepare to meet those expectations?

Animation: Fade, By Paragraph

Notes: Point out that Riverfront Enterprises simply represents many employers. Our expectations are very similar to those of other employers.

Explain that the best employees are the ones whose skills match the requirements of the particular job they seek. You need to focus on what type of job you want and then get the skills you need for that job.

Slide 3 (Title and Content)

Title: Our Expectations as an Employer

- Technical skills (critical at entry level)
- Soft skills (critical at every level)
- Conceptual skills (critical for advancement)
- Experience (past performance is a good—but not great—indicator of future performance)

Convert bulleted text to Target List SmartArt graphic.

Animation: Fade, One by One

Notes: Each of these points will be presented in some detail in the next three slides. This slide provides an overview of the package of skills that most employers consider requisites for success.

READ, REPLY, FORWARD, AND DELETE MESSAGES

Messages that are sent to you are stored on an e-mail server and then downloaded to your Inbox folder. From there, you can read, reply, or forward the message to someone else. You can also delete messages from the Inbox.

To Receive and Read E-mail Messages:

Send/Receive/Send & Receive/Send/Receive All Folders

TIP

You can also click the Send/ Receive All Folders button in the Quick Access Toolbar.

1. Click the Send/Receive All Folders button to update all items to be sent or received in all folders.
2. Click the Inbox folder in the Navigation Pane to display the contents of the Inbox. The Inbox folder displays the sender's name, the subject line, and the date the message was received. Messages that have not been opened are marked with a closed envelope icon.
3. Click the message you want to read to display its contents in the Reading Pane, or double-click the message to open the message in its own window.

Reply to a Message

You can reply to the message from the Inbox screen (Home/Respond/Reply) or from the Message screen (Message/Respond/Reply) if the message is open in its own window. The sender's name becomes the recipient name, and *RE:* is inserted at the beginning of the subject line to indicate that the message is a reply. The insertion point appears in the message window above a copy of the message you received. Key your reply; it will display in a different color. When you finish the reply, click Send. Close the message window to display your Inbox.

An open envelope icon now displays next to the message in the Inbox, indicating that you have read the message. An arrow displays on the envelope indicating that you have replied to the message.

Forward a Message

If you would like other people to have a copy of the e-mail you received, you can forward a copy to them by clicking the Forward button (Home/Respond/ Forward). Key the recipient's e-mail address; *FW* is inserted in the subject line to indicate that this is a forwarded message. You can add your comments in the message window, if needed. Click the Send button, and then close the window if necessary to return to the Inbox screen.

Delete a Message

Messages remain in your Inbox and Sent Items folders until you delete them. Delete a message by selecting the message and tapping DELETE.

The message moves to the Deleted Items folder. Messages in the Deleted Items folder can be opened, replied to, or forwarded to someone else. To delete all items in the Deleted Items folder, click the Empty Folder button (Folder/Clean Up) and confirm the deletion. The messages are now permanently deleted.

TIP

The Quick Check on page 80 contains a thumbnail of each slide. Try to obtain the same clip art shown for slide 4. If you cannot locate it, look for something similar. Position images in the same order and drag image to about the same size as shown.

Slide 4 (Title and Content)

Title: Technical Skills

- Knowledge
- Expertise
- Ability to do the job

Insert the *manager* picture from the data files (Insert/Picture). Crop about .5" from the right side and then size to a height of 2.5". Position the picture on the right side of the bulleted text. Compress the picture using all defaults. Search clip art (Insert/Clip Art/Search for) for three clips and position them below the bulleted text. Keywords for search: clip on left: *medical*; clip at the center: *artist*; clip on the right: *brick*.

Animation: Animate in following order—bulleted text, Fade, By Paragraph; manager, Fade; doctor, Fade; artist, Fade; bricklayer, Fade.

Notes: Every job has technical skills—they differ depending on the job. A manager in the Marketing Division has different skills using Excel to analyze data and prepare a graphic to present the advertising budget using PowerPoint than a consulting physician who advises us on health benefits. An artist in the Commercial Art Department has different skills than a bricklayer in our Construction Division.

In the technology area, the technical skills are Word, PowerPoint, Excel, Publisher, Access, and Outlook. Technical skills are more than knowing the functions of the software—employees must be able to integrate these skills and apply them to solving business problems.

Slide 5 (Title Only)

Title: Meeting Expectations for Technical Skills (Decrease font size to fit on one line)

Knowledge is one thing—applying skills to solve problems is different!

Draw a Rounded Rectangle (Insert/Shapes/Rectangles/Rounded Rectangle) about 3.5" high and 6.75" wide, and key the text shown above. Apply bold and increase font size to 40 point.

Animation: Fade, All at Once

Notes: This slide reinforces that applying technical skills to solving problems is the requisite for success—not punching buttons or clicking commands.

Slide 6 (Title and Content)

Title: Soft Skills—Our "Top Five" List

1. Honesty and integrity
2. Interpersonal skills
3. Communication skills
4. Motivation, initiative, and work ethic
5. Teamwork skills

Animation: Fade, By Paragraph

Notes: These are the most important to Riverfront Enterprises: however, many soft skills are needed to be successful in a career.

To Compose and Send E-mail:

Home/New/New E-mail

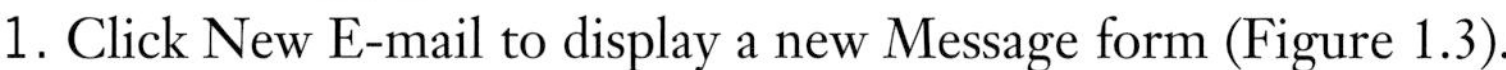

1. Click New E-mail to display a new Message form (Figure 1.3).
2. Key the e-mail address of the person to whom you are sending the e-mail. If he or she is on the same mail server as you, you need to key only the username. You can also click the To button and find the names of the people on your network listed in the Select Names box. If you are sending the message to someone outside your network, key the person's full e-mail address. If you are sending a copy of the message to someone else, key that e-mail address in the Cc box.

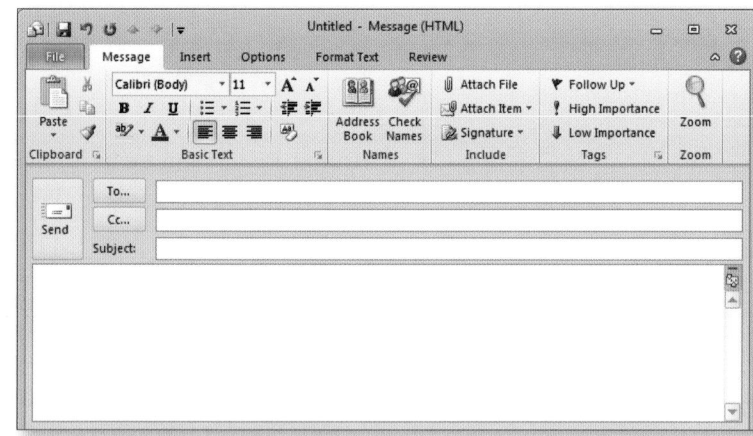

Figure 1.3 Message Form

3. Key the subject line in the Subject box.
4. Key the message in the message body box. Click the Format Text tab to access the formatting features. The Spelling & Grammar feature is located on the Review tab.
5. You can indicate whether a message is of high or low importance by clicking the appropriate button in the Tags group of the Message tab.
6. To create a draft of a message you can edit at a later time, click the Save button and close the message. To retrieve the message, select the Drafts folder in the Navigation Pane and double-click the saved message. (*Outlook* used your subject line to name the message.)
7. Proofread and use the spell-checker. Click the Send button when finished.

DRILL 2 SEND MESSAGE

You normally send messages to other people. In this lesson, you send messages to yourself so that you can practice sending and receiving messages.

1. Click New E-mail to display the Untitled-Message window; address a message to yourself.
2. Key **Meeting with Suni Engineering** in the Subject box.
3. Key the following message:

> I would like to arrange a meeting with Suni Engineering at 2:00 on [insert a date that is one week from today]. The meeting will be held in one of our conference rooms. Will you be able to attend? Let me know by [insert the day after tomorrow] so that I can make the necessary arrangements.

4. Indicate that the message is urgent by clicking the High Importance button.
5. Print the e-mail message (File/Print/Print).
6. Click the Send button.

Slide 7 (Title and Content)

Title: Our Expanded Soft Skills List

Adaptability and flexibility	Creativity	Communication—oral, written, and listening
Honesty and integrity	Interpersonal skills	Know how to learn and continue learning
Leadership	Motivation, initiative, and work ethic	Organizational skills
Problem solving and analytical skills	Teamwork and collaboration	Time management and productivity

The Quick Check on page 80 contains a thumbnail of each slide. Try to obtain the same clip art shown for slide 8. If you cannot locate it, look for something similar. Insert the Cloud callouts from Shapes and position in the same order; drag each to about the same size as shown.

Apply Medium Style 4 – Accent 1 to the table; use 20-point font and bold all text. Row Height: 1.2"; Column Width: 2.8".

Animation: Fade

Notes: Many more soft skills could be listed; these are on the "wish list" of most companies.

Slide 8 (Title Only)

Title: Points to Ponder

Text for Cloud callouts: Left: Honesty and integrity are near the top of most companies' soft skills lists! Center: Would you exaggerate to get a better job? Right: Many students we interview "pad" skills and qualifications.

Search Clip Art using the keyword *thinker*. Format the text in the callouts using 20-point font and apply bold. Click the callout and drag the yellow adjustment diamond to change the position of the small bubbles to point them toward the thinker.

Animation: Thinker, Fade; Left callout: Fade, All at Once; Center callout: Fade, All at Once; Right Callout: Fade, All at Once

Notes: This slide illustrates just one of the key soft skills. Similar analogies could be made for all of the key soft skills.

Slide 9 (Two Content)

Title: Conceptual Skills

- Ability to see the big picture
- Apply what you know to our business
- Understand how your job fits into the total business strategy
- Understand that businesses operate in a global context

1. Click on a segment of the puzzle to select it. Then right-click the selected segment and click Format Shape. Make sure you do not select the entire puzzle.
2. Then click Solid fill and select the appropriate color.

Search clip art using *conceptual* as the keyword, and select the puzzle for the content on the right side. Format the puzzle by changing the colors of each shape as follows: Top left: Gold, Accent 1; top right: Gold, Accent 1, Darker 25%; bottom left: Gold, Accent 1, Darker 50%; bottom right: Gold, Accent 1, Lighter 40%.

Animation: Right content area, Fade; then left content area, Fade, By Paragraph

Notes: Technical skills are most critical at the entry level. The person doing the job must have excellent technical skills. As you move up the career ladder, technical skills are not as important because someone else does the technical part that you manage and supervise. The skills needed to be effective at a higher level are conceptual skills.

USE THE NAVIGATION PANE

The Navigation Pane (Figure 1.2) provides quick access to all *Outlook* components: Mail, Calendar, Contacts, Tasks, and Notes. *Outlook* stores all of its data in folders. You can quickly display another component by clicking the component button in the button bar at the bottom of the Navigation Pane ❶ or by clicking on the folder in the Folder List ❷. When you click a different button, such as Calendar, the top portion of the Navigation Pane displays items related to calendaring.

The button bar displays icons across the bottom for Notes, Folder List, Shortcuts, and Configure buttons. These buttons are an extension of the button bar. When the button bar pane is enlarged, the Notes button displays below Tasks. Reducing the pane will result in more buttons displaying in miniature view across the bottom.

Figure 1.2 Navigation Pane

DRILL 1 USE THE NAVIGATION PANE

1. Start *Outlook*. Click Mail in the Navigation Pane to display the Mail window, if necessary.
2. Click the Calendar button in the Navigation Pane to display the Calendar window. The Navigation Pane now displays items relating to Calendar.
3. Click the Contacts button in the Navigation Pane to display the Contacts window. Lowercase letters display at the right; click a letter to display contacts that begin with that letter. No contacts display because none have been entered.
4. Click the Tasks button to display your To-Do List window.
5. Click the Notes button to view Notes. The folder is empty because you have not yet created any notes.
6. Click the Folder List button to display the folders at the top of the Navigation Pane. Notice the different folders that are listed. Click Inbox to display the contents of the Inbox folder. Click Calendar to display the daily calendar. Clicking the folder in the Folder List is another way in which you can move to other *Outlook* components.
7. Click the Mail button to display the Mail folders in the Navigation Pane.
8. Shrink the pane containing the Navigation buttons: Move the mouse to the top border of the Mail button; when the mouse changes to a two-headed arrow, drag the border down. Notice that the Tasks button moves to the bottom row with the Notes and Folder List buttons. Enlarge the pane so that the Notes button displays in a row by itself.

SEND E-MAIL

Electronic mail (e-mail) has risen in popularity because of its low cost and speed in delivery. Messages can be sent around the world in seconds. As a result, the business community has adopted e-mail as a standard method of communication.

The Mail window is divided into three panes, as shown in Figure 1.1. The Navigation Pane displays the folders that pertain to e-mail. The middle pane is the Inbox Pane. This pane contains a two-line presentation of messages. The Reading Pane appears on the right; this pane allows you to view the message without having to open it. You can also display the People Pane as shown in Figure 1.1.

Slide 10 (Title and Content)

Title: Path to Promotion

Insert a Pyramid List SmartArt graphic. Then insert a Block Up Arrow from Shapes at the left side of the three text boxes beginning at the bottom of the lowest text box and ending at the top of the highest text box.

Text for the text boxes:

Top: Conceptual skills are critical for moving up the career ladder

Middle: Conceptual training often includes rotation to a variety of departments to understand what each does and how they fit together

Bottom: Conceptual skills replace technical skills as one moves up the career ladder

Animation: None

Notes: Conceptual skills are hard to develop, but are critical for promotion.

DISCOVER

Home/Paragraph/Bullets

1. Click the down arrow on Bullets, and then click Bullets and Numbering.
2. Click Color at the bottom of the Bullets and Numbering dialog box and select the desired color.

Slide 11 (Title and Content)

Title: Experience

- Relevant job experience
- Other types of experience
  - Internships/co-op in field or related area
  - Part-time/temporary job in field
  - Unrelated job experience
  - Volunteer project work

Change the color of the second-level bullets from blue to Green, Accent 4, Darker 25%.

Animation: Fade, By Paragraph

Notes: Relevant experience can be defined as three to five years of employment in a job similar to the job you seek.

Slide 12 (Title Only)

Title: Student's Nightmare

Copy the "thinker" from slide 8 and position it at the lower-left corner of the slide. Add a Cloud callout. Position it at the top right corner of the slide. Format text 20-point bold.

Text for callout: How can I get relevant experience when I am applying for my first job?

Animation: Thinker, Fade; Cloud callout, Fade, All at Once

Notes: You cannot.

Slide 13 (Title and Content)

Title: Make the Most of What You Have

- Emphasize what you have learned in internships and co-op programs
- Package the experience you do have effectively
- Describe the skills you gained in any type of job and relate what was learned that is transferable to the job you seek.

Animation: Fade, By Paragraph

Notes: Students need to learn how to demonstrate that even though they may not have relevant work experience, they have other experiences that enable them to be effective employees.

Getting Started with Outlook and E-mail

LESSON 1

OBJECTIVES

- Launch *Outlook*
- Use the Navigation Pane
- Work with e-mail messages

GETTING STARTED

Launch *Outlook* by clicking the *Outlook* icon on your desktop, or click the Start button, click All Programs, *Microsoft Office*, and then select *Microsoft Outlook 2010*. If "Inbox" is not displayed in the title bar of your screen, click the Mail button in the left pane. Your Inbox screen will not look exactly like the screen shown below in Figure 1.1.

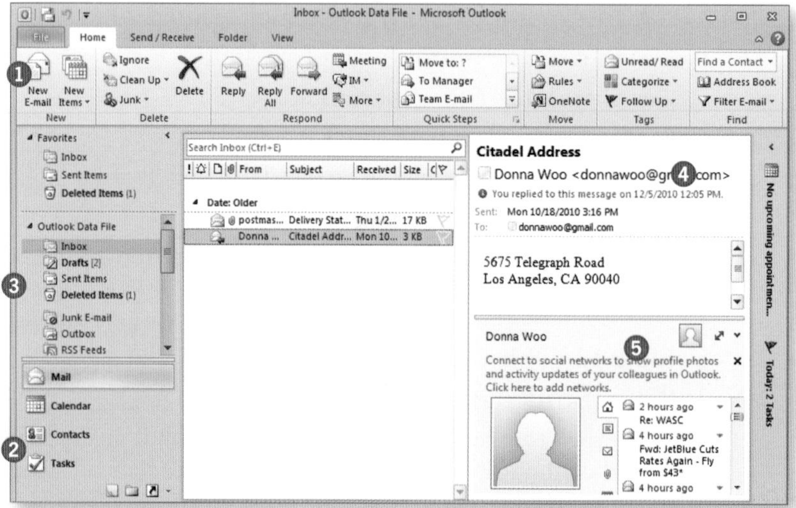

Figure 1.1 Mail Screen

OUTLOOK SCREEN

All the *Outlook* components display the tab and Ribbon interface and the Navigation Pane on the left side of the screen. The contents to the right of the Navigation Pane vary according to component.

❶ **Ribbon and tabs:** The Ribbon displays five tabs at the top of the *Outlook* window. Groups and commands on the tabs may change according to component.

❷ **Navigation Pane:** The Navigation Pane provides quick access to *Outlook* components and folders.

❸ **Folder List:** Displays the folders you can use to work with *Outlook*.

❹ **Reading Pane:** Displays the contents of the selected message.

❺ **People Pane:** Displays recent messages from the sender as well as social media updates on the person.

Slide 14 (Title Only)

Title: Tips for Career Success

Insert a Smiley Face from Shapes and position at the top center of the slide. Center it. Then insert a Horizontal Scroll Banner below the Smiley Face.

Add the text: Refer to the | *Tips for Career Success* Handout

Animation: Smiley Face, Fade; Banner, Fade, All at Once

Notes: Review the *Tips for Career Success* handout. Give students the slide handouts you printed.

(Check to see that you have followed the standard operating procedures on page 74.)

QUICK ✓ Use the slides in Figure P3.1 to prepare your slides and check your final results.

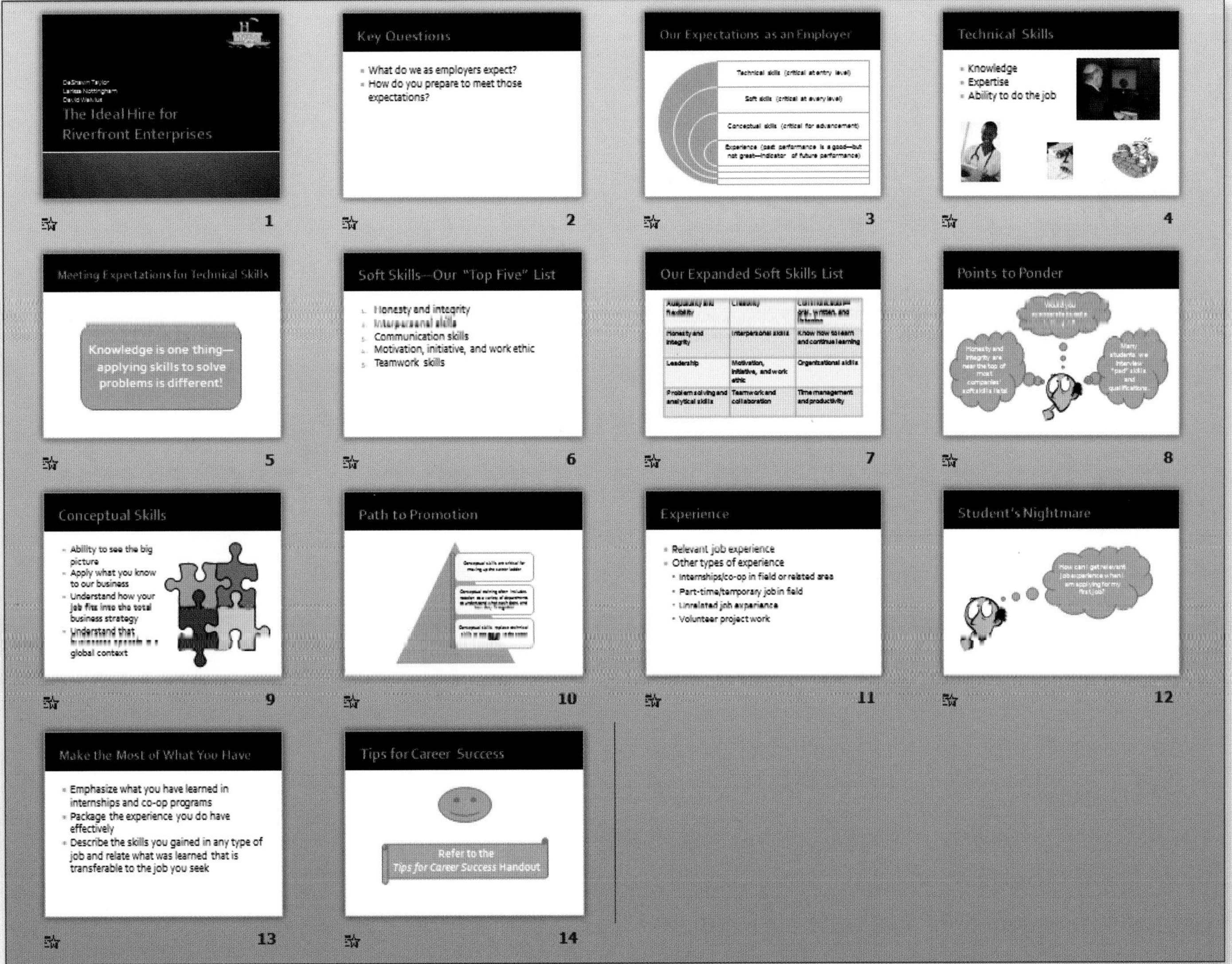

Photo (man at computer): Susie VanHuss

Figure P3.1 Quick Check

module 7

INFORMATION MANAGEMENT WITH OUTLOOK

overview

***O**utlook* is a full-featured personal information management program that provides the tools you need to be organized in today's electronic world. The major components of *Outlook* that will be covered in the module are:

- Mail—provides a tool for sending, receiving, and managing your e-mail
- Contacts—an electronic address book that holds names, addresses, phone numbers, and other pertinent information
- Calendar—keeps track of your appointments and schedule
- Tasks—an electronic "to-do" list
- Notes—sticky notes, or a notepad for your computer
- Journal—record activities based on contact

Outlook has the ability to integrate all of its components and link them. It can keep you organized with its ability to help you track and find activities pertaining to a particular person, topic, location, date, or event.

ESSENTIALS

1. Getting Started with Outlook and E-mail
2. Create and Manage Contacts
3. Use Calendar to Schedule Appointments
4. Create and Use Tasks
5. Use Notes and Journal
6. Manage Messages

Project 10—Aldrin Glenn Aircraft: Integrating Outlook and Word

Job 4

Report with Cover Page

ADDITIONAL TIPS

DISCOVER

To change the color of the pinstripe or line, right-click it and select Format AutoShape; then select the desired color.

The Cover Page gallery does not include a built-in cover page for the Module document theme. Therefore, use Pinstripes and modify it by changing the color of the blue stripes at the top and bottom to Black and the color of the vertical bars on the right and left to Gold. Add the Riverboat logo at the center near the bottom. Use today's date and no author name.

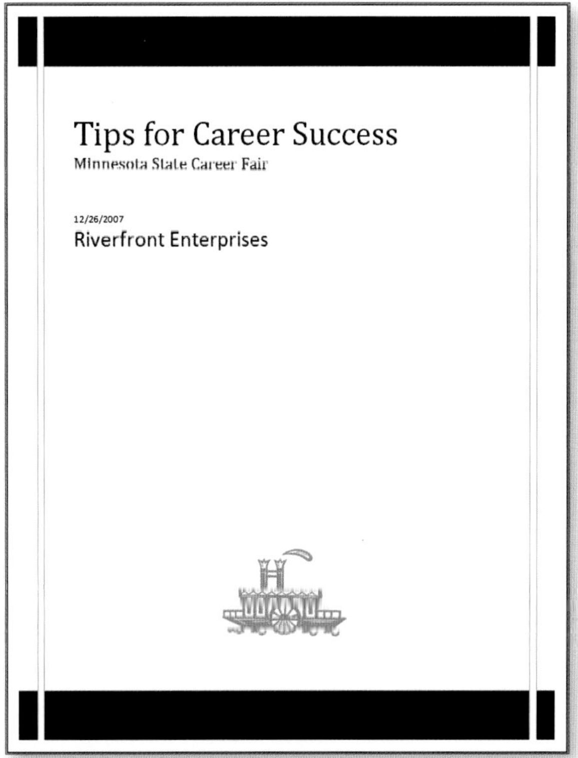

Title: Tips for Career Success

Subtitle: Minnesota State Career Fair

Company: Riverfront Enterprises

Use unbound report format for the handout. Insert the footnote where shown in the text. Insert the data file *additional tips* at the end of the document where noted. Use Motion Even Page header for the title and page number with a different first page. Apply title format and use the title **Tips for Career Success**.

TIP

Remember to insert a section break between the cover page and the first page of the report and to break the link between sections for the header and footer before inserting the header to number pages.

Employers including *Riverfront Enterprises* seek to hire employees who look, act, and are professionals who can do the job, represent the company effectively, and be productive immediately. Very few employers including *Riverfront Enterprises* are willing to hire bright students with great potential and wait for them to grow up, mature, and be effective. Several years of successful, relevant work experience (employed in a position similar to the one you seek) provide evidence of employability. Students without that experience must demonstrate (not talk about) that they are ready to be productive now if they expect to convince employers to hire them. The following tips suggest ways you can show an employer that you are ready to launch a successful career.[1] (Footnote text: These tips enhance your opportunities for employment even if you already have three to five years of relevant work experience.)

Job 7,
continued

To add a table to the Relationships window, click Relationship Tools Design/Relationships/Show Table; then select the desired table and create the relationship.

4. Create a relationship between the Owners and Property Listings tables. Enforce referential integrity.
5. Create a new form using the Owners table. *Access* recognizes that the Owners table is related to the Property Listings table and automatically displays the Property Listings table on the Owners form.
6. On 9/2/2012, agent Tyler Wheeler announced his listing of properties owned by John Lambert. In the Owners form, select New (blank) record, and enter Mr. Lambert as a new owner. Use Owner ID LAM-534. Mr. Lambert lives at 132 Castleoaks Drive, Castle Hills, TX 78213-2303.
7. Mr. Lambert, who owns a home rental business, has decided to sell two of his properties. Mr. Lambert agreed on 9/4/2012 to 3-month listings of the following properties in Castle Hills: listing 2004-Z2, 142 Wisteria Drive, 78213-2106, for $165,000; and listing 2009-Z2, 164 Moss Drive, 78213-1916, for $185,000.
8. Print the Current Listings query showing unsold properties.

Job 8
Word Report

STATUS
MLS SALES

Remember to use the Civic theme for all M&D's documents.

DISCOVER

Insert/Object/Text from File

1. Click Object down arrow, and select Text from File.
2. Browse and select *status* from your data files.
3. Click Insert.

You have been asked by Jan H. Martin, the chief operating officer, to format and finalize the confidential report that the two of you drafted using information from the *Access* database and several *Excel* files. Jan added a number of comments to the document containing information for data to be inserted and formatting instructions.

1. Begin by opening a new *Word* document, saving it as *p9-j8*, and inserting a Sideline cover page. Key the company name in the provided placeholder. At the bottom of the page, add Jan's name as the author, and pick the date September 6, 2012. You will complete the information for the title page in step 2. Reserve the blank page for the table of contents.
2. On page 2, tap ENTER several times to insert blank paragraphs, and then insert a Next Page section break near the bottom of page 2. Insert *status* from the data files on page 3. Use the information on the first page of the body of the report to complete the cover page. Then make all of the changes in the comments.
3. Insert the following sentence before the last sentence in the report:

   Fully integrating the Commercial Real Estate Division and the Property Management Division will enable McMullan & Donovan Realty to consolidate operations and reduce the cost of operations and to build synergies among the three divisions of the company.
4. Use the following directions to insert and adjust a footer beginning on the first page of the report (first page of Section 2):
   a. Click in the header area, and break the link to the previous section; do the same for the footer.
   b. Insert a Sideline footer; key the following text on the right side of the vertical bar:

      Confidential Assessment prepared for Mark Donovan and Carol McMullan
   c. Show the footer on all pages of the body of the report. On the first page of the body of the report, format the page number so that it is set to begin at 1.
5. On the blank page following the cover page, position the insertion point at about 2" and insert a table of contents using the second option. Format the title using Title style.
6. Insert a Plain Number 2 page number at the bottom of the table of contents page; format using lowercase Roman numerals.
7. Check to see that all instructions for inserting data and formatting in the comments have been followed; then delete all comments.
8. Preview the document carefully and resave it.

- ☑ Plan for employment early enough to ensure that you have the technical skills needed to get the job you want. Determine the technical skills that are needed and make sure you have them or that you have time to acquire them.
- ☑ Participate in activities that provide the skills that are obtained through experience if you do not have relevant work experience. Internships are a major source of jobs and a major plus with other companies. Part-time, temporary, or volunteer jobs are also valuable. Package experience effectively to demonstrate specific skills learned such as dealing with difficult customers, managing time effectively, or being responsible for money.
- ☑ Research a company thoroughly before submitting an application or going to an interview. Know as much about the company as possible and know what the job requires. Package your core competencies to show that they match the job requirements. Making it evident that extensive research about the company has been done also demonstrates initiative, motivation, and work ethic.
- ☑ Demonstrate good communication skills in every phase of the process—the application letter, resume, interview, and thank-you letter are opportunities to showcase your written and oral communication skills. Write a thank-you letter immediately after an interview. You will demonstrate courtesy that few applicants show (less than 20 percent of applicants write thank-you notes). A keying, spelling, or grammatical error will undo all assertions about having excellent communication skills. Organize and format documents carefully. Companies are concerned about image; if your documents do not represent you well, the company will think that you may not prepare documents that represent the company well.

(Insert the data file *additional tips* after the text shown above. Make sure the format is consistent and check to make sure bullet points are consistent.)

DISCOVER

Insert/Text/Object/Text from File

1. Position the insertion point where you wish to insert a file.
2. Click Text from File and browse to find the file.
3. Double-click the file to insert it.

Job 5
Print Notes Pages and Handouts

Print Notes Pages

Print a set of notes pages for the *PowerPoint* presentation you prepared in Job 3. The team would like to review the notes prior to delivering the presentation.

Print Handouts

Print a set of handouts using four slides to a page and landscape format to make the handouts easy to read. The handouts will be attached to the report you prepared in Job 4.

Job 5,
continued

6. Create a PivotTable on the current worksheet, selecting cell A11 for the location. Add the Last Name to the row labels and specify the sum of the Sales Price in the values. Format the number values as currency with 0 decimal places.
7. Create a pie chart on the same worksheet using the PivotTable data that presents the sum of the sales price for each agent. Include the amount of sales in the data labels. Right-click on the Last Name button on the PivotChart and select Hide All Field Buttons on Chart. Key the chart title **Total Sales by Agent | August 2012**.
8. Save the *Excel* workbook as *p9-j5b*.

Job 6

PowerPoint Presentation with Embedded Charts

MONTHLY UPDATE
MLS SALES

M&D prepares a monthly update for the meeting with all agents the first week of the following month. In this job, you will prepare the August Update.

1. Open the *PowerPoint* data file *monthly update*, and save it as *p9-j6*.
2. Use the following instructions to prepare the slides:

   Slide 1: Update title and key your name in the subtitle.

   Slide 2: Search clip art photos using the keywords *business woman* (use two words), and select one of the pictures of the woman giving the thumbs-up sign; insert it in the right content area. Use the information in the query August Listings that you prepared in Job 5 to complete the information on the slide.

   Slide 3: Search clip art photos using the keywords *business man* (use two words), and select the picture of the man giving the thumbs-up sign; insert it in the right content area. Use the information in the worksheet data and in the PivotTable of *p9-j5b* to complete the information on the slide.

   Slide 4: Key the headings **M&D August Sales** (left) and **MLS August Sales** (right). Copy and paste the *Excel* pie chart you created in Job 5 in the left content area. Open the *Excel* data file *mls sales*, copy the pie chart, and paste it in the right content area.

   Slide 5: New slide using Title and Content layout; key the following content:

   Title: August Points of Interest

   - M&D properties sold were on the market for an average of [insert # of days from *p9-j5b Excel* file]
   - Sales of M&D properties exceeded sales of MLS properties
   - MLS sales decreased by more than 15% compared to July sales

Convert the bulleted text to a Target List SmartArt graphic.

Job 7

Maintain Database

OWNERS

Having information about the owners of listed properties will improve the information available to M&D's employees. A list of owners is currently maintained in an *Excel* file.

1. Save the *p9-j5a* database as *p9-j7*.
2. Import Sheet1 of the *Excel* data file *owners* into a new *Access* table. In the second import window, select First Row Contains Column Headings. Choose the Owner ID field as the primary key. Key **Owners** as the name for the new table and finish the import. Open the Owners table to view the data that has been imported.
3. Modify the field properties on the Owner ID field to remove the @ symbol in the Format property box and include the input mask LLL-000. Modify the field properties on the ZIP field to remove the @ symbol and include the standard nine-digit Zip Code input mask. Close the table.

LESSON
5

Customize Presentations

OBJECTIVES

- Create effective presentations
- Customize themes
- Customize layout
- Customize handout master
- Save as template

CUSTOMIZE PRESENTATIONS

View/Master Views/Slide Master

The slide master is used to personalize and customize presentations. You can make a variety of changes including placeholders, layout, and theme. Making changes on the slide master affects all slides in the presentation. Customized presentations can be saved as templates for future use. Note that handouts and notes pages can be customized as well.

Figure 5.1 illustrates the tools that are available for customizing slides in Slide Master view. When you display Slide Master view, the slide master ❶ appears as the first slide in the slide thumbnail pane at the left side of the window. Slide layouts ❷ display below the slide master. The Slide Master tab ❸ has six groups of commands that enable you to perform a variety of tasks.

Edit Master—insert a new master or layout, or rename or preserve a master.

Master Layout—insert or rearrange placeholders and change the title and footers.

Edit Theme—edit the theme in the same way that you can edit it on the Design tab.

Background—change the background of slides.

Page Setup—change the page setup and orientation.

Close—close the Master view and return to Normal view.

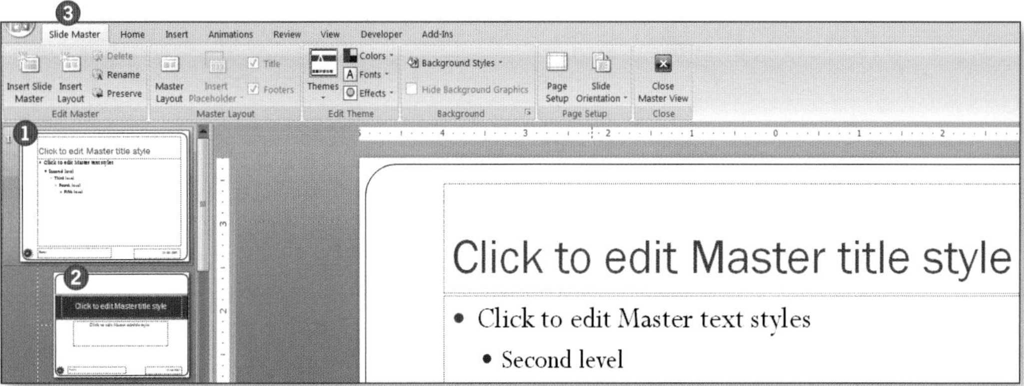

Figure 5.1 Slide Master View

Job 4, continued

Property No.	1356-Z2	1442-Z1
Address	2001 Colorado Street	2301 Rosita Place
City	San Antonio, TX 78207-2001	San Antonio, TX 78207-2301
Listing Price	$745,000	$695,000
Listing Term	6 months	6 months
Listing Renewal Date	you compute	you compute
Listing Agent ID	K1188N	K1188N
Owner ID	MAR-509	PFI-784

3. Use the Property Listings form to update the following properties that were sold on August 20 by agent Devin Neaves.

   1643-Z1 | 6732 N. Fredericksburg Street | San Marcos | Sold for $348,000

   1907-Z2 | 1875 Garden View Drive | Castle Hills | Sold for $158,000

Job 5

Export Access Query to Excel PivotTable and Chart

Ms. McMullan is preparing various reports of August activity and asks you to create an *Access* query and export it to *Excel*. In *Excel*, you will then create a PivotTable and a chart.

1. Save the *p9-j4* database as *p9-j5a*. Create an *Access* query to determine the properties listed during August.
   a. Include the Agent ID, First Name, Last Name, and Mobile Phone Number fields from the Agents table. Include the Street Address, City, Date Listed, and Listing Price fields from the Property Listings table.
   b. Key the criteria **between 8/1/2012 and 8/31/2012** in the Date Listed field to show only those properties that were listed during August. Sort the list in ascending order by Last Name. Run the query and save it as **August Listings**.
2. Create an *Access* query to determine the properties that have sold in August.
   a. Create a copy of the August Listings query, naming the new query **August Sales**.
   b. In query Design view, remove the existing relationship between the Agents and Property Listings tables by right-clicking on the join line and selecting Delete. Drag the Agent ID field in the Agents table to the Selling Agent ID field in the Property Listings table to create a new relationship between these fields.
   c. Add the Selling Agent ID, Sales Date, and Sales Price fields from the Property Listings table.
   d. Move the *between 8/1/2012 and 8/31/2012* criterion from the Date Listed field to the Sales Date field to list only those properties that have sold during August.
3. Export the August Sales query to *Excel*. Open the file in *Excel*, and wrap text in the headings in row 1. Apply the Civic theme to the worksheet.
4. Calculate the number of days required to sell each property: Key the heading **Days Listed** in cell L1. Create a formula in cell L2 that subtracts the Date Listed value from the Sales Date value. Apply comma format with no decimal places to numbers.
5. Insert a function in cell L10 to calculate the average days listed for all properties sold during August. Add a descriptive label adjacent to the function. Format the label and the cell containing the average with the Total cell style.

You can also modify or add placeholders to an existing layout in the same way that you add placeholders to a new layout.

To Insert a New Layout

View/Master Views/Slide Master

1. Click the layout in the slide thumbnail pane that will be above the new master; then in the Edit Master group, click Insert Layout to display a new layout.
2. Click Insert Placeholder to display the types of placeholders that you can insert, as shown in Figure 5.2. Note that the Content placeholder can be used to insert any of the items listed on the gallery of placeholders.
3. Click the type of placeholder and then draw it the desired size and at the location desired. For example, you may want to draw two content placeholders positioned one above the other.
4. Click Rename to display the Rename Layout dialog box and key the desired name, such as *Two Horizontal Content.*
5. Make other desired changes to the slide master or layouts or click Close Master View.

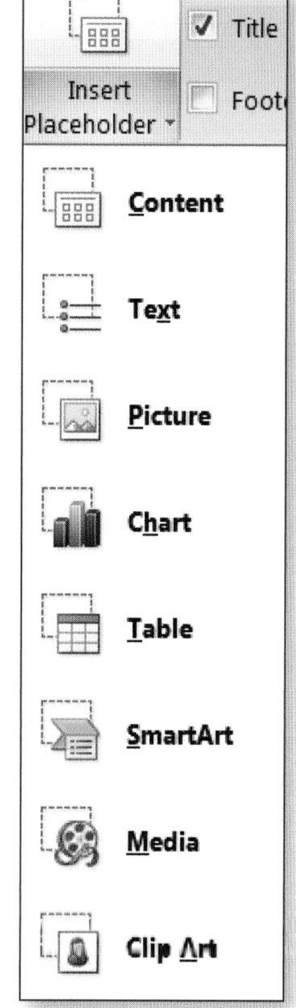

Figure 5.2 Placeholder Gallery

To Add Pictures to the Slide Master:

View/Master Views/Slide Master

1. In Slide Master view, click Slide Master Layout, the first slide in the slide thumbnail pane.
2. To add the same picture to all slides, copy the picture desired and paste it in the desired location on the slide master.
3. Select the picture and then under Picture Tools, click Format to size and align the picture.
4. Close Slide Master view when you have finished all changes.

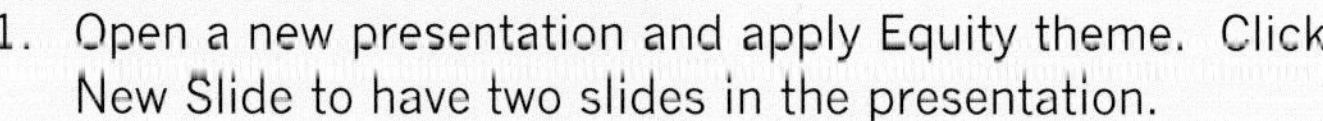

DRILL 1 ADD SLIDE LAYOUT

FARBE LOGO

1. Open a new presentation and apply Equity theme. Click New Slide to have two slides in the presentation.
2. Use Slide Master view to insert a new layout. Click the Comparison layout to insert the new layout below it.
3. Insert two horizontal content layout placeholders with one below the other.
4. Size the placeholders 8.5" wide × 2.25" high; align at left with the title placeholder.
5. Rename the layout **Two Horizontal Content**.
6. Click Slide Master (the first slide) in the slide thumbnail pane, and select the footer. Change the width to 2.5" (Drawing Tools/Format/Size/Width).
7. Right-click the *farbe logo* file, and click Copy.
8. Paste the logo in the space between the footer and the date placeholders. Size it .5" high. After it is sized, copy the logo.
9. Click Title Slide Layout directly below Slide Master in the slide thumbnail pane and paste the logo in the upper-left corner of the slide.
10. Save as *pp5-drill1* and leave the presentation open.

For ease in adjusting column widths in the table, view the gridlines (Home/Paragraph/Border, click View Gridlines).

3. Open the *Word* data file *m&d memo* and save as *p9-j2b*. Key the subject line **Listings to Expire in September**. Key the memo shown below. Paste the Renewal Before 9/30/2012 query after the first paragraph, merging formatting. Copy the memo to the three agents listed in the query. Remove the extra spacing between the agents' names.

   Our database indicates that three property listings will expire on or before September 30. The table below identifies the listing agent's name, street address and city of the property, the listing renewal date, and the listing price. The three agents are being copied on this memo and according to operating procedures will contact the respective owners to request renewal of the property listing with McMullan & Donovan Realty.

   [Paste the Renewal Before 9/30/2012 query results here. Format according to standard operating procedures and adjust formats as necessary to present data attractively. Change the table heading to the one shown in Figure P9.1.]

Listings to Expire in September						
First Name	Last Name	Property Number	Street Address	City	Listing Renewal Date	Listing Price

Figure P9.1 Adjust Column Width and Align Headings at Bottom

Job 3

Access Report Exported to Word

Prepare an *Access* report that presents the properties listed by each agent. You will create a query, and then create the report using the query. Finally, you will export the *Access* report to *Word* for final editing.

1. Save the *p9-j2a* database as *p9-j3a*.
2. The query for the report is almost identical to the Renewal Before 9/30/2012 query. Rather than designing a new query, create a copy of the Renewal Before 9/30/2012 query (right-click the query in the Navigation Pane, click Copy, then right-click the Navigation Pane and click Paste). Name the new query **Properties by Agent**.
3. Modify the query as follows: Remove all criteria and sorts, and remove the First Name and Listing Renewal Date fields; show the Sales Date field; and add Sales Price. Sort by the listing agent's last name in ascending order.
4. Use the Report Wizard to create a report using all of the fields in the Properties by Agent query.
   a. Group the report by Agents, sort by Property Number, use the Block layout and Landscape orientation, and name the report **Agent Listings**.
   b. In Layout view, adjust columns to make sure all text is visible in the report. Save layout changes and close the report.
5. Export the report to *Word* with formats. Save as *p9-j3b* and choose to open *Word* after the export. Save as a *Word* document with the same name and convert from Compatibility Mode. Change the margins to Moderate, convert the text to a table, and format the table according to standard operating procedures. Adjust formats as necessary to improve appearance.

Job 4

Update Database

You have two new listings and two sold properties to enter in the database.

1. Save the *p9-j3a* database as *p9-j4*.
2. Use the Property Listings form to add two new properties that were listed today (August 25). Compute the renewal date for each listing.

All slides have a theme—even the Office theme that is black and white. It is easier to select a theme that has features you like and edit it.

Once you have set up a custom color, it displays in Recent Colors. Click it to apply it.

To Customize Theme Colors on the Slide Master:

Slide Master/Edit Theme/Colors

1. Click Slide Master to display the Slide Master view, and then click Colors to display the gallery of theme colors.
2. Click Create New Theme Colors to display the Create New Theme Colors dialog box shown in Figure 5.3. Then click the down arrow next to the color that you wish to change such as Accent 4 to display the Theme Colors palette. Select the desired color. Repeat this step until all desired colors have been changed.
3. To use a custom color, such as a company logo color, click More Colors to display the Colors dialog box as shown in Figure 5.4. On the Custom tab, specify the RGB colors, such as Red 40, Green 25, and Blue 180; then click OK.

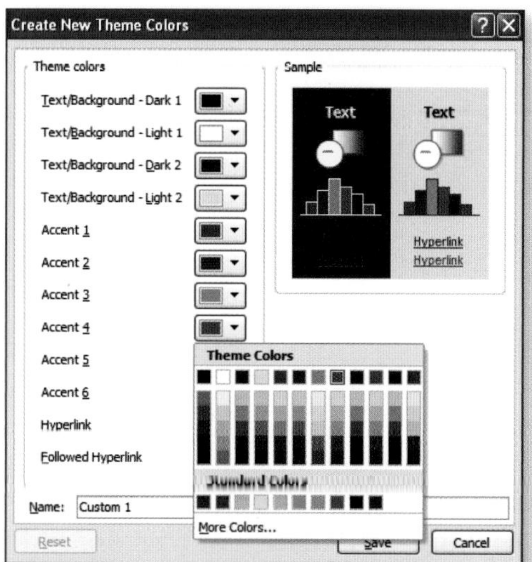

Figure 5.3 Create New Theme Colors

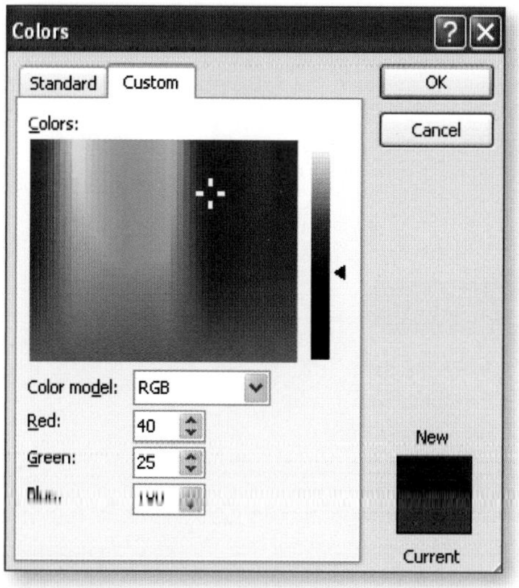

Figure 5.4 Set Custom Colors

4. After all color changes have been made, key a name for the custom theme colors, such as the company name, and click Save.

DRILL 1, continued EDIT THEME COLORS

1. In the open presentation, in Slide Master view, edit the theme colors, making the changes shown at the right.
2. Save the custom colors with the company name, **Farbe**. Leave Slide Master view open.
3. Click Slide Master in the slide thumbnail pane, and then select the shape containing the slide number at the bottom left. Under the Drawing Tools, select Format, and then change the Shape Fill color to the custom blue color.
4. Click Title Slide Layout and click the Orange bar shape. Change the color to the custom blue color. In the Master Layout group, remove the check from Footers so that the footers do not show on the title slide.
5. Resave as *pp5-drill1* and leave the presentation open.

Text/Background – Dark 2: Blue custom (40, 25, 180)

Accent 3 – Gold, Hyperlink

Accent 5 – Blue custom (40, 25, 180)

Hyperlink – Blue custom (40, 25, 180)

Followed Hyperlink – Gold, Hyperlink, Darker 50%

Job 1,
continued

August 20, 2012

«Title» «First_Name» «Last_Name»
«Agency»
«Address»
«City», «State» «ZIP»

Remove extra space after paragraphs

«GreetingLine»

Agents at McMullan & Donovan Realty are pleased to invite you to a special preview showing on Tuesday, August 28, of our two newest San Antonio listings. The table shown below outlines our tour with time and listing addresses. Please arrive promptly at the first listing at 11 a.m. Our second visit begins at 12:30 with a light lunch catered by JD Forde Eatery.

[Paste the two newest listings from the filtered Current Listings query result here, merging formatting. Then create the following table. Copy the street addresses from the query to the table, then delete the query results from the *Word* document. Format with the appropriate table style, changing font color to black.]

> **TIP**
> To remove the extra spacing after the table, click No Spacing from the Quick Styles.

Tour Schedule	
Time	Street Address
11:00 a.m.	
12:30 p.m.	

Please confirm your attendance of this special tour by Wednesday, August 22. Simply browse to www.mcdonrealty.com/confirm and complete the tour confirmation form.

We look forward to this preview showing and will welcome your recommendations in selling these fine listings.

Sincerely

4. Prepare mailing labels (Avery 5160) for the letters using the *Access* Labels report. Sort in the same order as the merged letters.

Job 2
Memo

M&D MEMO

You learn today (August 20) that it is your responsibility to determine which listings have a renewal date set to expire on or before 9/30/2012. Prepare a memo to Ms. McMullan listing properties with expiring listing agreements.

1. Save the *p9-j1a* database as *p9-j2a*.
2. Create a query that uses data from the Agents and Property Listings tables.
   a. Include the First Name and Last Name from the Agents table and the Property Number, Street Address, City, Date Listed, Listing Renewal Date, Listing Price, and Sales Date from the Property Listings table. Do not show the Date Listed and Sales Date fields.
   b. In the Sales Date field, key **Is Null** as the criteria to display unsold properties. In the Listing Renewal Date, key **<=9/30/2012** as the criteria.
   c. Sort the properties in ascending order by the date listed. Run the query and save it as **Renewal Before 9/30/2012**.

> **TIP**
> *Access* automatically adds a pound sign (#) in the criteria to denote dates.

To Change the Slide Background:

Slide Master/Background/Background Styles

1. Click Slide Master to display the Slide Master view, and then click Background Styles to display the gallery of styles. Note that the styles gallery changes depending on the theme used.
2. Click the style desired, such as Style 2 shown in Figure 5.5.

Figure 5.5 Background Styles

To Save as a Template:

File/Save As

1. Click Save As to display the Save As dialog box.
2. Key the filename and in the Save as type box, select PowerPoint Template. See Figure 5.6.
3. A template is saved in the Templates folder by default. Your instructor may direct you to save this template in the same folder as your solution files.

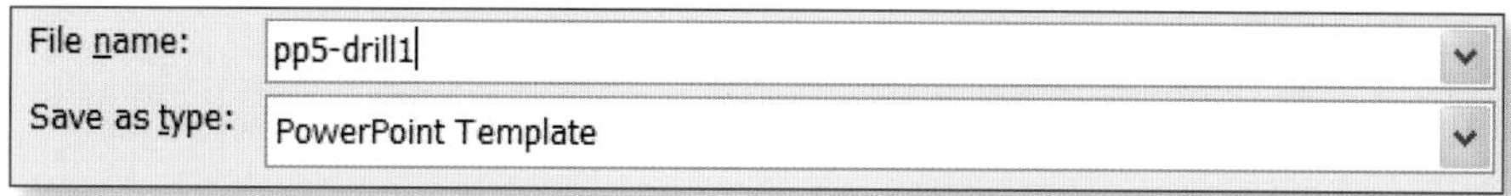

Figure 5.6 Save as Template

Note: The Save As dialog box looks slightly different depending on whether *Windows 7*, *Windows Vista*, or *XP* is used.

DRILL 1, continued — CHANGE BACKGROUND STYLES AND SAVE AS TEMPLATE

1. In Slide Master view, click Slide Master and change the background style of the open presentation to Style 2 on all slide layouts.
2. Rename the slide master **Farbe**. Use Figure 5.7 to check your Slide Master slides. Then close Slide Master view.
3. Click Save As and save the presentation as a PowerPoint Template in your solution files. Name the template *pp5-drill1* and close it.

Check your slide master layouts.

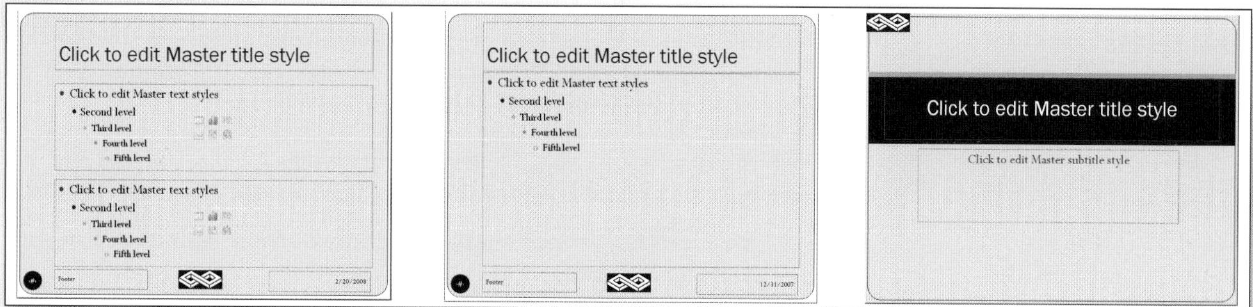

Figure 5.7 Two Horizontal Content, Slide Master, Title Slide Layout

project 9

McMullan & Donovan Realty: Integrating Access, Word, PowerPoint, and Excel

OBJECTIVES

- Update company database with imported data
- Create *Access* queries
- Create relationships between *Access* tables
- Prepare effective documents integrating data from *Word*, *PowerPoint*, *Excel*, and *Access*
- Work with limited supervision

SETTING

In Project 9, you continue your work for McMullan & Donovan Realty. You will expand the database you created in Project 8 by importing data from text and *Excel* files. More queries are needed as you create *Word* documents and *PowerPoint* presentations. *Access* reports and forms will also be required.

JOBS

1. Mail merge letters using *Access* query
2. Memo with *Access* query
3. *Access* data exported to *Word* and *Excel*
4. *PowerPoint* presentation with *Excel* and *Access* data
5. Report created in *Word*

STANDARD OPERATING PROCEDURES

Use these procedures for all documents you prepare.

1. Use the Civic document theme for all documents and *Access* forms and reports.
2. Use the *m&d letterhead* and *m&d memo* templates from the data files to prepare all letters and memos. Save as *Word* documents and not as templates.
3. Format tables imported from a query with the Light Shading – Accent 1 table style. Center tables horizontally.
4. Set up a folder named AC-WD-PP-EX Project 9 to store project files. Name all solution files *p9-j* (plus the job number, *j1*, *j2*, etc.) unless directed otherwise.

Job 1

Form Letters and Form Labels Using Access

P9-J1-DATA
M&D LETTERHEAD
MULTIPLE LISTINGS AGENTS

Ms. McMullan has asked you to prepare form letters inviting a small group of agents from other agencies to tour M&D's two newest listings in San Antonio. You will also prepare labels for mailing the letters using the *Access* Labels report.

1. Open the Access database *p9-j1-data* and save as *p9-j1a*. Import the *multiple listings agents* text file as a table. Save the table as **Multiple Listings Agents**.
2. Filter the Current Listings query to identify current listings in San Antonio. Copy the two newest listings in the filtered records.
3. Open the *Word* data file *m&d letterhead* and save as *p9-j1b main*. Use the Multiple Listings Agents table from the *Access* database as your recipient list, and sort ascending by ZIP. Key the letter shown on the next page as the mail merge main document. Insert the fields as indicated. Merge the letters and save as *p9-j1b*.

DRILL 2 CREATE PRESENTATION FROM TEMPLATE

Insert/Text/Header & Footer

1. Check Date and time; then click Update Automatically. Select desired date format.
2. Check Slide Number.
3. Check Footer and key **Farbe Industries**.
4. Leave check in Don't show on title slide.
5. Click Apply to All.

1. Open the template you created in Drill 1 (*pp5-drill1*) and save as a PowerPoint Presentation named *pp5-drill2*.
2. Use the information below to key the three slides. Show the date, slide numbers, and the footer *Farbe Industries* on all slides except the title slide.
3. Check slides carefully, resave as *pp5-drill2*, and close the file.

Slide 1 (Title slide)

Title: National Sales Report Subtitle: Student's Name | National Sales Manager

Slide 2 (Title and Content layout)

Title: Goals Met

- All regions met goals
  - Regions 2 and 4 exceeded goals by 10%
  - Regions 1 and 3 exceeded goals by 20%
- Fourth quarter stronger than expected
- Region 3 had exceptional 3rd and 4th quarters
- Region 1 had its strongest 4th quarter ever

Convert the bulleted text to a SmartArt graphic; use Chevron List.

Slide 3 (Two Horizontal Content layout)

Title: National Sales

Key the table in first content area with all content centered as shown below. Key bulleted text in second content area.

Region	1st Quarter	2nd Quarter	3rd Quarter	4th Quarter
1	$350,000	$325,000	$375,000	$450,000
2	$325,000	$354,000	$386,000	$420,000
3	$360,000	$328,000	$430,000	$490,000
4	$320,000	$310,000	$376,000	$410,000

- Valerie Maxwell—top sales manager for the year
- Jeff Johnson—top sales representative for the year
- Twenty sales representatives qualified for President's Club

CUSTOMIZING HANDOUTS

View/Master Views/Handout Master

TIP

View/Master Views/Notes Master

The notes master can be changed in the same way as the handout master.

Handouts can be customized using Handout Master view. Typical ways to customize the handout master are to add a logo, use the same background as the slides, and customize the text and color of the headers and footers.

To Customize the Handout Master:

Handout Master/Page Setup/Orientation

1. Click Handout Master to display the Handout Master view, and then make desired changes.
2. Close Handout Master view.

5. Sort ascending by Advisor Last Name and Last Name, and key a criterion that will show all students who have not yet applied to college. Do not show the Applied to College field. Run the query and save it as **College Calls**. Close the query.
6. Create a report using all the fields from the College Calls query. Group by Advisor Last Name, do not add any sorting, and use the default layout and orientation. Save as **College Calls**. Apply a theme of your choice, and adjust columns to show all data. Close the report.
7. Export the report to *Word*, and then save the document as a *Word* document with the name *ac7-db13c*. Convert from Compatibility Mode. Modify formats as desired to create an attractive document that advisors can use to contact students who have not yet applied for college.
8. Print, save, and close the document. Close all open applications.

College Calls

Advisor Last Name	First Name	Last Name	SAT Score	ACT Score	Phone
Choi					
	Cebell	Hewlett	1010	29	513-555-0108
	Chris	Jones	1275	26	513-555-0153
Perry					
	Sandy	Stark	1240	22	513-555-0154
Sengupta					
	Brad	Darling	1085	18	513-555-0141
St. Simon					
	Kenyatta	Escalera	1210	20	513-555-0146

Figure 7.5 College Calls Document

CAREER FOCUS

© asiseeit/iStockphoto.com

A quick Internet search for database careers produces a tremendous number of "hits." Some of the positions are highly technical and require significant amounts of education. Others, particularly those in small companies, require less technical education. Many of the jobs specify two skills of the prospective employee—critical thinking and creativity. Your ability to critically analyze data to develop creative solutions is an excellent career skill regardless of whether you choose a career in database administration or in any other field.

DRILL 3 CUSTOMIZE HANDOUT AND NOTES MASTER

FARBE LOGO

1. Open *pp5-drill2* and save it as *pp5-drill3*.
2. Open the handout master and apply the Farbe colors to it. Copy the *farbe logo* file from the data files and paste it in the Header placeholder; change the text of other headers and footers to the Farbe custom color.
3. Use the same background style as slides. Close Handout Master view.
4. Click Notes Master and paste logo in the Header placeholder. Then change the text color of the number at the bottom to the custom color and use the same background style as slides.
5. Close Notes Master view and key the following notes:

   Slide 2: Review goals for next year.

   Slide 3: Recognize top sales manager, the top sales representative, and the 20 President's Club sales representatives.

6. Preview and print one copy of handout and notes pages, using landscape orientation and four slides per page for the handout and portrait orientation for the note pages.
7. Resave as *pp5-drill3* and close.

Apply It

Presentation 6

Customized Presentation with Handouts

TLG LOGO

1. Open a new presentation and apply Median design. Use the information below to create a customized design for The Leadership Group. Add a new slide. Make all changes in Slide Master view.
2. Click on Comparison Layout (two content areas with a title placeholder above each) and insert a new slide layout with two content areas positioned one above the other. Size each one 2.2" × 8.9"; name the layout **Two Horizontal Content.**
3. Click on Slide Master, the first slide in the slide thumbnail pane; then copy the *tlg logo* file from the data files and paste it in the top right corner of the slide. Make sure it extends from the top to the blue bar. See Figure 5.8.

Figure 5.8 Slide Master

4. Create new theme colors with these changes:
   Text/Background – Dark 2: Gold, Accent 4
   Accent 1: Ice Blue, Accent 1, Darker 25%
   Accent 3: Olive Green, Accent 3, Darker 25%
   Hyperlink: Ice Blue, Accent 1, Darker 25%.
   Name the colors **TLG.**
5. Click on Title Slide Layout on the slide thumbnail pane, and drag the title placeholder to about the vertical and horizontal center of the main slide area. Center the text in the placeholder. Paste the TLG logo in the top right corner of the slide. Deselect the footer so that it will not show on the title slide. See Figure 5.9.

Figure 5.9 Title Layout

Design/Themes/More

1. Click More in Themes gallery
2. Click Save Current Theme at bottom of gallery.
3. Key the name of the theme and click Save.

6. Save the theme you customized with the name **TLG**; also save the presentation as a template named **TLG**.
7. Open *pp3-p4* that you prepared in Lesson 3; save as *pp5-p6*. Apply the TLG theme to it; make any necessary adjustments in the slides.
8. Print handouts four per page using landscape orientation for the handouts. Resave as *pp5-p6* and close.

You may want to delete the standard report footer before you convert the text to a table.

13. Change the margins for the document to Moderate. Then apply a table style of your choice, and adjust formats and column widths to create an attractive table.
14. Print the table, save, and close the document, and close the *Access* database.

Apply It

Database 12
Import and Link Data

AC7-DB12-DATA
STUDENT DATA
ADVISEES

1. Open the data file *ac7-db12-data*. Save the database as *ac7-db12*.
2. Import the text data file *student data* as a new table. Choose Student ID as the primary key, and name the table **Students**. In Design view, change data types for Student ID and Advisor ID to Text. Save and close the Students table.
3. Copy the *Excel* data file *advisees* to your solutions folder, and then import the file from that folder, choosing to link to the file. Name the new linked table **Scores**.
4. Create a query using the Students and Scores tables. Use the following fields: Student ID (Students), Last Name (Students), Class (Scores), SAT Score (Scores), ACT Score (Scores), Phone (Students). Sort by Class in ascending order. Run the query and save it as **Student Scores**. Close the query.
5. Open the *advisees* workbook in *Excel*, and make the following changes.
   a. Peter Olsen's SAT score was keyed incorrectly. Change it to **1190**.
   b. Delois Pierce took the SAT a second time and improved her score to **1105**.
6. Save the workbook and close it. In *Access*, run the Student Scores query to see the changes from the linked table. Print and close the query.
7. Create a relationship between the shared fields of the Advisors and the Students tables. Enforce referential integrity.
8. Leave the database open for the next exercise.

Database 13
Export Data

1. With *ac7-db12* open, save the database as *ac7-db13a*.
2. Export the Student Scores query to *Excel* with the name *ac7-db13b*, and save to your solutions folder. In *Excel*, insert a blank row below the last 2011 entry and below the last 2012 entry. In cell C9, key **Average**. In cell D9, average the SAT scores of the class of 2011. Copy the function to E9 to average the ACT scores.
3. Repeat this process to average the scores for the 2012 class and the 2013 class. Apply cell styles and other formatting to improve the look of the worksheet. Print, save, and close.
4. Create a new query and add the Advisors, Students, and Scores tables, in that order. (Note that all three tables are related.) Use the following fields in the query: Advisor Last Name (Advisors); First Name, Last Name (Students); SAT Score, ACT Score (Scores); Phone (Students); and Applied to College (Scores).

LESSON 6

Embed and Link Files

OBJECTIVES

- Create effective presentations
- Embed videos and audio
- Compress media
- Embed and link graphics

EMBED VIDEO AND AUDIO

Insert/Media/Video or Audio

Video and audio can be linked or embedded from files or clip art. In this lesson, you will embed video and audio from files. Media files tend to be large; therefore, always compress the files as you did with photographs.

To Embed Video:

1. Click in the slide; then click the arrow under Video and select Video from File.
2. In the Insert Video dialog box, locate the video you want to embed and click Insert.

DISCOVER

Audio Tools Options/Audio Options/Hide During Show

If a audio is set to start automatically, you can hide the audio icon during the show.

1. Click the audio icon.
2. Click Hide During Show.

To Embed Audio:

1. Click in the slide; then click the arrow under Audio and select Audio from File.
2. In the Insert Audio dialog box, locate the audio you want to embed and click Insert.

To Format Video or Audio:

Video or Audio Tools/Format or Playback/Video or Audio Options or Editing

The Format and Playback tools for video and audio are very similar.

Figure 6.1 Video Tools

DISCOVER

Compress Media

File/Info/Compress Media

Click the arrow under Compress Media and select Presentation Quality.

1. To start the media, select Automatically or On Click.
2. Check options desired such as Rewind after Playing, Hide During Show (audio icon), or Trim Video or Trim Audio.
3. To shorten video or audio, select the media and click Play. Then click Trim Video or Trim Audio and drag the beginning green marker or ending red marker inward to reduce the amount of time.

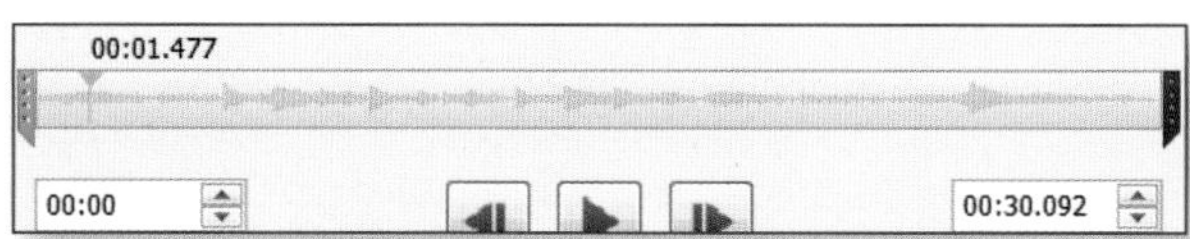

Figure 6.2 Trim Video

Figure 7.4 Export Group

To Export Data from *Access*:

External Data/Export

1. Select the object to export in the Navigation Pane.
2. Click the desired export option to open an Export dialog box. You will see the object name at the end of a path in the File name box. Use Browse, if necessary, to navigate to a new location and supply a new filename, and then click Save.
3. Click the *Export data with formatting and layout* option if desired to preserve formats and layouts. Selecting this checkbox activates another checkbox that lets you choose to open the destination file after the export.
4. Click OK and click Close.

TIP

To save and convert an RTF file:

1. Click File/Save As, click the Save as type drop-list arrow, and click Word Document.
2. Click Save.
3. Click File/Info, and then click Convert button.
4. Click OK.

Data exported to other applications may need format adjustments to look the way you want it to. In *Excel*, you may need to apply font formatting directly, even if you apply a theme. Data exported to *Word* is saved in Rich Text Format. To use many *Word 2010* features, such as themes, you must save the file as a *Word 2010* document and then convert the document from Compatibility Mode.

DRILL 2 EXPORT DATA TO EXCEL AND WORD

1. With *ac7-drill1* open, save the database as *ac7-drill2a*.
2. Open the List of Sold Items query in Design view. Drag the Date field in the query design grid to the left of the Product # field, and then sort ascending on both Date and Product #. Run the revised query and then save it as **Value of Items Sold**.
3. Close the query and then export it to *Excel* with the name *ac7-drill2b*. Save the file in your solutions folder. Export with formats, and choose to open *Excel* after the export.
4. In cell F1, key **Total Sale**. In cell F2, key a formula to multiply Quantity times Unit Price. Copy the formula down the column.
5. Use the Format Painter to copy the format from cell E2 to F2:F26. Apply the Civic theme; apply the 40% – Accent3 and Heading 3 cell styles to the column headings. Adjust column widths as necessary.
6. Use a SUM function to calculate total sales in cell F27. Format the cell using the Total cell style.
7. Print, save, and close the *Excel* workbook.
8. In *Access*, create a report from the Staff table, using all fields, no grouping, no sorting, Tabular layout and Landscape orientation, and the default title **Staff**. Apply the Civic theme.
9. In Layout view, adjust columns to make sure all text is visible in the report. Save layout changes and close the report.
10. Export the report to *Word* (External Data/Export/More/Word) with the same name, saving in your solutions folder. Choose to open *Word* after the export.
11. Save the document as a Word Document with the name *ac7-drill2c* and then use File/Info/Convert to convert from Compatibility Mode. Apply the Civic theme.
12. Select all the staff data, and convert the tabbed data to a table. Delete the first column, which should be empty; merge cells in the first row for the heading.

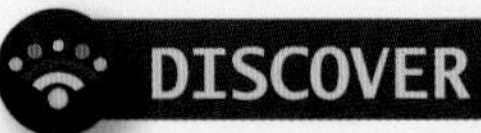

DISCOVER

Insert/Tables/Table

1. Click the Table arrow.
2. Click Convert Text to Table.
3. Accept default rows and columns and click OK.

DRILL 1 ADD VIDEO AND AUDIO

WILDLIFE, MARKETING MUSIC

1. Open *wildlife* from the data files and save as *pp6-drill1*.
2. Click in slide 2 Contents section and select Video from File. Browse to Libraries/Videos/Sample Videos and insert *Wildlife*.
3. Click Video Tools Playback and select Start Automatically; then check Play Full Screen and Rewind after Playing.
4. Click Play and then click Trim Video. Trim the video by dragging the red end marker to approximately 25 seconds and click OK.
5. Click in slide 3 and insert *marketing music* from the data files.
6. Click Audio Tools Playback and select Start Automatically, click Hide During Slide Show, and Rewind after Playing.
7. Click Play and then Trim Audio. Trim the audio to approximately 20 seconds and click OK.
8. Click File, Info, Compress Media, and select Presentation Quality.
9. Preview and resave as *pp6-drill1*.

LINK AND EMBED EXCEL CHARTS

TIP

Always copy the source of any linked file, including an *Excel* chart, to the folder in which the presentation is stored before you link the files.

TIP

If the linked chart has been changed in the *Excel* file but has not updated in the *PowerPoint* slide, right-click the chart and select Edit Data. The chart will update.

When a chart is pasted or embedded in a presentation, any changes made in the *Excel* chart must be made separately in the chart in a presentation. When a chart is linked, changes in the *Excel* chart are also made in the chart in the presentation. In Lesson 8 of the *Word* module, you pasted (embedded) an *Excel* chart as a picture. In this lesson, you will embed and link an *Excel* chart.

To Embed or Link an Excel Chart:

Home/Clipboard/Copy

1. Copy the *Excel* file to the same folder as will be used to store the presentation.
2. Open the *Excel* file, select the borders of the *Excel* chart, and click copy.
3. To embed the chart in a slide, click in the content area and click Paste. Select Use Destination Theme & Embed Workbook from the Paste Options.
4. To link the chart to a slide, click in the content area and click Paste. Select Use Destination Theme & Link Data from the Paste Options.

Figure 6.3 Paste Option

Figure 6.4 Link Option

DRILL 2 EMBED AND LINK CHARTS

NATIONAL SALES PRESENTATION, NATIONAL SALES

1. Open *national sales presentation* and save as *pp6-drill2*.
2. Copy the *Excel* data file *national sales* to your solution folder.
3. Open the *Excel* file; click the borders of the chart; then click copy. Note the colors of the chart.
4. Switch to the open presentation and click the last slide; add a new slide (4) with Title and Content layout. Key the title **National Sales**.
5. Click in the content area and then click Paste; select the Use Destination Theme & Embed Workbook option to paste the chart. Note the colors of the chart on the slide.
6. Add slide 5; key the same title and paste the same chart in the content section. Select the Use Destination Theme & Link Data option.
7. Right-click the *PowerPoint* chart and click Edit Data. Note that *PowerPoint* opens *Excel* in a split screen. Change the first-quarter data for Region 1 from $350,000 to $250,000. Note the change in the chart.
8. Resave as *pp6-drill2* and close both the *PowerPoint* and the *Excel* applications. Save the changes made in the worksheet.

To Link an *Excel* Worksheet to an *Access* Table:

External Data/Import & Link/Excel

1. In an open database, click Excel. Use Browse to select the file to which you wish to link.
2. Click the *Link to the data source by creating a linked table* option and click OK.
3. In the Link Spreadsheet Wizard, select the worksheet that contains the data to link to and click Next.
4. Make sure the First Row Contains Column Headings box is selected and click Next. Key a name for the table and click Finish.
5. A message will appear that *Access* is finished linking the *Excel* data to the file. Click OK.

The linked table appears with the list of other tables in the *Access* Navigation Pane. The arrow and *Excel* icon (Figure 7.3) indicate that the linked data is stored in *Excel*.

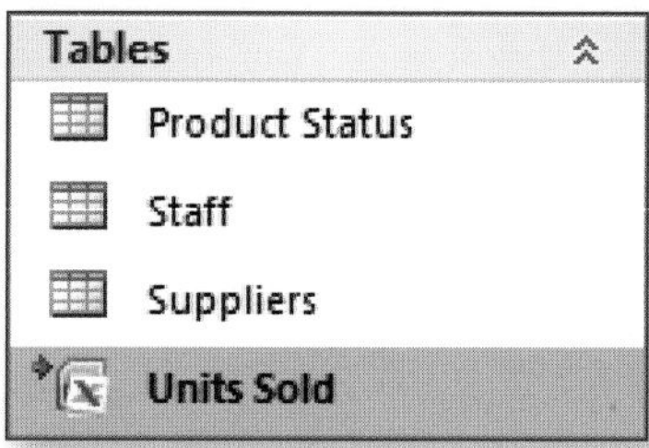

Figure 7.3 Linked Worksheet

DRILL 1 IMPORT AND LINK DATA

AC7-DRILL1-DATA, STAFF, UNITS SOLD

1. Open the data file *ac7-drill1-data*. Save the database as *ac7-drill1*.
2. Import the *staff* text file into a new table in the database. Accept the default Delimited option in the first import window; in the second import window, select First Row Contains Field Names. Choose the Staff ID field as the primary key.
3. Accept the default name for the new table and finish the import. Open the Staff table to view the data that has been imported. Print the table and close it.
4. Copy the *Excel* data file *units sold* to your solutions folder. Then import the *units sold* workbook into *Access*, choosing to link to the *Excel* file that you copied to your solutions folder. Accept all default options in the import windows, and name the linked table **Units Sold**.
5. Create a query that uses the Product Status table and the Units Sold table. Insert the Product # (Units Sold), Product Name (Product Status), Quantity (Units Sold), Unit Price (Product Status), and Date (Units Sold) fields.
6. Sort in ascending order by Product # and run the query. Notice there are 24 records in the query dynaset. Save the query as **List of Sold Items** and then close.
7. Open the *units sold* workbook in your solutions folder in *Excel*. Key the following data in cells A27:D27: **3229** | **6/21/2012** | **401** | **5**.
8. Save and close the workbook. In *Access*, run the List of Sold Items query to see the new record that has been added from the linked table.
9. Print and close the query, and leave the database open for the next drill.

TIP

You can reduce the number of both import steps and export steps to save time when you import or export the same kind of data on a regular basis.

EXPORT DATA TO OTHER APPLICATIONS

You may wonder why you would need to export data from *Access*. The chief reason is to use tools in another application to manipulate the *Access* data. You may find it easier to modify a report's appearance, for example, if you export it to *Word* and use *Word*'s table tools to adjust formats. Likewise, when you export data to *Excel*, you have access to *Excel*'s sophisticated number-crunching features to manipulate numerical data.

Although you can transfer data from *Access* tables to other applications simply by copying and pasting, you also have the choice to export using options in the Export group (Figure 7.4). These export commands give you more control over the process of sharing data.

Apply It

Presentation 7
Presentation with Charts

PORTFOLIO STRUCTURE

1. Open a new presentation, apply the Angles theme, and save as *pp6-p7*.
2. Key the title **Excel Charts** and subtitle *Your Name*; add two new slides with Title and Content layout.
3. On slide 2, key the title **Link Chart**; and on slide 3, key the title **Embed Chart**.
4. Copy the *Excel* data file *portfolio structure* to your solutions folder. Double-click the file you copied to open it, and select the pie chart borders.
5. Copy and paste the pie chart to the content area of slide 2. Use Destination Theme & Link Data option.
6. Paste the pie chart to the content area of slide 3. Embed the chart by selecting the Use Destination Theme and Embed Workbook option.
7. Switch to the *Excel* file *portfolio structure*. In the worksheet area, make the following changes:
   - Select the 20% for Large Cap, Value (Figure 6.5) and change it in the formula bar to 15%.
   - Select the 20% for Alternatives and change it in the formula bar to 25%.
8. Check slides 2 and 3 in the *PowerPoint* presentation. The linked chart in slide 2 should be updated, but the embedded chart in slide 3 should be the same.
9. Resave *pp6-p7* and close both applications. Save the changes made to the worksheet.

B3 ▾ ✗ ✓ fx 15%

	A	B
1		
2	Fixed Income	25%
3	Large Cap, Value	15%
4	Alternatives	20%
5	Large Cap, Growth	15%
6	International	10%
7	Small Cap, Value	5%
8	Small Cap, Growth	5%

Figure 6.5 Edit Data File

Presentation 8
Presentation with Video and Audio

VIDEO AND AUDIO, BROTHERS

1. Open *video and audio* from the data files and save as *pp6-p8*. You may use your own video clip if you wish to do so. Apply Box transition to all slides.
2. On slide 2, insert the *brothers* video. Key the title **Brothers** and the following text: **Hanging out and shooting a few baskets with Dad coordinating the activity**. Start video automatically and rewind when completed. Trim video to about 20'.
3. On slide 3, insert a clip of a manual typewriter and the sound of typing from clip art. Key the title **Manual Typewriter** and text: **Sights and sounds of the past**! Start the audio automatically, loop it until stopped, and hide the icon during the show.
4. Compress the media using presentation quality. If Optimize Media displays, click it to optimize the video or audio.
5. Preview and resave as *pp6-p8*.

Optimize Media
File/Info/Optimize Media
Click Optimize Media.

CAREER FOCUS

In the business world, frequently teams prepare presentations that require the use of multiple *Office* applications, including, among others, *Word*, *PowerPoint*, and *Excel*. Developing the ability to work effectively on a presentation as a team member and the ability to integrate applications in the *Office* suite are two important upward mobility career skills. When you devote time to developing and applying these skills, you are making a very wise investment in your future.

3. Select the *Import the source data into a new table in the current database* option if necessary and click OK.
4. Specify how information is organized, if necessary, by selecting Delimited or Fixed Width. Select Delimited unless you know the data is fixed width.
5. The next window asks you to specify the delimiting character and whether the first row in the file contains column headings that can be used for field names when the data is placed in a table. Select this checkbox to set the column headings as field names and click Next.
6. The next window lets you edit field names and data types for the new table. Because these changes can also be made in the table Design view, you can click Next to bypass this window.
7. The next window asks whether you want the Wizard to create a primary key for the new table or you want to choose your own primary key. If a field contains a unique value for each record, designate that field as the primary key (Figure 7.2). Otherwise, let *Access* create a new primary key field for the table. Make your selection and click Next.

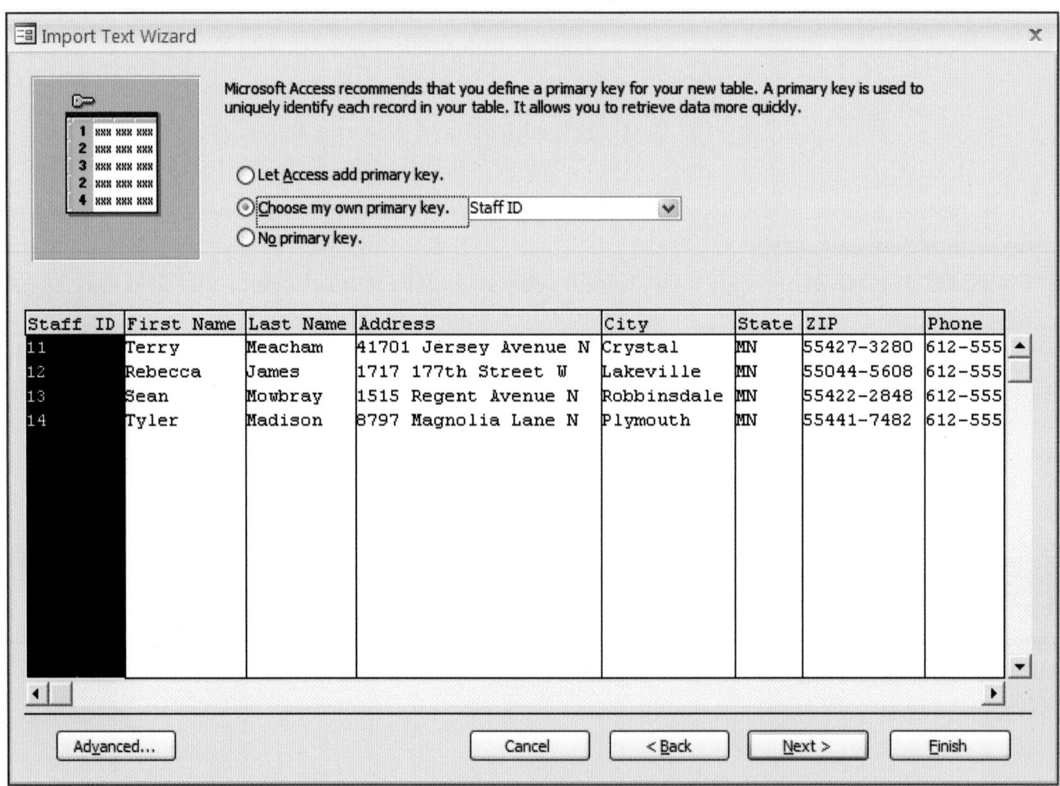

Figure 7.2 Choose Primary Key

8. Key the name of the new table, and then click Finish and Close. Your new table appears alphabetically in the list of tables. You can now create queries, forms, or reports based on the imported data.

After you import data into an *Access* database, check data types in table Design view. Numeric data will have the Number data type applied automatically, but you may need to change this data type to Text.

LINK DATA FROM EXCEL

When you import data into *Access*, you can choose to link the data. Linking an object to your database creates a connection between the source application file and *Access*. If you change the data in the linked application, the data in the database is updated. It is common to link an *Excel* file to an *Access* database to enable *Access* to use current data stored in the *Excel* workbook for queries. The process for linking is almost identical to the process for importing.

Manage and Deliver Presentations

LESSON 7

OBJECTIVES

- Create effective presentations
- Review and finalize presentations
- Prepare self-running presentations

Remember to copy linked audio and video files to your solution folder.

File/PowerPoint Options/User Name

Before you add comments, make sure your name and initials are listed in the User Name box. Note that comments display in Normal view, but not in Slide Show view.

REVIEW A PRESENTATION

Review presentations carefully using a systematic process: (1) preview slides and notes pages, edit content, and correct errors; (2) add action buttons or hyperlinks if needed; and (3) ask team members to review; then make revisions.

To Add, Review, Edit, and Delete Comments:

Review/Comments/New Comment

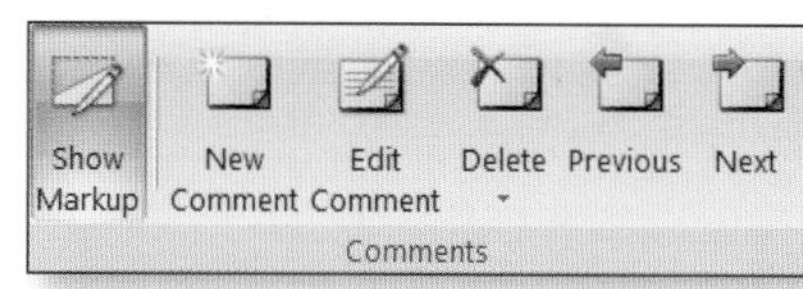

Figure 7.1 Comment Group

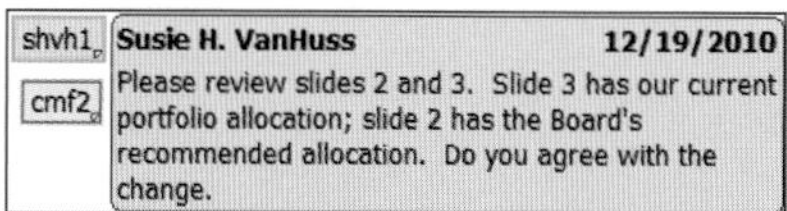

Figure 7.2 Comment

1. Click in the slide to which you want to add a comment; then click New Comment (Figure 7.1).
2. Key the text in the Comment balloon that displays. The comment thumbnail will be marked with the author's initials on the screen; hover the mouse over it to display the comment as shown in Figure 7.2.
3. To navigate from one comment to the next, click Previous or Next.
4. To edit a comment, display it and click Edit Comment; to delete a comment, display it and click Delete.

DRILL 1 ADD COMMENTS

PORTFOLIO REVIEW

1. Open *portfolio review* and save as *pp7-drill1*.
2. Review the first two comments. Respond to comment 1 by adding the following comments.

Slide 2: I support the Board's recommendation. This structure is better in today's market.

Slide 3: The problem with this allocation is that large cap value and large cap growth should be balanced.

3. Follow Connie Forde's instructions in comment 2; delete the VanHuss comment.
4. Preview, resave as *pp7-drill1*, and close.

HYPERLINKS

Insert/Links/Hyperlink

A hyperlink is used to connect to a slide, presentation, file, e-mail address, or Web page. Hyperlinks are active only in Slide Show view. On a slide, a hyperlink has a color controlled by the theme and is underlined.

LESSON 7

Import and Export Data

OBJECTIVES

- Import data from other applications
- Export data to other applications

DATA SHARING OPTIONS

Access has a number of options built into the program for sharing data with other *Office 2010* applications. The easiest way to share data is to use familiar Copy and Paste options that you have already used in other modules. Select records by dragging across the row selectors or column headings of a table or a query dynaset. Then copy the selected records, and paste them in other applications such as *Word* documents or *PowerPoint* slides. Use the options on the Paste Options button or in the Paste Special dialog box to control the appearance of the pasted records.

Another method of sharing *Access* data that you should find familiar is to select an *Access* database as the data source for a mail merge that you begin in *Word*. At the point where you are prompted to select recipients, navigate to the *Access* database and then choose the table or query that contains records you will use in the merge.

Access also includes commands on the External Data tab specifically for importing or linking data from sources such as *Excel* workbooks and text files, and for exporting data to *Excel* and *Word*. You will learn about some of these options in this lesson.

IMPORT DATA FROM OTHER APPLICATIONS

The process of importing data takes information from another application and copies it into an *Access* table—the data becomes part of your *Access* database. *Access* offers commands for importing data from a variety of sources, as shown in Figure 7.1. The import procedure varies according to the source. The following steps describe how to import a text file.

TIP

Before importing data from an *Excel* workbook or a text file, ensure the data resembles the structure of an *Access* table, including field names in the first row of the worksheet or document.

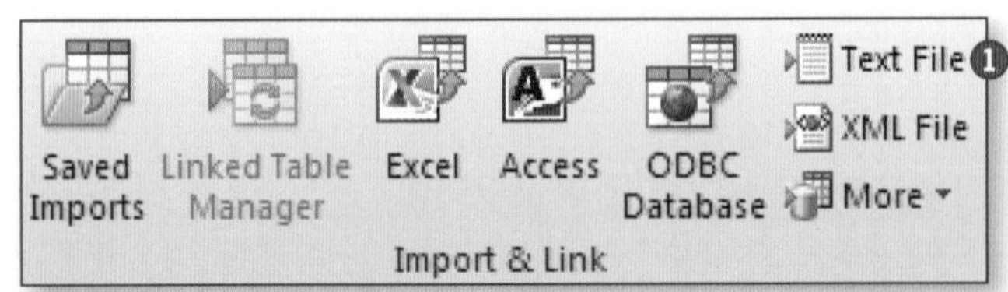

Figure 7.1 Import & Link Group

TIP

A text file must be saved in Plain Text format with the .txt extension.

To Import a Text File into *Access*:

External Data/Import & Link/Text File

1. In an open database, click Text File ❶. The Get External Data – Text File dialog box opens.
2. Click Browse and navigate to the location of the file. Select the file in the File Open window and click Open.

To Add and Follow a Hyperlink:

Insert/Links/Hyperlink

1. In Normal view, select the text or object on the slide to which you want to add a hyperlink.
2. Click Hyperlink to display the Insert Hyperlink dialog box as shown in Figure 7.3.

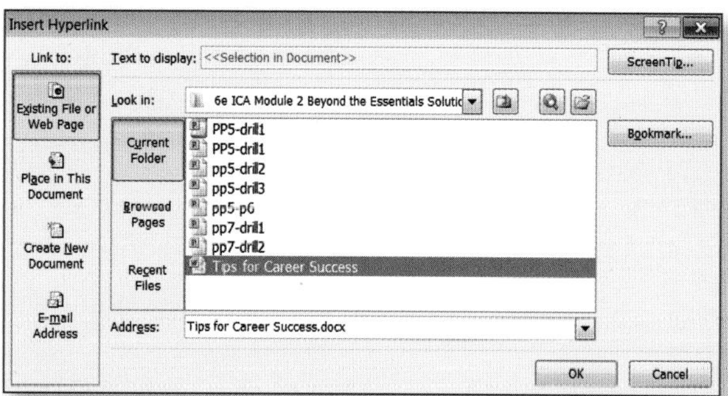

Figure 7.3 Add Hyperlink

3. In the Link to box, select what to link to, then select where it is located, and select the item to link to. Click OK.
4. In Slide Show view, click the hyperlink (Figure 7.4) to follow it.

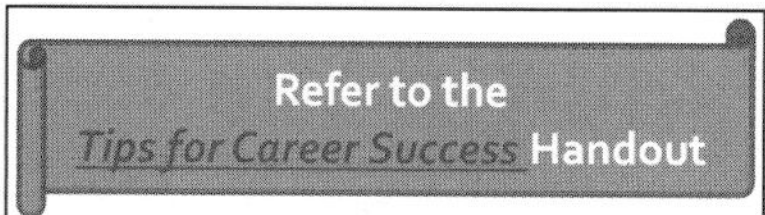

Figure 7.4 Click Hyperlink

ACTION BUTTONS

Insert/Illustrations/Shapes

DISCOVER

1. To rename a file, right-click it and select Rename.
2. Key the new name.

Action buttons function in the same way that hyperlinks do. They connect you to other locations within or external to the presentation, or perform other actions. Action buttons appear on the Shapes gallery (Figure 7.5).

Figure 7.5 Action Buttons

To Add and Follow an Action Button:

1. Display the Shapes gallery and hover the mouse over action buttons to see their functions. Click the desired action button and draw it on the slide. Click OK in the Action Settings dialog box (Figure 7.6).
2. In Slide Show view, click the action button to follow it.

Figure 7.6 Action Settings

DRILL 2 ADD A HYPERLINK AND ACTION BUTTON

1. Open *p3-j3* (from Project 3) and save as *pp7-drill2*.
2. Copy the *Word* file *p3-j4* to your solution folder and rename it *Tips for Career Success*.
3. Go to the last slide in the presentation, select *Tips for Career Success* on the banner, and add a hyperlink to the *Word* file *Tips for Career Success*.
4. In Slide Show view, click the hyperlink to open the file. Close it and return the presentation to Normal view.
5. Add an action button to the last slide to return to the first slide: click the Home button and draw it in the lower-right corner. Click OK in the Action Settings dialog box.
6. In Slide Show view, click the action button to return to the first slide.
7. Resave as *pp7-drill2* and close the presentation.

Database 10,
continued

Team 2:

575 | Peters | Marshall | 142 E Main Street | Columbus | OH | 43215-5015 | 614-555-0168 | 11/14/1984 | Today's date

8. Print the record for Team 5 in landscape orientation.
9. Close the form. Keep the database open for the next application.

Database 11
Multiple-Table Query

1. With *ac6-db10* open, save the database as *ac6-db11*.
2. Create a new query selecting the Team and Employee tables. Insert the following fields:

   Team Name (Team) | Last Name (Employee) | First Name (Employee) | Home Phone (Employee) | Team Leader (Team)
3. Sort by Team Name and Last Name in ascending order.
4. Run the query and then print it. Save the query as **Team Information**.
5. Close the query. Close the database.

JOB KNOWLEDGE

To keep *Access* running efficiently, you should compact your database files on a regular basis. Compacting a database reclaims unused space and makes most operations faster. When you compact the database, you reorganize records so that they are stored in adjacent spaces, making retrieval faster. Additionally, compacting a database updates its data statistics, helping queries run faster.

To compact a database, begin with an open database. On the Database Tools tab in the Tools group, click Compact and Repair Database. This process happens almost instantaneously.

Like car maintenance, performing routine file maintenance is well worth the time it takes. Make it part of your regular duties to keep your computer running smoothly.

SELF-RUNNING PRESENTATIONS

Self-running presentations are often broadcasted or used at trade shows or on kiosks. When setting up a self-running presentation, you must set the time before each slide advances. You can set timings automatically by rehearsing the presentation before you set up the show. Self-running shows will automatically "loop" to present the slides over and over.

> **TIP**
> Be ready to start delivering your presentation as soon as you click Rehearse Timings. You may have to rehearse several times before you are comfortable setting timings.

To Set Up a Self-running Slide Show:

Slide Show/Set Up/Set Up Slide Show

1. With the presentation open, click Set Up Slide Show to display the Set Up Show dialog box.
2. In Show type, click Browsed at a kiosk (full screen) and click Show without animation. Then click OK.

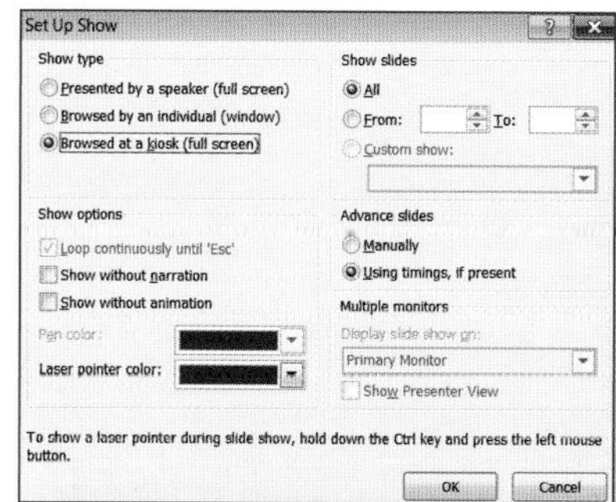

Figure 7.7 Set Up Slide Show

To Rehearse and Time the Delivery:

Slide Show/Set Up/Rehearse Timings

1. Click Rehearse Timings. The first slide opens in Slide Show view and displays the Rehearsal toolbar.
2. Use the Rehearsal toolbar as follows:
   ❶ Next—Move to the next slide.
   ❷ Pause—Stop recording time temporarily and restart recording.
   ❸ Slide Time—View time for current slide.
   ❹ Repeat—Restart recording for the current slide.
   ❺ Total Time—View time for entire show.
3. Rehearse each slide by viewing content, and then end the show.
4. Respond Yes to the prompt *Do you want to keep the new slide timings to use when you view the slide show?* if you are satisfied with them. If not, click No.

> **TIP**
> Tap ESC to end a self-running presentation.

DRILL 3 CREATE SELF-RUNNING PRESENTATION

1. Open *pp7-drill1* and save it as *pp7-drill3*.
2. Set up as a self-running presentation for a kiosk without animation.
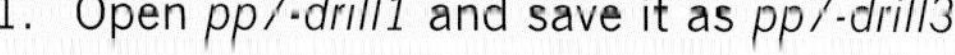
3. Rehearse the presentation, allowing about 30 seconds for slides 1 and 4 and 60 seconds for slides 2 and 3.
4. Accept the timings when you are satisfied. Your timings display below the slides in Slide Sorter view, as shown in Figure 7.8.
5. View the slides in Slide Show view; tap ESC when the title slide appears for the second time.
6. Resave as *pp7-drill3*.

Check the timing of slides.

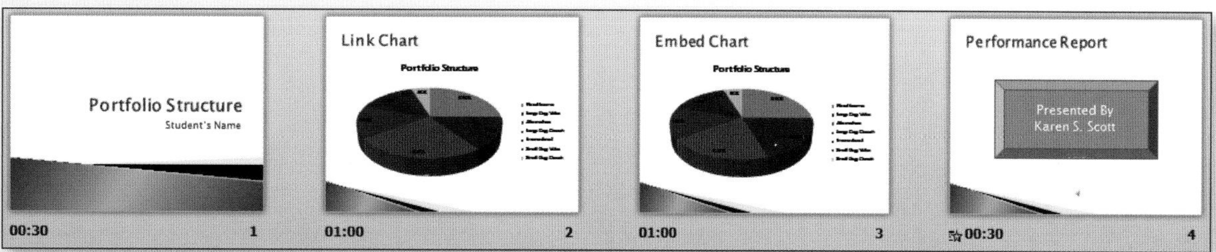

Figure 7.8 Slide Layout View with Timings

To Create Queries Using Related Tables:

1. Create a new query in Design view.
2. Add each table you want to include in the query. Then click the Close button. The joined tables appear in the Table pane of the query Design window as shown in Figure 6.2.
3. Select the fields to be used, the criteria, and the sort parameters for the selected fields. The Table row ❶ shows the name of the table from which each field was inserted.

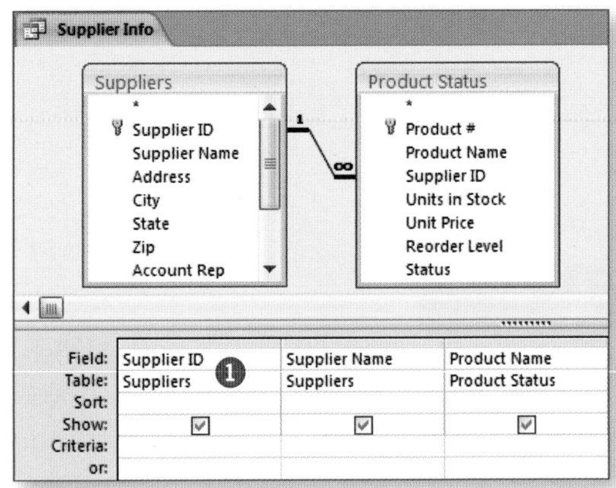

Figure 6.2 Multiple Table Query

DRILL 2 QUERY USING MULTIPLE TABLES

1. With *ac6-drill1* open, save the database as *ac6-drill2*.
2. Create a new query in Design view, and add the Suppliers and Product Status tables. Notice the join line between the Supplier ID field in each table.
3. Add the following fields to the query design grid: Supplier ID (from Suppliers table); Supplier Name (from Suppliers table); Product Name (from Product Status table); and Status (from Product Status table).
4. Add the criterion of Yes to the Status field. Deselect the Show box for Status. Sort the fields ascending by Supplier ID.
5. Run the query and then print it. Save the query as **Supplier Info**.
6. Close the query and the database.

Apply It

Database 10
Data Relationships

AC6-DB10-DATA

TIP

Notice there are two navigation bars in the form. Be sure to select New (blank) record at the bottom of the form to add a new team record in step 5. Use the navigation bar for the Employee table to add the new employees in step 7.

1. Open the data file *ac6-db10-data*. Save the database as *ac6-db10*.
2. Create a relationship between the Team ID fields of the Employee and Team tables. Enforce referential integrity.
3. Create a new form using the Team table. *Access* recognizes that the Employee table is related to the Team table and automatically displays the Employee table on the Team form.
4. Use the navigation buttons at the bottom of the form to display each team, noting that the members of the team are displayed in the Employees table.
5. Select New (blank) record and key the following data in the form for a new team: Team ID, **5**; Team Name, **Digital Imaging**; Team Leader, **Warner**.
6. Save the form as **Team Related**.
7. Use the Team Related form to add the following new employees:

Team 5:

470 | Warner | Sally | 3786 Fairview Avenue | Cincinnati | OH | 45219-3434 | 513-555-0132 | 04/30/1986 | Today's date

Apply It

Presentation 9
Self-Running Presentation

1. Open *pp7-drill2* and save it as *pp7-p9*.
2. Print a copy of the notes pages so that you can use them in rehearsing the presentation.
3. Set the presentation up as a self-running presentation without animation.
4. Rehearse the presentation and set the timings. Click Yes if you are comfortable with keeping the timings you set; if not, repeat the process.
5. Preview the presentation as a self-running presentation.
6. Resave the presentation as *pp7-p9* and close it.

Presentation 10
Presentation with Linked and Embedded Files, Hyperlink, and Action Button

COMMUNICATION TIME

On slide 6, the Communication Time *Excel* chart should be animated the same way as the clip art that you deleted (Wipe; From Bottom).

1. Open *pp4-drill1* and save it as *pp7-p10*.
2. Right-click slide 4 in the Slides tab, click Copy. Then click slide 5 and click Paste to paste the copied slide as slide 6. Hide slides 4 and 5.
3. Delete the clip art from the content area on the right side of slide 6, and link the *Excel* chart from the *communication time* data file.
4. Add a new slide 7 with Title and Content layout. Title: **Questions**. In the content area, embed the audio *Clap Cheers* from clip art. Choose to start When Clicked. Move the icon to the bottom center of the slide. Add a Home action button to return to the first slide.
5. Add the following notes on slide 7:

After all questions have been answered, thank the audience for their interest in the presentation and tell them that you applaud them for their attentiveness; then click the audio icon. Use the Home action button to return to the title slide.

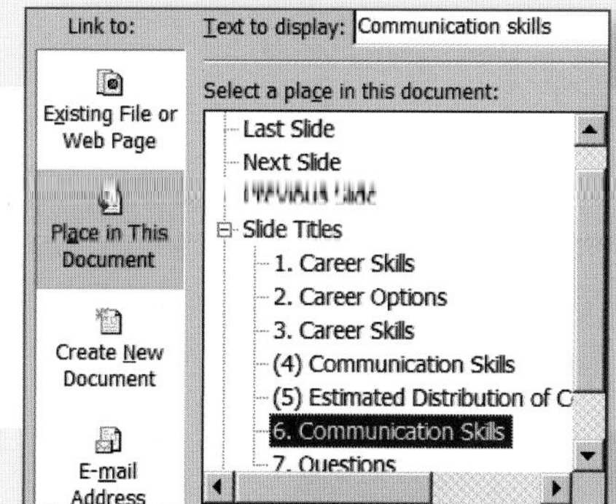

Figure 7.9 Hyperlink to Slide

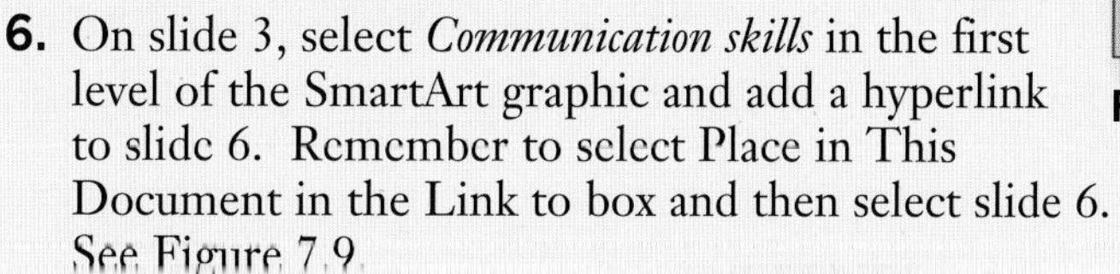

6. On slide 3, select *Communication skills* in the first level of the SmartArt graphic and add a hyperlink to slide 6. Remember to select Place in This Document in the Link to box and then select slide 6. See Figure 7.9.
7. Add the following to the notes on slide 3:

Review the entire graphic; then click the hyperlink to go to slide 6.

8. Resave as *pp7-p10* and close.

The join line between the tables is marked with special symbols. A 1 indicates a field is on the *one* side of the relationship. An infinity sign (∞) indicates that the field is on the *many* side of the relationship.

3. Select the table for which you want to create a relationship; then click the Add button. Repeat this step until each table you want to create relationships between appears in the Relationships window. Then close the Show Table dialog box.
4. If necessary, size the field lists so that all field names are visible.
5. Select the shared field in the table in which the field serves as the primary key, preceded with a key. Drag the field (a small field box appears), and drop it on the shared field in the other table. The Edit Relationships dialog box opens (Figure 6.1).
6. Select the Enforce Referential Integrity checkbox. Notice that the relationship type is now One-To-Many.
7. Click Create to establish the relationship. Close the Relationships window, saving changes when prompted.

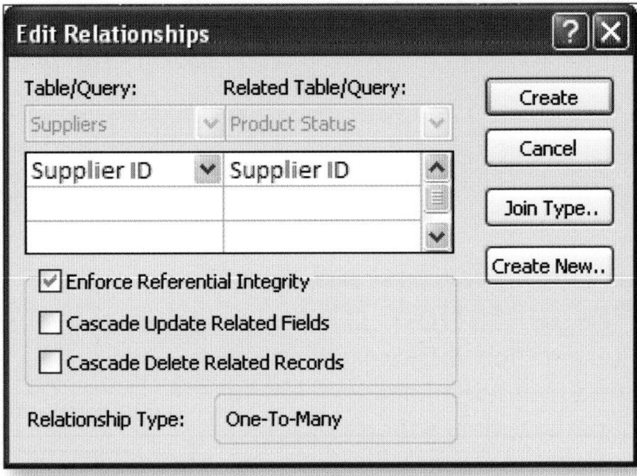

Figure 6.1 Edit Relationships Dialog Box

DRILL 1 SET TABLE RELATIONSHIP

AC6-DRILL1-DATA

1. Open the data file *ac6-drill1-data*. Save the database as *ac6-drill1*.
2. Create a relationship between the Supplier ID fields of the Suppliers and Product Status tables. Enforce referential integrity.
3. Enter the following information as a new record in the Product Status table using the Product Status form.

Product #	Product Name	Supplier ID	Units in Stock	Unit Price	Reorder Level	Status
401	TruePod MP3 Player	6	100	$149.99	50	✓

4. Notice the error message that appears when you complete the record, indicating that there is no Supplier ID of 6 in the Suppliers table.
5. Click OK and edit the Supplier ID of the new record to 5. Close the Product Status form, and leave the database open for the next drill.

CREATE AN OBJECT USING RELATED TABLES

Once you have created a relationship between tables in a database, you can create objects that draw data from all related tables. For example, you can create a single form that shows related tables so that you can enter records for both the *one* and the *many* tables. A common business example is keying data into a sales transaction form created from two tables: Data unique to the sale is entered in an Invoice table, and the items sold are entered in a Parts Sold table.

You can also create queries that display data from fields in related tables. When you add related tables to a query, a join line automatically appears between the two occurrences of the shared field in the two tables. For automatic joining to occur, the field shared by the two tables must be the primary key in one of the tables and the fields must have the same name.

project 4

The Leadership Group: Integrating PowerPoint and Word

OBJECTIVES

- Create effective *PowerPoint* presentations
- Prepare effective *Word* documents
- Work with very limited supervision

SETTING

In this project, you are employed by The Leadership Group (TLG). At the Spring Retreat of The Leadership Group, group leaders made several presentations. During informal sessions, several self-running presentations were available for individuals to view based on their particular interests. The Executive Committee was impressed with the quality of both the speaker-delivered and the self-running presentations. The Executive Committee decided that all managers could benefit from learning more about effective presentations. The Executive Committee asked your team members to develop a seminar and a white paper as a handout on effective presentations that featured both speaker-delivered and self-running presentations. Remember to use the custom TLG theme colors and the *PowerPoint* template that you developed in Lesson 5 for Presentation 6 (*pp5-p6*).

The Leadership Group refers to reports on general topics as *white papers*. A white paper is an in-depth report on a topic of interest. The team decided to prepare the white paper first and then use the information in developing the *PowerPoint* presentation. Some of the handout has been drafted, and you will use it to complete the white paper.

TIP

When you insert the table of contents, remember to use a Next page section break and to break the link between sections for both the header and the footer. Reset the number of the first page of the white paper to 1. Note that items with Title style will not be listed in the table of contents.

Jobs

1. Report with Cover page
2. *PowerPoint* presentation with notes and handouts
3. Self-running *PowerPoint* presentation

TLG STANDARD GUIDES FOR WHITE PAPERS

1. Apply TLG custom theme colors. Position the title at approximately 2" and apply Title style. Use Heading 1, 2, and 3 styles for first-, second-, and third-level headings.
2. Add a Gold, Text 2, 25% Darker page border to all pages.
3. Use Medium Shading 2 – Accent 4 design for tables.
4. Insert a table of contents if the paper is five or more pages long. Do not number it unless you have several preliminary pages.
5. Insert a Transcend (Odd Page) footer; add the company name and a vertical bar before the page number. Apply White text color to the name.

   The Leadership Group | 2

6. Set up a folder named PP-WD Project 4 and save all project files in it. Name all solution files *p4-j* (plus the job number, *j1*, *j2*, etc.).

LESSON 6

Create Table Relationships

OBJECTIVES

- Create table relationships
- Enforce referential integrity
- Create a query using related tables

TABLE RELATIONSHIPS

One of the advantages of using a relational database such as *Access* is its capability to use several tables with related information and to pull that information together through the use of related fields. By managing data in a relational way, data redundancy is avoided, thereby reducing the risk of errors and minimizing the size of the database.

As you create tables and fields within each table, identify and include fields that can potentially link two or more tables. Each table must have at least one shared field in its table structure. The shared field is usually the primary key for one of the tables. In the second table, the shared field is referred to as the foreign key. The joined fields must have the same data type.

The relationship is called a *one-to-many* because *Access* can match each record of one table to many records of another table. Think of a database that contains a Customers table and an Orders table. A unique customer number (primary key) identifies each customer. Each customer can place any number of orders for products. Therefore, *Access* can match each record (one) in the Customers table to an infinite number of records (many) in the Orders table.

ENFORCE REFERENTIAL INTEGRITY

TIP

Databases that contain related tables need to guarantee data integrity. Methods to guarantee data integrity include limiting field size to control the amount of data entered into a field and use of input masks to ensure correct formats for dates, postal codes, and phone numbers.

Referential integrity is a set of rules that *Access* uses to ensure that relationships between records in related tables are valid. For example, suppose a user tried to enter an employee number in the Team table (many) that was not in the Employee (one) table. Referential integrity would prevent the user from entering any employee number that was not already in the Employee table. If you update or delete a record in the Employee table, all associated records are also updated or deleted in the Team table. Using referential integrity as a strategy to enforce data validity means that you must enter the data into your tables in a particular order. Enforcing referential integrity also prevents orphan (unmatched) records in the many table.

CREATE TABLE RELATIONSHIPS

The ideal database is made up of simple tables that hold subsets of the complete data. Establishing relationships between the tables using common fields enables you to integrate the information with your queries, forms, and reports. Relationships are created in the Relationships window.

To Create a Relationship

Database Tools/Relationships/Relationships

1. Click Relationships.
2. In the Relationships window, the Show Table dialog box displays a list of the tables in your database.

Job 1

Report

EFFECTIVE PRESENTATIONS
VISUALS
TLG COVER PAGE

1. Open *effective presentations* and save it as *p4-j1*. Format the white paper using the standard TLG guides on the previous page.
2. Begin making all changes noted in the comments of the open file. When you get to the comment that instructs you where to position insertion #1, key the following text. All headings in insertion #1 are second-level headings.

   Slide Text

   Speakers usually limit text on slides to a few key words or phrases. The speaker then uses complete sentences to elaborate on the points listed on the slide. This technique helps to avoid the appearance of a speaker reading from the slide. Self-running presentations must ensure that the text itself conveys a clear message. An alternative is to record voice narration.

   Graphics

   Graphics help speakers to explain and illustrate concepts. The speaker amplifies the points made in the graphic representation and specifies the significant aspects of the graphic. Self-running presentations require that each graphic conveys the message intended clearly without interpretation or amplification. Presentations with heavy graphics often consist of large files that may present a variety of technical problems for viewers of the presentation.

   Audio

   Sound often competes with speakers and distracts the audience. Therefore speakers tend to use sound to add variety and interest—particularly in the introduction and at the end of the presentation—and to limit the types and quantity of sound used. Often speakers use background music as an introduction or at the end of the presentation. Rarely do they record sound for a live presentation. Sound does not compete with self-running presentations and can be used effectively to call attention to particular points made in the presentation. The message can be recorded and voice narration provided; however, Audio requires extensive memory and adds substantial volume to the file size.

   Notes and Handouts

   Speaker notes often consist of brief reminders of points to make about the content of the slide or of additional information to present while the slide is being displayed. Notes may be in very rough form because only the speaker sees them. Presentations published on a website may display notes as well. If so, the notes must be in final form and must convey the intended message or additional information clearly.

   Speakers often provide the audience with copies of the slides for future reference. Generally, handouts are provided at the end of the presentation so the audience does not read them during the presentation. Handouts tend not to be provided for self-running presentations.

3. When you get to the comments that indicate the position of insertion #2, key the tables shown on the next page.

Check your report with Figure 5.12.

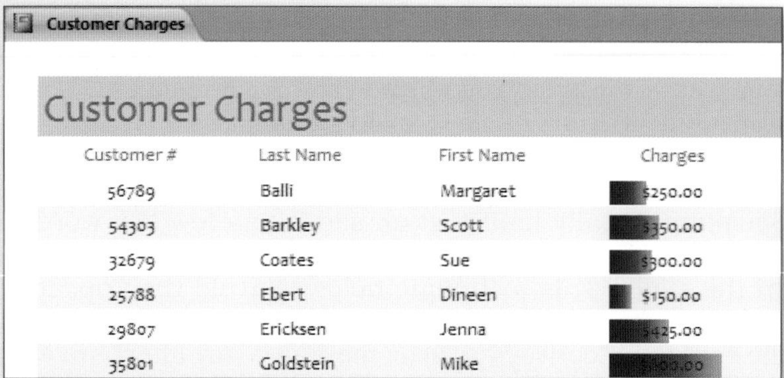

Figure 5.12 Customer Charges Report Format

Database 9
Labels

1. With *ac5-db8* open, save the database as *ac5-db9*. Create labels for the data in the Customers table: Select the Avery C2160 address label, and use a font size of 10.
2. Set up the label to show First Name, Last Name, Address, City, State, and ZIP with standard spacing and punctuation.
3. Sort the labels by ZIP, then Last Name, and then First Name.
4. Leave the default label name, Labels Customers.
5. Print and close the Labels Customers report, and close the database.

Format both tables so that information in a cell does not wrap to a second line. Check the standard guides and the comments in the data file for table formatting information.

Decision Factor	Select More Formal Style	Select Less Formal Style
Stakes or importance	High	Low
Audience disposition	Hostile	Friendly
Complexity	Complex	Simple
Audience size	Large	Small
Audience rank/status	High	Low
Repeat presentations	Likely	One time
Organization norms	Traditional	Casual

Reconciling Factors	Decision Criteria
High stakes vs. small group	Importance overrides size
Repeat performance vs. informal norms	Repeat performance because of consistency
Large audience vs. friendly audience	Large size requires careful structure
Small audience vs. **hostile audience**	Hostility overrides small size
Formal norms vs. low stakes	Use midrange between formal and informal

4. After you have carefully proofread the document and checked all comments to ensure that you have followed all directions, delete all comments in the document.
5. Check to make sure you have followed all of the TLG guides for formatting white papers.
6. Create the table of contents and use the Insert File command to insert the TLG cover page at the beginning of the document. Complete the cover page as follows:

   Select today's date.

   Title: Effective Presentations

   Subtitle: Speaker-Delivered and Self-Running Presentations
7. Print the white paper; you will need it to prepare the *PowerPoint* presentation.
8. Save as *p4-j1* and close.

Job 2
Presentation

Create a new presentation that you and your team members will present for company managers at the Effective Presentations Seminar. Read the white paper you prepared in Job 1 carefully, as you will use it as you prepare the presentation. Use the TLG custom template you prepared in Lesson 5. As you prepare each slide, compose at least two sentences of notes to help you present the information on that slide. Use the white paper as a reference for your notes. Save the presentation as *p4-j2*.

4. Select the specific label product number, and click Next.
5. The next screen lets you select the font, size, text color, and other options. Make any desired changes, and click Next.
6. Choose the fields to include from the Available fields list ❷. Click the Add ❸ button to move the field to the Prototype label ❹ (Figure 5.10).

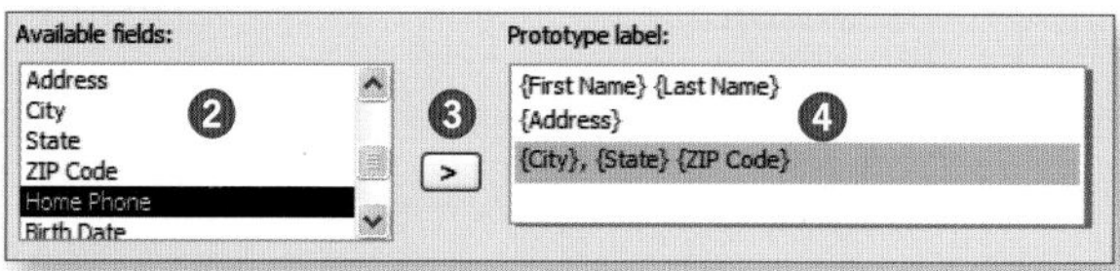

Figure 5.10 Add Fields in Label Wizard

7. Continue adding fields to complete the prototype label. Tap the Space Bar to add spaces between field names or ENTER to make a new line. Key necessary characters such as commas in their appropriate locations. Click Next to continue.
8. Indicate the Sort field(s), and click Next.
9. Key a name for your label report (or use the default name supplied). Click Finish.
10. The report is displayed in Print Preview. To make changes to the report, click Close Print Preview and change to Layout view.

DRILL 2 LABELS

1. With *ac5-drill1* open, save the database as *ac5-drill2*.
2. Create mailing labels using data in the Employee table: Select the Avery J8560 address label; change font size to 11, leaving the remaining default font attributes.
3. Set up your label as shown in Figure 5.11, including spaces and punctuation as indicated. Sort by ZIP Code, then by Last Name, and then by First Name.
4. Accept the default label name, Labels Employee.
5. Print the labels, close the report, and close the database.

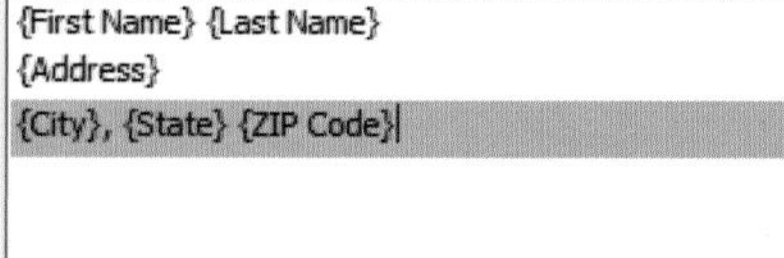

Figure 5.11 Prototype Label

Apply It

Database 8
Create and Modify a Report

AC5-DB8-DATA

1. Open the data file *ac5-db8-data*. Save as *ac5-db8*.
2. Use the Report Wizard to create the report shown in Figure 5.12 based on the Customer Charges query. Do not group; sort by Last Name and then by First Name (both ascending). Use the Tabular layout and Portrait orientation.
3. Name the report **Customer Charges**. Preview each page of the report.
4. Modify the Customer Charges report layout: Apply the Waveform theme. Move the Customer # field to the left of the Last Name field. Change the font size of all labels and text boxes to 10 point. Center the Customer # and Charges text boxes and labels. Apply conditional formatting to the Charges field. Choose to compare to other records and accept the default bar color. Change text box widths to achieve the spacing in Figure 5.12.
5. Print and close the report, saving the changes. Keep the *ac5-db8* database open for the next exercise.

General Guides

1. Apply Fade Smoothly transition to all slides. Start all animations on slide click for 2:00 duration. Animate only the content areas indicated; do not animate titles.
2. Use the white paper as your reference and key at least two sentences of notes for each slide. For example, on the first slide your notes might be: *Thank you for coming to today's seminar. At the end of the presentation, you will be given a white paper with additional information.*
3. Preview and proofread each slide and notes page carefully. Check to see that notes have been keyed on each slide. Compress pictures.
4. Print handouts four to a page and use landscape orientation. Print notes pages.
5. Resave as *p4-j2* and close.

Remember to compress pictures and media.

Slide 1 (Title Slide)

Title: Effective Presentations

Subtitle: Speaker-Delivered and Self-Running Presentations

Animation: None

SPEAKER
SLIDE STAR

Slide 2 (Comparison)

Title: Who Is the Star?

Left title: Speaker-Delivered Presentation | Content: Insert the *speaker* data file.

Right title: Self-Running Presentation | Content: Insert the *slide star* data file.

Animation: Left content: Fade | Right content: Fade

Picture Tools/Format/Adjust

1. Click Compress Pictures.
2. Click OK.

Slide 3 (Title and Content)

Title: Role of the Audience

Content: Use the Process List SmartArt graphic. Add an additional shape below the last shape on each side and key the following information:

Press SHIFT + ENTER to move to the next line in a shape without the 10 points after the paragraph spacing.

Passive Model	Interactive Model
Speaker gives presentation Audience listens	Speaker gives brief opening Audience listens
Questions Answers	Speaker solicits input Audience offers input
Follow up	Speaker summarizes Audience provides feedback

Animation: Fade, By Level at Once

The first clip art can be inserted by clicking the clip art icon; the second can be inserted by deselecting the first clip on the slide and using the open Clip Art task pane to search for the next clip.

Slide 4 (Comparison)

Title: Select Type of Presentation

Left side heading: Objectives | Right side heading: Cost (Figure P4.1)

Left content—bulleted text: What is the feasibility of accomplishing objectives? | What best meets the needs of the audience?

Right content—clip art: use keywords *time* and *money*; size about 1.5" high.

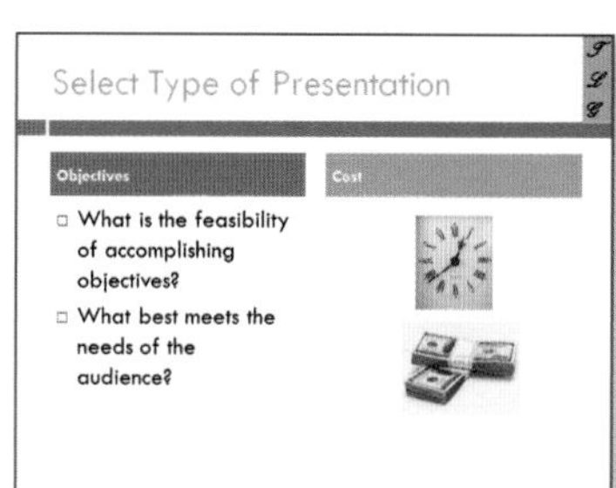

Figure P4.1 Slide 4 Illustration

To Apply Conditional Formatting:

Report Layout Tools Format/Control Formatting/Conditional Formatting

1. Click on any of the text boxes for a field.
2. Click on Conditional Formatting and click the New Rule button.
3. In the Select a rule type box, select Compare to other records.
4. Select the desired bar color and click OK twice.

DRILL 1 REPORT WIZARD

AC5-DRILL1-DATA

1. Open the data file *ac5-drill1-data*. Save the database as *ac5-drill1*.
2. Use the Report Wizard to create the report in Figure 5.8 using all fields from the Seniority List query. Group the report by Team, sort by Hire Date in descending order, use the Stepped layout and Portrait orientation, name the report **Seniority List**, and apply the Angles theme.
3. The spacing of the columns could be more attractive. Change to Layout view and center the Team ID, Team Name, Hire Date, and Employee ID labels and text boxes. Increase the size of all labels to 12 point. Boldface the Team ID label. Increase the Team ID and Team Name text boxes to 14 point. Change text box widths to achieve the spacing in Figure 5.8.
4. Save, print, and close the report, and leave the database open for the next drill.

Check your report with Figure 5.8.

Seniority List

Seniority List

Team ID	Team Name	Hire Date	Employee ID	First Name	Last Name
1	Solutions				
		3/26/2008	505	Shannon	Hayes
		12/3/2001	209	Michael	Richardson
		6/9/1998	657	Jacob	Smith
2	MP3s				
		1/12/2010	437	Chinh	Pham
		6/19/2001	339	Michelle	Rowe
		5/20/2000	465	Than	Nguyen

Figure 5.8 Seniority List Report

CREATE MAILING LABELS

Labels can be created easily in *Access* using a labels report. *Access* provides a Label Wizard to guide you through this process.

Report Wizard
Labels ❶
Report Report Design Blank Report
Reports

Figure 5.9 Label Wizard

To Use the Label Wizard:

Create/Reports/Labels

1. In an open database, select the table or query in the Navigation Pane that contains the data to be used for the labels.
2. Click Labels ❶ (Figure 5.9). The Label Wizard opens.
3. Change the Unit of Measure if necessary, and select the label brand in the Filter by manufacturer box.

Animation: Left content: Fade, By Paragraph | Right content: clock—Fade; money—Fade

Slide 5 (Two Horizontal Content)

Title: Formality—A Delicate Balance

Top content: (Figure P4.2) Line with double-headed arrow; weight 1 point. Shape text: Very Informal | Very Formal

Insert scales similar to the illustration and position below the line.

Bottom content—bulleted text: Informality encourages audience participation | Formality enhances audience control

Animation: None

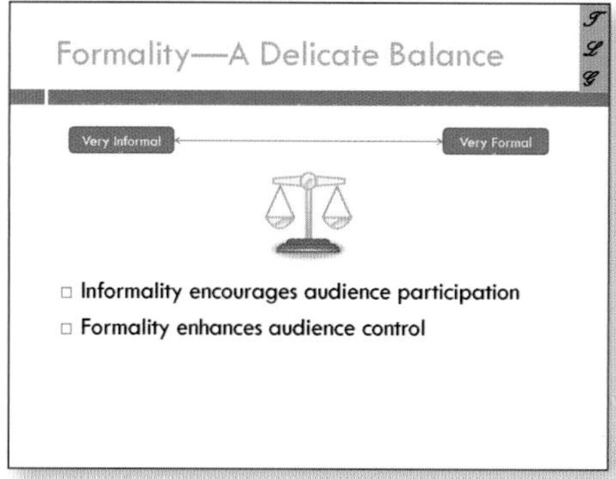

Figure P4.2 Slide 5 Illustration

Slide 6 (Title and Content)

Title: Level of Formality

Content: Insert a three-column, eight-row table; increase height of all rows to .5" and align all text at the left. Key the Decision Factor table from page 3 of the white paper.

Animation: Fade

Slide 7 (Title and Content)

Title: Prepare the Contents

Content: SmartArt Basic Chevron Process List. Text: Opening | Body | Closing

Animation: Fade, One by One

Slide 8 (Title and Content)

Title: Opening

Content—bulleted text: Use the opening to: | Convey the purpose of the presentation | Set a positive tone | Get audience's attention | Get audience involved | Build credibility | Establish rapport (Remove bullet from first item.)

Animation: Fade, By Paragraph

Slide 9 (Title and Content)

Title: Body

Content—bulleted text: Present information dynamically | Provide essential information—but not excessive details | Use illustrations and anecdotes effectively | Use effective visuals

Convert bulleted text to Target List Smart Art graphic.

Animation: Fade, One by One

Home/Views

The Views group is also available on the Home tab.

MODIFY A REPORT DESIGN

As with *Access* forms, you can modify the layout of an existing report design to customize it to your needs. *Access* offers you two methods to modify the report design—Layout view and Design view. Design view gives you the most control over layout of labels and text boxes. Layout view lets you make changes while still viewing the data. This view is typically easier for making minor design changes.

To Modify Report Design:

Report Design Tools Design

1. In the Print Preview tab, click Close Print Preview. The report displays in Design view.
2. On the Report Design Tools Design tab, select View to switch to the Layout view.
3. Click the Themes button to display the themes gallery and select a theme. A report created using the Newsprint theme is shown in Layout view in Figure 5.6.

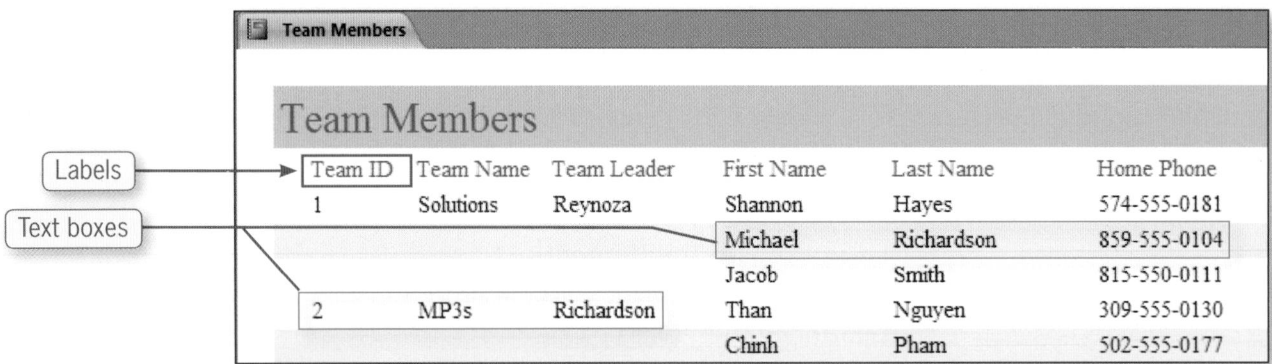

Figure 5.6 Report Using Newsprint Theme

Like form Layout view, report Layout view displays a series of labels and text boxes. You can change label text and apply new formats to both labels and text boxes. Change font formats or text alignment to improve the appearance of the report. Apply conditional formatting to a report field to supply a graphic means of comparing data.

To Modify a Label:

1. Click on the label.
2. Change the characters in the label using standard editing tools.
3. Use the tools on the Report Layout Tools Format tab in the Font group to change the appearance of the label (e.g., center, bold, italic, or color).

Report Layout Tools Format/Font

You can select the font type and color; apply bold, italic, or underline style to characters; change the alignment; and select a shading. These tools are also available on the Home tab.

To Modify a Text Box:

1. Click on any of the text boxes for a field. All the text boxes in that column will be highlighted (Figure 5.7), indicating any changes made to one text box will affect all text boxes in the column.
2. Use the tools on the Report Layout Tools Format tab in the Font group to change the appearance of the characters (e.g., center, bold, italic, or color).
3. To change the size of each text box, position the size handle anywhere on the right or left border. Click and drag the line to adjust the width of the text boxes.

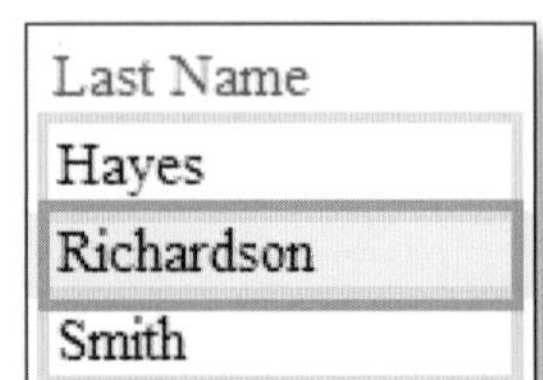

Figure 5.7 Format Text Boxes

MOSQUE
HUMOR

TIP

To animate the picture and the text box in each area to Fade at the same time, click the picture, press CTRL, and click the text box. Then apply the animation.

Figure P4.3 Original Clip Art

TIP

Adjust clip art to complement a slide. For example:

To recolor:
Picture Tools Format/Adjust/Color/and select desired color.

To Flip Horizontal:
Picture Tools Format/Arrange/Rotate/Flip Horizontal.

DISCOVER

Home/Paragraph/Numbering

1. Click content area; then Numbering down arrow, and click Bullets and Numbering.
2. In the Start at box, use the up arrow to begin at 6.

Slide 10 (Comparison)

Title: Visuals

Left heading: Pictures Enhance Descriptions | Right heading: Add Humor with Visuals

Content: Left: Insert the *mosque* data file picture | Right: Insert the *humor* data file picture | Use Picture Tools Format to size each picture about 2.9" high. From Shapes, draw a text box under each picture and key the following text:

Left: How many words would it take to describe this architecture? | Right: The secret of giving good presentations is to stay calm and cool on top and paddle like heck underneath. | Bold the text and decrease font size to 16 point.

Animation: Left content: Fade; then select text and click Fade As One Object | Right content: Same as left

Slide 11 (Title and Content)

Title: Closing

Content: Clip art: hook; add Line Callout 1 from Shapes; key the following text: Use the closing as the last chance to achieve your objectives. Think of it as a hook—keep the audience on the line. | Format: apply bold; increase font to 20 point.

Animation: None

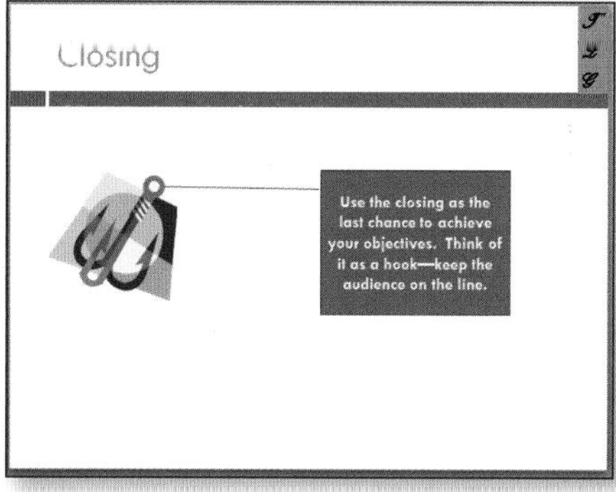

Figure P4.4 Slide 11 Illustration

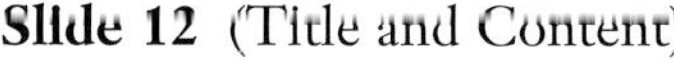

Slide 12 (Title and Content)

Title: Deliver a Dynamic Presentation

Content—numbered text: 1. Engage the audience and establish rapport | 2. Use body language effectively | 3. Pace the presentation appropriately | 4. Use your voice effectively | 5. Use smooth transitions

Animation: Fade, By Paragraph

Slide 13 (Title and Content)

Title: Deliver a Dynamic Presentation

Content—numbered text: 6. Use an energetic style | 7. Use humor appropriately | 8. Use visuals to support you | 9. Avoid vocal noise (uh, uh, you know) | 10. Facilitate discussion effectively

Animation: Fade, By Paragraph

Slide 14 (Title and Content)

Title: Self-Running Presentations

Content—bulleted text: Set up the self-running presentation | Avoid the use of animation | Add hyperlinks and action buttons to facilitate navigation | Rehearse to set the pace of the slides appropriately | Start the presentation

Animation: Fade, By Paragraph

The Report Wizard shows you where each of the fields will be presented on the report.

A grouping window like the one in Figure 5.3 appears if you use a query that has fields from two tables.

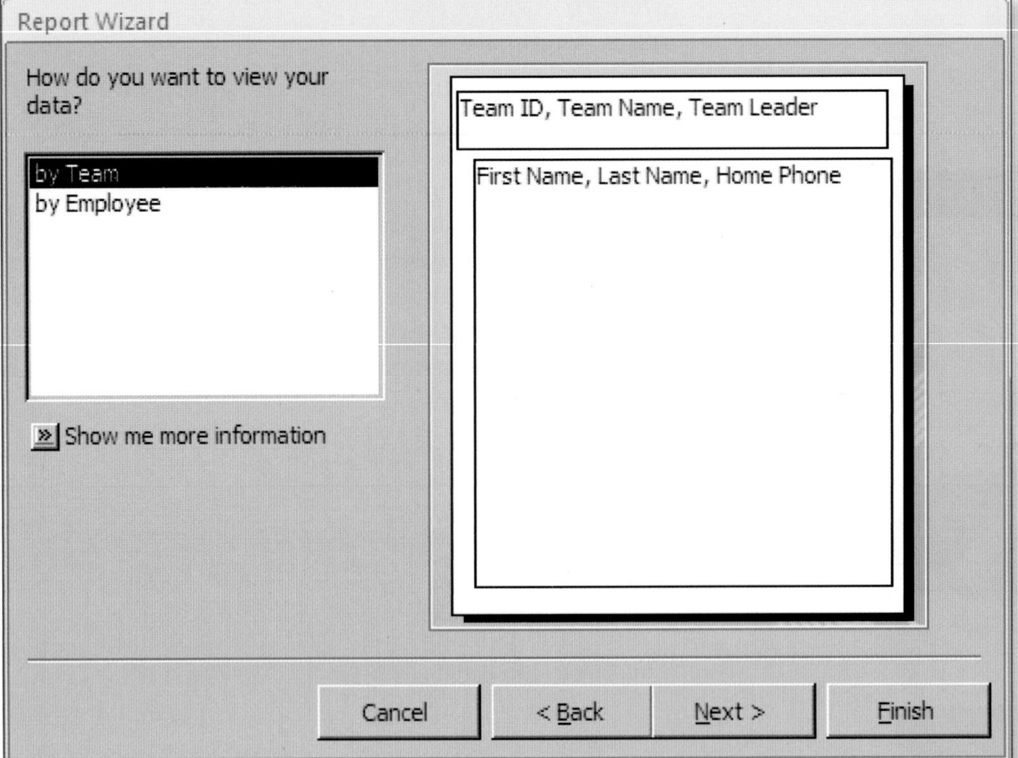

Figure 5.3 Grouping Options

5. The next screen allows you to select additional grouping levels. Select the field and click the Add button. Click Next to continue.
6. Click the level 1 Sort box ❶ (Figure 5.4) to select the field used to sort your data within each group. Click the Ascending button to change the sort to descending order. You can sort by up to four levels. Choose other Sort boxes to select additional sort levels. Click the Next button to continue.

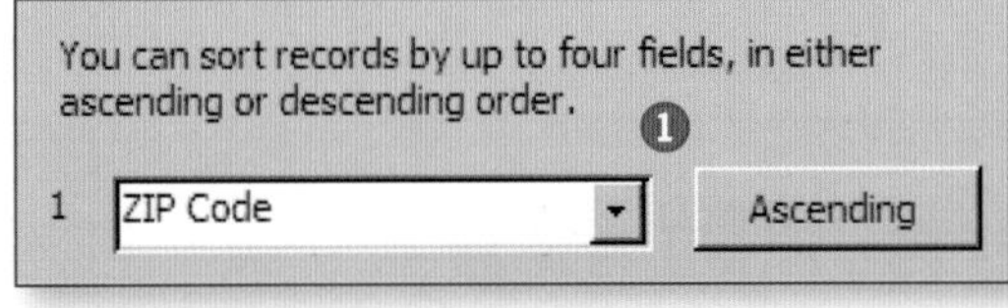

Figure 5.4 Sorting Options

The layout screen of the Wizard has an option to fit all fields on the page. Select this option if it is not already selected to make sure your report shows all fields on one page.

7. Click each layout option (Figure 5.5) to see a preview. Select the layout ❷ and paper orientation ❸ for your report, and then click Next.
8. Key an appropriate name for your report and click Finish. The new report appears in Print Preview, and the report is listed in the Navigation Pane.

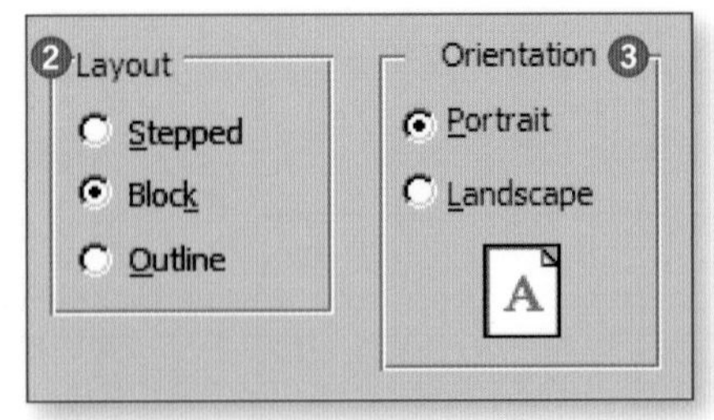

Figure 5.5 Layout and Orientation Options

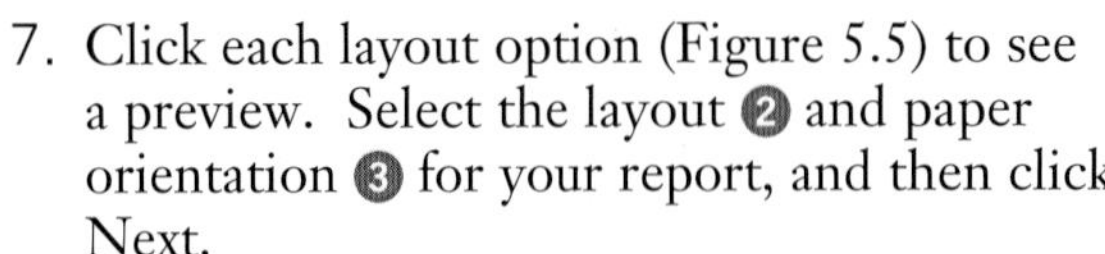

Access reports are designed to be printed. The Print Preview tab contains a variety of tools you can use to adjust the report printout. If you are not quite satisfied with the appearance of the report, you can modify it.

Slide 15 (Title only)

Title: Effective Presentations

Content:

1. From Shapes, draw a Rounded Rectangle about 2" high and 8"wide; add text: **Thank you for being a great audience!**
2. Add a hyperlink from the slide 15 title to the Effective Presentations document that you prepared in *p4-j1*; add a Home action button on the bottom of the last slide.
3. Insert *Clap Cheers* audio from clip art below the title; start the sound automatically; and hide the icon during the slide show.

Animation: None

Use Quick Check below to check presentation. Resave presentation as *p4-j2*. Leave open.

QUICK ✓ Check the 15 slides.

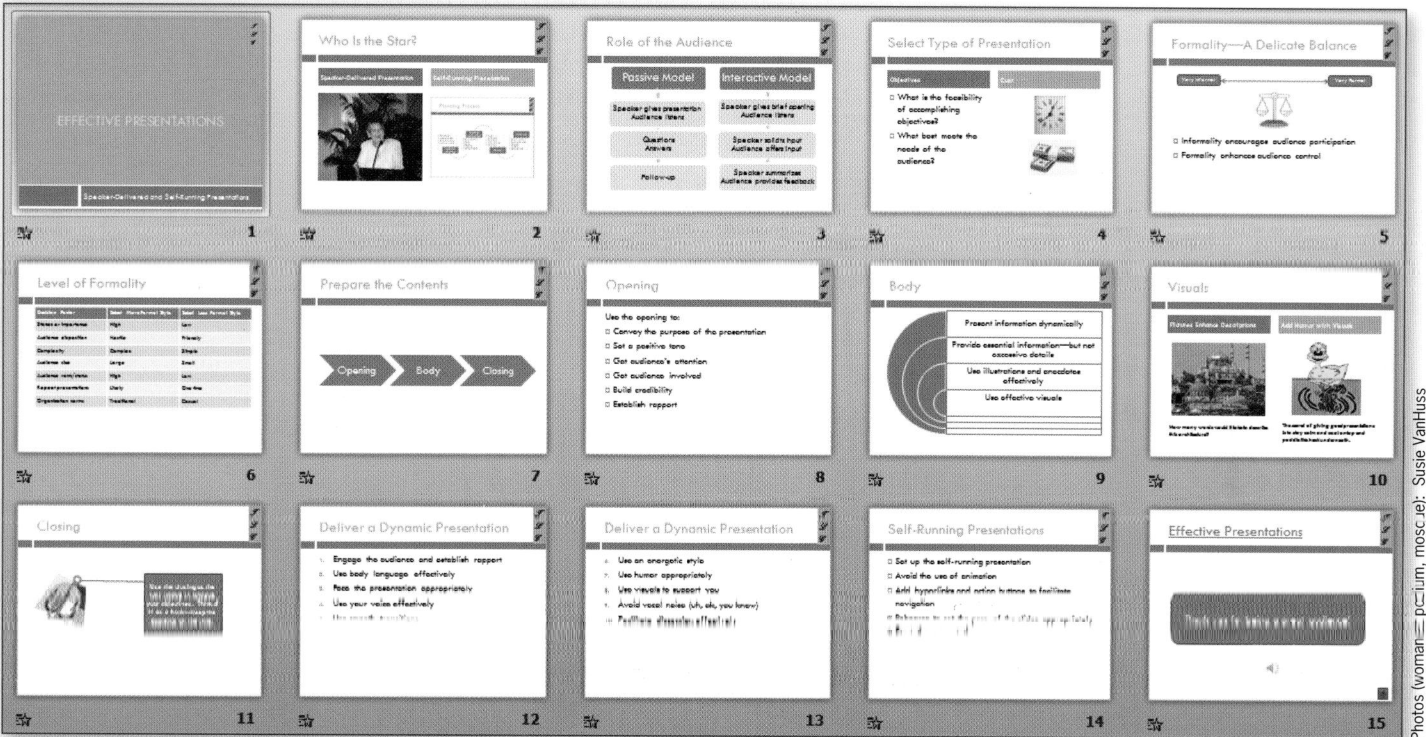

Figure P4.5 Quick Check

Job 3

Self-Running Presentation

1. Save open presentation as *p4-j3*.
2. Set up a self-running presentation; rehearse the presentation; and use your judgment to set appropriate timings. Preview the presentation.
3. Resave as *p4-j3* and close.

LESSON 5

Create Simple Reports

OBJECTIVES

- Use the Report Wizard
- Modify a report design
- Create mailing labels

USE THE REPORT WIZARD

Access provides many tools for creating reports. Reports are designed to summarize information from tables or queries in an attractive printed format that is easy to read.

Several methods exist for creating a report. This lesson focuses on the Report Wizard to create tabular reports or mailing labels. The Report Wizard asks you a series of questions and then creates a report based on your answers. You can use data in a table or a query to create a report.

To Use the Report Wizard to Create a Report:

Create/Reports/Report Wizard

1. In an open database, click Report Wizard ❶ (Figure 5.1). The Report Wizard (Figure 5.2) opens.

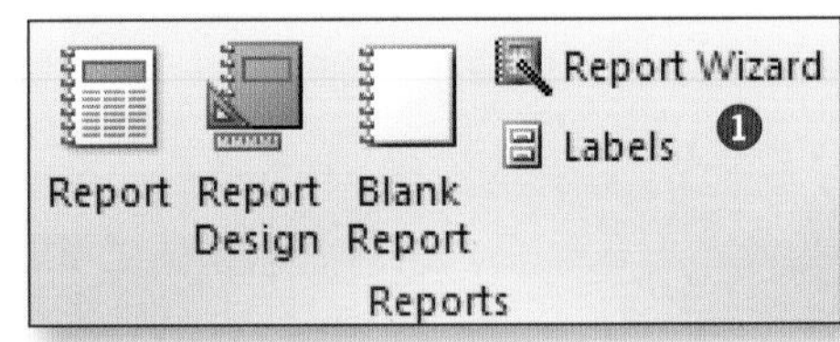

Figure 5.1 Reports Group

If you change your mind during the Wizard, click the Back button to return to the previous step.

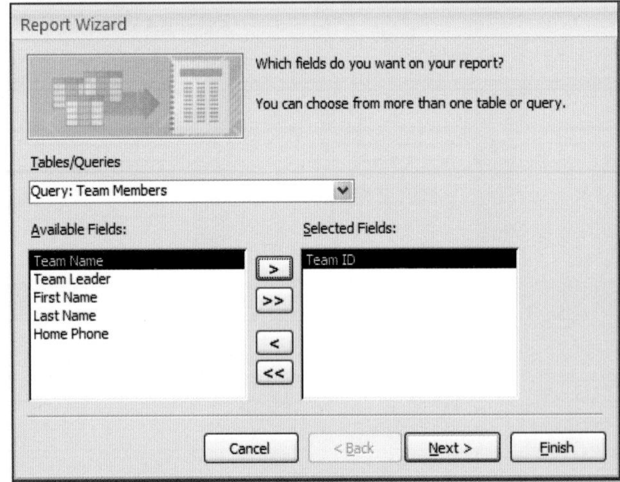

Figure 5.2 Report Wizard

Click the Add All Fields button to include all the available fields in the report.

2. From the Tables/Queries drop-down list, select a table or query.
3. Select the field(s) you want to include in the report from the Available Fields box and click the Add button. Repeat the process until all the fields you want to include in the report appear in the Selected Fields list, and then click Next.
4. The next screen allows you to select how you want the report grouped. Figure 5.3 shows a grouping of employees by Team. Select the desired grouping and click Next.

module 3

SPREADSHEETS WITH EXCEL

overview

Excel is a powerful software application that provides its users the tools they need to manage, present, and analyze numeric information. You may be familiar with some of the basic functions of *Excel*. If so, you will be able to work through the lessons quickly. However, this module assumes that you have had very little or no formal instruction in using *Excel*.

In this module, you will learn to create a wide variety of worksheet content by entering text, values, formulas, and functions. You will learn to format worksheets using many *Excel* formats as well as the *Word* formats you already know. In the Beyond the Essentials lessons, you will learn to create and modify charts, sort and filter worksheet data, create PivotTables, and combine data in more than one worksheet.

ESSENTIALS

1. Create Worksheets
2. Edit Worksheets
3. Insert Formulas and Functions
4. Print Worksheets
Project 5—The Bookstore, Inc.: Integrating Excel and Word

BEYOND THE ESSENTIALS

5. Create and Modify Charts
6. Sort and Filter
7. Create PivotTables
8. Insert 3-D Cell References
Project 6—The Bookstore, Inc.: Integrating Excel, Word, and PowerPoint

Job 4

Business Cards

DONOVAN BUSINESS CARDS

Create business cards for the three new agents hired in Job 3.

1. Open the *Publisher* data file *donovan business cards*.
2. Edit Mark Donovan's business card for Michelle Cox: Change the name, change the title to **Agent**, and change the e-mail address to **mcox@mcdonrealty.com**. Save the card as *p8-j4a*. Follow the same procedure to create cards for Felix Santos and Hannah Cato, using the same title (Agent) and the following e-mail addresses: **fsantos@mcdonrealty.com** and **hcato@mcdonrealty.com**. Save as *p8-j4b* and *p8-j4c*.

Job 5

Memo with Access Query

M&D MEMO

Prepare a memo for Carol McMullan to all agents requesting a meeting to discuss marketing ideas for the three longest-listed unsold M&D properties. You first must create an *Access* query, copy the results, and then paste in the appropriate location in the memo.

1. Save the *p8-j3* database as *p8-j5a*. Create an *Access* query that includes the Property Number, Street Address, City, Listing Price, Date Listed, and Sales Date.
   a. In the Sales Date field, key **Is Null** as the criteria and hide the field. Sort by Date Listed (ascending).
   b. Run the query and then save it as **Oldest Listings**. Copy the records of the three oldest listings.
2. Open the *Word* data file *m&d memo* and save as a *Word* document named *p8-j5b*. Key the memo heading information, using a date of August 19, 2012. Key the memo shown below. Paste the query results where indicated below, using the Merge Formatting paste option. Apply the Light Shading – Accent 1 table style, and adjust formats to display the table data attractively.

The three properties shown below are our oldest unsold listings. As you know, our next staff meeting is scheduled one week from today. One of the main topics on the agenda is a discussion of what we can do to make these three properties more salable.

[Paste the Oldest Listing query data here]

Each of you is being asked to visit the three properties and examine them carefully to determine the following:

- What barriers or obstacles might exist to sales?
- What might be done to improve the curb appeal?
- What investments in upgrading the property could be justified and might improve the odds of selling it soon?
- Is the home priced appropriately based on your evaluation of it and the comparables available in the files for each property?

Also please consider ideas we might use to market these properties more effectively. To provide incentive to work on these three properties, M&D will change the commission split on the three properties to 1 percent for the agency and 2 percent for the selling agent.

After the meeting, the listing agent and I will meet with the property owners to discuss options we believe will help sell these properties in the near future.

xx

LESSON 1

Create Worksheets

OBJECTIVES

- Create a worksheet
- Change column width
- Add and rename sheet tabs
- Move within a worksheet
- Select cells

OVERVIEW

When you launch *Excel*, a new blank workbook opens. This workbook contains three worksheets by default; however, worksheets can be added. A worksheet organizes information in rows and columns and is used to crunch numbers and perform automatic calculations. By compiling related worksheets in one *Excel* workbook, the user can manage data more effectively. Additionally, to display the data pictorially, users can create a wide variety of charts. Businesses use the organized data to visualize, understand, and predict data patterns. If data changes, *Excel* automatically recalculates and updates the worksheet data and any charts that have been created.

Worksheets are valuable and time-saving whether you are a business owner, manager, teacher, or student. Worksheets are useful when data is organized in rows and columns, when calculations are needed, and when changes may affect those calculations. In this module, you will create a wide variety of worksheets as you complete the drills and applications.

GETTING STARTED

You can launch *Excel* in the same way that you launch *Word*. Click the *Excel* icon on your desktop, or click the Start button, then click All Programs, and select *Microsoft Office Excel 2010*. The opening screen consists of a ribbon that is very similar to the Ribbon you used in *Word* and *PowerPoint* and a workspace that you will use to create worksheets. Note in Figure 1.1 below how similar the *Excel* Home tab is to the *Word* Home tab. The Clipboard and Font groups are identical. The File menu and the Quick Access Toolbar are also identical. You will be expected to apply these basic commands that you have already learned without additional instruction.

PATH

Home/Cells/Format

In the *Word* and *PowerPoint* modules, you were provided with the path to help you locate new commands quickly and easily. The path is also provided to help you locate commands in *Excel*. If you are directed to format cells, you automatically know by following the path that it will be located on the Home tab in the Cells group.

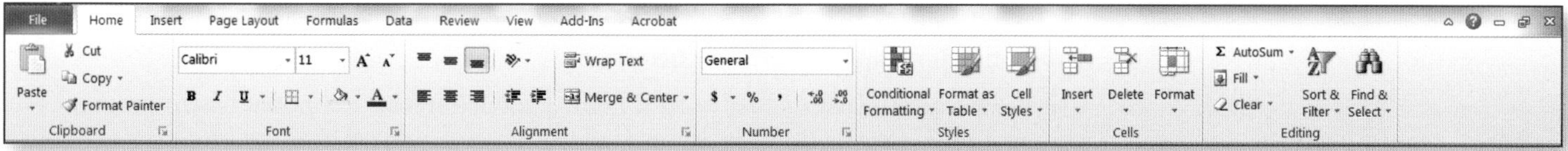

Figure 1.1 *Excel* Home Tab

Job 2

Presentation Handout with Access Query

To identify every record that has nothing entered in a field, key **Is Null** in the Criteria row of the QBE query grid.

For ease in adjusting column width, view the gridlines (Home/Paragraph/Border and click View Gridlines).

Ms. McMullan has just texted you, requesting that you design an attractive handout listing all property listings as of today, August 18, 2012. Query the *Access* database for the up-to-date data, select the query results, copy to a *Word* document, and use the *Word* tools to format attractively as a presentation handout.

1. Save the *p8-j1* database as *p8-j2a*. Create an *Access* query using the Property Listings table that includes the Property Number, Street Address, City, Date Listed, Listing Price, Listing Renewal Date, and Sales Date. In the Sales Date field, key **Is Null** in the Criteria row, and hide the field. Sort by Date Listed (ascending) and Listing Price (ascending). Save the query as **Current Listings**.
2. Select the query results, copy, and paste to a blank *Word* document, choosing the Merge Formatting paste option.
3. Edit by applying the Medium Shading 1 – Accent 1 table style. Change font size of all text except the title to 10 point. Delete the decimal places in the Listing Price column. Adjust column widths so that all entries in the body of the table fit on one line. Center data in the last three columns. Align the column headings using Align Bottom Center. See Figure P8.1 below for column heading arrangement.
4. Center the title of the table and change the title to **M&D Property Listings | August 18, 2012**. Insert the Puzzle (Even Page) footer; key the company name where indicated in the footer. Save the document as *p8-j2b*.

Property Number	Street Address	City	Date Listed	Listing Price	Listing Renewal Date

Figure P8.1 Column Headings for Table

Job 3

Create Form and Update Database

The hiring of several new agents and the sale of a property require that you update the data in the tables.

1. Save the *p8-j2a* database as *p8-j3*.
2. Create a form for the Agents table. Save the form as **Agents**. Apply the appropriate theme.
3. Three new agents were hired today, August 19, 2012. Use the Agents form to update the *Access* database using the data shown below.

C-4817-M	S-7522-F	C-7856-H
Michelle Cox	Felix Santos	Hannah Cato
199 S. Santa Rosa Street	8391 Dolorosa Street	43 College Street
San Antonio, TX 78207-3634	San Antonio, TX 78205-7209	San Antonio, TX 78205-7260
210-555-0136	210-555-0129	210-555-0152
Birth: 6/4/1958	Birth: 7/31/1973	Birth: 10/21/1988

4. Create a form for the Property Listings table. Save the form as **Property Listings**. Apply the appropriate theme, if necessary.
5. Use the Property Listings form to update a record in the Property Listing table. The property on Grissom Road in Leon Valley sold today for $294,000. Selling agent was Samuel Page. Use a filter to quickly locate the record to be updated.

WORKSHEET PARTS

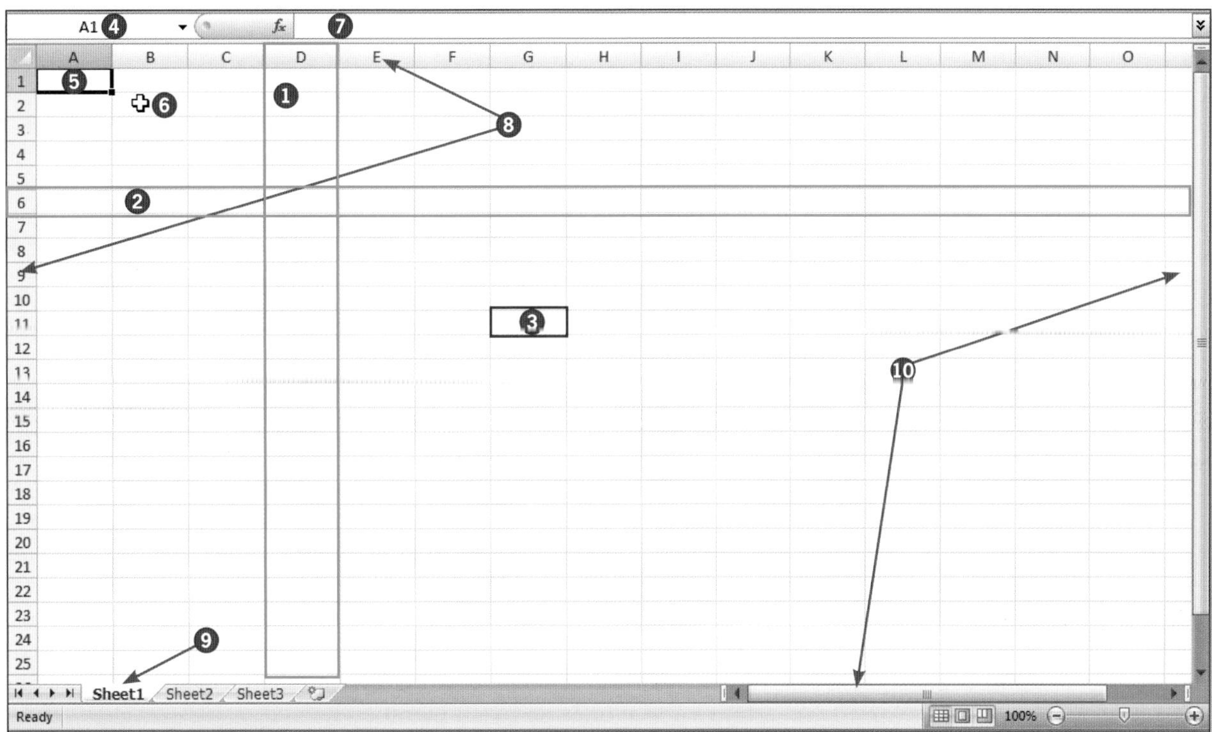

Figure 1.2 Worksheet Parts

The parts of a worksheet are explained below and illustrated in Figure 1.2.

❶ **Column:** Vertical list of information. Columns are labeled alphabetically from left to right; up to 16,384 columns are contained on one worksheet (A through XFD). Note the column heading that labels each column with the appropriate letter.

❷ **Row:** Information arranged horizontally. Rows are numbered from top to bottom; 1,048,576 rows are available on one worksheet (1 through 1,048,576). Note the row heading that labels each row with the appropriate row number.

❸ **Cell:** An intersection of a column and row. Each cell has its own address consisting of the column letter and the row number, such as A1 or AB36. A1 refers to column A, row 1; AB36 refers to column AB, row 36.

❹ **Name box:** The Name box displays the address of the active cell, which is the cell that is ready for information to be entered.

❺ **Active cell:** The active cell is surrounded by a dark border.

❻ **Cell pointer:** Cross-shaped pointer that appears when the mouse pointer is over a cell. Similar to the arrow in *Word*, the cell pointer does not indicate the active cell. Remember that the cell that is highlighted with the dark border is the active cell. To select a specific cell, click inside it.

❼ **Formula bar:** Displays the content of the active cell.

❽ **Row/column headings:** A heading labeling each row and column.

❾ **Sheet tab:** Labels each worksheet in the workbook.

❿ **Scroll bars:** Allow navigation of the worksheet.

project 8

McMullan & Donovan Realty: Integrating Access, Word, and Publisher

OBJECTIVES

- Create and update *Access* database
- Create *Access* queries
- Prepare effective *Word* documents and *Publisher* publications
- Work with limited supervision

SETTING

In Projects 8 and 9, you are employed as an assistant with McMullan & Donovan Realty located in San Antonio, Texas. You report directly to Carol McMullan, one of the owners. This small but growing agency has all of its records in *Word* documents and paper-based files. The company has 12 agents selling primarily residential real estate. However, it is currently recruiting new agents and would like to hire several more agents in the next few weeks. The company does subscribe to the multiple listing service that provides a listing and description of all real estate for sale or lease by all member agencies.

Your first responsibility in Project 8 is to create an *Access* database and update it as the new agents are hired. You will use data from the database to prepare various *Word* documents and business cards using *Publisher*.

JOBS

1. *Access* database
2. Presentation handout with *Access* query
3. Business cards in *Publisher*
4. Memo with *Access* query

STANDARD OPERATING PROCEDURES

Use these procedures for all documents you prepare. You will not be reminded to do these things during the project.

1. Use the Civic document theme for all *Word* documents and *Access* forms and reports.
2. Use the data file *m&d memo* template to prepare memos. Proof and print all documents and database objects.
3. Set up a folder named AC-WD-PB Project 8, and save all project files in it. Name all solution files *p8-j* (plus the job number, *j1*, *j2*, etc.) unless another solution name is provided.

Job 1

Create Database Tables

DB DESIGN

You have been asked to create the *Access* database for McMullan & Donovan Realty. Name the new database *p8-j1*. You will begin by creating the Agents and the Property Listings tables.

Open the *Word* data file *db design*, print the file, and follow the directions to design the two tables. Input the data for the 12 agents in the Agents table and the 12 property listings data in the Property Listings table.

Use arrow keys to move the insertion point in the cell to position properly for editing.

Create a new folder named Module 3 Solutions and save all workbooks and documents from this module in it.

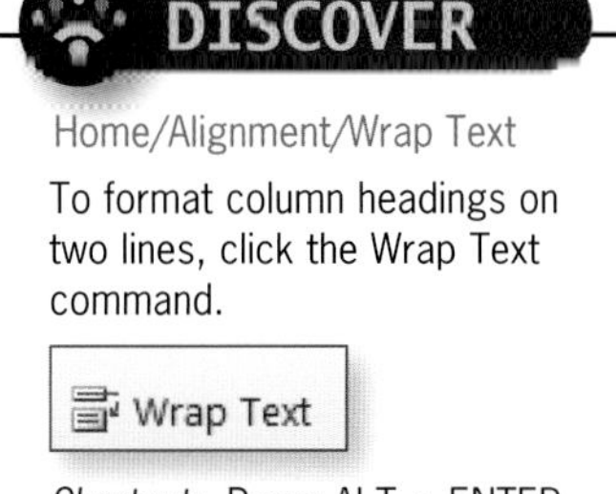

Home/Alignment/Wrap Text

To format column headings on two lines, click the Wrap Text command.

Wrap Text

Shortcut: Press ALT + ENTER after the text to be displayed on the first line.

ENTER DATA

When text or numbers are keyed in a cell, they appear both in the cell ❶ and in the formula bar ❷. Data is entered by keying the data and then tapping ENTER, tapping TAB, or clicking the Enter button ❸ on the formula bar (Figure 1.3). Use the BACKSPACE or DELETE key to edit while entering data in a cell. After data has been entered, double-click the cell. A flashing insertion point in the cell allows editing in the cell or editing in the formula bar.

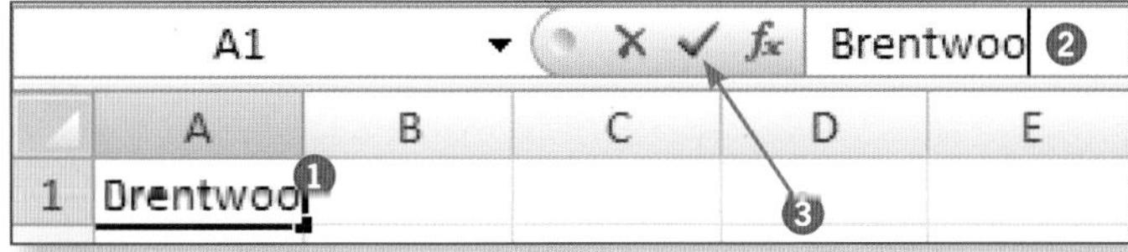

Figure 1.3 Enter and Edit Cell Data

Information is entered in a spreadsheet as either text (words), values (numbers), or formulas. See Figure 1.4 for illustrations of these data types. Tap ENTER after keying the data to make the cell below active; tap TAB to make the cell to the right active.

Text: ❶ Any combination of numbers, spaces, and non-numeric characters. For example, Sales Staff, 1991 Woodlake Drive, 206-555-0122, and 239TXY are all examples of text. Text automatically aligns at the left.

Number: ❷ A constant value that can include numeric characters as well as +, – , ( ), /, S, %, ., E, and e. If the cell is not large enough to display a number, #### will display. The data will display on the screen when you increase the column width. A very large number will be displayed in scientific notation (1.57E+17). Numbers automatically align at the right.

Formulas and functions: Sets of instructions for calculating values in cells. For example, the formula =C2+C4 would add the numbers in those two cells. Note in Figure 1.4 the SUM function is entered in F4; the function =SUM(B4:E4) displays in the formula bar ❸ and the result in F4 ❹. Drag the fill handle ❺ at bottom right of F4 to copy the formula to F5 and subsequent cells.

If a cell contains more characters than space allows, the excess characters spill over into the next cell if the next cell is blank ❻. If the next cell is not blank, the screen displays only the width of that column ❼. Default column width is 8.43 characters.

Column headings can be displayed on two lines ❽ by clicking the Wrap Text command.

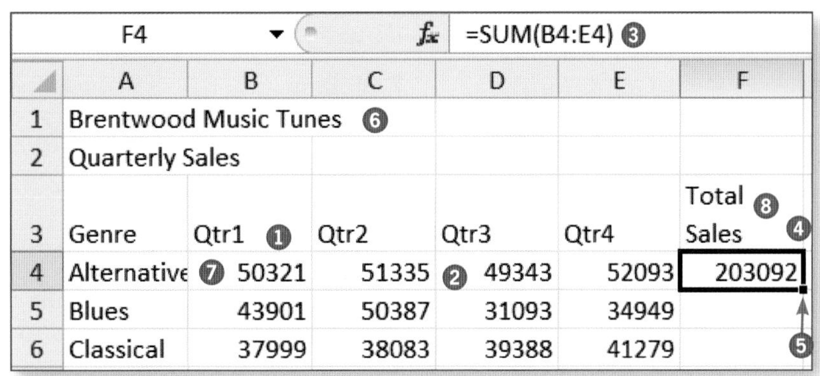

F4 | =SUM(B4:E4) ❸

	A	B	C	D	E	F
1	Brentwood Music Tunes ❻					
2	Quarterly Sales					
3	Genre	Qtr1 ❶	Qtr2	Qtr3	Qtr4	Total Sales ❽ ❹
4	Alternative ❼	50321	51335 ❷	49343	52093	203092
5	Blues	43901	50387	31093	34949	
6	Classical	37999	38083	39388	41279	❺

Figure 1.4 Data Types

Database 6, continued

Employee ID	180	226	505
Team ID	4	3	1
Last Name	DelRefugio	Morris	Hayes
First Name	Juan	Jack	Shannon
Address	37 W Main Street	187 E Locust Way	2004 Diamond Lane
City	Columbus	Bloomington	South Bend
State	OH	IL	IN
ZIP Code	43215-5015	61701-3006	46628-2407
Home Phone	614-555-0136	309-555-0190	574-555-0181
Birth Date	09/29/1989	01/05/1982	06/24/1978

Database 7
Change a Form

AC4-DB7-DATA
CAR

1. Open the data file *ac4-db7-data*. Save the database as *ac4-db7*.
2. Create a form based on the Donations – Autos table.
3. Apply the Austin theme.
4. Change the form title to **Automobile Donations**.
5. Change the logo to the graphic in the *car* data file and resize the logo to show the entire car.
6. Change the *Donated Value* label to **Donation Value**.
7. Add three new records to the Donations – Autos table:

Because the ID field is an AutoNumber field, *Access* will enter the ID number for you as you key these records.

Type	Car	Car	Van
Make	Honda	Mercury	Toyota
Model	Accord	Marquis	Sienna
Model Year	2005	2000	2000
Mileage	37,900	97,500	120,000
Color	Blue	Silver	Red
Condition	Excellent	Very Good	Good
Donation Value	14,950	6,995	7,990
Comments	Alloy wheels		New transmission

8. You have found some mistakes in the records while working with them. Filter by form to show all the Toyotas and change *Corrolla* to **Corolla**. Then find the Ford Escort and change *Escort* to **Escape**.
9. Find the record for the BMW and delete it.
10. Save the form as **Automobile Donations**, close the form, and close the database.

AutoFit Column Width

Home/Cells/Format/AutoFit Column Width

CHANGE COLUMN WIDTH

Use one of the two methods below to change column width (Figure 1.5), or use the AutoFit option to fit column width to the longest entry.

To Change the Width of a Column to Fit the Longest Entry:

1. Double-click the column border ❶ to fit the contents of the selected columns. -or-
2. Drag the column border ❶ to the desired column width.

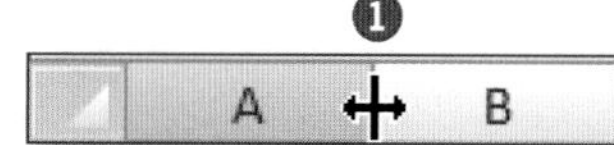

Figure 1.5 Adjust Column Width

DRILL 1 CREATE A WORKSHEET

1. Launch *Excel*.
2. In A1, key the worksheet title **Invoice**; bold, and increase font size to 14.
3. In A2, key the column heading **Quantity**; tap TAB. In B2, key **Description;** tap TAB.
4. In C2, key **Unit Price**, tap ENTER, click the cell again, and click the Wrap Text command to display text on two lines.
5. In D2, key **Total**.
6. Enter the remaining data in columns A through C as shown in Figure 1.6. Fit the column width to the longest entry in column D. Center and bold the headings in row 2.
7. In D3, key the formula **=A3*C3**. Point to the fill handle in D3 and drag to D5 to copy the formula.
8. Double-click A5 and change the quantity to **12**. Tap ENTER to accept the change. Note the total recalculates automatically in D5.
9. Save as *ex1-drill1*. Use Figure 1.7 to check your worksheet. Leave the worksheet open.

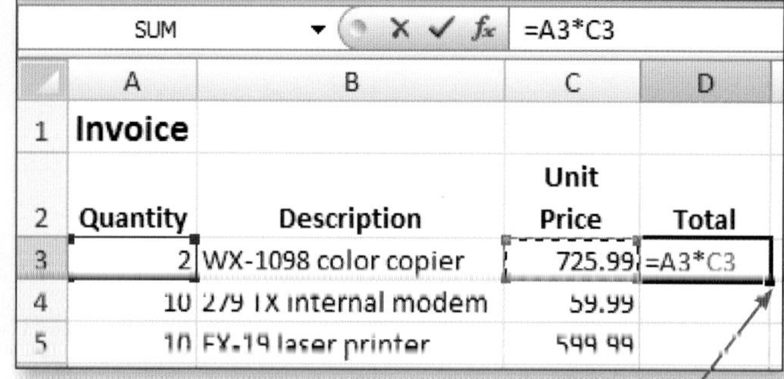
SUM =A3*C3

	A	B	C	D
1	**Invoice**			
2	**Quantity**	**Description**	**Unit Price**	**Total**
3	2	WX-1098 color copier	725.99	=A3*C3
4	10	279 TX internal modem	59.99	
5	10	FX-19 laser printer	599.99	

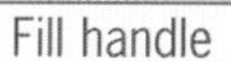

Figure 1.6 Drill 1 Source

	A	B	C	D
1	**Invoice**			
2	**Quantity**	**Description**	**Unit Price**	**Total**
3	2	WX-1098 color copier	725.99	1451.98
4	10	279 TX internal modem	59.99	599.9
5	12	FX-19 laser printer	599.99	7199.88

Figure 1.7 Quick Check

JOB KNOWLEDGE

To be more effective and more productive, *Excel* users quickly learn key principles of worksheet design.

1. What is the objective of the worksheet? Will this worksheet save me time?
2. What information is needed on this worksheet? Draft the worksheet on paper before entering it in the software.
3. How can I ensure the worksheet calculations are correct? Manually calculate any formulas and functions to ensure that the formulas are correct.

Changing a form label does not change the related field name in the underlying table.

A label is typically the same as the name of the field in a table. You may want to change a label to make it more descriptive.

To Change a Label:

1. Click once on a label to select it and then click again to set the insertion point.
2. Use standard editing commands to change the label (Figure 4.9).
3. Click off the label to save the change. If the edited label extends into the text box area, *Access* will automatically reformat the form.

Units in Stock:	322
Unit Price:	$49.00
Reorder Level:	100
Reorder Status:	☑

Figure 4.9 Edit a Label

DRILL 2 CUSTOMIZE A FORM

COMPUTER

1. With *ac4-drill1* open, save the database as *ac4-drill2*.
2. Create a form for the Suppliers table.
3. Apply the Austin theme.
4. Change the form title to **Update Supplier Information**.
5. Change the logo to the graphic in the *computer* data file. Resize to show the entire computer image.
6. Change the *Shipping Method* label to **Shipper**.
7. Switch to Form view. Edit the record of supplier 3, changing the account rep's name to **Jim Peterson**.
8. Add the following new record: supplier 5 is **Jackman Data Source**, located at **2699 Oak Court**, **Naperville**, **IL 60565-2411**. Their account rep is **John Matthews**, whose phone number is **630-555-0157**. The company's website is **www.jackdatasource.com**, terms will be **net 30**, and shipper is **FedEx**.
9. Using a landscape orientation, print the form for the new record only.
10. Save the form as **Supplier Information**, close the form, and close the database.

Apply It

Database 6

Simple Form

AC4-DB6-DATA

1. Open the data file *ac4-db6-data*. Save the database as *ac4-db6*.
2. Create a form for the Employee table.
3. Enter the information on the next page for three new employees hired today (use today's date).
4. Find the record for Nancy Judd, and change her team ID to 3.
5. Using landscape orientation, print the Employee form record for Jack Morris.
6. Save the form as **Employee List**, close the form, and close the database.

ADD AND RENAME SHEET TABS

An *Excel* workbook contains three worksheets by default. Each worksheet is identified by a sheet tab at the lower-left corner. Worksheets can be related to each other. For example, sales for each month can be captured in separate worksheets, and all monthly worksheets can be related to one summary worksheet. Each worksheet has 16,384 columns and 1,048,576 rows. To make a worksheet active, click its sheet tab. The sheet tab label for the active worksheet is displayed in bold.

To Insert and Rename Worksheets:

1. Click the Insert Worksheet button ❶ to the right of the last sheet tab.
2. Double-click the sheet tab ❷ to select the default name (Figure 1.8).
3. Key a new name.

Figure 1.8 Sheet Tabs

DRILL 2 WORK WITH WORKSHEETS

Right-click a sheet tab and use commands to edit tabs, e.g., Delete, Tab Color, Rename, or Protect Sheet.

1. With *ex1-drill1* open, insert a worksheet after Sheet3.
2. Rename Sheet1 as 2012, Sheet2 as 2011, Sheet3 as 2010, and Sheet4 as 2009.
3. Change the colors of the sheet tabs.
4. Move the sheet tabs to appear in lowest to highest numeric order. *Hint*: Point to sheet tab and drag and drop the tab in desired location.
5. Save as *ex1-drill2* and keep open for next drill.

MOVE WITHIN A WORKSHEET

When working with a large worksheet, you must learn to move quickly within the worksheet—both vertically and horizontally.

To Move within a Worksheet:

1. Click the scroll box ❶ and drag it any distance. -or-
2. Click the up and down arrows ❷ or left and right arrows ❷ to move one row or column. -or-
3. Click the area on either side of the scroll box to move one window ❸ (Figure 1.9). The active cell does not move to the area displayed when the scroll bars are used. To activate a cell, you must click it.

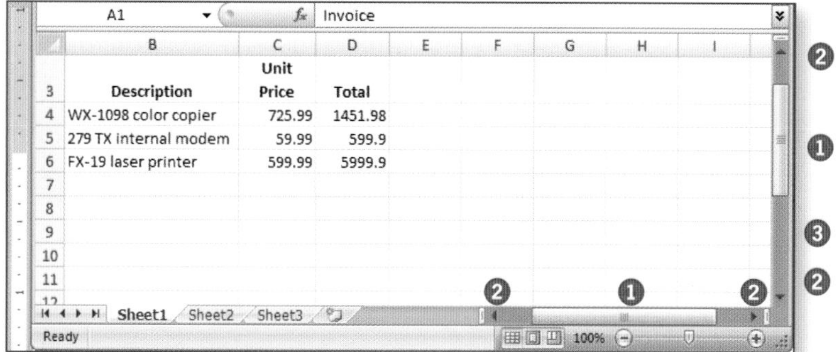

Figure 1.9 Scroll Bars

DRILL 1 CREATE A FORM AND EDIT RECORDS

AC4-DRILL1-DATA

1. Open the data file *ac4-drill1-data*. Save the database as *ac4-drill1*.
2. Create a form for the Product Status table.
3. Switch to Form view.
4. Use Filter By Form to view all products with zero (0) in the Reorder Level field.
5. Edit each of the filtered records, changing the reorder level to 10.
6. Remove the filter.
7. Find and delete the record for Product #899.
8. Save the form as **Product Status**, and close the form. Leave the database open for the next drill.

Another design option, Design view, is available to make more sophisticated changes not available in the Layout view.

CUSTOMIZE A FORM

The more a form will be used, the more effort you should expend to ensure the form is both easy and pleasant to use. Switch to form Layout view to customize a form by changing its design or appearance. When in Form view, you can click the View button shown at left to switch to Layout view.

Your forms should be attractive and easy to read. The colors should be pleasant and reflect the branding of your organization. Use themes to quickly apply colors and graphics that match those of themes in other *Office 2010* applications.

By default, a theme applies to all objects in the database. To apply a theme to only one object, right-click the theme and select Apply Theme to This Object Only.

To Apply a Theme:

Form Layout Tools Design/Themes/Themes

1. Open the form in Layout view.
2. Click the Themes button ❶ (Figure 4.7) to display the themes gallery and select a theme.

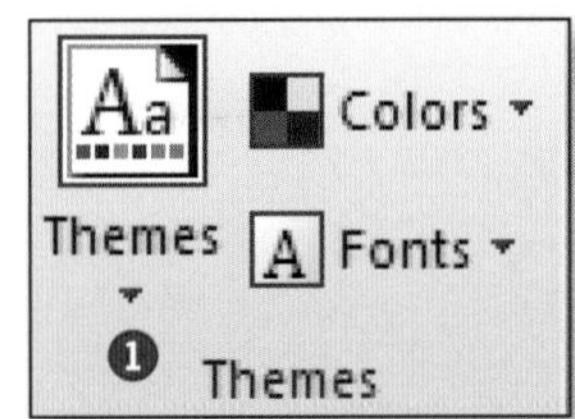

Figure 4.7 Themes Group

The form title should clearly communicate the purpose of the form. The form title is located in the form heading section of the form. The title is stored in a label and initially is the same as the table from which the form was created. In most cases, a more descriptive title should be substituted.

To Change the Form Title:

Form Layout Tools Design/Header / Footer/Title

1. Click Title ❷ (Figure 4.8).
2. Use standard editing commands to change the title.
3. Click off the label to save the changes.

Figure 4.8 Header / Footer Group

Access displays a default logo in the upper-left corner of the form heading. Changing the logo to a company graphic is a quick way to improve the appearance of the form.

To Change the Logo:

1. Click Logo ❸ in the Header / Footer group.
2. Navigate to the location of the graphic file, select the file, and click OK.
3. Resize the graphic object as desired by dragging its selection box.

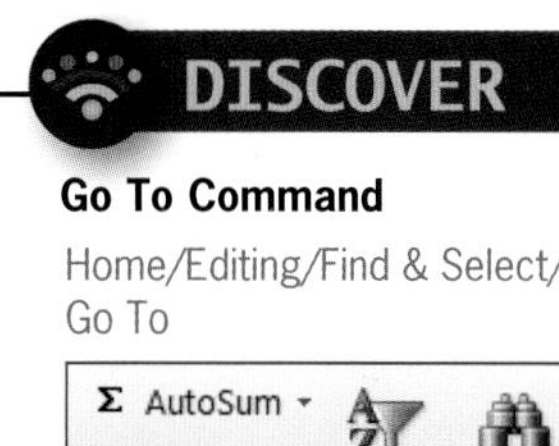

DISCOVER

Go To Command

Home/Editing/Find & Select/ Go To

Shortcut: CTRL + G

Keystrokes also help you move quickly in a worksheet. Refer to the table below as you learn this method. When keystrokes are used, the active cell moves. You can also use the Go To command to move quickly to specified parts of the worksheet.

To Move:	Press:
Up, down, left, or right one cell	↑, ↓, ←, →
Up or down one window	PgUp or PgDn
Beginning of a row	HOME
Beginning of the worksheet	CTRL + HOME
Last cell containing data	CTRL + END

SELECT CELLS

You have learned to select a single cell by clicking it to make it the active cell. A range of cells is two or more cells selected on a worksheet. The range reference A2:C2 identifies the first cell in the range as A2 and the last cell as C2; the range cell references are separated by a colon. After a range is selected, you can perform one or more operations on all cells within that range; e.g., bold, center, copy.

To Select a Range of Cells:

1. Adjacent cells: Click the first cell and drag to the last cell ❶ (Figure 1.10).

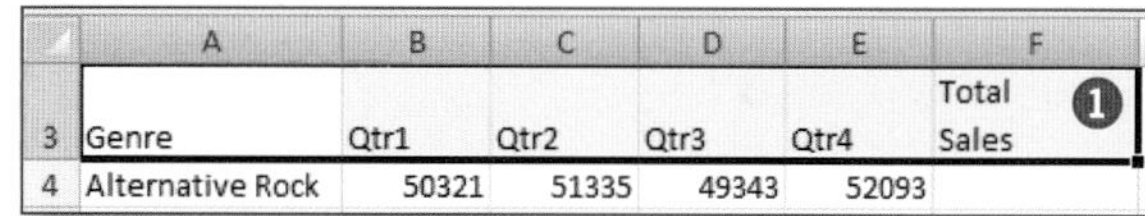

	A	B	C	D	E	F
3	Genre	Qtr1	Qtr2	Qtr3	Qtr4	Total Sales
4	Alternative Rock	50321	51335	49343	52093	

Figure 1.10 Adjacent Range A3:F3

2. Nonadjacent cells: Select the first range of cells and then hold down CTRL and select the nonadjacent cells ❷ (Figure 1.11).

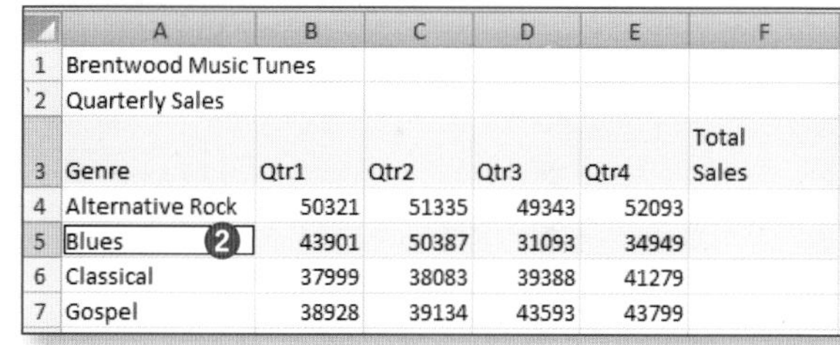

	A	B	C	D	E	F
1	Brentwood Music Tunes					
2	Quarterly Sales					
3	Genre	Qtr1	Qtr2	Qtr3	Qtr4	Total Sales
4	Alternative Rock	50321	51335	49343	52093	
5	Blues	43901	50387	31093	34949	
6	Classical	37999	38083	39388	41279	
7	Gospel	38928	39134	43593	43799	

Figure 1.11 Nonadjacent Range A3:F3, A5:F5

3. All worksheet cells: Click the Select All button ❸ (Figure 1.12).

	A	B	C
1	Brentwood Music Tunes		
2	Quarterly Sales		

Figure 1.12 Range A1:XFD1,048,576

4. Column or row of cells: Click the column heading ❹ to select an entire column or a row heading ❺ to select an entire row (Figure 1.13).

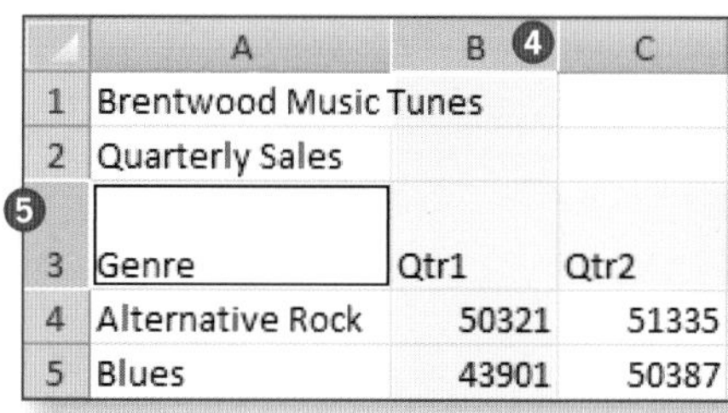

	A	B	C
1	Brentwood Music Tunes		
2	Quarterly Sales		
3	Genre	Qtr1	Qtr2
4	Alternative Rock	50321	51335
5	Blues	43901	50387

Figure 1.13 Column B and Row 3

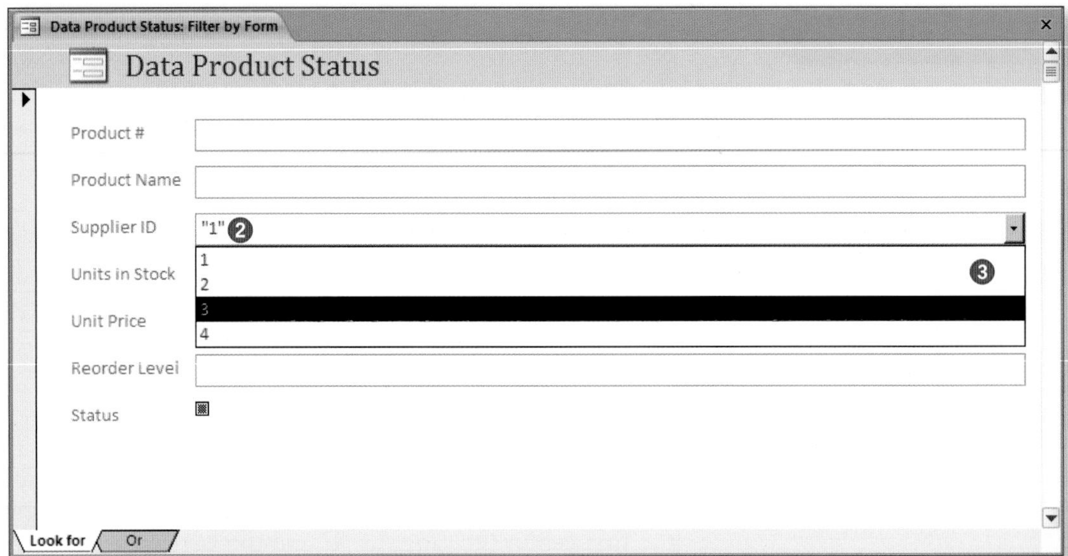

Figure 4.4 Filter by Form

3. Key data in the appropriate field ❷ to find the record, or select the data using the list box ❸ visible when you select a field.
4. On the Home tab in the Sort & Filter group, click Toggle Filter to apply the filter. The desired record is now visible.
5. Edit the record by clicking on the desired field and using standard editing methods to add and delete characters.
6. More than one record may be selected by the filter. The number of filtered records appears on the form's navigation bar, as shown in Figure 4.5. Use the navigation buttons to select any other record.

Figure 4.5 Navigation Bar Indicates Three Filtered Records

7. Click Toggle Filter again to remove the filter.

DELETE A RECORD

You may need to delete a record from a table. As when you edit records, you should delete records from a table using the form related to the table.

TIP

Be careful when deleting records—there is no Undo button to restore records deleted accidentally.

To Delete a Record:

Home/Records/Delete

1. Open the form related to the table containing the record to be deleted.
2. Use the navigation buttons or filter the data to view the record to be deleted.
3. Click the down arrow next to Delete ❶ (Figure 4.6), and select Delete Record.
4. Click Yes to confirm that you want to delete the record.

Figure 4.6 Records Group

DRILL 3 WORKING WITH WORKSHEETS

With *ex1-drill2* open, practice moving within the worksheet and selecting cells.

Move by Scrolling

1. Click the area below the vertical scroll box to move down one window and then click above the vertical scroll box to move up one window.
2. Click the down arrow three times on the vertical scroll bar to move down three rows.
3. Click the right arrow on the horizontal scroll bar to move right one column.
4. Scroll left one column.
5. Drag the vertical scroll box up any distance.
6. Click the area to the right of the horizontal scroll box to scroll right one window.

Move with Go To Command

7. Press CTRL + G and key **C6**. Click OK.

Move with Keystrokes

8. Tap HOME to move to the beginning of the row.
9. Press CTRL + END to move to the last cell with data.
10. Press CTRL + HOME to move to the beginning of the worksheet.

Select Range

11. Select the range A4:F4: Click A4 and drag to F4. Click away from the range to deselect.

Select Nonadjacent Ranges

12. Select the range A5:F5. Hold down the CTRL key and select A9:F9. Deselect.

Select Rows, Columns, and All

13. Select column B: Click column B heading.
14. Select row 1: Click row 1 heading.
15. Select all cells in the worksheet: Click the Select All button.
16. Close the file without saving.

Apply It

Worksheet 1
New Worksheet

DISCOVER

Quick Print
File/Print/Print

Shortcut: Click arrow on Quick Access Toolbar and add Quick Print.

1. Key the worksheet shown in Figure 1.14. Format *Tickets Sold* in B2 on two lines.
2. Format cell A1 in 14-point bold; apply bold and center alignment to A2:D2.
3. Adjust the column widths to display all text as shown in Figure 1.14.
4. In D3, key the formula **=B3*C3**. Using the fill handle in D3, copy the formula to D4:D7.
5. Increase the number of tickets sold for the City Tour by 12. Change *Regal* to **Regis**.
6. Add two worksheets. Rename the sheet tabs as follows: Sheet1, **Events**; Sheet2, **Registration**; Sheet3, **Program**; Sheet4, **Awards**; and Sheet5, **Budget**.
7. Rearrange the sheet tabs in alphabetical order. Change sheet tabs to a desired color.
8. Save as *ex1-w1* and print. Close the file.

	A	B	C	D	E	F
1	**Summary Special Events Participation and Sales Report**					
2	**Event**	**Tickets Sold**	**Price**	**Total**		
3	Kick-off Breakfast	164	25			
4	Delegates Luncheon	78	45			
5	Dinner Banquet	223	70			
6	City Tour	125	45			
7	Regal Dinner Cruise	200	75			

Figure 1.14 Worksheet 1 Source

CHANGE FORM VIEWS

Home/Views/View

A new form displays in Layout view so that you can make changes to the form design if necessary. You will learn later in this lesson how to modify form design in Layout view. To enter records and work with data, use Form view.

To switch to Form view, click the View command that displays the icon shown above, or click the down arrow and select Form View. The form displays in Form view (Figure 4.2).

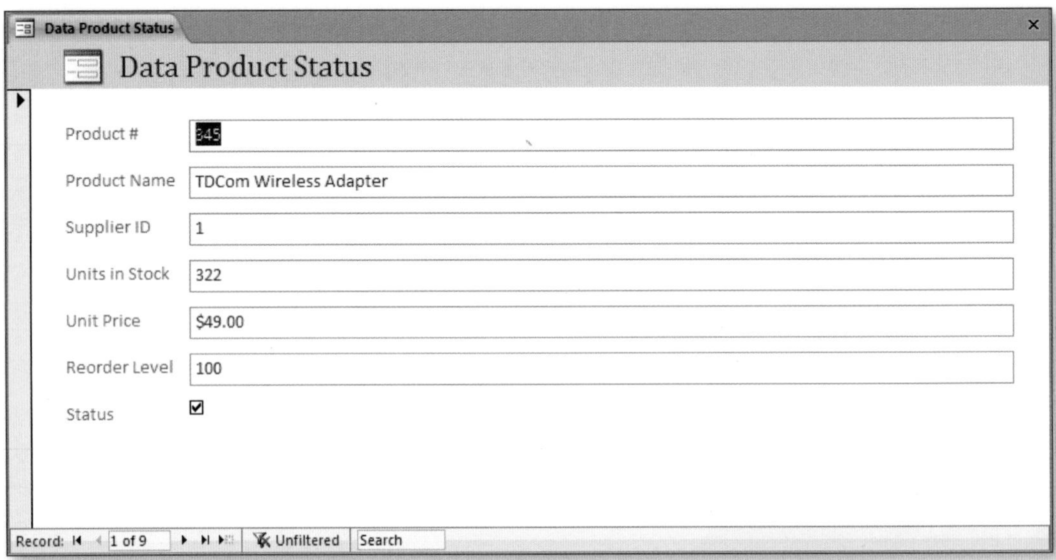

Figure 4.2 Form in Form View

File/Print/Print

Print Current Record

1. Display the record to print.
2. In the Print dialog box, click Selected Record(s).
3. Click OK.

Print All Records

1. In the Print dialog box, click All.
2. Click OK.

Change Orientation

1. In the Print dialog box, click Properties.
2. Click the Printing Shortcuts tab and click the desired orientation.
3. Click OK.

Note that Form view looks very similar to Layout view. You know you are in Form view if you do not see a heavy orange border displayed around a text box when you click in it.

Insert records using Form view by displaying a new record—click the New (blank) record button in the navigation bar—and keying text in each field. Tap TAB to move to the next field or press SHIFT + TAB to move to the previous field.

You can print a form for a single record or forms for all records in the table.

FILTER AND EDIT RECORDS

You can use a form not only to add records to a table but also to edit the data in the table. If the table has a small number of records, you might find it easy to use the navigation buttons to find the record to be edited. For large tables, however, you can filter the data using Filter By Form to find one or more records in the table.

Once the desired record is displayed on the form, you can make any required changes. Your changes are saved when you navigate to another record or close the form.

To Find a Record Using Filter By Form:

Home/Sort & Filter/Advanced

1. Open the form.
2. Click Advanced ❶ (Figure 4.3) and select Filter By Form. A blank copy of the form appears (Figure 4.4).

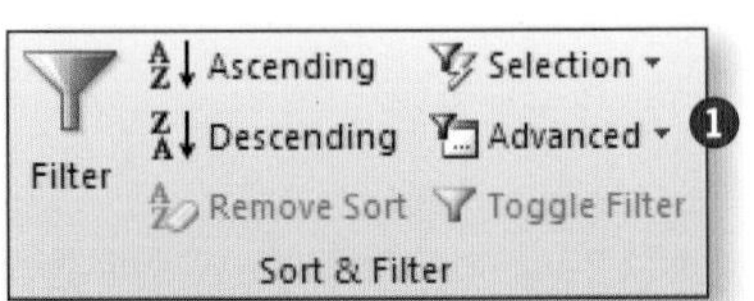

Figure 4.3 Sort & Filter Group

LESSON 2

Edit Worksheets

OBJECTIVES

- Merge and center cells
- Insert and delete rows, columns, and cells
- Format cells and numbers
- Insert sparklines

MERGE AND CENTER CELLS AND CHANGE VERTICAL ALIGNMENT

The Merge & Center command allows the user to spread and center the content of one cell over many cells. The worksheet in Figure 2.1 shows the title in A1 merged and centered across columns A–F. The title in A2 is merged and centered as well.

	A	B	C	D	E	F
1	Brentwood Music Tunes					
2	Quarterly Sales					
3	Genre	Qtr1	Qtr2	Qtr3	Qtr4	Total Sales
4	Alternative Rock	50321	51335	49343	52093	

Figure 2.1 Title Merged and Centered

To further enhance the format of the title in A1, the designer used Book Antiqua font, 20 point and bold, increased the row height to 39.00 points, and middle aligned the title in the cell.

To Merge and Center Cell Content:

Home/Alignment/Merge & Center

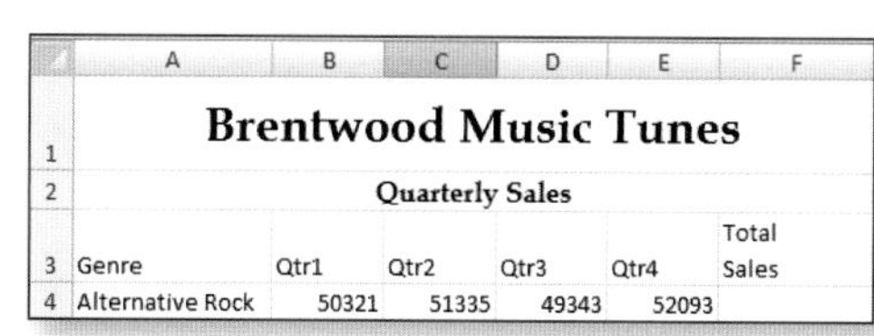

1. Select the cells you want to merge, e.g., A1:F1.
2. Click Merge & Center ❶.

To split or uncombine merged cells, select the merged cell and click Merge & Center. When cells are merged, the Merge & Center command is selected. *Note:* To only merge cells and not center the content, click the arrow next to the Merge & Center command and click Merge Across or Merge Cells.

TIP

Always follow the path to locate the new command you are directed to use.

To Select Vertical Cell Alignment:

Home/Alignment/Top, Middle, or Bottom Align

1. Click in the cell.
2. Click the desired cell alignment from the Alignment group: Top Align ❷, Middle Align ❸, or Bottom Align ❹. Bottom alignment is the default cell alignment.

DRILL 1 MERGE AND CENTER CELLS

To adjust row height:
1. Point to row border.
2. Drag to desired height.

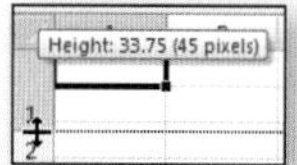

1. Open *ex1-drill2*. Save as *ex2-drill1* and display the 2012 worksheet.
2. Select the range A1:D1. Click the Merge & Center command. Change the font for the heading to Book Antiqua, 20 point, bold.
3. Drag the row border to increase the row height to 36.00 points. Change the vertical alignment to Middle Align.
4. Resave as *ex2-drill1* and close.

Create and Customize Forms

LESSON 4

OBJECTIVES

- Create a form
- Add, edit, and delete data in a form
- Customize a form

CREATE A FORM

Although you can enter data directly into an *Access* table, you may find that this task becomes more difficult as the number of records increases. Forms usually make data entry more convenient. Forms also make it easier to modify and view the information stored in one or more tables.

To Create a Form:

Create/Forms/Form

1. In an open database, highlight the table or query in the Navigation Pane for which you want to make a form.
2. Click Form. The new form appears in its Layout view (Figure 4.1).
3. Save the form as you save other database objects. The form is added to the Navigation Pane.

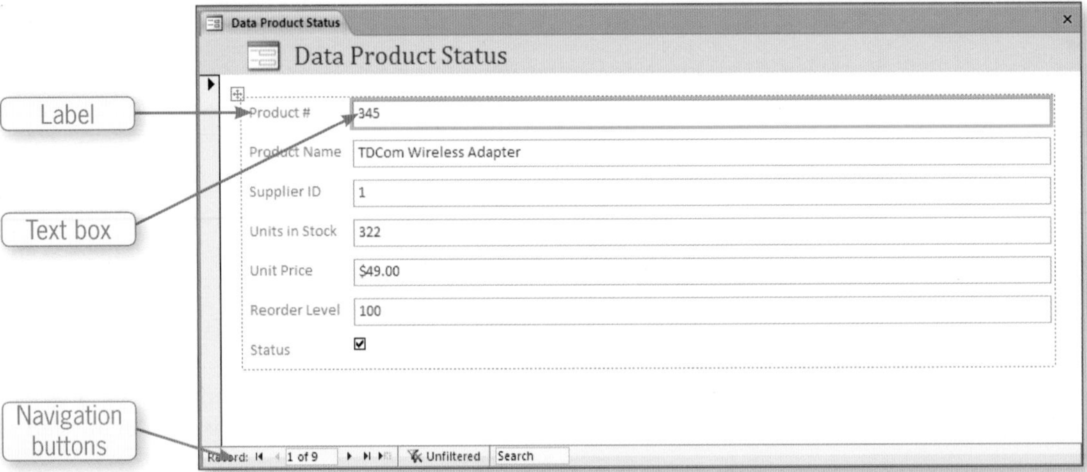

Figure 4.1 Form in Layout View

★ TIP

Although Layout view shows data in the text boxes, you must use Form view to edit, add, or delete data.

As shown in Figure 4.1, a form displays a label and text box for every field in the table. Labels are static, meaning that they stay the same regardless of what record is displayed. Text boxes display the data from the table used to create the form. Labels and text boxes are presented in the same order that they appear in the related table. The order can be changed on the form to improve your efficiency when entering data.

Note that a form also displays the navigation bar you saw in table Datasheet view. Use these buttons in the same way as in Datasheet view to navigate from one record to another, go to the first or last record, or display a new blank record for data entry.

INSERT ROWS, COLUMNS, AND CELLS

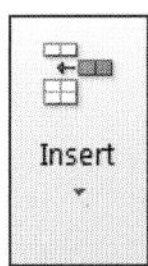

If you find you need to insert data in an area of a worksheet that already contains entries, you can add rows, columns, or blank cells. To save time, insert multiple rows, columns, or cells at the same time.

To Insert a Row or Column:

Home/Cells/Insert

Single row or column

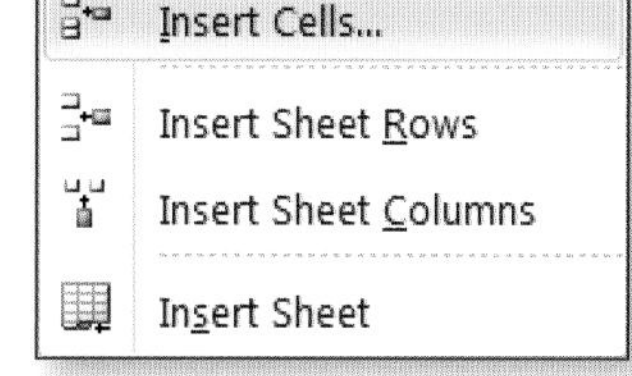

Figure 2.2 Insert Rows or Columns

1. Click a cell in the row immediately below where the new row is to be inserted, or click in a column to the right of where a new column is to be inserted.
2. Click the Insert drop-list arrow and click Insert Sheet Rows to insert a row or Insert Sheet Columns to add a new column (Figure 2.2). Figure 2.3 shows a worksheet with a new row and column.

   Shortcut: Click the row or column heading, right-click, and click Insert.

> **TIP**
>
> If you insert a cell, row, or column next to a cell, row, or column that contains formatting, the Insert Options button displays with the inserted object. Click the Insert Options button to choose the formatting of the inserted cell, row, or column.

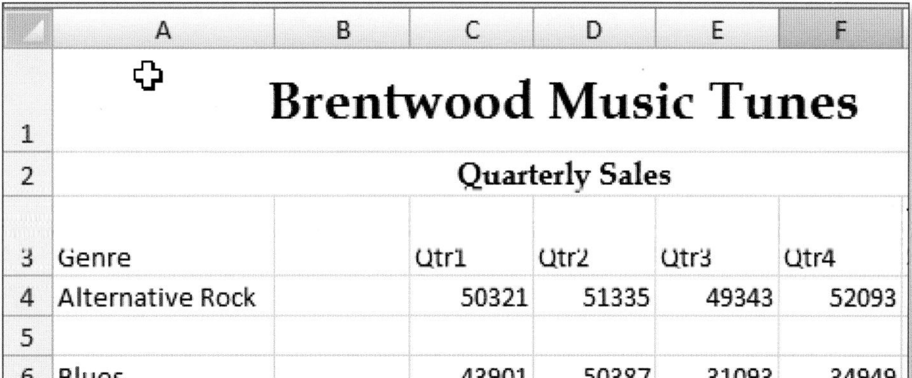

	A	B	C	D	E	F
1	Brentwood Music Tunes					
2	Quarterly Sales					
3	Genre		Qtr1	Qtr2	Qtr3	Qtr4
4	Alternative Rock		50321	51335	49343	52093
5						
6	Blues		43901	50387	31093	34949

Figure 2.3 Inserted Row 5 and Inserted Column B

Multiple rows or columns

1. Multiple rows—Select rows immediately below where the new rows are to be inserted. Click Insert Sheet Rows from the Cells group. Be sure to select the same number of rows you want to insert.
2. Multiple columns—Select columns to the right of where the new columns are to be inserted. Click Insert Sheet Columns. Be sure to select the same number of columns to be inserted.

   Shortcut: Drag the row or column headings to select the number to insert; then right-click and click Insert.

To Insert Blank Cells:

Home/Cells/Insert

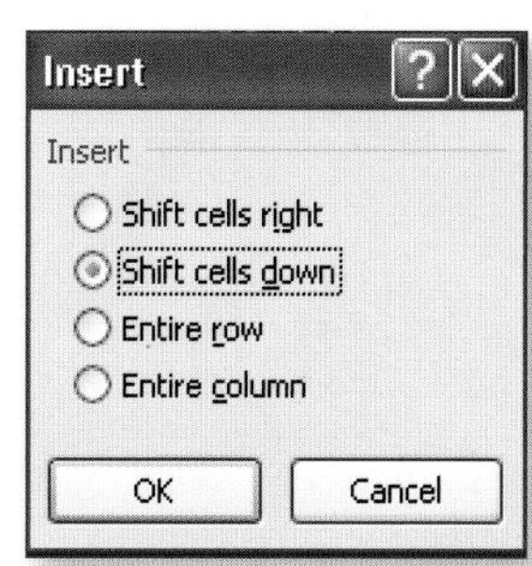

Figure 2.4 Insert Dialog Box

1. Select a range of cells at the place where the new blank cells are to be inserted. Be sure to select the same number of cells to be inserted.
2. Click the Insert drop-list arrow and click Insert Cells.
3. Choose Shift cells right or Shift cells down. Refer to Figure 2.4.

Database 5
Queries Using Filters

1. With *ac3-db4* open, save the database as *ac3-db5*.
2. Create the following queries and filter as indicated.
   a. Using the Employee List table, display Title, First Name, Last Name, City, and State for all employees. Sort in ascending order by City. Filter the dynaset to show the employees in Massachusetts or Connecticut. Print the list and remove the filter. Save the query as **Employees** and close it.
   b. Create a query using all fields in the Mgr by Depart table. Show records for departments that have more than 30 employees. Filter by selection to display departments that have 5 managers. Print the list, remove the filter, save the query as **Employees > 30**, and close the query.
   c. Using the Employee List table, display First Name, Last Name, Job Title, and Department for all employees who are attending the conference (Attending equals "Yes"). Do not display the Attending field, and sort in ascending order by Last Name. Filter the query results to display only employees who have the word *Manager* anywhere in their job title. Your filtered query should look like Figure 3.5. Print the filtered list and remove the filter. Save the query as **Conference** and close it.
3. Close the database.

Conference

First Name	Last Name	Job Title	Department
Maria	Cabera	Manager	Customer Relations
Karen	Cho	Assistant Manager	Finance
Claudia	Dalamangus	Account Manager	Customer Relations
Chris	Dowd	Manager	Legal Affairs
William	Janiak	Manager	Finance
Alex	Kaplan	Manager	Customer Relations
Jim	Levenson	Manager	Information Systems
Daniel	McCarthy	Assistant Manager	Human Resources
Raisa	Talkov	Manager	Marketing

Figure 3.5 Filtered Conference Query

CAREER FOCUS

© erwinova/Shutterstock.com

Understanding how to create databases and how to find, organize, and use data in an existing database effectively are important career skills. In small organizations, employees are more likely to create databases than in large ones. Most large organizations have existing company-wide databases. Because employees are likely to use data from a database for presentations and publications, they must be able to export data to and import data from other software applications such as *Word* and *Excel*. You will learn about importing and exporting in Lesson 7.

DELETE ROWS, COLUMNS, AND CELLS

Editing a worksheet often includes deleting unneeded cells, rows, or columns. The procedure to delete is very similar to inserting rows, columns, and cells.

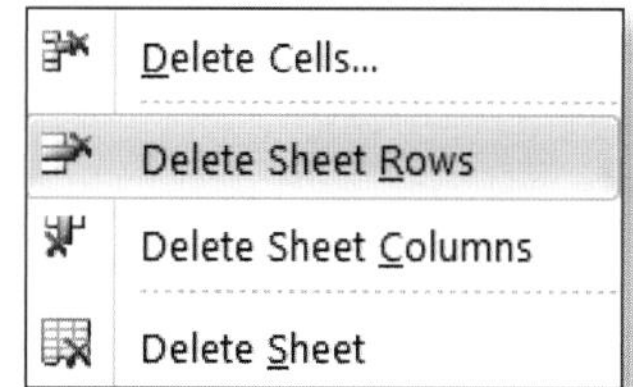

Figure 2.5 Delete Rows or Columns

To Delete a Single Row or Column:

Home/Cells/Delete

1. Click a cell in the row or column to be deleted and click the Delete drop-list arrow (Figure 2.5).
2. Click Delete Sheet Rows to delete a row or Delete Sheet Columns to delete a column.

   Shortcut: Click the row or column heading, right-click, and click Delete.

To Delete Cells:

1. Select a cell or a range of cells to be deleted. Click the Delete drop-list arrow.
2. Click Delete Cells.
3. Choose Shift cells left or Shift cells up. Refer to Figure 2.6.

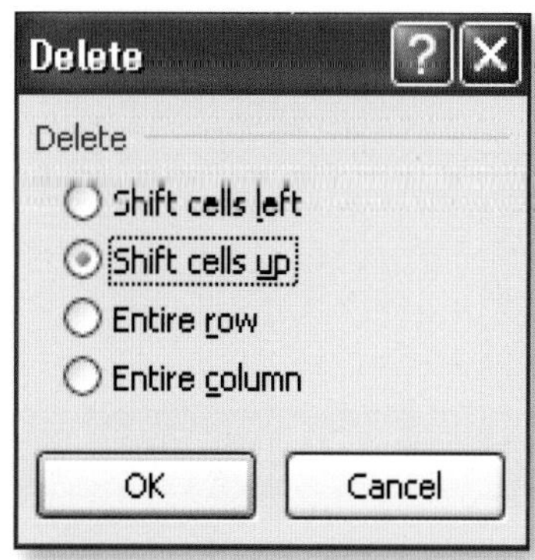

Figure 2.6 Delete Dialog Box

DRILL 2 INSERT AND DELETE ROWS, COLUMNS, AND CELLS

1. Open the data file *insert*. Save as *ex2-drill2a*.
2. Insert a row immediately before row 4, Travel. Add the following entry in the new row 4.

   Legal Fees 95332 97000
3. Select B1:C1; insert cells and choose to shift cells down.
4. Select A2; insert cells and choose to shift cells down.
5. Insert two columns immediately to the left of column B, 2010.
6. In B2, key **2008**, and in C2, key **2009**. Bold and center-align the column headings in the range B2:E2.
7. Save your changes so far.
8. Delete columns B and C.
9. Save as *ex2-drill2b* and close.

CAREER FOCUS

© Stockbyte/Getty Images

Companies are investing large sums of money in the sophisticated automated workplace. Interestingly, training consultants report that only a small percentage of the functions of software are used by most people. If companies are to earn a return on investment, employers will be inclined to hire employees who possess expert levels of software expertise and who know how to maximize the value of software. Set a goal to learn the powerful functions of the software and look for smarter ways to accomplish tasks to save time and energy.

Access's filter options make it easy to display only records matching specific criteria. You can use the common filters in field headers, which are very similar to *Excel* filters, to select criteria on which to filter. Use this filtering option to filter for more than one criterion in a datasheet.

You can also use the field header list to sort a field at any time or to sort the filtered data to make it easier to understand.

To Apply Common Filters in Datasheet View:

1. In Datasheet view, click the down arrow next to a field name to display the list of values you can use to filter the data (Figure 3.4).
2. Check the boxes that contain the criteria you want to filter for, or click Text (or Number) Filters to see more options for filtering.
3. Click OK to apply the filter.
4. Click Toggle Filter in the Sort & Filter group to remove the filter.

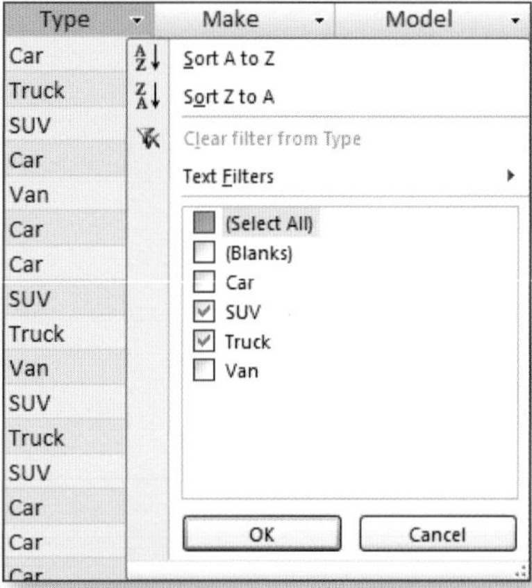

Figure 3.4 Filter Options

DRILL 3 FILTER QUERY RESULTS

1. With *ac3-drill2* open, save the database as *ac3-drill3*.
2. Create a query to display the Type, Make, Model, Model Year, Condition, and Comments fields. Sort in ascending order by Model. Add a criterion to show only the Ford donations. Save the query as **Ford**.
3. Filter the Ford query to print answers to each of the following questions. Clear the filter after printing each dynaset:
   a. Which vehicles are from model years 2003, 2004, or 2005?
   b. Which vehicles are in excellent condition?
   c. Is there anything special or particularly wrong with any of these vehicles, as recorded in the Comments field?
4. Clear the filter if necessary, close the Ford query without saving, and close the database.

Apply It

Database 4

Simple Queries Using Criteria

AC3-DB4-DATA

1. Open the data file *ac3-db4-data*. Save the database as *ac3-db4*.
2. Create the following queries from the Employee List table. Print the results of each query before closing.
   a. Display the Title, First Name, Last Name, Job Title, and Department fields. Sort in ascending order by Last Name. Add a criterion to display only records for employees with the job title Manager. Save the query as **Managers**.
   b. Save the Managers query with the new name **New York**. Remove the Manager criterion. Add the State field to the query. Add a criterion to display only records for employees in New York. Save and close the query.
3. Leave the database open for the next exercise.

FORMAT NUMBERS

Home/Number

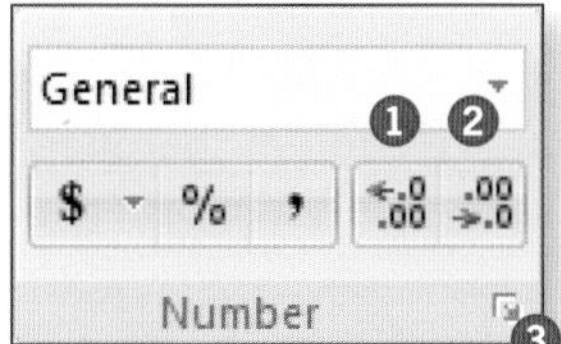

Formatting numbers is very easy when you use the number formats commands on the Number group on the Home tab. The following formats are available in this group:

Accounting ($): Displays fixed dollar sign at the left of the cell.
Percent (%): Displays % sign.

Comma (,): Numbers display commas for ease in reading large numbers, e.g., 1,353,813.
Decimal places: Click Increase ❶ or Decrease Decimals ❷ to select the number of decimal places to display.

For more advanced formatting, click the Number Dialog Box Launcher ❸ to display the Format Cells dialog box. Click the Number tab ❹ to display additional formatting categories. For example, Figure 2.7 shows the Currency format (floating dollar sign that appears at the left of the first digit) and negative numbers displayed in red.

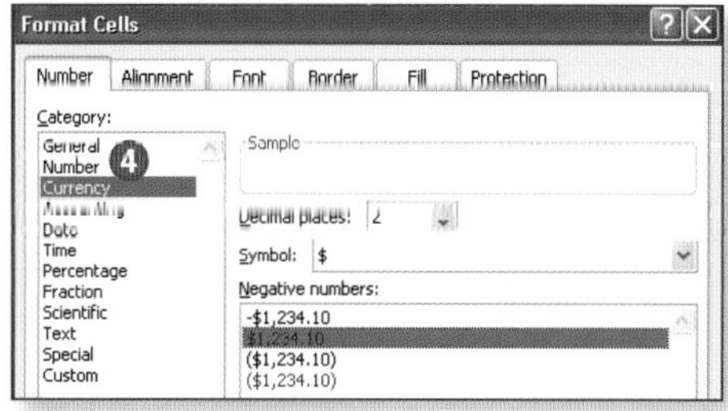

Figure 2.7 Format Cells Dialog Box

DRILL 3 FORMAT NUMBERS

STATEMENT

DISCOVER

Check Spelling

Review/Proofing/Spelling

1. Open the data file *statement* and save as *ex2-drill3*.
2. Format the number in B2 as Accounting, 0 decimal places, B3:C6 as Comma, 0 decimal places, and C7 as Currency with dollar sign, 0 decimal places, and negative number formatted to display in red in parentheses.
3. Check the spelling on the worksheet and make the needed changes.
4. Resave as *ex2-drill3* and close.

CELL STYLES

Home/Styles/Cell Styles

You can apply formats to worksheet cells just as you apply styles to text in a *Word* document. Applying a cell style results in consistent formatting and saves valuable time. Study Figure 2.8 for the various cell styles categories to mark Good, Bad, or Neutral data; to identify Data and Model data types; to format Titles and Headings; to apply Themed Cell Styles; and to apply Number Formats. Click Normal ❶ to remove cell styles.

DISCOVER

Modify Cell Style

Home/Styles/Cell Styles

Select the style and right-click. Click Modify and then Format. Make the desired changes.

To Apply a Cell Style:

1. Select the cells to be formatted.
2. Click the arrow next to Cell Styles and click the desired style.

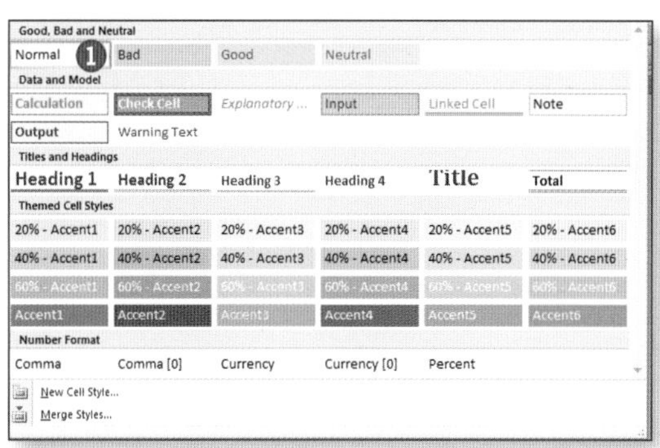

Figure 2.8 Cell Styles Gallery

DRILL 2 ADD CRITERIA TO A QUERY AND SORT

1. With *ac3-drill1* open, save the database as *ac3-drill2*.
2. Create the following queries using the Donations – Autos table. Unless otherwise instructed, show all the fields that are used in the query, sort by Make and Model in ascending order, and print each query before closing.
   a. Display the Make, Model, and Condition of SUVs that are in Very Good condition. Save the query as **Very Good SUVs**.
   b. Display the Make, Model, and Mileage of cars that have greater than 100,000 miles (>100000). Save the query as **Cars > 100,000**.
   c. Display the Make, Model, Model Year, and Donated Value of vehicles with a model year before 2000 (<2000) that have a donated value less than $10,000. Save the query as **Vehicles < 2000**.
   d. Display the Make and Model of all vehicles from 2005 or later that have a donated value greater than $15,000. Save the query as **Late Model > $15,000**.
   e. Display the Make, Model, Model Year, Color, and Condition of all Toyotas. Sort as desired. Save the query as **All Toyotas**.
   f. Display Make and Model of all vans with a model year earlier than 2005. Sort by Model Year in descending order, and do not show the Type field. Save the query as **Older Vans**.
   g. Display Make and Model of all trucks that are *not* Chevrolets. Do not show the Type field. Sort as appropriate, and save the query as **Trucks Not Chevrolet**.
3. Leave the database open for the next drill.

> **TIP**
> Do not include the comma when keying number criteria such as 100,000.

FILTER RECORDS

A filter is a selected criterion placed on records in a datasheet (such as a query dynaset) or a form to temporarily display a subset of the records. Unlike a query, a filter cannot be saved. After you have viewed filtered records, remove the filter to see all records again.

A simple technique for filtering records is to filter by selection—select any entry in a field as the criterion on which to filter.

> You will learn about filtering in a form in Lesson 4.

To Filter by Selection:

Home/Sort & Filter/Selection

1. In Datasheet view, click on a field of any record containing the desired value. For example, to select all records where the Type entry is "Car," click on Car in any record.
2. Click Selection ❶ (Figure 3.3) to display a list of selection options.
3. Select any of the available options, such as Equals "Car."
4. Click Toggle Filter ❷ to remove the filter.

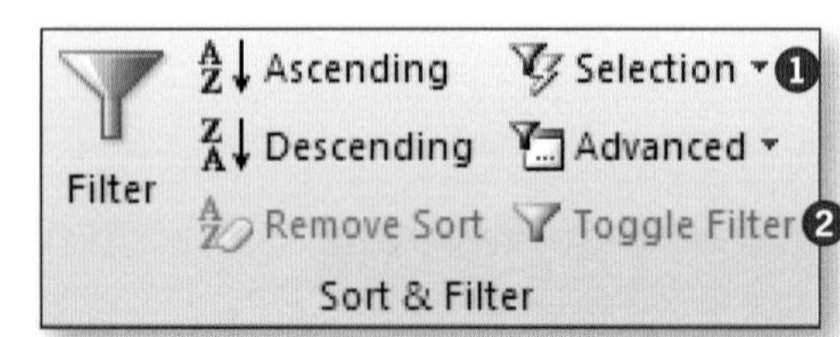

Figure 3.3 Sort & Filter Group

DRILL 4 CELL STYLES

1. Open *ex2-drill2b*. Save as *ex2-drill4*.
2. Select A1:C1 and merge and center the title. Increase the row height of row 1 to 45.00 points and middle-align the text in the row.
3. Select A1 and apply the Title cell style and the Accent1 themed cell style.
4. Select the column headings A2:C2 and apply the Heading 2 cell style.
5. Select A3:C10 and apply the Calculation style. Select A3:A10 and apply the Normal style to remove the style.
6. Select B3:C10 and apply the Comma [0] cell style.
7. Key the word **Total** in A11. Select A11:C11 and apply the Total cell style.
8. Modify the Calculation cell style by changing the font to blue and the font size to 10. Apply the modified cell style to cells B3:C10.
9. Change the theme to Foundry. Note the cells where themed cell styles were applied updated to the new theme.
10. Print; resave the file as *ex2-drill4* and close.

Use Figure 2.9 to check the format.

	A	B	C
1	Expenses		
2		2010	2011
3	Salaries	198,736	250,789
4	Office Supplies	8,458	8,547
5	Legal Fees	95,332	97,000
6	Travel	9,873	9,105
7	Communication	999	1,089
8	Printing	1,089	1,309
9	Insurance	5,983	5,977
10	Utilities	6,991	7,988
11	**Total**		

Figure 2.9 Quick Check

SPARKLINES

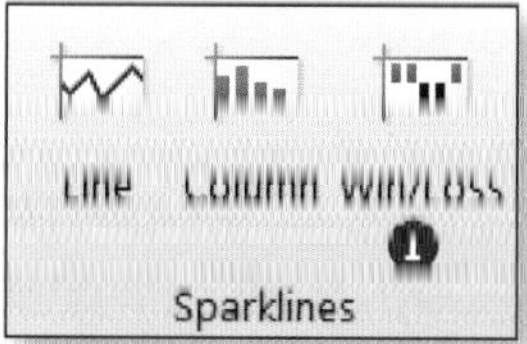

A sparkline is a miniature chart (line, column, or win/loss) that displays in a cell. Note the chart is simple—it does not contain titles, legends, or axes. Users find sparklines helpful to show valuable information in little space.

To Insert Sparklines:

Insert/Sparklines/Line, Column, or Win/Loss

1. Select the desired cell or range of cells where the sparkline is to display.
2. Follow the path above and select either the Line, Column, or Win/Loss chart ❶. The Create Sparklines dialog box displays. The appropriate location range displays ❷.
3. Click in the Data Range box and then select the data range B3:E5 ❸.
4. Click OK.

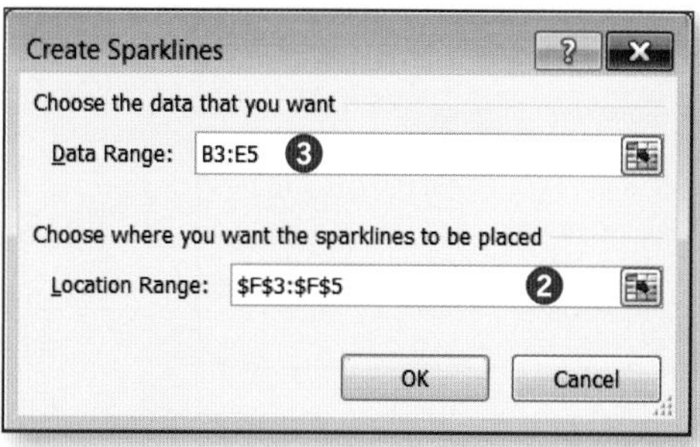

Figure 2.10 Create Sparklines

DISCOVER

You can key a criterion in the Or line ❷ to specify that *Access* will find records that contain either the value shown in the Criteria line OR the value shown in the Or line.

ADD CRITERIA TO A QUERY

After you select the fields that you want to include in the query, you can add criteria to choose the records to appear in the query results. Criteria are a set of conditions that limit the records included in a query. Use the Criteria row ❶ in the query design grid to add one or more criteria to a query.

A query criterion can be one of the values in the records you are searching. For example, to find only Fords in the auto donations table, key Ford in the Criteria row for the Make field, as shown in Figure 3.2. You can also use comparison operators to compare values in a field to a value you key in the Criteria row. Comparison criteria can also be used to display those values that do not match given criteria. Comparison operators include the following:

>	Greater than	>=	Greater than or equal to
<	Less than	<=	Less than or equal to
<>	Not equal to		

You can use comparison criteria with both alphabetic and numeric fields. Figure 3.2 shows a query that will display all Fords *except* trucks that are later than 2003 and that have fewer than 100,000 miles.

TIP

If you see a blank dynaset after running your query, it means that *Access* found no matching records. Sometimes this is because no records actually match your criteria. Other times, it means you have mistyped the criteria in the query design grid. Proofread carefully!

In some cases, you may want to include a field in the query but not want to see the field's data in the dynaset. To exclude a field from the dynaset, deselect the checkbox in the Show ❸ row, as shown for the Type field in Figure 3.2.

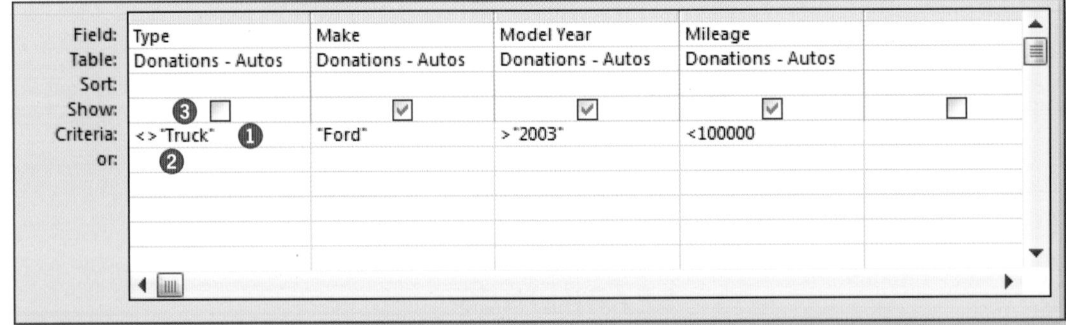

Figure 3.2 Query with Criteria and Hidden Field

To Add Criteria for a Field:

1. Once you have added the desired fields to the query design grid, click the Criteria row in the desired field's column.
2. Key the criterion you want to use. For example, to list all 2003 vehicles, key 2003 on the Criteria row of the Model Year column. If you have additional criteria, key them on the Criteria row of the appropriate field.

SORT RECORDS IN A QUERY

You can add a sort to the query by selecting an option in the Sort row of the query design grid. This can be more efficient than having to sort the dynaset each time you run a query.

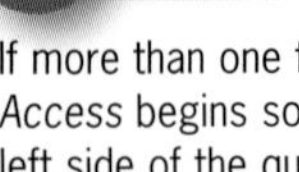

TIP

If more than one field is sorted, *Access* begins sorting from the left side of the query design grid. Make sure you place the field you want sorted first to the left of the other fields to be sorted.

To Sort Records:

1. In the query design grid, click the Sort row for the field you want to sort. A down arrow appears.
2. Click the down arrow and select Ascending or Descending from the list.

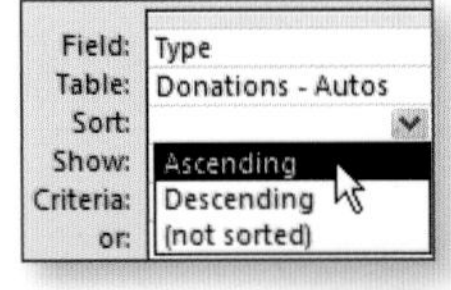

To Edit Sparklines:

Sparkline Tools Design

1. Click the Sparkline Tools Design tab and browse the commands in each group (Figure 2.11). You will apply these in Drill 5.

   Type—Use to change sparkline type or edit data ❶.

   Show—Display the various points noted and show markers ❷.

   Style—Select from a gallery of styles; change sparkline color and marker colors ❸.

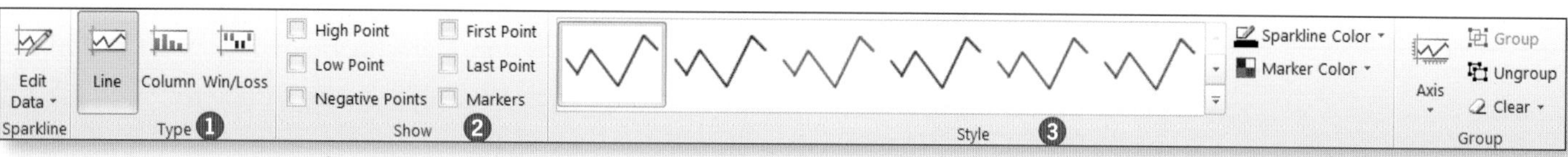

Figure 2.11 Edit Sparklines

DRILL 5 SPARKLINES

REQUESTS

1. Open the data file *requests*. Save as *ex2-drill5*.
2. Select the range F3:F5. Click Insert and then click the Line sparkline. In the Create Sparklines dialog box, select B3:E5 as the data range. Click OK.
3. In F2, key the column title **Quarterly Record**. Use the Format Painter to copy the format of E2, and wrap text in cell F2.
4. Change the sparkline type to Column, then to Win/Loss, and back to Line.
5. Apply the Accent 5, Darker 50% sparklines style.
6. Click the Marker Color drop-list arrow and choose Standard Purple for the marker color, Green for the High Point, and Dark Red for the Low Point.
7. Resave as *ex2-drill5* and close.

Apply It

Worksheet 2

Format Worksheet

ADDRESS FILE

1. Open the data file *address file* and save as *ex2-w2*. Key your name in A1. Key information for at least five people you would add to your address file. Apply the Equity theme.
2. Merge and center the worksheet title; apply the 20% Accent1 style and then apply the Title style. Increase the row height to 45.00 points and middle-align the title.
3. Insert two rows above row 2; click the Insert Options button and select Format Same As Below. Key your full address in A2. Move cell phone data in A11 to A3. Merge and center both rows. Apply same accent cell style used in A1 for new rows.
4. Apply Heading 4 style to A2.
5. Modify Heading 3 style by changing horizontal alignment to center.
6. Apply Heading 3 style to A3 and to A4:G4.
7. Change column heading *Phone* to **Work Phone** and click Wrap Text to display text on two lines. Insert a new column to the left of Work Phone. Key the heading **Cell Phone** on two lines.
8. Delete the column containing e-mail addresses. Change to the Module theme.
9. Check spelling, resave as *ex2-w2*, and close.

Move Selected Cells

1. Select cells to be moved.
2. Point to the border and drag to the new location and drop.

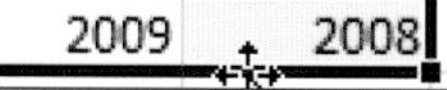

You can also drag and drop fields from the field list to the query design grid. Select adjacent fields as a group by clicking the first field name and then SHIFT + clicking the last field name. Use the CTRL + click method to select nonadjacent fields. Then use drag and drop to move the selected fields.

4. To increase the viewing size of the table pane or the field list, position the mouse pointer on the split between the two panes or on the bottom border of the field list box and drag down.
5. Add a field name to the query design grid by double-clicking it in the field list. The field name appears in the first open Field box of the query design grid. The table name shows in the Table row, and a check mark appears in the checkbox of the Show row, indicating that this field will be displayed in the query results.
6. Double-click additional field names necessary for the query. Each field will appear in the query design grid to the right of the previous field.
7. On the Query Tools Design tab in the Results group, click Run ❶. The dynaset (query results table) is displayed in Datasheet view.
8. On the Home tab in the Views group, click View and Design View to return to the Query Design view.

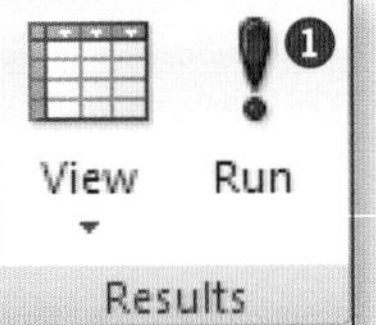

You can save a query by closing the object window. *Access* will ask you if you want to save the query.

SAVE A QUERY

A query can be saved for future use. As new records are entered in the tables, you can run a saved query to obtain an up-to-date list of records that meet the criteria.

To Save a Query:

File/Save

1. Click Save.
2. Key the query name and click OK.

After saving a query, you may want to make a change in the query, or you may want to base a new query on an existing one. After making any changes, you can elect to save the revised query using a different object name.

You can save any database object with a new name by selecting the object in the Navigation Pane and following these steps.

To Save a Query Using a New Name:

File/Save Object As

1. Click Save Object As.
2. Key the query name in the Save to box.
3. Click OK.

DRILL 1 SIMPLE QUERY

AC3-DRILL1-DATA

To remove a field from the query design grid, position the mouse pointer just above the Field row so it becomes a black, down-pointing arrow. Click to select the column, and then tap DELETE.

1. Open the data file *ac3-drill1-data*. Save the database as *ac3-drill1*.
2. Create a new query using the Donations – Autos table:
   a. Double-click the Make, Model, and Donated Value fields to add them to the query design grid.
   b. Run the query to see a list of all makes, models, and values.
   c. Save the query as **Makes Models Values**. Print the dynaset.
3. Switch back to Design view, and add the Condition and Comments fields to the query.
4. Run the query; then save the new version of it as **Makes and Comments**.
5. Expand columns as necessary by double-clicking field header borders to see all data, and then print the Makes and Comments dynaset.
6. Close the query and leave the database open for the next drill.

QUICK

Use Figure 2.12 to check *ex2-w2*.

	A	B	C	D	E	F	G	H
1	Address File for Your Name							
2	Your Address, City, State ZIP							
3	Cell Phone: xxx-xxx-xxxx							
4	Last	First	Street	City	State	ZIP	Cell Phone	Work Phone

Figure 2.12 Quick Cheek

Worksheet 3

Format Worksheet

SALES STATS

1. Open the data file *sales stats* and save as *ex2-w3*. Apply the Module theme.
2. Apply the Normal cell style to clear the formatting in range A1:A2.
3. Delete the blank row 3. Delete column B, ID Number.
4. Insert a blank row and key your name so it will appear in alphabetical order. Your sales figures are as follows: 1458381, 1442321, 1331333, 1467928.
5. Brian Brooks has moved to another city; delete the row that contains Brian's stats.
6. The manager changed his mind about recording the ID. Insert a column before Qtr 1 and label it **ID Number**. Key the ID numbers from the data file. Your ID is 25-00-73.
7. In G3, key the column title **Trend**. Insert Line sparklines in cells G4:G8 to show the sales trends for the range C4:F8. Apply the sparkline style Accent 2, Darker 50%. Display the High Point and Low Point. Change the marker color to Green for the High Point and Red for the Low Point.
8. Format as follows:
   a. Row 1—Merge and center, Accent2 and Title cell styles, row height 39.00 points, middle-align text.
   b. Row 2—Merge and center, 40% Accent2 and Heading 3 cell styles, row height 24.00 points.
   c. Column headings (A3:G3)—20% Accent5 and Heading 3 cell styles.
   d. Selected cells—Select A5:F5; press CTRL and select A7:F7. Apply the 40% Accent4 cell style.
   e. C4:F8—Format Comma [0] cell style.
9. Check the spelling, resave, and print. Close the file.

Use Figure 2.13 to check *ex2-w3*.

	A	B	C	D	E	F	G
1	Sales Report						
2	Prepared by: David Slaughter						
3	Representative	ID Number	Qtr 1	Qtr 2	Qtr 3	Qtr 4	Trend
4	Leung, Kelly	25-12-93	1,458,921	1,459,981	1,458,882	1,438,921	
5	Marion, Abigail	25-41-01	1,318,926	1,298,932	1,279,363	1,258,921	
6	Uriz, Michael	25-45-37	1,242,387	1,198,792	1,298,297	1,268,293	
7	West, Samantha	25-23-22	1,258,976	1,294,729	1,308,789	1,327,894	
8	Student's Name	25-00-73	1,458,381	1,442,321	1,331,333	1,467,928	
9							
10	*Student's name should be included in the proper location.						

Figure 2.13 Quick Cheek

LESSON 3

Create Simple Queries

OBJECTIVES

- Create simple queries
- Add criteria to a query
- Sort and filter records in a query

CREATE QUERIES IN DESIGN VIEW

A query is a question that you ask the database. In this lesson, you will work with select queries, the most common type of query. A select query finds and lists the records that satisfy the criteria you set. For example, you might want to display only the first and last names of all customers from Illinois. The select query results are displayed in a table format called a *dynaset.*

Queries are based on one or more tables or on other queries. Although *Access* offers a Query Wizard, it is easy to create a query using the Query Design command. Designing queries in Design view is called *query by example* (often abbreviated QBE), because you use a graphical interface to designate the fields and the query parameters desired.

To Create a Query Using Design View:

Create/Queries/Query Design

1. In an open database, click Query Design. The Show Table dialog box appears, containing a list of the database's tables and queries.
2. Select each table or query you want to use in your query and click Add.
3. Click Close to close the Show Table dialog box. The Query Design view appears. Figure 3.1 shows one field added to the query design grid.

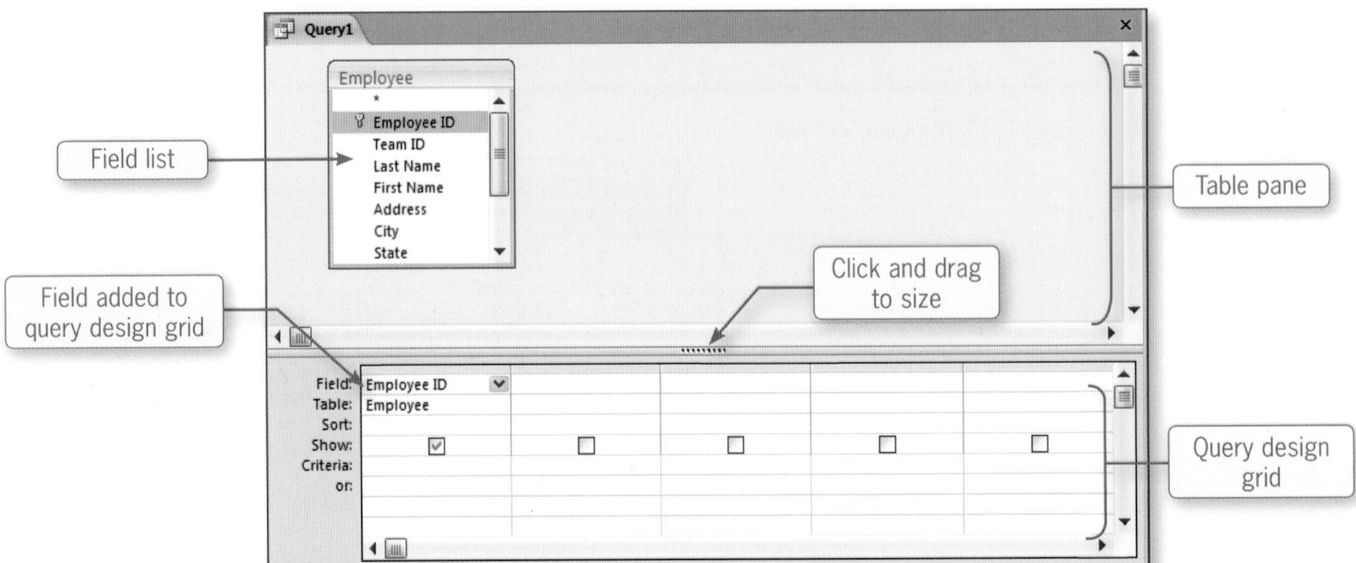

Figure 3.1 Query Design View

LESSON 3

Insert Formulas and Functions

OBJECTIVES

- Create formulas in a worksheet
- Insert functions in a worksheet
- Use relative and absolute cell references

CREATE FORMULAS

A formula is a set of instructions to perform calculations in a cell. All formulas begin with an equals sign (=) and consist of a number or cell reference (e.g., A5) and a calculation operator that indicates what to do. In the formula =A5+C2, the values in A5 and C2 are added. The cell reference may be a cell address, such as D4, or a range of cells (D4:D8). Study the calculation operators in Table 3.1; substitute 10 for B4 and 2 for D4.

Operation	Example	Meaning	Result
Addition (+)	=B4+D4	Adds the values in B4 and D4	10 + 2 = 12
Subtraction (-)	=B4-D4	Subtracts the value in D4 from the value in B4	10 – 2 = 8
Division (/)	=B4/D4	Divides the value in B4 by the value in D4	10 / 2 = 5
Multiplication (*)	=B4*D4	Multiplies the values in B4 and D4	10 * 2 = 20
Percent (%)	=B4*8%	Calculates 8% of the value in B4	10 * 8% = .8
Exponentiation (^)	=B4^3	Increases the value of B4 to the third power	10^3 = 1000

Table 3.1 Formula Operations

In the worksheet titled Invoice shown in Figure 3.1, the formula =A3*C3 is displayed in the active cell, D3 ❶. An efficient way of entering this formula is to key the =; then point to A3 and click; key the *; then point to C3 and click. Note the formula displays in the active cell and the formula bar. Tap ENTER or click the Enter button ❷ to the left of the formula bar to complete the operation.

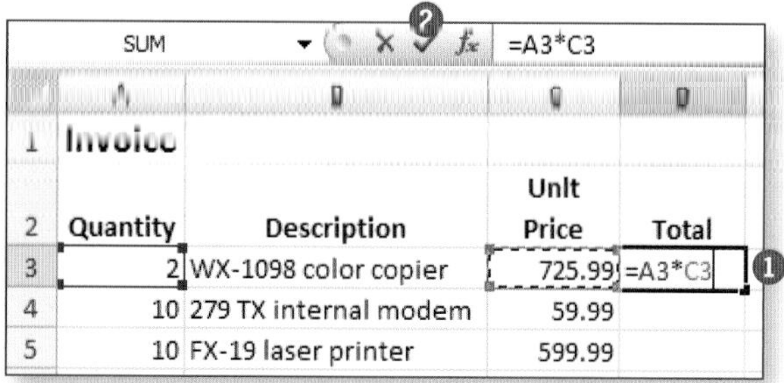

Figure 3.1 Formula in Active Cell and Formula Bar

If several calculation operators are included in one formula, *Excel* performs the operations in the following order of precedence: (1) negation, e.g., –1; (2) percent; (3) exponentiation; (4) multiplication and division, whichever comes first left to right; and (5) addition or subtraction, whichever comes first left to right. In the formula =6+4/2, division has precedence over the addition, so the result is 8—not 5.

To change the order of precedence, enclose the part of the formula to be calculated first in parentheses. The formula =(6+4)/2 would result in the answer 5 because the addition is performed first within the parentheses.

Database 2,
continued

1. Create a new, blank database in your solutions folder named *ac2-db2*.
2. Create a table named **Employees** from the data shown in Figure 2.8, using data types, field sizes, and properties appropriate for each field. Create an input mask for the Phone field that does not have parentheses around the area code.
3. Key the records displayed in Figure 2.8.
4. Print and close the table. Close the database.

Database 3
New Database and Table

The names, addresses, and positions of selected board members of your company are shown in Figure 2.9.

Janice Edwards Compensation Committee Chair 311 Greenbriar Street Starkville, MS 39759-4455	Adam Hyde Audit Committee Chair 111 7th Avenue South Columbus, MS 39701-1768
Samuel Glenn Treasurer 290 Tomlinson Road Starkville, MS 39759-4121	Matthew Stephens President 1140 Nottingham Road Starkville, MS 39759-8915

Figure 2.9 Records for Board Table

TIP

Do not key any data in the ID field; Access will automatically enter a number in this field for you.

1. Create a new, blank database in your solutions folder named *ac2-db3*.
2. Create a table named **Board** from the data shown in Figure 2.9. Assign field names and use data types appropriate for each field. Use the default ID field as the primary key, and accept the default AutoNumber data type.
3. Change the field properties to assign a field size and use the required value, default value, and input mask properties as appropriate.
4. Key the records displayed in Figure 2.9.
5. Print and close the table. Close the database.

JOB KNOWLEDGE

In recent years, several well-publicized database hacking incidents have brought computer security to the forefront of issues facing database users and administrators. Databases are designed to promote open and flexible access to data, but it is this same ready access that makes them vulnerable to many kinds of malicious activity.

Businesses must develop database security plans to protect the confidentiality and integrity of their information. The threats to the security of database information are varied. Computer hackers, disgruntled employees, and careless workers all pose risks to database integrity. A database security program should include employee management and training; secure network and software design; storage, transmission, and disposal of data; and emergency contingencies, including preventing, detecting, and responding to a security breach.

TO COPY A FORMULA:

1. Point to the fill handle ❶ at the bottom right corner of the active cell until the crosshair appears (Figure 3.2).
2. Drag down through the range ❷ to copy the formula to the remaining cells.

   Alternate method: Click the Copy command; select the range of cells where the formula is to be copied; and click the Paste command.

D3 | fx =A3*C3

	A	B	C	D
1	**Invoice**			
2	**Quantity**	**Description**	**Unit Price**	**Total**
3	2	WX-1098 color copier	725.99	1451.98 ❶
4	10	279 TX internal modem	59.99	
5	10	FX-19 laser printer	599.99	❷

Figure 3.2 Drag Fill Handle to Copy Formula

DRILL 1 ENTER FORMULAS

FORMULAS

1. Open the data file *formulas*. Save as *ex3-drill1*.
2. On Sheet1, in D2 (Difference column), enter the formula **=C2-B2**. Remember to key =, point to C2 and click; then key -, point to B2, and click.
3. In E2 (% Change column), key the formula **=D2/C2**.
4. Select D2:E2. Copy both formulas by dragging the fill handle through the remaining expenses.
5. Click Sheet2. In E20, enter the appropriate formula for Quantity times Unit Price.
6. Copy the formula to the remaining items being ordered.
7. Rename Sheet1 as % **Change** and Sheet2 as **Purchase Order**.
8. Save the file and leave open for the next drill.

INSERT FUNCTIONS

Formulas/Function Library

Formulas may also include functions, which are predefined formulas that perform calculations by using specific values, called arguments, in a particular order, or syntax. Each function has a specific structure: (1) equals sign (=), (2) function name, and (3) arguments. If the argument consists of more than one part, separate each part with a comma. Table 3.2 shows common *Excel* functions and their arguments.

Function	Syntax	Meaning
SUM	=SUM(A5:A12)	Adds all cells from A5 through A12
	=SUM(A5,A12)	Adds only A5 and A12
AVERAGE	=AVERAGE(C5:F5)	Averages all values in the range C5:F5
COUNT	=COUNT(A2:A20)	Counts the number of cells that contain numbers in the range A2:A20
MIN	=MIN(A2:A20)	Returns the smallest number in a set of values
MAX	=MAX(A2:A20)	Returns the largest number in a set of values
PMT	=PMT(rate,nper,pv,fv,type)	Calculates the payment for a loan based on constant payments and a constant interest rate
	=PMT(12%/12,36,20000)	The 12% rate is divided by 12 to determine monthly payment; 36 is the number of months, and $20,000 is the amount of the loan. (The last two parts of this argument are optional.)

Table 3.2 Function Arguments

Excel has many functions, which are arranged in categories ❶ in the Function Library group (Figure 3.3). Begin with the AutoSum category, click the arrow next to each category, and browse the various functions available.

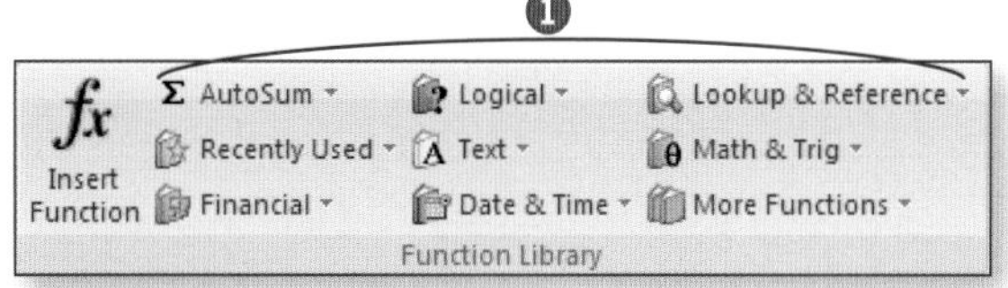

Figure 3.3 Function Library Group

DRILL 3 CREATE AN INPUT MASK

DISCOVER

Create/Tables/Table

Follow this path to create a new table in an open database.

1. With *ac2-drill2* open, save the database as *ac2-drill3*.
2. Create a new table in Design view named **Suppliers** with the following fields, data types, and properties. Supplier ID is the primary key.

Field Name	Data Type	Field Size	Other Properties
Supplier ID	Text	2	Required
Supplier Name	Text	50	Required
Address	Text	50	
City	Text	40	
State	Text	2	Default value: OH
ZIP	Text	10	
Telephone	Text	12	

TIP

In an input mask, a 0 requires that you enter a digit (0–9). Using a 9 in the area code makes entering a digit optional.

3. In the ZIP field, use the Input Mask Wizard to insert the Zip Code input mask. Accept all defaults and choose to store the data with symbols.
4. In the Telephone field, use the Input Mask Wizard to insert the Phone Number input mask. Change the input mask format to **!999-000-0000**. Choose to store the data with symbols.
5. Save changes to the table design, and switch to Datasheet view. Key the records shown in Figure 2.7.
6. Print the table, close it, and close the database.

TIP

Business communication standards now prefer that area codes not use parentheses.

Suppliers

Supplier ID	Supplier Name	Address	City	State	ZIP	Telephone
1	Jordan Fine Art Supply	7404 Beechmont Avenue	Cincinnati	OH	45230-1245	513-555-0189
2	Kloppinger Artwerks	48 E Main Street	Lexington	OH	44904-1222	419-555-0122
3	Belle Epoch Arts	67 Springfield Street	Dayton	OH	45403-1157	937-555-0176
4	Muybridge & Co	74 Eden Park Drive	Cincinnati	OH	45202-6031	513-555-0144
*				OH		

Figure 2.7 Records for Suppliers Table

Apply It

Database 2
New Database and Table

The data shown in Figure 2.8 is currently maintained on a paper schedule.

Employee #	First Name	Last Name	Hourly Wage	Phone	CPE Complete
188	Brad	Rost	$25.25	662-555-0145	Yes
218	Penny	Li	$16.25	662-555-0148	No
226	Peter	Zimble	$18.50	601-555-0132	No
286	Chris	Dowd	$16.20	601-555-0163	Yes
294	Karen	Cho	$18.50	662-555-0121	Yes

Figure 2.8 Records for Employees Table

Home/Editing

Five frequently used functions, including the SUM function, are located on the Home tab.

To Insert a Function:

Formulas/Function Library

1. Click in the cell where the result of the function is to display ❶.
2. Click the arrow next to a category, e.g., AutoSum, and click the desired function, e.g., Sum ❷ (Figure 3.4).

Figure 3.5 shows the function displayed in F4 with a scrolling marquee marking the cells used in the function.

3. Tap ENTER or click the Enter button.

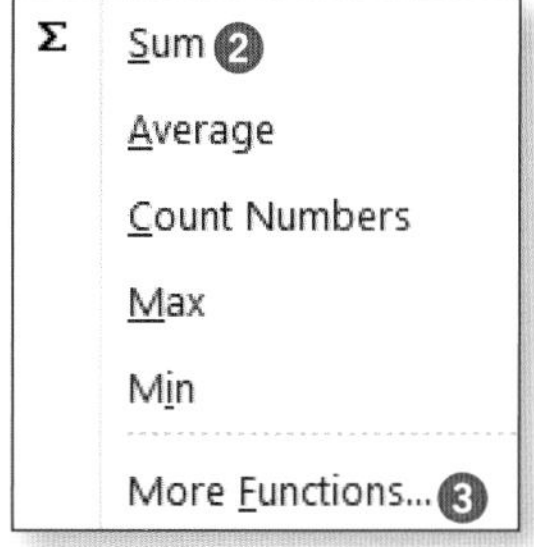

Figure 3.4 AutoSum Functions

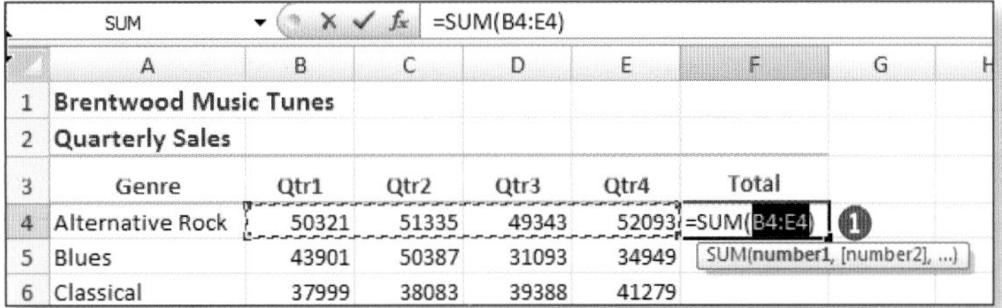

	A	B	C	D	E	F	G	H
1	**Brentwood Music Tunes**							
2	**Quarterly Sales**							
3	Genre	Qtr1	Qtr2	Qtr3	Qtr4	Total		
4	Alternative Rock	50321	51335	49343	52093	=SUM(B4:E4)		
5	Blues	43901	50387	31093	34949			
6	Classical	37999	38083	39388	41279			

Figure 3.5 SUM Function Displayed in F4

Note: If you cannot find the function you want to use, click More Functions ❸ or click Insert Function in the Function Library group. The Insert Function dialog box displays (Figure 3.6).

In the Search for a function box, key the desired function name. Click the Help on this function hyperlink to go directly to Help information on the desired function. Note the description provided for the selected function.

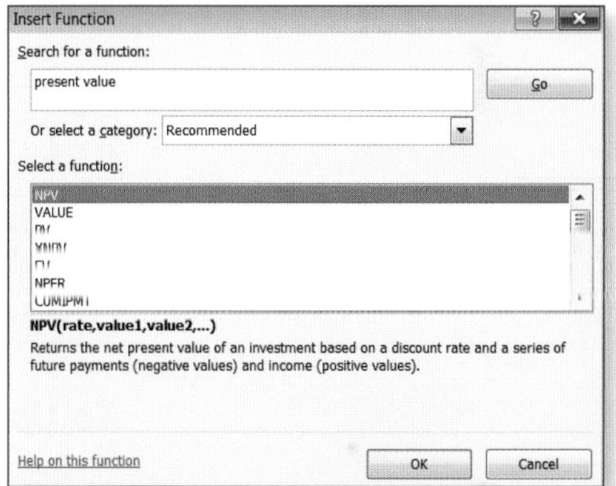

Figure 3.6 Insert Function Dialog Box

DRILL 2 INSERT FUNCTIONS

1. Save *ex3-drill1* as *ex3-drill2*.
2. On the Purchase Order sheet, click D28. Key **Total** and apply the Total cell style to D28:E28.
3. Click in E28 and insert the SUM function to sum (E20:E27).
4. On the % Change sheet, key **Total** in A9 and apply the Total cell style to A9:E9. Change the B1 and C1 headings to text data by keying an apostrophe in front of the heading ('2010 and '2011).
5. Click in B9 and insert the SUM function to sum (B2:B8). Drag the fill handle to copy the formula in C9.
6. In D9, compute the total difference, and in E9, compute the total % change. *Hint:* For D9, copy formula from D8; for E9, copy formula from E8.
7. Apply the Percent cell style to E2:E9.
8. Resave as *ex3-drill2*, print, and close the file.

If you do not add the apostrophe to the dates 2010 and 2011, *Excel* will attempt to include them in the SUM function's range of values.

Field Name	Data Type	Field Size	Other Properties
Product ID		3	Required
Supplier ID		2	Required
In Stock	Number		
Unit Price	Currency		
Reorder Level	Number		

6. Save your changes. A warning message will appear that tells you some data may be lost. Click Yes to continue. A second warning message will appear to tell you that data integrity rules have changed. Click Yes to continue.
7. Switch to Datasheet view. For each product, check to see if the current In Stock number is less than the Reorder Level number. If it is, click in the Reorder Now checkbox. In the Reorder Date field, pick the following Monday as the reorder date and use 2012 as the year.
8. Preview, adjust column widths as necessary to fit the table on one page, print, and close the Supplies Inventory table. Leave the database open for the next drill.

CREATE AN INPUT MASK

The Input Mask Wizard helps you to create an input mask. You can select from pre-designed input masks for common fields, such as social security number, phone number, and ZIP code. For unique fields, you can create a custom input mask using a variety of available tools.

To Use the Input Mask Wizard:

1. In Design view, select the field to contain the input mask, and click the Input Mask property box.
2. Click the Mask button visible in the Input Mask property box. Save the table if prompted.
3. The Input Mask Wizard window shown in Figure 2.6 opens, displaying a list of input masks.
4. Use the vertical scroll bar to view the pre-existing mask choices. Select the desired mask, and click Next.
5. The next window displays the input mask format and asks whether you want to change the default input mask. Key any changes to the mask format, if necessary, and click Next.
6. The next window asks if you want to store symbols with the data. It is usually a good idea to do this, so select With the symbols in the mask. Then click Next.
7. Click Finish. The mask format appears in the Input Mask property box.

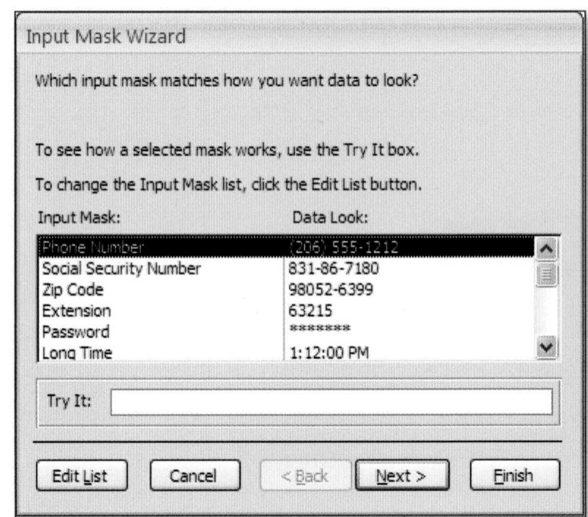

Figure 2.6 Input Mask Wizard

USE CELL REFERENCES

Using cell references in formulas rather than using the actual values in cells is essential because when a cell value changes, each formula or function that contains the cell reference is automatically recalculated. Relative and absolute cell references are shown in Figure 3.7.

A relative cell reference ❶ changes relative to the cell from which the formula is being copied. Note that when the formula in D4 is copied down, =B4*C4 changes to =B5*C5; the row 4 cell references adjust for their new location in row 5.

An absolute cell reference ❷ does not adjust if copied and is designated with the dollar symbol ($) before the column and the row, e.g., $B$2. When the formula in cell E4 is copied, the reference to cell $B$2 stays the same in each new row. Note that the D4 reference in E4 is a relative cell reference and changes when copied to E5.

	A	B	C	D	E
1	Commission Report for Product 23-934				
2	Commission Rate:	5%		❶	❷
3	Name	Units	Price $	Total Sales	Commission
4	Davis, Bonnie	175	$ 250	=B4*C4	=D4*$B$2
5	Ferguson, George	250	250	=B5*C5	=D5*$B$2
6	Kline, Mary	110	250	=B6*C6	=D6*$B$2

Figure 3.7 Relative and Absolute Cell References

TIP

After keying a cell reference, tap F4 and the $ symbols will be added to the cell reference. Repeat tapping F4 to cycle to the desired cell reference.

DRILL 3 USE ABSOLUTE AND RELATIVE CELL REFERENCES

BAKERY

1. Open the data file *bakery*. Save as *ex3-drill3*.
2. In G4, enter the formula for calculating the total due from each customer. Use the cell references in the Price List (A14:B19). *Hint:* Include all cells in the range B4:F4 in the formula because you will copy the formula down. The formula will include a relative and absolute cell reference.
3. Copy the formula in G4 to the other customers.
4. In B12, enter the function to determine the total coffee cakes sold. Be sure the scrolling marquee marks B4:B11; drag to select that range if necessary.
5. Copy the formula in B12 to columns C through G. Apply the Accounting [0] cell style to cell G12.
6. Resave as *ex3-drill3*, print, and close the file.

QUICK ✓ Use Figure 3.8 to check the worksheet.

G4 | =B4*$B$15+C4*$B$16+D4*$B$17+E4*$B$18+F4*$B$19

	A	B	C	D	E	F	G
1	Bakery Fundraiser						
2			Cakes			Pies	
3	Customer	Coffee Cake	Carrot Cake	Pound Cake	Pecan Pie	Egg Custard	Total Due
4	Ron Atkins	1				1	32.00
5	Gail Barr				2		30.00
6	Andrew Dennison		1			1	37.00
7	Vanessa King	3					60.00
8	Chien Lee		1	1			50.00
9	Tom Robinson		1		2		55.00
10	Wanda Walden	1	1				45.00
11	Jim Zakkak			1		3	61.00
12	Total	5	4	2	4	5	$ 370
13							
14	Price List						
15	Coffee Cake	$20.00					
16	Carrot Cake	25.00					
17	Pound Cake	25.00					
18	Pecan Pie	15.00					
19	Egg Custard	12.00					

Figure 3.8 Quick Check

Format: Defines how the data should display once entered; e.g., choose percent format for a Number field or select a date or time format for a Date/Time field.

Input Mask: Establishes the pattern for information; e.g., a ZIP Code has a hyphen between the first five digits and the last four digits. By setting an input mask, you do not have to key the hyphen—it displays automatically as you key the number.

Default Value: Specifies a value that is automatically inserted in the field when you create a new record.

> **TIP**
> If a field usually contains the same value, set a Default Value. For example, if most of your customers are located in Illinois, you can enter IL as the default value of the State field.

Required: Requires that an entry be made in this field before you can save the record. If you want data to be required in a field, select Yes.

Although you should set field properties when you create the table, you may decide after the table structure has been saved that you need to change field properties. For example, you may decide that a particular default State field should be inserted.

To Set or Change Field Properties:

1. In Design view, click anywhere in the field's row in the Field Grid pane.
2. The field properties for the field appear in the Field Properties pane (Figure 2.5) at the bottom of the window. Set all desired properties for the field, and continue until properties have been set for all fields.
3. Switch to Datasheet view when finished changing field properties. Click Yes to save changes in field properties.

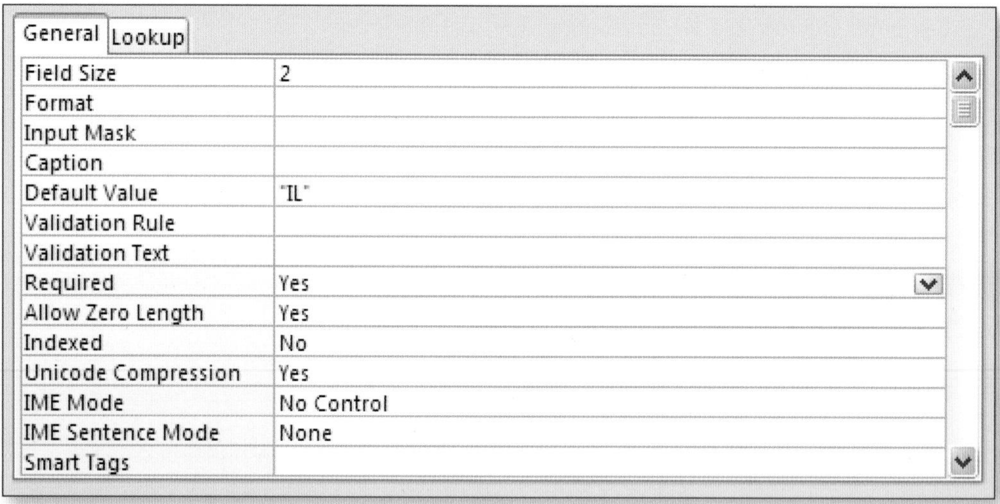

Figure 2.5 Field Properties Pane for State Field

DRILL 2 CHANGE DATA TYPES AND FIELD PROPERTIES

1. Open the data file *ac2-drill2-data*. Save the database as *ac2-drill2*.
2. Display the Supplies Inventory table in Design view.
3. Make the changes shown in the table on the next page to field properties in the table.
4. Add a new field at the bottom of the field list with the name **Reorder Now** and the Yes/No data type.
5. Add another new field with the name **Reorder Date** and the Date/Time data type. Change the Format property to Medium Date.

Apply It

Worksheet 4
Payroll Worksheet

SIMPLE PAYROLL

1. Open the data file *simple payroll* and save as *ex3-w4*. Rename Sheet1 as **June 1-5**.
2. Select column headings B–F; right-click, select Column Width, and key **5**.
3. Enter the following formulas and copy to the remaining employees:
   a. Total Hours—In G4, enter a function to add the hours worked M–F.
   b. Gross Pay—In I4, key a formula that multiplies total hours and hourly rate.
   c. Stock Deduction—In J4, enter an absolute cell reference to the cost of Stock Option 1 (B16) in the table shown in A15:B18. Stock Option numbers display in parentheses after each employee name. Enter the correct Stock Option cost for each employee.
   d. Net Pay—In K4, key a formula that subtracts the Stock Deduction from Gross Pay.
   e. Total—In G13, enter a function to add total hours; copy the formula to I13 and K13.
4. Format the following cells using cell styles:
   A1—Title, merge and center; A2—Heading 4, merge and center
   A3:K3—Heading 3; H4:K4, I13, and K13—Accounting, 2 decimals
   H5:K12—Comma, 2 decimals; A15:B18—Note
   A13:K13—Total
5. Resave as *ex3-w4*, print, and close the file.

Use Figure 3.9 to check the worksheet.

	A	B	C	D	E	F	G	H	I	J	K
1	**Payroll**										
2	Week of June 1-5, 20--										
3	Employee	Mon	Tue	Wed	Thu	Fri	Total Hours	Hourly Rate	Gross Pay	Stock Deduction	Net Pay
4	Merritt, Terry (1)	8	8	7	5	4	32	$ 6.00	$ 192.00	$ 10.00	$ 182.00
5	Newsome, Dianna (2)	8	8	8	8	8	40	6.25	250.00	15.00	235.00
6	Pankasemsuk, Girish (1)	8	7	8	8	4	35	7.00	245.00	10.00	235.00
7	Skaggs, Greg (3)	5	5	8	4	8	30	7.50	225.00	25.00	200.00
8	Wakefield, Derrick (2)	8	7	4	8	8	35	6.25	218.75	15.00	203.75
9	Jackson, Jolynn (1)	6	8	8	8	8	38	7.50	285.00	10.00	275.00
10	Ingram, Enyo (2)	6.5	6	8	8	7	36.5	10.50	372.75	15.00	357.75
11	[illegible] (1)	7	7.5	[illegible]	[illegible]	[illegible]	[illegible]	[illegible]	[illegible]	10.00	[illegible]
12	Aycock, Melody (3)	0	0	0	0	0	40	7.10	204.00	25.00	[illegible]
13	**Total**						320		$ 2,279.50		[illegible]
14											
15	Stock Option Type	Cost									
16	1	10									
17	2	15									
18	3	25									

Figure 3.9 Quick Check

Worksheet 5
Gradebook

GRADEBOOK

1. Open the data file *gradebook* and save as *ex3-w5*. Enter the following functions from the AutoSum category of the Function Library:
   G4—Compute the average on the four tests; copy the formula to each student.
   C16—Average scores for Test 1 (C4:C14).
   C17—Count the number of students taking Test 1 (C4:C14).
   C18—Find the minimum score made on Test 1 (C4:C14).
   C19—Find the maximum score made on Test 1 (C4:C14). Select C16:C19 and use the fill handle to copy the four formulas in one efficient step to D16:F19.

You can preview an *Access* table to see how it will appear when printed. Select printing options such as orientation and margins on the Print Preview tab. After previewing, you may want to adjust column widths to fit data on one page.

DISCOVER

Select options in the Page Layout and Zoom groups on the Print Preview tab based on the width of the table.

To Preview and Print a Table:

File/Print/Print Preview

1. In Datasheet view, click Print Preview.
2. Change any print properties as needed and click Print.
3. Select the printer and pages to print. Click OK.

DRILL 1 NEW DATABASE AND TABLE

1. Create a new, blank database in your solutions folder.
2. Name the file *ac2-drill1*, click OK, and then click Create.
3. Switch to Design view and, when prompted, key the table name **Sept Orders**.
4. Use the following information to insert the fields and data types in the Sept Orders table.
   a. Select the default ID field name and key **Order #**. Select Text as the data type. Note that this field remains the primary key in the table even after you change the field name and data type.
   b. Key the following field names and data types:

TIP

When a field has the Date/Time data type, a calendar displays next to the cell when you key data so that you can pick a date from the calendar rather than key it, if desired.

Customer ID	Text
Order Date	Date/Time
Ship Date	Date/Time
Account Rep	Text

5. Save your changes, switch to Datasheet view, and key the four records shown in Figure 2.4. (You must key the slashes in the dates.)

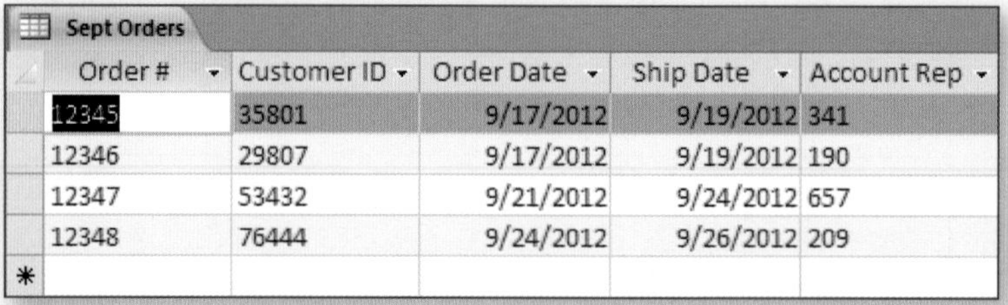

Sept Orders

Order #	Customer ID	Order Date	Ship Date	Account Rep
12345	35801	9/17/2012	9/19/2012	341
12346	29807	9/17/2012	9/19/2012	190
12347	53432	9/21/2012	9/24/2012	657
12348	76444	9/24/2012	9/26/2012	209
*				

Figure 2.4 Sept Orders Data

6. Preview, print, and close the Sept Orders table. Close the database.

SET AND MODIFY FIELD PROPERTIES

Setting field properties establishes rules or guidelines for entering data and helps to prevent data from being entered incorrectly or inconsistently. The most common options available for setting field properties include the following:

Field Size: Defines the maximum number of characters that can be entered in a Text field. The default is 255, but that can be reset for fewer characters; e.g., setting a State field to a field size of 2. For Number fields, use Long Integer as the field size; for fractional numbers with decimal places, choose Double field size.

2. In H4, insert the IF function from the Logical category to determine who qualifies for the President's List (95 or better). In the cell you will see the three parts of the argument separated by commas. Figure 3.10 shows the function arguments. Enclose text statements in quotation marks. Key two quotation marks ("") to display a blank for a false statement. The result of H4 is blank because the average did not meet the criteria. Copy the formula in H4 to the remaining students. Two students qualify for the President's List. Adjust the width of column H.

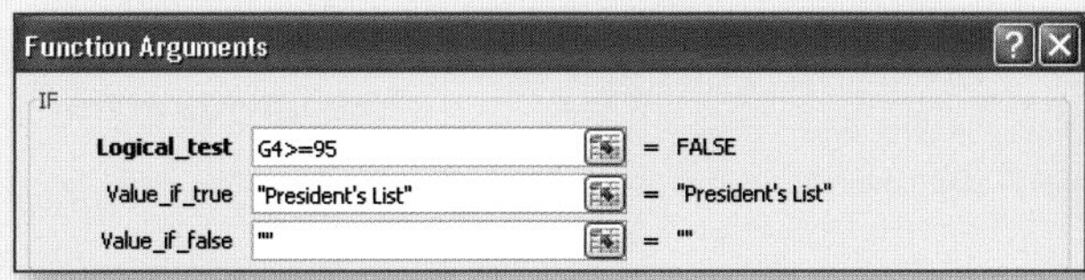

Figure 3.10 Function Arguments

3. In I4, key an IF statement that would determine students who are exempt from the final exam (98 and above). The word *Exempt* should display if eligible. Copy the formula to the remaining students. One student is exempt from the final.
4. Check the spelling. Resave as *ex3-w5*, print, and close the file.

Worksheet 6

Edit Gradebook

1. Open *ex3-w5* and save as *ex3-w6*.
2. Make H4 the active cell. Click the formula bar and edit the formula so that students with averages of 94.5 or higher may be eligible for the President's List. Copy the formula to the remaining students.
3. Double-click I4 and edit the formula so that students with an average of 94.5 or higher may be exempt from the final exam. Three students are eligible for the President's List and exempt from the final exam.
4. In L4:M8, key the table at right; you will use it to compute the final grade in J4.

0	F
60	D
70	C
80	B
90	A

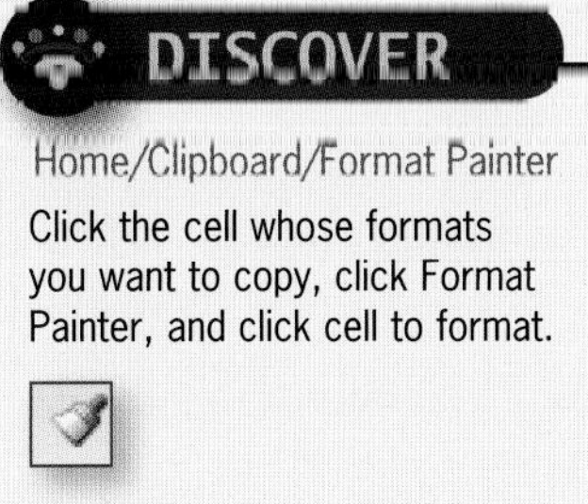

5. In J3, key **Final Grade** on two lines. Use the Format Painter button to copy the formats needed for J3.
6. In J4, key the following vertical lookup function: **=VLOOKUP(G4,$L$4:$M$8,2)**. Copy the formula to the remaining students. *Note*: The logical test is G4, the student average in G4 is then located in the table L4:M8, and the value in the second column is recorded in J4. The reference to the table was keyed as an absolute cell reference because it was copied down to the other students.
7. Resave as *ex3-w6*, print, and close the file.

Worksheet 7

Advanced Payroll Worksheet

ADVANCED PAYROLL

1. Open the data file *advanced payroll* and save as *ex3-w7*. Display the June 1-5 worksheet.
2. Write an IF function for I3 that will compute net pay for those employees working 40 hours per week and those working overtime at 1.5 times their regular hourly rate. The argument for the IF statement is =IF(logical_test, value_if_true,value_if_false).
   a. Logical test: G3<=40
   b. True statement: G3*H3 (formula to compute net pay if <=40 hours)
   c. False statement: 40*H3+(G3-40)*H3*1.5 (formula if >40 hours)

   In I3, key the following IF statement: **=IF(G3<=40,G3*H3,40*H3+(G3-40)*H3*1.5)**. Copy the formula for all employees.
3. In I12, enter a function to compute the total net pay.
4. Click Sheet2 to check your worksheet. Resave, print, and close the file.

Text: Alphabetic or numeric characters that do not require calculations; e.g., a name or telephone number.

Memo: Used for lengthy text that does not follow a particular format; e.g., notes or comments about a record.

Number: Numbers used in mathematical calculations.

Date/Time: Dates and times can be used in calculations. For instance, an employee start date could be subtracted from the current date to determine an employee's length of employment. All dates and times should be defined with the Date/Time data type.

Currency: Numbers that include the currency symbol and might be calculated.

AutoNumber: Consecutive numbers that are assigned automatically by *Access*. AutoNumbers cannot be changed.

Yes/No: Requires a Yes/No, True/False, or On/Off value. Yes/No would be appropriate to indicate memberships or dues paid.

Hyperlink: Stores a path and filename that enable you to jump from the current field to another file or to a location on the Internet.

Attachment: *Word*, *Excel*, *PowerPoint*, and other supported file types can be attached to a record. Multiple files can be attached to a single record.

Lookup Wizard: Creates a field that allows you to choose a value from another table or from a list of values. The Lookup Wizard is not really a data type but a tool that helps provide a list of values for this field.

While *Access* automatically saves changes to data when you close an *Access* object, you must manually save changes to an object's design (or layout) by clicking Save on the Quick Access Toolbar.

To Insert Field Names and Data Types:

1. Click in the first empty Field Name row (or select an existing field entry such as ID).
2. Key the field name and tap TAB.
3. Accept the default data type or click the down arrow in the Data Type column and select another data type option.
4. Tap TAB and, if appropriate, key a description in the Description column.
5. Tap TAB to position the insertion point in the next blank Field Name.
6. Enter field names and select data types for each desired field. Save your changes.

Once you have saved your table structure in Design view, you need to switch to Datasheet view in order to enter records into the table. Click the View button, and choose Datasheet View.

After you change views several times, you'll notice that *Access* changes the View button. The View button alternates between the two most common views—Design and Datasheet.

You may find when you begin to key data in a new table that fields are not wide enough to show all data. Adjust the width of fields in Datasheet view by dragging the field borders, similar to the way you adjust column width in an *Excel* worksheet.

PREVIEW AND PRINT A TABLE

A printout of an *Access* table is not the ideal way to display your data because large tables may print on multiple sheets, making it difficult to get an overall picture of the significance of the data. For an attractive and well-organized printout, it is best to create a report. However, you may want to print the data in a table so that you can check the accuracy of the records.

Print Worksheets

LESSON 4

OBJECTIVES

- Add a header and footer to a worksheet
- Make page adjustments for professional printing

ADD HEADER AND FOOTER

Insert/Text/Header & Footer

Before printing worksheets, you may add a header to appear at the top of every page of the worksheet and a footer to appear at the bottom of every page. You can key the header or footer text yourself or use one of *Excel*'s predefined headers or footers.

To Add a Header and Footer:

1. Click Header & Footer. The worksheet now displays in Page Layout view with a blinking insertion point in the center header box ❶ (Figure 4.1). If desired, click in the left ❷ or right ❸ header box.
2. Key text for the header and click any desired elements from the Header & Footer Elements group on the Header & Footer Tools Design tab (Figure 4.2).
3. Scroll to the bottom of the worksheet and click in the footer box. Repeat steps 1 and 2 to insert footer information.

Figure 4.1 Key Header Text

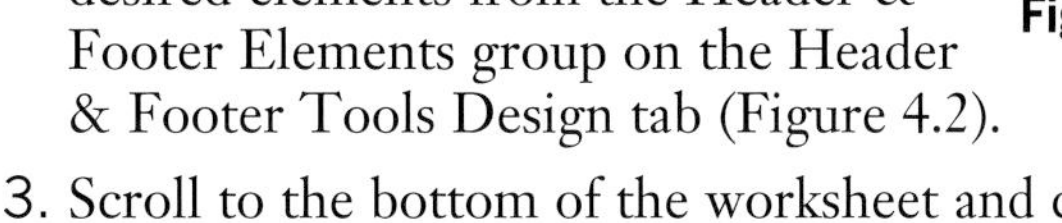

Figure 4.2 Select Header Elements

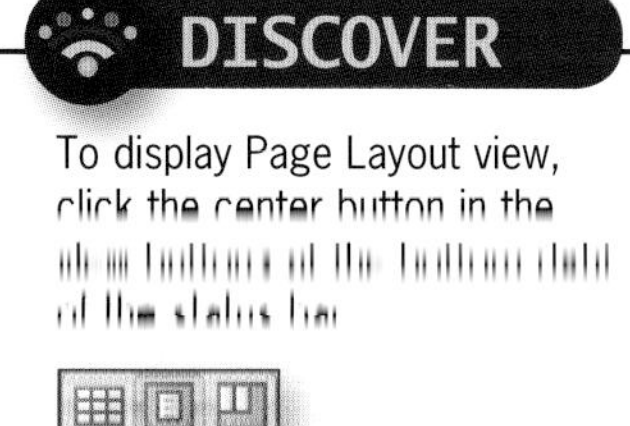

DISCOVER

To display Page Layout view, click the center button in the [illegible] of the status bar.

To close the header or footer, click in the worksheet. To edit the header or footer, double-click in the header or footer area when in Page Layout view.

To Add a Predefined Header or Footer:

Header & Footer Tools Design/Header & Footer/Header or Footer:

1. Click Header to insert a predefined header, or click Footer to insert a predefined footer.
2. Click the desired predefined header or footer from the list. Figure 4.3 shows predefined headers you can insert.

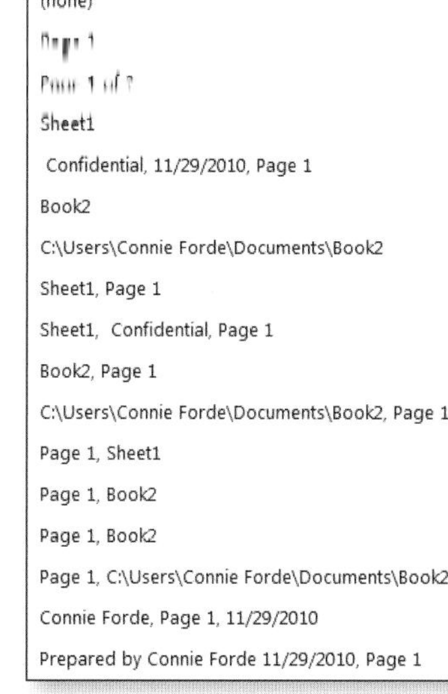

Figure 4.3 Predefined Headers

To Change Views:

Table Tools Fields/Views/View

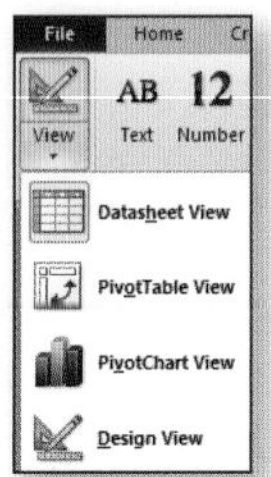

1. With the table in Datasheet view, click View and select Design View.
2. Kcy a namc for thc tablc.
3. Click OK. The table is now shown in Design view. The Design view for an existing table is shown in Figure 2.3.

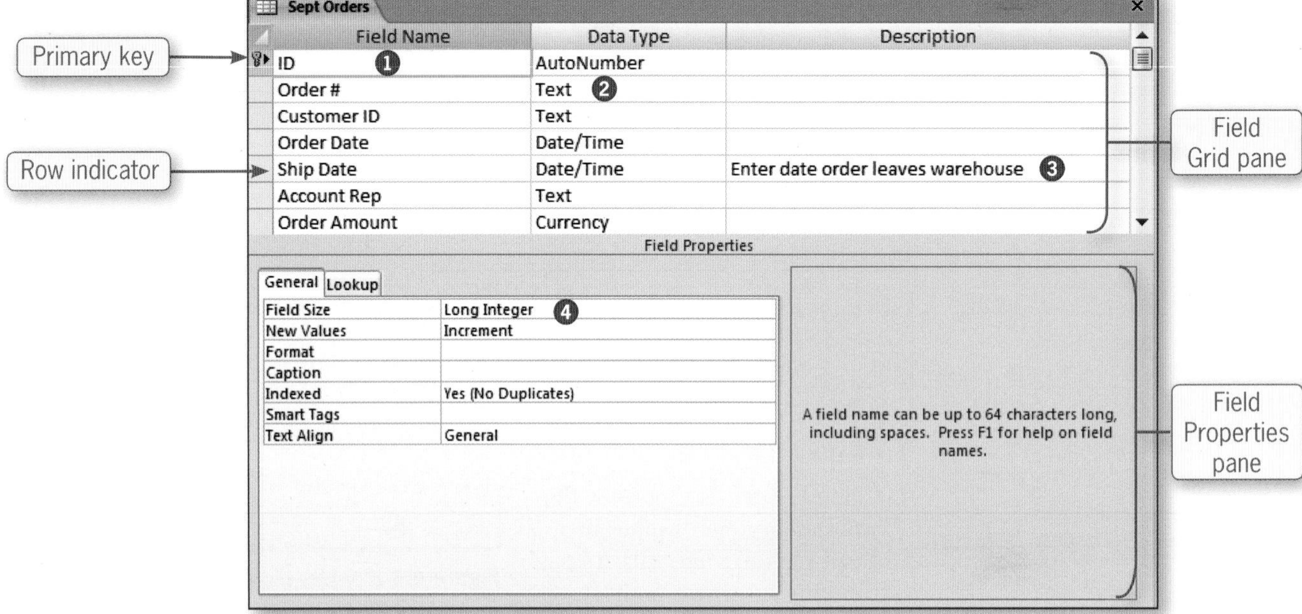

Figure 2.3 Table in Design View

Table Design view is composed of two panes. The Field Grid pane displays field names, data types, and descriptions, while the Field Properties pane is where you set field-related items. Each field has the following four qualities:

❶ **Field Name:** Should be short and descriptive.

❷ **Data Type:** Defines the kind of information to be stored in a field.

❸ **Description:** Should be meaningful so that others can easily use and understand the organization of the database. Entering a description is optional.

❹ **Field Properties:** Define the characteristics of data to be entered in a field.

Choose a Primary Key

In a new table, *Access* automatically creates a field named ID with the AutoNumber data type, as shown in Figure 2.3. This field is designed to number records automatically and to create a unique value for each record. A field that uniquely identifies a record is called a *primary key*. The primary key is identified by a key symbol in the row indicator (Figure 2.3) and is usually the first field in the table. You can change the name of the ID field to a name that better identifies your data, such as Customer ID or Student #. Data for the primary key field must consist of unique values.

Select Data Types

As you insert additional fields in the table, your choice of data type will depend on the nature of the data. You can choose from several data types, including:

DRILL 1 HEADERS AND FOOTERS

PERSONAL BUDGET

1. Open the data file *personal budget* and save as *ex4-drill1*.
2. Rename Sheet1 as **Current Year**.
3. Go to Page Layout view. Add the predefined header *Current Year, Confidential, Page 1*.
4. Add a footer as follows: Left: Key **Prepared by Mitzi Jackson**; right: Click Current Date from Header & Footer Elements group. Click in the worksheet to close the header and footer.
5. Go to Normal view. Format the worksheet quickly using shortcuts:

   A2:B2—Heading 2; click Format Painter and copy to A6:B6.

   A5—Heading 4; copy to A33 and A34.

   Select the nonadjacent range A3:A5 and A7:A33—click Increase Indent button. *Hint:* Use CTRL key to select nonadjacent ranges.

   Select the nonadjacent range B5, B33, B34 and the Calculation cell style.
6. In B5, insert a function to add the income. In B33, total the expenses.
7. In B34, insert a formula to subtract the expenses from the income. If the result is within the budget, apply the Good cell style; if bad, the Bad cell style.
8. Save. Click on the Last Year sheet tab. Experiment with the different predefined headers and footers and the various elements on the Header & Footer Elements group.
9. Resave and print the Current Year worksheet. Close the workbook.

PREPARE WORKSHEET TO PRINT

Page Layout/Page Setup

Before you print a worksheet, you may want to adjust page setup options on the Page Layout tab. Options in this group can make your worksheet more attractive and easier to read. Refer to Figure 4.4 as you study the needed adjustments on this page and the next page. Before you begin, display Page Layout view.

TIP

Add Print Preview to the Quick Access Toolbar.

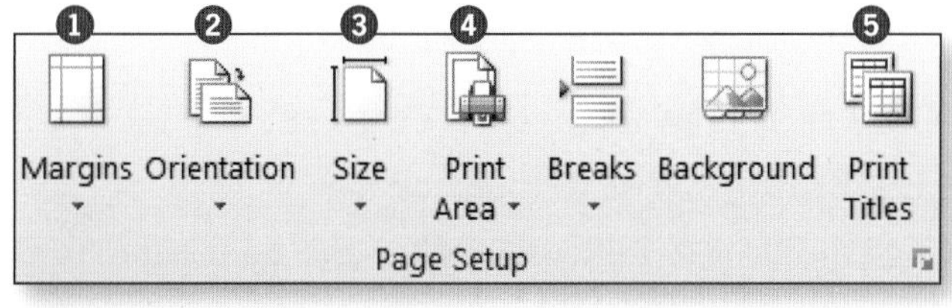

Figure 4.4 Page Setup Group

DISCOVER

Alternate method: In Print Preview, select Show Margins; then drag the margin lines to adjust.

To Change Margins:

1. Click Margins ❶ and select Normal, Wide, or Narrow.
2. Click Custom Margins to set specific top, bottom, left, and right margins.

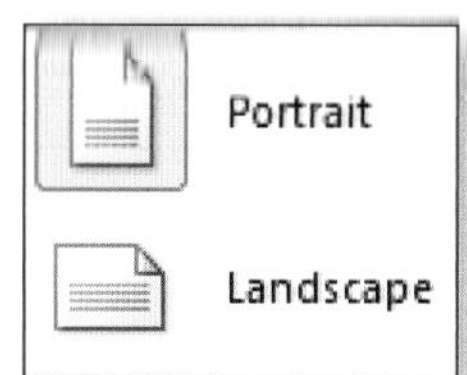

Figure 4.5 Orientation

To Change Orientation and Paper Size:

1. Click Orientation ❷ and choose Portrait or Landscape (Figure 4.5).
2. Click Size ❸ and choose desired paper size.

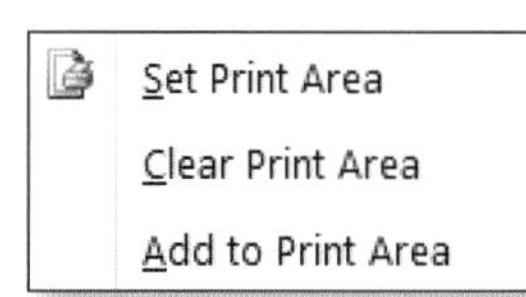

Figure 4.6 Print Area

To Select Print Area:

1. Select the cells to be printed and click Print Area ❹.
2. Click Set Print Area (Figure 4.6).
3. To add more cells to the print area, select those and click Add to Print Area. Click Clear Print Area to clear all print areas.

LESSON 2

Create and Modify Tables

OBJECTIVES

- Plan and create a database
- Create, preview, and print a table
- Modify field properties and create an input mask

PLAN AND CREATE A DATABASE

Before you create a new database, you should spend some time planning. Consider what types of information you want to organize and how you intend to use that information. It is sometimes helpful to make a list on paper of the fields you need. You can then organize the fields into tables.

TIP

Unlike other *Microsoft Office* products, *Access* requires a file to be created before you begin entering data.

Each table in the database should store data on only one subject, such as employee information, products, or inventory. Each table should include a field that contains a value unique to each record, such as an ID number field.

If you find that you are storing too much information in a single table—such as employee contact information *plus* employee insurance information—you should split fields into separate tables. You can then insert common fields in both tables, such as an employee ID number, to create a relationship between the tables.

When you have an idea how you are going to organize your data, you are ready to create the database.

TIP

You will learn more about table relationships in Lesson 6. Databases that allow you to relate tables are called *relational databases.*

To Create a New *Access* Database:

1. Click Blank database in the Backstage view.
2. Click the Browse folder icon ❶ in the right pane of the window (Figure 2.1).
3. Navigate to the location where the database will be stored, and key a name for the new database file.
4. Ensure that Microsoft Office Access 2007 Databases is selected in the Save as type box. Click OK.
5. Click Create ❷ to open the new database.

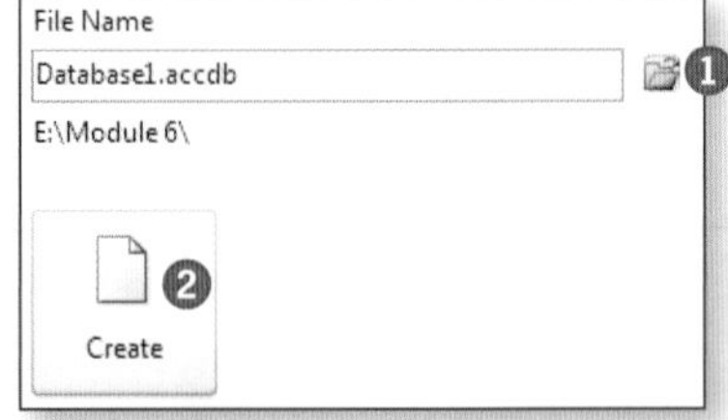

Figure 2.1 Create Blank Database

CREATE TABLES IN A NEW DATABASE

When you create a new database, *Access* expects that the next thing you will do is create a table. Thus, *Access* automatically displays a new table called Table1 in its Datasheet view, as shown in Figure 2.2.

You can create a table in Datasheet view by keying field names in the Click to Add boxes ❶, but it is preferable to create a new table in Design view because Design view gives you more control over how you set up the table. You use the View command ❷ to switch between views for any database object.

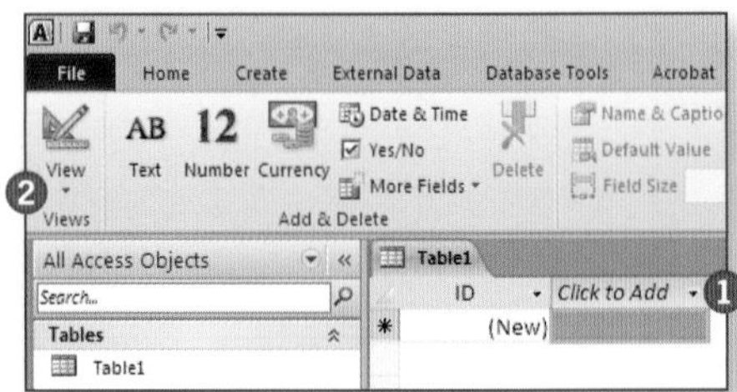

Figure 2.2 New Table in Datasheet View

To Print Titles on Multiple Page Worksheets:

Page Layout/Page Setup/Print Titles

Use the Collapse Dialog button to reduce a dialog box so that you can select a range of cells. After selecting the range, click the button again to restore the full dialog box size.

1. Click Print Titles ❺ to display the Page Setup dialog box.
2. Click the Collapse Dialog button at the right of the Rows to repeat at top and Columns to repeat at left, and select the row and column to repeat on each page (Figure 4.7). *Note:* You may also key the desired rows and columns in the box.

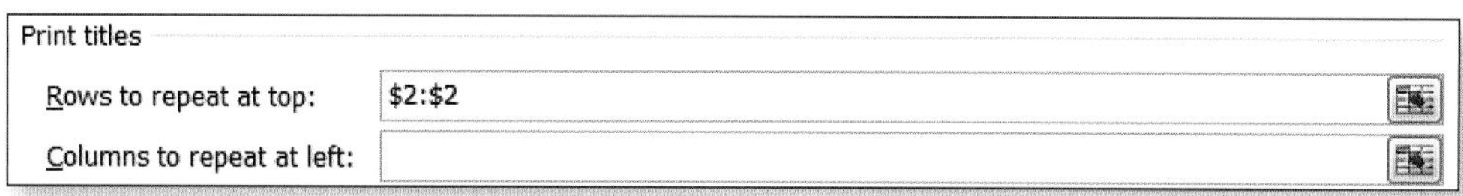

Figure 4.7 Enter Rows and Columns to Repeat

3. Click the Collapse Dialog button again and then click OK to return to the worksheet.

To Move, Insert, or Delete a Page Break:

Page Layout/Page Setup/Breaks

To display Page Break Preview, click the right button in the view buttons at the bottom right of status bar.

1. Switch to Page Break Preview to view the location of page breaks (Figure 4.8). Dashed lines are automatic page breaks inserted by *Excel;* solid lines are manual page breaks inserted by user.

29	Nisbett	Jill	31-999	3/6/2002	1940	jnisbett@company.com
30	Pankasemsuk	Girish	11-331	6/7/2002	6627	gpankasemsuk@company.co
31	Perry	Brittney	21-735	6/16/2008	4193	bperry@company.com
32	Piacentino	Blair	21-553	8/27/2007	1192	bpiacentino@company.com
33	Price	Darcy	31-016	8/2/2004	1271	dprice@company.com
34	Pulliam	Michael	21-966	2/23/2004	4953	mpulliam@company.com
35	Qualls	Crystal	11-016	6/7/2002	6513	cqualls@company.com
36	Quinn	Brian	11-367	11/23/2004	4800	bquinn@company.com
37	Scott	Desten	21-887	7/14/2003	3957	dscott@company.com
38	Segrest	Kenny	31-553	6/2/2003	9560	ksegrest@company.com
39	Sullivan	Andrew	31-444	6/30/2004	8823	asullivan@company.com
40	Taylor	Wayne	21-957	4/14/2002	4428	wtaylor@company.com
41	Thomas	Amanda	21-856	2/28/2007	7134	athomas@company.com
42	Williams	Ben	31-198	7/10/2003	8472	bwilliams@company.com
43	Yue	Cetin	31-783	1/15/2008	5072	cyue@company.com
44	Zhang	Hongzheng	21-306	4/5/2003	8930	hzhang@company.com

Figure 4.8 Worksheet in Page Break Preview

2. Move a page break: Drag the page break line (vertical or horizontal) to the desired location. A dashed line becomes solid when moved.

Alternate method: Drag the page break outside of the print area to delete it.

3. Insert a vertical or horizontal page break: Select a row or column below or to the right of the desired page break location, click Breaks, and then Insert Page Break (Figure 4.9).
4. Delete or remove a page break: Click in a cell below the page break and click Remove Page Break.
5. Reset all page breaks: Click Reset All Page Breaks.

Insert Page Break
Remove Page Break
Reset All Page Breaks

Figure 4.9 Breaks

DRILL 2 ADJUSTMENTS BEFORE PRINTING

EMPLOYEE DATABASE

1. Open the data file *employee database* and save as *ex4-drill2*. In Page Layout view, change to landscape orientation to fit the worksheet on the page horizontally.
2. Repeat row 2 titles on the second page.
3. Set custom margins as follows: Left 1.5" and Top 1.5".
4. In Page Break Preview, move the bottom page break just below Quinn. Insert a page break to the right of the Extension column.
5. Reset all page breaks. Move bottom page break below Quinn.
6. Set the print area to print employees on page 3. Click Print Preview to check.
7. Add page 2 to the print area. Clear print area. Set print area to print page 1 and print the page.
8. Resave as *ex4-drill2* and close.

Field	Record 11	Record 12	Record 13
Employee ID	556	385	339
Team ID	4	3	2
Last Name	Judd	Barkley	Rowe
First Name	Nancy	Liz	Michelle
Address	10 Shelby Street	8806 Mark Avenue	2077 Newtown Road
City	Florence	Dayton	Cincinnati
State	KY	OH	OH
ZIP Code	41042-1613	45424-3213	45244-4011
Home Phone	859-555-0121	937-555-0118	513-555-0125
Birth Date	10/15/1978	06/12/1968	09/21/1985
Date Hired	01/01/2000	11/28/2009	06/19/2001

Apply It

Database 1
Access Database Objects

AC1-DB1-DATA

1. Open the data file *ac1-db1-data.* Save the database as *ac1-db1.*
2. Add the following new records to the Customers table.

Field	Record 36	Record 37
Customer #	44343	56495
Title	Ms.	Mr.
First Name	Illiana	Marcus
Last Name	Rodriguez	Williams
Address	32 Washington Street	3670 Palm Drive
City	Elgin	Dayton
State	IL	OH
ZIP	60123-0401	45449-2926
Home Phone	847-555-0136	937-555-0147
Account Rep	984	437

3. Locate the record for Mr. Skirvin. Edit his record by changing the area code from 606 to **859**. Then close the table.
4. Open the Customer Charges query. Identify the number of records in the query. Close the Customer Charges query.
5. Open the Customers form. The records are sorted by the Customer #. Use the navigation buttons to move to the following locations: last record, previous record, and first record. Close the Customers form.
6. Open and print the Customers report. Close the report.
7. Close the database.

Apply It

Worksheet 8
Format for Printing

BALANCE SHEET

1. Open the data file *balance sheet* and save as *ex4-w8*. Rename Sheet1 as **Balance Sheet**.
2. Format as follows:
   a. Row 1—Merge and center across A and B, Heading 4 style, increase font to 16 point and row height to 24.00 points.
   b. Row 2—Merge and center, Heading 1 style.
   c. A3, A10, and A16—Heading 4 style.
   d. A8:B8 and A:14:B14—Bold.
   e. A18:B18—Total style.
   f. B4:B18—Comma [0].
   g. B8 and B14—Calculation style.
   h. Click Increase Indent to indent the assets listed under Assets and the liabilities listed under Current Liabilities.
3. Key the following formulas:
   a. B8—Sum the assets.
   b. B14—Sum the current liabilities.
   c. B16—Subtract the total liabilities from the total assets.
   d. B18—Add total liabilities and owners' equity.
4. Insert the following header using the Header & Footer Elements:

   Sheet Name   Page #   Date

   Hint: Key the word **Page** followed by a space.
5. Key the following footer:

   Prepared by Your Name   Time
6. Set the print area to include the asset section (A3:B8). Print and resave as *ex4-w8*.
7. Clear the print area. Change the left margin to 2.0" and the top margin to 1.5".
8. Edit the header by deleting the page number in the middle header box.
9. Save as *ex4-w8revised*; print and close the file.

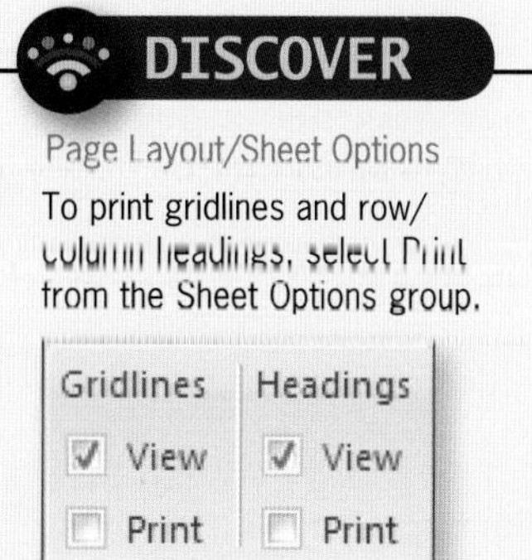

Worksheet 9
Format for Printing

INVENTORY

1. Open the data file *inventory* and save as *ex4-w9*.
2. Insert the predefined header *Page 1 of ?*. Insert the date in the middle footer box.
3. Change margins to Wide. Repeat row titles on the second page.
4. In Page Break Preview, move the page break after the items located in the garage.
5. Set print area to print kitchen items; then select office items and add to the print area.
6. Print gridlines and row/column headings.
7. Resave as *ex4-w9;* print and close the file.

4. To edit a record, click in the field that needs to be changed, position the insertion point, and insert or delete text as required.
5. To delete a record, click the Select All button ❶ (Figure 1.6) to select the entire record.
6. Tap DELETE and click Yes when *Access* warns you that you are deleting a record.

Employee

Employee ID	Team ID	Last Name
190	4	Reynoza
209	1	Richardson
222	4	Thompson

Figure 1.6 Select a Record to Delete

To prevent file errors, never copy or move an open *Access* database. Always close *Access* files before performing these tasks.

SAVE A DATABASE WITH A NEW NAME

In *Access 2010*, you can use the Save Database As command to save a file with a new name or location. Saving a database is a good way to create a backup of important data or preserve an original set of data while you manipulate a copy of that data.

To Save a Database with a New Name or Location:

File/Save Database As

1. Close any open database objects.
2. Follow the path and click Save Database As to open the Save As dialog box.
3. Key a name for the database, navigate to the location where it is to be stored, and click Save.

File/Close Database

Follow this path to close a database without closing *Access*.

Note that you do not have to save objects such as tables or forms after you enter or delete records. *Access* automatically saves data in these objects for you when you close them.

DRILL 2 SAVE A DATABASE AND ENTER RECORDS

1. With *ac1-drill1-data* open, save the database in your solutions folder as *ac1-drill2*. Identify the folder as a trusted location.
2. Open the Employee table. Click the New (blank) record button on the navigation bar to move the insertion point to the first field in the empty row at the bottom of the table (record 11).
3. Enter the three new records shown on the next page. *Note:* You do not have to key the hyphens in the telephone numbers or ZIP Codes, or the diagonals in the birth or hire dates.
4. Find the record for Jacob Smith. In the Address field, key the word **Avenue** after the street name.
5. Locate the record for Laura Nelson and delete it.
6. Quick print the Employee table, and then close it. Close the *ac1-drill2* database.

An input mask has been applied to the ZIP Code, Home Phone, and date fields to make data entry easier and more accurate. You will learn about input masks in Lesson 2.

project 5

The Bookstore, Inc.: Integrating Excel and Word

OBJECTIVES

- Create and format professional *Excel* worksheets
- Prepare effective *Word* documents
- Coordinate themes and designs in documents and worksheets
- Work with very limited supervision

SETTING

Project 5 integrates *Excel* and *Word*. In this project, you are an assistant to Derek Bradberry, Training Director of The Bookstore, Inc., a national chain of bookstores that is experiencing significant growth. To meet the needs of its many clients, the company staffs a large training department. Your position will allow you to showcase your *Word* and *Excel* skills.

Your first responsibility is to design and implement the Software Mastery Training Series scheduled for November 15 and 19. Mr. Bradberry has shared with you the need for staff members to master their software completely, not just a few functions. Knowing the software will increase efficiency in completing tasks and will allow more time to serve clients and for other creative endeavors. Schedule your time wisely, and remember the documents you create will be published as training materials. Proofread carefully to ensure error-free documents, and consider the importance of an attractive design.

JOBS

1. Edit letterhead template and create memo Quick Part
2. Worksheet
3. Memo
4. Training design sheet
5. Worksheet
6. Block letter

STANDARD OPERATING PROCEDURES

Use these procedures for all documents you prepare. You will not be reminded to do these things during the project.

1. Use Solstice document theme for all *Word* and *Excel* documents.
2. Use the Bookstore letterhead from the data files, block letter format with open punctuation, an appropriate salutation and closing, and prepare envelopes.
3. Insert the memo heading you will create in Quick Parts below the letterhead template.
4. Use the Light Shading – Accent 1 table style.
5. Proofread, preview, and print all documents.
6. Set up a folder named EX-WD Project 5 and save all project files in it. Name all solution files *p5-j* (plus the job number, *j1*, *j2*, etc.).

DRILL 1 DATABASE OBJECTS

AC1-DRILL1-DATA

TIP

Always maximize the main *Access* window to take full advantage of the Ribbon and other available *Access* tools.

TIP

The database file remains open when you close any object. If you accidentally close *Access*, simply reopen the database file.

1. Launch *Access* and open the data file *ac1-drill1-data*. Maximize the window.
2. Identify the folder containing this file (and the other data files used in this module) as a trusted location.
3. Open the Employee table. Note the fields used to organize the data and the number of records in the table. Then close the Employee table.
4. Open the Team 4 query. The query datasheet looks similar to the table but contains only the Employee ID, Last Name, First Name, Home Phone, and Team ID fields, and only Team 4 employee records. Close the query.
5. Open the Employee form. Notice that the information for the first record is presented in an attractive form. Close the Employee form.
6. Open the Team 4 report. Notice that the information from the Team 4 query is presented in an attractive report that will look good when printed.
7. Quick print the Team 4 report.
8. Close the report, leaving the *ac1-drill1-data* database open for the next drill.

NAVIGATE IN AN ACCESS OBJECT

You can navigate in an *Access* object just as you would in a *Word* table. In *Access* tables and queries, the arrow, TAB, END, and HOME keys move your insertion point to the next field or up and down one record. In an object such as a form or report, the navigation buttons at the bottom of the object screen make it easy to display records and pages.

Figure 1.5 shows navigation buttons that appear at the bottom of an *Access* table, query, or form. Use these buttons to move to the next record, previous record, the first or last record, or to a blank row for a new record. The total number of records is also displayed, as well as the current record number.

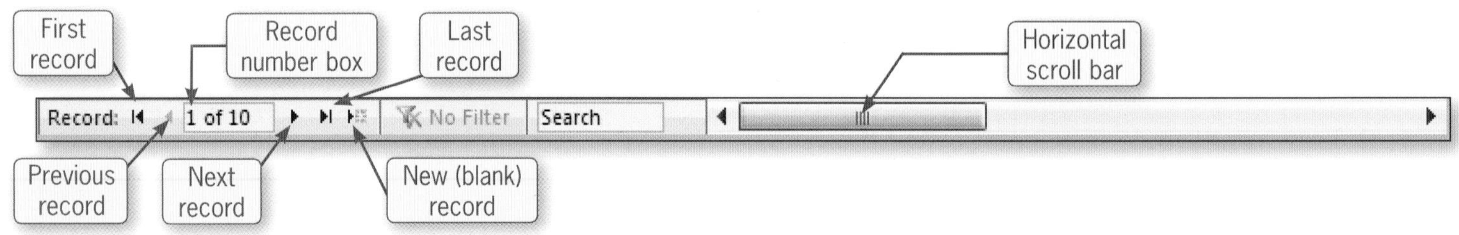

Figure 1.5 Navigation Buttons

ENTER, EDIT, AND DELETE RECORDS IN A TABLE

TIP

Although you can enter, edit, and delete records from a table, it is a better practice to do these tasks using a form. You will learn how to work with forms in Lesson 4.

Entering data in a database table is similar to entering data in an *Excel* worksheet—key data in the first field and move to the remaining fields to complete the record. Records in a database often need to be updated or changed, so editing is a common task. Delete records to remove them permanently from the database.

To Enter, Edit, and Delete Records:

1. Click the New (blank) record button on the navigation bar, if necessary, to move the insertion point to the first field of an empty row. Key the data for the first field.
2. Tap TAB to move to the next field, and key data for that field.
3. Continue to tap TAB to move from field to field. Tapping TAB at the end of a record starts a new record.

Job 1

Edit Letterhead Template and Create Memo Quick Parts

TBI LETTERHEAD

You will begin your work by completing two time-saving tasks.

1. Open the data file *tbi letterhead*, update the theme to the Solstice theme, and save as *tbi letterhead* in your solutions folder. Close the file.
2. Learning the Quick Parts feature of *Word 2010* recently, you realize you can save major time by creating the memo heading as a Quick Part. Key the memo heading in a new blank document. Save the memo heading as a Quick Part to be inserted when keying a memo.

Job 2

Worksheet

Mr. Bradberry asked you to prepare the budget for the Software Mastery Training Series. Key the worksheet as shown in Figure P5.1; edit as directed below.

1. Insert a new row as the fourth item in the Salaries category. Select A14:C14 (Staff) and move to the new row. Indent A7, like the three other salary categories above. Move C7 to B7. Delete the blank row remaining where the Staff entry was originally.
2. Enter the needed formulas:
   a. C7—Compute the total salaries.
   b. C8—Compute total benefits (15% of total salary). *Hint:* Reference the percent entered in A19.
   c. C16—Compute the total budget.
3. Format the worksheet as follows:
   a. A1—Merge and center over columns A–D, apply Heading 2 style, row height 37.5 points, middle align text vertically in cell; Gold, Accent 4, Lighter 60% fill color.
   b. A2:D2—Heading 3 style, row height 24 points, center.
   c. A16:D16—Total style.
   d. B7—Bottom border, choose color of total lines.
   e. All number cells—Comma [0] style.
   f. A19—Percent style.
   g. A18:A19—40% Accent6 cell style; add outside cell border.
   h. Select the range C7:C15 and apply the Blue – White – Red Color Scale conditional formatting.
4. Create a header that displays *Training Department* at the center. Create a footer that displays *Software Mastery Training Series* at the left and *Page #* of total pages at the right.
5. Change the left margin to 2.0", top margin to 1.0", header and footer margins to 0.5", and print gridlines.

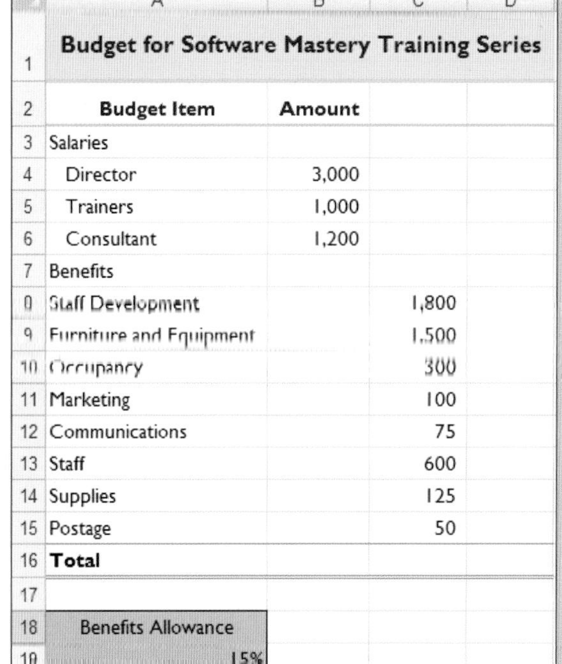

	A	B	C	D
1	Budget for Software Mastery Training Series			
2	Budget Item	Amount		
3	Salaries			
4	Director	3,000		
5	Trainers	1,000		
6	Consultant	1,200		
7	Benefits			
8	Staff Development		1,800	
9	Furniture and Equipment		1,500	
10	Occupancy		300	
11	Marketing		100	
12	Communications		75	
13	Staff		600	
14	Supplies		125	
15	Postage		50	
16	Total			
17				
18	Benefits Allowance			
19	15%			

Figure P5.1 Key Budget for Training Series

Home/Styles/Conditional Formatting

Use conditional formatting to see differences in a range of data.

As you can see, *Access* does not have a standard work screen like the other *Microsoft Office* applications.

You will learn about queries in Lesson 3, forms in Lesson 4, and reports in Lesson 5.

5. Click the Add new location button to view the Microsoft Office Trusted Location dialog box.
6. Click Browse and select the folder you want to trust. Click OK.
7. Click OK to close each dialog box and return to the main *Access* window.

WORK WITH ACCESS OBJECTS

The Navigation Pane at the left side of the *Access* workspace displays the primary objects of a database: tables, queries, forms, and reports. These objects are grouped in the Navigation Pane; all tables are stored under the Tables heading, for example, and all queries under the Queries heading (see Figure 1.2).

Tables are the main data storage containers in any database, with each table holding a specific type of information. Queries are structured questions used to extract specific information from tables. Forms provide a convenient way to enter and edit data in tables. Reports are used to summarize data from the database's tables or queries and are designed to be printed.

All *Access* database files must contain at least one table. Other database objects do not store data—they simply give you different ways to view or work with the existing data stored in tables. You will learn more about tables and how to create and modify them in Lesson 2.

As shown in Figure 1.4, tables are composed of rows and columns of related data, similar to the way data is displayed in an *Excel* worksheet. The columns are called fields; each field contains an individual piece of information about an item, such as a person's last name. A complete set of *fields* is called a *record.*

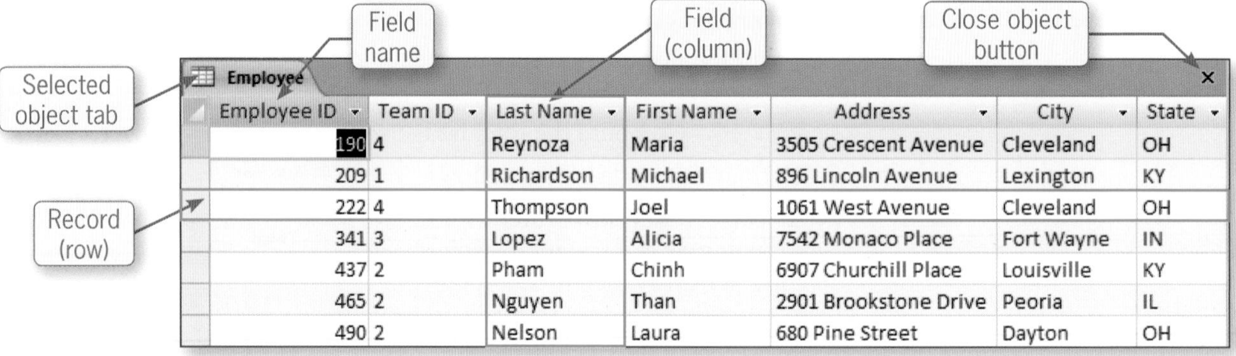

Figure 1.4 Components of a Database Table

Open any database object by double-clicking its name in the Navigation Pane. The object opens in a new window, with a tab containing the name of the object above the window (see Figure 1.4). If the object window contains more information than can be displayed in the *Access* window, horizontal and vertical scroll bars display so you can scroll to see all data.

Close an object by clicking the Close object button (see Figure 1.4). After you close an object, the database remains open so you can continue to use other objects in the same database.

You can have several objects open at one time. To ensure you are closing the correct object, the ScreenTip for the Close object button contains the name of the active object, such as Close 'Employee.'

You can print any open object as you would print any other *Microsoft Office* application document. You can also print an object from the Navigation Pane.

File/Print/Quick Print

Follow this path with an object open to print that object. Or click an object in the Navigation Pane and follow the path to print the object.

Job 3
Memo

Open the *tbi letterhead* template and insert the memo heading you saved as a Quick Part. Compose a memo to Derek Bradberry that requests him to review the budget for the Software Mastery Training Series. If possible, you would like the changes a week from today. Refer to the documents that are to be enclosed and add the proper enclosure notation. *Reminder*: Save the file as a *Word* document and not a template.

Job 4
Word Training Design Sheet

Create the training design sheet for the first module of the Software Mastery Training Series as a five-column table. Refer to Figure P5.2 as you follow the directions below.

Become Efficient in Your Job—Master Your Software

Training Design Sheet: for Module #1 Calendar Template

Leader: Tarase Lowry — Facilitator: Kelly Easley

Objectives	Procedures	Time	Materials	Evaluation
The participant will: 1. understand the benefits of using *Word* templates. 2. create a calendar using the *Word* calendar template. 3. change font color to add emphasis. 4. insert a graphic. 5. decrease size of text box. 6. create text box and key special notes.	**The trainer will:** 1. check the session roster. 2. complete icebreaker to introduce training participants and leader. 3. distribute Handout #1 (yellow) to participants and demonstrate accessing the various *Word* templates (memo, agenda, Web page, etc.). 4. instruct participants to save calendars. 5. distribute Handout #2 (blue) and demonstrate creating November calendar while participants work along with leader. 6. assist students in completing the independent practice to reinforce training objectives. 7. close and check for understanding through oral questioning.	2 min. 10 min. 7 min. 15 min. 2 min. 20 min. 4 min.	15 laptop computers for participants 1 demonstration workstation with computer and projection device **Handouts:** a. #1 Sample Template (yellow) b. #2 Using the Calendar Template (blue)	**Independent Practice** See Handout #2 Dec calendar **Observation** **Student Participation** **Check for Understanding** 1. Click ______, ______ to open the *Word* templates. 2. Would a picture of a duck be a relevant graphic for February's calendar? 3. What is the path for finding • text box button? • font color button? • insert clip art button? **Out-of-Session Application** See Handout #2 Jan–Oct calendars

Figure P5.2 Key the Design Sheet

1. Insert a footer with *Module #1* printed at left and *Page 1* of total pages at right; bold, 10 point.
2. In the Procedures columns, switch items 4 and 5.
3. Insert a column to the left of the Evaluation column. Label it **Cost**; center the heading. Center the following costs in the new column, aligned with the materials items in the Materials column:

Laptops	$1,000
Demonstration workstation	$500
Handout 1	$20
Handout 2	$25

Create a new folder named Module 6 Solutions, and save all databases and documents from this module in it.

OPEN AN EXISTING DATABASE

Use the list of recent databases to open an existing database you have worked with recently. You can also open a database using the Open command on the File menu.

TO OPEN AN EXISTING *ACCESS* DATABASE:

File/Open

1. Click Open to view the Open dialog box.
2. Choose the location and file you wish to open.
3. Click Open. The main *Access* window opens, as shown in Figure 1.2.

Click the Recent command on the File menu to display more files and to change the number of files to be displayed in the short list.

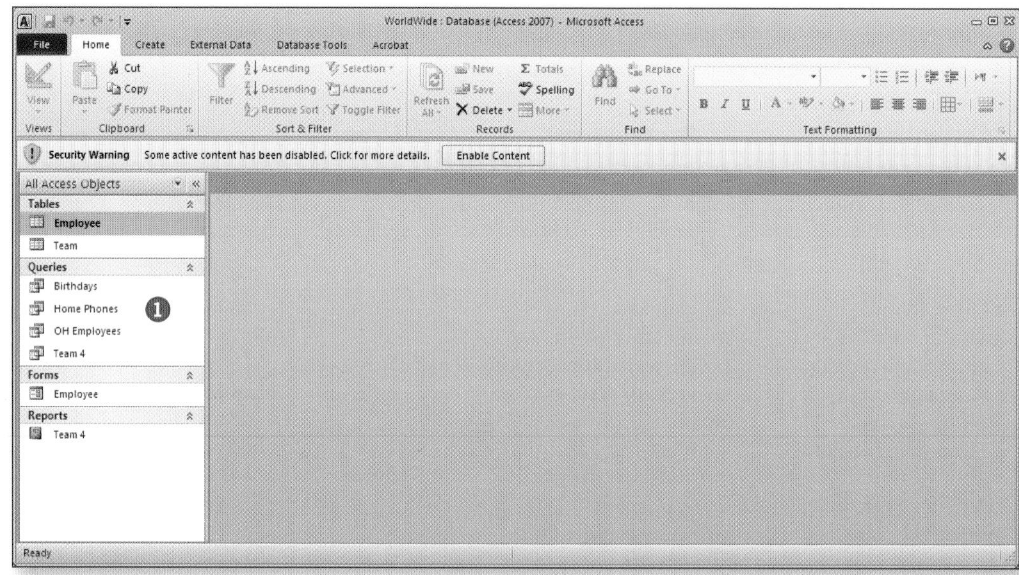

Figure 1.2 Main *Access* Window

Maximize the *Access* window using the Maximize button in the title bar to provide the largest possible area for viewing *Access* objects.

Notice that *Access* has the same Fluent interface you have seen in *Word*, *PowerPoint*, and *Excel*. *Access* also has an additional feature, the Navigation Pane ❶, that you use to work with *Access* objects. You will learn more about *Access* objects later in this lesson.

CHANGE SECURITY SETTING

Access analyzes every database it opens to detect possible threats to your computer. The Security Warning bar shown in Figure 1.3 indicates that *Access* has detected a possible threat. If you are confident the file came from a trustworthy source, you can enable the content for all files opened from that location.

To trust individual *Access* files, click the Enable Content button on the Security Warning bar.

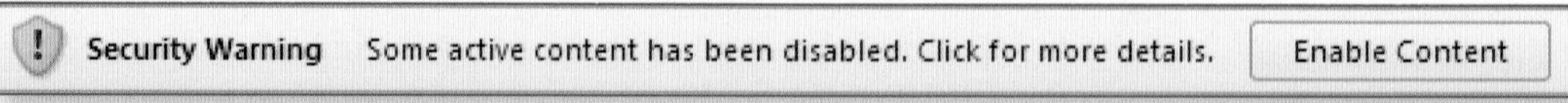

Figure 1.3 Security Warning Bar

TO CHANGE THE SECURITY SETTING FOR A LOCATION:

File/Options

1. Follow the path to open the Access Options dialog box.
2. Click Trust Center in the left pane.
3. Click the Trust Center Settings button.
4. Click Trusted Locations in the left pane.

4. Add a row at the end of the table. Merge the cells so the row is one cell. Insert the following content in the row:

   Teacher Reflection

   Were the participants at ease in the learning environment?

   Did the participants understand the time-saving capability of using *Word* templates?

   Did each participant successfully complete the November and December calendars?

   Were the participants motivated to return to their offices and complete the Jan–Oct calendars for mastery of this objective?

   Do you perceive that the participants will call you if additional assistance is needed?

5. Insert a row above the Teacher Reflection row. Enter a formula to total the Time and Cost columns.

Job 5
Worksheet

You are pleased to have Caleb Smith, an intern from the local university, working with you this semester. Using the *Excel* time sheet template, create a time sheet for the week of 9/11/2012. (To open this template, click File/New/Sample templates/Time Card.) Refer to Figure P5.3 and edit as shown. Point out to Caleb the preinserted formulas that calculate the time card automatically as the data is entered. After watching you create this one, Caleb will be able to create the remaining time cards.

Time Card

Employee	Caleb Smith
[Street Address]	3893 North Elm Street
[Address 2]	
[City, ST ZIP Code]	Germantown, TN 38138-3893
Week ending:	9/11/2012

Manager:	Derek Bradberry
Employee phone:	555-0193, Ext. 35
Employee e-mail:	Caleb.Smith@tbi.net

Day	Date	Regular Hours	Overtime	Sick	Vacation	Total
Monday	9/5/2012	8.00				8.00
Tuesday	9/6/2012	8.00				8.00
Wednesday	9/7/2012	8.00				8.00
Thursday	9/8/2012	8.00	1.00			9.00
Friday	9/9/2012	8.00				8.00
Saturday	9/10/2012					
Sunday	9/11/2012					
Total hours		40.00	1.00			41.00
Rate per hour		$ 8.00	$ 16.00			
Total pay		$ 320.00	$ 16.00	$ -	$ -	$ 336.00

Figure P5.3 Time Card

Work with Access

LESSON 1

OBJECTIVES

- Open an *Access* database and change security settings
- Work with *Access* objects
- Enter, edit, and delete records in a table
- Save a database with a new name

OVERVIEW

Think of a database file as a container that holds a collection of objects used to store and manipulate data. *Object* is a generic term that refers to any component stored in an *Access* database, such as a table, query, form, or report. You use objects to work with data. Objects are grouped by type in the database file so that they are readily available for use.

GETTING STARTED

Launch *Access* in the same way that you launch other *Microsoft Office 2010* applications. Click the *Access* icon on your desktop, or click the Start button, click All Programs, Microsoft Office, and then select *Microsoft Access 2010*. The Backstage view shown in Figure 1.1 appears after you start *Access*.

The Backstage view contains a list of available templates ❶, Office.com templates ❷, and a list of recently used databases ❸. You may also select Blank database ❹ to create a new database. This view also provides access to a variety of helpful resources ❺.

Figure 1.1 *Access* Backstage View

Job 6

Block Letter

Mr. Bradberry asked you to prepare the following letter to Ms. Fulton, whose contact information is shown in Figure P5.4. Include her title in the address. Save as a *Word* document—not template.

Figure P5.4 Contact Information

To remove the extra space after the paragraph with short lines, such as the inside address, use the keyboard shortcut SHIFT + ENTER to move directly to the next line.

The design of our Software Mastery Training Series is well underway with delivery on November 15 and 19. The initial response from our employees is quite good, and we are expecting a capacity audience size.

As consultant for this training series, you are responsible for the following elements of the program:

- Initial and final review of the design and all training materials
- Development of the course management site
- Two-hour presentation on November 15 and November 19

A contract further outlining your responsibilities is enclosed. Please sign the four copies of the contract and return to us in the stamped envelope. You will receive a final copy for your records.

The first meeting for reviewing the initial design is July 15 at 10 a.m. in Conference Room 2058. Rough drafts will be posted to our company ftp site by July 1 for your review. We look forward to working with you on this training program.

DATABASES WITH ACCESS

overview

Have you ever thought about how your favorite retail store keeps track of the different clothing items available? How does a company track inventory quantities and reorder information so that it is kept up to date and easily retrievable? Do you think someone manually handles these tasks? Not only would this process be time-consuming, it could also result in problems caused by human error.

Data such as inventory or customer information can be organized, managed, and manipulated using a database software program such as *Access 2010*. *Access* uses many common features that you learned in other *Microsoft Office 2010* applications. This module assumes that you have had little or no formal instruction in using *Access*.

ESSENTIALS

1. Work with Access
2. Create and Modify Tables
3. Create Simple Queries
4. Create and Customize Forms

Project 8—McMullan & Donovan Realty: Integrating Access, Word, and Publisher

BEYOND THE ESSENTIALS

5. Create Simple Reports
6. Create Table Relationships
7. Import and Export Data

Project 9—McMullan & Donovan Realty: Integrating Access, Word, PowerPoint, and Excel

LESSON 5

Create and Modify Charts

OBJECTIVES

- Create a chart as a new sheet and as an embedded object
- Format a chart attractively

CREATE EXCEL CHARTS

Insert/Charts

Information from a worksheet can be illustrated in a more meaningful way by displaying the data as a chart. Use *Excel*'s Charts group to create column, line, pie, bar, area, scatter, and other chart types. Study the parts of a chart as labeled in Figure 5.1.

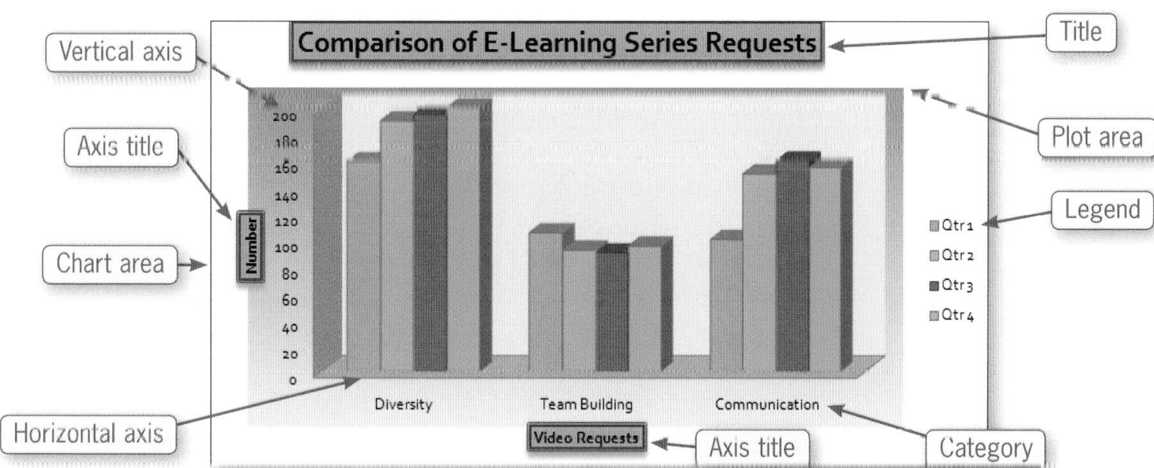

Figure 5.1 Parts of a Chart

To Create a Column Chart:

Insert/Charts/Column

1. Select the data to be included in the chart. If cells are not adjacent, hold down the CTRL key to select.
2. Click Column ❶ and then click the desired type of column, e.g., 3-D Clustered Column ❷ (Figure 5.2).

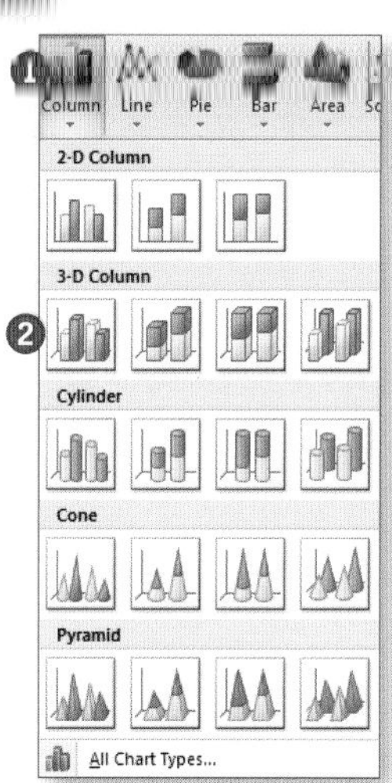

Figure 5.2 Types of Column Charts

Add Space Between Columns

Format Text Box/Text Box/ Columns

1. Right-click the text box; then click Format Text Box.
2. On the Text Box tab, click Columns and increase the spacing to about .3".

3. Draw a text box from the first text box to the right margin. Key and right-align **Edition**; apply 28-point Script MT Bold font with Accent 2 font color.
4. Draw a text box below the name and edition boxes that extends from left margin to right margin and to the bottom margin. Format the text box using Calibri 12-point font and apply two-column format. Add about .3" space between the columns.
5. Draw text boxes for the three story headings shown in Figures P7.3 and P7.4. Size them .5" high and the width of the column. *Note:* Allow about .3" for the spacing at the left of the column in the right panel. Key the headings shown below; apply 24-point Cambria bold font with Accent 1 font color, and Align Center Left. Apply Top and Bottom text wrap to the text boxes.

   Looking Back | Enjoying the Present | Looking Ahead

SCHOOL SPIRIT
ANDY

6. Insert a picture placeholder about the center of the text box and size it 2.3" high × 3.3" wide; apply Square text wrapping. Insert clip art of a movie camera in the placeholder. If clip art or a picture does not fit in the placeholder, apply Fit to it (Picture Tools Format/Crop/Fit).
7. Save as a template named *cdp critique* in your solution files and close.
8. Open the template and prepare the newsletter.
9. Add **School Spirit** to *Edition* in the top right text box.
10. Change the text in the main text box to text from the file *school spirit*. Text should fit as shown in Figure P7.4.
11. Replace the picture with the one from the *andy* file and save as a *Publisher* file named *p7-j4*.

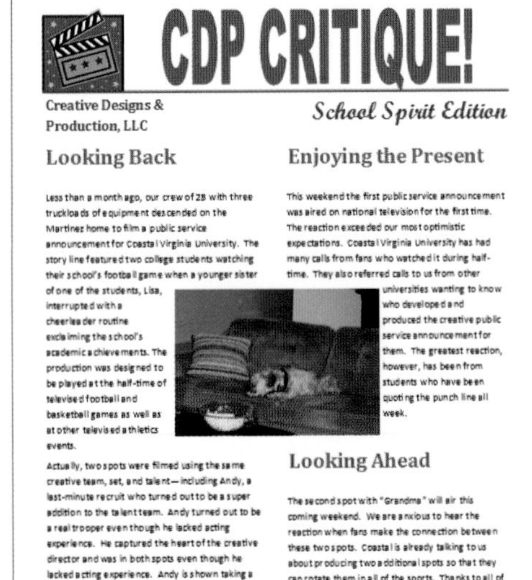

CDP CRITIQUE!

Creative Designs & Production, LLC

School Spirit Edition

Looking Back

Less than a month ago, our crew of 28 with three truckloads of equipment descended on the Martinez home to film a public service announcement for Coastal Virginia University. The story line featured two college students watching their school's football game when a younger sister of one of the students, Lisa, interrupted with a cheerleader routine exclaiming the school's academic achievements. The production was designed to be played at the half-time of televised football and basketball games as well as at other televised athletics events.

Actually, two spots were filmed using the same creative team, set, and talent—including Andy, a last-minute recruit who turned out to be a super addition to the talent team. Andy turned out to be a real trooper even though he lacked acting experience. He captured the heart of the creative director and was in both spots even though he lacked acting experience. Andy is shown taking a power nap on the set while Lisa made the wardrobe and makeup conversion from Jim's younger sister to his grandmother. Incidentally, Todd still thinks Jim's sister and his grandmother are both awesome.

Enjoying the Present

This weekend the first public service announcement was aired on national television for the first time. The reaction exceeded our most optimistic expectations. Coastal Virginia University has had many calls from fans who watched it during half-time. They also referred calls to us from other universities wanting to know who developed and produced the creative public service announcement for them. The greatest reaction, however, has been from students who have been quoting the punch line all week.

Looking Ahead

The second spot with "Grandma" will air this coming weekend. We are anxious to hear the reaction when fans make the connection between these two spots. Coastal is already talking to us about producing two additional spots so that they can rotate them in all of the sports. Thanks to all of you we think we have another award-winning production—only time will tell.

Photo: Susie VanHuss

Figure P7.4 Newsletter

Job 5
Compose and Format Block Letter

CDP LETTERHEAD

You worked closely with Mr. and Mrs. Esteban Martinez on the School Spirit project. Compose a letter of at least three paragraphs to them explaining how much you enjoyed working on the project with them and send them a copy of the School Spirit Edition you prepared. Express appreciation for being able to film the public service announcement in their home. Make appropriate comments about Andy being in the production. Edit the letter carefully. Use *cdp letterhead* and the Martinez home address: One Cedardale Lane | Irvington, VA 22480-1001. Save as *p7-j5* and close.

Job 6
Business Cards

Prepare business cards for yourself using the Marker template and your new title.

1. Edit the business information to use your name and your title, Events and Printed Products Coordinator.
2. Adjust the size of the company name to 8-point Cambria.
3. Save as *p7-j6* and close.

To display the Chart Tools Design and Layout tabs, click in the chart.

MODIFY THE DESIGN AND LAYOUT OF CHARTS

Use the commands on the Chart Tools Design and Layout tabs to customize a chart. Learn the commonly used commands presented below, but browse the many capabilities.

To Edit the Chart Design:

Chart Tools Design

1. Click the Chart Tools Design tab and browse the commands in each group (Figure 5.3). You will apply these in Drill 1.

   Type—Use to change chart type or to save as a template ❶.

   Data—Switch data in rows and columns; select data from the worksheet ❷.

   Chart Layouts—Select from a gallery of layouts ❸.

   Chart Styles—Select from a gallery of styles ❹.

   Location—Move to a new location (embedded or a new chart sheet) ❺.

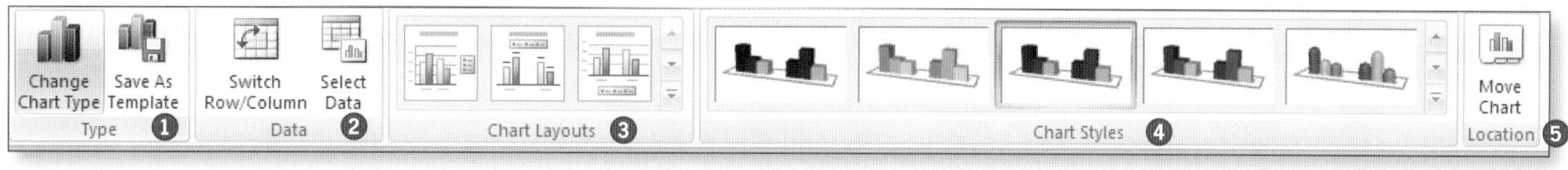

Figure 5.3 Chart Tools Design Tab

DRILL 1 CREATE CHART AND REVISE DESIGN

REQUESTS

1. Open the data file *requests* and save as *ex5-drill1*. Select the Module theme.
2. Select A2:E5 and create a 3-D Bar chart. Change the chart type to 3-D Clustered Column.
3. Switch the rows and columns and observe the difference.
4. Click Select Data; click the Collapse Dialog button, select the range A3:E4, click the button again, and click OK. Change the data range back to A2:E5.
5. Browse the chart layouts and then select Layout 1. Browse the chart styles and select Style 34.
6. Move the chart to display as a new sheet. Rename the sheet as **3-D Column Chart**.
7. Resave as *ex5-drill1* and leave the file open for the next drill.

Use Figure 5.4 to check

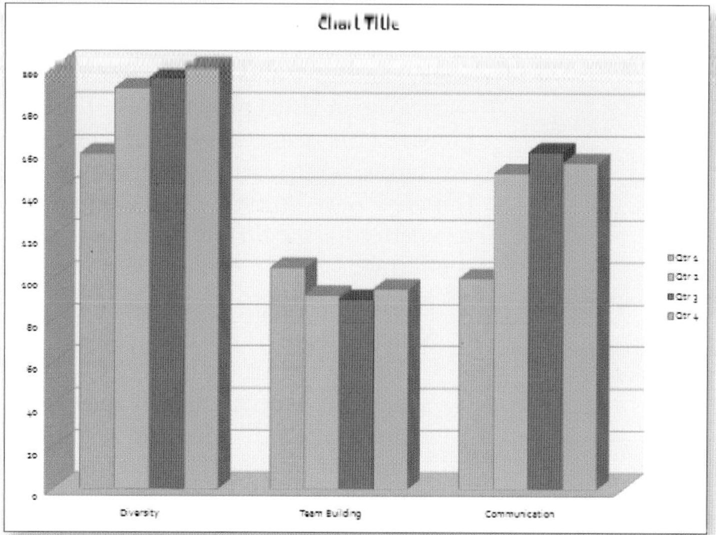

Figure 5.4 Quick Check

DISCOVER

Insert a File

Insert/Text/Object/Text from File

1. Position the insertion point where the file is to be inserted. Then click the down arrow on Object and select Text from File to browse and select the file to insert.
2. Click Insert.

Outlook for Third and Fourth Quarters [use Heading 1 style]

The total number of projects signed during the second quarter was 80 with a value of $4,397,010. The increase in audio and print products is encouraging as shown in Figure 2 on the next page. Since the resource allocation on print products has changed, no real basis exists for making projections for the remainder of the year.

9. Link the Projects Signed chart below the last paragraph in your document; add the caption **Figure 2** below the chart.
10. Insert the data file *outlook* below Figure 2. Apply Heading 2 style to product headings and Heading 1 style to the final heading.
11. Insert the Motion (Odd Page) header and key the title **CDP Project Report**; use a different first page.
12. Use Quick Check to check your document; save as *p7-j3* and close.

QUICK ✓ Use Figure P7.2 to check Job 3.

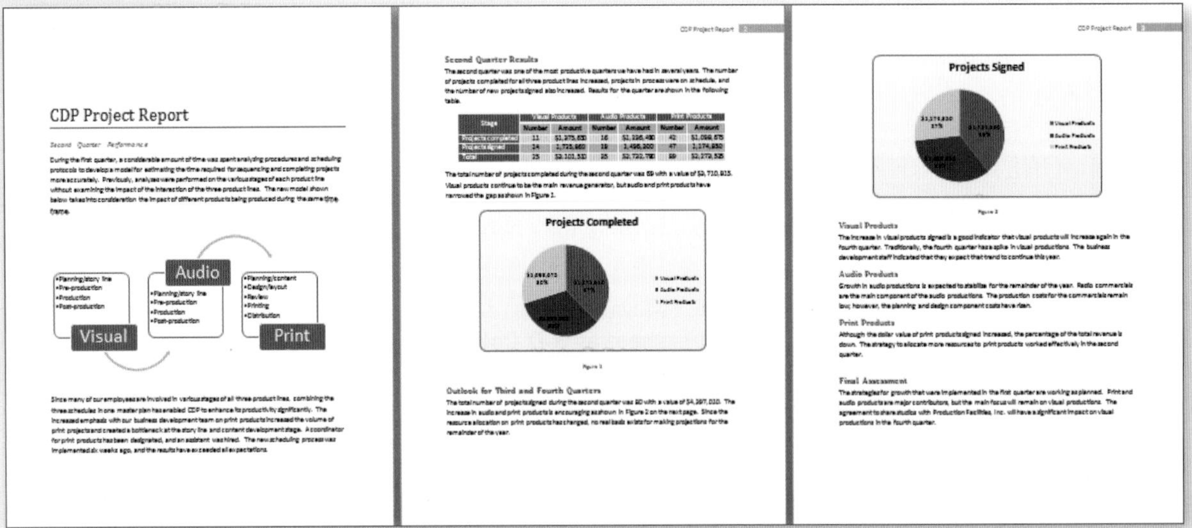

Figure P7.2 Quick Check

Job 4

Customized Template and Newsletter

CDP wants to send a newsletter to all contractors who participate in visual productions. Lori has asked you to prepare a one-page customized template with a heading, text boxes, three story headings, and a picture placeholder (Figure P7.3). You will use the template to create a newsletter for the School Spirit project to ensure that it is effective.

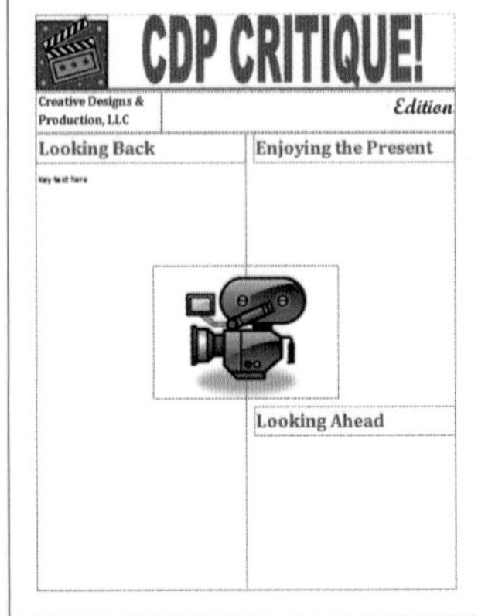

Figure P7.3 Template Illustration

TIP

Remember to display boundary lines, compress pictures, and turn hyphenation off.

1. Create the heading with the CDP logo and WordArt. Size the logo 1.3" × 1.3". Insert Fill – White, Outline – Gray WordArt style. Key **CDP CRITIQUE!** Apply Shape Fill Accent 1 and Shape Outline Accent 2. Size approximately 5" wide and as tall as the logo. Draw a 3-point line below the logo from margin to margin; apply the CDP Accent 1 color.
2. Draw a text box about .7" × 2.25" for the CDP name. Key the full name in the box; format with Accent 2 font color; apply bold 16-point Cambria font.

To Edit Chart Layout—Labels, Axes, and Plot Area:

Chart Tools Layout

TIP

To display the Chart Elements box on the Quick Access Toolbar, right-click the Chart Element box's drop-list arrow, and click Add to Quick Access Toolbar.

1. From the Chart Tools Layout tab, click a command in the Labels, Axes, or Background group and select the desired layout. For example, click Chart Title ❶ (Figure 5.5) and select one of the three layouts: None, Centered Overlay Title, or Above Chart. -or- Click a command such as More Title Options ❷ to display a Format dialog box for that particular element.
2. In the Current Selection group (Figure 5.6), note that the chart area currently selected displays in the Chart Elements box ❸. If needed, click the arrow and select the desired chart element.
3. Click Format Selection ❹. The Format dialog box for the selected element displays, such as the Format Chart Title dialog box shown in Figure 5.7. Use options in the Format dialog box to modify fill, change border color and style, add a shadow, add glow and soft edges, adjust 3-D format, or change alignment.
4. Click Reset to Match Style ❺ to clear the custom formatting.

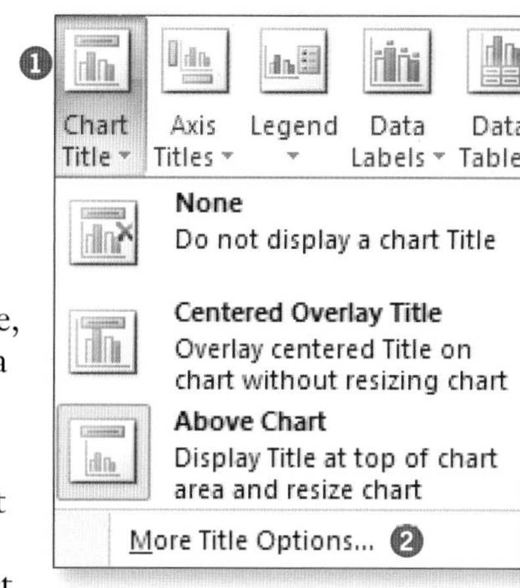

Figure 5.5 Chart Title Options

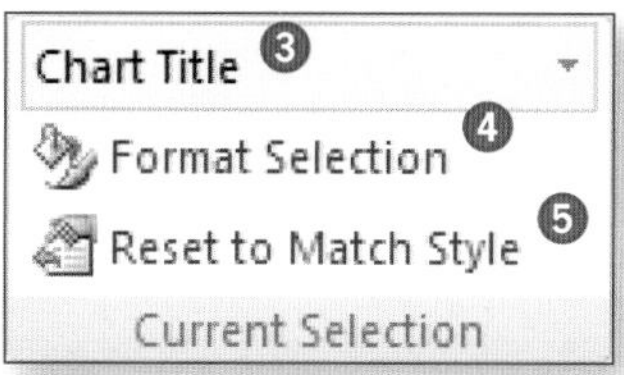

Figure 5.6 Current Selection Group

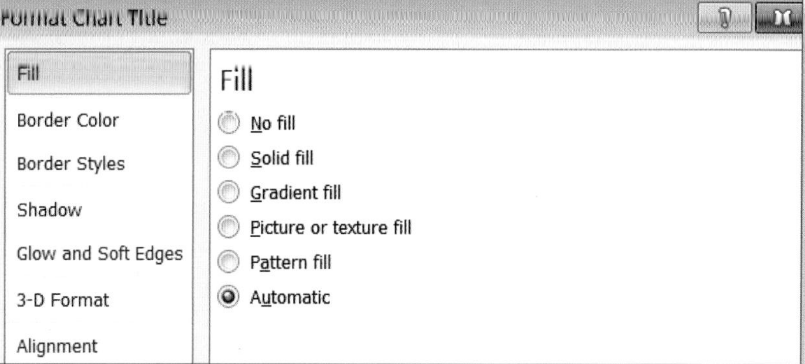

Figure 5.7 Format Chart Title

DRILL 2 REVISE CHART LAYOUT

1. With *ex5-drill1* open, move the chart back to Sheet1. Move the chart's upper-left corner to A8 and drag the lower-right corner to fit the range A8:J29.
2. Use Chart Tools Layout commands to edit the chart as directed below.
   a. Chart Title—Key **Comparison of E-Learning Series Requests** and format as follows: Solid fill, Gold, Accent 1; Solid line border, Red, Accent 6; Border style, 3-point width and Thin Thick style; Shadow, Green, Accent 4; and Glow, Preset Orange, 18 pt glow, Accent color 5.
   b. Primary Horizontal Axis Title—Select Title Below Axis and key **Video Requests** in the text box. Choose the same format options as the chart title, except change size of glow to 3 pt.
   c. Primary Vertical Axis Title—Select Rotated Title. In the formula bar, key **Number**. Choose the same format options as the chart title, except change size of glow to 3 pt.
   d. Gridlines—Do not display horizontal or vertical gridlines.
   e. Plot Area—Select Plot Area in the Chart Elements box and format with Gradient fill and Daybreak as the preset colors. Your chart should look similar to Figure 5.8.
3. Save as *ex5-drill2* and leave the file open for the next drill.

SmartArt Tools Design/Create Graphic/Text Pane

Display the Text pane to key the text rather than keying directly in the shapes.

Visual

- Planning/story line
- Pre-production
- Production
- Post-production

Audio

- Planning/story line
- Pre-production
- Production
- Post-production

Print

- Planning/content
- Design/layout
- Review
- Printing
- Distribution

4. Key the following text:

Since many of our employees are involved in various stages of all three product lines, combining the three schedules in one master plan has enabled CDP to enhance its productivity significantly. The increased emphasis with our business development team on print products increased the volume of print projects and created a bottleneck at the story line and content development stage. A coordinator for print products has been designated, and an assistant was hired. The new scheduling process was implemented six weeks ago, and the results have exceeded all expectations.

Second Quarter Results [use Heading 1 style]

The second quarter was one of the most productive quarters we have had in several years. The number of projects completed for all three product lines increased, projects in process were on schedule, and the number of new projects signed also increased. Results for the quarter are shown in the following table.

5. Format the table using AutoFit and apply Medium Grid 3 – Accent 1 design. Adjust column widths so all entries fit on one line. Bold and center all headings vertically and horizontally; center all text vertically. Align column 1 at the left, columns 2, 4, and 6 centered, and 3, 5, and 7 at the right. Sum all columns. Center the table horizontally.

Stage	Visual Products		Audio Products		Print Products	
	Number	Amount	Number	Amount	Number	Amount
Projects completed	11	$1,375,650	16	$1,236,490	42	$1,098,675
Projects signed	14	1,725,860	19	1,496,300	47	1,174,850
Total						

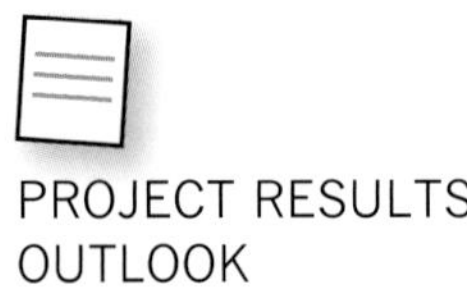

PROJECT RESULTS OUTLOOK

6. Key the following paragraph:

The total number of projects completed during the second quarter was 69 with a value of $3,710,815. Visual products continue to be the main revenue generator, but audio and print products have narrowed the gap as shown in Figure 1.

7. Open the *Excel* file *project results*; select the three products and their revenue; create a 2-D pie chart for each worksheet. Use the sheet tab title as chart title and position the title above the chart. Show legend at the right and use best fit for data labels; display both percentage and dollar value. Use a new line separator and format the numbers using currency with a dollar sign and no decimal places. Add the Subtle Effect – Light Yellow, Accent 3 shape style to the chart area. Add a Brown, Accent 1 1 pt. border with rounded corners. Save the file as *project charts* in your solution files.

8. Embed the Projects Completed chart below the last paragraph in your document; add the caption **Figure 1** below the chart; then key the heading and paragraph shown on the next page. Center the caption and the chart.

Use Figure 5.8 to check.

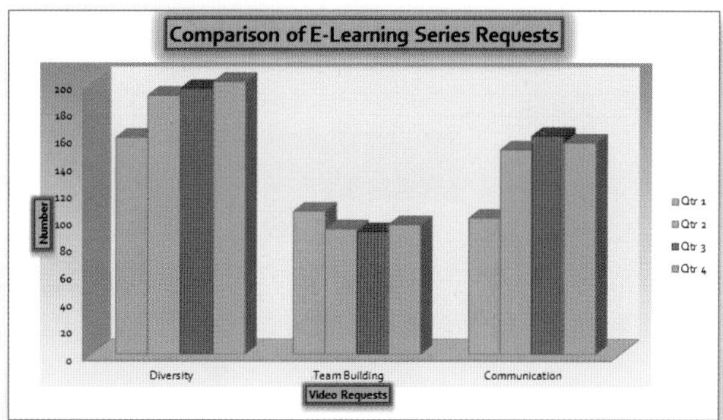

Figure 5.8 Quick Check

To display the Drawing Tools Format tab to edit shapes and text boxes, click the object on the chart.

MODIFY THE FORMAT OF SHAPES

Chart Tools Format

To insert a picture, shape, or a text box on a chart, click the desired object on the Chart Tools Layout tab (Figure 5.9). After the object is inserted, the Drawing Tools Format tab displays (Figure 5.10). Follow the same steps you used in *Word* to customize these objects using the commands in the Shape Styles group ❶ and the WordArt Styles group ❷. You can find the same commands on the Chart Tools Format tab.

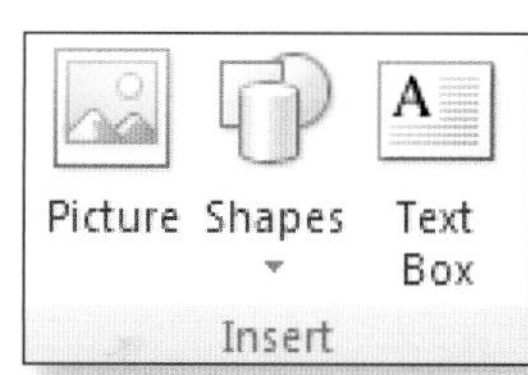

Figure 5.9 Insert Objects

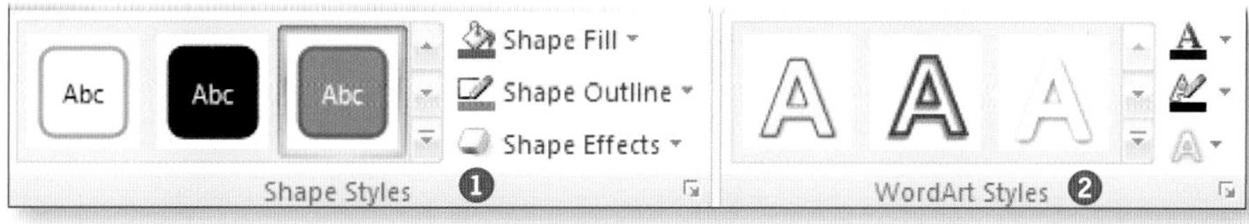

Figure 5.10 Modify Shape Styles and WordArt Style

DRILL 3 REVISE CHART FORMAT

1. With *ex5-drill2* open, select the chart title and apply the WordArt Fill – White, Drop Shadow style.
2. Decrease the size of the plot area slightly. Move the chart title to center attractively over the plot area.
3. Show data labels. Insert a down arrow pointing to 90 in the Team Building category; add Preset 2 effect. Add a text box and key **Low Demand**.
4. Save as *ex5-drill3* and print. Close the file.

Use Figure 5.11 to check.

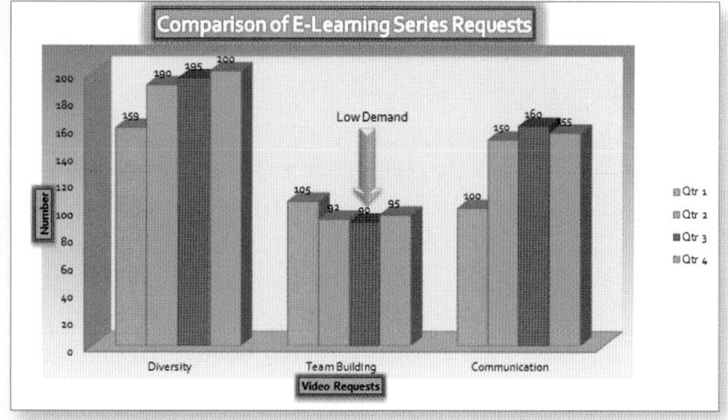

Figure 5.11 Quick Check

QUICK ✓ Use Figure P7.1 to check Job 1.

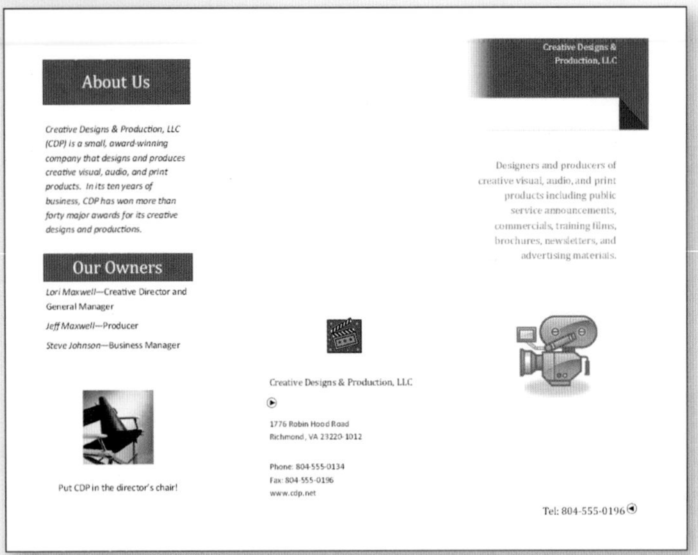

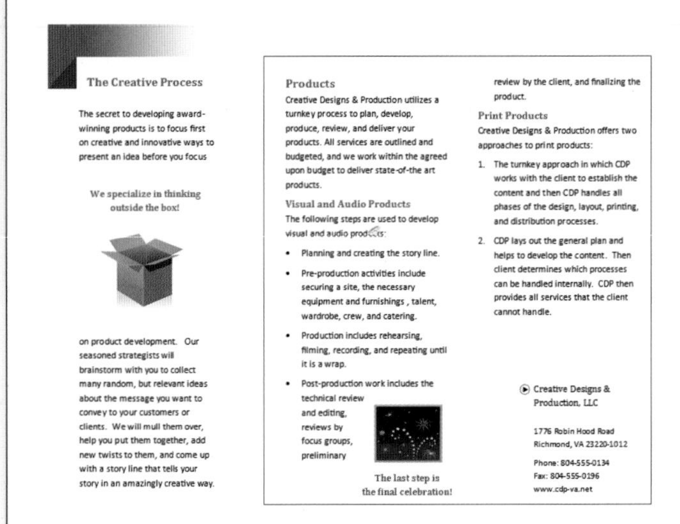

Figure P7.1 Job 1 Illustration

Job 2

Memo

Remember to use the CDP theme in all documents.

Prepare a memo to Lori Maxwell from you about the CDP brochure you have drafted. Insert the CDP memo head you saved as a Quick Part in Project 1. If necessary, open the memo you prepared in Project 1 and save the heading as a Quick Part. Key the memo below. Attach a copy of the brochure to the memo. Save as *p7-j2* and close.

The first draft of the brochure that you asked me to prepare is attached. Please review it at your convenience and offer suggestions for improving it. If you like the format and general content, I will work with Bill in photo archives to find more creative graphics for the final copy.

A copy of the brochure has been saved on our shared drive using the name *CDP brochure* if you wish to have an online version. I look forward to receiving your reaction to the first draft.

Job 3

Report with Excel Charts

1. Prepare a report using title, subtitle, and heading styles.

   Title: CDP Project Report | Subtitle: Second Quarter Performance

2. Key the first paragraph:

   During the first quarter, a considerable amount of time was spent analyzing procedures and scheduling protocols to develop a model for estimating the time required for sequencing and completing projects more accurately. Previously, analyses were performed on the various stages of each product line without examining the impact of the interaction of the three product lines. The new model shown below takes into consideration the impact of different products being produced during the same time frame.

3. Insert the Alternating Flow SmartArt graphic, and key the text shown on the next page.

Apply It

Worksheet 10
Create Column Chart

SALES

Click Reset to Match Style to return to the original style.

1. Open the data file *sales* and save as *ex5-w10*. Apply the Civic theme.
2. Select the appropriate cells and create a column chart as an embedded object. Use the default Layout 1 and Style 2. Refer to Figure 5.12 for text for the chart title, horizontal axis title, and vertical axis title. *Note:* Key **Units** for vertical axis title. You will display units in thousands in step 5.
3. Move the chart to A10. Size to fill the range A10:J30.
4. Format the chart area as a texture fill using Parchment; border color Brown, Accent 4 with 3.5 pt Double border style with rounded corners.
5. Format the chart title as WordArt Gradient Fill – Orange, Accent 6, Inner Shadow. Format vertical axis options to display units in thousands.
6. Insert a text box to recognize the Sales Award. Format with Ice Blue, Background 2 fill; add Green, Accent 5 border with 2¼ pt weight; and add a Red, 11 pt glow, Accent color 1 glow effect. Select the text and apply the Orange, Accent 6, Darker 50% font color.
7. Resave as *ex5-w10*, click on chart to print the chart only, and close the file.

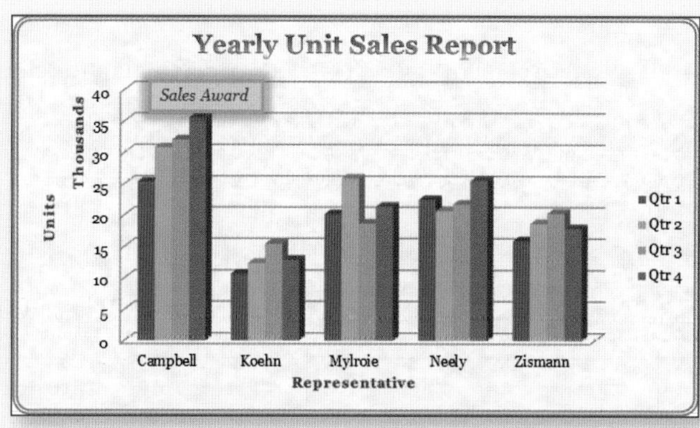

Figure 5.12 Column Chart

Worksheet 11
Create Pie Chart

ADVERTISING

1. Open the data file and save as *ex5-w11*. Apply the Paper theme.
2. Create a pie chart in 3-D similar to Figure 5.13. Move to a new sheet named **Pie Chart**. Choose Layout 1 and Style 40.
3. Click on the largest pie slice; then click the largest pie slice again and drag away from pie to explode for emphasis.
4. Format the chart title attractively using a WordArt style; add shape effects. Increase font size and position attractively.
5. Format the chart area attractively, adding a fill, border color, style, shape effects, etc.
6. Insert a text box at the bottom left and format attractively. Key **Prepared by Brad Tyner, 4-1-2012**.
7. Select the data labels. Change the font to Arial Bold and increase the font size to 14 point.
8. Resave as *ex5-w11* and print the chart and the worksheet. Close the file.

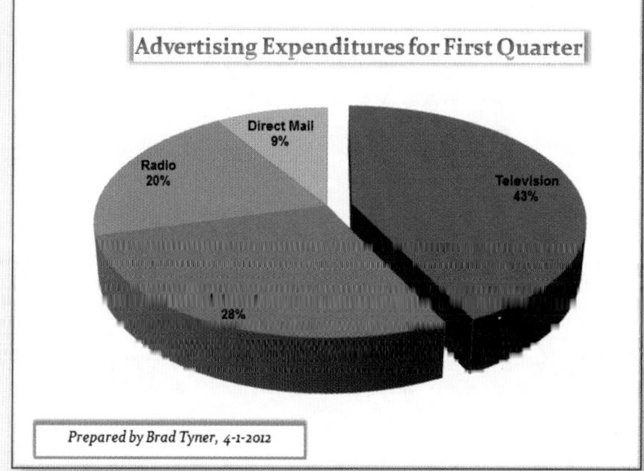

Figure 5.13 Pie Chart

Job 1,
continued

Page 1

1. Key the following text in the Product/Service information text box:

   Designers and producers of creative visual, audio, and print products including public service announcements, commercials, training films, brochures, newsletters, and advertising materials.

2. Increase the Cambria font size to 12 point. Adjust the size of the text box to fit the text.
3. Replace the clock with clip art featuring a movie camera. Recolor the clip to complement the CDP color scheme.
4. Key the correct telephone number at the bottom of the panel. Apply 12-point font size.
5. In the center panel, increase Cambria font size to 11 point for the CDP name and Calibri font size to 10 point for the remainder of the information. Adjust the size and position of the text boxes if necessary to display all of the information. Center the logo horizontally in the column. Apply this same format to the CDP information on page 2.
6. Replace the Back Panel Heading with **About Us**; increase the font size to 20 point, apply White text color, and fill the text box with the Accent 1 color.
7. Select the text in the box below the heading, increase the font to 11 points, left-align it, and replace it with the following text:

   Creative Designs & Production, LLC (CDP) is a small, award-winning company that designs and produces creative visual, audio, and print products. In its ten years of business, CDP has won more than forty major awards for its creative designs and productions.

8. Insert a text box below the text and format it the same as the About Us text box. Use the title **Our Owners**. In the text box below the heading, key Lori, Jeff, and Steve's names followed by an em dash and their titles. Apply italic to the names and increase the font size of all text to 11 point.
9. In the picture frame, replace the briefcase with a director's chair from clip art and add the caption **Put CDP in the director's chair!** Increase the font size of the caption to 11 point. Adjust the placeholder size as needed.

Turn off hyphenation in all text boxes including title boxes.

Page 2

1. Format all body text on page 2 using 11-point Calibri font.
2. Extend the rectangle with the fill above the main inside heading to the width of the text box below it.
3. Key **The Creative Process** as the main heading. Increase font size to 14 point; apply bold.
4. Extend the caption text box and picture frame to the full width of the text box; apply Top and Bottom wrapping. Replace the picture with a box from clip art.
5. Key the caption **We specialize in thinking outside the box!** Format using 11-point bold Cambria font and the same color as the headings.
6. Replace the text with the file *creative process*. Make sure the text wraps around the box and fits in the left panel.
7. Replace the text in the two panels on the right with the file *products*. Use 14-point bold font for the Products heading and 12-point bold font for the other two headings.
8. Follow the directions in step 5 for page 1 to format the CDP information.
9. Replace the picture with the *celebration* file and add the caption: **The last step is the final celebration!** Format the caption as directed in step 5, adjusting text box size as necessary.
10. Check using Quick Check in Figure P7.1, save as *p7-j1*, and close.

CREATIVE PROCESS
PRODUCTS
CELEBRATION

LESSON 6

Sort and Filter

OBJECTIVES

- Sort data in a worksheet
- Filter data in a worksheet

SORT

Home/Editing/Sort & Filter

Data becomes more useful when it is sorted. For example, a human resource director may need to sort data by ID number, birth date, date of employment, or department.

To Sort a Single Column:

1. Click in the column to be sorted.
2. Click the Sort & Filter drop-list arrow ❶. Select sorting option as determined by data type.

   Numbers: Smallest to Largest (ascending) or Largest to Smallest (descending). Figure 6.1 shows options for sorting numbers.

   Text: A to Z (ascending) or Z to A (descending).

   Dates and times: Oldest to Newest or Newest to Oldest.

Sort & Filter ❶ · Find & Select
Sort Smallest to Largest
Sort Largest to Smallest
Custom Sort... ❷
Filter
Clear
Reapply

Figure 6.1 Sort Numbers

Data in a worksheet sometimes does not sort correctly if a merged heading appears above the data set. If you find that data is not sorting the way it should, insert a blank row above the data set.

To Sort by More Than One Criterion:

Home/Editing/Sort & Filter

1. Click the Sort & Filter drop-list arrow ❶ and click Custom Sort ❷. The Sort dialog box displays, as shown in Figure 6.2.
2. In the Sort by box, click the arrow ❸ and select the column to be sorted. Click the arrows in the boxes below Sort On ❹ and Order ❺ to further define sort.
3. Click Add Level ❻ to add the Then by ❼ column. Make the desired selections.
4. Repeat step 3 for additional criteria. Click OK.

An alternate way to sort is to use the Quick Sort commands (Data/Sort & Filter).

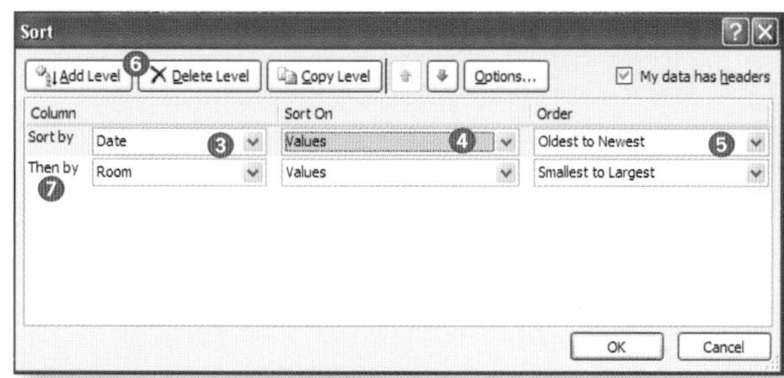

Figure 6.2 Sort Dialog Box

project 7

Creative Designs & Production III: Integrating Publisher, Word, and Excel

OBJECTIVES

- Create effective *Publisher* publications
- Prepare effective *Word* documents
- Work independently with few instructions

SETTING

In Project 7, you will assume new responsibilities. An assistant who reports to you now handles some events coordination duties, and you are now responsible for coordinating the print products as well as serving as events coordinator. You may wish to refer to Project 1 on page 24 and Project 2 on page 48 to refresh your memory about Creative Designs & Production and for contact information. You may still have the customized document theme and the Quick Parts you developed in the earlier projects that you can use in this project. If not, you will have to recreate them. One of the important things to learn is when to use *Word* and when to use *Publisher*. It should be obvious to you that three of the documents in this project should be prepared using *Word* and the other three should be prepared using *Publisher*.

Jobs

1. Brochure
2. Memo
3. Report
4. Newsletter
5. Block letter
6. Business cards

Job 1

Brochure

CDP LOGO

Duplicate a Font Scheme

Page Design/Schemes/Fonts

1. In the Scheme Fonts list, click the down arrow on Office 1 and select Duplicate Scheme.
2. Name the font scheme **CDP** and apply it.

Lori Maxwell has asked you to design and draft a threefold brochure printed on both sides to provide information about Creative Designs & Production to potential clients. You have decided to use the Marker template. Use the information from Project 1 to create new business information. Use the Web address rather than the e-mail address for this brochure. Include the *cdp logo* from the data files

CDP color scheme (RGB color model):

Accent 1: Red—204 | Green—102 | Blue—0
Accent 2: Red—50 | Green—50 | Blue—255
Accent 3: Red—255 | Green—205 | Blue—100
Accent 4: Red—153 | Green—153 | Blue—245

Hyperlink: Red—0 | Green—0 | Blue—255

Followed Hyperlink: Red—204 | Green—102 | Blue—0

CDP font scheme: After you create the publication, display the Scheme Fonts list on the Page Design tab. Then right-click and duplicate the Office 1 font scheme; name it **CDP**.

Instructions and text to insert are provided on the next page.

DRILL 1	SORT A WORKSHEET	SESSIONS

1. Open the data file *sessions* and complete the following sorts. Save each sort as instructed.
   a. Sort by instructor in ascending order. Save as *ex6-drill1a*.
   b. Sort by room in ascending order. Save as *ex6-drill1b*.
   c. Sort by fee in descending order. Save as *ex6-drill1c*. Highlight the fees greater than 450 (Home/Styles/Conditional Formatting/Highlight Cells Rules/Greater Than).
   d. Clear the conditional formatting rules set in 1c. Use the Sort dialog box to sort first by Date (oldest to newest) and then Room (smallest to largest). Select the fees and use one of the conditional formatting icons sets (rating category) to show a rating of the fees. Save as *ex6-drill1d*.
   e. Compose a multiple sort of your own. Be sure to include conditional formatting for more practice in this helpful tool. Save as *ex6-drill1e*.
2. Close the file.

AUTOFILTER

Home/Editing/Sort & Filter

Filtering is a feature used to locate and work with a subset of data in a worksheet. Useful filter applications include locating employees who worked over 40 hours, locating students whose average is greater than 95, or identifying all clients with January birthdays.

To Select from a List to Filter:

1. Click a cell in the list to be filtered. Click the Sort & Filter drop-list arrow ❶ and click Filter. Arrows display next to the column headings, as shown in Figure 6.3. *Note:* Click Filter again to toggle between filter and no filter.

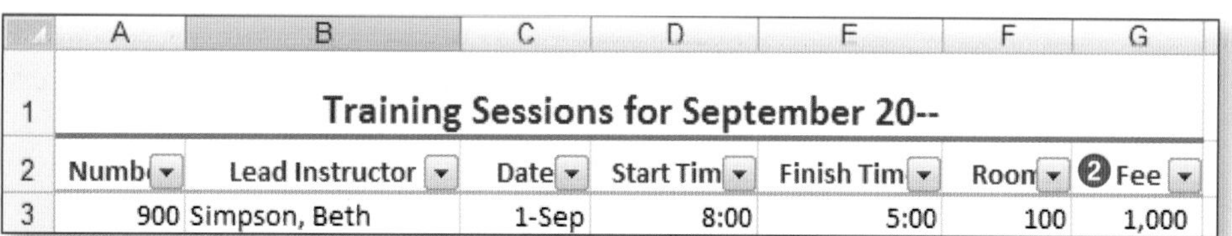

	A	B	C	D	E	F	G
1	Training Sessions for September 20--						
2	Numb	Lead Instructor	Date	Start Tim	Finish Tim	Room	Fee
3	900	Simpson, Beth	1-Sep	8:00	5:00	100	1,000

Figure 6.3 Filter a List

DISCOVER

Alternate way to clear a filter: Home/Editing/Sort & Filter/Clear

2. Click the arrow in the column that contains the data to filter—e.g., if you want to locate all sessions in Room 100, click the arrow in the Room ❷ column.
3. In the list of text filters ❸, select one or clear one or more text values to filter by (Figure 6.4). Click OK. *Excel* displays only those rows meeting the filter criteria.
4. Click Clear Filter From "..." ❹ to clear the filter.

Clear Filter From "Lead Instructor" ❹
Filter by Color
Text Filters ❸
(Select All)
Rankin, Jill
Watkins, Russ
Yielding, David
Zhag, Yin

Figure 6.4 Select Criteria

As shown in Figure 6.5, the row headings remaining after the filter is applied display in blue. The blue row headings indicate a filtered subset. You may edit, format, chart, and print this subset.

2	Numb	Lead Instructor	Date	Start Tim	Finish Tim	Room	Fee
8	905	Yielding, David	8-Sep	8:00	10:00	100	600
17	915	Yielding, David	30-Sep	9:00	11:30	102	150

Figure 6.5 Rows That Meet the Filter Yielding, David

To add another criterion, click the arrow in the desired column and choose one of the options. Note that the filtered subset must meet both of the criteria, which results in an AND search—e.g., Yielding, David AND Room 100.

Apply It

Publication 7

Newsletter from Template

BROTHERS
ARTICLE-BROTHERS
HEADQUARTERS
ARTICLE-HEADQUARTERS
ACQUISITION
EMPLOYEE NEWS

1. Open the *Klienwood Newsletter* template you prepared and save it as a *Publisher* file named *pb4-p7*.
2. Turn off hyphenation in all text boxes.
3. Select *Newsletter Date* in the masthead and replace it with Friday of this week's date.
4. Key the title **Brothers Honored in Starkville** for the lead article on page 1. Select *Article* and replace it with the text from the *article-brothers* data file.
5. Copy the quote from the Committee Chair; paste it in the pull quote text box. Apply 10-point font to the quote.
6. Change the picture in the first article by inserting *brothers* from the data files.
7. Key the title **New Orleans Headquarters Office Completed** for the second article on page 1. Select and replace *Article* with text from the *article-headquarters* file. Adjust text boxes so that both articles fit on the page.
8. Change the picture by inserting *headquarters* from the data files.
9. On page 2, key the title **Klienwood Acquires NetGen Commercial Printers** for the first article. Replace *Article* with text from the *acquisition* data file.
10. On page 2, key the title **Employee News** for the second article. Replace *Article* with text from the *employee news* data file.
11. Search clip art for a photograph of a woman who has the appearance of a professional customer service representative. If necessary, click Fit (Picture Tools Format/Crop/Fit) so that it will fit in the placeholder.
12. Key the bullet points shown below in the sidebar:

- The comprehensive benefits study should be completed within the next two or three weeks. From the preliminary analysis, it appears that we may be able to lower the cost of benefits by changing our provider.
- Currently The Klienwood Group has 861 employees in 12 states. More than 20 professional-level positions are posted on our intranet. We encourage all employees to recommend qualified individuals to us for these positions. If we hire an individual you recommend for a professional-level position, you will receive a $500 bonus.

13. Resave and close the publication.

Publication 8

Design Newsletter and Create Template

Design a template for a two-page newsletter for an organization to which you belong. If you do not belong to any organizations, design the newsletter template for one of your classes. Use your creativity as you prepare the template with the design elements of your choice:

1. Create a custom color scheme and font scheme of your choice.
2. Create new business information for the organization including a logo that you designed.
3. Design and format text boxes for articles that will be written.
4. Add placeholder graphics.
5. Create a second-page header using the style and design elements you prefer.
6. Save the template in the Templates folder as *my newsletter* and in your solutions folder as *pb4-p8*. Compose at least two articles for the newsletter.

The column containing a filter displays [filter icon]. If you have applied a sort to a column, the column displays a sort symbol [sort icon].

To Create Criteria for a Filter:

Home/Editing/Sort & Filter

1. Click the arrow in the column to be filtered. If text data, click Text Filters. If numerical data, click Number Filters.
2. Click one of the comparison operator commands or click Custom Filter (Figure 6.6).
3. Choose the criteria from the Custom AutoFilter dialog box shown in Figure 6.7. Click OK.

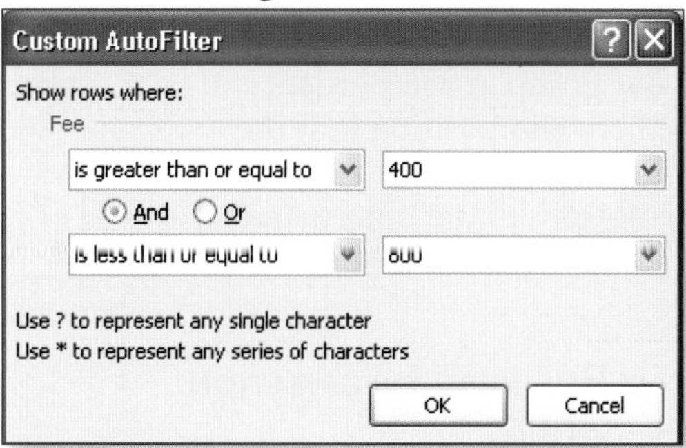

Figure 6.7 Custom AutoFilter Dialog Box

Figure 6.6 Choose Comparison Operator or Click Custom Filter

DRILL 2 FILTER A LIST

SESSIONS

1. Open the data file *sessions* and complete the following filters. Save each filter as instructed and clear it before starting the next filter.
   a. Display sessions listed with David Yielding as the instructor. Save as *ex6-drill2a*.
   b. Display all sessions in Room 101. Save as *ex6-drill2b*.
   c. Display sessions on September 15. Save as *ex6-drill2c*.
   d. Add a second criterion to item c that displays sessions in Room 102. The subset displays two sessions on September 15 in Room 102. Save as *ex6-drill2d*.
   e. Display sessions with fees between $400 and $800. Use Number Filters. After filtering, click the down arrow by Fee and sort largest to smallest. Save as *ex6-drill2e*.
   f. Display sessions led by Beth Simpson or Jill Rankin on September 1 or September 11. Save as *ex6-drill2f*.
   g. Create a custom filter of your choice. Save as *ex6-drill2g*.
2. Close the file.

JOB KNOWLEDGE

Using *Excel* to display data is a common use of the program, but the power of *Excel* is when it is used for problem solving and decision making. Here are a few examples:

1. Instructors use the vertical lookup function to assign grades to their students. Instead of looking at each average and keying the grade, instructors can use the lookup function to compare the student's average to a table of grades and then generate the grade.
2. Accountants use *if* statements to quickly generate data. For example, if sales in B2 are greater than $10,000, multiply the amount in B3 by 125%. The gross pay for the sales representative is generated in B5. Nested *if* statements can even compute the gross pay if sales are less than $10,000.
3. PivotTables are used to analyze related totals in a long list of numbers. You are able to view different summaries using various *Excel* functions.
4. Scenarios are used as what-if analysis tools and used to forecast the outcome of a proposed plan.
5. Charts are used to show comparisons and trends in worksheet data.

To Create a Second-Page Header:

1. Add a .5" × .5" logo in the top left corner and a .5" × .5" text box with Accent 1 (207C) fill in the top right corner (Figure 4.8). Select the text box and insert the page number in it in 11-point Cambria. Format the text White and center it vertically and horizontally.
2. Insert a Double Check design object from the Bar group in the Borders and Accents gallery and position it at the center of the header. Draw a 3-point line at the bottom of the objects in the header and use the same color (Accent 1, 207C).

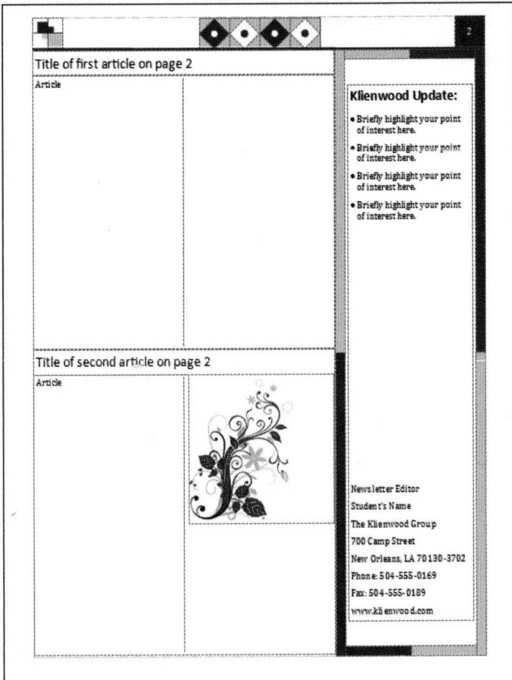

Figure 4.8 Page 2 of Newsletter Template

To Transfer Business Information to the Publication:

Insert/Text/Business Information

1. Display the business information fields.
2. Click each field you want to use to add it to the page. Tap ENTER between each item.

DRILL 2, continued — ADD HEADER AND TRANSFER BUSINESS INFORMATION TO SIDEBAR

1. In the open publication, add a second page and create the header shown in Figure 4.8.
2. Insert a Borders sidebar that extends from the header to the bottom margin and sized 2.25" wide.
3. Select *Special Points of Interest* and replace the text with **Klienwood Update**; format the text as a heading.
4. About 2.5" from the bottom of the sidebar, key:

   Newsletter Editor | Your Name

   Then display the business information and click each field except the name and title fields to add it to the sidebar. Draw text boxes that end at the sidebar for the title of both articles. Key **Title of first article on page 2 | Title of second article on page 2**. Format all text boxes the same as you did for page 1.
5. Draw text boxes about 4.4" high with two columns. Key **Article** in both text boxes.
6. Add the picture placeholder as shown in Figure 4.8.
7. Save as a *Publisher* template in the Templates folder with the name **Klienwood Newsletter**. Also save as a template in your solutions folder named *pb4-drill2* and close the publication.

Apply It

Worksheet 12
Sort and Filter

APPLICANT TRACKING

View/Window/Freeze Panes

For ease in keying data in a large worksheet, freeze or lock the row and/or column heading. As you scroll, the headings remain visible.

To unfreeze, click View/Window/Freeze Panes. Choose Unfreeze Panes.

1. Open the data file *applicant tracking*.
2. Click in C3 and freeze the worksheet panes for both columns and rows. Scroll down until row 21 displays just below the column headings. Key your name and related information as an applicant for the management trainee position, recruited by Johnson at a college visit. Your application is complete and your resume was received on 9/23/2012.
3. Click in C10 and scroll until column H (Alternate Phone) is next to column B. Key Hayden's alternate phone as **662 555-0138**. Unfreeze the panes.
4. Sort the worksheet by recruiter in ascending order. Save as *ex6-w12a*.
5. Sort the worksheet using a multiple sort: Sort first by Position Applied For, then by Last Name, and then by First Name. All sorts are ascending order. Save as *ex6-w12b*.
6. Sort the worksheet using a multiple sort: Sort first by Position Applied For (ascending), then by Date Resume Received (newest to oldest order), and then by Last Name and First Name (both ascending). Save as *ex6-w12c*.
7. Filter the worksheet to display only those applicants with complete applications. Sort by last name and then first name (ascending order). Save as *ex6-w12d*.
8. Filter the worksheet and display only those applicants for the management trainee position whose application is complete. Then sort in ascending order by last name. Save as *ex6-w12e*.
9. Create a filter of your own choice. Save as *ex6-w12f*. Close the file.

Worksheet 13
Sort and Filter

INVENTORY

1. Open the data file *inventory* and save as *ex6-w13a*.
2. Select row 3; freeze panes. Scroll down the worksheet so that row 60 displays immediately below the column headings on row 3.
3. Key the new inventory shown below.

Bonus room	Pool table		3000
Bonus room	HD television	SS-39-03-T	3000

4. Sort the inventory by room in ascending order. Save.
5. Sort the inventory by room in ascending order and then by item in ascending order. Save as *ex6-w13b*.
6. Sort the inventory by cost with smallest to largest. Apply conditional formatting using a directional icon set of your choice. Save as *ex6-w13c*.
7. Filter the worksheet to display only items in the den. Sort by item in ascending order. Save as *ex6-w13d*.
8. Filter the worksheet to display items in all the bedrooms. Sort by bedroom and then by item (ascending order). Save as *ex6-w13e*.
9. Clear all filters to display all the inventory. Sort by room and then by item in ascending order. Unfreeze the panes. Select the costs and edit conditional formatting rules by changing the percents to 50% and 25% (Home/Styles/Conditional Formatting/Manage Rules/Edit Rules). Save as *ex6-w13f*. Close the file.

INSERT AND FORMAT PLACEHOLDERS

When creating a template from scratch, you will need to insert and position the text boxes in which headings and stories will be positioned and the picture placeholders for graphics. Use tools tabs such as Drawing Tools Format to modify placeholders.

TIP

Check each text box to make sure that the custom font scheme is applied. All headings should be Calibri font. Apply 16-point bold to each heading. Body text should be formatted using 11-point Cambria unless directed otherwise.

To Add and Format Placeholders:

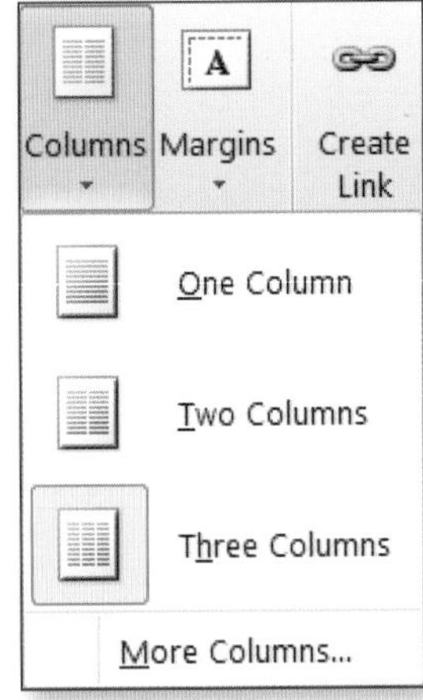

Figure 4.7 Columns

1. Use the Insert/Text/Draw Text Box command to draw text boxes. Size the text box as desired. Key directions in the text box, such as Title of lead article, and format the text the way it should be formatted in the newsletter.
2. To create columns in a text box, follow the path Text Box Tools Format/Alignment/Columns and select the desired number of columns as shown in Figure 4.7. The text box will be divided into equal-sized columns, and text will flow from one column to the next.
3. Use the Insert/Illustrations/Picture Placeholder command to draw placeholders for graphics. -or- Insert a graphic directly on the template as a sample; a user can then use the Picture Tools Format/Adjust/Change Picture command to replace the sample.
4. To insert pull quotes or sidebars, follow the path Insert/Building Blocks/Page Parts, and in the Pull Quotes or Sidebars group, select the pull quote or sidebar desired and position it where desired.
5. When objects (pull quotes or pictures) are positioned in text boxes, apply the wrapping style desired such as Tight or Top and Bottom (Drawing Tools Format or Picture Tools Format/Arrange/Wrap Text).
6. To center text vertically in a text box, follow the path Text Box Tools Format/Alignment. Select the desired alignment such as Align Center Left or Align Center.

To Add a Second Page and Page Number to a Newsletter:

- Follow the path Insert/Pages/Page and click Insert Blank Page.
- To insert a page number, follow the path Insert/Header & Footer/Page Number; then select Insert in Current Text Box and remove the check from Show Page Number on First Page.

DRILL 2, continued — ADD TEXT BOXES AND PICTURES

1. In the open publication (*pb4-drill2*), add and format all the elements on page 1 of the template as shown in Figure 4.6 and described below.
2. Draw a text box for the title; size it .4" high × 7.5" wide. Key **Title of lead article** in the text box and apply 16-point Calibri font. Center the title vertically.
3. Draw a text box 3.8" high for body text; format it in three columns. Key **Article** at the top of the first column, and format the text with 11-point Cambria.
4. Insert a picture from clip art at the bottom of the first column using the keyword *design* as a placeholder; size it 2" × 2.4".
5. Insert the Accessory Bar pull quote from the Page Parts gallery in the center of the third column. Size it 1.5" × 2.5".
6. Follow steps 2 and 3 to add and format text boxes for the title and the body text of the second article. Use the remaining space on the page.
7. Follow step 4 to insert a picture placeholder at the bottom of column 3.
8. Resave the file as *pb4-drill2* and leave it open.

LESSON 7

Create PivotTables

OBJECTIVES

- Create a PivotTable
- Filter a PivotTable

PIVOTTABLE

Insert/Tables/PivotTable

Worksheets compile much data, but often they do not provide answers needed for effective decision making. A PivotTable report can be created in a few mouse clicks to answer questions such as which representative or which region generated the most revenue for which product, and on which day of the month.

TIP

If a correct range is not selected, click the Collapse Dialog button and select the desired range. Click the Collapse Dialog button to return to the Create PivotTable dialog box.

To Create a PivotTable:

1. Click in the worksheet data. Click the PivotTable drop-list arrow and click PivotTable. The Create PivotTable dialog box displays (Figure 7.1).
2. The correct range should be automatically entered.
3. Click New Worksheet ❶. Click OK.

   Figure 7.2 shows the display of the blank PivotTable report on the left side of the new worksheet.

   Figure 7.3 shows a list of column headings ❷ (now referred to as fields), which displays on the right side of the new worksheet.
4. Click the box ❸ to the left of the field to add a field to the PivotTable report on the left side -or- click on the field and drag to areas ❹ below.

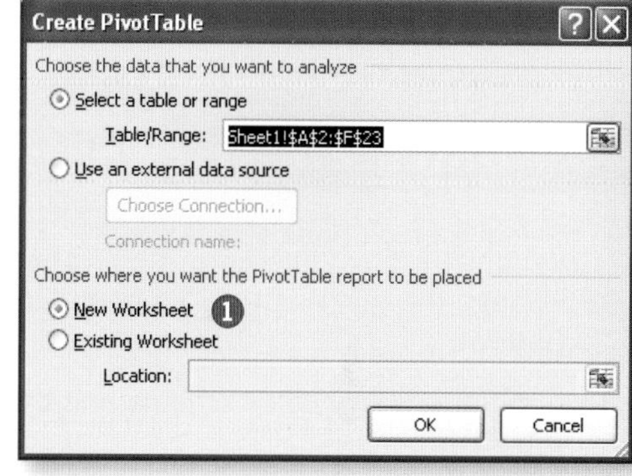

Figure 7.1 Create PivotTable Dialog Box

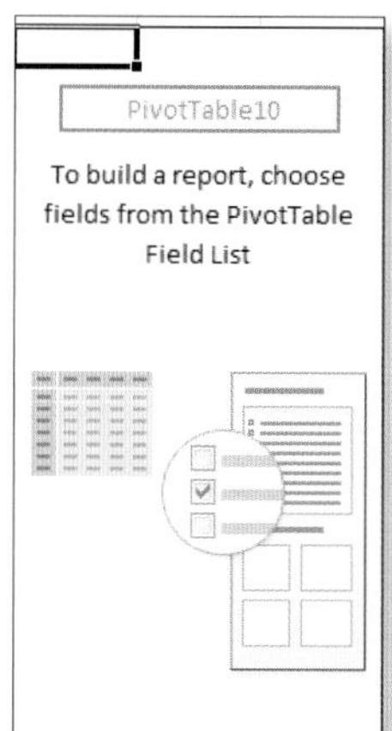

Figure 7.2 Build a PivotTable Report

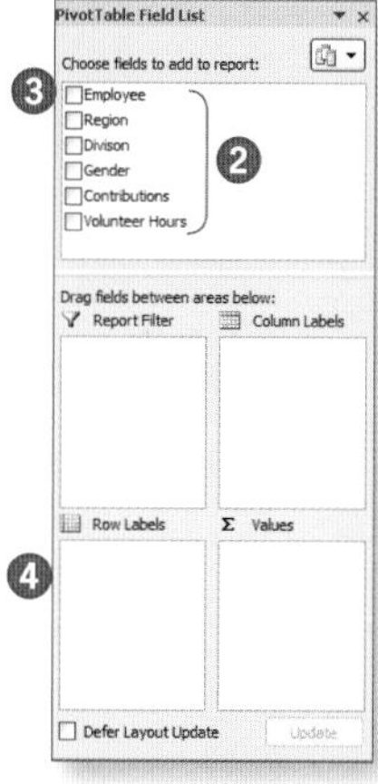

Figure 7.3 PivotTable Field List

View/Show/Boundaries

Displaying the boundaries of text boxes and frames makes it easier to design a template from a blank page.

If the design object you are looking for is not displayed, click More . . . (such as More Page Parts) at the bottom of the gallery to find more items. If the design element in a particular group is not displayed, click the folder at the end of the group named All . . . (such as All Headings).

Figure 4.6 shows the first page of the template that you will prepare in Drill 2 of this lesson. Note the elements that have been placed on the template. Also note that the formatting is part of the template. The design objects were inserted after the custom color and font schemes were applied and new business information was created. Refer to Figure 4.6 as you work on the drill.

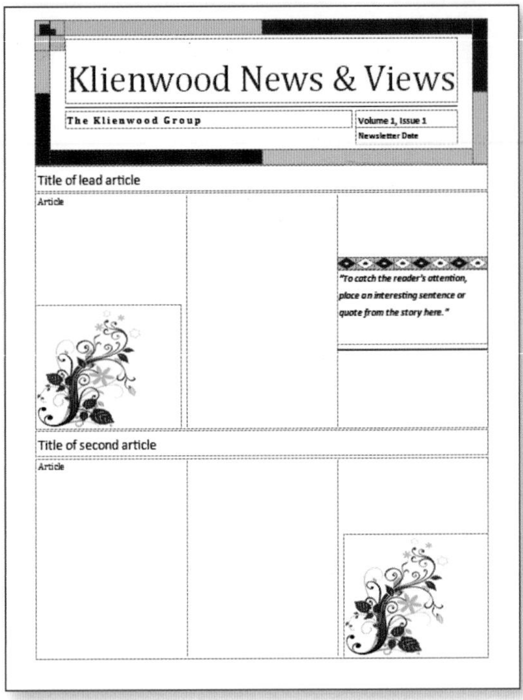

Figure 4.6 Page 1 of Newsletter Template

DRILL 2 CREATE A TEMPLATE FROM A BLANK PAGE

1. Select a blank page size 8.5 × 11" with portrait orientation.
2. Change the margins to .2" top, and .5" right, left, and bottom.
3. Apply Cranberry color scheme and change the colors to PANTONE colors:

   Accent 1: 207C | Accent 3: 7425C | Accent 4: 671C | Followed Hyperlink: 690C; name the color scheme **Klienwood** and apply it.
4. Create a new font scheme using Calibri as the heading font and Cambria as the body font; name the font scheme **Klienwood** and apply it.
5. Create a logo for The Klienwood Group by inserting the building block object Layered Boxes from the Borders & Accents category. Right-click the object and select Format Object. On the Colors and Lines tab, change the line color to Accent 1 (207C).
6. Save the logo as a picture named *klienwood logo* in your solutions folder. Also add the picture to the Borders & Accents gallery in the General category so it can be used in other ways.
7. From Building Blocks in the Page Parts gallery in the Headings group, insert a Borders heading and position it at the top of the page. Key the title **Klienwood News & Views**.
8. Create new business information; add the logo that you saved in your solution files to your business information. (Note that for the newsletter the Web address was substituted for the e-mail address.)

   Patrick R. Hess | President and CEO | The Klienwood Group | 700 Camp Street | New Orleans, LA 70130-3702 | 504-555-0169 | 504-555-0189 | www.klienwood.com
9. Insert the *klienwood logo* from your solution files or use the one you inserted in the publication; position it at the top left corner of the masthead so that the cross bar touches the left and top side of the beige border. Size it about .5" by .5". (See Figure 4.6.)
10. Save the newsletter as *pb4-drill2* and leave it open. (Do not save as a template until you are instructed to save it when both pages have been completed.)

Dragging the fields down to the area below the fields allows the user flexibility in choosing to display as a row label, column label, or values.

Figure 7.4 shows three fields added to a newly created PivotTable. Region and Division are added as row labels ❶ and Volunteer Hours is added as values ❷. Click the minus sign ❸ by a row label to collapse or click the plus sign ❹ to expand it.

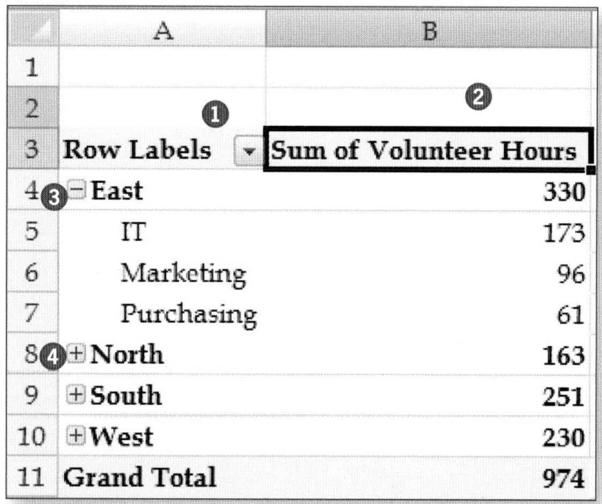

	A	B
1		
2	❶	❷
3	Row Labels	Sum of Volunteer Hours
4	❸ ⊟ East	330
5	IT	173
6	Marketing	96
7	Purchasing	61
8	❹ ⊞ North	163
9	⊞ South	251
10	⊞ West	230
11	Grand Total	974

Figure 7.4 Completed PivotTable Using Three Fields

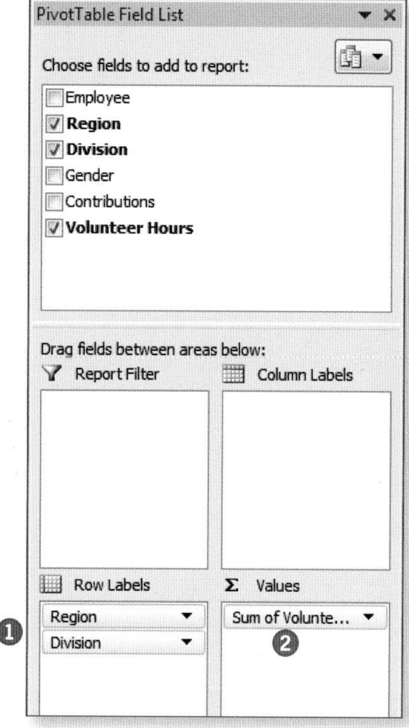

Figure 7.4 shows how a PivotTable can be used to sum values to create totals. You can edit value field settings to summarize data using a different function, such as Count, Average, Max, or Min.

To Edit Value Field Settings:

1. Double-click the column heading showing the sum (B3 in Figure 7.4). The Value Field Settings dialog box displays (Figure 7.5).

   Shortcut: Point to the field and right-click.

2. In the Custom Name box, key a new column label if desired, e.g., Total Volunteer Hours.
3. In Summarize value field by, click a new calculation from the list.
4. Click Number Format and select the desired format for that value column.
5. Click OK.

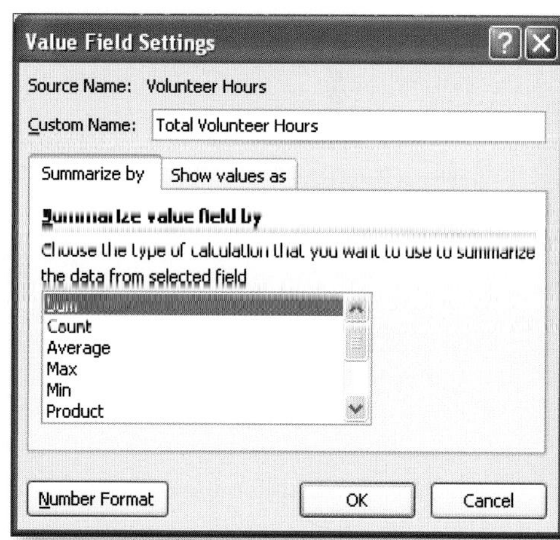

Figure 7.5 Value Field Settings

To Apply a PivotTable Style:

PivotTable Tools Design/PivotTable Styles

1. Click in the PivotTable to select it.
2. Click the desired PivotTable style.

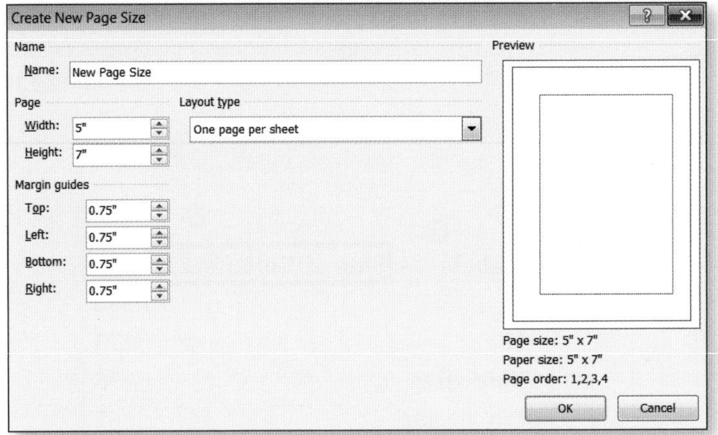

Figure 4.3 Create New Page Size Dialog Box

4. Select or create a new color scheme, font scheme, and business information; then click Create.
5. To create a second page for the template, with the same size and margins, use the Insert Page command (Insert/Pages/Page). Click the down arrow on Page and select Insert Duplicate Page.

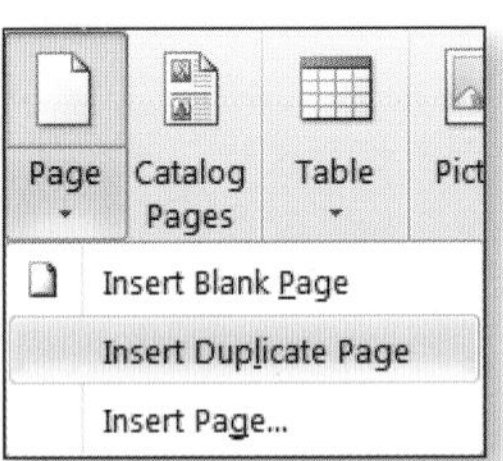

Figure 4.4 Duplicate Page

DRILL 1 CREATE A CUSTOM-SIZED BLANK PAGE

FISATTO, INC. LOGO

1. Create a custom page sized 5" × 7".
2. Change the margin guides to .75" for all four sides.
3. Apply the Fisatto color and font schemes.
4. Apply a Border 4 frame from Borders & Accents to the publication. Drag the border so that it frames the publication.
5. Insert the Fisatto logo, size it, and center it at the top of the page as shown in the illustration.
6. Draw a text box as shown by the blue dotted lines in the illustration.
7. Key the text shown below. Apply 16-point Brush Script MT font for the text of the invitation and 12-point font for the R.S.V.P. (Press SHIFT + ENTER for the second line to remove the extra space after the paragraph.) Apply Accent 1 (PANTONE 2738C) color to all text.
8. Save as *pb4-drill1*. Then save as a template named *invitation* and close.

Chef Tyler LeBlanc | Cordially invites you | To join him for a complimentary | Customer Appreciation Dinner | At | Le Fisatto | March 15, 7:30 p.m.

R.S.V.P. 717-555-0134

By March 10

Figure 4.5 Drill 1 Illustration

DRILL 1 CREATE PIVOTTABLE BY CLICKING FIELDS

1. Open the data file *pivottable* and save as *ex7-drill1*. Create a new PivotTable and name the new worksheet **PivotTable 1**. Change the theme to Apex.
2. Add the Region and Division fields to display as row labels.
3. Add the Volunteer Hours field to display as values in a column.
4. Collapse all regions except the East region.
5. Change the calculation from Sum to Min to determine the minimum number of volunteer hours.
6. Change the calculation to Max to determine the maximum number of volunteer hours.
7. Change the calculation to Average to determine the average number of volunteer hours. Format as a number with 2 decimal places.
8. Apply the Light 19 PivotTable style.
9. Resave as *ex7-drill1* and leave the file open for the next drill.

DRILL 2 CREATE PIVOTTABLE BY DRAGGING FIELDS

1. Save the open file as *ex7-drill2*. Create a new PivotTable on a new worksheet using the dragging method of adding fields.
   a. Drag the Gender field and the Region field to the Row Labels box below the field names and the Division field to the Column Labels box.
   b. Drag the Contributions field to the Values box below the field names.
   c. Format the range B5:G15 as Accounting and 2 decimal places. Adjust column widths if needed.
   d. Rename the sheet tab as **PivotTable 2**. Apply the Medium 3 PivotTable style.
2. Resave as *ex7-drill2* and leave the file open for the next drill.

TIP

To filter a field that displays in the PivotTable, click the arrow by Row Labels or Column Labels. Select the desired criteria.

DISCOVER

Use a Slicer for Alternate Method of Filtering

PivotTable Tools Options/Insert Slicer

1. Follow path to open Insert Slicers dialog box.
2. Select one or more fields to filter PivotTable by field(s).
3. To remove the filter, click the Clear Filter button.

FILTER A PIVOTTABLE

Insert/Tables/PivotTable

Use the Filter command to display a subset of the data that meets established criteria.

1. Create a PivotTable and select the desired fields to display.
2. Drag the desired filter field to the Report Filter ❶ box in the area below the fields (Figure 7.6).
3. In the PivotTable, click the arrow by All and select the filter criteria from the drop down list (Figure 7.7).

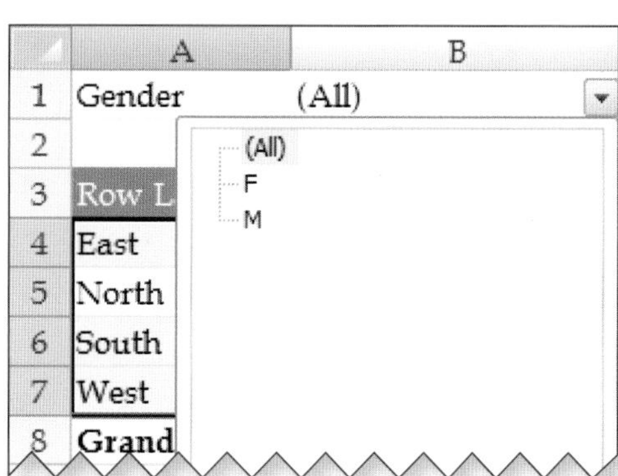

Figure 7.7 Select Filter Criteria

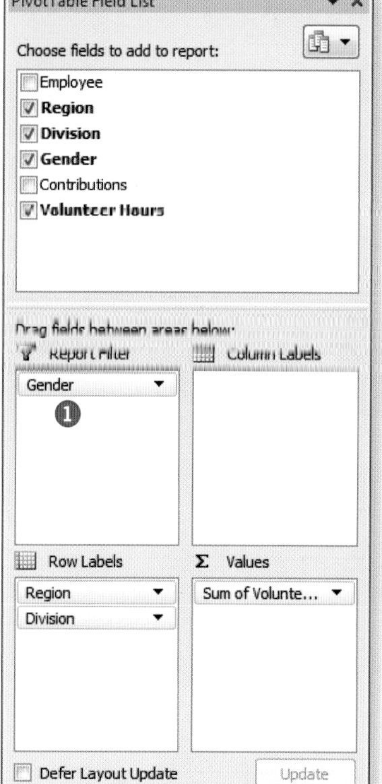

Figure 7.6 Filter Field Selected

Create a Template from a Blank Page

LESSON 4

OBJECTIVES

- Create a template for a weekly newsletter from a blank page
- Design a template using objects from the Building Block Library
- Create custom colors and font schemes to match branding

DESIGNING TEMPLATES

This lesson concentrates on designing a two-page newsletter template for a company that wants to send the newsletter out to all its employees by e-mail every Friday. This is a very inexpensive way to communicate effectively with employees on a regular basis. Because of its frequency, the newsletter will be limited to four short articles or fewer articles if one extends to the second page.

TEMPLATE FROM BLANK PAGE

In previous lessons, you designed publications by applying and then modifying a template. In this lesson, you will start with a blank page and create the design and format that will make the desired publication effective. You can use one of *Publisher*'s standard blank page sizes or create a custom page size. Custom page sizes are often used for electronic rather than printed publications because of the high cost of nonstandard paper.

To Create a Template from a Blank Page:

File/New

1. If the desired page size and orientation, such as 8.5 × 11", displays, select it. You can change the margins of the page using the Margins option on the Page Design tab if necessary.
2. If you do not see the size you need, click More Blank Page Sizes to display the gallery of standard sizes and the option to create custom sizes (Figures 4.1 and 4.2).

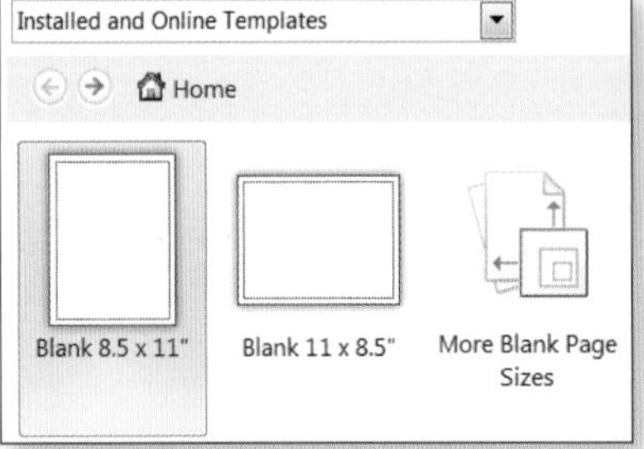

Figure 4.1 Blank Page Sizes

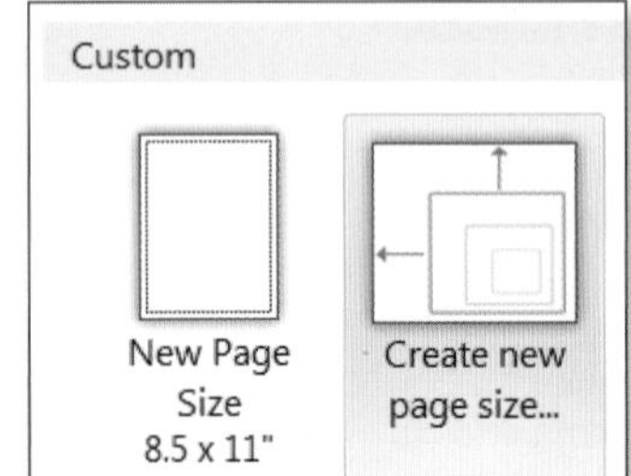

Figure 4.2 Create New Page Size

3. To create a new page size, click Create new page size to display the Create New Page Size dialog box. See Figure 4.3 on the next page. Use the arrows in the Page boxes to set the width and height of the page. You can also change the margin guides. Click OK.

DRILL 3 FILTER A PIVOTTABLE

1. Save the open file as *ex7-drill3a*. Filter PivotTable 2 to display the contributions of all female employees in the East or South regions employed in the Executive or Marketing division.
   a. Drag the Gender field in the Report Filter box below the field names. In B1, select F as the criterion.
   b. Click the arrow by Row Labels and select East and South.
   c. Click the arrow by Column Labels and select Executive and Marketing. Close the file.
2. Open *ex7-drill2*. Complete the same filter, but use the slicer feature. Click in the PivotTable; insert slicer for Gender and click F. Repeat for Region and then for Division. Use the CTRL key to select more than one item. Position the slicers attractively next to the PivotTable for easy view.
3. Resave as *ex7-drill3b* and close.

Apply It

Worksheet 14
PivotTable

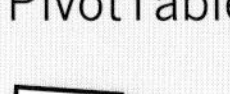

APPLICANT TRACKING

TIP

To clear a field from the PivotTable, deselect the field's checkbox in the field list.

1. Open the data file *applicant tracking* and complete the following PivotTables as new worksheets. When finished, close the file.

a. Create a PivotTable that displays the following fields as row labels: Recruiter Name, Last Name, Status of Application, and Date Resume Received. Rename the sheet tab as **PivotTable A**. Save as *ex7-w14a*.

b. Filter the PivotTable created in step 1a to display only the recruiter Emmons' applications. Which applications are complete? Rename sheet tab as **PivotTable B**. Save as *ex7-w14b*.

c. Clear all fields from the PivotTable. Select Source of Application as the row label. Drag the field Position Applied For to the Column Labels box and also to the Values box. What were the two leading sources of applications? What was the primary source for the management trainee position? Rename sheet tab as **PivotTable C**. Save as *ex7-w14c*.

d. Clear all the fields in the PivotTable. Select Last Name and First Name as row labels. Drag the field Status of Application to the Column Labels box and also to the Values box. How many complete applications do you have? How many total applications? Rename sheet tab as **PivotTable D**. Save as *ex7-w14d*.

e. Using the slicer feature, filter the PivotTable created in step 1d to display the documents needed by Younger. Rename sheet tab as **PivotTable E**. Save as *ex7-w14e*.

Worksheet 15
PivotTable

SALES ANALYSIS

1. Open the data file *sales analysis*. Create the following PivotTables as new worksheets. Apply the Medium 9 PivotTable style. When finished, close the file.

a. Display the State field in the Row Labels box; display the Commercial, Residential, and Student fields in the Values box. Choose the Average calculation. What were the average sales for each customer type by state? Format the customer sales as Currency and 0 decimals. Rename sheet tab **PivotTable A**. Save as *ex7-w15a*.

b. Add the field Representative as a row label. Use a slicer to filter to show TN only. Choose the MAX calculation. Which sales representative had the maximum sales for each customer type? Rename sheet tab as **PivotTable B**. Save as *ex7-w15b*.

c. Clear all the fields in the PivotTable. Select the field State as the row label and S-1, S-2, S-3, and S-4 in the Values box. In the slicer, press CTRL and click the two states not selected to show all states. Which of the four types of service did most students purchase overall? Rename sheet tab as **PivotTable C**. Save as *ex7-w15c*.

d. Repeat step c for commercial users. Which service did most commercial customers purchase? Rename sheet tab as **PivotTable D**. Save as *ex7-w15d*.

JOB KNOWLEDGE

This module focuses on using *Publisher* to produce attractively designed publications. However, it is important to remember that effective design is only one element of producing excellent publications. The content has to be carefully selected to achieve the objectives of the publication and to meet the needs of the reader; the writing has to be clear, crisp, and appropriate to convey the message effectively; and the visual design has to create a consistent, professional appearance that appeals to the reader. Being able to visualize the kind of graphic elements that best present a message and the way to position those elements on the page requires both creativity and technical knowledge. Effective design is both an art and a science.

Publication 5
Save As Template

1. Open *pb3-p4* and save it as a template file named *Menu*; create a category named **Menu**.
2. Do not delete any of the text because many items can be reused each week.
3. Resave the file as a template named *pb3-p5* in your solutions folder.

Publication 6
Create Personal Letterhead

1. Select a template of your choice and create personal letterhead that you can use for personal-business correspondence.
2. Customize a color scheme and a font scheme using colors that you like and that you think would be appropriate for business letters.
3. Create your own logo using objects from Borders & Accents building blocks, clip art, or other design elements and create your own business information.
4. Preview and save the file as a template named *My Letterhead* in the Templates folder.
5. Save the file as a template named *pb3-p6* in your solutions folder.

CAREER FOCUS

© Rubberball Productions/Jupiter Images

Preparing effective publications for organizations can be a very exciting and rewarding career. Planning and designing the layout and appearance of the newsletter are only part of the process of preparing effective publications. Both technical knowledge and creativity are required to design effective publications. The second facet of preparing publications is the ability to write content that is interesting, clear, and easy to read. It also involves knowing what graphics to use and how to use them to simplify complex content. Good communication skills will serve you well in any career.

LESSON
8

Insert 3-D Cell References

OBJECTIVE

- Create 3-D cell references in formulas

3-D CELL REFERENCES IN FORMULAS

Workbook users often want to combine data from multiple worksheets in a workbook on a summary worksheet. For example, a user may sum quarterly totals to show yearly totals.

In the example shown in Figure 8.1, the budget requests for three departments are shown on sheet tabs labeled Dept 1, Dept 2, and Dept 3. These three budgets are combined to prepare the total budget request on the Summary worksheet.

Figure 8.1 Summary Worksheet Uses 3-D Cell References

In B3, a formula containing a 3-D reference is entered to combine or add the three departments' requests for salaries, as shown in Figure 8.2. The formula =SUM('Dept 1:Dept 3'!B3) indicates the addition of values in cell B3 in the range beginning with the Dept 1 worksheet and ending with the Dept 3 worksheet. The ! is used to separate the sheet reference and the cell or range of cells. The formula actually adds the values in B3 on all three worksheets to generate the value in B3 on the Summary worksheet.

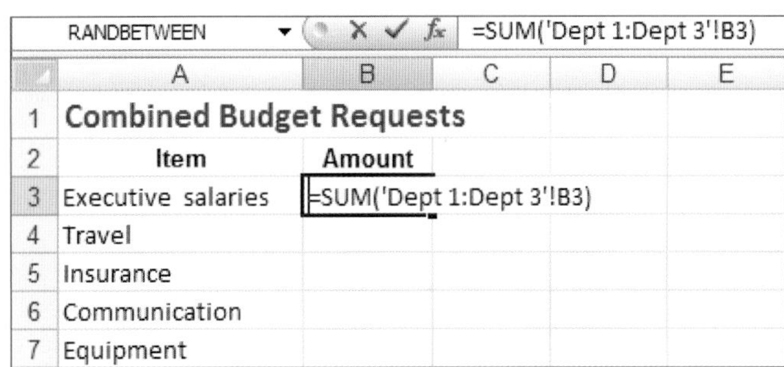

Figure 8.2 Cell B3 Displays a 3-D Reference

To Share Data Among Worksheets Using a 3-D Reference:

1. Click the cell on the Summary worksheet where the formula is to be entered.
2. Key =, the function to be used in the 3-D reference, and the opening parenthesis, e.g., =sum(.
3. Click the sheet tab for the first worksheet to be referenced, e.g., Dept 1.
4. Hold down the SHIFT key and click the last worksheet to be referenced, e.g., Dept 3. The sheet tabs will display as shown in Figure 8.3 when selected.

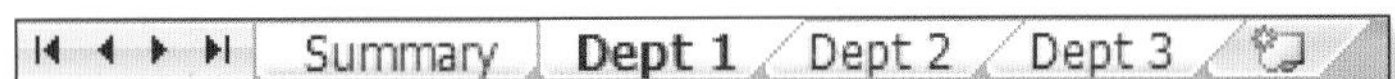

Figure 8.3 Sheet Tabs in a 3-D Cell Reference

5. Click the cell or range of cells to be referenced, e.g., B3. *Hint:* Do not click the cell until all sheet tabs have been selected.
6. Complete the formula and tap ENTER. See Figure 8.4 on the next page.

Page 2, Panel 1

Category Name: Amuse-Gueule
These items are small, special treats from the chef that are served at various times during the meal. The two or three items selected vary from day to day. Additional amuse-gueule main course items may also be offered.

Gougères
Miniature cheese puffs

Amuse-Gueule Soup
A demitasse of one of the soups prepared that day

Quenelle
An egg-shaped spoon of ice cream, custard, or sorbet

Amuse-Gueule au Chocolat
An assortment of chocolates

Category Name: Entrées
Select one of these appetizers or starters.

Carpaccio de Boeuf
Beef carpaccio

Soupe à l'Oignon
French onion soup

Gratinée de Coquille St. Jacques
Scallops served with shrimp

Page 2, Panel 2

Category Name: Le Plat Principal
Select one of the main courses.

Sautéed Atlantic Halibut
Cold water halibut sautéed with onions

Dover Sole Grillée
Grilled Dover Sole

Petit Filet Mignon Medallions
Beef tenderloin

Magret de Canard
Duck breast

Category Name: La Salade
Select one salad which will follow the main course.

Salade Niçoise
Salad with seafood

Salade d'Endive, Noix et Roquefort
Salad with walnuts and Roquefort cheese

Salade du Printemps
Mixed green salad

Page 2, Panel 3

Category Name: Les Fromages
The cheese course features a full cheese cart with both soft and hard cheese and with cheese made from both goat and cow's milk. Many more varieties are available.

Comté, Beaufort

Valençay, Chèvre, Sainte-Maure de Touraine

Boursin, Brie, Camembert

Category Name: Le Dessert
Dessert is followed by coffee including Café au Lait, Cappuccino, and Espresso.

Farandole de Crepes
Sweet crepes with assorted fillings

Crème Caramel
A caramel cream custard

Soufflé au Chocolat
Chocolate soufflé

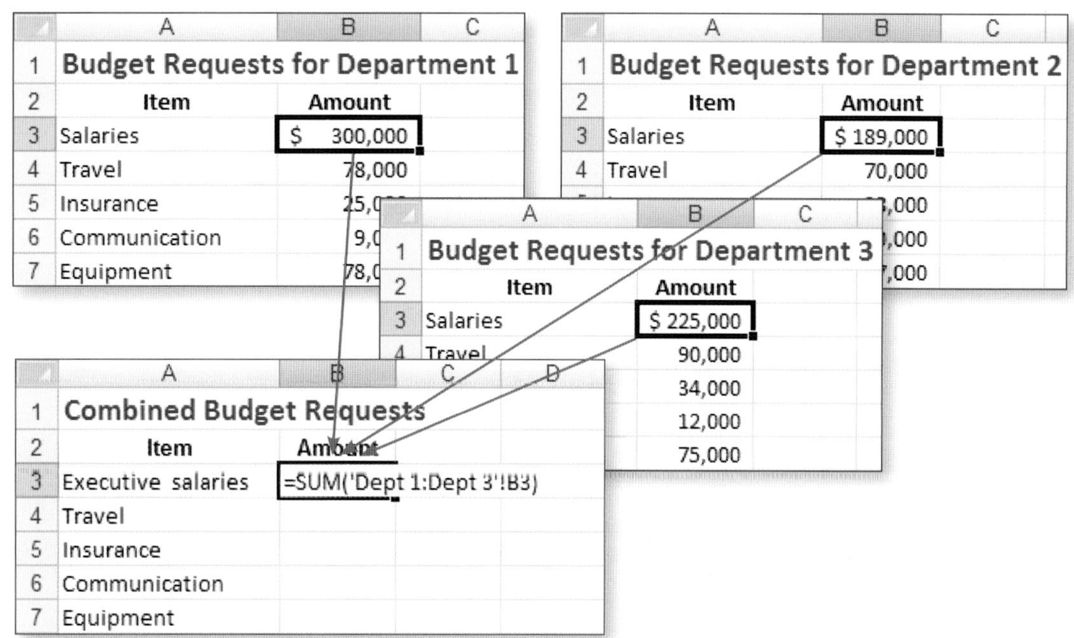

Figure 8.4 Values in Cell B3 on Each Sheet Are Summed in Cell B3 on Summary Worksheet

DRILL 1 USE 3-D CELL REFERENCES

3-D REFERENCE

1. Open the data file *3-D reference* and save as *ex8-drill1*.
2. Click the Summary worksheet. In B3, enter the formula using a 3-D reference to sum the amount for salaries in Dept 1, Dept 2, and Dept 3.
3. Copy this formula to the remaining budget items.
4. Resave as *ex8-drill1*; print the Summary worksheet. Close the file.

Apply It

Worksheet 16

Combine Worksheets

STATS

1. Open the data file *stats* and save as *ex8-w16*.
2. Click the Summary sheet tab. Click B5 and enter a formula to compute the combined statistics for At Bats for the three games played by the Madison All Stars.
3. Copy the formula in B5 to C5 through M5 to sum the remaining statistics for each play.
4. Select B5:M5 and copy to the remaining players.
5. Click N5. Enter the formula **=C5/B5** to compute the batting average for the three games. Copy the formula to the remaining players. Format with three decimal places if necessary.
6. Enter a formula in B17 to determine total At Bats. Copy formula to columns C–M. Format B17:M17 with the Total cell style.
7. Apply conditional formatting using a data bar of your choice to highlight the data in the appropriate columns to determine the following awards: Most Home Runs, Most RBIs, and Highest Batting Average. *Optional:* E-mail your instructor the recipient's name for each award.
8. Move the Summary sheet tab to display as the last sheet. Color the tab green.
9. Resave as *ex8-w16;* print the summary sheet. Close the file.

2. Select the text in the bottom text box and replace it with the text shown below; format it using 9-point font.

Call 717-555-0134 for reservations | $100 per person including gratuities | All major credit cards accepted

3. Note all text on page 1, the front cover, is centered.

Page 1, Panel 2

1. Delete the sample object at the bottom of the panel, insert the *map* picture from the data files, and size it about 2.5'' wide. Apply Picture Style 4.
2. Note that the logo and the address are inserted automatically with the business information.
3. Select all of the text in the Hours placeholder and replace with the following information:

Hours | Monday–Saturday 6:00 p.m.–10:45 p.m.

4. Select the text boxes and drag them higher to position them as shown in the illustration.

Page 1, Panel 3

1. Note that the tag line, restaurant name, graphic, and menu are part of the template and business information.
2. Click before *MENU* and key **LE** so the name will be *LE MENU*. Tap ENTER after *MENU* and key **Week of March 15**; format the week using 11-point font.
3. Select the text in the text box below *LE MENU* and key the following text:

This menu features the six-course, fixed-price menu and changes weekly.

Formatting Guides for Page 2

Use the Zoom feature to make text easier to read when you are keying menu items.

1. Use the default font and size for the Category Name.
2. Format the description under each Category Name using 8-point font.
3. Select the column with the numbers under each Category and delete the column (Table Tools Layout/Rows & Columns/Delete/Columns).
4. Adjust the table column width to fit the items and descriptions as needed.
5. Format the menu items using 9-point font and the descriptions under the items using 6-point font. *Note:* You can delete unused rows in the menu item tables if needed to position text.
6. Adjust the position of the text boxes so that the category names will be about even and the bottom of the page will be about even.
7. Check the alignment of each table and adjust the position if necessary.
8. Key the text shown on the next page. Turn off hyphenation if necessary.
9. For items with accents, insert the letters with the accent from Symbols (Insert/Text/Symbol); select the symbol; click Insert.

project 6

OBJECTIVES

- Create and format professional *Excel* worksheets
- Prepare effective *Word* documents
- Link *Excel* chart in *PowerPoint* presentation
- Work with very limited supervision

The Bookstore, Inc.: Integrating Excel, Word, and PowerPoint

SETTING

Project 6 integrates *Excel*, *Word*, and *PowerPoint*. In this project, you continue your work as assistant to Derek Bradberry, Training Director of The Bookstore, Inc. You continue the development of the documents required to implement the two software training mastery workshops on November 15 and 19. Refer to Project 5 on page 128 to refresh your memory about the setting.

Your responsibilities in this project require advanced *Excel* skills as you create professional charts with callouts and embed them in *Word* and *PowerPoint* documents and as you use data in *Excel* to create rosters, PivotTables, and mail merge documents.

JOBS

1. Column charts
2. Memo with chart
3. Worksheets with sparklines and chart
4. PivotTables
5. Mail merge with *Excel* worksheet
6. Link chart and worksheet data to *PowerPoint* slide
7. E-mail

STANDARD OPERATING PROCEDURES

You will continue using the procedures outlined in Project 5 on page 128 and the additional procedures shown below. You will not be reminded to do these things during the project.

1. *Excel* charts are created as embedded charts unless requested as a chart sheet or linked. Format column charts as follows:

   Clustered Cylinder column chart, Layout 1, Style 26

   Chart area—Gradient fill Tan, Background 2; Border: Aqua, Accent 1, Darker 50%, 3.75 pt

   Thick Thin style with rounded corners

   Insert text box with source note in italics at the lower-left corner of chart. Decrease the plot area slightly and move up slightly to allow room for the note.
2. PivotTables—Apply Medium 7 style.
3. Proofread, preview, and print all documents.
4. Set up a folder named EX-WD-PP Project 6 and save all project files in it. Name all solution files *p6-j* (plus the job number, *j1*, *j2*, etc.).

Apply It

Publication 4

Menu from Customized Template

FISATTO, INC. LOGO
MAP

In Publication 4, you will customize a template to match a company's brand and prepare a weekly menu for a fixed-price dinner for Le Fisatto, an upscale French restaurant. The template is a three-panel publication that is designed to be printed on the front and back of one page.

1. Open a new publication and create a menu using Gingham in the Regular menu category.
2. Study the format of the menu shown in Figure 3.10. Directions for preparing the menu follow the illustration.
3. Preview, proofread, check spelling, and print.
4. Save as *pb3-p4* and close.

Figure 3.10 Cover of Menu (Page 1)

Inside of Menu (Page 2)

Business Information

Name: Tyler LeBlanc

Job Position: Owner and Chef

Organization: Le Fisatto

Address: 250 Walnut Street
Harrisburg, PA 17101-1710

Phone: 717-555-0134
Fax: 717-555-0186
E-mail: tyler.leblanc@fisatto.com

Tagline: Superior food cooked to the point of perfection!

Logo: *fisatto, inc. logo*

1. Click Default template colors and create a new customized color scheme with PANTONE colors. Save it as **Fisatto**.

   Accent 1: Blue 2738C | Accent 2: Gold 116C | Accent 3: Red 1797C | Hyperlink: Blue 293C | Followed Hyperlink: Purple 696C
2. Create a new font scheme using French Script MT as the heading font and Calibri as the body font. Save it as **Fisatto**.
3. Create new business information as shown at left and save it as **Fisatto**.

Page 1, Panel 1

1. Select the text in the top text box and replace it with the following text; format it using 11-point font. Turn hyphenation off in each box and adjust box size and position if needed.

Le Fisatto is owned by the family of Chef Tyler LeBlanc and has served its customers for more than forty years at the current location. Prior to that, it was owned by the Fisatto family. Le Fisatto is part of Fisatto, Inc., which also owns and operates Fisatto Bistro, Fisatto Catering, and Fisatto Fresh Market.

Job 1
Column Chart

Your first assignment is to prepare a column chart that shows the breakdown of the Salaries budget item that you prepared in Project 5. Open your file *p5-j2*. Refer to operating procedures and to Figure P6.1 as you work.

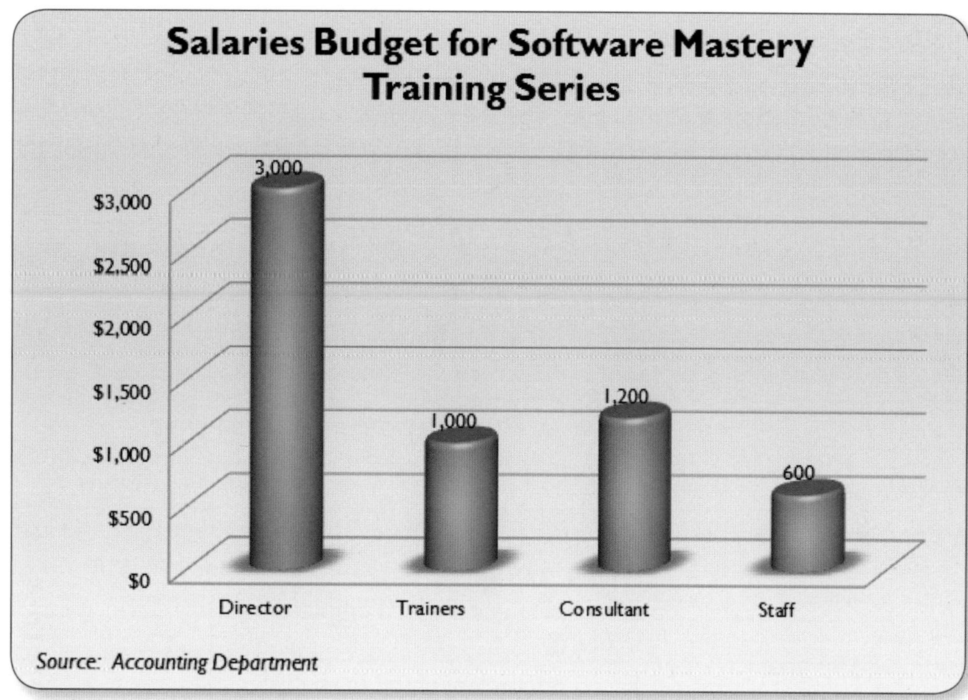

Figure P6.1 Salaries Budget

Job 2
Memo with Chart

TBI LETTERHEAD

Immediately after clicking the Paste command in *Word*, click the Paste Options button near the lower-right corner of the chart and select Use Destination Theme & Embed Workbook.

Mr. Bradberry has asked you to send a memo from him to Tara Lanford, Vice President. Use the subject line **Update on Training Program for Software Mastery Series**. Use the Quick Parts memo heading created in Project 5 and the company letterhead (see data files). Key the text below.

Copy the budgeted salaries chart prepared in Job 1. Paste the chart after the last paragraph of the memo and use the Paste Options button to embed the chart. Size the chart to 3.5" by 5.2" and center align. *Reminder:* The Solstice theme is used for *Excel*, *Word*, and *PowerPoint* documents to ensure document consistency.

The training program titled Software Mastery Training Series is designed as a result of the outcome of a needs assessment conducted by the Training Department last week. The needs assessment showed that more than three-fourths of our staff only know and use one-fourth of the capabilities of their software. When asked about time-saving features such as mail merge, Quick Parts, templates, styles, index, bookmarks, macros, and hyperlinks, very few were using these efficiency features.

Upon evaluation of the learning outcomes determined by the needs assessment, I have hired a consultant to identify the software competencies needed by our staff to increase efficiency in completing administrative tasks. The chart below shows the breakdown of the salaries budgeted for this training program. As training director, I will be responsible for designing the training program upon receipt of the consultant's report. My trainers are very qualified to lead the instructional sessions.

DRILL 2 CREATE LOGO AND ADD IT TO BUSINESS INFORMATION

1. Open *pb3-drill1* and save as *pb3-drill2*.
2. Follow the path Insert/Building Blocks/Borders & Accents/ More Borders and Accents.
3. Select 3-D Button and click Insert.
4. Right-click the picture and save it as *children's center logo* in your solution files. Note that the object has the custom colors you created.
5. Delete the picture from the document so that you can learn to add it to business information and insert it automatically as a logo.
6. Edit the business information for the children's center and add the logo.
7. Update the publication to include the logo.
8. Resave as *pb3-drill2* and close.

SAVE AS TEMPLATE

Publications may be saved as templates in the Templates folder. If you already have a publication completed, you may want to delete the text and put text directions in its place before saving it as a template.

To Save a Publication as a Template:

File/Save As/Template

1. In the Save As dialog box, change Save as type to Publisher Template (Figure 3.8) ❶. Note the Save in box changes to the Templates folder ❷.
2. Key the template name in the File name box.
3. Click Change ❸ to specify a category for the template.
4. If the category is not listed in the category box (Figure 3.9), key the category name; then click OK.
5. Click Save.

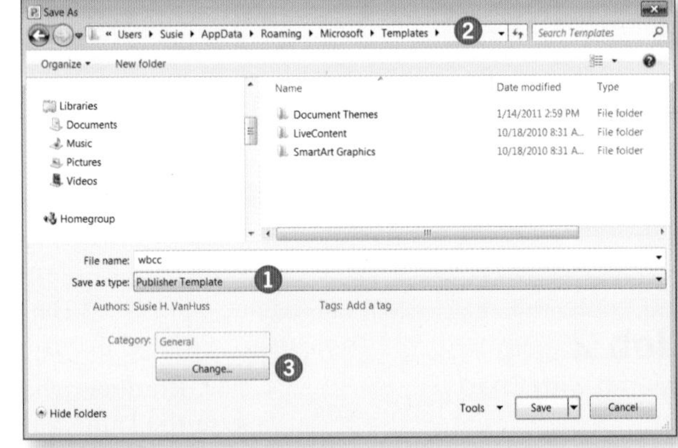

Figure 3.8 Save As Template

To Open a Template from My Templates:

File/New/My Templates

1. Click My Templates and then select the desired template (Figure 3.9).
2. Click Create to open the new publication based on the template.
3. Complete the publication and save.

Figure 3.9 Category

DRILL 3 SAVE AND USE A TEMPLATE

1. Open *pb3-drill2*.
2. Delete the title and key the word **Title** in the placeholder.
3. Delete the body text and key the following directions: **Key text about the subject of the flyer here**.
4. Save as a template in the Templates folder; use the name **WBCC field trips**.
5. Save the template as a *Publisher* file named *pb3-drill3*. Close the file.

Job 3

Participation Worksheets

ROSTER TEMPLATE
LIST

Maintaining a record of participation in the training sessions is very important. Mr. Bradberry has asked you to prepare the worksheets for the November 15 and November 19 training sessions. He alerts you to edit the standard template used in the company. On Sheet1, add the appropriate heading information and rename the sheet tab as **Nov 15**. Copy the heading and paste on Sheet2 and edit for the November 19 session. Remember you are using the Solstice theme for all documents. Save this edited template as an *Excel* workbook (*p6-j3*).

Using the *Word* data file *list*, add the data to the November 15 and 19 worksheets. Sort in ascending order by last name and then first name.

Job 4

Edit Rosters

You have just received a payment of $25 for each participant from Departments 4 and 6. Update the roster completed in Job 3. Add a column in each roster to display as column C; label **Fee Paid**.

Filter each roster to display Departments 4 and 6. Then enter the amount paid in each cell displayed. Remember to use the fill handle to copy that amount.

Job 5

Assign Groups, Name Ranges, Create PivotTables

You now must assign each participant to either the Blue, Yellow, Green, or Orange group. Update the workbook you completed in Job 4. First remove the filter on each roster worksheet. Enter the column heading **Group** in cell F5. In F6:F20, assign the first person to Blue, second to Yellow, and so forth. Start over with Blue for the fifth person. Sort both worksheets by Department, then Group, then Last Name, and finally First Name.

To make it easier to create name badges in later jobs, name the range that contains the participant information. On the Nov 15 worksheet, select the range A5:F20, right-click, select Define Name, and key the name **Database_15**. Click OK. Repeat the process on the Nov 19 worksheet, naming the range **Database_19**.

The group leaders have requested a list of the employees assigned to their groups. Create a PivotTable as a new worksheet for each session. Rename the sheet tabs as **Nov 15 Groups** and **Nov 19 Groups**. Design the PivotTable to display the Group and Last Name as rows.

Job 6

Financial Report

Mr. Bradberry needs to know which departments have paid fees for the two training sessions. Prepare a PivotTable for both sessions that displays the Department and Last Name in the Row Labels column and Sum of Fee Paid in the Values column. Rename the sheet tabs as **Nov 15 Fees** and **Nov 19 Fees**.

Job 7

Name Badges for November 15 Session

You have been asked to prepare the name badges for the participants in the November 15 training session. You will complete this job by merging a *Word* document and *Excel* data. For your main document, use Avery label #5147 (name badge). For your data source, navigate to the *Excel* file *p6-j5* and select the *Database_15* source. See Figure P6.2 for a suggested design.

Save the main document as *p6-j7 main Nov 15*. Save the merged labels as *p6-j7*. Check each label with the *Excel* file to be sure groups were assigned correctly. Note that having the teams assigned prior to the training session will save time during the session.

CREATE A LOGO FROM BUILDING BLOCKS

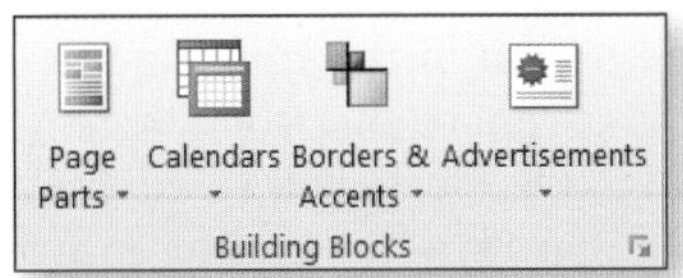

The Building Block Library contains a variety of page parts, calendars, borders, accents, and advertisements. The borders and accents are quite useful in creating logos. Some of the logos you used in previous publications were created from borders and accents. You can also use other graphics to create a logo.

To Create a Logo from Borders and Accents:

Insert/Building Blocks/Borders & Accents

1. With the publication open, click Borders & Accents and then More Borders and Accents at the bottom of the gallery to display all of the borders and accents in the Building Block Library (Figure 3.5).
2. Select an accent, such as 3-D Button, or other design object and click Insert.
3. For future use, right-click the object and save it as a picture. It can then be inserted as a logo with your business information.
4. To edit business information and add the logo, follow the path Insert/Text/Business Information/Edit Business Information/Edit/Add Logo. Then select the logo and click Save.

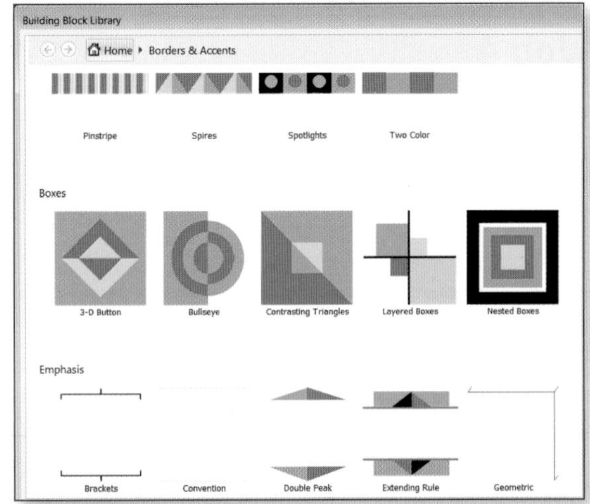

Figure 3.5 Building Block Library

5. Click Update Publication to add it to the current document.
6. You can also create a new building block accent using clip art or a logo you have designed with graphic elements. Right-click the object, click Save as Building Block (Figure 3.6), and complete the Create New Building Block dialog box (Figure 3.7). Key the name of the logo, select the Gallery, key the keywords, and click OK.

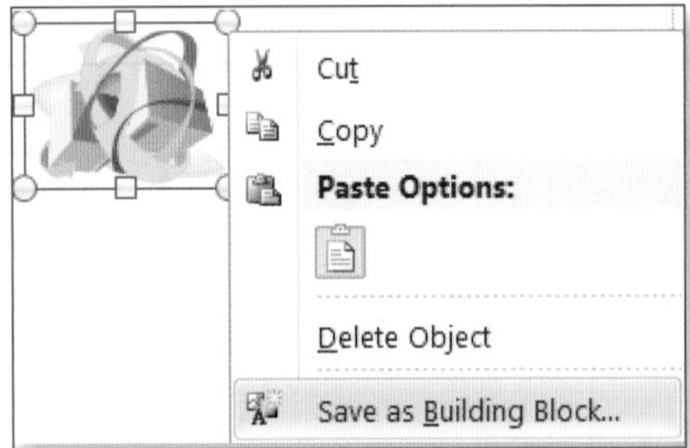

Figure 3.6 Save as Building Block

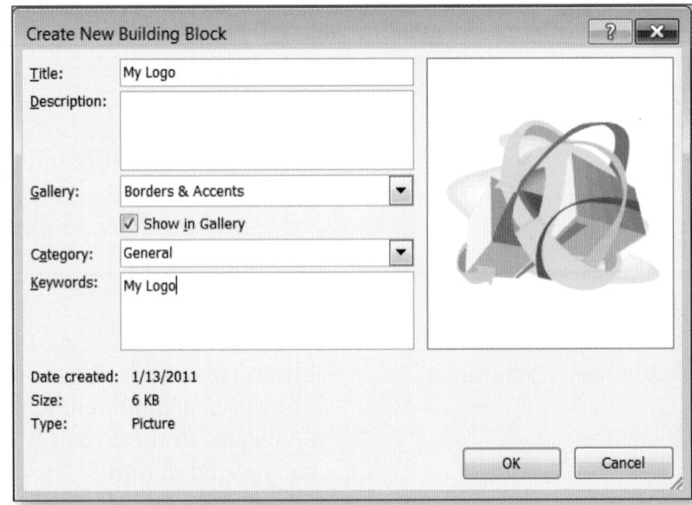

Figure 3.7 Create New Building Block

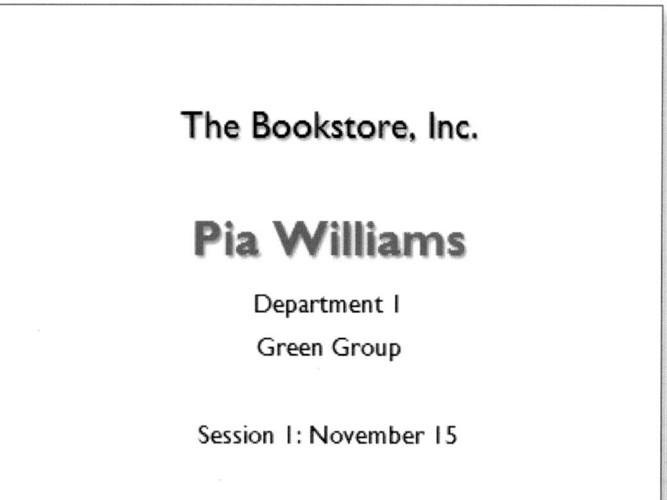

Figure P6.2 Sample Name Badge

Job 8
Name Badges for November 19 Session

You must now prepare the labels for the November 19 session. Follow the same procedures as in Job 7. However, the training instructor has asked that the name badges be sorted alphabetically by last name. *Hint:* Sort the names in the Mail Merge Recipients dialog box. Be sure to update the label to Session 2: November 19.

Job 9
Chart and Sparklines

COMPARISON

Mr. Bradberry e-mails you the worksheet *comparison* and asks you to add Line sparklines to the Trend column. He also asks you to prepare a column chart to compare the cost of the three types of training offered during the fourth quarter. Refer to P6.3 to guide you in the design and the standard operating procedures on page 148. Add a shape to highlight the October software training series. The star was rotated with a 3-D command, and the text is formatted as WordArt.

Sparklines
Insert/Sparklines/Line

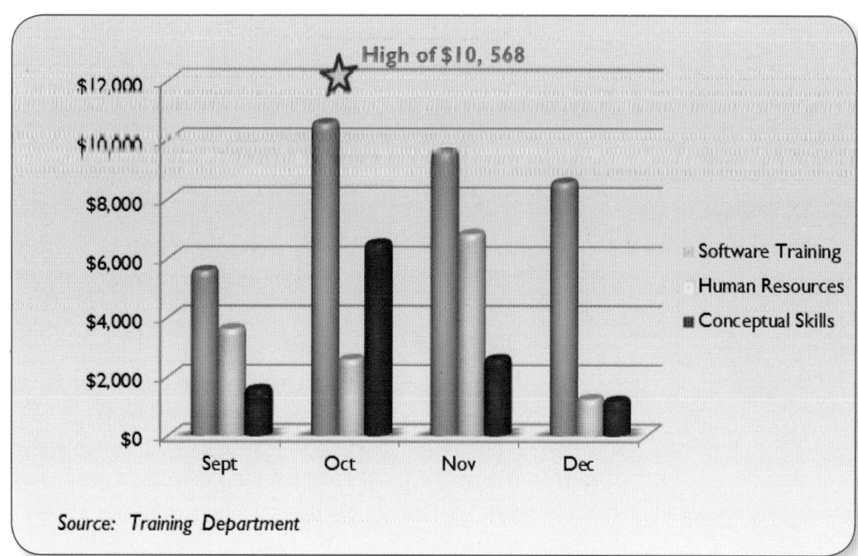

Figure P6.3 Column Chart

CUSTOMIZE FONT SCHEME

In this lesson, you will create a new font scheme. Fonts should match the tone of the organization. For example, a children's center might use a more casual font than a bank.

To Create a New Font Scheme:

Page Design/Schemes/Fonts

1. Click Create new at the bottom of the Font scheme gallery to display the Create New Font Scheme dialog box (Figure 3.3).

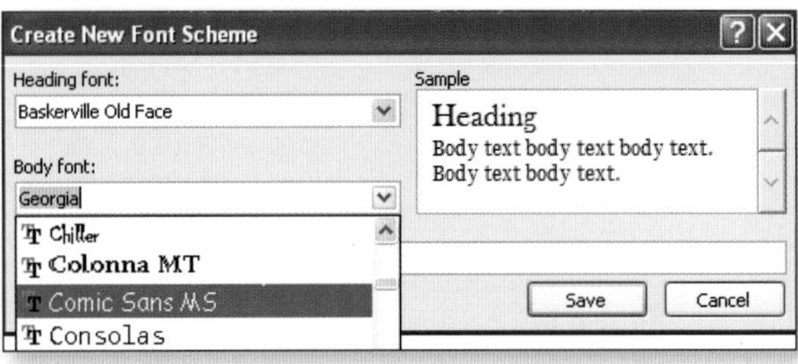

Figure 3.3 Create New Font Scheme Dialog Box

2. Select the Heading font and the Body font desired; key desired name and click Save.

TIP

To turn hyphenation off, click in the text box and follow the path Text Box Tools Format/Text/Hyphenation. Then remove the check from the Automatically hyphenate this story box.

DRILL 1 CUSTOMIZE COLOR AND FONT SCHEMES

1. Create a flyer using the Color Band template from the New Event folder and apply the Reef color scheme.
2. Create new business information and name it Children's Center.

Student's Name | Director of Activities | Westbrook Children's Center | 374 Rena Drive | Lafayette, LA 70503-4968 | Telephone: 337-555-0192 | Fax: 337-555-0186 | studentname@wbcc.com | no logo

3. Change colors to the PANTONE colors indicated below; name the scheme **Children's Center** and save it.

   Accent 1: 7458C | Accent 3: 602C | Accent 4: 643C | Hyperlink: 3262C | Followed Hyperlink: 7424C

4. Create a new font scheme using the Gill Sans MT font for headings and Comic Sans MS font for body text; name the scheme **Children's Center** and save it.
5. Apply the new color and font schemes to the flyer.
6. Increase the company name heading to 14-point and the text box to .3" high; delete the tagline; then key the text below; increase body font to 12 point; do not hyphenate.

Zoo Trip for Four-Year-Olds

The annual zoo trip for four-year-olds is scheduled for Friday, May 8. The activities bus will leave at 12:45 p.m. and return to the Children's Center no later than 4:45 p.m. The costs of zoo admission and a snack were included in the Field Trip Activity Fee. Please complete the parent's permission sheet and drop it in the Activities Box no later than Thursday.

7. Remove the picture placeholder and insert a clip art picture depicting a zoo scene. Use *zoo* as the keyword. Apply Picture Style 3 to the clip. See Figure 3.4.
8. Save as *pb3-drill1* and close the document.

Figure 3.4 Flyer

Job 10

PowerPoint Slides Linked with Chart and Worksheet Data

DISCOVER

Link Data

Home/Clipboard/Paste

1. Select chart or worksheet range and copy.
2. In *PowerPoint*, follow path and click Paste drop-list arrow, and then click Paste Special.
3. Click Paste link and click OK.

Your next assignment is to create two *PowerPoint* slides that contain a linked chart and linked worksheet from Job 9. Mr. Bradberry asked you to link the data because he is still verifying figures with the Accounting Department. After reviewing the two slides, he will select one for the final presentation.

Slide 1: On a Title Only slide, add the slide title **Fourth Quarter Trends**. In *p6-j9*, select the worksheet range A2:F5, copy, and paste as a link on the *PowerPoint* slide. Size and position attractively and add an Aqua, Accent 1, 3 pt border.

Slide 2: Add the slide title **Software Training Leads in Cost** and link the chart completed in Job 9. Size and position appropriately.

If you make design changes once the chart is inserted in *PowerPoint*, right-click the chart and click Update Link.

Job 11

E-mail

Compose an appropriate e-mail message and e-mail to Mr. Bradberry (your instructor). Use the following outline to compose the e-mail:

1. Thank Mr. Bradberry for the experiences you have gained as his assistant.
2. Briefly summarize your experiences at The Bookstore, Inc.
3. Explain your strengths in completing the assigned tasks.
4. List areas of responsibility that were most challenging for you. Explain how you handled the challenge in order to complete the assigned task.
5. Identify at least two areas of professional development you will begin focusing on as a result of this internship.

CAREER FOCUS

© Stockbyte/Getty Images

This project has introduced you to the job responsibilities and tasks of a training department. A training program is not designed and implemented unless a need has been researched and established. As the training program is designed, the method of evaluation is designed as well. The training manager must be able to report to management the return on the resources invested in the training program.

An important skill for you to acquire as you advance in your career is the ability to evaluate. You may begin now by learning to evaluate resources, e.g., data you will use in a research paper, whether it is published in a journal or on the Web. Learn to evaluate your professional traits, such as attendance, punctuality, and appearance. Have friends and mentors assist you in your self-evaluation and develop a plan to improve based on your evaluation. Your return on this investment will surely result in advancement and the fulfillment of a rewarding career.

LESSON
3

Customize Templates

OBJECTIVES

- Create a flyer and a menu from customized templates
- Customize a color scheme
- Customize a font scheme
- Use building blocks

CUSTOMIZE TEMPLATES

Each template includes text boxes and picture placeholders, a color scheme, a font scheme, and a design that is suitable for a particular purpose, such as a business card. Each template can be modified and saved as a new template in the Microsoft Templates folder (or your solution files folder).

CUSTOMIZE COLOR SCHEME

In this lesson, you will create a new theme to match a company's branding. You can apply a color scheme that has similar colors and then change colors to create a new color scheme, or you can create a new one without applying another scheme. Usually, it is easier to modify a similar theme. In *Word*, you used the RGB color model. Company branding often specifies colors using the PANTONE® color model. You will work with this color model in this lesson.

TIP

You can customize color and font schemes when you first open a presentation in the Customize box that displays on the right side of the screen.

-or-

You can customize color and font schemes using the commands on the Page Design tab in the Schemes group.

To Customize a Color Scheme:

Page Design/Schemes/Click More button

1. Select and apply a color scheme with colors similar to those desired. Click the More button to display the gallery of color schemes. Then click ❶ Create New Color Scheme at the bottom of the gallery (Figure 3.1) to display the Create New Color Scheme dialog box ❷ (Figure 3.2). Click each color you want to change and select More Colors.
2. On the Colors dialog box ❸, select the PANTONE tab ❹. If the desired color is displayed, click it. If not, key the color desired in the Lookup box ❺ and click Find. When it displays in the New ❻ preview box, click OK.
3. Repeat step 2 for each color you wish to change.
4. Key a name for the new color scheme ❼ and click Save to add the new custom scheme to the gallery of color schemes.

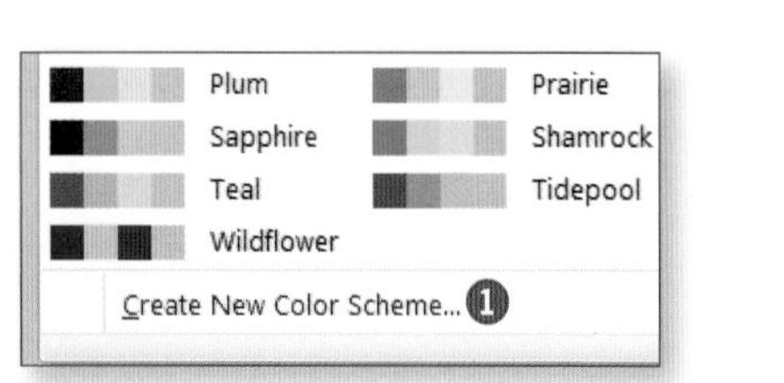

Figure 3.1 Create New Color Scheme

Figure 3.2 New Color Scheme

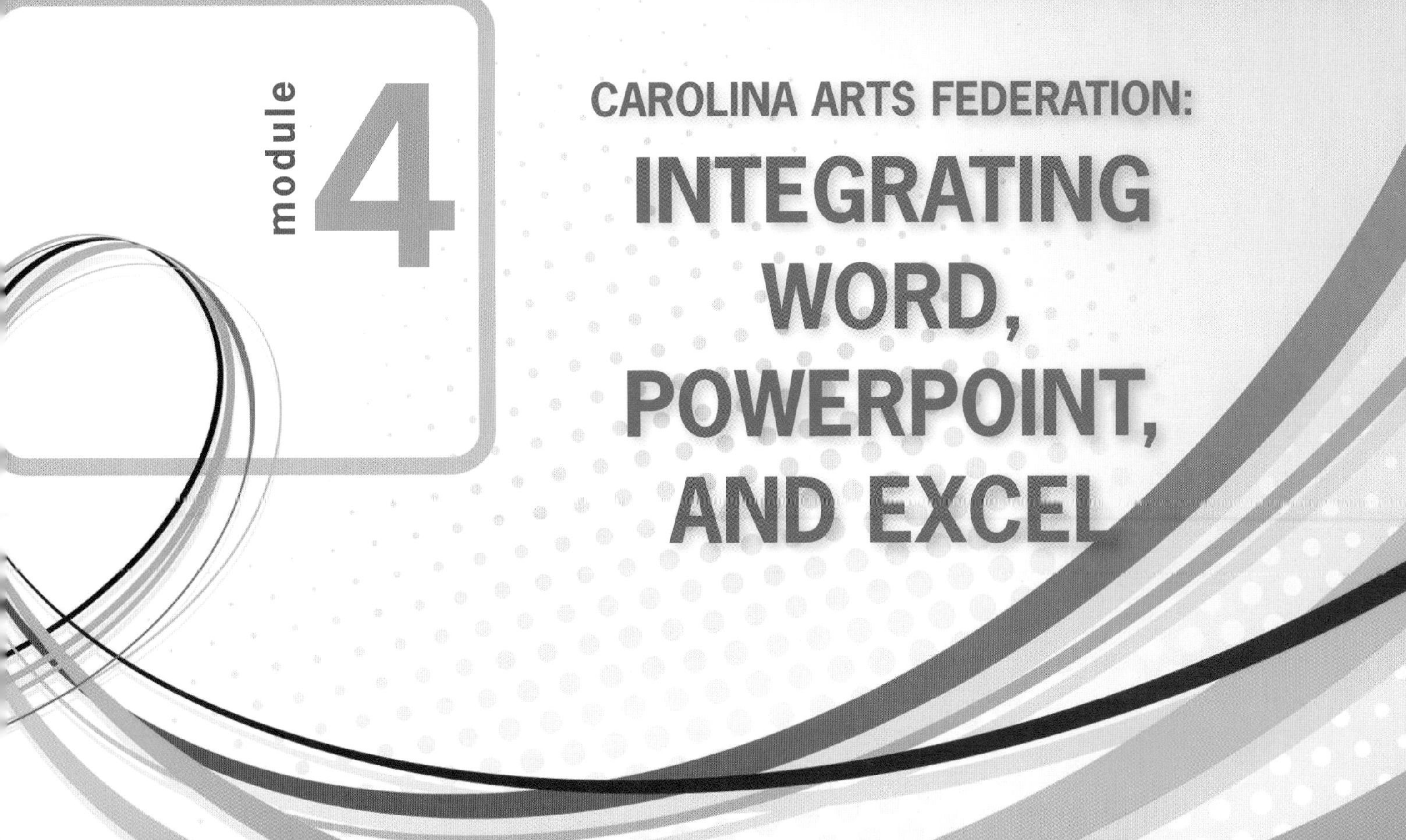

overview

Integrated Project 1 is designed to reinforce your mastery of *Word*, *PowerPoint*, and *Excel*. This project demonstrates how integrating a coordinated theme with multiple applications (*Word*, *PowerPoint*, and *Excel*) facilitates problem solving, enhances productivity, establishes and promotes the branding and identity of the organization, and creates a powerful communication impact.

JOBS

1. Word Contact Information Sheet
2. Word Memo with Excel Data
3. Word Table
4. PowerPoint Presentation with Excel Chart
5. Word Mail Merge Letter
6. Excel Worksheet with PivotTables and PivotCharts
7. Word Report with Excel Data
8. PowerPoint Presentation

Page 4—Back Cover Story

1. Drag the right black border of the text box in the left column to widen it. In the text box, key **Check our intranet for more information**; then apply Calibri 9-point font.
2. Key and format appropriately the headline **Why Place Emphasis on Health and Fitness?** for the back page story.
3. Delete the object in the story. Use the keywords *medical professionals* and search for a diverse group of medical professionals. Insert the clip art in the upper-right corner of column 3.
4. Replace the text in the placeholder with the file *health and fitness*.
5. Delete the text from the business tagline or motto box.

Table

1. Delete the text box at the top of page 4 and insert a two-column, six-row table (Insert/Tables/Table/Insert Table). Adjust size if necessary. Key the table shown below.
2. Format the table as follows, using Table Tools Design and Layout tools. Apply Table Style 7. Apply 20-point Calibri to the title and center title. Apply 9-point Cambria font to remaining text and left-align text. Center all text vertically. Select the table and apply a 2¼ point Accent 2 (Gold) Outside Border.

Employee Enhancement Task Force	
Lynn Blackmon, Director, Marketing	Ann Cox, V.P., Human Resources, Chair
Jeff DeMars, Production Manager	Mark Fox, Executive Assistant
Julie Grayson, Chief Financial Officer	Leslie Hayes, Purchasing Associate
Rhett Jameson, Sales Associate	Pam Lester, Manager, Employee Benefits
Pat Ray, Executive Vice President	Brenda Woods, Executive Assistant

Preview your newsletter and use the following illustration to check it.

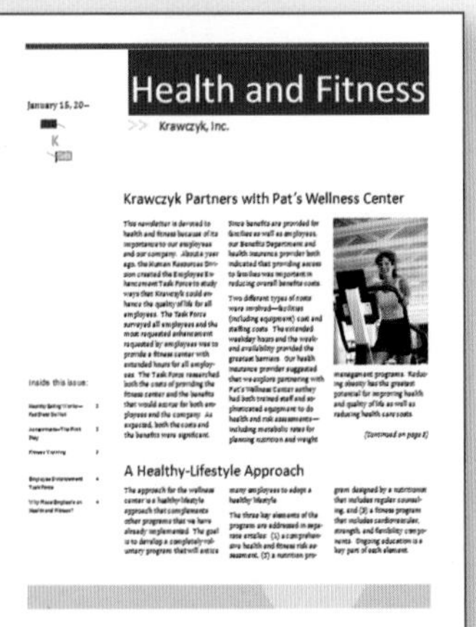

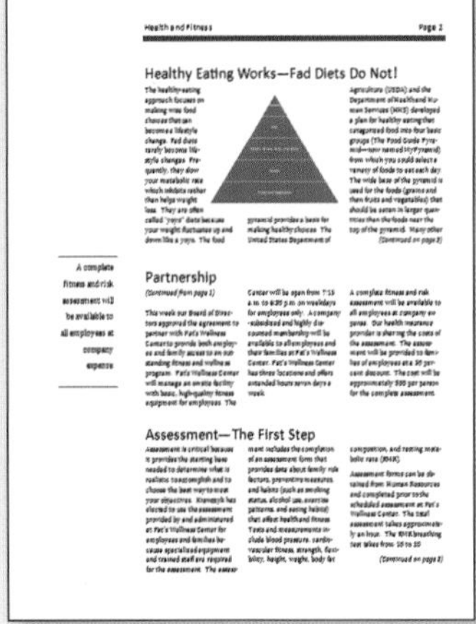

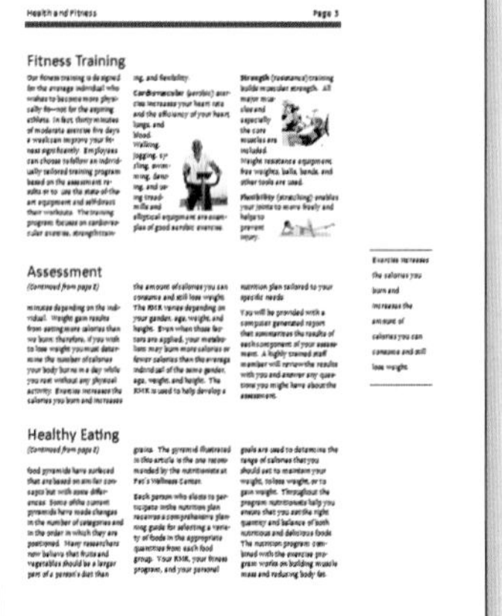

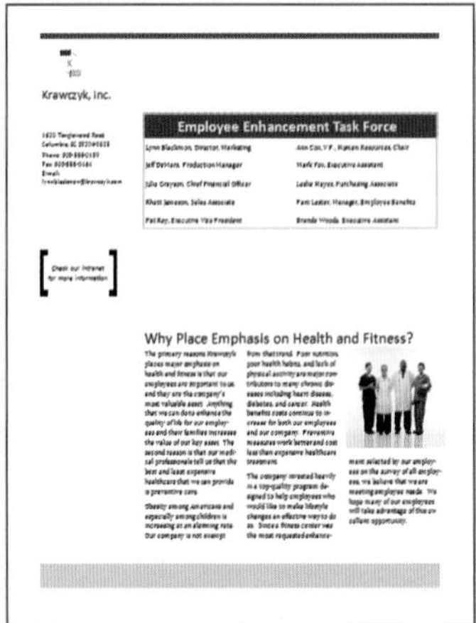

Figure 2.8 Quick Check

integrated project 1

Carolina Arts Federation: Integrating Word, PowerPoint, and Excel

OBJECTIVES

- Prepare *Word* documents, *PowerPoint* presentations, and *Excel* worksheets with a coordinated theme
- Integrate two or three of the applications in a job
- Work independently with few instructions

SETTING

Integrated Project 1 integrates *Word*, *PowerPoint*, and *Excel*. The Carolina Arts Federation (CAF), headquartered in Charlotte, North Carolina, is designed to promote and support the arts (visual and performing) and artists in North Carolina and South Carolina. A key component of its mission is its Arts in Education program in K-12 schools. CAF is a private organization with extensive support from companies and individuals throughout North Carolina and South Carolina. Your position in the organization is Events Coordinator, and the entire project will focus on an event you are managing—the 50th Anniversary Gala, which includes an Art Auction featuring the works of leading North Carolina and South Carolina artists. This fundraising event supports Arts in Education and other programs. You will complete jobs for the CAF Board of Directors and staff. Many of the board members are corporate executives from major companies in both states.

Company Information

Address:	Carolina Arts Federation 4300 Sharon Road Charlotte, NC 28211-3519
Telephone:	704-555-0164
Fax:	704-555-0163
Website:	www.carartsfed.org
E-mail:	Firstname.Lastname@carartsfed.org

Jobs

1. *Word* contact information document with custom theme used in *PowerPoint* and *Excel.*
2. *Word* memo with data extracted from *Excel* worksheet and *Excel* attachment.
3. *Word* table that will be used in a *PowerPoint* presentation and a report.
4. *PowerPoint* presentation with *Word* table and *Excel* chart.
5. *Word* mail merge letter.
6. *Excel* worksheet with data and charts used in *Word* report and *PowerPoint* presentation.
7. *Word* report with data and graphics from *Excel.*
8. *PowerPoint* presentation with *Excel* charts and *Word* tables.

STANDARD OPERATING PROCEDURES

1. Use the CAF theme for all jobs. Use the CAF letterhead and memo head for letters and memos. Use block letter format for letters.
2. Create a folder named Integrated Project 1 for all job solutions. Name the files *ip1-j* plus the job number (*ip1-j1*, *ip1-j4*, etc.) unless another solution name is provided.
3. Proofread, preview, and print all documents. Save and close all open files.

11. Delete the picture placeholder in the story on the bottom of page 3. You will need that space for the continued text.
12. Click at the bottom of the first article on page 2 and connect it to the text box at the bottom of page 3.
13. Add the "continued on" and "continued from" notices for the article, and key the headline **Healthy Eating** on page 3.

Page 3

1. Key and format appropriately the headline **Fitness Training** for the first story on page 3.
2. Delete the object in the text area of the story. You will add clip art.
3. Key the following story:

TIP

Using the Zoom feature to enlarge the text to 150% makes it easier to see what you are keying and to fit the text and clip art appropriately.

Our fitness training is designed for the average individual who wishes to become more physically fit—not for the aspiring athlete. In fact, thirty minutes of moderate exercise five days a week can improve your fitness significantly. Employees can choose to follow an individually tailored training program based on the assessment results or to use the state-of-the-art equipment and self-direct their workouts. The training program focuses on cardiovascular exercise, strength training, and flexibility.

Cardiovascular (aerobic) exercise increases your heart rate and the efficiency of your heart, lungs, and blood. Walking, jogging, cycling, swimming, dancing, and using treadmills and elliptical equipment are examples of good aerobic exercise.

Strength (resistance) training builds muscular strength. All major muscles and especially the core muscles are included. Weight resistance equipment, free weights, balls, bands, and other tools are used.

Flexibility (stretching) enables your joints to move freely and helps to prevent injury.

4. Use the following keywords and insert a small clip illustrating each type of exercise as shown in Figure 2.7: Cardiovascular—*exercise bicycle*; Strength—*exercise*; and Flexibility—*stretching*.
5. Make sure the story fits on page 3 with no text overflow. If you have text overflow, adjust the size and position of the clip art to fit it in the space available.

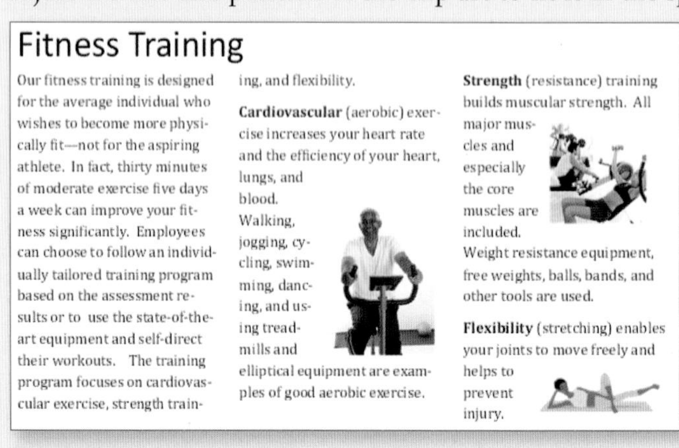

Fitness Training

Our fitness training is designed for the average individual who wishes to become more physically fit—not for the aspiring athlete. In fact, thirty minutes of moderate exercise five days a week can improve your fitness significantly. Employees can choose to follow an individually tailored training program based on the assessment results or to use the state-of-the-art equipment and self-direct their workouts. The training program focuses on cardiovascular exercise, strength training, and flexibility.

Cardiovascular (aerobic) exercise increases your heart rate and the efficiency of your heart, lungs, and blood. Walking, jogging, cycling, swimming, dancing, and using treadmills and elliptical equipment are examples of good aerobic exercise.

Strength (resistance) training builds muscular strength. All major muscles and especially the core muscles are included. Weight resistance equipment, free weights, balls, bands, and other tools are used.

Flexibility (stretching) enables your joints to move freely and helps to prevent injury.

Figure 2.7 Page 3 Illustration

Job 1

CAF Information

CAF INFORMATION

Your first job is to create a theme for CAF, and then you will finalize the CAF information document that will be enclosed with many documents CAF prepares.

1. Open a new document with the default Office theme. Then modify the colors as indicated to create new theme colors. Name the new theme colors *CAF* and save them.

   Accent 2: Red, Accent 2, Lighter 40%; Accent 4: Tan, Text 2, Darker 50%
   Hyperlink: Dark Blue, Background 2

   Create new theme fonts using Lucida Sans for headings and Lucida Bright for body text; name the fonts *CAF*, and save them.
2. Name the current theme *CAF* and save it. Use it for all jobs in this project.
3. Open the data file *caf information*, and add your name to the Key Staff section where indicated.
4. Key the following information below your name; fit the text on one page.

   Contact Information [Format as a shaded heading]

   The letterhead contains contact information for everyone listed. The e-mail address is FirstName.LastName@carartsfed.org.
5. Select the entire page including the letterhead and save as a Quick Part using *CAF* for both the name and description. Create a new category named *CAF*. Choose the option to insert the Quick Part in its own page.
6. Insert the *CAF* Quick Part in a new document; check and save it appropriately.

Use the Format Painter to format the heading.

Job 2

Memo

BID PRICES
CAF LETTERHEAD

1. Open the *Excel* data file *bid prices* and make the following changes to the worksheet. You will use information from the worksheet in the memo you are preparing for the Planning Team and staff about the artists who are participating and the bid prices they have submitted for the silent auction.
2. Use a two-level sort to sort the data by state (A–Z) and then by bid price (largest to smallest). Insert two rows between the last North Carolina entry and the first South Carolina entry. In the first new row, key **Total** in A23, **NC** in C23, and total the bid prices in D23. Format total as currency with 0 decimal places. Apply Blue, Accent 1, Lighter 80% shading to the row. Leave the next row blank.
3. Insert two rows between the last South Carolina entry and the Carolinas Total row. In the first row, key **Total** in A53, **SC** in C53, and total the bid prices in D53. Use the same shading and number formats as you did for the NC Total. In cell D55, use a formula to add the two state totals, and format the row with shading as for the other total rows.
4. In row 2, key **Artist List with Bid Prices**, merge and center the title, and apply Title style.
5. Apply Heading 1 style to the column headings, and repeat them on the second page; center the page horizontally. Select D5:D22 and apply Blue Data Bars, Solid Fill conditional formatting. Repeat for SC.
6. Rename the sheet tab **Bid Prices**; save the workbook as *ip1-j2a*, and leave it open.
7. Use the *caf letterhead* template to create a new memo form. Add the To, From, Date, and Subject headings formatted appropriately. Save as a Quick Part named *CAF Memo*. Use the same name for the description, and select the *CAF* category.
8. Use the new memo form to prepare the memo shown on the next page. Replace the blanks in the memo with the appropriate information from the worksheet that is open. Attach a copy of the worksheet (*Attachment: Artist List and Bid Prices*) and copy Patrick V. Hess. Save as *ip1-j2b* and close all files.

Center Page Horizontally
Page Layout/Page Setup dialog box launcher

1. Click Margins tab in Page Setup dialog box.
2. Click Horizontally in Center on page area.
3. Click OK.

Apply It

Publication 3
Newsletter from Template

HEALTHY LIFESTYLE
ASSESSMENT
FOOD PYRAMID
HEALTHY EATING
HEALTH AND FITNESS

When you insert text from a file for the body of a story, format the text with 9-point Cambria if it is not already used.

1. Open *pb2-drill2* and save it as *pb2-p3*.
2. Use the instructions below to complete the four-page newsletter you worked on in Drills 1 and 2.
3. Use 20-point Calibri font for all story headlines and 9-point Cambria font for the body text and continued lines.
4. Preview, proofread, check spelling, and print.
5. Resave as *pb2-p3* and close.

Page 1

1. Delete the *Special Points of Interest* placeholder.
2. Insert the file *healthy lifestyle* in the placeholder at the bottom of page 1. Cancel autoflow when the warning appears.
3. Key and format appropriately the headline **A Healthy-Lifestyle Approach**.
4. Apply 11-point Calibri font to the heading *Inside this issue*; format the stories listed using 7-point Cambria font. List the headline stories; delete unused text.

Healthy Eating Works—Fad Diets Do Not!	2
Assessment—The First Step	2
Fitness Training	3
Employee Enhancement Task Force	4
Why Place Emphasis on Health and Fitness?	4

Page 2 and Stories Continued on Page 3

Displaying the boundaries in a publication makes it easier to fit graphics.

View/Show/Boundaries

1. Key the following sentence to complete the last paragraph of the partnership article on page 2:

   The cost will be approximately $30 per person for the complete assessment.
2. Delete the picture and insert the file *assessment* in the placeholder at the bottom of page 2.
3. Key the headline **Assessment—The First Step.**
4. Connect the third column at the bottom of page 2 to the center story on page 3. Key and format appropriately the headline **Assessment** on page 3.
5. Add a "continued on" notice below the text in the third column on page 2 and a "continued from" notice at the beginning of the story on page 3.
6. Copy the last sentence in the first column of page 3 (beginning with *Exercise increases the calories you burn . . .*) and paste it in the pull quote placeholder. Use 9-point font.
7. Enlarge the picture placeholder in the top story on page 2 by dragging it to the right border of the second column. Select the picture and ungroup it. Then delete the caption placeholder.
8. Right-click the picture, select Change Picture, and insert the picture *food pyramid* in the placeholder. Use Picture Tools Format/Crop/Fit to fit the picture in the placeholder, and then change the size of the image to 2.4'' wide by 2.2'' high. Adjust the position if necessary.
9. Insert the file *healthy eating* in the placeholder at the top of the page. This file will not fit in this placeholder; click Cancel to the query about autoflowing text.
10. Key the headline **Healthy Eating Works—Fad Diets Do Not!**

Job 2, continued

TIP

Key 50th as shown; *Word* will automatically apply superscript to the *th.*

To: Planning Team and CAF Staff | From: Your Name | Date: March 1, 20-- | Subject: Artist List and Bid Prices

The judges on the Artist Selection Panel finalized the list of artists who were invited to participate in the Art Auction for the 50th Anniversary Gala. Of the 60 artists (30 from each state) invited to participate, 46 have accepted the invitation. Each artist was limited to entering one piece of original artwork in the auction and was asked to submit the bid price for the work selected.

The artists understand that this benefit auction is designed to support the arts in North Carolina and South Carolina and agreed to the terms and conditions for participation. Each artist will receive 70 percent of the bid price listed. The Carolina Arts Federation will receive the difference between the sales price at the auction and the 70 percent of the bid price paid the artist.

The bid prices from the ___ North Carolina artists totaled $_____, and the bid prices from the ___ South Carolina artists totaled $______ for a total of $133,950. The judges have previewed all of the artwork, and they believe that the work is marketable and of high artistic quality. The outlook is very good for a very successful event. The list of artists with the bid prices for their work is attached.

Job 3
Table

1. Prepare the table shown below. You will use it in a presentation and a report in later jobs.
2. Apply Medium Grid 3 – Accent 1.
3. Merge row 1; center the title vertically and horizontally; use the heading font and increase the font size to 16 point; increase row height to .5".
4. Increase row 2 height to .4". Apply Align Center to row 2 and Align Center Left to the remaining entries in column A. Apply bold to B2.
5. Apply AutoFit Contents and center the table.

TIP

Position bullets in tables at the left edge of the column rather than indenting them. Center all headings in tables vertically and horizontally.

Gala Celebration Sponsorships	
Sponsorship Level	Benefits of Sponsorship
Platinum—$25,000	• Presenting sponsor at event • Full page ad in program • Recognition in all print materials • 16 event tickets
Gold—$15,000	• Half-page ad in program • Recognition in all print materials • 12 event tickets
Silver—$10,000	• Quarter-page ad in program • Recognition in all print materials • 10 event tickets
Bronze—$5,000	• Recognition in all print materials • 8 event tickets

7. Add a "continued from" notice at the beginning of the story on page 2. Change the font size of the continued line to 9 point.
8. Add the heading **Partnership** on page 2, and increase the font size to 20 point.
9. On page 2, select the sentence *A complete fitness and risk assessment will be available to all employees at company expense*. Copy the sentence and paste it in the pull quote box in the left margin. Use 10-point font in the pull quote box.
10. Format the second and third page headers using Calibri 12-point font.
11. Use Print Preview and the Quick Check in Figure 2.6 to check your work.
12. Resave as *pb2-drill2* and close.

QUICK ✓ Use Figure 2.6 to check pages 1 and 2 of Drill 2.

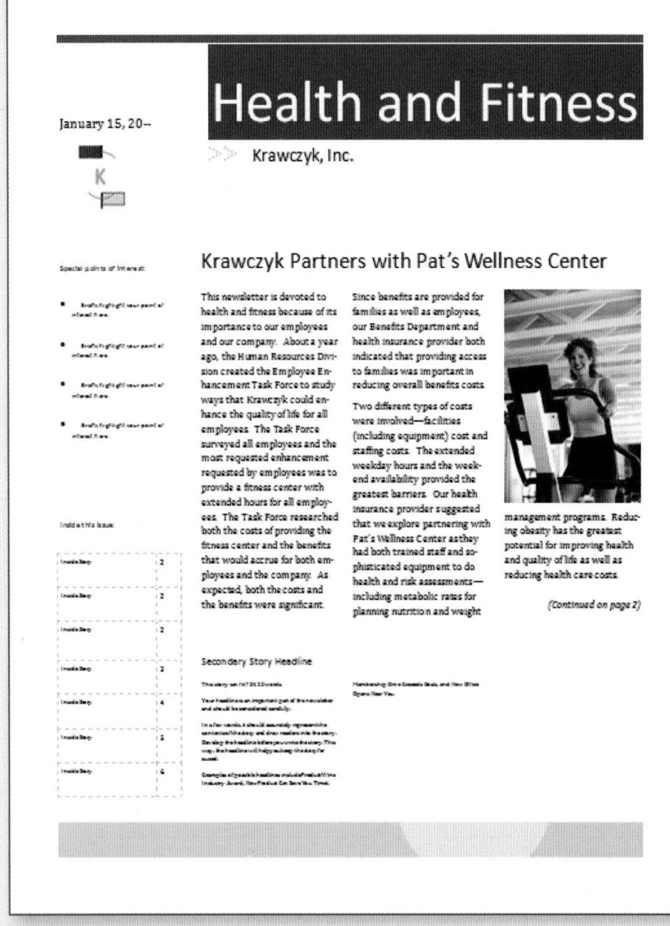

Figure 2.6 Page 1

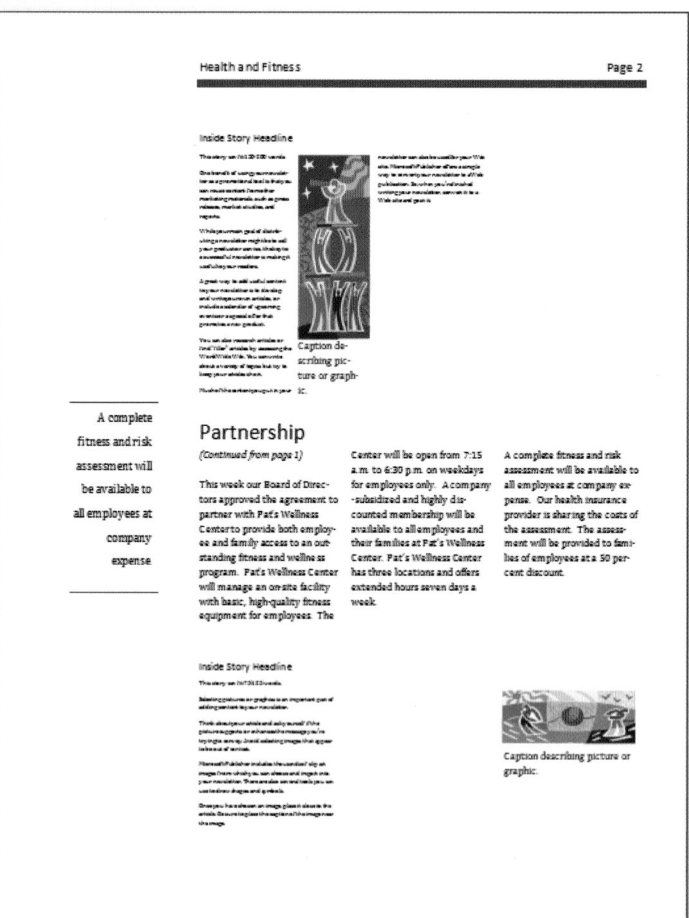

Page 2

Job 4

Presentation

In this job, you will save a custom theme for presentations and prepare a presentation to update the Board on the revenue outlook for the Gala Celebration.

1. Open a new *PowerPoint* presentation and apply Clarity theme. Then apply the CAF colors and font scheme to the presentation. Click More in the Themes group, click Save Current Theme, and save it as *CAF*. Use this theme for all CAF presentations.
2. Copy the logo from the letterhead and paste it in the upper-right corner of the slide master below the blue bar at the top of the slide so that it will appear on all slides.
3. Save as *ip1-j4a*. Prepare the eight slides shown below.

Slide 1 (Title Slide)
Title: Gala Update
Subtitle: Revenue Outlook
Animation: None

Slide 2 (Title and Content)
Title: Revenue Sources
Slide content:

- Revenue
  - Auction profits
  - Corporate sponsorships
  - Ticket sales

Convert bulleted text to SmartArt Converging Radial.
Animation: Fade, One by One

Slide 3 (Title and Content)
Title: Silent Auction Update
Slide content:

- Excellent response—46 artists participating
- Good geographical representation—18 from NC and 28 from SC
- Top artists exhibiting some of their best work
- Bid values exceeded expectations

Convert bulleted text to SmartArt Segmented Process.
Animation: Fade, One by One

Slide 4 (Title and Content)
Title: Bid Values
Slide content: Pie Chart

1. Open *ip1-j2a* and save it as *ip1-j4b*.
2. Select the cells in row 23, columns C and D, and in row 53, columns C and D; create an Exploded Pie in 3-D chart in the same sheet.
3. Position the title Total Bid Values above the chart, and apply Rose, Accent 2 font color.
4. Show data labels in the center, and format to show the value and percentage separated by a new line.
5. Copy the chart. In *PowerPoint*, click the content area and click Paste.

Animation: Fade, By Category

Chart Tools Layout/Labels/ Data Labels

1. Click More Data Label Options.
2. Check Value and Percentage.
3. Select Center option.
4. Click Separator down arrow and select (New Line).

DISCOVER

Work with Picture Groups

1. Right-click the group (picture and caption) and select Ungroup.
2. To change a picture, right-click it and select Change Picture.
3. To delete a caption, right-click and select Delete Object.

INSERT OR CHANGE PICTURES

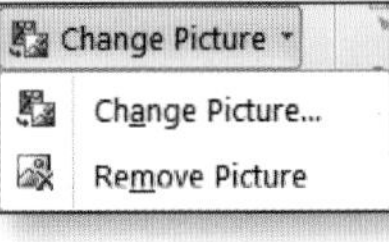

Pictures from files can be inserted and formatted in the same way that you inserted them in *Word* or *PowerPoint*. Pictures can be changed and replaced with a picture of the same size, position, and format by using the Change Picture command. A picture can also be removed, leaving an empty picture placeholder for future use. If a picture is grouped with a caption, you must ungroup the objects before you can change the picture or delete the caption. You can also insert and format picture placeholders for future use. The picture placeholder reserves space for a picture but looks like a blank space. It will display when you hover the mouse over it.

To Insert a Picture:

Insert/Illustrations/Picture

1. Click Picture and browse in the Insert Picture dialog box to locate the picture you wish to insert.
2. Click Insert.

To format a picture that has already been inserted, select it and click the Picture Tools Format tab.

To Change or Remove a Picture:

Picture Tools Format/Adjust/Change Picture

1. Select the picture to change.
2. Follow the path, click Change Picture, and browse to select the picture to insert.
3. To remove a picture, follow the path and select Remove Picture.

To Insert a Picture Placeholder:

Insert/Illustrations/Picture Placeholder

1. Click Picture Placeholder to insert it.
2. Size and position the picture placeholder as desired.

DRILL 2 CONNECT TEXT BOXES AND ADD PICTURES

KRAWCZYK LOGO

DISCOVER

Shortcut: Use CTRL + A to select all text in a story.

If you drag the mouse over the text to select it, be extremely careful not to drag the text box.

1. Open *pb2-drill1* and save as *pb2-drill2*.
2. Select the text in the lead story that you inserted, and increase the font size to 9 point. Note the Text in Overflow icon will be displayed.
3. Click the picture and caption group in the third column of the lead story and delete it. Use the keyword *fitness* to search for clip art and insert it in that column. Size the clip about 1.7" wide.
4. Insert a picture placeholder below the newsletter date; size it about .75" wide and center it below the date. Insert the *krawczyk logo* from the data files in the placeholder.
5. Connect the text box with the clip art to the first text box of the center inside story on page 2.
6. Add a "continued on" notice below the text in the third column on page 1. Change the font size of the continued line to 9 point.

Job 4,
continued

Slide 5 (Title Only)

Title: Corporate Sponsorships

Slide content: Table

Open *ip1-j3*, copy table, and paste table in the content area, using the Keep Source Formatting Paste option. Use 20-point heading font for heading and 16-point body font for other rows. Set row 1 height to .6" and row 2 to .5". Animation: Fade

Slide 6 (Title and Content)

Title: Sponsorship Update

Slide content:

- More than 50 personalized solicitations have been made
- Pledges are being received
- Approximately $100,000 has been pledged at this point

Convert bulleted text to SmartArt Segmented Process. Animation: Fade, One by One

Slide 7 (Title and Content)

Title: Ticket Sales

Slide content:

- Sales are primarily to individuals
- Mailing list with 500 names has been prepared
- Solicitation delayed until corporate sponsorship phase has been completed

Convert bulleted text to SmartArt Segmented Process. Animation: Fade, One by One

Slide 8 (Title and Content)

Title: Gala Site—Art Museum

Slide content: Search clip art for art museum and insert the clip shown at the right.

Recolor the clip art: Rose, Accent color 2 Light. Size 4.5" high and center. Animation: Fade

Figure IP1.1 Clip Art

Job 5
Mail Merge

CAF LETTERHEAD

1. You will use the *caf letterhead* from the data files, the information below, and the Mail Merge Wizard to prepare letters to sponsors of the Gala.
2. Use the fields and records shown on the next page to key the address list. Save it as *caf sponsors list.*
3. Key the letter on the next page; insert the fields. Format the letter appropriately.
4. Save the main document as *caf sponsors main.*
5. After you have edited all letters, save the final merged document as *ip1-j5.*

CONNECT TEXT BOXES

If more text is placed in a box than fits in it, *Publisher* will ask if you want to overflow the text to another box. Answer Cancel to the query each time it occurs in this lesson. You will learn to handle the overflow by linking text boxes later.

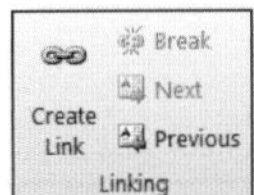

Text boxes can be connected by creating a link between them. Most templates contain some connected text boxes. Note that the text box into which you inserted text in Drill 1 is connected to the other two text boxes to its right. The Go to Next arrow displays at the lower-right side of a text box that is linked to another text box. If there is more text in the story than will display in the linked text boxes on page 1, the Text in Overflow icon will display to indicate the story still has text that is not displayed.

To display overflow text, you either have to enlarge the text box or create a link to another text box so it can flow from one text box to the next. Typically, text flows to another page so that more than one story receives first-page attention.

To Connect Text Boxes:

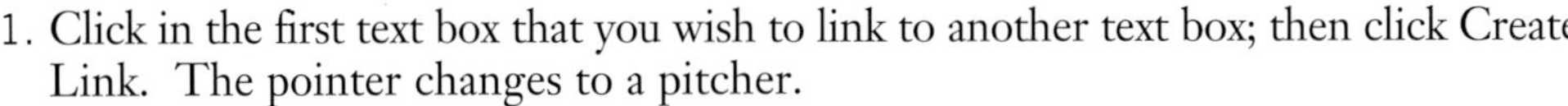

1. Click in the first text box that you wish to link to another text box; then click Create Link. The pointer changes to a pitcher.
2. Click in the text box on the page (such as page 2) that you want the text to flow to and the text will display. *Note:* If the box you click in is connected to other boxes, the text will flow into those boxes as well.

CONTINUED NOTICE

Articles that are continued on a different page generally have a "continued on" notice to inform the reader where to find the remainder of the article. On the page where an article is continued, a "continued from" notice tells the reader where to locate the previous part of the article.

The default size of "continued on" and "continued from" notices is small. You will be instructed to increase font size of these lines when you insert them.

To Add a Continued to or from Notice:

1. Position the insertion point at the end of the article on the first page it appears. Right-click and select Format Text Box to display the Format Text Box dialog box (Figure 2.5).
2. Click the Text Box tab ❶ and then select the Include "Continued on page" checkbox ❷. Click OK.
3. Position the insertion point at the beginning of the article on the page where it is continued. Select the Include "Continued from page" checkbox ❸. Click OK.

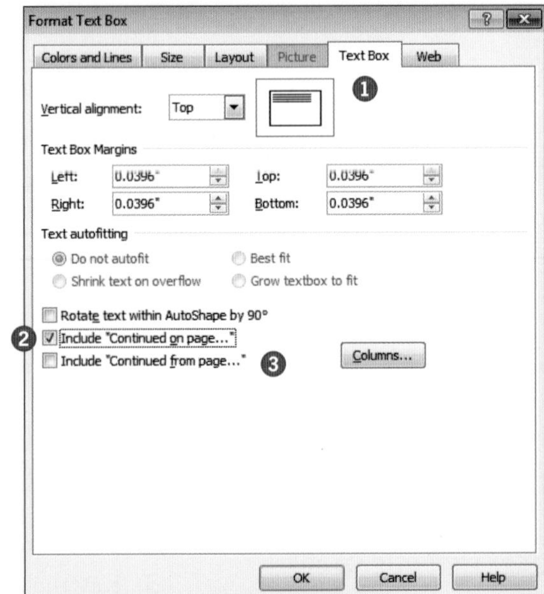

Figure 2.5 Format Text Box Dialog Box

Job 5,
continued

Field Name	Record 1	Record 2	Record 3
Title	Mr.	Ms.	Mr.
First Name	William	Norma	Charles
Last Name	Holder	Timmons	Mann
Company Name	Holder & Holder	Jeansonne Designers	Mann & Rex, PA
Address Line 1	100 Broad Street	1915 Rexford Road	1029 Wade Avenue
City	Charleston	Charlotte	Raleigh
State	SC	NC	NC
ZIP Code	29401-2206	28211-4247	27605-1160
Sponsorship	Platinum	Gold	Silver
Ad Size	full-page	half-page	quarter-page

March 15, 20--

«AddressBlock»

«GreetingLine»

Thank you for your «Sponsorship» sponsorship of the 50th Anniversary Gala. We are very excited to have you and your guests participate in this memorable event. Your sponsorship entitles you to a «Ad_Size» ad in the program.

The digital art specifications for your ad are enclosed. As you will note, our printer prefers that a high-resolution PDF, print-ready file be submitted. Other acceptable formats are listed on the ad specification sheet.

Net proceeds from the event will be used to promote and support the visual and performing arts throughout North Carolina and South Carolina. The Arts in Education program in K 12 schools will be a major beneficiary of your generosity

Please provide us by May 5 the names and addresses of your guests who will be attending as part of your sponsorship. We will send them information about the event and a color catalog of the art featured in the silent auction. You may e-mail the list to Jan.Miller@carartsfed.org or use the enclosed form.

We look forward to celebrating the 50th anniversary of the Carolina Arts Federation with you and your guests.

Sincerely | Student's Name | Events Coordinator | Enclosures

Remember to remove the hyperlink in letters.

To Insert Text from Another File:

1. Right-click the placeholder text to select it and display a shortcut menu (Figure 2.4).
2. Point to Change Text ❶.
3. Click Text File ❷ and then browse and select the file. Click OK.

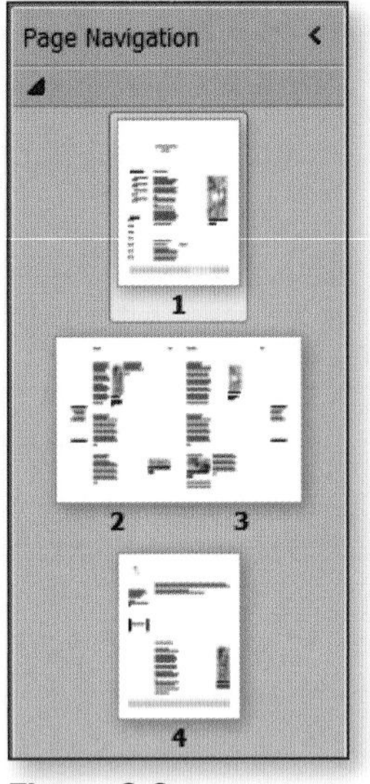

Figure 2.3 Page Navigation Pane

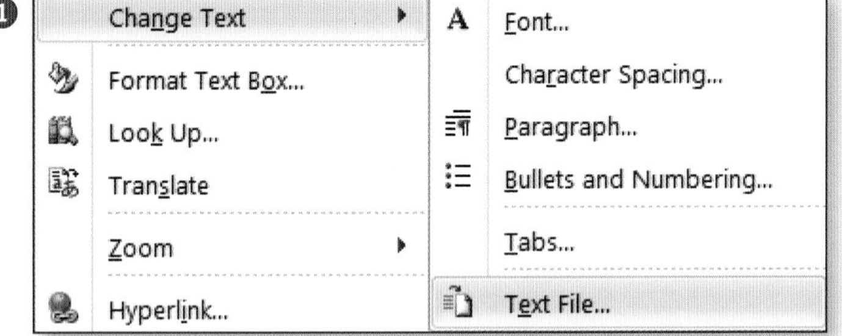

Figure 2.4 Insert Text from File

TIP

You can also find text-formatting options on the Text Box Tools Format tab.

FORMAT TEXT AND TEXT BOXES

Apply text formats from the Home tab as in previous applications. Format text boxes using Text Box Tools or Drawing Tools Format tabs.

DRILL 1 ENTER AND FORMAT TEXT

PARTNERSHIP

TIP

Note that *Publisher* generally refers to articles as stories. Either term is acceptable.

1. Create a newsletter using the Arrows template.
2. Use the Bluebird color scheme, Office 2 font scheme, and the Krawczyk 1 business information. Select the One-page spread page size.
3. Key the title **Health and Fitness**; apply Title style; format the title box using Accent 1 (Blue) fill and change text color to White.
4. Key the date **January 15, 20--** and increase the font size to 12 point. Increase the size of *Krawczyk, Inc.* that was automatically entered from the business information to 16 point.
5. Key the lead story headline **Krawczyk Partners with Pat's Wellness Center**. Increase the font size as large as will fit on one line.
6. Right-click in the first story text box, click Change Text, click Text File, and insert the *partnership* data file. The text will fill the first text box and automatically flow to the next one. Click Cancel when you see the autoflow warning.
7. Save as *pb2-drill1* and close the publication.

PULL QUOTES

A "pull quote" is text such as a quotation that has been "pulled" out of an article to emphasize the text. A pull quote is usually inserted in a text box with special formatting that is positioned in the margins or the center of a column or story. (Figure 2.6, page 2, at the left margin.) You may also draw and format a text box for a pull quote.

Job 6

Worksheet with PivotTables and PivotCharts

ART AUCTION

Mr. Hess, Chair of the Board of Directors, asked you to complete the *art auction* worksheet. These analyses will provide data and charts for the report to the Board of Directors (Job 7). Complete the worksheet and create six PivotTables and two PivotCharts.

WORKSHEET

1. In F5, insert a formula to compute the artist share, which is 70 percent of the bid price. Copy the formula to remaining entries.
2. In G5, insert a formula to compute the CAF share by subtracting Artist Share from Sale Price. Copy the formula to remaining entries.
3. Sort the worksheet by state, then city, and then artist, all in ascending order.
4. In D51, insert the SUM function to total the Bid Price column. Copy across to the other columns.
5. Format the worksheet as follows:
   a. Row 1—20% Accent5, Title style, and row height 30 points. Merge and center the heading.
   b. Row 2—20% Accent5, Heading 1 style, and row height 21 points. Merge and center the heading.
   c. Row 4—Heading 3 style and center column headings; repeat headings on all pages.
   d. D51:G51—Total style.
   e. Format D5:G5 and D51:G51 as Accounting style with 0 decimals. Format all other numbers as Comma style with 0 decimals.
   f. Apply landscape orientation and center the worksheet horizontally.

PIVOTTABLES (AS NEW WORKSHEETS) AND PIVOTCHARTS

Be sure you do *not* include the totals row in the data range for the PivotTables.

Table 1—Drag the State and City fields to the Row Labels box. Drag the Artist and CAF Share fields to the Values box. Use the default Count field setting for Artist and keep Sum for CAF Share. Format numbers in the CAF Share column as Number, 0 decimal places, and include the comma separator. Sort the Sum of CAF Share column in ascending order. Rename sheet tab **PivotTable 1**. Insert a slicer that filters to display the cities of Charlotte and Raleigh.

Table 2—Drag the State and City fields to the Row Labels box. Drag the Artist Share and CAF Share fields to the Values box. Change field setting to Average for both Artist Share and CAF Share columns. Format the numbers the same as PivotTable 1. Rename sheet tab **PivotTable 2**.

Table 3—Drag the State and City fields to the Row Labels box. Drag the Bid Price and Sale Price fields to the Values box. Change field settings to Max for both columns. Format the numbers the same as before. Rename sheet tab **PivotTable 3**.

PivotTable Tools Options/ PivotChart

1. Click in the PivotTable.
2. Click PivotChart.
3. Format chart as desired.

Table 4 and Column Chart—Drag the State field to the Row Labels box. Drag the Bid Price and Sale Price fields to the Values box. Keep Sum field settings for both columns. Format the numbers the same as before. Rename sheet tab **PivotTable 4 & Chart**.

Click PivotChart and choose the Clustered Column chart. Click the close button to close the PivotTable Field List. Use the following directions and Figure IP1.2 to guide you in formatting the chart.

a. Apply Layout 9 and delete legend. Apply the Style 15 chart style.
b. Choose Inside End for format of data labels.
c. Format the Vertical (value) axis in thousands.

Work with Text Boxes and Picture Placeholders

LESSON 2

OBJECTIVES

- Create a newsletter with extensive text and graphics
- Work with text boxes
- Work with picture placeholders

TEXT BOXES AND PICTURE PLACEHOLDERS

Publisher treats each text block or graphic as an independent object. Text is positioned in text boxes, and graphics are positioned in placeholders. Text boxes and placeholders can be moved, sized, and formatted in a variety of ways. Text boxes can be linked so that when one box is full, the remaining text can flow to another box on the same or a different page. Most of the commands used to insert text boxes and graphics are located on the Insert tab. Objects are formatted with Drawing Tools, Text Box Tools, and Picture Tools (Figure 2.1).

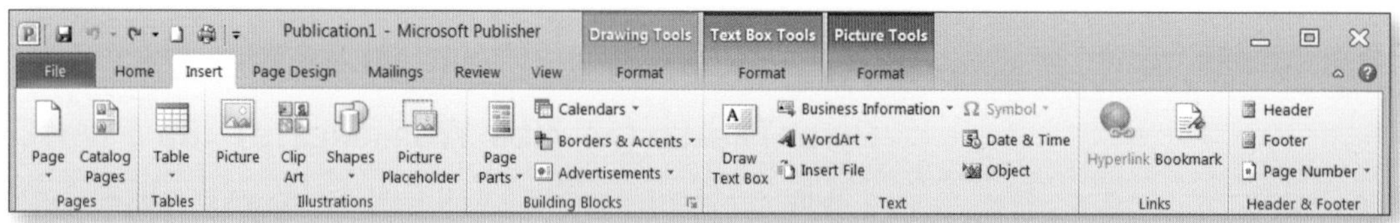

Figure 2.1 Insert Tab

To Create a Newsletter:

File/New/Newsletters

1. Preview templates and select one (such as Arrows).
2. Change the color and font schemes if desired.
3. Select the business information you wish to use or create a new set.
4. Under Options, select a page size as shown in Figure 2.2. Note that a two-page spread is designed for newsletters that will be printed on both sides of the paper or that will use oversize paper folded.
5. Click Create to display the first page of the newsletter. Note that the Page Navigation pane displays on the left side and the illustration displays in the main workspace.

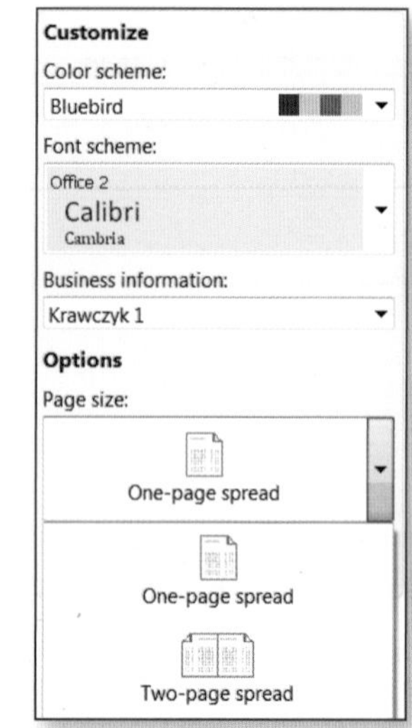

Figure 2.2 Page Size Options

Insert/Text/Business Information

You can always create new business information, add information, or change information by following the path and clicking Edit Business Information. Then select the Edit, Delete, or New button.

NAVIGATE PAGES AND ADD TEXT

To navigate from one page to another, click the desired page in the Page Navigation pane (Figure 2.3). Normally, to add text, you will select the text shown in the template and replace it by keying new text or by inserting text from another file.

d. Apply the Subtle Effect – Aqua, Accent 5 style (from the Shape Styles gallery) to the chart area and Subtle Effect – Orange, Accent 6 to the plot area.

e. Format chart area border as Olive Green, Accent 3 color, 2.75 Thick Thin border style with rounded corners.

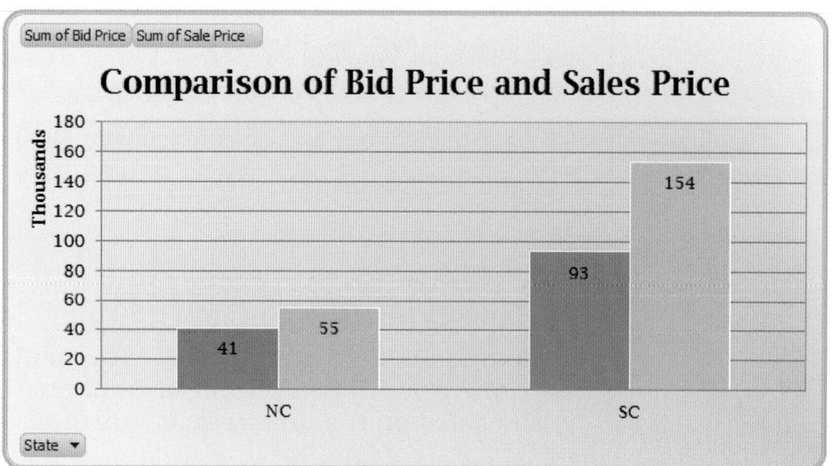

Figure IP1.2 Bid Price and Sales Price PivotChart

Table 5—Drag the State, City, and Artist fields to the Row Labels box. Drag the Sale Price to the Values box. Keep the Sum field setting for the Sale Price column. Format as before. In B6, right-click and click Sort; sort in descending order. Rename sheet tab **PivotTable 5**.

Table 6 and Column Chart—Drag the State field to the Row Labels box. Drag the Artist field to the Values box. Field settings should be set to Count to determine the number of artists in each state. Rename the sheet tab **PivotTable 6 & Chart.**

Click PivotChart and choose Clustered Column. Format as you did Chart 4 above and refer to Figure IP1.3. Insert a text box for source note; format italics, Aqua, Accent 5 color, and 10 point.

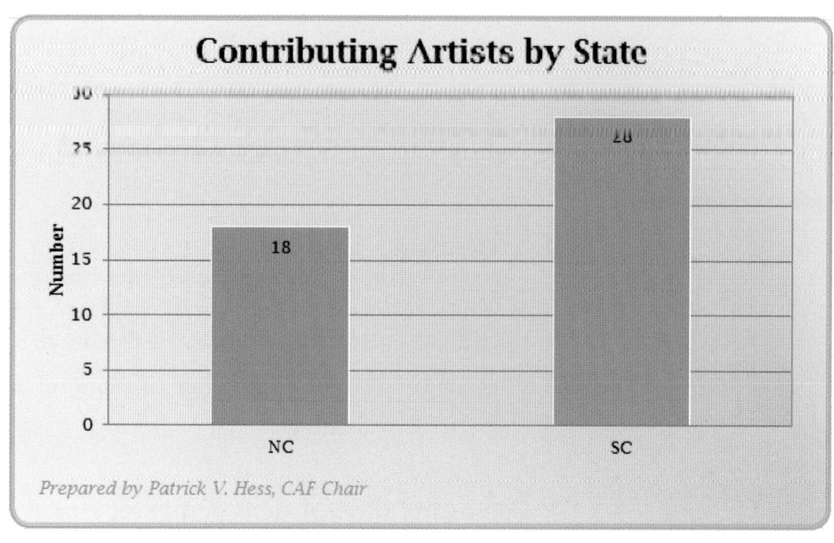

Figure IP1.3 Contributing Artists PivotChart

TIP

To hide field buttons, right-click the Field Button on the chart and click Hide All Field Buttons on Chart.

If necessary, select the plot area and resize to fit the chart area attractively.

Move the Art Auction worksheet to display as the first sheet. Arrange the remaining sheets in numeric order.

DRILL 2

CREATE A CALENDAR

DISCOVER

Turn Off Hyphenation

Text Box Tools Format/Text/Hyphenation

1. Click in the event text and follow the path.
2. In the Hyphenation dialog box, remove the check from Automatically hyphenate this story.

1. Create a Calendar using the Borders template and the Krawczyk 1 business information.
2. Select Bluebird color scheme and Office 2 font scheme.
3. In the Options, select One year per page, use the current year to set the calendar dates, and check Include schedule of events. Click Create.
4. Select the event column text and key the events shown below. Add **Marketing Committee Schedule** to the year as the main title.
5. Select event text and increase font size to 10 point. Do not hyphenate.
6. Preview and print.
7. Save as *pb1-drill2* and close.

- January 16, 9:30 a.m. to 11:30 a.m. Marketing Conference Room.
- March 16, 2:15 p.m. to 4:45 p.m. (tentative) Meeting will be at the Krawczyk Annual Retreat in Bluffton. Note the time and meeting room will be listed on the final retreat schedule.
- June 18, 9:30 a.m. to 11:30 a.m. Marketing Conference Room.
- September 17, 9:30 a.m. to 4:30 p.m. Joint meeting with the six Krawczyk Division Committees. Agenda will focus on review of the current year and planning for next year.

Apply It

Publication 1
Business Cards

1. Prepare business cards for yourself using the Accent Box template. Create new business information using your school name as the organization, your name, and student as your title. Use the school address, telephone, and fax numbers. Save the business information with your name. Click Remove on the Business Information Set dialog box to clear the previous logo. Select and copy the Contrasting Triangles accent next to the school name and paste it below your name and title. Size it about .5" × .5". Use the e-mail address FirstLast@school.edu. Use the Burgundy color scheme and the Basis font scheme.
2. Preview and print one page of cards.
3. Save as *pb1-p1* and close.

Publication 2
Calendar

1. Create a one-page calendar for the current year with schedule of events. Select the Accent Box template. Use the same business information, color scheme, and font scheme you used in Publication 1. Paste the Contrasting Triangles object from the top of the calendar centered below the calendar. Delete the business tag line.
2. Key the items indicated below in the schedule of events section.
3. Save as *pb1-p2* and close.

- Beginning date of next semester or quarter
- All holidays during the semester or quarter
- Beginning and ending dates of final examinations

Job 7

Report with Excel Data

GALA REPORT

Open the data file *gala report*, and follow the directions in the comments in the document and on this page to format the report. Directions are provided for formatting charts, tables, and captions; apply them to all examples of these.

Charts—Copy the charts indicated in the comments, and paste them using the default Paste option. Format charts using Top and Bottom wrapping style. Size charts to about 2.7" high by 5.2" wide. Center the charts horizontally.

Tables—Format all tables using the same format you used in *ip1-j3*. Apply Medium Grid 3 – Accent 1 table style. Merge the cells in the top row and format the title using 16-point bold heading font; increase the row height to .5"; apply Align Center. Increase the row height for column heads to .4"; apply Bold to column heads if they are not already bold. Center column headings vertically and horizontally. Center all tables horizontally on the page.

Captions— Add captions for all charts and tables. Use Figure for charts and Table for tables; note figure captions are positioned below the chart and table captions above the table. Center table captions and left-align figure captions.

Number Pages—Insert a Conservative footer to number pages. Use Different First Page for the body of the report so that the footer does not show on the first page. Format page numbers to start at 1 on the first page of the body of the report.

On the blank page after the cover page, insert a table of contents and change the format of the page number in the footer to lowercase Roman numerals. Use Automatic Table 2 and apply Title style to the title.

Comments—Follow all directions in the comments. Then delete all comments.

DISCOVER

References/Captions/Insert Caption

1. Click Insert Caption and select Figure or Table from the Label box.
2. Key the title of the caption.

QUICK ✓

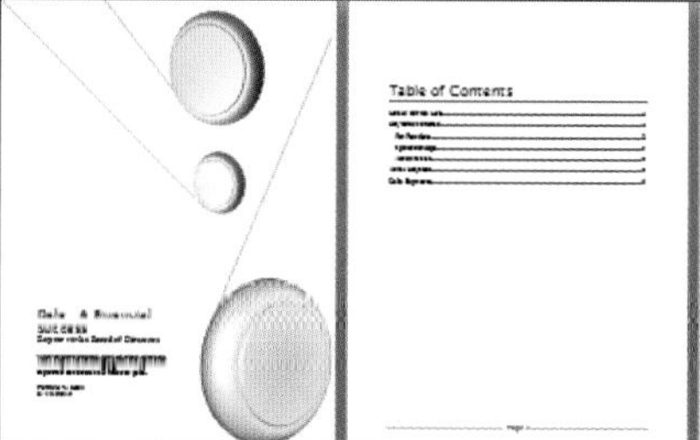

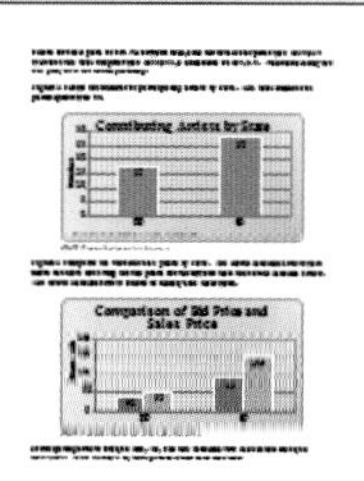

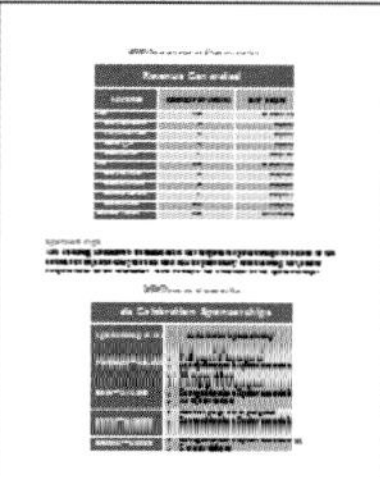

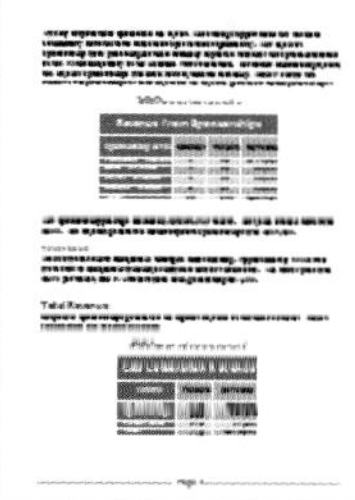

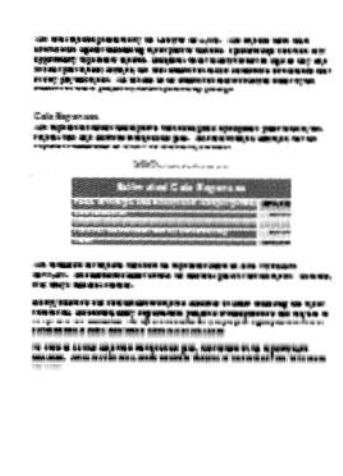

Figure IP1.4 Job 7 Quick Check

Job 8

Presentation

Open *ip1-j4a* and save as *ip1-j8*. You will modify the presentation to include final information about the Gala. Make the following changes on the slides.

Slide 1

Change title to **Gala—A Financial Success** and subtitle to **Report to the Board of Directors**.

Slide 3

In the slide title, delete *Update*. In the first shape, change *participating* to **participated**. In the third shape, change *exhibiting* to **exhibited**. In the fourth shape, change *Bid values* to **Bid and sales values**.

5. Key the information in each of the text boxes, as shown in Figure 1.4 on page 166.
6. To add a logo, click Add Logo ❺ to browse for the logo file, select it, and then click Insert.
7. Key the Business Information set name ❻ and click Save ❼.
8. To create the publication, click Create. Preview the publication (File/Print) if desired.
9. Save and close the publication.

DRILL 1 CREATE BUSINESS CARDS

Print on plain paper to check business cards before printing on prescored card sheets. For class purposes, you will probably print only on plain paper.

1. Launch *Publisher*.
2. Click the Business Cards publication type; select the Arrows template.
3. Select the Bluebird color scheme.
4. Create new business information; key the information shown below. Add the *krawczyk logo*.
5. Name the business information **Krawczyk 1**; then click Create.
6. Check the card that displays. Preview the sheet of cards (File/Print) and then print it (File/Print).
7. Use Save As (File/Save As) to save the publication as *pb1-drill1* in your *Publisher* solutions folder. Close the publication.

Name: Lynn C. Blackmon
Title: Director, Marketing
Organization: Krawczyk, Inc.
Address: 1620 Tanglewood Road | Columbia, SC 29204-3325
Phone: 803-555-0159
Fax: 803-555-0161
E-mail: lynnblackmon@krawczyk.com

USE OTHER TEMPLATES

Once you become familiar with using a template for one type of publication, it is easy to use other available templates. Some templates (such as the Calendar templates) have additional features.

To Create a Calendar:

File/New

1. Click on the Calendars publication type and select the desired template (such as Borders). Use existing business information or add new information.
2. Select a new color scheme and font scheme if desired.
3. Complete the options indicating the timeframe and dates and whether to include a schedule of events (see Figure 1.5). Then click OK.
4. Key the text for the events. Key additional information for title if desired.

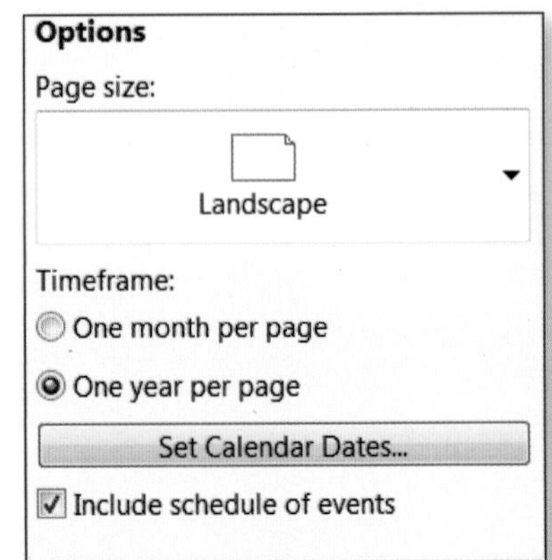

Figure 1.5 Calendar Options

Job 8,
continued

Format all tables using the same format you used for Job 4, slide 5. Center tables horizontally on the slide. Make any other changes that improve the appearance of the tables, such as increasing row height and centering text vertically. Use Keep Source Formatting when you paste tables.

Slide 5 (New slide, Title Only)

Title: Bid and Sales Prices

Paste the chart (Comparison of Bid Price and Sales Price) in PivotTable 4 on this slide. Click the corner and drag to increase the size so that it extends to about 1" from each side of the slide.

Slide 6 (New slide, Title Only)

Title: Revenue from Art Auction

Copy and paste Table 1 from the report in *ip1-j7* to this slide. Choose the Keep Source Formatting Paste option. Drag the table to increase the size to about 4.6" high.

Slide 8 (New slide, Title Only)

Title: Sponsorship Revenue

Copy and paste Table 3 from the report in *ip1-j7* to this slide.

Animate tables and charts in the same way they were animated on the slides from Job 4. Do not animate slides 13 and 14.

Slide 9

Delete Slide 9 Sponsorship Update and make changes below in the new Slide 9, Ticket Sales.

Change second shape text to **Approximately 500 solicitation letters mailed**

Change third shape text to **Individuals bought 378 tickets at $100 each**

Add a fourth shape and key text **Total revenue from sales was $37,800**

Slide 11 (New slide, Title Only)

Title: Revenue Summary

Copy and paste Table 4 from the report in *ip1-j7* to this slide.

Slide 12 (New slide, Title Only)

Title: Estimated Gala Expenses

Copy and paste Table 5 from the report in *ip1-j7* to this slide.

Slide 13 (New slide, Title Only)

Title: Estimated Net Revenue

Draw a text box and key the text shown in Figure IP1.5.

Slide 14 (New Slide, Blank)

Use keyword celebration to find appropriate clip art. Insert and add an artistic effect to the clip.

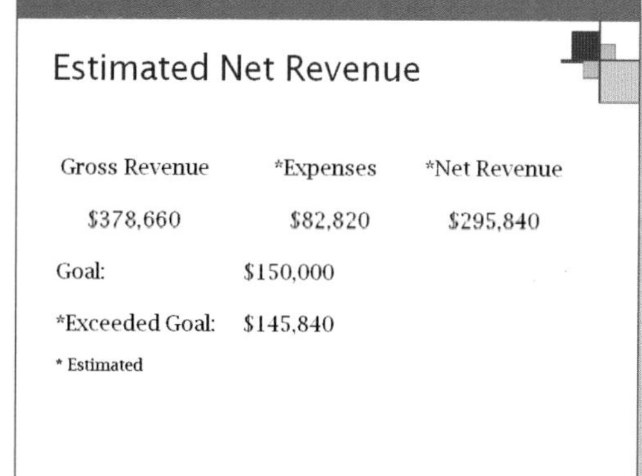

Figure IP1.5 Slide 13 Estimated Net Revenue

Figure IP1.6 Slide 14 Celebration

Use 24-point font for all text except the **Estimated* footnote; use 18-point font for it.

Note in Figure 1.2 that the groups and commands on the Home tab are basically the same as those on the Home tab of *Word*, *PowerPoint*, and *Excel*. The main workspace is on the right, and the Page Navigation pane is on the left side. Publications frequently are multiple-page documents with text flowing from one page to the next. The Page Navigation pane makes it easy to move from one page to another.

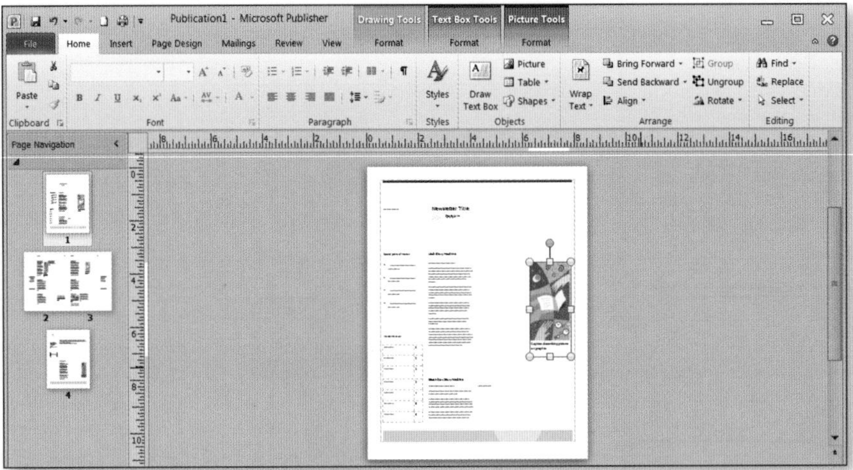

Figure 1.2 Publisher Workspace

In a *Publisher* publication, all text is placed in text boxes and all graphics are placed in picture placeholders. When you click in a text box or placeholder, Text Box Tools, Drawing Tools, or Picture Tools tabs display at the top of the Ribbon. You already have experience using these tools to format text boxes, shapes, pictures, and other objects.

TIP

Create a new folder named Module 5 Solutions and save all publications and documents from this module in it. Remember to close and save all publications, even if you are not directed to do so.

To Create a New Publication:

1. Click on a template option. A preview of the publication ❶ displays in the right pane. (See Figure 1.3.)
2. To change the color scheme, click the down arrow in the Customize Color scheme box ❷ and select a different color scheme.
3. To change the font scheme, click the down arrow ❸ and select the desired font scheme.
4. If you have entered business information in the system, the preview will display it. If you have not entered business information, the Create new option ❹ displays. Click Create new to display the Create New Business Information Set dialog box as shown in Figure 1.4.

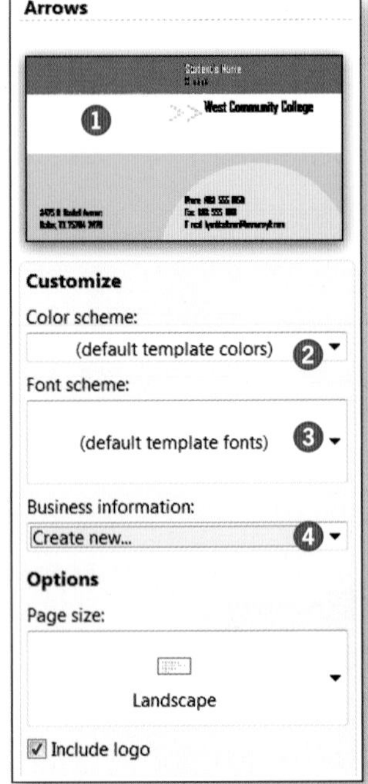

Figure 1.3 Publication Preview

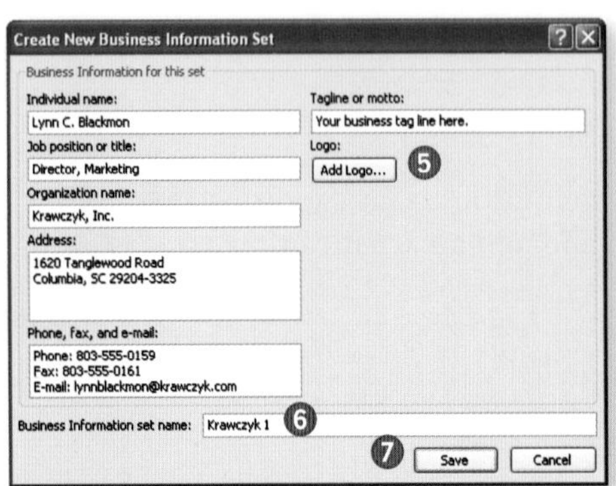

Figure 1.4 Create New Business Information

PUBLICATIONS WITH PUBLISHER

overview

Publisher 2010 is a powerful and easy-to-use software application that facilitates creating, designing, and publishing documents with extensive graphics and layouts. Both *Publisher* and *Word* focus on document production; however, *Word* is best used for documents such as letters, memos, reports, legal documents, and documents requiring collaboration, whereas *Publisher* is best used for documents such as business cards, newsletters, brochures, and flyers. Many of the commands you used in *Word*, *PowerPoint*, and *Excel* will be applied in *Publisher*. This module assumes that you have had little or no formal instruction in using *Publisher*.

ESSENTIALS

1. Create Publications Using Templates
2. Work with Text Boxes and Picture Placeholders
3. Customize Templates
4. Create a Template from a Blank Page

Project 7—Creative Designs & Production III: Integrating Publisher, Word, and Excel

Create Publications Using Templates

LESSON 1

OBJECTIVES

- Create effective publications
- Use templates
- Store business information for repetitive use

OPENING SCREEN

You launch *Publisher* the same way that you launched *Word*, *PowerPoint*, and *Excel*. Note that *Publisher* opens with the File menu displayed (Figure 1.1). You are already familiar with the information and commands contained on the File menu. You will also see the familiar Ribbon tabs and the Quick Access Toolbar.

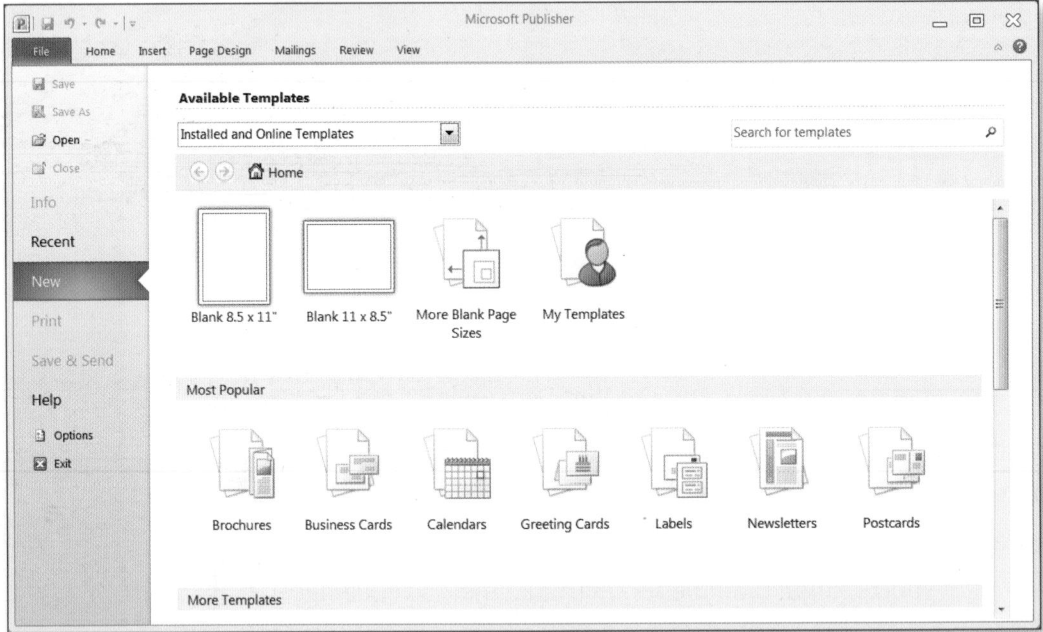

Figure 1.1 Opening Screen

GETTING STARTED

File/New

Generally, publications prepared using *Publisher* are based on templates. The New tab in Backstage view displays categories of templates from which you can choose to create a new publication. Templates available are either installed or available from Office.com.

To create a new publication, select the desired template. A pane opens to the right to give you options for customizing the template by selecting a color scheme, font scheme, and other options that relate to the type of template. Click Create to create the new publication and display it in the *Publisher* window, as shown in Figure 1.2 on the next page.

Microsoft Windows 7

OVERVIEW

Windows 7 is the newest operating system software released by Microsoft. The operating system software controls the operations of the computer and works with the application software. *Windows* 7 works with *Word* in opening, printing, deleting, and saving files. It also allows you to work with photos and pictures, play music, and access the Internet.

When you turn on your computer, *Windows* displays a login screen followed by a password screen. See your instructor for login and password information. The *Windows* 7 desktop displays after you have logged in.

MICROSOFT WINDOWS 7 DESKTOP

TIP

The Windows desktop and its components are described on the next page.

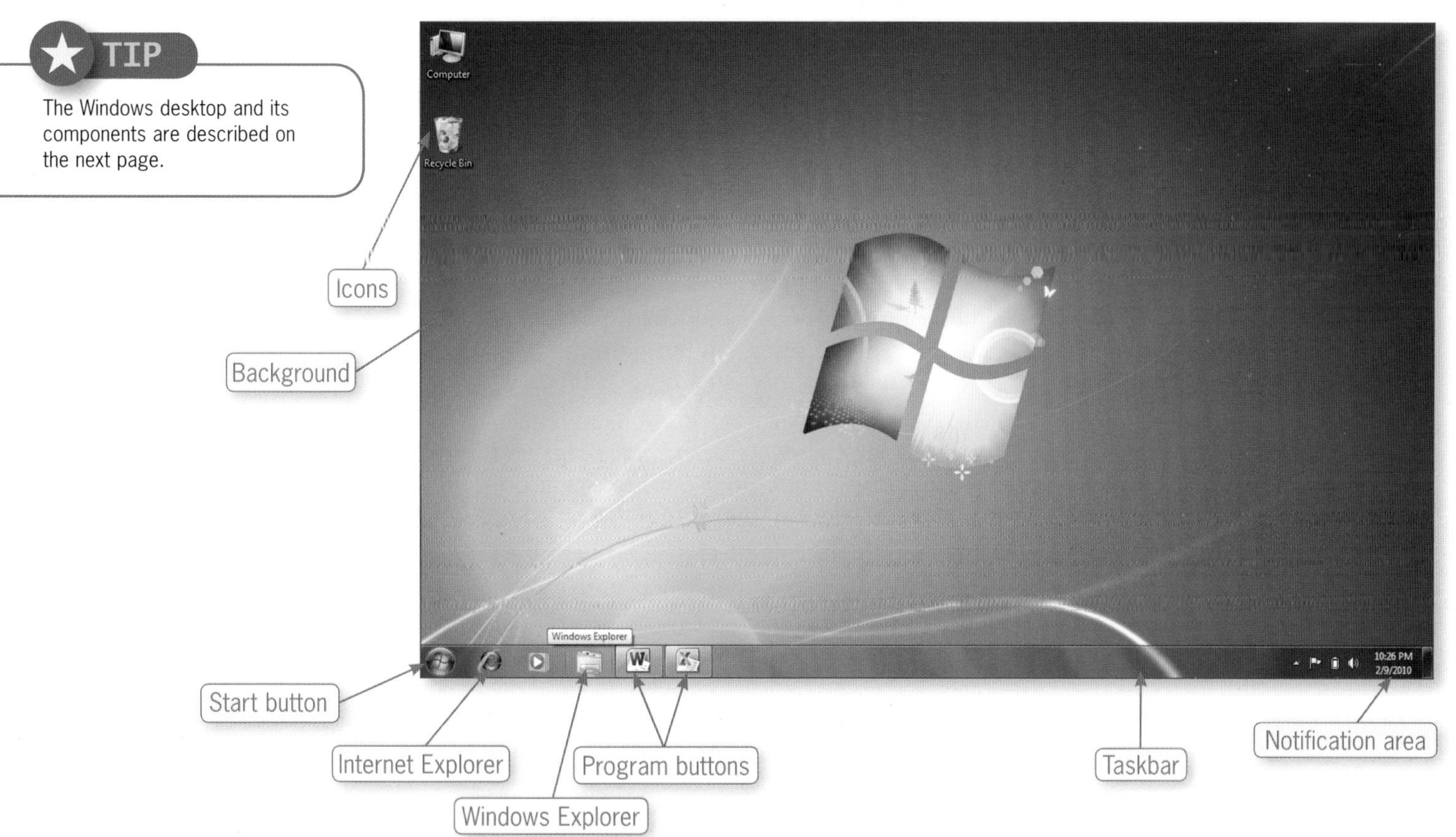

WINDOWS DESKTOP COMPONENTS

The illustration on the previous page shows the default *Windows* 7 Aero desktop. The Aero theme has a semitransparent glass design that gives a three-dimensional appearance. In order to see the graphical enhancements of the Aero theme, your computer hardware and version of *Windows* 7 must support it. Your screen may have the *Windows* 7 Basic theme.

Read the description of each component and hover the mouse over each object to display the ScreenTip that identifies each element.

- *Taskbar*. The taskbar displays across the bottom of the screen and contains the elements listed below.
  - *Start button*. Click the Start button to display the Start menu. The Start menu provides access to programs and files on your computer.
  - *Program and file buttons*. Buttons display for the programs that are open or pinned to the taskbar and allow you to switch between them easily. The illustration shows that *Internet Explorer*, *Windows Explorer*, *Word*, and *Excel* either are open or have been pinned to the taskbar so that they remain on the desktop.
  - *Notification area*. The notification area provides helpful information, such as the date and time and the status of the computer. When you plug in a USB drive, *Windows* displays an icon in the notification area letting you know that the hardware is connected.
- *Icons and shortcuts*. Icons, small pictures representing certain items, may be displayed on the desktop. The Recycle Bin, which represents a wastepaper basket, displays when *Windows* is installed. Other icons and shortcuts may be added.
- *Background*. The default background is the *Windows* logo on a blue background. The background can be changed or customized to include a personal picture or a company logo.

START MENU

The Start menu enables you to access all programs, documents, and other computer resources. The programs listed in the left pane of the Start menu vary depending on which programs you have used recently. However, all programs can be located by clicking All Programs. The right pane contains links to files and resources on your computer. One of the key links that will be useful is Help and Support. Note that the Shut down button is also located on the Start menu.

To display the Start menu, click the Start button. The Start menu is illustrated on the next page. Review the callouts on the illustration on the next page.

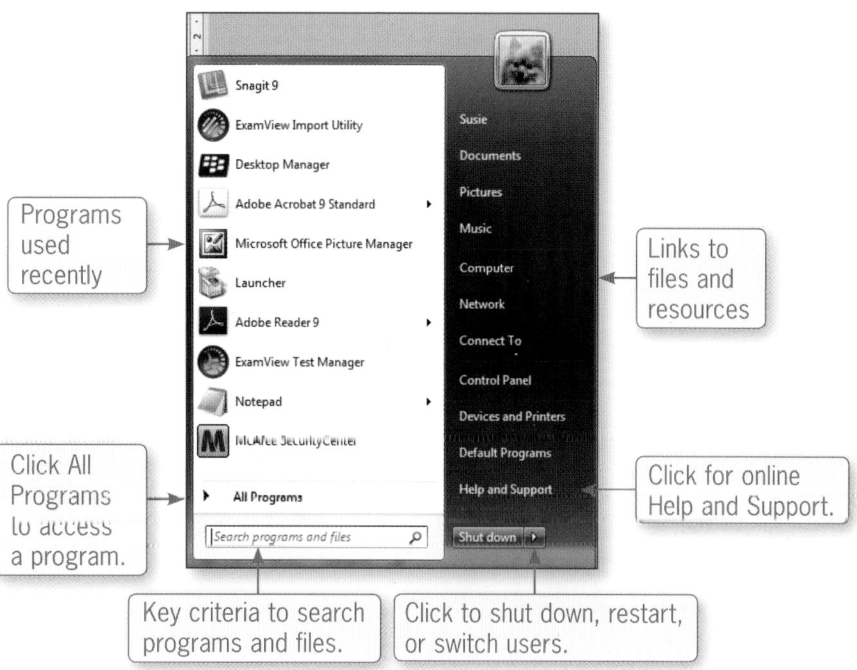

TIP

You will be able to access both the Help files stored on your computer and those stored on the Microsoft website if your computer is connected to the Internet.

WINDOWS 7 HELP AND SUPPORT

The fastest way to get help is to key a word or phrase in the Search Help box and tap ENTER; all the Help pages that contain the word or phrase will display. You can also click the Browse Help topics link and then click an item in the contents listing of subject headings that appear. Some subject headings contain Help topics within a subheading. Click the Help topic to open it, and click the subheading to narrow your search.

COMPUTER DRIVES

You will be working with auxiliary drives, including CD/DVD and universal serial bus (USB) flash drives. USB flash drives vary in size and shape and can hold gigabytes of information. They are also called thumb drives, memory keys, pen drives, and key drives. The USB drive needs to be plugged into a USB port in order for the computer to read the drive. Your computer may have several USB ports.

To access drives on your computer:

1. Click the Start button to display the Start menu.
2. Click Computer in the right pane to view the drives and storage devices connected to your computer.

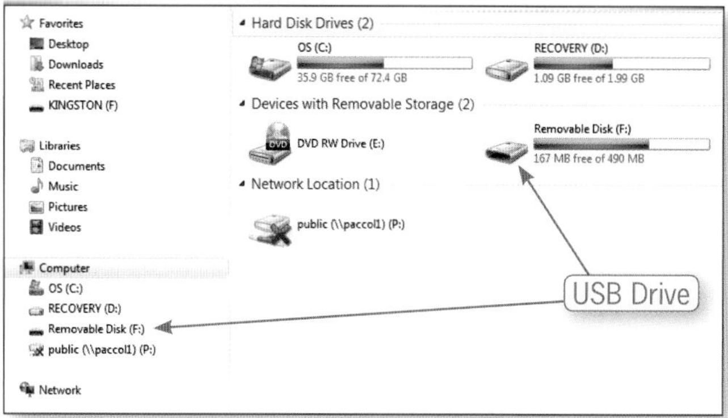

Formatting Decisions

Decisions regarding document formats require consideration of four elements: (1) attractiveness of the format, (2) readability of the format, (3) effective use of space on the page, and (4) efficiency in producing the format. Please note several formatting decisions made in this text regarding defaults in *Word 2010*.

Styles

Word 2010 offers a quick gallery of styles on the Home tab, and a gallery of cover pages. Using these styles and cover pages results in efficient production of an attractive report and title page.

Default 1.15 Line Spacing

The default line spacing of 1.15 in *Word 2010* provides readers with a more open and more readable copy.

Space after the Paragraph

The default space after a paragraph in *Word 2010* is 10 points after the paragraph. This automatic spacing saves time and creates an attractive document.

In some situations, the additional 10 points of space after each paragraph consumes too much space and should be removed. For example, the layout is more attractive when the extra spacing is removed between the lines in the letter address or between the writer's name and title. Remove the extra space by clicking on options of the Line and Paragraph Spacing command.

Margins

The default margins for *Word 2010* are 1" top, bottom, left side, and right side. With side margin defaults of 1", additional space is needed for the binding of leftbound reports.

Custom Themes Across Applications

Themes can be used in all applications to match corporate branding and identity. Color printing has becoming increasingly popular and more cost effective. See the illustration below that features coordinated custom themes in a *Word* report with a *Word* SmartArt graphic, a *Word* table, *Excel* graphics, and a *Publisher* newsletter.

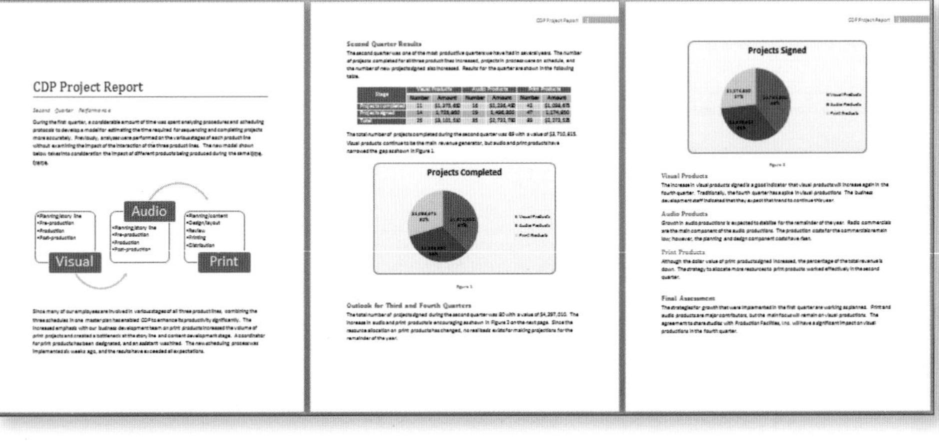

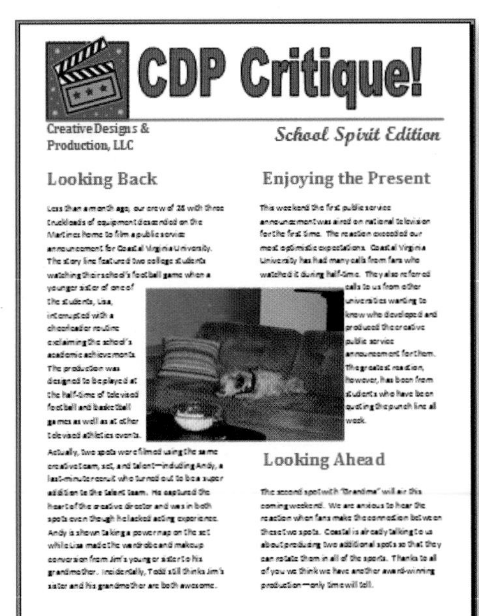

CDP Critique!

Creative Designs & Production, LLC

School Spirit Edition

Looking Back

Less than a month ago, our crew of 28 with three truckloads of equipment descended on the Martinez home to film a public service announcement for Coastal Virginia University. The story line featured two college students watching their school's football game when a younger sister of one of the students, Lisa, interrupted with a cheerleader routine exclaiming the school's academic achievements. The production was designed to be played at the half-time of televised football and basketball games as well as at other televised athletics events.

Actually, two spots were filmed using the same creative team, set, and talent—including Andy, a last-minute recruit who turned out to be a super addition to the talent team. He captured the heart of the creative director and was in both spots even though he lacked acting experience. Andy is shown taking a power nap on the set while Lisa made the wardrobe and makeup conversion from Jim's younger sister to his grandmother. Incidentally, Todd still thinks Jim's sister and his grandmother are both awesome.

Enjoying the Present

This weekend the first public service announcement was aired on national television for the first time. The reaction exceeded our most optimistic expectations. Coastal Virginia University has had many calls from fans who watched it during half-time. They also referred calls to us from other universities wanting to know who developed and produced the creative public service announcement for them. The greatest reaction, however, has been from students who have been quoting the punch line all week.

Looking Ahead

The second spot with "Grandma" will air this coming weekend. We are anxious to hear the reaction when fans make the connection between these two spots. Coastal is already talking to us about producing two additional spots so that they can rotate them in all of the sports. Thanks to all of you we think we have another award-winning production—only time will tell.

Photo: Susie VanHuss

Letter Parts

Letterhead. Company name and address. May include other data.

Date. Date letter is mailed. Usually in month, day, year order. Position at 2" (3 hard returns).

Letter address. Address of the person who will receive the letter. Include personal title (*Mr.*, *Ms.*, *Dr.*), name, professional title, company, and address. Remove the extra spacing in the letter address.

Salutation. Greeting. Corresponds to the first line of the letter address. Usually includes name and courtesy title; use *Ladies and Gentlemen* if letter is addressed to a company name.

Body. Message. Key in default 1.15 line spacing; tap ENTER once between paragraphs.

Complimentary close. Farewell, such as *Sincerely*.

Writer. Name and professional title. If the name and title are keyed on two lines, remove the extra spacing between the lines.

Initials. Identifies person who keyed the document (for example, *tr*). May include identification of writer (*ARB:tri*).

Enclosure. Copy is enclosed with the document. May specify contents. If more than one line is used, align at 1" and remove the extra spacing between the lines.

Copy notation. Indicates that a copy of the letter is being sent to person named. If more than one line is used, align at 0.5" and remove the extra spacing between the lines.

Note: To remove extra spacing between lines, click the down arrow on the Line and Paragraph Spacing command and select Remove Space After Paragraph.

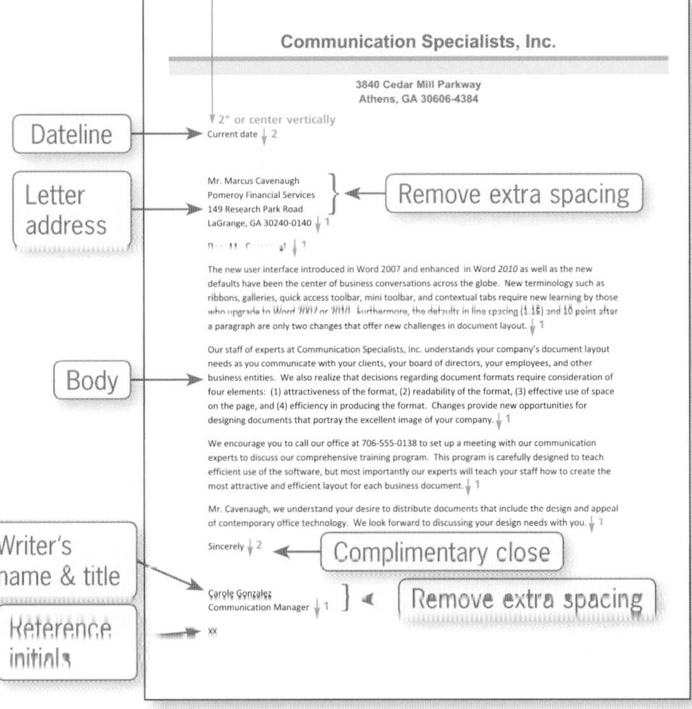

Communication Specialists, Inc.

3840 Cedar Mill Parkway
Athens, GA 30606-4384

Current date ↓ 2

Mr. Marcus Cavenaugh
Pomeroy Financial Services
149 Research Park Road
LaGrange, GA 30240-0140 ↓ 1

[illegible] ↓ 1

The new user interface introduced in Word 2007 and enhanced in Word *2010* as well as the new defaults have been the center of business conversations across the globe. New terminology such as ribbons, galleries, quick access toolbar, mini toolbar, and contextual tabs require new learning by those who upgrade to Word 2007 or 2010. Furthermore, the defaults in line spacing (1.15) and 10 point after a paragraph are only two changes that offer new challenges in document layout. ↓ 1

Our staff of experts at Communication Specialists, Inc. understands your company's document layout needs as you communicate with your clients, your board of directors, your employees, and other business entities. We also realize that decisions regarding document formats require consideration of four elements: (1) attractiveness of the format, (2) readability of the format, (3) effective use of space on the page, and (4) efficiency in producing the format. Changes provide new opportunities for designing documents that portray the excellent image of your company. ↓ 1

We encourage you to call our office at 706-555-0138 to set up a meeting with our communication experts to discuss our comprehensive training program. This program is carefully designed to teach efficient use of the software, but most importantly our experts will teach your staff how to create the most attractive and efficient layout for each business document. ↓ 1

Mr. Cavenaugh, we understand your desire to distribute documents that include the design and appeal of contemporary office technology. We look forward to discussing your design needs with you. ↓ 1

Sincerely ↓ 2

Carole Gonzalez
Communication Manager ↓ 1

xx

Block Letter (Open Punctuation)

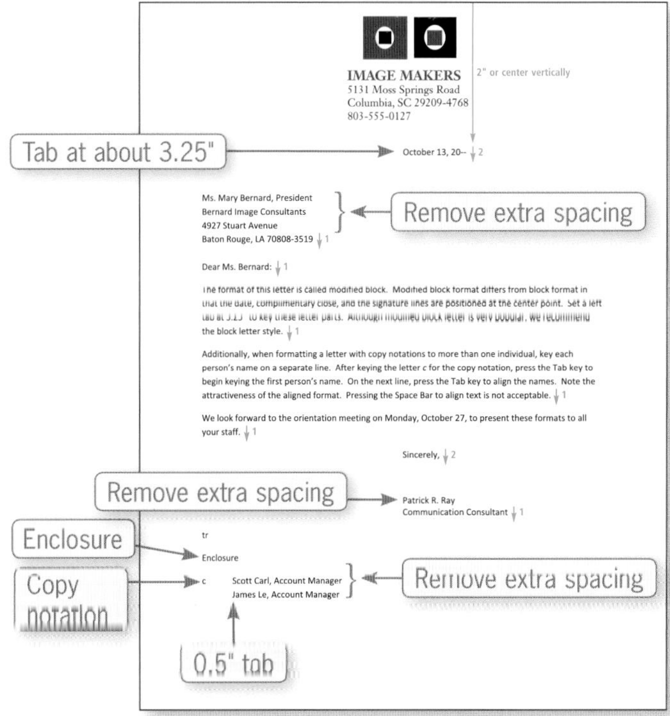

IMAGE MAKERS
5131 Moss Springs Road
Columbia, SC 29209-4768
803-555-0127

October 13, 20-- ↓ 2

Ms. Mary Bernard, President
Bernard Image Consultants
4927 Stuart Avenue
Baton Rouge, LA 70808-3519 ↓ 1

Dear Ms. Bernard: ↓ 1

The format of this letter is called modified block. Modified block format differs from block format in that the date, complimentary close, and the signature lines are positioned at the center point. Set a left tab at 3.25" to key these letter parts. Although modified block letter is very popular, we recommend the block letter style. ↓ 1

Additionally, when formatting a letter with copy notations to more than one individual, key each person's name on a separate line. After keying the letter *c* for the copy notation, press the Tab key to begin keying the first person's name. On the next line, press the Tab key to align the names. Note the attractiveness of the aligned format. Pressing the Space Bar to align text is not acceptable. ↓ 1

We look forward to the orientation meeting on Monday, October 27, to present these formats to all your staff. ↓ 1

Sincerely, ↓ 2

Patrick R. Ray
Communication Consultant ↓ 1

tr

Enclosure

c Scott Carl, Account Manager
James Le, Account Manager

Modified Block Letter (Mixed Punctuation)

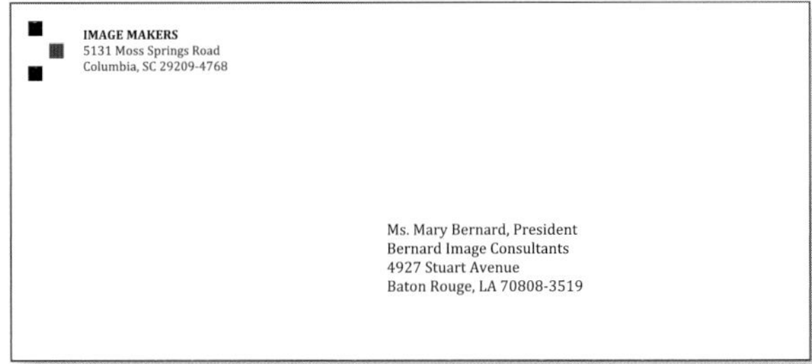

IMAGE MAKERS
5131 Moss Springs Road
Columbia, SC 29209-4768

Ms. Mary Bernard, President
Bernard Image Consultants
4927 Stuart Avenue
Baton Rouge, LA 70808-3519

Envelope

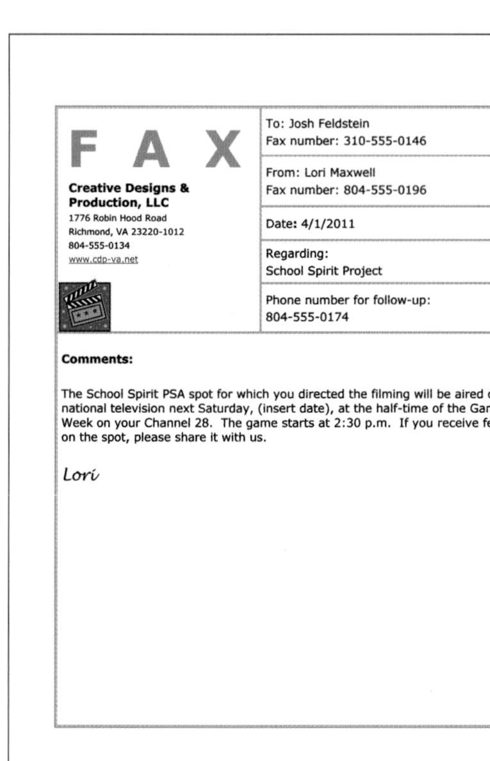

TO: Parents

FROM: Lynn Marshall

DATE: May 15, 201-

SUBJECT: Tuition

The Board of Directors has reviewed our financial statements, the proposed budget for next year, and our current tuition plan. Although we have tried to maintain tuition at the current rate, it is not possible to do so. Our costs for utilities, food, supplies, and gasoline for the buses have increased substantially. Therefore, we have applied a 2.5% increase in tuition for next year. The following table summarizes our new weekly rates.

Age Group	Single-Child Rate	Multi-Child Rate	Half-Day Rate
Infant/Toddler	$268	$245	$150
Preschool 2	$253	$233	$140
Preschool 3	$240	$230	$125
Preschool 4	$237	$228	$122
Preschool 5	$235	$225	$122

The new rates take effect on July 1 and will be guaranteed not to change for one full year. The Children's Center will continue to accept credit cards and personal checks as it has always done. Tuition may be paid weekly, monthly, and annually.

If you wish to pay the annual tuition at one time prior to July 1, you may pay the current rates rather than these new rates with the 2.5% increase shown in the table. If you have any questions about tuition or other financial issues, please check with our business manager at the Children's Center.

We look forward to seeing all of you at the annual picnic next week.

xx

Memo with Table

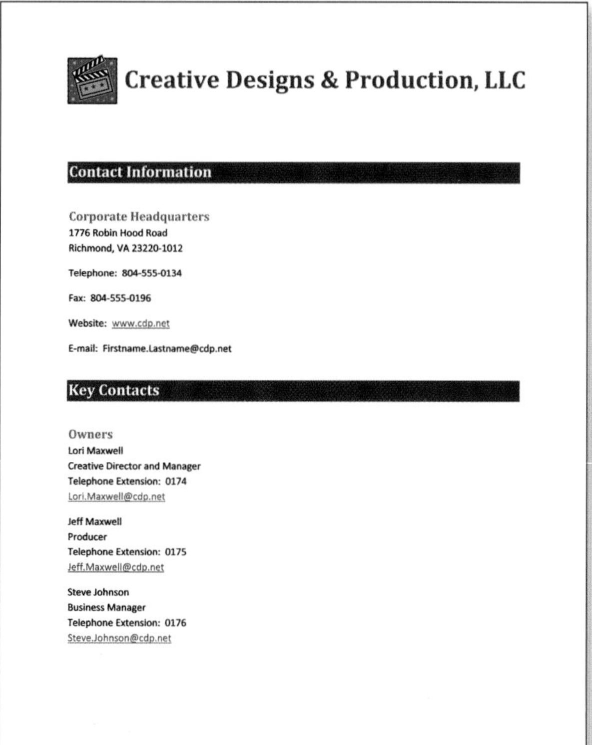

The Bookstore, Inc.

3893 North Elm Street * Germantown, TN 38138-3893 * Telephone 901-555-0193 * Fax 901-555-0112

TO: Tara Lanford, Vice President

FROM: Derek Bradberry

DATE: Current date

SUBJECT: Update on Training Program for Software Mastery Series

The training program titled Software Mastery Training Series is designed as a result of the outcome of a needs assessment conducted by the Training Department last week. The needs assessment showed that more than three-fourths of our staff only know and use one-fourth of the capabilities of their software. When asked about time-saving features such as mail merge, Quick Parts, templates, styles, index, bookmarks, macros, and hyperlinks, very few were using these efficiency features.

Upon evaluation of the learning outcomes determined by the needs assessment, I have hired a consultant to identify the software competencies needed by our staff to increase efficiency in completing administrative tasks. The chart below shows the breakdown of the salaries budgeted for this training program. As training director, I will be responsible for designing the training program upon receipt of the consultant's report. My trainers are very qualified to lead the instructional sessions.

xx

Memo with Linked Chart

Creative Designs & Production, LLC

Contact Information

Corporate Headquarters
1776 Robin Hood Road
Richmond, VA 23220-1012

Telephone: 804-555-0134

Fax: 804-555-0196

Website: www.cdp.net

E-mail: Firstname.Lastname@cdp.net

Key Contacts

Owners
Lori Maxwell
Creative Director and Manager
Telephone Extension: 0174
Lori.Maxwell@cdp.net

Jeff Maxwell
Producer
Telephone Extension: 0175
Jeff.Maxwell@cdp.net

Steve Johnson
Business Manager
Telephone Extension: 0176
Steve.Johnson@cdp.net

Contact Information Quick Part

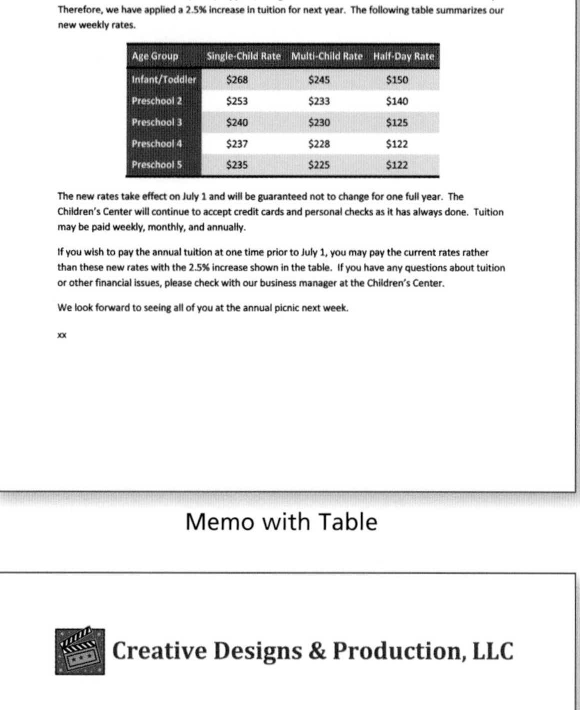

F A X **Creative Designs & Production, LLC** 1776 Robin Hood Road Richmond, VA 23220-1012 804-555-0134 www.cdp-va.net	To: Josh Feldstein Fax number: 310-555-0146
	From: Lori Maxwell Fax number: 804-555-0196
	Date: 4/1/2011
	Regarding: School Spirit Project
	Phone number for follow-up: 804-555-0174

Comments:

The School Spirit PSA spot for which you directed the filming will be aired on national television next Saturday, (insert date), at the half-time of the Game of the Week on your Channel 28. The game starts at 2:30 p.m. If you receive feedback on the spot, please share it with us.

Lori

Fax

Business Reports

Margins. Tap ENTER three times to begin first page of report at 2"; default 1" top margin for succeeding pages; default 1" for bottom margin.

Unbound report: Side margins 1"

Leftbound report: Left margin 1.5"; right margin 1"

Titles. Title style. Main words capitalized.

Spacing. Default 1.15 line spacing; paragraphs blocked. Tap ENTER once between paragraphs.

Page numbers. Second and subsequent pages are generally numbered at top right of the page, but custom headers and footers can be used with either one including the page number.

Side headings. Heading 1 style. Main words capitalized.

Report of Industrial Space in Fayette and Clark Counties

Introduction

In long-term planning, the management of Kisner Industrial Co. identified the immediate need to determine current space being used in Fayette and Clark counties for (1) industrial manufacturing, (2) warehouse space, and (3) distribution space. Two internal studies of industrial distribution and warehouse space had been conducted. The study completed in [illegible] focused on properties over 10,000 square feet, while the [illegible] study examined properties ranging from 2,000 to 10,000 square feet.

Kisner Industrial Co. authorized MarketAnalysis, Inc. to conduct an expanded market study to include manufacturing sites, in addition to distribution and warehouse space. Because long-term plans of Kisner Industrial Co. include expanding into Clark County, the study also included Clark County as well as Fayette County.

Purpose of the Study

The purpose of the study was to determine the key real estate attributes, such as size, location, rental rate, availability, and construction of all industrial sites located in Fayette and Clark counties. The following information was desired:

- **Property location data:** Tax map number, real estate zone (based on ZIP Code), full street address, and county.
- **Owner and contact data:** Owner's name, address, and telephone number; contact person's name, address, and telephone number.
- **Availability data:** Whether the property was available for sale or lease; whether property was owner-occupied or leased; and lease expiration data.
- **Property description data:** Total square footage of property, subdivided by warehouse, manufacturing, and office space; rent per square foot per year; and building quality. Building quality included such factors as year built, type of construction (metal, concrete, etc.), roof height, and utilities present.

Methods and Procedures Used

Consultants divided Fayette and Clark counties into three zones for reporting real estate information. Table 1 shows the three zones.

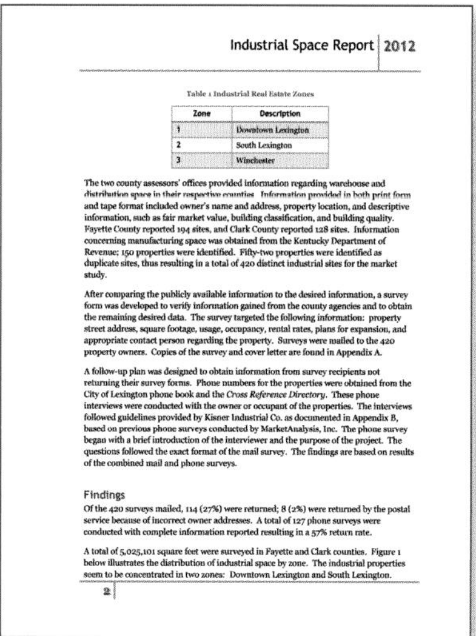

Industrial Space Report | 2012

Table 1 Industrial Real Estate Zones

Zone	Description
1	Downtown Lexington
2	South Lexington
3	Winchester

The two county assessors' offices provided information regarding warehouse and distribution space in their respective counties. Information provided in both print form and tape format included owner's name and address, property location, and descriptive information, such as fair market value, building classification, and building quality. Fayette County reported 194 sites, and Clark County reported 128 sites. Information concerning manufacturing space was obtained from the Kentucky Department of Revenue; 150 properties were identified. Fifty-two properties were identified as duplicate sites, thus resulting in a total of 420 distinct industrial sites for the market study.

After comparing the publicly available information to the desired information, a survey form was developed to verify information gained from the county agencies and to obtain the remaining desired data. The survey targeted the following information: property street address, square footage, usage, occupancy, rental rates, plans for expansion, and appropriate contact person regarding the property. Surveys were mailed to the 420 property owners. Copies of the survey and cover letter are found in Appendix A.

A follow-up plan was designed to obtain information from survey recipients not returning their survey forms. Phone numbers for the properties were obtained from the City of Lexington phone book and the *Cross Reference Directory*. These phone interviews were conducted with the owner or occupant of the properties. The interviews followed guidelines provided by Kisner Industrial Co. as documented in Appendix B, based on previous phone surveys conducted by MarketAnalysis, Inc. The phone survey began with a brief introduction of the interviewer and the purpose of the project. The questions followed the exact format of the mail survey. The findings are based on results of the combined mail and phone surveys.

Findings

Of the 420 surveys mailed, 114 (27%) were returned; 8 (2%) were returned by the postal service because of incorrect owner addresses. A total of 127 phone surveys were conducted with complete information reported resulting in a 57% return rate.

A total of 5,025,101 square feet were surveyed in Fayette and Clark counties. Figure 1 below illustrates the distribution of industrial space by zone. The industrial properties seem to be concentrated in two zones: Downtown Lexington and South Lexington.

2

Reports with Preliminary Pages

Preliminary pages are numbered at the bottom center using small Roman numerals (except the cover page). A section break must be inserted to include two different page numbering formats in one document. A table of contents, list of figures, list of tables, bibliography page, and index can be generated automatically.

MarketAnalysis, Inc.

Industrial Space Report

Fayette and Clark Counties

Melanie Winters

2012

P.O. Box 5643, Lexington, KY 40515-5643

Title Page Using Cover Page Feature

[illegible]

Mr. Jerry Chitturi, President
Kisner Industrial Co.
1783 Portland Drive
Lexington, KY 40503-1783

Dear Mr. Chitturi

The market study authorized by Kisner Industrial Co. is now complete.

The report presents data for 249 properties in Fayette and Clark counties. The market information was collected through an initial mail survey and finally a phone survey. The rate of return was rather high at 59 percent. Data were then analyzed to determine trends in industrial real estate.

After careful consideration of the data, MarketAnalysis, Inc. recommends expansion to the South Lexington area. This area is a prime area for industrial use, has the lowest average rental rate, and was second only to the downtown area in terms of vacant space available at the present time.

Thank you for allowing our organization the opportunity to conduct this market study. Our project staff will be happy to discuss any part of this report and wish you the best in making long-term plans for Kisner Industrial Co.

Sincerely

Melanie Winters
Project Coordinator

xx

Attachment

ii

Letter of Transmittal

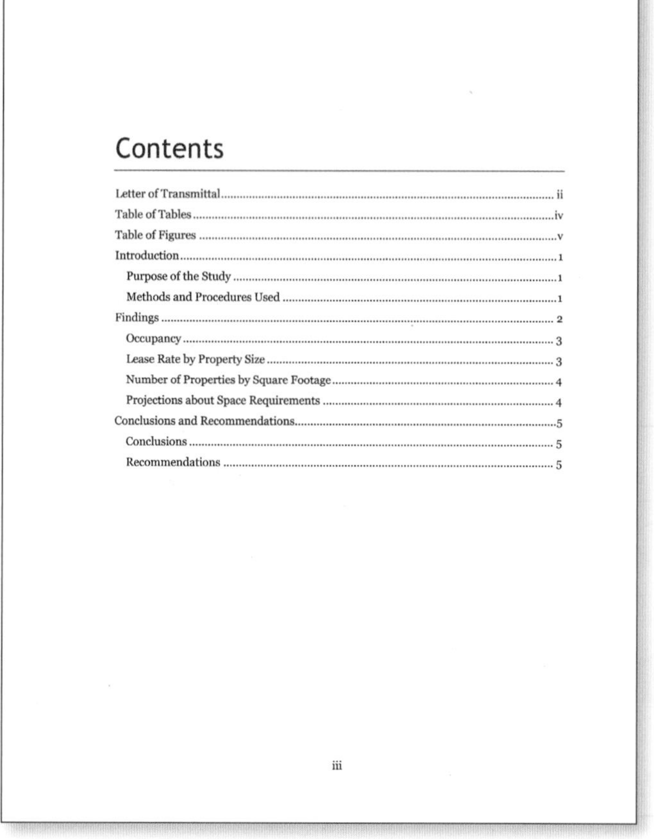

Contents

iii

Table of Contents

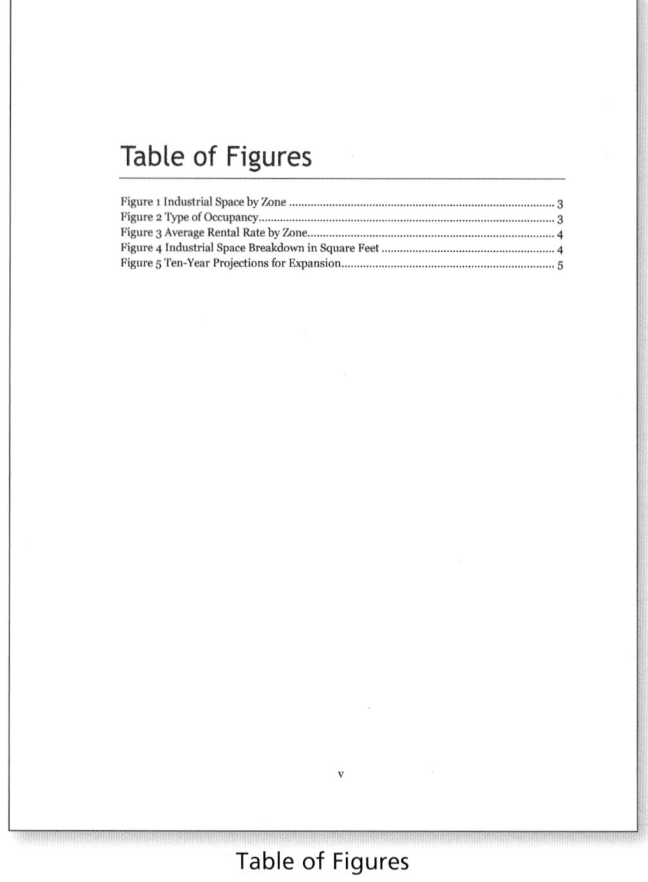

Table of Figures

v

Table of Figures

Charts

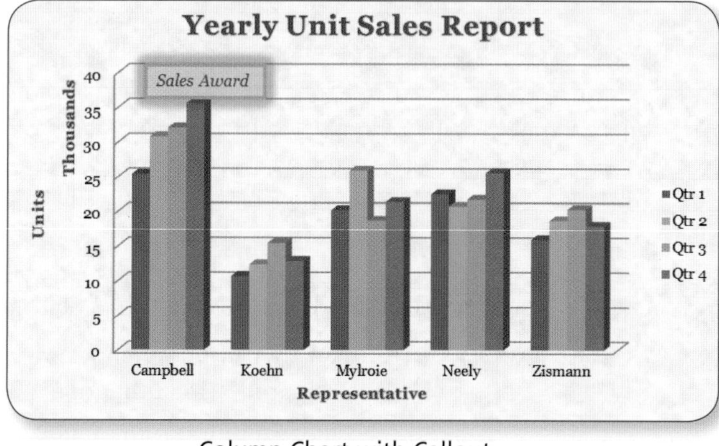

Column Chart with Callout

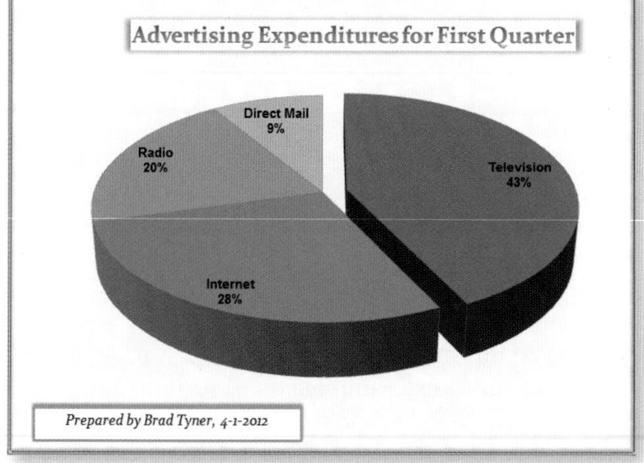

Pie Chart with Source Note

Lynn C. Blackmon
Director, Marketing
Krawczyk, Inc.
1620 Tanglewood Road
Columbia, SC 29204-3325
Phone: 803-555-0159
Fax: 803-555-0161
E-mail: lynnblackmon@krawczyk.com

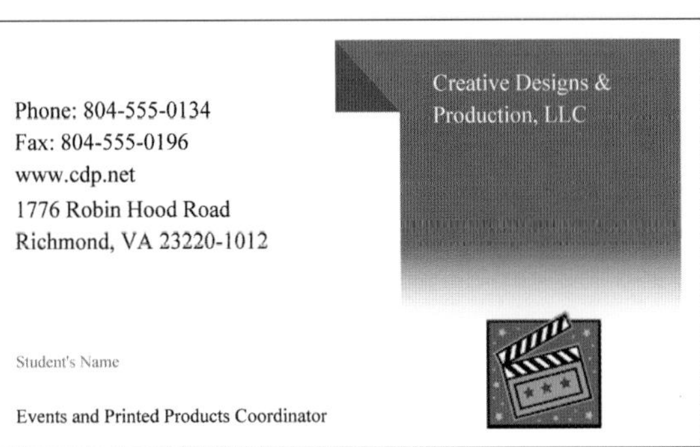

Phone: 804-555-0134
Fax: 804-555-0196
www.cdp.net
1776 Robin Hood Road
Richmond, VA 23220-1012
Creative Designs & Production, LLC
Student's Name
Events and Printed Products Coordinator

Publisher Business Cards

The Creative Process

The secret to developing award-winning products is to focus first on creative and innovative ways to present an idea before you focus

We specialize in thinking outside the box!

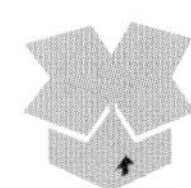

on product development. Our seasoned strategists will brainstorm with you to collect many random, but relevant ideas about the message you want to convey to your customers or clients. We will mull them over, help you put them together, add new twists to them, and come up with a story line that tells your story in an amazingly creative way.

Products

Creative Designs & Production utilizes a turnkey process to plan, develop, produce, review, and deliver your products. All services are outlined and budgeted, and we work within the agreed upon budget to deliver state-of-the art products.

Visual and Audio Products

The following steps are used to develop visual and audio products:

- Planning and creating the story line.
- Pre-production activities include securing a site, the necessary equipment and furnishings , talent, wardrobe, crew, and catering.
- Production includes rehearsing, filming, recording, and repeating until it is a wrap.
- Post-production work includes the technical review and editing, reviews by focus groups, preliminary review by the client, and finalizing the product.

Print Products

Creative Designs

The last step is

& Production offers two approaches to print products:

1. The turnkey approach in which CDP works with the client to establish the content and then CDP handles all phases of the design, layout, printing, and distribution processes.
2. CDP lays out the general plan and helps to develop the content. Then client determines which processes can be handled internally. CDP then provides all services that the client cannot handle.

Creative Designs & Production, LLC

1776 Robin Hood Road
Richmond, VA 23220-1012
Phone: 804-555-0134
Fax: 804-555-0196
www.cdp.net

Publisher Three-Panel Duplex Brochure (inside)

Sidebar

Klienwood News & Views
The Klienwood Group
Volume 1, Issue 1
Newsletter Date

Brothers Honored in Starkville

Ten employees in our Starkville, Mississippi office nominated two brothers for the Klienwood monthly *Making a Difference Award*. The Awards Committee selected Michael and Eric Bass from more than a dozen nominees in six states.

Both young men are academic stars—Michael at the college level and Eric at the high school level. They belong to numerous organizations and are very well-rounded and talented. Michael is very creative in the visual arts and performing arts. Eric is an excellent young athlete who excels as a baseball pitcher.

Christopher Martin, Committee Chair, said, "The Committee was most impressed with the creative way in which they used their talents to benefit both youth with special needs and senior citizens in their community."

Michael's band frequently performs at facilities for senior citizens, and he has been able to get many senior citizens involved in art and music projects.

"The Committee was most impressed with the creative way in which they used their talents to benefit both youth with special needs and senior citizens in their community."

Pull Quote

Eric has been successful in getting youth with special needs involved in athletic programs and in raising funds for the support of those programs.

New Orleans Headquarters Office Completed

The new headquarters office has been completed, and all staff from the old headquarters building at 250 Camp Street moved in last weekend. The staff from the offices in Metairie and in Kenner will move this weekend. For the first time in more than five years, all of our staff in the New Orleans area will be in one facility.

Our work environment for all New Orleans employees will be significantly improved. In addition, the consolidation of staff will enable us to provide better service to all of our regional offices.

We look forward to hosting our annual sales meeting in our new headquarters next month. Special events showcasing the various departments and divisions as well as tours of the new facility are on the agenda.

Our facilities staff is to be commended for the seamless move from the old facilities to the new facilities without inconveniencing our clients by closing down for a single day. The moving crew worked double shifts Friday night, Saturday, and Sunday to get the job done. The move for next weekend will be handled in the same way.

Newsletter, page 1 with Pull Quote

Photos: (brothers) Connie Forde, (business structure)

2

Klienwood Acquires NetGen Commercial Printers

Klienwood completed its acquisition of NetGen Commercial Printers this week. NetGen currently has facilities in New Orleans, Atlanta, and Charlotte. This acquisition should dramatically improve client services and enable us to shorten client deadlines on many of the complex reports that we produce. Often it has been difficult for us to schedule commercial printing jobs if we had a tight schedule. Having our own operation will eliminate a major bottleneck in our work flow process.

In addition, we expect the commercial printing operation to become a major profit center for Klienwood. Our cost of doing business will be significantly reduced, and we believe that many of our current clients will use our professional printing services for a substantial portion of their printing needs.

Our Board of Directors will make a final decision at their next meeting on whether we will retain the name and branding of NetGen Commercial Printers or whether we will use the Klienwood branding and rename the company Klienwood Professional Printers.

Information on how to access printing services and on opportunities for increasing new business by offering professional printing services will be provided after the Board meeting.

Employee News

Please join us in congratulating Alena, pictured at the right. She was named Customer Service Representative of the year by the Association of Sales and Marketing Executives of New Orleans. Alena has been with our group for eight years and developed our training program for new customer service representatives.

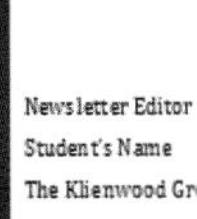

Brianna Westcliffe from the Atlanta office has been named regional manager for Business Development. Brianna has led the company in new business development for the past three years. Please congratulate Brianna on her promotion. Human Resources is accepting applications for Brianna's replacement in the Atlanta office. Information has been posted on our intranet.

President Ray confirmed today that we will offer the highly successful Summer Internship Program again this summer in all offices. Qualified children of employees will be given priority for the positions. Check our intranet for more information.

Klienwood Update:

- The comprehensive benefits study should be completed within the next two or three weeks. From the preliminary analysis, it appears that we may be able to lower the cost of benefits by changing our provider.
- Currently The Klienwood Group has 861 employees in 12 states. More than 20 professional-level positions are posted on our intranet. We encourage all employees to recommend qualified individuals to us for these positions. If we hire an individual you recommend for a professional-level position, you will receive a $500 bonus.

Newsletter Editor
Student's Name
The Klienwood Group
700 Camp Street
New Orleans, LA 70130-3702
Phone: 504-555-0169
Fax: 504-555-0189
www.klienwood.com

Newsletter, page 2 with Sidebar

Agent Listings

Last Name	Property Number	Street Address	City	Listing Price	Sales Date	Sales Price
Alvarez	1907-Z2	1875 Garden View Drive	Castle Hills	$175,000.00	8/20/2012	$158,000.00
Horton	1227-Z4	227 E. Nueva Street	San Antonio	$150,000.00		
	1290-Z1	48 N. Crockett Street	San Antonio	$220,000.00	8/15/2012	$200,000.00
	1861-Z1	2493 Grissom Road	Leon Valley	$250,000.00	8/19/2012	$294,000.00
Kaase	1356-Z2	2001 Colorado Street	San Antonio	$745,000.00		
	1442-Z1	2301 Rosita Place	San Antonio	$695,000.00		
O'Neal	1816-Z2	82 Alamo Plaza	San Antonio	$800,000.00	8/2/2012	$750,000.00
Page	1285-Z3	250 Villita Street	San Antonio	$375,000.00	7/15/2012	$365,000.00
	1438-Z2	5 Colter Road	San Antonio	$500,000.00		
	1726-Z4	2208 Tamworth Drive	San Antonio	$700,000.00	8/1/2012	$690,000.00
	1912-Z1	34 E. Hutchison Street	San Marcos	$425,000.00	8/14/2012	$410,000.00
Palfreyman	1643-Z1	6732 N. Fredericksburg S	San Marcos	$400,000.00	8/20/2012	$348,000.00
Wheeler	2004-Z2	142 Wisteria Drive	Castle Hills	$165,000.00		
	2009-Z2	164 Moss Drive	Castle Hills	$185,000.00		
Wilbanks	1807-Z2	151 Frio City Road	San Antonio	$295,000.00	8/10/2012	$290,000.00
	1809-Z3	31 Guadalupe Street	San Antonio	$350,000.00		

Saturday, April 02, 2011 Page 1 of 1

Report Created in Access

Agents

Agent ID	A-8931-C
First Name	Carmen
Last Name	Alvarez
Street Address	156 Chestnut Street
City	San Antonio
State	TX
ZIP Code	78202-5156
Mobile Phone Numbe	210-555-0138
Date of Birth	5/3/1942
Hire Date	2/1/2012

Property Number	Street Address	City	State	ZIP Code	Date Listed	Listing
1907-Z2	1875 Garden View Drive	Castle Hills	TX	78213-1875	6/10/2012	$175,0

Form Created in Access

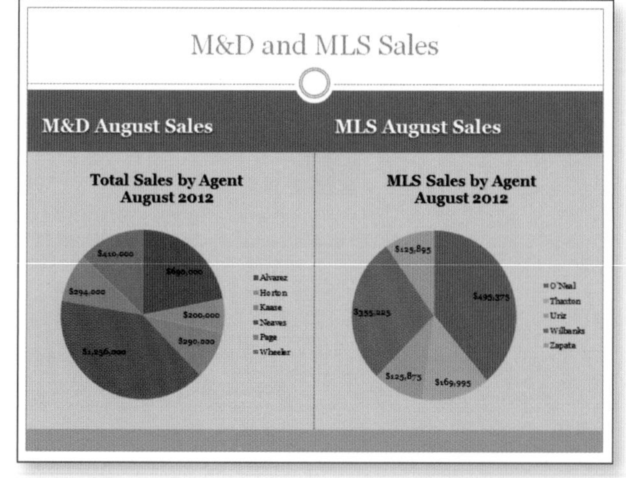

PowerPoint Slide with Linked Excel Charts

Index